LEADERSHIP

For Lawrence

Who has
taught me
so much about
leadership
& so much
else

With deepest
affection, appreciation
and respect

Deborah

ASPEN ELECTIVE SERIES

LEADERSHIP: LAW, POLICY, AND MANAGEMENT

Deborah L. Rhode
Ernest W. McFarland Professor of Law
Director, Center on the Legal Profession
Stanford Law School

Amanda K. Packel
Associate Director
Center on the Legal Profession
Stanford Law School

Wolters Kluwer
Law & Business

Published by Wolters Kluwer Law & Business in New York.

Wolters Kluwer Law & Business serves customers worldwide with CCH, Aspen Publishers, and Kluwer Law International products. (www.wolterskluwerlb.com)

To contact Customer Service, e-mail customer.service@wolterskluwer.com, call 1-800-234-1660, fax 1-800-901-9075, or mail correspondence to:

Wolters Kluwer Law & Business
Attn: Order Department
PO Box 990
Frederick, MD 21705

Printed in the United States of America.

1 2 3 4 5 6 7 8 9 0

ISBN 978-1-4548-0217-4

Library of Congress Cataloging-in-Publication Data

Rhode, Deborah L.
  Leadership : law, policy, and management / Deborah L. Rhode, Amanda K. Packel. — 1st ed.
    p. cm. — (Aspen elective series)
  Includes bibliographical references.
  ISBN 978-1-4548-0217-4 (perfectbound : alk. paper)
1. Executives. 2. Leadership. 3. Social responsibility of business. I. Packel, Amanda K. II. Title.

HD38.2.R47 2011
658.4′092—dc22

2011009908

About Wolters Kluwer Law & Business

Wolters Kluwer Law & Business is a leading global provider of intelligent information and digital solutions for legal and business professionals in key specialty areas, and respected educational resources for professors and law students. Wolters Kluwer Law & Business connects legal and business professionals as well as those in the education market with timely, specialized authoritative content and information-enabled solutions to support success through productivity, accuracy and mobility.

Serving customers worldwide, Wolters Kluwer Law & Business products include those under the Aspen Publishers, CCH, Kluwer Law International, Loislaw, Best Case, ftwilliam.com and MediRegs family of products.

CCH products have been a trusted resource since 1913, and are highly regarded resources for legal, securities, antitrust and trade regulation, government contracting, banking, pension, payroll, employment and labor, and healthcare reimbursement and compliance professionals.

Aspen Publishers products provide essential information to attorneys, business professionals and law students. Written by preeminent authorities, the product line offers analytical and practical information in a range of specialty practice areas from securities law and intellectual property to mergers and acquisitions and pension/benefits. Aspen's trusted legal education resources provide professors and students with high-quality, up-to-date and effective resources for successful instruction and study in all areas of the law.

Kluwer Law International products provide the global business community with reliable international legal information in English. Legal practitioners, corporate counsel and business executives around the world rely on Kluwer Law journals, looseleafs, books, and electronic products for comprehensive information in many areas of international legal practice.

Loislaw is a comprehensive online legal research product providing legal content to law firm practitioners of various specializations. Loislaw provides attorneys with the ability to quickly and efficiently find the necessary legal information they need, when and where they need it, by facilitating access to primary law as well as state-specific law, records, forms and treatises.

Best Case Solutions is the leading bankruptcy software product to the bankruptcy industry. It provides software and workflow tools to flawlessly streamline petition preparation and the electronic filing process, while timely incorporating ever-changing court requirements.

ftwilliam.com offers employee benefits professionals the highest quality plan documents (retirement, welfare and non-qualified) and government forms (5500/PBGC, 1099 and IRS) software at highly competitive prices.

MediRegs products provide integrated health care compliance content and software solutions for professionals in healthcare, higher education and life sciences, including professionals in accounting, law and consulting.

Wolters Kluwer Law & Business, a division of Wolters Kluwer, is headquartered in New York. Wolters Kluwer is a market-leading global information services company focused on professionals.

For Christine and Gus

SUMMARY OF CONTENTS

TABLE OF CONTENTS

ACKNOWLEDGEMENTS

This book grows out of research and teaching supported by Stanford Law School's Center on the Legal Profession. We are deeply grateful for the support provided for this and other Center projects from Stanford Law School Dean Larry Kramer, and from Stanford University President John Hennessy and Provost John Etchemendy. We also owe great debts to Columbia Law School Professor Philip Bobbitt, who co-taught with Deborah Rhode one of the first Leadership courses, and whose insights inspired much of what is best in this collection. Our gratitude for research assistance goes to Columbia law students Katherine Scully and Vivek Mohan, to Stanford Law School students Ashley Hannebrink, Stephanie Lake, Erin Michelle Mohan and, and to the staff of Stanford Law Library, particularly Paul Lomio, Sonia Moss, Rich Porter, Rachel Samberg, Sergio Stone, George Vizvary, Erika Wayne, George Wilson, and Sarah Wilson. Suzanne Peterson at Stanford Law School gave invaluable assistance in preparing the manuscript. We are also indebted to John Devins, Doug Gallaher, and Carol McGeehan at Aspen Publishers.

The book is dedicated to Christine Rhode and Gus Araya, who have taught us so much about leadership, and so much else.

We gratefully acknowledge the permission granted by the authors, publishers, and organizations to reprint portions of the following copyrighted materials.

Adut, Ari, On Scandal: Moral Disturbances in Society, Politics, and Art (2008). Copyright © Ari Adut. Reprinted with the permission of Cambridge University Press.

American Bar Association Commission on Women in the Profession, "Visible Invisibility: Women of Color in Law Firms, Executive Summary" (2006). © 2006 by the American Bar Association. Reprinted With permission. All rights reserved. This information or any or portion thereof may not be copied or disseminated in any form or by any means or stored in an electronic database or retrieval system without the express written consent of the American Bar Association.

Dean, John W., Blind Ambition by John W. Dean, originally published with *Simon & Schuster* (1976). Copyright © 2006 by John W. Dean, used with permission of The Wylie Agency LLC.

Dezenhall, Eric and Weber, John, Damage Control. Reprinted by permission of International Creative Management, Inc. Copyright © 2007 by Eric Dezenhall and John Weber. All rights reserved.

Dobbin, Frank and Kalev, Alexander, and Kelly, Erin, "Diversity Management in Corporate America," in *Contexts* vol. 6, no. 4 (Fall 2007), pp. 21-27. © 2007 by The American Sociological Association. Published by the University of California Press. Reprinted with permission by the University of California Press.

Goleman, Daniel. Reprinted by permission of *Harvard Business Review*. [Excerpt/Exhibit] From "Leadership that Gets Results" by Daniel Goleman, Mar.-Apr. 2000. Copyright © 2000 by the Harvard Business School Publishing Corporation; all rights reserved.

Goleman, Daniel, Boyatzis, Richard, and McKee, Annie. Reprinted by permission of Harvard Business School Press. From Primal Leadership: Realizing the Power of Emotional Intelligence by Daniel Goleman, Richard Boyatzis, and AnnieMcKee. Boston, MA 2002, pp 38-40 and 45-52. Copyright © 2002 by the Harvard Business School Publishing Corporation; all rights reserved.

Heath, Chip and Heath, Dan. From MADE TO STICK by Chip Heath and Dan Heath, copyright © 2007 by Chip Heath and Dan Heath. Used by permission of Random House, Inc.

Heifetz, Ronald A. Reprinted by permission of the publisher from LEADERSHIP WITHOUTH EASY ANSWERS by Ronald A. Heifetz, pp. 16-23; 88-98; 129-139, 141-149; Cambridge, Mass.: The Belknap Press of Harvard University Press, Copyright © 1994 by the President and Fellows of Harvard College.

Heineman, Jr., Ben W. Reprinted by permission of Harvard Business School Press. From High Performance with High Integrity by Ben W. Heineman Jr. Boston, MA 2008, pp 1-3, 9-11, 25, 31-35, 39-42, 89-90, 96-98, 109-111, and 138-139. Copyright © 2008 by the Harvard Business School Publishing Corporation; all rights reserved.

Heineman, Jr., Ben W., "Law and Leadership," 56 J. Legal Educ. 596 (2006). Copyright © 2006 Association of American Law Schools. Reprinted with permission by Journal of Legal Education.

Ibarra, Herminia, and Obodaru, Otilia. Reprinted by permission of *Harvard Business Review*. [Excerpt/Exhibit] From "Women and the Vision Thing" by Herminia Ibarra and Otilia Obodaru, Jan. 2009. Copyright © 2009 by the Harvard Business School Publishing Corporation; all rights reserved.

Janis, Irving L. Irving L. Janis—Groupthink © Copyright 1971 www. Psychologytoday.com.

Johnson, David W., and Johnson, Frank P. Johnson & Johnson, JOINING TOGETHER, pp. 43-48, © 1994 by Allyn & Bacon. Reproduced by permission of Pearson Education, Inc.

Kellerman, Barbara. Reprinted by permission of Harvard Business School Press. From Followership: How Followers Are Creating Change and

Wiley & Sons, Inc. All rights reserved. Reproduced with permission of John Wiley & Sons, Inc.

Rhode, Deborah L, "Moral Character: The Personal and the Political," 20 Loy. U. Chi. L.J. 1 (1988-1989). Copyright © 1989 The Loyola University of Chicago Law Journal. Reprinted with permissions by The Loyola University of Chicago Law Journal.

Rhode, Deborah L., "Rethinking the Public in Lawyers' Public Service: Pro Bono, Strategic Philanthropy, and the Bottom Line," 77 Fordham L. Rev. 1435 (2008-2009). Copyright © 2010 Fordham University School of Law. Reprinted with permission by Fordham Law Review.

Rhode, Deborah L., and Kellerman, Barbara, "Women and Leadership: The State of Play," in Barbara Kellerman and Deborah L. Rhode (eds.)," Women and Leadership: The State of Play and Strategies for Change. Copyright © 2007 by Wiley & Sons, Inc. All rights reserved. Reproduced with permission of John Wiley & Sons, Inc.

Rhode, Deborah L. and Luban, David, "A Case Study: The Hewlett Packard Pretexting Scandal," in Deborah L. Rhode and David Luban (eds.), Legal Ethics (5th ed.). Copyright © 2009 By Thomson Reuters/Foundation Press. Reprinted with permission by West, a Thomson Reuters business.

Rhode, Deborah L. and Packel, Amanda K., "Diversity on Corporate Boards: How Much Difference Does Difference Make?." Rock Center for Corporate Governance at Stanford University Working Paper No. 89, (September 2010). Copyright © 2010 by Deborah L. Rhode and Amanda K. Packel. Reprinted with permission by the authors.

Rubenstein, William B., "Divided We Litigate: Addressing Disputes Among Group Members and Lawyers in Civil Rights Campaigns," 106 Yale L.J. 1623 (1996-1997). Copyright © 2011 by The Yale Law Journal Company, Inc. Reproduced with permission of Yale Law Journal Company, Inc. in the format of Textbook via Copyright Clearance Center.

RUNCIMAN, DAVID; *POLITICAL HYPOCRISY.* © 2008 by Princeton University Press. Reprinted by permission of Princeton University Press.

Sahlman, William A., Management and the Financial Crisis, Harvard Business School Working Paper No. 10-033, Oct. 28, 2009. Copyright © 2009 by William A. Sahlman. Reprinted with permission by the author.

Shklar, Judith N. Reprinted by permission of the publisher from ORDINARY VICES by Judith N. Shklar, pp. 47-48 and 77-78; Cambridge, Mass.: The Belknap Press of Harvard University Press, Copyright © 1984 by the President and Fellows of Harvard College. Permission was also sought from MIT Press Journals, Judith Shklar, "Let Us Not Be Hypocritical," Daedalus, 108:3 (Summer, 1979), pp. 1-25. © 1979 by the American Academy of Arts and Sciences.

Sunga, Lyal S., "Dilemmas Facing NGOs in Coalition-Occupied Iraq," in Daniel A. Bell, Jean-Marc Coicaud (eds.), Ethics in Action: The Ethical Challenges of International Human Rights Nongovernmental Organizations (2007). Copyright © 2007 Cambridge University Press. Reprinted with the permission of Cambridge University Press.

Svetvilas, Chuleenan, "Anatomy of a Complaint: How Hollywood Activists Seized Control of the Fight for Gay Marriage," California Lawyer, Jan.

THE NATURE
OF LEADERSHIP

CHAPTER 1

DEFINING LEADERSHIP

A. INTRODUCTION: WHY STUDY LEADERSHIP?

The most crucial challenges of our times involve issues of leadership. Increasing competitive pressures and global interdependence make the consequences of decision making play out on a wider stage. Society faces problems of growing scale and complexity in areas such as human rights, national security, environmental degradation, poverty, corporate governance, economic development, and social justice. Leaders in law, policy, and business make decisions affecting thousands of individuals whose views are imperfectly registered in market, political, and regulatory processes.

In this context, our need for leaders with vision, values, and technical competence has never been greater. Yet their ability to meet this need is in serious question. Recent financial scandals and implosions have reinforced long-standing concerns about the quality of American leadership. Confidence in business leaders is at the lowest ebb since polls started measuring their standing a half century ago, and they are now the least trusted group in American society.[1] Only 11 percent of the public has "a great deal of confidence . . . in people in charge of running law firms," and almost a third has "hardly any."[2] Less than a quarter of surveyed Americans trust the government in Washington "almost always" or "most of the time," one of the lowest measures in the last fifty years.[3]

In this context, leadership education takes on a new urgency. Although a traditional assumption was that leaders are "born, not made," contemporary research is to the contrary.[4] Studies of twins suggest that about 70 percent of leadership skills are acquired, not genetically based, and decades of experience with leadership development indicate that its major capabilities can be learned.[5] Indeed, as one expert notes, "It would be strange if leadership were the one skill that could not be enhanced through understanding and practice."[6]

It is, of course, true that for thousands of years, leaders have developed without formal education the qualities that made them effective. But informal methods of learning have been common, and many leaders have learned from history, example, and experts in related fields. Civil rights leaders in many countries have borrowed techniques of non-violent resistance pioneered by Mahatma Gandhi in his campaign against British colonial rule in India.

Barack Obama looked for guidance in Franklin D. Roosevelt's first 100 days in office.[7] Great political leaders have learned not only from their predecessors but also from masters in communication. John F. Kennedy famously worked hard on developing the personal magnetism that he observed among Hollywood actors.[8]

Moreover, the value of formal leadership education is gaining increased recognition. Leadership development is roughly a fifty-billion-dollar industry, and at least 700 academic institutions have leadership programs.[9] Courses in this area are now a staple in management and policy schools, and are attracting increased interest in law and other professional programs. Attorneys who head law firms and nonprofit organizations are participating in a growing range of leadership development initiatives.

This book is a response to these trends, and it builds on several premises. The first is that leadership involves core competencies that cut across traditional occupational and academic boundaries. Leaders in any context need skills involving vision, influence, innovation, decision making, ethical reasoning, and conflict management. Leaders also confront common challenges, including those arising from competition, cognitive bias, and organizational dynamics. To develop necessary leadership skills, students can benefit from a wide range of disciplines including psychology, philosophy, management, economics, communication, organizational behavior, political science, and dispute resolution.

A second organizing premise is that effective leadership education requires an integration of theory and practice. To that end, this text situates foundational scholarship in the context of actual leadership problems and case histories. It draws not only on conventional sources but also on portraits from literature and the media that can broaden and deepen analysis. Each chapter includes references to short media clips that highlight particular leadership issues, and one chapter focuses on books and films that could be discussed in their entirety.

A third core assumption is that the materials in this volume can benefit leaders in all occupations and all spheres of civic life, but hold special value for those interested in law, management, and policy. Why focus on these fields? One reason is that they together account for a large proportion of individuals holding formal leadership positions, and insufficient interdisciplinary teaching materials have been available to meet their needs. The inadequacy is particularly striking in legal education. Even law schools that explicitly present themselves as preparing leaders rarely offer a course on the subject; two-thirds offer no instruction on practice management, and this is the first text expressly designed for a leadership class.[10] The omission is an odd one, given the career paths of law graduates. The legal profession has supplied a majority of American presidents, and in recent decades, almost half of Congress, and 10 percent of the CEOs of S&P 500 companies.[11] Lawyers also serve as governors, state legislators, judges, prosecutors, general counsel, law firm managing partners, and heads of government agencies and nonprofit organizations. Moreover, even lawyers who do not hold top positions often exercise leadership roles as heads of teams and advisors to clients exercising managerial authority. And leadership skills are generally viewed as critical in promotion decisions.[12]

Not only does it make sense to target lawyers, managers, and policy makers as key audiences for leadership education, it makes sense to do so in ways that bridge these occupational boundaries. Leaders in these fields require similar skill sets: running a company, a public agency, or a law firm poses many comparable challenges. So too, the career paths of lawyers, managers, and policy makers frequently intersect. Particularly in the United States, the revolving door between public and private sectors means that leaders often rotate in and out of legal, business, government, and nonprofit organizations over the course of their professional lives. Whatever their role, lawyers, managers, and policy makers will often interact. Most attorneys spend time working for or with businesses, government, and nonprofits in some capacity. Corporate officers frequently interface with lawyers, regulators, and politicians in both their business and charitable activities. Government and nonprofit leaders necessarily navigate the worlds of law and business in pursuit of policy objectives. Indeed, the major social problems in today's world require partnerships among these groups. Effectively regulating financial institutions, promoting environmental sustainability, and ensuring fundamental rights are impossible without such collaborative efforts. Helping future leaders see such challenges from multiple disciplinary viewpoints is an increasingly critical skill in today's complex, interconnected world.

To provide the necessary educational background, this book proceeds in five parts. This introductory chapter explores the nature of leadership. What defines a leader? To what extent does leadership involve traits and styles that are generalizable across situations? What is the role of values? What common and distinctive challenges do leaders face in law, management, and policy settings? Chapter 2 focuses on the challenges, styles, and contexts of leadership, and on how it can be learned. What can individuals do to prepare themselves for future challenges and what obstacles will they confront as lifelong learners?

Part II of the book explores key leadership skills. Chapter 3 looks at what makes effective decision making and the cognitive biases and group dynamics that get in the way. Chapter 4 focuses on the exercise of influence: the relationship between leaders and followers, and the strategies necessary to foster change, resolve conflicts, and communicate persuasively.

Part III focuses on ethical issues in leadership. Chapter 5 surveys the personal qualities and organizational structures that foster moral leadership, and the forces that undermine it. Chapter 6 looks more closely at the dynamics of authority and accountability that influence ethical conduct and help explain how the good go bad. Chapter 7 turns attention to scandals: financial, political, and sexual. At what point does "personal" conduct become a political or professional issue, and what strategies of crisis prevention and management are most effective?

Part IV of the book explores leadership in context. Chapter 8 examines the composition of leadership and the difference it makes in practice. How much does gender, racial, and ethnic diversity matter, and how can it be fostered? Chapter 9 focuses on leadership for social change. How can leaders motivate and mobilize followers in pursuit of social justice? How do they resolve competing views of what justice requires? Chapter 10 explores those issues from a global perspective. What challenges confront leaders in law, government, business, and nonprofit organizations in promoting human rights and corporate social responsibility? Chapter 11 analyzes related issues in charitable contexts. What constitutes strategic philanthropy and how can corporate giving programs and lawyers' pro bono activities most effectively serve the public interest?

Part V looks at leadership through a broader lens. Chapter 12 reviews literature and films that explore leadership in law, political, and business contexts. Such fictional portraits highlight the central themes of the book and provide models for dealing with recurrent leadership challenges. Chapter 13 concludes the discussion by reviewing core insights and their relationship to individuals' own leadership aspirations and values.

B. WHAT MAKES LEADERS: CHARACTERISTICS AND CIRCUMSTANCES

1. DEFINITIONS

A threshold question involves what exactly we mean by leadership. That issue has generated a cottage industry of commentary, and by some researchers' accounts, over 1500 definitions and forty distinctive theories.[13] The term "lead" comes from the Old English word "leden," "laedan, or "loeden," which meant to make go, guide, or show the way, and the Latin word "ducere," which meant to draw, drag, pull, guide, or conduct. "Leader" dates to the thirteenth century, but "leadership" only appeared in the nineteenth century.[14]

Although popular usage sometimes equates leadership with power or position, most contemporary experts draw a distinction. They view leadership in terms of traits, processes, skills, and relationships. John Gardner, founder of Common Cause, famously noted that heads of public and private organizations often mistakenly assume that their status "has given them a body of followers. And of course it has not. They have been given subordinates. Whether the subordinates become followers depends on whether the executives act like leaders."[15] Moreover, just as many high officials are not leaders, many leaders do not hold formal offices. Mahatma Gandhi, Eleanor Roosevelt, Martin Luther King Jr., and Osama bin Laden led from the outside. In essence, "leadership requires a relationship, not simply a title. Leaders must be able to inspire, not just compel or direct their followers."[16] As former army chief of staff Eric Shinsek once noted, "You can certainly command" without commitment from followers, "but you cannot lead without it."[17]

2. EARLY THEORIES AND CONTEMPORARY CRITIQUES: TRAITS AND CHARISMA

The question then becomes, how do leaders forge such commitment? Do they share identifiable personal characteristics and styles that are effective across varying situations? Early Greek philosophers such as Plato, Aristotle, and Socrates all assumed that leadership required exceptional personal qualities, particularly intelligence. Abu Mohammad Al Farabi, a tenth-century Persian scholar, summarized Greek, Roman, and Chinese theorists to distill a list of leadership traits that are remarkably similar to those cited in contemporary accounts.[18] The importance of such traits gained currency during the Enlightenment, and Thomas Carlyle subsequently elaborated the view in *On Heroes, Hero Worship, and the Heroic in History* (1902). From his perspective, behind every great institution and social movement was the shadow of a "great man."

The noted social theorist Max Weber also stressed personal qualities and styles, most importantly "charisma." The term came from Catholic theologians, who borrowed it from St. Paul's concept of gifts manifesting God's grace.[19] Weber used the term in a secular sense to convey the magnetism and persuasiveness that enabled individuals to attract a wide following, particularly in times of turbulence:

> [T]he further back we look in history, the more we find . . . that the "natural" leaders — in times of psychic, physical, economic, ethical, religious, political distress — have been neither officeholders nor incumbents of an "occupation" in the present sense of the word, that is, men who have acquired expert knowledge and who serve for remuneration. The natural leaders in distress have been holders of specific gifts of the body and spirit; and these gifts have been believed to be supernatural, not accessible to everybody. The concept of "charisma" is here used in a completely "value-neutral" sense. . . .
>
> In contrast to any kind of bureaucratic organization of offices, the charismatic structure knows nothing of a form or of an ordered procedure of appointment or dismissal. It knows no regulated "career." . . . Charisma knows only inner determination and inner restraint. The holder of charisma seizes the task that is adequate for him and demands obedience and a following by virtue of his mission. . . . His charismatic claim breaks down if his mission is not recognized by those to whom he feels he has been sent. If they recognize him, he is their master — so long as he knows how to maintain recognition through "proving" himself.[20]

Weber distinguished charismatic leadership from other forms of authority based on tradition (as with monarchies) or law and "technical rationality" (as with bureaucracies).

Building on Weber's insight, modern theorists have defined charisma in terms of qualities such as emotional expressiveness, empathy, competence, self-confidence, and control.[21] However, unlike Weber, contemporary theorists view these traits as acquired, rather than God given or innate. Charismatic leaders make inspirational appeals that tap into followers' values and identity.[22] Some commentators also stress leaders' commitment and self-sacrifice.[23] Others focus on the needs of followers. When circumstances evoke feelings of uncertainty, powerlessness, and alienation, the stage is set for charismatic appeals.[24]

These "trait" and "style" theories of leadership have attracted widespread criticism, much of it summarized in the excerpt below from Heifetz's *Leadership without Easy Answers*. The first systematic critique of the "great man" approach to leadership came from social theorist Herbert Spencer, who famously argued that the times produce great leaders rather than the converse.[25] A prominent case in history is Winston Churchill. In *The Power to Lead*, excerpted below, Joseph Nye argues that Churchill was widely viewed as a "washed up backbench member of Parliament" until Hitler invaded France in May of 1940. Then, Churchill became the "man of the moment."[26] His personal characteristics "did not change in 1940: the situation did."[27]

The same individual with the same traits may be a superb leader in some contexts but not in others. The tactics that made Bismarck so successful in nineteenth-century Prussia would not have won him election as mayor of Los Angeles.[28] Sir Ernest Shackleton won worldwide acclaim for leading his crew back from a perilous attempt to cross Antarctica on foot, but in normal business ventures, he was spectacularly ineffective.[29] Another leading example is Jimmy Carter, who failed to win reelection after a single frustrating term as president, but subsequently received a Nobel Peace Prize for his efforts to secure peace and international human rights. The commitment to principle that made him effective in some global contexts ill suited him for the horse trading necessary to accomplish his domestic agenda.[30] By contrast, Lyndon Johnson's adeptness at congressional logrolling made possible his landmark "Great Society" antipoverty and civil rights legislation, but his lack of foreign policy expertise contributed to a disastrous escalation of the Vietnam War. The kind of backroom dealing that enabled Johnson to pressure congressional opponents was unproductive in a context of greater transparency, in which failures in Southeast Asia became staples of television news.[31] John Gardner notes both that history makes leaders and that leaders make history; no single pattern of styles and traits is apparent in leaders as different as Lenin and Gandhi. What produces leadership is "great opportunities greatly met."[32]

Systematic research confirms what those examples reflect. Over the last half century, leadership scholars have conducted more than 1000 studies in an attempt to determine the definitive personal styles or traits of great leaders. Yet, as a *Harvard Business Review* summary notes, none of these studies has produced a clear profile of the ideal leader.[33] Nor has research identified consistent relationships between personality and leadership effectiveness.[34]

Even the much celebrated quality of charisma is not necessarily related to performance. Indeed, some studies find that the leaders of the most continuously profitable corporations have tended to be self-effacing and lacking in the qualities commonly considered charismatic.[35] Peter Drucker famously denounced efforts to find a "boardroom Elvis Presley." Real leadership, he argued, has little to do with such qualities. It is "mundane . . . and boring. Its essence is performance."[36] Some research suggests that charismatic leaders can impair performance because followers rely too heavily on such leaders' judgment and fail to challenge erroneous decisions.[37] So too, according to experts such as historian James McGregor Burns, "charisma" is so ambiguously and inconsistently used that "it is impossible to restore the word to analytic duty."[38] Often it seems to function as a conclusory label that fails to specify what exactly accounts for the appeal described.

3. THE IMPORTANCE OF LEADERS

Moreover, focusing on the individual traits of leaders deflects attention from organizational factors and institutional structures that may be more consistent drivers of performance.[39] Contemporary experts caution against the "leader attribution error": the tendency to overvalue the contribution of leaders to organizational performance.[40] Although findings are mixed, most research suggests that leadership makes only a modest impact on corporate performance. Other factors such as the competitive circumstances within the industry and the organization's fixed assets and entrenched structures play a dominant role.[41]

However, because leadership is one of the few important factors within management control, it makes sense to make the most of its potential contributions. And in other contexts, such as those involving government and nonprofit organizations, professional firms, and social movements, leadership often makes a highly significant difference in effectiveness.[42] Particularly in contexts involving policy reform, similar initiatives under similar circumstances have quite different impacts depending on the strength and competence of leaders.[43]

4. THE ROLE OF CIRCUMSTANCE: SITUATIONS, CONTINGENCY, AND CONTEXT IN LEADERSHIP THEORY

The inadequacies of trait-based theories of leadership have led to a wide variety of alternatives.[44] The most influential have been frameworks that acknowledge the importance of context. Beginning in the 1960s, contingency theories began to explore what would make leadership effective under particular conditions.[45] The first and best known of these approaches focused on leaders' need to consider factors such as their relationship to followers, the amount of power and resources conferred by their position, and the structure of the task at hand. Later models included additional considerations such as the importance of the decision, the availability of information, and the likelihood and importance of its acceptance by followers.[46] Some circumstances require controlling, autocratic behavior and others benefit from participatory styles. As a general matter, these approaches advocate more directive styles when subordinates had clearly defined tasks and low-level skills and motivation, but more supportive styles when well-educated employees had challenging assignments and significant intrinsic motivation.[47] Situational theories have similarly related leadership styles to followers' readiness. The ability and confidence that subordinates have in carrying out tasks dictates whether directive, consultative, participatory, or delegating strategies make the most sense.[48] Contemporary policy experts have also emphasized timing as a key contextual factor. Successful reform efforts often require waiting until policy windows open, that is, a need for action appears urgent, and effective political alliances and plausible proposals are available.[49]

Under these approaches, the key to effective leadership is a match between what the circumstances require or enable, and the strengths that an individual has to offer.[50] But, as Nye points out in the excerpt below, what is relevant in a situation and what is the appropriate way of handling it turn out to be "interpretative and contestable issues" that cannot be determined by objective criteria.[51] Nor does contingency theory explain exactly how leaders acquire and exercise power in light of the relevant considerations, and why some of them seem consistently effective in different situations.[52] Moreover, as Harvard Business School professors Nitin Nohria and Rakesh Khurana note, "It is hard to imagine what leadership is if there isn't a core set of leadership functions or behaviors that cut across different situations and persons."[53] One way to bridge these theoretical tensions is to think of leadership in terms that Princeton professor Nan Keohane describes as "overlapping similarities" or "family resemblances."[54] Leading involves certain core functions and competencies, but the styles and traits that are most effective will vary to some extent depending on the circumstances.

5. VALUES IN LEADERSHIP

One other limitation in both trait and contingency theories is the inattention to values. That is not to suggest that these approaches are value free. Rather, as Nye suggests, the value they privilege is impact; leaders are assessed in light of their effect on history, followers, and organizations. Yet missing or marginal in such frameworks is the morality of means and ends. Does an effective leader need to be an ethical leader? Ethical in what sense? Chapter 5 explores those issues in greater depth. Our question here is simply what role values play in the definition of leadership.

For some commentators, good leadership depends on the ends being pursued. Theorists beginning with James MacGregor Burns have distinguished between transactional and transformational leadership. Transactional approaches focus on the relationship between leaders and subordinates and on what each gains or loses from the exchange. Such frameworks assume that people are motivated primarily by rewards and punishments and need financial, psychological, and status-related incentives to comply with specified rules and goals.[55] Yet these approaches fail to capture the complexity of human motivation and the importance of values. Accordingly, transformational approaches stress the capacity not simply to influence followers' behaviors through rewards and sanctions but also to transform their objectives and, in the process, to elevate leaders' own sense of purpose. Transformational leadership inspires individuals to transcend their immediate self-interest in the service of the greater good of the organization or society. Such leadership is "moral in that it raises the level of human conduct and ethical aspiration of both leader and led."[56] Techniques include providing an inspirational vision and role model, and responding to followers' capacities for creativity and commitment.[57]

Other theorists have similarly argued for values-based leadership. Servant leadership focuses on the capacity to meet the needs of others, and to help them support the organizational mission.[58] Strategic leadership and visionary leadership stress the ability to transform institutions in ways that better enable them to address change and pursue their mission.[59] Such approaches are considered superior to laissez-faire leadership, in which those in positions of authority fail to take a stand on issues implicating fundamental values.[60]

Many contemporary theories of leadership have been subject to criticism on normative grounds. Some theories pay no attention to the moral content of leaders' objectives, and even some values-based approaches give insufficient attention to the content of the values at issue, and how to resolve conflicts among them. Yet, without some focus on the ultimate moral purpose or effect of influence, Hitler and Osama bin Laden are in the same general category as Gandhi and Mother Teresa. Moreover, the transformational objectives that Burns identified for political leaders do not translate smoothly into business contexts in which what constitutes the greater good is subject to dispute. Leadership that gives priority to shareholder profits and market dominance is value driven, but many business ethics experts argue that these values are inadequate metrics. On this view, transformational leadership needs to take into account other stakeholder concerns and societal interests, but the theory says little about how to weigh these competing goals.

Another concern with values-based approaches is that their focus on transformative ends can obscure the significance of ethical means and the need for transactional strategies in ensuring compliance. When interviewed about their understanding of ethical leadership, senior American executives and ethics officers stress the importance not only of communicating moral values but also of implementing them through appropriate incentives. Ethical leaders are "known for setting ethical standards and holding people accountable . . . via the [organizational] reward system."[61] So too, in political contexts, theorists have noted the danger in relying on transformational or charismatic leadership at the expense of procedural values. As Michael Keeley points out, not everyone is attracted to the same leaders or the same ultimate values. Without institutional checks and balances along the lines that framers of the United States Constitution envisioned, a majority led by a charismatic leader may oppress the minority. "Might," as Keeley puts it, is an unreliable "guide to right," and countries that have given too much authority to leaders such as Mao or Stalin have paid an enormous price in human life and liberty.[62]

For the most part, argues Nan Keohane, "good" and "bad" are terms more useful in judging specific acts than leaders themselves.[63] Even our most revered leaders often have some toxic qualities or blots on their records. Franklin D. Roosevelt's court-packing plan is one of Keohane's examples. Moreover, as Chapter 5 notes, "dirty hands" are a common, and some believe endemic, aspect of political governance. Moral leadership may require moral trade-offs that defy categorical judgments.

6. LEADING AND MANAGING

Values also play a role in the distinction many contemporary theorists draw between leading and managing. In a widely quoted phrase, Warren Bennis and Burt Nanus summarized the difference: "Managers are people who do things right; leaders are people who do the right things."[64] The term "management" comes from the Latin "manus," meaning hand. It originally referred to handling things and gained currency during the Industrial Revolution in the nineteenth century. Contemporary scholars generally distinguish between leaders, who chart a destination, and managers, who enable individuals and institutions to get there. Managers administer; leaders envision, inspire, and innovate.[65]

In his *Harvard Business Review* article "What Leaders Really Do," John Kotter claims that most American corporations are "overmanaged and underled" and that companies need to develop individuals who have both leadership and management skills.[66] According to Kotter, the fundamental difference is that management is about coping with complexity while leadership is about coping with change. The latter capability has become increasingly important because "the business world has become more competitive and more volatile. Faster technological change, greater international competition, the deregulation of markets, . . . and the changing demographics of the work force are among the many factors that have contributed to this shift."[67]

Kotter analogizes to the military. An army can usually survive in times of peace with good administration at all levels of the hierarchy and good leadership at the very top. A "wartime army, however, needs competent leadership at all levels. No one yet has figured out how to manage people effectively into battle; they must be led." Organizations manage complexity through planning, budgeting, organizing, staffing, and problem solving. Leading involves setting direction, which according to Kotter is often mistakenly confused with planning.

> Leaders gather a broad range of data and look for patterns, relationships, and linkages that help explain things. What's more, the direction-setting aspect of leadership does not produce plans; it creates vision and strategies. These describe a business, technology, or corporate culture in terms of what it should become over the long term and articulate a feasible way of achieving this goal.
>   Most discussions of vision have a tendency to degenerate into the mystical. The implication is that a vision is something mysterious that mere mortals, even talented ones, could never hope to have. But developing good business direction isn't magic. It is a tough, sometimes exhausting process of gathering and analyzing information. People who articulate such visions aren't magicians but broadbased strategic thinkers who are willing to take risks.[68]

Achieving the vision "requires *motivating and inspiring*—keeping people moving in the right direction, despite major obstacles to change, by appealing to basic but often untapped human needs, values, and emotions."[69]

Yet the distinction between leading and managing should not be overstated. Joanne Ciulla questions the normative assumption underlying Bennis and Nanus's formulation—that managers do things right and leaders do the right thing. If the implication is that leaders are virtuous and managers are "morally flabby," does that make Hitler a manager, not a leader?[70] Moreover, as many commentators have noted, managers need leadership skills to get things done, and leaders need management skills to ensure that systems are in place to realize organizational objectives. Although leaders' primary role is to see over the horizon and formulate long-term goals, they also remain responsible for short-term performance.[71] In organizations of professionals, such as law firms, managerial and leadership roles are typically combined and shared. Firm chairs work with management committees and chief financial officers to make key operational decisions, and with equity partners to set policy directions. So too, a growing trend in many other large corporate and public-sector organizations is toward diffused and collaborative leadership structures.[72]

Theories of management and leadership also overlap and cover some of the same ground concerning how to motivate subordinates. In the corporate sector, popularized frameworks proliferate, leading to what *Fortune Magazine* described as "management by fad."[73] A similar literature exists for "leadership lite," with titles ranging from *Leadership Lessons from Attilla the Hun, Toy Box Leadership: Leadership Lessons from the Toys You Loved as a Child,* and *Make It So: Leadership Lessons from Star Trek.* One recent overview listed sixty leadership "brands," including alpha leadership, connected leadership, directive leadership, enlightened leadership, emergent leadership, formative leadership, generative leadership, inspired leadership, integral leadership, quantum leadership, and synergistic leadership.[74] Many of these accounts repackage similar insights. Yet sensationalized titles and niche marketing should not obscure the importance of the fundamental goals of these publications: to extend core insights from the leadership field to management of common business dilemmas.

7. THE LEADER'S LEGACY

One paradox of power is that leaders who are most effective in building a positive legacy that outlasts them are those least interested in exercising power for its own sake, or in establishing their own place in history. Building on this insight, J. Patrick Dobel cautions individuals to "beware of pigeons on your monuments. . . . Insisting on credit [for your achievements] invites disappointment and distortion of personal energy and aspirations."[75] He also advises that aspiring leaders "begin sooner rather than later[; a] person's legacy unfolds every day," and that priorities and relationships formed early in a career create the foundations for later achievements. People cannot control how history will judge them, but they can be conscious of how their daily interactions and priorities affect individuals and institutions.[76] Unless their priorities include support for others' careers as well as their own, their legacy is likely to be limited. As Noel Tichy, a former director of executive development, notes, "[T]he ultimate test of a leader is not whether he or she makes smart decisions . . . but whether he or she teaches others to be leaders and builds an organization that can sustain its success even when he or she is not around."[77]

The excerpts that follow explore the meaning of leadership and the qualities associated with its exercise. Based on these approaches, how would you define leadership? Are there any characteristics that seem generalizable?

JOSEPH S. NYE JR., THE POWERS TO LEAD

(New York: Oxford University Press, 2008),
pp. 3-7, 10-11, 14-16, 18-22, 24, 53, and 56-64

Do Leaders Matter?

Skeptics deny that leaders matter all that much. People easily make the mistake of "leader attribution error." We see something going right or wrong with a group or organization and then attribute the result to the leader. He or she becomes a scapegoat, even while being more a symbol of failure than its cause. Sports teams fire coaches after a losing season whether or not they are blameworthy. Business executives lose their jobs after profits turn down; others get credit for success in bull markets. Voters reward and punish politicians for economic conditions that often were created before the leaders took office.

In the presence of multiple causes and random events, attributing blame or praise to a person can provide a sense of psychological comfort and reassurance about our ability to understand and control events in a complex and confusing world. ... "Belief in a political leader's ability to alter affairs may generate a feeling of indirect control. The ability to reward or punish incumbents through the vote implies this influence." Various experiments have shown that the desire to make sense of confusing events leads to a romanticized, larger-than-life role for leaders, particularly in extreme cases of very good or very bad performance.

How much do leaders really matter? ... A Harvard Business School study of the effects of CEOs on corporate performance in forty-two industries shows that on average the effect of the CEO accounted for about 14 percent of the difference in performance, ranging from 2 percent in the meat processing industry to 21 percent in telecommunications. A study of forty-six college and university presidents found that the role of the leader was largely a myth, and a study of the effects of mayors on city budgets came to a similar conclusion. Another study of service teams at Xerox found that the way teams were designed accounted for 42 percent of the variance in success; less than 10 percent was attributable to the qualities of their leaders' coaching abilities. On the one hand, any variable (such as leadership) that accounts for 10 percent of the variation of complex social phenomena is a factor to be reckoned with. On the other hand, these findings hardly support the magical view of causation popularly attributed to leaders!

Of course, such studies have their limits. They tell us about averages over numerous cases, but sometimes a leader can make a large difference and beat the averages in a particular case. Moreover, these studies focus on institutions with well-established procedures for recruitment and promotion, and leaders who already hold positions of authority. Leaders are already well sorted before they reach the top, and the oddballs, deviants, and geniuses have been excluded well before that. Social movement leaders like Gandhi and Martin Luther King, Jr. would not have made it to the top of GE, nor is it likely they would have done well if by some chance they had. Formal organizations are an important slice of life, but only a slice. Many leadership contexts are far more fluid, whether they are political groups, street gangs, universities, or online communities. Leading inside an institution is different from leading a movement without institutions. A prophetic style fits well with a loosely organized social movement, whereas managerial competence is important in an organization. In social movements, we might expect leaders to count for more (and in the case of online communities, less) than in corporate life. Conclusions drawn from studies of organizational behavior (which is the focus of the majority of academic and business studies) may not tell us much about these other dimensions of leadership.

History Lessons

This raises the age-old question of the role of leaders in history. For centuries, history was written as the record of the doings of great men. Thomas Carlyle wrote in 1840, "The history of what man has accomplished in this world, is at bottom the History of the Great Men who have worked here" (although a skeptical Herbert Spencer pointed out in 1873, "Before he can re-make his society, his society must make him"). Perhaps the best summary of this insoluble problem came from Karl Marx: "Men make their own history, but they do not make it as they please . . . but under circumstances existing already, given and transmitted from the past."

It seems obvious that Alexander the Great, Julius Caesar, Genghis Khan, Louis XIV, and Winston Churchill all made a difference in history, but it is much harder to say how much. History is an imperfect laboratory, and controlled experiments that hold other variables constant are impossible. Time and context have a huge impact. For example, President George W. Bush frequently refers to Churchill, whom many historians describe as one of the greatest leaders of the twentieth century. But at the beginning of 1940, Churchill was widely regarded as a washed-up backbench member of Parliament. As a conservative British prime minister said in 1936, "While we delight to listen to him in this House, we do not take his advice." Churchill would have been a minor figure in the history books if Hitler had not invaded France in May 1940. Then Churchill became the man who fit the moment. Churchill did not change; the context changed. Without Hitler's actions, Churchill would not be seen today as a great leader. Or to take a more recent example, Rudolph Giuliani (who also takes Churchill as his role model) has enjoyed a reputation for leadership (and written a book with that title) based on his actions following September 11, 2001. Before that tragedy, he was known as a mayor with a mixed record. He did well on crime but poorly on race relations. On September 10, he seemed to have little political future. But his ability to interpret events and calm a fearful public after the attack, particularly in the absence of the president, projected him as a great leader and helped to relaunch a political career that includes a run for the presidency.

The philosopher Sidney Hook once tried to sort out this question by distinguishing "eventful vs. event-making" leaders. An eventful leader influences the course of subsequent developments by his actions. In Hook's metaphor, the mythical little Dutch boy who stuck his finger in a leaking dike and saved his country was an eventful leader, but any little boy or any finger could have done the trick. An event-making leader, on the other hand, doesn't just find a fork in the historical road: he helps to create it. Such leaders are called *transformational* in the sense of changing what would otherwise be the course of history. They raise new issues and new questions. "Good politicians win the argument. Every now and then someone comes along and changes it." Margaret Thatcher and Tony Blair were not universally liked as prime ministers in Britain, but both were credited with changing the political weather. . . . Many opportunities for change go unfulfilled. Leaders matter when they have the intuition and skills to take advantage of those windows while they are open.

Heroic and Alpha Male Approaches to Leadership

The fact that history has been written in terms of heroes constrains our imagination and understanding of the enormous potential of human leadership that ranges from Attila the Hun to Mother Teresa. Most everyday leaders remain unheralded. . . . Humans seek heroes, but not all heroes are leaders, and not all leaders are heroic.

Neither the ancient Greeks nor the Romans who influenced Western civilization had an abstract noun that denoted "leadership" as we use it today. To lead (*agein* in Greek; *ducere* in Latin) was originally a military term meaning "to be general of soldiers." Western civilization's paradigmatic ideal of a leader grew out of Homer's *Iliad* and *Odyssey*, an ideal of the brave warrior leading by example in the Trojan War. The role of heroic leadership in war led to overemphasis of command and control and hard military power. The ancient image of the leader as warrior persists to this day. A study of twentieth-century rulers found that more than half "had a chance to show their military prowess either as aggressors or defenders." Even in modern America, presidential greatness (and failure) has been correlated with wartime presidencies. . . .

Nature and Nurture

Another effect of the traditional heroic approach to leadership has been to support the belief that leaders are born rather than made, and that nature is more important than nurture. . . . Physical traits such as physique, intellectual traits such as IQ, and personality traits such as extroversion have been extensively examined by researchers, but with poor explanatory results. "While studies might find a certain trait to be significant, there always seemed to be considerable evidence that failed to confirm that trait's importance." Context is often more important than traits. The athletic child who is the natural leader on the playground may lose that dominant position when the group returns to a well-structured classroom. As we saw earlier, Churchill's traits did not change in 1940; the situation did.

The traits-centered approach has not vanished from studies of leadership, but it has been broadened and made more flexible. Traits have come to be seen as consistent patterns of personality rather than inherited characteristics. This definition mixes nature and nurture and means that traits can to some extent be learned rather than merely inherited. We talk about leaders being more energetic, more willing to take risks, more optimistic, more persuasive, and more empathetic than other people, but these traits are affected partly by a leader's genetic makeup and partly by the environments in which the traits were learned and developed. A nice experiment recently demonstrated the interaction between nature and nurture. A group of employers was asked to hire workers who had been ranked by their looks. If the employers saw only the individuals' resumes, beauty had no impact on hiring.

Surprisingly, however, when telephone interviews were included in the process, beautiful people did better even though unseen by the employers. A lifetime of social reinforcement based on their genetic looks may have encoded into their voice patterns a tone of confidence that could be projected over the phone. Nature and nurture became thoroughly intertwined. . . .

Defining Leaders and Leadership

. . . I define a leader as someone who helps a group create and achieve shared goals. . . . Some leaders act with the formal authority of a position such as president or chair; others act without formal authority, as Rosa Parks did. . . . Holding a formal leadership position is like having a fishing license; it does not guarantee you will catch any fish.

Leadership is not just who you are but what you do. The functions that leaders perform for human groups are to create meaning and goals, reinforce group identity and cohesion, provide order, and mobilize collective work. In a careful study of work teams, Richard Hackman found that the functions of leaders are setting a compelling direction, fine-tuning a team's structure, and providing resource support and expert coaching: "Team leadership can be—and, at its best, often is—a *shared* activity. Anyone and everyone who clarifies a team's direction, or improves its structure, or secures organizational supports for it, or provides coaching that improves its performance processes is providing team leadership."

The test of a leader is whether a group is more effective in both defining and achieving its goals because of that person's participation. . . . We can think of leadership as a process with three key components: leaders, followers, and contexts. The context consists of both the external environment and the changing objectives that a group seeks in a particular situation. As we have seen, the traits that are most relevant to effective leadership depend on the context, and the situation creates followers' needs that lead them to search for particular leaders. A group of workers that wants someone to organize a weekend party may turn to a fun-loving member to take the lead. The same group will probably want a very different member to lead in negotiating a benefits package with management.

Rather than think of a leader as a particular type of heroic individual, we need to think of all three parts of the triangle together constituting the process of leadership. Leaders and followers learn roles and change roles as their perceptions of situations change. One of the key issues is for leaders and followers to understand how to expand and adapt their repertoires for different situations. They can learn to broaden their bandwidth and thus provide for a more effective leadership process in a wider range of situations. Because learning is possible, leadership studies, though not a science, is still a valid discipline. . . .

Charismatic Leadership

. . . Does charisma originate in the individual, in the followers, or in the situation? Some theorists say all three. . . . [One] study looked at seven major political spellbinders of the twentieth century: Hitler, Mussolini, and Roosevelt in industrialized countries; Gandhi, Sukarno, Castro, and Khomeini in less developed countries. The author concluded that in all cases "charisma is found not so much in the personality of the leader as in the perceptions of the people he leads." Ann Ruth Willner found that to locate the sources of charisma, she needed to look for the factors that called forth those perceptions and that they varied by culture and by time. She speculated that culture may explain why so few women charismatic leaders appear in political history; followers in most cultures have denied them the opportunity. Joan of Arc and Evita Peron are rare exceptions.

Social crises cause followers' distress, which leads them to turn to a leader and attribute charisma to him or her. But knowing that, leaders sometimes help to enlarge a crisis and exacerbate the distress that triggers the process of charisma creation. . . .

The power that charismatic leaders unleash among their followers can do great good or great harm. Some theorists categorize "negative charismatics" as those who are prone to grandiose projects, inattention to details, unwilling-ness to delegate, failure to create institutions that empower followers, and lack of planning for their succession. On the other hand, there have been historical moments when "positive" or "reparative" charismatic leaders like Gandhi, King, and Nelson Mandela have released energies among their followers that have transformed social and political situations for the better. . . .

Charismatic leaders are adept at communication, vision, confidence, being an exemplar, and managing the impressions they create. Some theorists dis-tinguish between "close" charismatics, who work best in small groups or inner circles where the effects of their personality are felt directly, and "distant" charismatics, who rely on more remote theatrical performance to reach and move the broader imagined communities that they aspire to lead. In the first case, the personal charm is felt directly; in the latter case, it is projected and mediated. Other theorists distinguish "socialized" charismatics, who use their power to benefit others, and "personalized" charismatics, whose narcissistic personalities lead to self-serving behavior.

Regardless of type, charisma is hard to identify in advance. . . . Searching for corporate saviors has increasingly produced what Rakesh Khurana of Harvard Business School calls "the irrational quest for charismatic CEOs." He reports that companies often search for white knights with attractive images created by the media rather than those with the most appropriate managerial experience. Yet their charismatic image, however poorly it fits the company's internal needs, often helps to recruit resources such as capital and people from the outside world. And resources help reinforce charisma. "In ancient times, leaders often wore special clothing, masks and ornaments that conferred on them a larger-than-life appearance"; for modern executives, "the same function is played by private planes, limousines, palatial homes, exclusive seats at sporting events, and other trappings of corporate power." . . .

Transformational and Transactional Leadership

Given the inadequate explanatory value of charisma alone, leadership the-orists have incorporated it into a broader concept of transformational leadership. . . . Transformational leaders empower and elevate their followers; they use conflict and crisis to raise their followers' consciousness and trans-form them. Transformational leaders mobilize power for change by appealing to their followers' higher ideals and moral values rather than their baser emo-tions of fear, greed, and hatred.

Transformational leaders induce followers to transcend their self-interest for the sake of the higher purposes of the group that provides the context of the relationship. Followers are thus inspired to undertake what Ronald Heifetz has termed "adaptive work" and do more than they originally expected based on self-interest alone. Charisma in the sense of personal magnetism is only one part of transformational leadership. As defined and operationalized by the leadership theorist Bernard Bass, transformational leadership also includes an element of "intellectual stimulation" (broadening followers' awareness of situations and new perspectives) and "individualized consideration" (providing support, coaching, and developmental experiences to followers rather than treating them as mere means to an end). Thus a leader can be charismatic without being transformational, and vice versa. Transformational leaders who succeed may remain respected, but they may lose their aura of charisma as followers' needs change. Alternatively, charismatic leaders who come to believe they are truly exceptional may become autocratic and intolerant and no longer remain transformational.

Transformational leaders are contrasted with transactional leaders, who motivate followers by appealing to their self-interest. Transactional leaders use various approaches, but all rest on reward, punishment, and self-interest. Transformational leaders appeal to the collective interests of a group or organization, and transactional leaders rely on the various individual interests. The former depend more on the soft power of inspiration, the latter on the hard power of threat and reward. Transactional leaders create concrete incentives to influence followers' efforts and set out rules that relate work to rewards. . . .

Although the term transactional is clear, the concept of transformation is confusing because theorists use it to refer to leaders' objectives, the styles they use, and the outcomes they produce. Those three dimensions are not the same thing. Sometimes leaders transform the world but not their followers, or vice versa, and sometimes they use a transactional style to accomplish transformational objectives.

Consider the example of Lyndon Johnson. In the 1950s, Senator Johnson deeply wanted to transform racial injustice in the South, but he did not use soft power to preach to or inspire a new vision in other senators. Instead, he misled his fellow southerners about his intentions and used a transactional style of hard power bullying and bargaining to achieve progress toward his transformational objectives in passing a civil rights bill in 1957 that was anathema to many of the supporters who had made him majority leader. He did not change his followers, but he did begin to change the world of African Americans in the South.

In the following excerpt, Ronald Heifetz similarly argues for viewing leadership as an activity, involving the interaction of ability, culture, and situation. He also recognizes the centrality of a leader's relationship with followers and the importance of adaptive work in advancing common goals.

RONALD A. HEIFETZ, LEADERSHIP WITHOUT EASY ANSWERS

(Cambridge, MA: Belknap Press of Harvard University Press, 1994), pp. 16-23

Hidden Values in Theories of Leadership

Perhaps the first theory of leadership—and the one that continues to be entrenched in American culture—emerged from the nineteenth-century notion that history is the story of great men and their impact on society. (Women were not even considered candidates for greatness.) . . . Although various scientific studies discount the idea, this *trait approach* continues to set the terms of popular debate. Indeed, it saw a revival during the 1980s. Based on this view, trait theorists since Carlyle have examined the personality characteristics of "great men," positing that the rise to power is rooted in a "heroic" set of personal talents, skills, or physical characteristics. As Sidney Hook described in *The Hero in History* (1943), some men are eventful, while others are event-making.

In reaction to the great-man theory of history, *situationalists* argued that history is much more than the effects of these men on their time. Indeed, social theorists like Herbert Spencer (1884) suggested that the times produce the person and not the other way around. In a sense, situationalists were not interested in leadership per se. "Historymakers" were interesting because they stood at the vortex of powerful political and social forces, which themselves were of interest. Thus, the more or less contemporaneous emergence of the United States' first great leaders—Jefferson, Washington, Adams, Madison, Hamilton, Monroe, Benjamin Franklin—is attributed not to a demographic fluke but to the extraordinary times in which these men lived. Instead of asserting that all of them shared a common set of traits, situationalists suggest that the times called forth an assortment of men with various talents and leadership styles. Indeed, many of them performed marvelously in some jobs but quite poorly in others. Thus, "What an individual actually *does* when acting as a leader is in large part dependent upon characteristics of the situation in which he functions."

Beginning in the 1950s, theorists began (not surprisingly) to synthesize the trait approach with the situationalist view. Empirical studies had begun to show that no single constellation of traits was associated with leadership. Although this finding did not negate the idea that individuals "make" history, it did suggest that different situations demand different personalities and call for different behaviors. Primary among these synthetic approaches is *contingency theory*, which posits that the appropriate style of leadership is contingent on the requirements of the particular situation. For example, some situations require controlling or autocratic behavior and others participative or democratic behavior.

The field of inquiry soon expanded into the specific interactions between leaders and followers—the *transactions* by which an individual gains influence and sustains it over time. The process is based on reciprocity. Leaders not only influence followers but are under their influence as well. A leader earns influence by adjusting to the expectations of followers. In one variant of the transactional approach, the leader reaps the benefits of status and influence in exchange for reducing uncertainty and providing followers with a basis for action. In another variant, bargaining and persuasion are the essence of political power, requiring a keen understanding of the interests of various stakeholders, both professional and public.

Each of these theories is generally considered to be value-free, but in fact their values are simply hidden. The great-man or trait approach places value on the historymaker, the person with extraordinary influence. Although the approach does not specify in what direction influence must be wielded to constitute leadership, the very suggestion that the mark of a great man is his historical impact on society gives us a particular perspective on greatness. Placing Hitler in the same general category as Gandhi or Lincoln does not render the theory value-free. On the contrary, it simply leaves its central value—influence—implicit.

The situational approach, ironically, does something similar. It departs radically from the great-man view by suggesting that certain people emerge to prominence because the times and social forces call them forth. Yet leaders are still assumed to be those people who gain prominence in society. The people that a trait theorist would select to study from history, the situational theorist would select as well.

Contingency theory, synthesizing the great-man and situational approaches, also began with a value-free image of itself. It examines which decisionmaking style fits which situational contingency in order for the decisionmaker to maintain control of the process. Sometimes a directive, task-oriented style is the most effective, and at other times a participative, relationship-oriented style is required. Yet even in this more specific rendition of the traditional view, the mark of leadership is still influence, or control.

Advocates of transactional approaches, focusing on how influence is gained and maintained, also see themselves as value-neutral. Although they describe elegantly the relational dynamics of influence, they do not evaluate the purpose to which influence is put or the way purposes are derived. By stating that the mark of leadership is influence over outcomes, these theorists unwittingly enter the value realm. Leadership-as-influence implicitly promotes influence as an orienting value, perpetuating a confusion between means and ends.

These four general approaches attempt to define leadership objectively, without making value judgments. When defining leadership in terms of prominence, authority, and influence, however, these theories introduce value-biases implicitly without declaring their introduction and without arguing for the necessity of the values introduced. From a research point of view, this presents no real problem. Indeed, it simplifies the analytic task. The problem emerges when we communicate and model these descriptions as "leadership" because "leadership" in many cultures is a normative idea — it represents a set of orienting values, as do words like "hero" and "champion." If we leave the value implications of our teaching and practice unaddressed, we encourage people, perhaps unwittingly, to aspire to great influence or high office, regardless of what they do there. We would be on safer ground were we to discard the loaded term leadership altogether and simply describe the dynamics of prominence, power, influence, and historical causation. . . .

Toward a Prescriptive Concept of Leadership

. . . Rather than define leadership either as a position of authority in a social structure or as a personal set of characteristics, we may find it a great deal more useful to define leadership as an *activity*. This allows for leadership from multiple positions in a social structure. A President and a clerk can both lead. It also allows for the use of a variety of abilities depending on the demands of the culture and situation. Personal abilities are resources for leadership applied differently in different contexts. As we know, at times they are not applied at all. Many people never exercise leadership, even though they have the personal qualities we might commonly associate with it. By unhinging leadership from personality traits, we permit observations of the many different ways in which people exercise plenty of leadership everyday without "being leaders."

The common personalistic orientation to the term leadership, with its assumption that "leaders are born and not made," is quite dangerous. It fosters both self-delusion and irresponsibility. For those who consider themselves "born leaders," free of an orienting philosophy and strategy of leadership, their grandiosity is a set-up for a rude awakening and for blindly doing damage. Minimally, they can waste the time and effort of a community on projects that go, if not over a cliff, then at least in circles. Conversely, those who consider themselves "not leaders" escape responsibility for taking action, or for learning how to take action, when they see the need. In the face of critical problems, they say, "I'm not a leader, what can I do?"

So, we ought to focus on leadership as an activity—the activity of a citizen from any walk of life mobilizing people to do something. But what is the socially useful something? What mode of leadership is likely to generate socially useful outcomes? Several approaches to these questions might work. We could imagine that a leader is more likely to produce socially useful outcomes by setting goals that meet the needs of both the leader and followers. This has the benefit of distinguishing leadership from merely "getting people to do what you want them to do." Leadership is more than influence.

Even so, setting a goal to meet the needs of the community may give no definition of what those needs are. If a leader personally wants to turn away from the difficulty of problems, and so do his constituents, does he exercise leadership by coming up with a fake remedy?

To address this problem, the leadership theorist James MacGregor Burns suggested that socially useful goals not only have to meet the needs of followers, they also should elevate followers to a higher moral level. Calling this *transformational leadership*, he posits that people begin with the need for survival and security, and once those needs are met, concern themselves with "higher" needs like affection, belonging, the common good, or serving others. This approach has the benefit of provoking discussion about how to construct a hierarchy of orienting values. However, a hierarchy that would apply across cultures and organizational settings risks either being so general as to be impractical or so specific as to be culturally imperialistic in its application.

We might also say that leadership has a higher probability of producing socially useful results when defined in terms of legitimate authority, with legitimacy based on a set of procedures by which power is conferred from the many to the few. This view is attractive because we might stop glorifying usurpations of power as leadership. But by restraining the exercise of leadership to legitimate authority, we also leave no room for leadership that challenges the legitimacy of authority or the system of authorization itself. No doubt, there are risks to freeing leadership from its moorings of legitimate authority. . . . Yet we also face an important possibility: social progress may require that someone push the system to its limit. . . . Hence, a person who leads may have to risk his moral state, and not just his health and job, to protect his moral state. Defining leadership in terms of legitimate authority excludes those who faced moral doubt and deep regret by defying authority. Vaclav Havel, Lech Walesa, Aung San Suu Kyi, Martin Luther King Jr., Margaret Sanger, and Mohandas Gandhi, to name a few, risked social disaster by unleashing uncontrollable social forces.

Business schools and schools of management commonly define leadership and its usefulness with respect to organizational effectiveness. Effectiveness means reaching viable decisions that implement the goals of the organization. This definition has the benefit of being generally applicable, but it provides no real guide to determine the nature or formation of those goals. Which goals should we pursue? What constitutes effectiveness in addition to the ability to generate profits? From the perspective of a town official viewing a local corporation, effectiveness at implementation seems an insufficient criterion. A chemical plant may be quite effective at earning a profit while it dangerously pollutes the local water supply. We are left with the question: Effective at what?

This study examines the usefulness of viewing leadership in terms of adaptive work. Adaptive work consists of the learning required to address conflicts in the values people hold, or to diminish the gap between the values people stand for and the reality they face. Adaptive work requires a change in values, beliefs, or behavior. The exposure and orchestration of conflict — internal contradictions — within individuals and constituencies provide the leverage for mobilizing people to learn new ways.

In this view, getting people to clarify what matters most, in what balance, with what trade-offs, becomes a central task. In the case of a local industry that pollutes the river, people want clean water, but they also want jobs. Community and company interests frequently overlap and clash, with conflicts taking place not only among factions but also within the lives of individual citizens who themselves may have competing needs. Leadership requires orchestrating these conflicts among and within the interested parties, and not just between the members and formal shareholders of the organization. Who should play a part in the deliberations is not a given, but is itself a critical strategic question. Strategy begins with asking: Which stakeholders have to adjust their ways to make progress on this problem? How can one sequence the issues or strengthen the bonds that join the stakeholders together as a community of interests so that they withstand the stresses of problem-solving?

. . . The implication is important: *the inclusion of competing value perspectives may be essential to adaptive success.* In the long run, an industrial polluter will fail if it neglects the interests of its community. Given the spread of environmental values, it may not always be able to move across borders. Conversely, the community may lose its economic base if it neglects the interests of its industry.

The point here is to provide a guide to goal formation and strategy. In selecting adaptive work as a guide, one considers not only the values that the goal represents, but also the goal's ability to mobilize people to face, rather than avoid, tough realities and conflicts. The hardest and most valuable task of leadership may be advancing goals and designing strategy that promote adaptive work. . . .

Warren Bennis, one of America's first prominent scholars of leadership, offers his definition of its key characteristics in the following excerpt, and draws a commonly cited distinction between leaders and managers.

WARREN BENNIS, ON BECOMING A LEADER

(Cambridge, MA: Perseus Publishing, 2002),
pp. 31-35, 39-40, 86, 89-91, and 108-109

... [Leaders] all seem to share some, if not all, of the following ingredients:

- The first basic ingredient of leadership is a *guiding vision*. The leader has a clear idea of what he or she wants to do—professionally and personally—and the strength to persist in the face of setbacks, even failures. Unless you know where you're going, and why, you cannot possibly get there. ...
- The second basic ingredient of leadership is *passion*—the underlying passion for the promises of life, combined with a very particular passion for a vocation, a profession, a course of action. The leader loves what he or she does and loves doing it. ...
- The next basic ingredient of leadership is *integrity*. I think there are three essential parts of integrity: self-knowledge, candor, and maturity.

"Know thyself" was the inscription over the Oracle at Delphi. And it is still the most difficult task any of us faces. But until you truly know yourself, strengths and weaknesses, know what you want to do and why you want to do it, you cannot succeed in any but the most superficial sense of the word. Leaders never lie to themselves, especially about themselves, know their faults as well as their assets, and deal with them directly. You are your own raw material. When you know what you consist of and what you want to make of it, then you can invent yourself.

Candor is the key to self-knowledge. Candor is based in honesty of thought and action, a steadfast devotion to principle, and a fundamental soundness and wholeness. ...

Even though I talk about basic ingredients, I'm not talking about traits that you're born with and can't change. As countless deposed kings and hapless heirs to great fortunes can attest, true leaders are not born, but made, and usually self-made. Leaders invent themselves. They are not, by the way, made in a single weekend seminar, as many of the leadership-theory spokesmen claim. I've come to think of that one as the microwave theory: pop in Mr. or Ms. Average and out pops McLeader in sixty seconds. ...

Leaders, Not Managers

I tend to think of the differences between leaders and managers as the differences between those who master the context and those who surrender to it. There are other differences, as well, and they are enormous and crucial:

- The manager administers; the leader innovates. ...
- The manager has a short-range view; the leader has a long-range perspective.
- The manager asks how and when; the leader asks what and why.
- The manager has his or her eye always on the bottom line; the leader's eye is on the horizon. ...
- The manager does things right; the leader does the right thing. ...

PROBLEM 1-1

One key quality of leaders is self-knowledge. Understanding your core values, aspirations, and identity can help guide you to positions in which you can develop as a leader. To that end, complete two of the following self-assessment exercises.

A. What are ten qualities that best define you on the dimensions relevant to leadership? Ask someone who knows you well the same question. Compare your lists.[78]

B. Name three leadership positions that you would like to have, or three organizations in which you would like a leadership position. What is distinctive about these work settings? What does creating the list tell you about your most important values?

C. Create a list of key personal values and preferences relevant to leadership. For example:
   - What are your professional goals?
   - What do you most want to accomplish in your career? What will make your work meaningful?
   - What is your tolerance for risk? For conflict?
   - What kind of work do you like most and least? In what professional contexts do you feel most challenged and effective?[79]
   - Complete either the Meyers-Brigg Types Inventory of personal characteristics, which rates individuals on four dimensions (introversion-extroversion, sensing-intuition, thinking-feeling, and judging-feeling), or the Five Factor Model of personality, which uses five factors (neuroticism, extraversion, openness, agreeableness, and conscientiousness).[80] What does this assessment suggest about the kinds of leadership positions in which you would be most effective?

NOTES AND QUESTIONS

1. How would you define leadership?

2. As you observe leaders, do you see characteristics that are particularly critical? Is it possible to generalize? Think of three individuals from history or personal experience whose leadership you particularly admire. What qualities were most important? Why?

3. What makes leaders effective in some contexts but not in others? Break into groups and identify a leader who both succeeded and failed. What accounts for the different outcomes?

4. Does effective leadership presuppose ethical leadership? Were Hitler, Mao, and Lenin effective leaders?[81] Is the ultimate test of leadership influence, or does it presuppose something more? Richard Nixon once claimed that in "evaluating a leader, the key question about his behavioral traits is not whether they are attractive or unattractive, but whether they are useful."[82] Do you agree? Does the research summarized below suggest that these criteria are related?

5. What is the relationship between power and leadership? Harvard Professor Rosabeth Moss Kanter claimed that power was "America's last dirty word."

And despite its importance for leaders, "it is easier to talk about money — and much easier to talk about sex — than it is to talk about power."[83] John Gardner famously observed that in most democracies "power has such a bad name that many good people persuade themselves they want nothing to do with it." Yet in Gardner's view, the negative connotations are undeserved. "To say a leader is preoccupied with power, is like saying that a tennis player is preoccupied with making shots his opponent cannot return. Of course leaders are preoccupied with power! The significant questions are: What means do they use to gain it[?] . . . To what ends do they exercise it?"[84] How comfortable would you be if someone accused you of being focused on power? Would you be satisfied giving Gardner's response?

Harvard psychologist David McClelland famously distinguished between power exercised to control others and power exercised to enable them. Building on that distinction, a growing number of leadership experts emphasize the value of using power to empower.[85] Have you observed that distinction? Consider its importance in light of the discussion of leadership styles in Chapter 2, and relationships with followers in Chapter 4.

6. Are the qualities necessary to gain leadership the same as those necessary to gain power? Stanford Business School professor Jeffrey Pfeffer maintains that power is a function of "will and skill." Will includes ambition, energy, and focus; skill includes self-knowledge, confidence, empathy, and capacity to tolerate conflict.[86] To what extent do these overlap with the qualities of effective leadership described below?

7. Are you persuaded by Bennis's distinctions between leaders and managers? Think of an organization in which you have worked. Which of the qualities that he identifies were most critical to its performance?

8. One interesting finding of some research on leadership traits is that typical leaders are only slightly more intelligent than the groups they lead, and the most intelligent person in a group is not the one most likely to become its leader. In general, people do not like to be led by those who seem very much smarter than themselves.[87] Nor is intelligence a good predictor of power.[88] This disconnect between leadership and intelligence is captured in titles of books about the leaders responsible for the Vietnam War (*The Best and the Brightest*) and the Enron scandal (*The Smartest Guys in the Room*). What accounts for this disconnect? Arrogance? Overconfidence? Inability to understand or value others' concerns and perspectives?[89] What implications do these findings have for aspiring leaders?

C. WHAT QUALITIES ARE CRITICAL FOR LEADERSHIP?

Although, as noted earlier, researchers have identified no single personality trait that correlates with successful leadership across all circumstances, they have identified qualities that tend to make leaders effective. Peter Northouse, after reviewing a century's worth of studies, clusters a wide range of characteristics into five main categories: intelligence, self-confidence, determination, integrity, and sociability (i.e., interpersonal skills).[90] Robert Hogan and Robert Kaiser's overview of research similarly found that self-esteem, integrity, and cognitive ability correlated with organizational effectiveness.[91]

Other experts have looked at leadership in particular fields. The federal Office of Personnel Management and experts on public administration emphasize integrity, decisiveness, self-direction, resilience, flexibility, emotional maturity, and an ethic of service.[92] Maureen Broderick's study of personal service firms, including law firms, identified the capacity to influence and build coalitions, to inspire and be visionary, and to listen and communicate effectively.[93] James Kouzes and Barry Posner's survey of some 7500 corporate leaders identified four key qualities: honest, forward-looking, inspiring, and competent.[94] The Harvard Good Work project, which interviewed some 1200 leaders from a range of professions, cited excellence in technical and professional competence, ethical orientation, an engaged sense of fulfillment, and meaning in work.[95]

At the abstract level, few would disagree about the desirability of these characteristics. At the practical level, however, they have not always been shown to correlate with outcomes or other measures of effectiveness.[96] Moreover, in many contexts, competing values and situational pressures tug in different directions. For example, is empathy always the best policy? Empathy for whom? To what extent do we want leaders to empathize with the inevitable civilian casualties of military operations — euphemistically identified as "collateral damage"? Many brutal leaders are selectively empathetic; Hitler, for example, was responsive to concerns of the great majority of the German people.

James Kouzes and Barry Posner's *The Leadership Challenge*, excerpted below, identifies practices that are key to effective leadership: model the way, inspire a shared vision, challenge the process, enable others to act, foster trust and collaboration, and encourage the heart. Do these seem adequate descriptions? Can you identify examples of such practices in leaders whom you admire?

JAMES M. KOUZES AND BARRY Z. POSNER,
THE LEADERSHIP CHALLENGE (4TH ED.)

(San Francisco: Jossey-Bass, 2007), pp. 14-23, 28-30, and 32-35

The Five Practices of Exemplary Leadership

. . . As we looked deeper into the dynamic process of leadership, through case analyses and survey questionnaires, we uncovered five practices common to personal-best leadership experiences. When getting extraordinary things done in organizations, leaders engage in these Five Practices of Exemplary Leadership:

- Model the Way
- Inspire a Shared Vision
- Challenge the Process
- Enable Others to Act
- Encourage the Heart . . .

Model the Way

Titles are granted, but it's your behavior that wins you respect. . . . Exemplary leaders know that if they want to gain commitment and achieve the highest standards, they must be models of the behavior they expect of others. *Leaders model the way.*

To effectively model the behavior they expect of others, leaders must first be clear about guiding principles. They must *clarify values.* . . . Leaders must forge agreement around common principles and common ideals.

. . . Sure, leaders had operational and strategic plans. But the examples they gave were not about elaborate designs. They were about the power of spending time with someone, of working side by side with colleagues, of telling stories that made values come alive, of being highly visible during times of uncertainty, and of asking questions to get people to think about values and priorities.

Modeling the way is about earning the right and the respect to lead through direct involvement and action. People follow first the person, then the plan.

Inspire a Shared Vision

. . . Every organization, every social movement, begins with a dream. The dream or vision is the force that invents the future. *Leaders inspire a shared vision.* . . . They *envision exciting and ennobling possibilities.* Leaders have a desire to make something happen, to change the way things are, to create something that no one else has ever created before. . . . Leaders cannot command commitment, only inspire it.

Leaders have to *enlist others in a common vision.* To enlist people in a vision, leaders must know their constituents and speak their language. People must believe that leaders understand their needs and have their interests at heart. Leadership is a dialogue, not a monologue. To enlist support, leaders must have intimate knowledge of people's dreams, hopes, aspirations, visions, and values. . . .

Challenge the Process

Leaders are pioneers. They are willing to step out into the unknown. They *search for opportunities to innovate, grow, and improve.* But leaders aren't the only creators or originators of new products, services, or processes. In fact, it's more likely that they're not: innovation comes more from listening than from telling. . . .

When it comes to innovation, the leader's major contributions are in the creation of a climate for experimentation, the recognition of good ideas, the support of those ideas, and the willingness to challenge the system to get new products, processes, services, and systems adopted. It might be more accurate, then, to say that leaders aren't the inventors as much as they are the early patrons and adopters of innovation.

Leaders know well that innovation and change involve *experimenting and taking risks.* Despite the inevitability of mistakes and failures leaders proceed anyway. One way of dealing with the potential risks and failures of experimentation is to approach change through incremental steps and small wins. . . . Claude Meyer, with the Red Cross in Kenya, put it to us this way: "Leadership is learning by doing, adapting to actual conditions. Leaders are constantly learning from their errors and failures." Life is the leader's laboratory, and exemplary leaders use it to conduct as many experiments as possible. Try, fail, learn. Try, fail, learn. Try, fail, learn. That's the leader's mantra. Leaders are learners. They learn from their failures as well as their successes, and they make it possible for others to do the same.

Enable Others to Act

Grand dreams don't become significant realities through the actions of a single person. It requires a team effort. It requires solid trust and strong relationships. . . . Leaders *foster collaboration and build trust.* . . . Leaders make it possible for others to do good work. They know that those who are expected to produce the results must feel a sense of personal power and ownership. . . .

Encourage the Heart

. . . Genuine acts of caring uplift the spirits and draw people forward. . . . *Recognizing contributions* can be one-to-one or with many people. It can come from dramatic gestures or simple actions. . . . It's part of the leader's job to show appreciation for people's contributions and to create a culture of *celebrating values and victories.* . . . [These are not] about pretentious ceremonies designed to create some phony sense of camaraderie. . . . Encouragement is, curiously, serious business. It's how leaders visibly and behaviorally link rewards with performance [and] . . . build a strong sense of collective identity and community spirit that can carry a group through extraordinarily tough times. . . .

What People Look for and Admire in Leaders

We began our research on what constituents expect of leaders more than twenty-five years ago by surveying thousands of business and government executives. We asked the following *open-ended* question: "What values, personal traits, or characteristics do you look for and admire in a leader?" . . .

From [the responses], we developed a survey questionnaire called "Characteristics of Admired Leaders." We've administered this questionnaire to over seventy-five thousand people around the globe, and we update the findings continuously. We distribute a one-page checklist and ask respondents to select the seven qualities that they "most look for and admire in a leader, someone whose direction they would willingly follow." We tell them that the key word in this question is *willingly.* What do they expect from a leader they would follow, not because they have to, but because they want to?

The results have been striking in their regularity over the years, and they do not significantly vary by demographical, organizational, or cultural differences. Wherever we've asked the question, it's clear, as the data in [the following t]able illustrate, that there are a few essential "character tests" someone must pass before others are willing to grant the designation *leader.*

Although every characteristic receives some votes, and therefore each is important to some people, what is most striking and most evident is that only four over time (with the exception of Inspiring in 1987) have always received over 60 percent of the votes. And these same four have consistently been ranked at the top *across different countries.* . . .

What people most look for in a leader (a person that they would be willing to follow) has been constant over time. And our research documents this consistent pattern across countries, cultures, ethnicities, organizational functions and hierarchies, gender, educational, and age groups. For people to follow someone willingly, the majority of constituents believe the leader must be

- Honest
- Forward-looking
- Inspiring
- Competent . . .

Honest

In almost every survey we've conducted, honesty has been selected more often than any other leadership characteristic; overall, it emerges as the single most important factor in the leader-constituent relationship. The percentages vary, but the final ranking does not. Since the very first time we conducted our studies honesty has been at the top of the list.

It's clear that if people anywhere are to willingly follow someone— whether it's into battle or into the boardroom, the front office or the front lines—they first want to assure themselves that the person is worthy of their trust. They want to know that the person is truthful, ethical, and principled. When people talk to us about the qualities they admire in leaders, they often use the terms *integrity* and *character* as synonymous with honesty. . . .

We want our leaders to be honest because their honesty is also a reflection upon our own honesty. Of all the qualities that people look for and admire in a leader, honesty is by far the most personal. More than likely this is also why it consistently ranks number one. It's the quality that can most enhance or most damage our own personal reputations. . . .

Forward-Looking

A little more than 70 percent of our most recent respondents selected the ability to look ahead as one of their most sought-after leadership traits. People expect leaders to have a sense of direction and a concern for the future of the organization. This expectation directly corresponds to the ability to envision the future that leaders described in their personal-best cases. Whether we call that ability vision, a dream, a calling, a goal, or a personal agenda, the message is clear: leaders must know where they're going if they expect others to willingly join them on the journey. . . .

We want to know what the organization will look like, feel like, and be like when it arrives at its destination in six quarters or six years. We want to have it described to us in rich detail so that we can select the proper route for getting there and know when we've arrived.

Clarity of vision into the distant future may be difficult to attain, but it's essential that leaders seek the knowledge and master the skills necessary to envision what's across the horizon. Compared to all the other leadership qualities constituents expect, this is the one that most distinguishes leaders from other credible people. Expecting leaders to be forward-looking doesn't mean constituents want their leaders to set out on a solitary vision quest; people want to be engaged in the search for a meaningful future. . . . But this expectation does mean that leaders have a special responsibility to attend to the future of their organizations.

Characteristics of Admired Leaders

Characteristic	Percentage of Respondents Selecting Each Characteristic (2007 ed.)
HONEST	89
FORWARD-LOOKING	71
INSPIRING	69
COMPETENT	68
Intelligent	48
Fair-minded	39
Straightforward	36
Broad-minded	35
Supportive	35
Dependable	34
Cooperative	25
Courageous	25
Determined	25
Caring	22
Imaginative	17
Mature	15
Ambitious	16
Loyal	18
Self-Controlled	10
Independent	4

Note: These percentages represent respondents from six continents: Africa, North America, South America, Asia, Europe, and Australia. The majority of respondents are from the United States. Since we asked people to select seven characteristics, the total adds up to more than 100 percent.

Inspiring

People expect their leaders to be enthusiastic, energetic, and positive about the future. It's not enough for a leader to have a dream. A leader must be able to communicate the vision in ways that encourage people to sign on for the duration and excite them about the cause. . . .

Inspiring leadership also speaks to constituents' need to have meaning and purpose in their lives. Being upbeat, positive, and optimistic about the future offers people hope. . . .

Competent

To enlist in a common cause, people must believe that the leader is competent to guide them where they're headed. They must see the leader as having relevant experience and sound judgment. If they doubt the person's abilities, they're unlikely to join in the crusade.

Leadership competence refers to the leader's track record and ability to get things done. . . .

Another key characteristic of effective leaders is what Daniel Goleman, Richard Boyatzis, and Annie McKee describe as "emotional intelligence": (1) personal competence, involving self-awareness and self-management; and (2) social competence, involving social awareness (i.e., empathy) and relationship management (i.e., persuasion, conflict management, and collaboration). Their research suggests that these skills enable individuals to find resonance with wide groups, identify common ground, build rapport, and move people toward a common vision.[97]

DANIEL GOLEMAN, RICHARD BOYATZIS, AND ANNIE MCKEE,
PRIMAL LEADERSHIP: LEARNING TO LEAD WITH EMOTIONAL INTELLIGENCE

(Boston: Harvard Business School Press, 2002), pp. 38-40 and 45-52

. . . Interestingly, no leader we've ever encountered, no matter how outstanding, has strengths across the board in every one of the many EI [(emotional intelligence)] competencies. Highly effective leaders typically exhibit a critical mass of strength in a half dozen or so EI competencies. Moreover, there's no fixed formula for great leadership: There are many paths to excellence, and superb leaders can possess very different personal styles. Still, we find that effective leaders typically demonstrate strengths in at least one competence from each of the four fundamental areas of emotional intelligence.

Self-Awareness

Simply put, self-awareness means having a deep understanding of one's emotions, as well as one's strengths and limitations and one's values and motives. People with strong self-awareness are realistic—neither overly self-critical nor naively hopeful. Rather, they are honest with themselves about themselves. And they are honest about themselves with others, even to the point of being able to laugh at their own foibles.

Self-aware leaders also understand their values, goals, and dreams. They know where they're headed and why. They're attuned to what "feels right" to them. For example, they're able to be firm in turning down a job offer that's tempting financially but doesn't fit with their principles or long-term goals. Conversely, a person lacking self-awareness will likely make decisions that trigger inner turmoil by treading on buried values. "The money looked good so I signed on," someone might say two years into a job, "but the work means so little to me that I'm constantly bored." Because the decisions of self-aware people mesh with their values, they more often find their work energizing.

Perhaps the most telling (though least visible) sign of self-awareness is a propensity for self-reflection and thoughtfulness. Self-aware people typically find time to reflect quietly, often off by themselves, which allows them to think things over rather than react impulsively. Many outstanding leaders, in fact, bring to their work life the thoughtful mode of self-reflection that they cultivate in their spiritual lives. For some this means prayer or meditation; for others it's a more philosophical quest for self-understanding.

All of these traits of self-aware leaders enable them to act with the conviction and authenticity that resonance requires. . . .

In short, intuition offers EI leaders a direct pipeline to their accumulated life wisdom on a topic. And it takes the inner attunement of self-awareness to sense that message.

The Leader's Primal Challenge: Self-Management

From self-awareness—understanding one's emotions and being clear about one's purpose—flows self-management, the focused drive that all leaders need to achieve their goals. Without knowing what we're feeling, we're at a loss to manage those feelings. Instead, our emotions control us. That's usually fine, when it comes to positive emotions like enthusiasm and the pleasure of meeting a challenge. But no leader can afford to be controlled by negative emotions, such as frustration and rage or anxiety and panic.

The problem is that such negative emotional surges can be overwhelming; they're the brain's way of making us pay attention to a perceived threat. The result is that those emotions swamp the thinking brain's capacity to focus on the task at hand, whether it's strategic planning or dealing with news of a drop in market share. . . .

Self-management, then—which resembles an ongoing inner conversation—is the component of emotional intelligence that frees us from being a prisoner of our feelings. It's what allows the mental clarity and concentrated energy that leadership demands, and what keeps disruptive emotions from throwing us off track. Leaders with such self-mastery embody an upbeat, optimistic enthusiasm that tunes resonance to the positive range. . . .

Similarly, leaders who can stay optimistic and upbeat, even under intense pressure, radiate the positive feelings that create resonance. By staying in control of their feelings and impulses, they craft an environment of trust, comfort, and fairness. And that self-management has a trickle-down effect from the leader. No one wants to be known as a hothead when the boss consistently exudes a calm demeanor. . . .

Social Awareness and the Limbic Tango

After self-awareness and emotional self-management, resonant leadership requires social awareness or, put another way, empathy. . . .

While empathy represents a necessary ingredient of EI leadership, another lies in leaders' ability to express their message in a way that moves others. Resonance flows from a leader who expresses feelings with conviction because those emotions are clearly authentic, rooted in deeply held values. . . .

Social awareness—particularly empathy—is crucial for the leader's primal task of driving resonance. By being attuned to how others feel in the moment, a leader can say and do what's appropriate—whether it be to calm fears, assuage anger, or join in good spirits. This attunement also lets a leader sense the shared values and priorities that can guide the group. By the same token, a leader who lacks empathy will unwittingly be off-key, and so speak and act in ways that set off negative reactions. Empathy—which includes listening and taking other people's perspectives — allows leaders to tune into the emotional channels between people that create resonance. And staying attuned lets them fine-tune their message to keep it in synch.

Empathy: The Business Case

Of all the dimensions of emotional intelligence, social awareness may be the most easily recognized. We have all felt the empathy of a sensitive teacher or friend; we have all been struck by its absence in an unfeeling coach or boss. But when it comes to business, we rarely hear people praised, let alone rewarded, for their empathy. The very word seems unbusinesslike, out of place amid the tough realities of the marketplace.

But empathy — the fundamental competence of social awareness — doesn't mean a kind of "I'm okay, you're okay" mushiness. It doesn't mean that leaders should adopt other people's emotions as their own and try to please everybody. That would be a nightmare — it would make action impossible. Rather, empathy means taking employees' feelings into thoughtful consideration and then making intelligent decisions that work those feelings into the response. . . .

Empathetic people are superb at recognizing and meeting the needs of clients, customers, or subordinates. They seem approachable, wanting to hear what people have to say. They listen carefully, picking up on what people are truly concerned about, and they respond on the mark. . . .

Finally, in the growing global economy, empathy is a critical skill for both getting along with diverse workmates and doing business with people from other cultures. Cross-cultural dialogue can easily lead to miscues and misunderstandings. Empathy is an antidote that attunes people to subtleties in body language, or allows them to hear the emotional message beneath the words.

Relationship Management

The triad of self-awareness, self-management, and empathy all come together in the final EI ability: relationship management. Here we find the most visible tools of leadership — persuasion, conflict management, and collaboration among them. Managing relationships skillfully boils down to handling other people's emotions. This, in turn, demands that leaders be aware of their own emotions and attuned with empathy to the people they lead.

If a leader acts disingenuously or manipulatively, for instance, the emotional radar of followers will sense a note of falseness and they will instinctively distrust that leader. The art of handling relationships well, then, begins with authenticity: acting from one's genuine feelings. Once leaders have attuned to their own vision and values, steadied in the positive emotional range, and tuned into the emotions of the group, then relationship management skills let them interact in ways that catalyze resonance.

Handling relationships, however, is not as simple as it sounds. It's not just a matter of friendliness, although people with strong social skills are rarely mean-spirited. Rather, relationship management is friendliness with a purpose: moving people in the right direction, whether that's agreement on a marketing strategy or enthusiasm about a new project.

That is why socially skilled leaders tend to have resonance with a wide circle of people — and have a knack for finding common ground and building rapport. That doesn't mean they socialize continually; it means they work under the assumption that nothing important gets done alone. Such leaders have a network in place when the time for action comes. And in an era when more and more work is done long distance—by e-mail or by phone—relationship building, paradoxically, becomes more crucial than ever.

Given the primal task of leadership, the ability to inspire and move people with a compelling vision looms large. Inspirational leaders get people excited about a common mission. They offer a sense of purpose beyond the day-to-day tasks or quarterly goals that so often take the place of a meaningful vision. Such leaders know that what people value most deeply will move them most powerfully in their work. Because they are aware of their own guiding values, they can articulate a vision that has the ring of truth for those they lead. That strong sense of the collective mission also leaves inspirational leaders free to direct and guide with firmness.

NOTES AND QUESTIONS

1. Not all leaders seem to have the emotional intelligence that Goleman, Boyatzis, and McKee describe. Many politicians, such as Margaret Thatcher or more recently Rahm Emanuel, President Obama's former chief of staff, have been portrayed as abrasive, arrogant, or lacking in interpersonal skills.[98] CEOs (including such legendary leaders as Steve Jobs) have frequently lost positions in part due to arrogance and inability to relate well to others.[99] Stanford Business School professor Roderick Kramer's portrayal of "great intimidators," excerpted in Chapter 2, describes others. What accounts for their success despite such personal failures?
2. Although some leaders, such as George H.W. Bush, have dismissed the "vision thing," most research underscores the importance of an inspiring mission—an appealing and credible image of the future.[100] How would you describe the vision of a leader or an organization that you admire?
3. Think of some examples of leadership behavior in literature and film. What characteristics of exemplary leadership or emotional intelligence seem present or lacking? Of those you come up with, which leaders do you most admire or would you most want to follow?

PROBLEM 1-2

Create a list of seven qualities that you think would be most useful for a leadership position that you could envision yourself occupying. Rate yourself from one to five on each of those characteristics. Ask several individuals who know you reasonably well to do the same on an anonymous form and develop a mean for each of these traits. How do your self-ratings compare with their ratings?[101] What areas of improvement do the ratings suggest?

MEDIA RESOURCES

Many films and television series offer useful snapshots of leadership. The opening scenes of *Primary Colors*, a film based on Bill Clinton's initial presidential primary campaign, shows the magnetism and empathetic responses that enabled him to connect so well with voters. Many episodes in the television series *The West Wing* offer interesting portraits of White House leadership. Jon Stewart satirizes Rahm Emanual's style in a January 26, 2011, *Daily Show* discussion of the Chicago mayoral battle. *Michael Clayton*, starring George Clooney as a fixer for a prominent corporate law firm, shows lawyers exercising a range of soft and hard power.

The BBC series *Yes Minister* provides a window on leadership issues through the experience of Ian Hacker, a fictional minister of Great Britain's Department of Administrative Affairs, and Sir Humphrey, the department's permanent undersecretary. The first episode on "open government" works particularly well as an introduction to the difference between hard and soft power, and between what makes a successful politician and a successful cabinet minister. To teach Hacker a lesson about the limits of transparency and his own fallibility, Sir Humphrey lets Hacker discover a confidential governmental contract to purchase computer equipment from American rather than British suppliers. On advice of his campaign director, Hacker prepares a press statement denouncing the deal. Sir Humphrey sees that a preliminary draft reaches the prime minister, who is furious that the criticism might jeopardize sensitive negotiations with the United States government on a far more important issue. Fortunately, the statement was not issued because of what Sir Humphrey claims was his own inadvertent "error." The scene ends with Hacker pompously forgiving Sir Humphrey because "we all make mistakes," and Sir Humphrey pointedly responding that indeed "we" do. The episode provides a classic illustration of why hard power, such as Hacker's command and control authority, is often less effective than soft power, such as Sir Humphrey's knowledge of how to lead in a bureaucracy. A particularly interesting question for discussion is why Sir Humphrey does not claim credit for saving Hacker from his own mistake. One possible answer involves what creates the most effective learning experience, which forms a natural bridge to the materials that follow.

END NOTES

1. See Rakesh Khurana, The Retreat of Professionalism in Business Education, University of St. Thomas Law Review 6 (2009):433; Edelman, 2009 Edelman Trust Barometer Executive Summary (2009); Pew Global Attitudes Project (2006).

2. Harris Poll, March 5, 2009; The Harris Poll Annual Confidence Index Rises 10 Points (March 5, 2009), available at http://www.harrisinteractive.com/harris_poll/pubs/Harris_Poll_2009_03_05.pdf.

3. The PEW Research Center for People and the Press, The People and Their Government: Distrust, Discontent, Anger, and Partisan Rancor (April 18, 2010), available at http://www.people-press.org/reports/pdf/606.pdf.

4. In his classic 1954 book on management, Peter Drucker summed up conventional wisdom: "Leadership cannot be taught or learned." Peter E. Drucker, The Practice of Management (New York: Harper Collins, 1954), 194. For contemporary research, see, e.g., Roger Gill, The Theory and Practice of Leadership (Thousand Oaks, CA: Sage, 2006), 271; for Drucker, see Peter Drucker, Foreword, The Leader of the Future (New York: Jossey-Bass, 1996), xi (noting that "leadership must be learned and can be learned").

5. For twins studies, see R. Avery, M. Rotundo, W. Johnson, and M. McGue, The Determinants of Leadership Role Occupancy: Genetic and Personality Factors, Leadership Quarterly 17 (2006):1;

Bruce Avolio, Pursuing Authentic Leadership Development, in Nitin Nohria and Rakesh Khurana, eds., Handbook of Leadership Theory and Practice (Cambridge, MA: Harvard Business Press, 2010), 739, 752. Warren G. Bennis and Bert Nanus, Leadership: Strategies for Taking Charge (New York: Harper Collins, 1997), 207.

6. Keith Grint, Leadership: Classical, Contemporary, and Critical Approaches (New York: Oxford University Press, 1997), 2.

7. Jacob Heilbrunn, Interim Report, New York Times Book Review, May 30, 2010, 12.

8. William A. Cohen, Drucker on Leadership (San Francisco: Jossey-Bass, 2010), 204.

9. For corporate expenditures, see Doris Gomez, The Leader as Learner, International Journal of Leadership Studies 2 (2007):280, 281. For courses, see Gregory Williams, Teaching Leaders and Leadership, AALS President's Message, April 1999, available at http://www.aals.org/presidents messages/leaders.html. The number has doubtless grown over the last decade. For growing recognition of the need for leadership education, see Richard Greenwald, Today's Students Need Leadership Training Like Never Before, Chronicle of Higher Education, December 6, 2010, http://chronicle.com/article/Todays-Students-Need/125604.

10. At last count, some thirty-eight schools had mission statements that included fostering leadership, but only two of these schools were actually offering a leadership course. Neil W. Hamilton, Ethical Leadership in Professional Life, University of St. Thomas Law Journal 62 (2009):362, 370. For practice management, see G.M. Filisko, Getting the Business, ABA Journal (August 2010):24.

11. Hamilton, Ethical Leadership in Professional Life, 361-362.

12. Over half of participants in one survey by the National Association for Law Placement (NALP) viewed leadership skills as very important in the decision to name equity partners. NALP Foundation, Navigating the Bridge to Partnership (Washington, D.C.: National Association for Law Placement Foundation, 2007), 86.

13. Bass and Stogdill's Handbook of Leadership: Theory, Research, and Managerial Applications (New York: Free Press, 3d ed. 1990); Gareth Edwards, In Search of the Holy Grail: Leadership in Management (Working Paper LT-GE-00-15 Ross-on-Wye, United Kingdom, Leadership Trust Foundation, 2000).

14. Roger Gill, Theory and Practice of Leadership (Los Angeles: Sage, 2006); Joseph C. Rost, Leadership for the Twenty-First Century (New York: Praeger, 1991), 38.

15. John W. Gardner, On Leadership (New York: Free Press, 1990), 3.

16. Deborah L. Rhode, Where Is the Leadership in Moral Leadership?, in Deborah L. Rhode, Moral Leadership: The Theory and Practice of Power, Judgment, and Policy (San Francisco: Jossey-Bass, 2006), 1, 4.

17. Thom Shanker, Retiring Army Chief of Staff Warns against Arrogance, New York Times, June 12, 2004, 32.

18. Montgomery Van Wart, Dynamics of Leadership in Public Service: Theory and Practice (Armonk, NY: M.E. Sharpe, 2005), 113.

19. John Gardner, On Leadership, 34.

20. Max Weber, The Sociology of Charismatic Authority, in H.H. Gerth and C. Wright Mills, trans. and ed., From Max Weber: Essays in Sociology (New York: Routledge, 2009), 245-246.

21. Gill, Theory and Practice of Leadership, 253; Ronald E. Riggio, The Charisma Quotient (New York: Dodd Mead, 1987) (chapters 2 and 3 discuss emotional and social sensitivity, expressiveness, and control).

22. See R.J. House, Path-Goal Theory of Leadership: Lessons, Legacy and Reformulated Theory, Leadership Quarterly 7 (1996): 323. Michael E. Brown and Linda K. Trevino, Is Values-Based Leadership Ethical Leadership?, in Gilliland, Emerging Perspectives on Values in Organizations (Charlotte, NC: Information Age Publishing, 2003), 151, 168.

23. J.A. Conger and R.N. Kanungo, Charismatic Leadership in Organizations (Thousand Oaks, CA: Sage, 1998).

24. R.N. Kanungo and M. Mendonca, Ethical Dimensions of Leadership (San Francisco: Jossey Bass, 1995), 20.

25. Herbert Spencer, The Great Man Theory Breaks Down, in Barbara Kellerman, ed., Political Leadership: A Source Book (Pittsburgh, PA: University of Pittsburgh Press, 1986), Chapter 13.

26. Joseph Nye, The Powers to Lead (New York: Oxford University Press, 2008), 5.

27. Nye, The Powers to Lead, 15.

28. Gardner, On Leadership, 65.

29. Joseph Badaracco, Questions of Character (Boston: Harvard Business Press, 2006), 82-83.

30. Walter R. Newell, The Soul of a Leader (New York: Harper Collins, 2009), 81-84.

31. Jeffrey Pfeffer, Managing with Power (Boston: Harvard Business Press, 1992), 305-306; David Halberstam, The Best and the Brightest (New York: Random House, 1972), 511; Newall, The Soul of a Leader, 65-66.

32. Gardner, On Leadership, 5-6, 47.

33. Nye, The Powers to Lead, 121-122.

34. Gill, Theory and Practice of Leadership, 39.

35. Jim Collins, Level 5 Leadership: The Triumph of Humility and Fierce Resolve, Harvard Business Review (January 2001):73; Gill, Theory and Practice of Leadership, 253.

36. Michael Hiltzik, Peter Drucker's Revolutionary Teachings Decades Old but Still Fresh, Los Angeles Times, December 31, 2009, http://articles.latimes.com/2009/dec/31/business/la-fi-hiltzik31-2009dec31.

37. Gary Yuki, Leading Organizational Learning: Reflections on Theory and Practice, Leadership Quarterly 20 (2010):49, 50.

38. James McGregor Burns, Leadership (New York: Harper and Row, 1978), 244. Robert Solomon argues that "charisma doesn't refer to any character trait or quality in particular, but is rather a general way of referring to a person who seems to be a dynamic and effective leader. And as a term of analysis in leadership studies, . . . it is more a distraction than a point of understanding." Robert C. Solomon, Ethical Leadership, Emotion and Trust: Beyond "Charisma," in Joanne B. Ciulla, ed., Ethics: The Heart of Leadership (Westport, CT: Praeger, 2d ed. 2004), 98. See also Gardner, On Leadership, 35.

39. James O'Toole, When Leadership Is an Organizational Trait, in Warren Bennis, Gretchen M. Spreitzer, and Thomas G. Cummings, The Future of Leadership (San Francisco: Jossey-Bass, 2001), 159.

40. J. Richard Hackman, What Is This Thing Called Leadership?, in Nohria and Khurana, Handbook of Leadership Theory and Practice, 110; Joel L. Podolney, Rakesh Khurana, and Max L. Besharov, Revisiting the Meaning of Leadership, in Noria and Khurana, Handbook of Leadership Theory and Practice, 53, 66.

41. Noria and Khurana, Advancing Leadership Theory and Practice, 9; Noah Wasserman, Bharat Anand, and Nitin Nohria, When Does Leadership Matter?, in Nohria and Khurana, Handbook on Leadership Theory and Practice, 27, 30-32, 49; Hackman, What Is This Thing Called Leadership?, 110.

42. For example, a recent statistical study by Laurie Bassi and Daniel McMurrer found that the most powerful predictor of large firm profitability is "the quality of the partners' leadership skills." Laurie Bassi and Daniel McMurrer, Leadership and Large Firm Success: A Statistical Analysis, March 2008, 5, available at http://www.mcbassi.com/resources/documents/WhitePaper-LeadershipAndLawFirmSuccess.pdf. For other evidence on the importance of leadership, see Jennifer A. Chatman and Jessica A. Kennedy, Psychological Perspective on Leadership, in Nohria and Khurana, Handbook of Theory and Practice, 159, 160.

43. Joe Wallis and Brian Dollery, Market Failure, Government Failure, Leadership, and Public Policy (London: MacMillan, 1999), 119, 125.

44. For overviews, see Gill, Theory and Practice of Leadership; Peter Guy Northouse, Leadership: Theory and Practice (Thousand Oaks, CA: Sage Publications, 3d ed. 2004).

45. For early development of the theory, see Fred E. Fiedler, A Theory of Leadership Effectiveness (New York: McGraw Hill, 1967); Fred E. Fiedler, Leadership: A New Model, in C.A. Gibb, ed., Leadership (New York: Penguin, 1969), 230-241.

46. Northouse, Leadership, 111-123; Hollander, Inclusive Leadership, 28.

47. Northouse, Leadership, 93-107; Hollander, Inclusive Leadership, 27.

48. Paul Hersey and Kenneth H. Blanchard, The Life Cycle Theory of Leadership, Training and Development Journal 23 (1969):26; Paul Hersey and Kenneth H. Blanchard, Management of Organizational Behavior: Utilizing Human Resources (Englewood Cliffs, NY: Prentice Hall, 6th ed. 1993); Northouse, Leadership, 89-90.

49. Wallis and Dollery, Market Failure, Government Failure, Leadership and Public Policy, 145.

50. For discussion of its influence, see Robert Goffee and Gareth Jones, Why Should Anyone Be Led by You?, Harvard Business Review (September-October 2000):63, 64; Jay Lorsch, A Contingency Theory of Leadership, in Nohria and Khurana, Handbook of Leadership Theory and Practice, 411-424.

51. Nye, The Powers to Lead, 22.

52. Gill, Theory and Practice of Leadership, 49; Northouse, Leadership, 115-116.

53. Nohria and Khurana, Advancing Leadership Theory and Practice, 17.

54. Nanerl O. Keohane, Thinking about Leadership (Princeton, NJ: Princeton University Press, 2010), 10.

55. Northouse, Leadership, 176, 185; Bernard M. Bass and Ronald E. Riggio, Transformational Leadership (Mahwah, NJ: Lawrence Earlbaum Associates, Inc., 2d ed. 2006), 3-4.

56. Burns, Leadership, 20. See also Bernard M. Bass and Paul Steidlmeier, Ethics, Character and Authentic Transformational Leadership Behavior, Leadership Quarterly 10 (1999):181, 181-183.

57. Bass and Riggio, Transformational Leadership, 6-7.

58. The leading texts are by Robert K. Greenleaf, Servant Leadership (New York: Paulist Press, 1977), and The Servant as Leader (Indianapolis, IN: The Robert K. Greenleaf Center, 1991). The term is used in many leadership contexts. The motto of Sandhurst, the United Kingdom's Royal Military College is "serve to lead," and its prayer states: "Help us to be masters of ourselves that we may be servants of others and teach us to serve to lead."

59. For an overview, see Gill, Theory and Practice of Leadership, 54, 59-60; Joan B. Ciulla, Leadership Ethics: Mapping the Territory, in Joan B. Ciulla, ed., Ethics: The Heart of Leadership (Westport, CT: Quorum Books, 1998). For visionary leadership, see Marshall Saskin, The Visionary Leader, in J.A. Conger and R.N. Kanungo, Charismatic Leadership: The Elusive Factor in Organizational Effectiveness (San Francisco: Jossey-Bass, 1988). For strategic leadership, see Gerry Johnson and Kevan Scholes, Exploring Corporate Strategy (Harlow, UK: Pearson Ed., 6th ed. 1998); Michael Hitt, R.D. Ireland, and R.E. Hoskisson, Strategic Management: Competitiveness and Globalization (Minneapolis/St. Paul: West Publishing, 1995); K. Beatty and L. Quinn, Strategic Command: Taking the Long View for Organizational Success, Leadership in Action 22 (2002):3.

60. Bernard Bass and Bruce Avolio, Introduction, in Bernard M. Bass and Bruce J. Violio, eds., Improving Organizational Effectiveness through Transformational Leadership (Thousand Oaks, CA: Sage Publications, 1994).

61. M.E. Brown and Linda K. Trevino, Is Values Based Leadership Ethical Leadership?, 168.

62. Michael Keeley, The Trouble with Transformational Leadership: Toward a Federalist Ethic for Organizations, in Joanne B. Ciulla, ed., Ethics: The Heart of Leadership (Westport, CT: Quorum Books, 1998), 111, 124.

63. Keohane, Thinking about Leadership, 43.

64. Bennis and Nanus, Leaders: Their Strategies for Taking Charge (New York: Harper & Row, 1985), 21.

65. Warren Bennis and Joan Goldsmith, Learning to Lead (New York: Basic Books, 2003), 8; Gill, Theory and Practice of Leadership, 26; Abraham Zaleznik, Managers and Leaders: Are They Different?, Harvard Business Review (1977): 74; John P. Kotter, A Force for Change: How Leadership Differs from Management (New York: Free Press, 1990), 3-8.

66. John P. Kotter, What Leaders Really Do, Harvard Business Review 68 (May-June 1990):103.

67. Kotter, What Leaders Really Do, 104.

68. Kotter, What Leaders Really Do, 104-105.

69. Kotter, What Leaders Really Do, 104.

70. Joanne B. Ciulla, Leadership Ethics: Mapping the Territory, in Ciulla, ed., Ethics: The Heart of Leadership (Westport, CT: Quorum Books, 1998), 1, 13.

71. Northouse, Leadership, 10.

72. Gill, Theory and Practice of Leadership, 28-30; Pasternak, T.D. Williams, and P.E. Anderson, Beyond the Cult of the CEO: Building Institutional Capacity, Strategy and Business (2001), 1; James O'Toole, When Leadership is an Organizational Trait, in Warren Bennis, G.M. Spreitzer, and T.G. Cummings, eds., The Future of Leadership (San Francisco: Jossey-Bass, 2001), 160.

73. William A. Cohen, Drucker on Leadership (San Francisco: Jossey-Bass, 2010), 167.

74. Herb Rosenthal, Leadership for Lawyers (Chicago: American Bar Association, 2004), 192.

75. J. Patrick Dobel, Managerial Leadership and the Ethical Importance of Legacy, in Denis Saint-Martin and Fred Thompson, eds., Public Ethics and Governance: Standards and Practices in Comparative Perspective (Oxford, UK: Elsevier, 2006), 201.

76. Doebel, Managerial Leadership, 202.

77. Ray Blunt, Leaders Growing Leaders for Public Service, reprinted in James L. Perry, ed., The Jossey-Bass Reader in Non-Profit Public Leadership (New York: Wiley & Sons, 2010), 41 (quoting Noel Tichy).

78. For similar exercises, see Robert E. Quinn, Sue R. Faerman, Michael P. Thompson, Michael R. McGrath, and Lynda S. St. Clair, Becoming a Master Manager (Hoboken, NJ: John Wiley & Sons, 5th ed. 2010), 37.

79. For a more complete list, see Mary C. Gentile, Giving Voice to Values (New Haven, CT: Yale University Press, 2010), Appendix Table 1.

80. See Quinn et al., Becoming a Master Manager, 40-41; Oliver P. John, Laura P. Naumann, and Christopher J. Soto, Paradigm Shift to the Integrative Five Factor Trait Taxonomy, in Oliver P. John, Richard W. Robins, and Lawrence A. Pervin, eds., Handbook of Personality: Theory and Research (New York: Guilford, 3d ed. 2008).

81. Leadership experts are divided. Burns claims Hitler was not a leader but a tyrant; Bass and Heifetz disagree. See Joanne Ciulla, Leadership Ethics, Mapping the Territory, 12-13, 74; Burns, Leadership, 27, 240. Bernard M. Bass, Leadership and Performance beyond Expectations (New York: Free Press, 1985), 183-185.

82. Richard Nixon, Leaders (New York: Warner, 1982), 324.

83. Rosabeth Moss Kanter, Power Failure in Management Circuits, Harvard Business Review 57 (July-August 1979):65.

84. Gardner, On Leadership, 55, 57.

85. Liz Wiseman with Greg McKeown, Multipliers: How the Best Leaders Make Everyone Smarter (New York: Harper Collins, 2010), 20-22, 100-121; Scott N. Spreier, Mary H. Gonaine, and Ruthy L. Malloy, Leadership Run Amok: The Destructive Potential of Overachievers, Harvard Business Review (June 2006):74-79.

86. Jeffery Pfeffer, Power: Why Some Have It — and Others Don't (New York: Harper Collins, 2010), 43-47.

87. Edwin P. Hollander, Inclusive Leadership: The Essential Leader-Follower Relationship (New York: Routledge, 2009), 25.

88. Pfeffer, Power, 55.

89. Pfeffer, Power, 56.

90. Northouse, Leadership, 19.

91. Robert Hogan and Robert B. Kaiser, What We Know about Leadership, Review of General Psychology 9 (2005):169, 172.

92. Montgomery Van Wart, Dynamics of Leadership in Public Service: Theory and Practice (Armonk, NY: M.E. Sharpe, 2005), 16, 92-119.

93. Maureen Broderick, The Art of Managing Professional Services (Upper Saddle River, NJ: Wharton Press, 2011), 267.

94. James M. Kouzes and Barry Posner, The Leadership Challenge.

95. Howard Gardner, Mihaly Csikszentmihalyi, and William Damin, Good Work: When Excellence and Ethics Meet (New York: Basic Books, 2001), 293. See also Lynn Barendsen and Howard Gardner, The Three Elements of Good Leadership in Rapidly Changing Times, in Frances Hesselbein and Marshall Goldsmith, eds., The Leader of the Future (San Francisco: Jossey-Bass, 2006), 266.

96. Northouse, Leadership, 27.

97. Daniel Goleman, Rischard Boyatzis, and Annie McKee, Primal Leadership: Realizing the Power of Emotional Intelligence (Boston: Harvard Business Publishing, 2002), 253-256.

98. For discussion of Thatcher's domineering, overconfident, and sometimes acerbic style, see Howard Gardner, Leading Minds (New York: Basic Books, 2005), 238; Ben Fenton, Damiel Pimlott, and Vanessa Houlder, Iron Lady Was Advised How to Dominate Cabinet, Financial Times (December 30, 2010):1. For Rahm Emanuel's volcanic style, see Pfeffer, Power, 141.

99. For descriptions of Jobs, see Pfeffer, Managing with Power, 109; Quinn et al., Becoming a Master Manager, 186.

100. Quinn et al., Becoming a Master Manager, 183.

101. For an example of such a rating form, see Northouse, Leadership, 34-35.

CHAPTER 2

DEVELOPING LEADERSHIP

Leadership is not simply matter of personal characteristics or formal position. It is, most importantly, a process of building relationships. Recall the metaphor by Harvard government professor Joseph Nye, quoted in Chapter 1: "[H]olding a formal title is like having a fishing license; it does not guarantee you will catch any fish."[1] This chapter begins by exploring the challenges confronting those who seek to exercise leadership and the styles that are most effective in addressing them. It then turns to the distinctive issues posed in law, management, and policy, and closes with an analysis of how the core competencies of leadership can be learned.

A. CONTEMPORARY CHALLENGES

Whatever their differences, experts on leadership generally agree that its exercise has grown in complexity over recent decades. To understand these increasing challenges, it is helpful to look at what Nye identified as the three crucial dimensions of the leadership process: leaders, followers, and context, that is, external circumstances and objectives.[2]

1. THE WORLD OF LEADERS: COMPETITION, SCALE, PACE, AND DIVERSITY

Although the contexts of contemporary leadership vary, most share some common features, including an increase in competition, complexity, scale, pace, and diversity. In law and business settings, competitiveness has escalated within and across organizations. Publicly traded corporations depend on investors who care about short-term profits and relative market share, and leaders who cannot produce results by these measures are forced out at escalating rates.[3] In private law firms, partnership means less and is harder to attain, and attention has increasingly centered on bottom-line financial performance. In the public sector, competition for attention, support, and resources has intensified, particularly during the recent economic downturn.[4] These pressures pose difficulties on both financial and interpersonal levels.

As one commentator quips, "[C]ompetition brings out the best in products and the worst in people."[5]

Other challenges arise from the growth in scale and complexity of professional, corporate, government, and nonprofit organizations, as well as the problems that they confront. In law, over the last half century, the size of the fifty largest firms has increased more than ten times and the staff in the most prominent public interest legal organizations have more than doubled.[6] In the private sector, the number of businesses with more than 500 employees has grown more than 40 percent over the last two decades.[7] Large corporations are operating in many countries and product markets, and they have more alliances, subsidiaries, and outsourcing arrangements. Summarizing these developments, the title of a prominent *Economist* article put it bluntly: it's "tough at the top."[8] In organizations with multiple offices and thousands of employees, the advantages that come from "leadership by walking around" and personal interactions are harder to realize. If, as John Gardner argued, "nothing can substitute for a live leader . . . listening attentively and responding informally," the challenges of achieving such responsiveness are daunting.[9]

This increase in size, together with other social, economic, legal, and technological changes, has significantly complicated the landscape of leadership. As the president of the Institute for the Future has noted, governments, markets, organizations, and professions are interacting in more complex ways, and leaders' decisions often play out on a larger social, international, and environmental stage.[10]

The technological advances that have encouraged such growth have also posed additional challenges. Over the last decades, both the pace of decision making and the accessibility of decision makers have dramatically increased. Leaders often face a barrage of information along with pressure to make complex decisions instantly.[11] As one former deputy attorney general noted, "if you don't like an issue before you, wait fifteen minutes. . . . Somebody will give you a new one."[12] Leaders remain tethered to their workplaces through electronic communication, and the personal costs can be substantial: stress, burnout, substance abuse, and related mental health difficulties.[13] The risks and consequences of bad decisions are also amplified by an ever more present media. A case in point is the rush to judgment involving Shirley Sherrod, an African American midlevel official in the Department of Agriculture who was forced to resign after a misleading clip of remarks she made about race went viral on the Internet. Once the entire video circulated, both the NAACP president and the Cabinet official who had condemned her statements faced a public relations disaster.[14]

Additional challenges involve increased diversity. Although this trend has had many payoffs for organizations along the lines described in Chapter 8, it has also complicated the lives of leaders. In the United States, organizations are focusing increased efforts on reducing barriers based on sex, race, ethnicity, age, disability, and sexual orientation. In virtually every industrialized nation, leaders of global corporations are attempting to accommodate cultural variations in leadership styles and preferences. The GLOBE study of some 17,000 managers in 62 societies identified some important cultural differences in perceptions of leaders' effectiveness. For example, more egalitarian societies valued participatory leadership styles, while cultures that attached high priority to empathy and altruism viewed those qualities as more essential in leaders.[15] Creating institutions that can deal productively with differences across race, ethnicity, gender, culture, and related factors is a crucial skill in an increasingly interconnected world.

2. RELATIONSHIPS WITH FOLLOWERS

Relationships with followers pose another cluster of challenges. Although the extent and complexity of demands on contemporary leaders often argues for shared authority, many stakeholders retain a desire for a single heroic figure at the helm. As Joseph Nye describes it, this "Mt. Rushmore syndrome" rests on a fundamental "leader attribution error" — a tendency to ascribe undue credit or blame for performance to the person at the top.[16] The problem is endemic in both the public and the private sectors. People often expect quick fixes to complex social problems and intractable market dynamics. Unrealistic expectations by followers encourage unrealistic promises by would-be leaders. The result is that those individuals often "fail upwards" because their grand visions inevitably fall short.[17]

A further difficulty is that although followers might want, or benefit from, the results of strong leadership, they may not like to be led, and may not welcome the changes and sacrifices that it demands. This problem is particularly common in legal- and public-sector workplaces. By training and temperament, lawyers tend to value independence and are well prepared to challenge authority when they disagree. As consultants note, lawyers are experts at locating loopholes and are attached to precedent; any new leadership proposal is likely to be met with skepticism and counterexamples — hardly a "recipe for a strategic advantage" or innovation.[18] In public-sector bureaucracies, rigid legal constraints, job protection for civil servants, insulation from market pressures, and potential political landmines can often foster resistance to innovation.[19] Policy settings also tend toward what experts describe as "organized anarchy." No one is in charge: power is dispersed across shifting coalitions and interest groups, which require considerable leadership skills to align in pursuit of societal goals.[20]

3. GAINING AND EXERCISING LEADERSHIP

A final set of challenges arises from the disconnect between motives and qualities that often enable individuals to achieve leadership positions and the qualities that are necessary to perform effectively once they get there. What makes individuals willing to accept the pressure, hours, scrutiny, and risks that come with leadership positions? For many leaders, it is not only commitment to a cause, an organization, or a constituency; it is also an attraction to power, status, admiration, and financial reward. Successful leadership requires subordinating these personal interests to a greater good. The result is often what some psychologists label the leadership paradox. Individuals reach top positions because of their high needs for personal achievement. Yet, to perform effectively once there, they need to focus on creating the conditions for achievement by others.[21]

If left unchecked, the ambition, self-confidence, and self-centeredness that often propel individuals to leadership positions may sabotage their subsequent performance. Research on personality and organizational effectiveness finds that narcissistic individuals often have an advantage in being selected for leadership positions because they project the confidence and charisma that makes a positive short-term impression. Yet over time those characteristics can translate into a sense of entitlement, overconfidence, and an inability to learn from mistakes.[22] Strong ego needs can also prevent leaders from letting go at times when an organization would benefit from change.[23] Yet, as the discussion below notes, the environments in which leaders function often fail to supply honest feedback about their weaknesses; subordinates may be understandably unwilling to deliver uncomfortable messages. And the perks that accompany leadership may inflate individuals' sense of self-importance and self-confidence. Being constantly surrounded by those with less ability or less opportunity to display their ability may also encourage what psychologists label the uniqueness bias: people's sense that they are special and superior. Such environments risk reinforcing narcissism and entitlement; leaders may feel free to disregard rules of ethics or norms of courtesy and respect that are applicable to others.[24] Yet when individuals "come to think of themselves as better than those, you know, those little people," leaders "cut themselves off from [followers'] good ideas and good graces."[25] The pressures to succeed and the rewards when it happens can result in what former Medtronic CEO Bill George describes as "CEO-itis": a willingness to compromise core values to "keep it going."[26] Yet, as Jim Collins's study of successful businesses makes clear, the most effective leaders are those who are self-aware, and more ambitious for their institutions than for themselves.[27]

B. STYLES OF LEADERSHIP

To meet these challenges, leaders need to develop diverse styles that can accommodate different leadership contexts. In the following excerpt, Daniel Goleman's research suggests six styles that can be effective under different circumstances. Consider which match best with your own leadership approach or with those occupying positions to which you might aspire.

DANIEL GOLEMAN, "LEADERSHIP THAT GETS RESULTS"

Harvard Business Review, March–April 2000

The mystery of what leaders can and ought to do in order to spark the best performance from their people is age-old. In recent years, that mystery has spawned an entire cottage industry: literally thousands of "leadership experts" have made careers of testing and coaching executives, all in pursuit of creating businesspeople who can turn bold objectives—be they strategic, financial, organizational, or all three—into reality.

Still, effective leadership eludes many people and organizations. One reason is that until recently, virtually no quantitative research has demonstrated which precise leadership behaviors yield positive results. Leadership experts proffer advice based on inference, experience, and instinct. Sometimes that advice is right on target; sometimes it's not.

But new research by the consulting firm Hay/McBer, which draws on a random sample of 3,871 executives selected from a database of more than 20,000 executives worldwide, takes much of the mystery out of effective leadership. The research found six distinct leadership styles, each springing from different components of emotional intelligence. The styles, taken individually, appear to have a direct and unique impact on the working atmosphere of a company, division, or team, and in turn, on its financial performance. And perhaps most important, the research indicates that leaders with the best results do not rely on only one leadership style; they use most of them in a given week — seamlessly and in different measure — depending on the business situation. . . . Imagine the styles, then, as the array of clubs in a golf pro's bag. Over the course of a game, the pro picks and chooses clubs based on the demands of the shot. Sometimes he has to ponder his selection, but usually it is automatic. The pro senses the challenge ahead, swiftly pulls out the right tool, and elegantly puts it to work. That's how high-impact leaders operate, too.

What are the six styles of leadership? None will shock workplace veterans. Indeed, each style, by name and brief description alone, will likely resonate with anyone who leads, is led, or as is the case with most of us, does both. *Coercive leaders* demand immediate compliance. *Authoritative leaders* mobilize people toward a vision. *Affiliative leaders* create emotional bonds and harmony. *Democratic leaders* build consensus through participation. *Pacesetting leaders* expect excellence and self-direction. And *coaching leaders* develop people for the future.

Close your eyes and you can surely imagine a colleague who uses any one of these styles. You most likely use at least one yourself. What is new in this research, then, is its implications for action. First, it offers a fine-grained understanding of how different leadership styles affect performance and results. Second, it offers clear guidance on when a manager should switch between them. It also strongly suggests that switching flexibly is well advised. New, too, is the research's finding that each leadership style springs from different components of emotional intelligence. . . .

The Styles in Detail

Executives use six leadership styles, but only four of the six consistently have a positive effect on climate and results. Let's look then at each style of leadership in detail. . . .

The Coercive Style. . . . It's easy to understand why of all the leadership styles, the coercive one is the least effective in most situations. Consider what the style does to an organization's climate. Flexibility is the hardest hit. The leader's extreme top-down decision making kills new ideas on the vine. People feel so disrespected that they think, "I won't even bring my ideas up — they'll only be shot down." Likewise, people's sense of responsibility evaporates:

unable to act on their own initiative, they lose their sense of ownership and feel little accountability for their performance. Some become so resentful they adopt the attitude, "I'm not going to help this bastard."

Coercive leadership also has a damaging effect on the rewards system. Most high-performing workers are motivated by more than money—they seek the satisfaction of work well done. The coercive style erodes such pride. And finally, the style undermines one of the leader's prime tools—motivating people by showing them how their job fits into a grand, shared mission. Such a loss, measured in terms of diminished clarity and commitment, leaves people alienated from their own jobs, wondering, "How does any of this matter?"

Given the impact of the coercive style, you might assume it should never be applied. Our research, however, uncovered a few occasions when it worked masterfully . . . , such as during a turnaround or when a hostile takeover is looming. In those cases, the coercive style can break failed business habits and shock people into new ways of working. It is always appropriate during a genuine emergency, like in the aftermath of an earthquake or a fire. And it can work with problem employees with whom all else has failed. But if a leader relies solely on this style or continues to use it once the emergency passes, the long-term impact of his insensitivity to the morale and feelings of those he leads will be ruinous.

The Authoritative Style. . . . Our research indicates that of the six leadership styles, the authoritative one is most effective, driving up every aspect of climate. Take clarity. The authoritative leader is a visionary; he motivates people by making clear to them how their work fits into a larger vision for the organization. People who work for such leaders understand that what they do matters and why.

Authoritative leadership also maximizes commitment to the organization's goals and strategy. By framing the individual tasks within a grand vision, the authoritative leader defines standards that revolve around that vision. When he gives performance feedback—whether positive or negative—the singular criterion is whether or not that performance furthers the vision. The standards for success are clear to all, as are the rewards. Finally, consider the styled impact on flexibility. An authoritative leader states the end but generally gives people plenty of leeway to devise their own means. Authoritative leaders give people the freedom to innovate, experiment, and take calculated risks.

Because of its positive impact, the authoritative style works well in almost any business situation. But it is particularly effective when a business is adrift. An authoritative leader charts a new course and sells his people on a fresh long-term vision.

The authoritative style, powerful though it may be, will not work in every situation. The approach fails, for instance, when a leader is working with a team of experts or peers who are more experienced than he is; they may see the leader as pompous or out-of-touch. Another limitation: if a manager trying to be authoritative becomes overbearing, he can undermine the egalitarian spirit of an effective team. Yet even with such caveats, leaders would be wise to grab for the authoritative "club" more often than not. It may not guarantee a hole in one, but it certainly helps with the long drive.

The Affiliative Style. If the coercive leader demands, "Do what I say," and the authoritative urges, "Come with me," the affiliative leader says, "People come first." This leadership style revolves around people — its proponents value individuals and their emotions more than tasks and goals. The affiliative leader strives to keep employees happy and to create harmony among them. He manages by building strong emotional bonds and then reaping the benefits of such an approach, namely fierce loyalty. The style also has a markedly positive effect on communication. People who like one another a lot talk a lot. They share ideas; they share inspiration. And the style drives up flexibility; friends trust one another, allowing habitual innovation and risk taking. Flexibility also rises because the affiliative leader, like a parent who adjusts household rules for a maturing adolescent, doesn't impose unnecessary strictures on how employees get their work done. They give people the freedom to do their job in the way they think is most effective.

As for a sense of recognition and reward for work well done, the affiliative leader offers ample positive feedback. Such feedback has special potency in the workplace because it is all too rare: outside of an annual review, most people usually get no feedback on their day-to-day efforts — or only negative feedback. That makes the affiliative leader's positive words all the more motivating. Finally, affiliative leaders are masters at building a sense of belonging. They are, for instance, likely to take their direct reports out for a meal or a drink, one-on-one, to see how they're doing. They will bring in a cake to celebrate a group accomplishment. They are natural relationship builders. . . .

The affiliative style's generally positive impact makes it a good all-weather approach, but leaders should employ it particularly when trying to build team harmony, increase morale, improve communication, or repair broken trust. For instance, one executive in our study was hired to replace a ruthless team leader. The former leader had taken credit for his employees' work and had attempted to pit them against one another. His efforts ultimately failed, but the team he left behind was suspicious and weary. The new executive managed to mend the situation by unstintingly showing emotional honesty and rebuilding ties. Several months in, her leadership had created a renewed sense of commitment and energy.

Despite its benefits, the affiliative style should not be used alone. Its exclusive focus on praise can allow poor performance to go uncorrected; employees may perceive that mediocrity is tolerated. And because affiliative leaders rarely offer constructive advice on how to improve, employees must figure out how to do so on their own. When people need clear directives to navigate through complex challenges, the affiliative style leaves them rudderless. Indeed, if overly relied on, this style can actually steer a group to failure. Perhaps that is why many affiliative leaders . . . use this style in close conjunction with the authoritative style. Authoritative leaders state a vision, set standards, and let people know how their work is furthering the group's goals. Alternate that with the caring, nurturing approach of the affiliative leader, and you have a potent combination.

The Democratic Style. Sister Mary ran a Catholic school system in a large metropolitan area. One of the schools — the only private school in an impoverished neighborhood — had been losing money for years, and the archdiocese could no longer afford to keep it open. When Sister Mary eventually got the order to shut it down, she didn't just lock the doors. She called a meeting of all the teachers and staff at the school and explained to them the details of the financial crisis — the first time anyone working at the school had been included in the business side of the institution. She asked for their ideas on ways to keep the school open and on how to handle the closing, should it come to that. Sister Mary spent much of her time at the meeting just listening.

She did the same at later meetings for school parents and for the community and during a successive series of meetings for the school's teachers and staff. After two months of meetings, the consensus was clear: the school would have to close. A plan was made to transfer students to other schools in the Catholic system.

The final outcome was no different than if Sister Mary had gone ahead and closed the school the day she was told to. But by allowing the school's constituents to reach that decision collectively, Sister Mary received none of the backlash that would have accompanied such a move. People mourned the loss of the school, but they understood its inevitability. Virtually no one objected.

Compare that with the experiences of a priest in our research who headed another Catholic school. He, too, was told to shut it down. And he did — by fiat. The result was disastrous: parents filed lawsuits, teachers and parents picketed, and local newspapers ran editorials attacking his decision. It took a year to resolve the disputes before he could finally go ahead and close the school.

Sister Mary exemplifies the democratic style in action — and its benefits. By spending time getting people's ideas and buy-in, a leader builds trust, respect, and commitment. By letting workers themselves have a say in decisions that affect their goals and how they do their work, the democratic leader drives up flexibility and responsibility. And by listening to employees' concerns, the democratic leader learns what to do to keep morale high. Finally, because they have a say in setting their goals and the standards for evaluating success, people operating in a democratic system tend to be very realistic about what can and cannot be accomplished.

However, the democratic style has its drawbacks, which is why its impact on climate is not as high as some of the other styles. One of its more exasperating consequences can be endless meetings where ideas are mulled over, consensus remains elusive, and the only visible result is scheduling more meetings. Some democratic leaders use the style to put off making crucial decisions, hoping that enough thrashing things out will eventually yield a blinding insight. In reality, their people end up feeling confused and leaderless. Such an approach can even escalate conflicts.

When does the style work best? This approach is ideal when a leader is himself uncertain about the best direction to take and needs ideas and guidance from able employees. And even if a leader has a strong vision, the democratic style works well to generate fresh ideas for executing that vision.

The Pacesetting Style. Like the coercive style, the pacesetting style has its place in the leader's repertory, but it should be used sparingly. That's not what we expected to find. After all, the hallmarks of the pacesetting style sound admirable. The leader sets extremely high performance standards and exemplifies them himself. He is obsessive about doing things better and faster, and he asks the same of everyone around him. He quickly pinpoints poor performers and demands more from them. If they don't rise to the occasion, he replaces them with people who can. You would think such an approach would improve results, but it doesn't.

In fact, the pacesetting style destroys climate. Many employees feel overwhelmed by the pacesetter's demands for excellence, and their morale drops. Guidelines for working may be clear in the leader's head, but she does not state them clearly; she expects people to know what to do and even thinks, "If I have to tell you, you're the wrong person for the job." Work becomes not a matter of doing one's best along a clear course so much as second-guessing what the leader wants. At the same time, people often feel that the pacesetter doesn't trust them to work in their own way or to take initiative. Flexibility and responsibility evaporate; work becomes so task focused and routinized it's boring.

As for rewards, the pacesetter either gives no feedback on how people are doing or jumps in to take over when he thinks they're lagging. And if the leader should leave, people feel directionless — they're so used to "the expert" setting the rules. . . .

[T]he pacesetting style isn't always a disaster. The approach works well when all employees are self-motivated, highly competent, and need little direction or coordination — for example, it can work for leaders of highly skilled and self-motivated professionals, like R&D groups or legal teams. And, given a talented team to lead, pacesetting does exactly that: gets work done on time or even ahead of schedule. Yet like any leadership style, pacesetting should never be used by itself.

The Coaching Style. . . . Coaching leaders help employees identify their unique strengths and weaknesses and tie them to their personal and career aspirations. They encourage employees to establish long-term development goals and help them conceptualize a plan for attaining them. They make agreements with their employees about their role and responsibilities in enacting development plans, and they give plentiful instruction and feedback. Coaching leaders excel at delegating; they give employees challenging assignments, even if that means the tasks won't be accomplished quickly. In other words, these leaders are willing to put up with short-term failure if it furthers long-term learning.

Of the six styles, our research found that the coaching style is used least often. Many leaders told us they don't have the time in this high-pressure economy for the slow and tedious work of teaching people and helping them grow. But after a first session, it takes little or no extra time. Leaders who ignore this style are passing up a powerful tool: its impact on climate and performance are markedly positive.

Admittedly, there is a paradox in coaching's positive effect on business performance because coaching focuses primarily on personal development, not on immediate work-related tasks. Even so, coaching improves results. The reason: it requires constant dialogue, and that dialogue has a way of pushing up every driver of climate. Take flexibility. When an employee knows his boss watches him and cares about what he does, he feels free to experiment. After all, he's sure to get quick and constructive feedback. Similarly, the ongoing dialogue of coaching guarantees that people know what is expected of them and how their work fits into a larger vision or strategy. That affects responsibility and clarity. As for commitment, coaching helps there, too, because the style's implicit message is, "I believe in you, I'm investing in you, and I expect your best efforts." Employees very often rise to that challenge with their heart, mind, and soul.

The coaching style works well in many business situations, but it is perhaps most effective when people on the receiving end are "up for it." For instance, the coaching style works particularly well when employees are already aware of their weaknesses and would like to improve their performance. Similarly, the style works well when employees realize how cultivating new abilities can help them advance. In short, it works best with employees who want to be coached.

By contrast, the coaching style makes little sense when employees, for whatever reason, are resistant to learning or changing their ways. And it flops if the leader lacks the expertise to help the employee along. The fact is, many managers are unfamiliar with or simply inept at coaching, particularly when it comes to giving ongoing performance feedback that motivates rather than creates fear or apathy. Some companies have realized the positive impact of the style and are trying to make it a core competence. At some companies, a significant portion of annual bonuses are tied to an executive's development of his or her direct reports. But many organizations have yet to take full advantage of this leadership style. Although the coaching style may not scream "bottom-line results," it delivers them.

Leaders Need Many Styles

Many studies, including this one, have shown that the more styles a leader exhibits, the better. Leaders who have mastered four or more—especially the authoritative, democratic, affiliative, and coaching styles—have the very best climate and business performance. And the most effective leaders switch flexibly among the leadership styles as needed. Although that may sound daunting, we witnessed it more often than you might guess, at both large corporations and tiny start-ups, by seasoned veterans who could explain exactly how and why they lead and by entrepreneurs who claim to lead by gut alone. Such leaders don't mechanically match their style to fit a checklist of situations—they are far more fluid. They are exquisitely sensitive to the impact they are having on others and seamlessly adjust their style to get the best results. . . .

Daniel Goleman identified a repertoire of styles that can be effective for leaders. In the following excerpt, Jack Zenger and Joseph Folkman identify styles that can be fatal. As you read their description, think about other characteristics that you might add and whether your leadership has fallen short in any of the ways that they describe.

JACK ZENGER AND JOSEPH FOLKMAN, "TEN FATAL FLAWS THAT DERAIL LEADERS"

Harvard Business Review, June 2009, p. 18

Poor leadership in good times can be hidden, but poor leadership in bad times is a recipe for disaster. To find out why leaders fail, we scrutinized results from two studies:

In one, we collected 360-degree feedback data on more than 450 Fortune 500 executives and then teased out the common characteristics of the 31 who were fired over the next three years. In the second, we analyzed 360-degree feedback data from more than 11,000 leaders and identified the 10% who were considered least effective.

We then compared the ineffective leaders with the fired leaders to come up with the 10 most common leadership shortcomings. Every bad leader had at least one, and most had several.

The worst leaders:

Lack energy and enthusiasm. They see new initiatives as a burden, rarely volunteer, and fear being overwhelmed. One such leader was described as having the ability to "suck all the energy out of any room."

Accept their own mediocre performance. They overstate the difficulty of reaching targets so that they look good when they achieve them. They live by the mantra "Underpromise and overdeliver."

Lack clear vision and direction. They believe their only job is to execute. Like a hiker who sticks close to the trail, they're fine until they come to a fork.

Have poor judgment. They make decisions that colleagues and subordinates consider to be not in the organization's best interests.

Don't collaborate. They avoid peers, act independently, and view other leaders as competitors. As a result, they are set adrift by the very people whose insights and support they need.

Don't walk the talk. They set standards of behavior or expectations of performance and then violate them. They're perceived as lacking integrity.

Resist new ideas. They reject suggestions from subordinates and peers. Good ideas aren't implemented, and the organization gets stuck.

Don't learn from mistakes. They may make no more mistakes than their peers, but they fail to use setbacks as opportunities for improvement, hiding their errors and brooding about them instead.

Lack interpersonal skills. They make sins of both commission (they're abrasive and bullying) and omission (they're aloof, unavailable, and reluctant to praise).

Fail to develop others. They focus on themselves to the exclusion of developing subordinates, causing individuals and teams to disengage.

These sound like obvious flaws that any leader would try to fix. But the ineffective leaders we studied were often unaware that they exhibited these behaviors. In fact, those who were rated most negatively rated themselves substantially more positively. Leaders should take a very hard look at themselves and ask for candid feedback on performance in these specific areas. Their jobs may depend on it.

One much debated leadership style is intimidation. Although frequently condemned, it can also achieve desired results. In the following excerpt, Stanford Business School professor Roderick Kramer explores the capacities and constraints of leading by intimidating.

RODERICK M. KRAMER, "THE GREAT INTIMIDATORS"

Harvard Business Review, February 2006

"Since when has being a difficult boss been a disqualifier for a job?" asked *Nightline*'s Ted Koppel after several abrasive, intimidating leaders of major corporations—Disney's Michael Eisner, Miramax's Harvey Weinstein, and Hewlett-Packard's Carly Fiorina—fell from their heights of power. Picking up on what seemed to be a new trend in the workplace, the business media quickly proclaimed that the reign of such leaders was over. From now on, the *Wall Street Journal* predicted, "tough guys will finish last."

But wait a minute, you might think. If they're just plain bad for their organizations, why have so many of these leaders made it to the top in the first place? Wouldn't the ones who've wreaked nothing but havoc have plateaued or been weeded out long before they could inflict too much damage? Yet many leaders who rule through intimidation have been doing just fine for a very long time. Before we proclaim their extinction, then, it's worth taking a close look at the pros as well as the cons of their tough-minded approach. Doing so might cast light on some subtle dimensions of effective leadership, especially in organizations or industries that were once rigid or unruly, stagnant or drifting—places where it took an abrasive leader to shake things up a little and provide redirection.

Consider Ed Zander, who's been hailed as "Motorola's modernizer." When Zander took over as CEO of Motorola in January 2004, the company was in steep decline. After being in the high-velocity world of Silicon Valley, Zander found himself at the helm of a company that seemed to be running, in his words, "on autopilot." In taking on the challenge of turning Motorola around, Zander described his guiding philosophy as, "Whack yourself before somebody whacks you." He observed, "A lot of companies have clogged arteries." In Motorola's case, Zander found that much of the problem was at the VP level. "I don't know how many dozens of VPs are no longer with us," he reported in one interview. "Some have left on their own accord, some have not." The transformation at Motorola is far from complete, but it is off to a good start. . . . A similar story can be told about Harvey Weinstein, also notorious for his abrasiveness. When he entered the Hollywood scene, a handful of major studios dominated the landscape. Independent picture producers limped along on the margins of power and influence. Weinstein almost single-handedly pulled the independent film industry out of the doldrums, in the process making Miramax one of the few widely recognized industry brand names. He didn't make a lot of friends over the years, and people who have worked with him often say that they find him hard to take. . . . [T]here is no contending with Weinstein's success: more than 240 Academy Award nominations and 60 wins.

Zander and Weinstein are examples of what I call *great intimidators*. They are not averse to causing a ruckus, nor are they above using a few public whippings and ceremonial hangings to get attention. And they're in good company. A list of great intimidators would read a bit like a business leadership hall of fame: Sandy Weill, Rupert Murdoch, Andy Grove, Carly Fiorina, Larry Ellison, and Steve Jobs would be just a few of the names on it. These leaders seem to relish the chaos they create because, in their minds, it's constructive. Time is short, the stakes are high, and the measures required are draconian.

But make no mistake — the great intimidators are not your typical bullies. If you're just a bully, it's all about humiliating others in an effort to make yourself feel good. Something very different is going on with the great intimidators. To be sure, they aren't above engaging in a little bullying to get their way. With them, however, the motivating factor isn't ego or gratuitous humiliation; it's vision. The great intimidators see a possible path through the thicket, and they're impatient to clear it. They chafe at impediments, even those that are human. They don't suffer from doubt or timidity.

They've got a disdain for constraints imposed by others. . . . Beneath their tough exteriors and sharp edges, however, are some genuine, deep insights into human motivation and organizational behavior. Indeed, these leaders possess what I call *political intelligence*, a distinctive and powerful form of leader intelligence that's been largely ignored by management theorists and practitioners. . . .

Political Intelligence at Work

. . . Over the past decade, management theorists and practitioners alike have come to appreciate the roles that different forms of human intelligence play in effective leadership. Psychologist Howard Gardner — who first articulated the theory of multiple intelligences — suggested, for example, that social intelligence is what makes some leaders so adept at getting others to follow them and at extracting maximum performance from subordinates. Gardner defined social intelligence in terms of leaders' interpersonal skills, such as empathy and the ability to influence others on the basis of that understanding.

There's no question that it's important for all leaders to have these skills. Indeed, social intelligence is the sort of competency leaders rely on every day to accomplish the routine work of an organization. However, it's not the *only* kind of intelligence they need. What's more, in some settings (a rigidly hierarchical organization, for example), other forms of intelligence may be more useful. That's when the application of political intelligence, the hallmark of great intimidators, can make the difference between paralysis and successful — if sometimes wrenching — organizational change.

In understanding the distinction between socially intelligent and politically intelligent leaders, it's important to realize that they share certain skills. Both types of leaders are adept at sizing up other people. Both possess keen, discriminating eyes—but they notice different things. For instance, socially intelligent leaders assess people's strengths and figure out how to leverage them, while politically intelligent leaders focus on people's weaknesses and insecurities. Speaking of President Lyndon B. Johnson, one of history's truly great intimidators, former press secretary Bill Moyers noted that he possessed "an animal sense of weakness in other men." As one political scientist elaborated, Johnson "studied, analyzed, catalogued, and remembered the strengths and weaknesses, the likes and dislikes, of fellow politicians as some men do stock prices, batting averages, and musical compositions. He knew who drank Scotch and who bourbon, whose wife was sick . . . who was in trouble . . . and who owed him."

Not only do socially intelligent and politically intelligent leaders notice different things; they also *act* differently on the basis of their divergent perceptions. While leaders with social intelligence use empathy and soft power to build bridges, politically intelligent leaders use intimidation and hard power to exploit the anxieties and vulnerabilities they detect. Both kinds of leaders are good judges of character. But instead of having empathy for others, the politically intelligent leader adopts a dispassionate, clinical, even instrumental view of people as resources for getting things done. This absence of empathy opens up branches of the decision tree, exposing options that other leaders might reject.

Perhaps the starkest point of contrast between these two kinds of leaders is how willing they are to use hard power. Politically intelligent leaders appreciate the power of fear and its close relation, anxiety. As Harvard University's president, Larry Summers, once observed: "Sometimes fear does the work of reason." He went to Harvard determined to shake up the institution—and whatever else may be said about him, he has succeeded in doing just that. Interviews with faculty, staff, and students at Harvard who've had close encounters with Summers reveal a common pattern in his interactions: initial confrontation, followed by skeptical and hard questioning. "Perhaps we don't really even need a department like this at Harvard," he is said to have told one group of faculty at a "let's get acquainted" session.

Such questions may not make a leader popular, but they certainly wake people up. And they sometimes compel people to think more deeply about their purpose in an organization and the value they add to it. In asking them to justify their existence, for instance, Summers has forced professors and administrators at Harvard to become more thoughtful about what they do. . . .

Summers' sentiments regarding the virtues of inculcating a little fear echo one of President Richard Nixon's convictions: "People react to fear, not love— they don't teach that in Sunday school, but it's true." For Nixon, leadership wasn't about inspiring others or being liked; it was about producing tangible results. And although too much fear or anxiety may induce trepidation and paralysis, too little may result in lackluster effort and complacency. . . .

The Intimidator's Tactics

. . . *Get up close and personal.* . . . In addition to aggressive physical demeanors, intimidators routinely use the weapons of language—taunts and slurs—to provoke their victims. This behavior is designed to throw others off balance. It's hard to think clearly and follow your own game plan when your buttons are being pushed. Clarence Thomas, associate justice of the U.S. Supreme Court, used this tactic to browbeat his Democratic opponents on the Senate judiciary committee during his nomination hearings. When accused by Anita Hill of sexual harassment, he asked the members of the committee how they would like to be so accused. The discomfort of the committee (which included an understandably subdued Ted Kennedy) was palpable. To complete the trick, he threw the race card down on the table, calling the procedure "a high-tech lynching for uppity blacks who in any way deign to think for themselves . . . [and don't] kowtow to an old order." By putting the committee on the defensive, Thomas pulled the moral high ground right out from under their feet.

Be angry. Most intimidators use anger and rage to get their way. A calculated "loss of temper" does more than help intimidators prevail in the heat of the moment, though. It also serves as a chilling deterrent for potential challengers. While in some instances they are clearly putting on an act, intimidators aren't always in full control of their emotions when they go off on tirades. But even then a loss of control can be useful. As political pundit Chris Matthews once said, "Don't have a reputation for being a nice guy—that won't do you any good." He cited his experience working with former Maine senator Ed Muskie: "Muskie was the best of them all, the absolute best, because nobody wanted to tangle with the guy. You know, why tangle with the guy? Why ruin your day?" . . .

Know it all. Mastery of the facts—or at least the appearance of it—can also be hugely intimidating. "Informational intimidators" always have facts and figures at their fingertips, while their opponents are still trying to formulate an argument or retrieve something from memory. British prime minister Margaret Thatcher was legendary for her ability to silence or paralyze her opponents with her superior command of whatever topic was being debated. As one observer noted, Thatcher was a "demon for information, for research, for numbers. She devoured them, [and] she remembered them. . . . No one could out-study or out-prepare her." In one famous confrontation in the House of Commons, Thatcher took on and "battered into submission" the able and respected Richard Crossman. "It was obvious," recalled John Boyd-Carpenter, the cabinet minister in charge at the time. "She had done her homework, and he had not done his."

Often, it doesn't even matter all that much whether the "facts" are right. When it comes to making a good impression or anchoring an argument, the truly great intimidator seizes the advantage. Even the misleading or inaccurate factoid—when uttered with complete confidence and injected into a discussion with perfect timing and precision—can carry the day. In a negotiation or board meeting, less confident individuals are likely to remain silent and avoid challenging someone presenting her case with assurance. It's only later, when there might be time to check out the accuracy of a statement, that people realize they've been hoodwinked. By then, however, it's too late: The moment is gone, and the informational intimidator has walked away with all the marbles. Robert McNamara raised this technique to the level of an art. When he and Lee Iacocca were at Ford, Iacocca once commented to another executive, "That son of a bitch [McNamara] always has an answer, and it always sounds good. But you know," he added, "I checked some of it out after a meeting, and some of it is really bullshit. Stuff he just made up." . . .

People may not like intimidators, but they do respect the truly great ones. The political intelligence of the great intimidator may have its downsides, but it can also be used creatively and toward great purpose, just like any other form of influence. One observer of Michael Eisner's recent travails at Disney had this to relate:

> What is lost in the stories about Mr. Eisner's arrogance, greed, and insensitivity is the more illuminating tale of how he transformed a faltering animation and amusement park company into one of the world's most successful entertainment companies. When he assumed command in 1984, Disney had a market value of $1.8 billion. Today its market value is $57.1 billion.

So before we throw out all the great intimidators—and turn the organizational helm over to those gentle, humble, self-effacing leaders who've apparently been waiting in the wings—we might stop to consider what we would lose. Great intimidators may create disharmony, but they also can create value.

NOTES AND QUESTIONS

1. Consider two leaders whom you have especially admired. How did their styles match up to Goleman's categories? What made their approaches effective?

2. Hay/McBer's research finds that "coaching" is the least common style of leadership. Why? Experts identify not only lack of time and interest but also interpersonal obstacles to candid feedback, such as the desire to be liked or to avoid conflict, and concerns about damaging the relationship. Even leaders who attempt to provide coaching may sabotage their efforts by lack of sensitivity. Common problems include becoming antagonistic or defensive; losing sight of others' needs; failing to be specific about what needs to change and why; getting locked into one approach and not being responsive to the impact of criticism or to new information and behavior; and failing to follow up on plans for improvement. Think about contexts in which you have given or received feedback. What has been most and least effective?

3. Ronald Heifetz describes effective leadership as an ability to move "back and forth between the dance floor and the balcony." Leaders not only have to guide their partners around the ballroom, they also need periodically to move above it and look for broader patterns.[28] Some distance is necessary to identify what is really going on in a situation and to understand when the problem of the moment is symptomatic of broader difficulties. Is that metaphor helpful in describing leadership challenges that you have faced or the ones confronting leaders in problems 2-1 and 2-2 below?

4. Are the "fatal flaws" of leadership that Zenger and Folkman identify ones that you have observed or studied? How might they be remedied? Revisit that question in light of problem 2-1 below.

5. A less extreme version of the intimidation style is what some consultants label a drive to "overachievement."[29] Leaders with this tendency focus on

their own achievement and the need to outperform not only competitors but subordinates. They do not listen or enable others; they soak up "all the oxygen in the room," by pushing their ideas and even answering their own questions.[30] Such an approach may yield some short-term advantages if the leader is gifted, but in the long term it creates dependency and disengagement. What strategies can leaders employ to overcome this tendency? How can subordinates help?

6. Kramer claims that the "great intimidators" are "not your typical bullies." What is the difference? How much does motive matter to those who are on the receiving end of abusive conduct? Most research suggests that pervasive bullying impairs performance, and that likeability is correlated with effective leadership. Surveys also find that about a third of employees report being bullied, and of these, about half leave their jobs as a result.[31] Women are particularly likely to be disliked for intimidating and domineering styles; indeed, some leadership development experts have developed a niche in coaching "bully broads."[32] Although some forceful female leaders manage to be viewed positively — Richard Nixon echoed Georges Pompidou's description of Golda Meir as a "femme formidable" — Chapter 8 notes the difficulty that women have in negotiating the "too assertive/not assertive enough" double bind.[33] What strategies might best enable female leaders to cope with this challenge?

7. For every example that Kramer cites of successful bullying, other experts offer counterexamples or disagree with his characterization of success. Kramer's assessment of Lawrence Summers differs sharply from those of many observers, including that of Harvard professor Howard Gardner, discussed in Chapter 4. In your view, what separates the successful from the unsuccessful intimidators? Have you ever worked for an individual with that style? How would you assess its effectiveness? What would you do if you worked for someone like Joe Cassano, described in the following problem?

PROBLEM 2-1

One of the organizations that played a pivotal role in the global financial crisis beginning in 2007 was A.I.G. Financial Products (A.I.G. F.P.), a unit of the A.I.G. insurance company. The unit's highly educated, extremely well-compensated traders made risky financial decisions that have been estimated to cost United States taxpayers something on the order of $182 billion when the Obama administration stepped in to prevent A.I.G.'s collapse. At the head of that unit was Joe Cassano, who by all accounts, was a classic great intimidator.

According to Michael Lewis's in-depth profile,

> Across A.I.G. F.P. the view of the boss was remarkably consistent: a guy with a crude feel for financial risk but a real talent for bullying people who doubted him. "A.I.G. F.P. became a dictatorship," says one London trader. "Joe would bully people around. He'd humiliate them and then try to make it up to them by giving them huge amounts of money." . . . [Another trader recalled:] "The fear level was so high that when we had these morning meetings you presented what you did not to upset him. And if you were critical of the organization, all

hell would break loose." . . . [Others agreed.] "The way you dealt with Joe was to start everything by saying, 'You're right, Joe.' "

According to traders, Cassano was one of those people whose insecurities manifested themselves in a need for obedience and total control. . . . Oddly, he was as likely to direct his anger at profitable traders as at unprofitable ones — and what caused him to become angry was the faintest whiff of insurrection.

Even more oddly, his anger had no obvious effect on the recipient's paycheck; a trader might find himself routinely abused by his boss and yet delighted by his year-end bonus, determined by that same boss. Every one of the people I spoke with admitted that the reason they hadn't taken a swing at Joe Cassano, before walking out the door, was that the money was simply too good. . . . [A.I.G. F.P. was] now run, roughly, by a man who didn't fully understand all the calculations and whose judgment was clouded by his insecurity. The few people willing to question that judgment wound up quitting the firm.[34]

This management style was a recipe for disaster when A.I.G. F.P. began to insure credit default swaps that consisted primarily of subprime mortgages. Cassano failed to appreciate the risks, or listen to those who did, until it was too late. Of course, as is clear from Chapter 5's discussion of moral leadership in the financial crisis, there is plenty of blame to go around for the factors that led to A.I.G.'s collapse, including irresponsibility on the part of regulators as well as Wall Street financiers. However, by Lewis's account, Cassano was "as responsible for a series of disastrous trades as a person in a big company can be. He discouraged the dissent of subordinates who understood them better than he did."[35]

The question then becomes, why did no one at A.I.G. see this coming? The employees Lewis interviewed felt that the problem began with Hank Greenberg, the A.I.G. CEO who put Cassano in charge because "he saw in him a pale imitation of his own tyrannical self and felt he could control him."[36] That worked as long as Greenberg was closely supervising Cassano's decisions. But when a scandal forced Greenberg to resign in the mid-1990s, his replacement thought the "money machine ran on its own, and Cassano did nothing to discourage the view. By 2005, A.I.G. F.P. was, in effect, his company."[37]

The traders who worked under Cassano had much to lose personally from his risky and ill-informed decisions. The company required them to defer about half of their pay, in order to intertwine their long-term interests with those of the organization. When A.I.G. imploded, some lost as much as half of what they had earned over the past decade. What might they have done to avert the crisis?

One other factor that contributes to problems such as A.I.G.'s is that leaders can become "victims of their own success." People can become complacent "once money starts rolling in" and then miss changes in the market environment.[38] Moreover, as Chris Argyris notes in the excerpt in section D below, successful leaders often lack experience with failure, and their desire to retain control and avoid looking inept keeps them from trying new approaches that might better adapt to evolving circumstances.[39] How can boards of directors and CEOs prevent these blind spots and the management styles that proved so problematic for A.I.G? What broader lessons does this problem suggest?

MEDIA RESOURCES

Examples of different styles of leadership abound. Models of effective coaching appear in *Invictus* and *A Man for All Seasons*, described in Chapter 12, as well as in movies about teachers or athletes, such as *A League of their Own*, *The Great Debates*, and *Chariots of Fire*. A particularly good example comes from season 4, episode 8 of the television series *Mad Men* ("The Summer Man"), in which Peggy, the female copywriter, asks her boss Don Draper to deal with sexual harassment and disrespect by a male freelance employee. Draper tells her to handle it herself and earn respect rather than a reputation as a tattletale. When she does so, she is told by the female office manager who was also a target of the harassment that the action succeeded only in establishing Peggy as a humorless bitch. The scene raises multiple issues of effective styles of coaching, as well as diversity and conflict management.

Profiles of intimidating leaders in television and film are in ample supply. Three examples that can spark useful discussion are *The Devil Wears Prada*, *The Proposal*, and "Executive Wrath," the pilot episode of *The West Wing*. In *The Devil Wears Prada*, Meryl Streep plays the fictionalized version of a legendary head of a women's fashion magazine who terrorizes subordinates without ever raising her voice. *The Proposal* features Sandra Bullock as the abusive head of a publishing company, whose morning entrance prompts an e-mail to the workforce that "the witch is on her broom." These portraits raise issues not only of effectiveness but also of gender stereotypes. As discussion in Chapter 8 indicates, behavior that appears assertive in male leaders often appears abrasive in their female counterparts. The segment from *The West Wing* shows a more productive example of intimidation. President Bartlett, played by Martin Sheen, upbraids right-wing leaders who were trying to bully his staff into accepting legislative concessions; the conservatives were seeking payback for an insult that an administration official had delivered on morning television. Bartlett undercuts the conservatives' moral high ground by denouncing their failure to disavow tactics of a fundamentalist group that had sent graphic hate mail to his twelve-year-old granddaughter. A key issue is how much motive matters. Does Bartlett's wrath seem more justified because larger social values are implicated? Another core question is whether intimidation works in the absence of hard power to back it up.

For those who prefer contemporary real-life examples, instructive parodies of congressional majority leader Nancy Pelosi and Obama's chief of staff Rahm Emanuel appeared in the fall of 2010 on *Saturday Night Live* and *The Daily Show with Jon Stewart*. Taken together, these portraits raise questions about what makes intimidation productive or abusive.

C. LEADERSHIP IN CONTEXT: LAW, POLICY, AND MANAGEMENT

1. COMPARING LAW, POLICY, AND MANAGEMENT

As the preceding discussion noted, much of what makes leaders effective depends on context. Although most core competencies of leadership are relevant in any workplace, different occupations pose their own distinctive challenges. Law, policy, and management offer representative illustrations of the differences that arise both across and within fields. So, for example, the challenges that arise in managing a 1000-person law firm with multiple branches in six countries differ from those involved in running a state attorney general's office, or a small disability rights organization. The United States Secretary for Housing and Urban Development and the head of a nonprofit community association are both exercising policy influence, but their roles and responsibilities are quite different. The CEO of IBM and the CEO of a small family start-up can hold the same job title, but their leadership opportunities and constraints vary considerably.

Consider the following contextual factors:

- Organizational characteristics: size, complexity, structure, resources, and competitive position;
- Stakeholder characteristics: expectations, needs, and values; and
- Positional characteristics: forms of hard and soft power, relationships with stakeholders (including clients), criteria for success, and structures of accountability.

How might these factors affect the qualities of leadership that will be most successful in a given context? Compare, for example, the variety of settings in which lawyers exercise leadership. This advisory role is often analogized to "servant leadership."[40] In effect, the lawyer serves clients by enabling them to realize their highest aspirations and their organizations' best interests. Much of lawyers' work, both as leaders and advisors to leaders, involves soft power. Unlike top executives in hierarchical corporate structures, these lawyer leaders often lack the structural power to make important decisions themselves. They need to rely on "persuasion, political currency, and shared interests to create conditions for the right decisions to happen."[41] Qualities essential to leadership in these contexts involve active listening, communication, and self-reflection.[42]

By contrast, leaders in more hierarchical corporate organizations may have greater hard power, but even CEOs are subject to a variety of constraints. Their autonomy is limited by boards of directors, government regulators, and investors. Often the tyranny of the balance sheet can serve as a greater limitation on power than many outsiders appreciate. Moreover, particularly in large, complex organizations, top management's capacity to oversee all aspects of performance is bounded by time, distance, and technical capacities. Leaders' effectiveness depends heavily on followers, and on their ability to develop leadership in others who will necessarily exercise oversight.

Those in public office face their own set of challenges. These leaders are expected to serve the public interest, often in contexts lacking consensus on what that interest in fact requires or clear metrics on how to measure or compare performance. How does a public official decide if he should spend less on health and more on sanitation?[43] A comprehensive overview of the distinctions between public and private sector organizations identified the following differences that are relevant to government leaders:

- Less market discipline results in less pressure for efficiency and less objective definitions of goals and results;

- More public accountability results in greater constraints on activities, more formal rules and controls, more disruptive turnover following elections, greater diversity and intensity of external influences, and greater need for support of multiple constituencies with competing agendas;
- Greater social impact and symbolic importance results in greater public scrutiny, and higher expectations of fairness, openness, honesty, and responsiveness; and
- Greater need for personal achievement and social impact, and greater civil service protections results in greater difficulty in devising incentives for efficient performance and more infighting over "power and glory."[44]

These dynamics often pose significant challenges even for those with substantial formal power. President Truman once famously expressed sympathy for his successor General Eisenhower, who would no longer be able to expect having his orders followed.[45]

Consider how contextual differences may demand corresponding differences in leadership style. Stanford Business School professor Jeffrey Pfeffer notes that even seemingly similar positions may require different approaches. He gives the example of a Minnesota school district superintendent who was widely acclaimed for her charismatic qualities and interpersonal skills in uniting diverse constituencies. Through broad collaboration, she managed to achieve budget reductions, administrative restructuring, and other innovative reforms. Her effectiveness led to an appointment as the head of the state Department of Education, where she pursued similar strategies with far less success. In her first year in office, she personally visited almost every one of Minnesota's 435 districts, held town meetings drawing over 15,000 citizens, sponsored opinion polls, and brought in nine outsiders to lead organizational change.[46] Yet the change met widespread resistance, half of the outsiders left or were fired within a year, and she became quickly mired in the "day to day details" of a large bureaucracy. Her new position involved a "much more complex web of relations among the legislature, state executive departments, constituents, interest groups and networks, and state and national educational communities," where personal contacts and a charismatic style counted for much less.[47] What lessons might her experience hold for others making similar career transitions?

2. LAWYERS IN LEADERSHIP ROLES: A CASE STUDY

In the excerpt below, Ben Heineman, a lawyer who has also held managerial and public-policy positions, describes what he sees as the primary leadership challenges for the legal profession. Are the capacities that he sees as desirable for lawyers different from those that would be relevant for business or policy leaders? How can the necessary talents for all these individuals be most effectively nurtured?

BEN W. HEINEMAN JR., "LAW AND LEADERSHIP"

Journal of Legal Education 56 (2006) 596.

My thesis is that law school graduates should aspire not just to be wise counselors but wise leaders; not just to dispense "practical wisdom" but to be "practical visionaries"; not just to have positions where they advise but where they decide. I wish to redefine, or at least reemphasize, the concept of lawyer explicitly to include "lawyer as leader." I do this with the hope that the law schools and the profession will more candidly recognize the importance of leadership and will more directly prepare and inspire young lawyers to seek roles of ultimate responsibility and accountability than is the case today. These are roles which those with core legal training have in fact assumed throughout our history and which Alexis de Tocqueville recognized and celebrated more than 150 years ago.

Why do I advance this thesis? First, our society—national and global—suffers from a leadership deficit. We need our brightest, toughest, most ethical, most broad-gauged to combine strong substantive visions with an ability to get things done. Surely, our law school graduates can try—and I emphasize try—to address that deficit if they are so motivated. The core competencies of law are as good a foundation for broad leadership as other training. . . .

Second, the legal profession, by many accounts, is suffering from a crisis that is "the product of growing doubts about the capacity of a lawyer's life to offer fulfillment. . . ." An important dimension of this problem is the disconnect between personal values and professional life, especially the possible amorality of serving clients' interests in an adversary mode. Providing leadership can certainly be an affirmation—and a testing—of one's vision and one's values. So providing leadership may serve both social and individual needs. . . .

Whatever the setting and whatever the style, the lawyer as leader is focused on making decisions for institutions or causes or ideas that . . . have as a driving force the desire to make our national or global society a "better place," however difficult that goal is to define, much less achieve. . . .

[What kind of lawyers should we be educating for leadership roles?] Most generally, we are seeking lawyers who *have a creative and constructive, not just a critical, cast of mind*, who relish asking "ought," not just answering "is," questions. How do we—how can we—build, not just deconstruct, an argument in a brief, a regulation, a complex piece of legislation, a business plan, the agenda of an NGO, a foreign policy, a cross-border strategy for global issues like energy and the environment?

We are seeking lawyers who, in asking the "what ought we to do" questions, *can articulate powerfully a set of systematic and constructive options that expose and explore the value tensions inherent in most decisions* . . . [and] *can find a fair balance . . . between legitimate competing values. . . .*

We are seeking lawyers who *think about the ethical, reputational, and enlightened self-interest of their client or the institution they are leading*, not just about what is strictly legal or advantageous in the short term. . . .

We are seeking lawyers who, in making recommendations or decisions, *are capable of assessing all dimensions of risk but who are not risk-averse*. Taking chances is not a quality of mind customarily associated with lawyers but is often vital to innovation and change in the public and private sectors.

We are seeking lawyers who *have the ability to understand how to make rules realities*: lawyers who understand, *inter alia*, institutions, history, culture, resources, and psychology and who can identify, and develop, strategies to mitigate the obstacles to meaningful implementation.

We are seeking lawyers who *understand and respect the hurly burly world of politics, media and power*, not just the more intellectual world of policy prescriptions and legal rules. . . .

We are seeking lawyers who are not just strong individual contributors but who *have the ability to work cooperatively and constructively on teams.* . . .

We are seeking lawyers who are not just strong team members but who *can lead and build organizations*: create the vision, the values, the priorities, the strategies, the people, the systems, the processes, the checks and balances, the resources, and the motivation. Working on teams and leading them are interconnected: much of leadership today is not command and control of the troops but persuasion, motivation, and empowerment of teams around a shared vision.

We are seeking lawyers who, in developing positions, whether in an article, brief, regulation, legislation, code of corporate conduct, or a myriad other rule-announcing activities, *have the ability to understand the value, and limits, of related disciplines*—including economics, anthropology, history, political science, psychology, statistics, sociology, [public policy management,] and organizational theory—to increase the accuracy and sophistication of those positions. Lawyers cannot all have joint degrees, but they need the aptitude and capacity to envision the relevance and then, through the expertise of others, mine these other fields of knowledge—to understand their strengths and the limitations inherent in their assumptions and methods.

Most importantly, we are seeking lawyers who *understand the methods of thinking and analysis taught in the business and public policy schools.* . . .

We are seeking lawyers who *have global understanding, intuition, and perspective.*

We are seeking lawyers who can *perform early in their careers as outstanding specialists* so that they truly understand what analytic rigor and excellence are, but can *then have the vision, breadth and inclination to be outstanding generalist/ leaders* later in life. The quintessential quality of the great generalist is envisioning and understanding the multiple dimensions of issues—to define the problem or issue properly—and the ability to comprehensively integrate those dimensions into the decision. . . .

QUESTIONS

1. How can the capabilities that Heineman describes be most readily acquired?
2. If Heineman is right about the qualities necessary for effective leadership, what does that suggest about necessary curricular reforms in legal, management, and policy education?

PROBLEM 2-2

You are the chairman of a major San Francisco firm. With the recent economic downturn, your firm's profits have taken a substantial dip. Rather than cut compensation for equity partners, the firm's leading rainmakers prefer deferred offers, layoffs of associates and staff, and pay cuts for underemployed non-equity partners, which will encourage their departures. None of these options is appealing. If the firm decreases profits per partner, it risks losing some of its highest-billing attorneys. If it downsizes the workforce, it will impose undeserved hardships on those least able to bear them, reduce the ranks of experienced employees necessary when the economy rebounds, and adversely affect morale, recruiting, and reputation.

If the firm decides that reductions are necessary, you are not sure whether to freeze all new hiring, layoff associates and non-equity partners who are seriously underemployed, and/or furlough new recruits with partial pay. Nor are you sure of what criteria to use in targeting cuts. Should layoffs and deferred hiring be based on the work available in individuals' specialty areas? Should you encourage high-performing associates to retool in a different field? You also face questions about whether to ask laid-off employees to leave immediately, or whether to allow them a period of transition in which they can look for another position. The latter is more humane, but it also imposes more salary and support costs for the firm, risks retaliation, and jeopardizes workplace morale.

A further difficulty is how forthcoming to be about the firm's financial position and the likelihood of further reductions. Full candor could damage the firm's reputation with clients and potential recruits, thus compounding its financial problems. Lack of transparency could also jeopardize the firm's standing and further sour workplace relationships.

If you were the managing partner of the firm, how would you handle its economic challenges?

NOTES

Layoffs pose challenges for leaders in any employment context, and the recent financial downturn has pushed the problems to new levels. Between September 2008 and 2010, over 5 million workers were subject to layoffs.[48] However, as noted in Chapter 1, leadership of lawyers poses some distinctive challenges, which become particularly pronounced during economic downturns. In a Hildebrandt Institute study of failed firms, about half had "fundamental flaws related to the internal dynamics of the firms themselves . . . [stemming] from a lack of clear strategies, of clearly articulated and compatible goals among their partners, and of strong leadership to achieve their mutually shared strategic visions."[49] Underlying these problems are the characteristics of individuals who choose legal careers, the qualities reinforced in legal practice, and the structures of legal workplaces.

One cluster of difficulties involves autonomy, skepticism, and distrust. Partners value their independence and are often skeptical of governance structures based on shared credit, collaboration, and subordination of their own interests to the greater good.[50] The result is a low-trust environment, which is exacerbated by lateral movement, mergers, and branch offices. Particularly during times of stress, partners are reluctant to make sacrifices that they are not confident will be reciprocated. A related set of problems involves decision-making styles. Most lawyers take a highly analytic view of management, which focuses on financial scorecards and devalues soft skills. Lawyers often rise to leadership positions because of their skills as lawyers, not as leaders. They are hampered by colleagues whose tendency in evaluating proposals is to look for loopholes, counterexamples, exceptions, and risks, the result can be strategic paralysis. According to consultant David Maister, the main reason many lawyers do so well financially is that they "compete only with other lawyers." But they fail to realize their potential in organizations by behaving as "bands of warlords, each with his or her followers . . . acting in temporary alliance — until a better opportunity comes along."[51]

Compounding these problems is the lack of importance that lawyers ascribe to leadership issues. Surveys find that only about a quarter of firms have succession plans, and that partners with significant management possibilities bill only about 10 percent fewer hours than their non-manager peers.[52] Less than a third of surveyed firms make chairs among their highest-paid partners.[53] And because firms almost always fill chair vacancies from within, individuals may be reluctant to invest too much effort in managerial roles because they will be unable to capitalize on their experience once they leave the position.

These problems came to a head as the economy worsened in the early twenty-first century. Many law firms found themselves confronting some variation of the facts described in problem 2-2. The legal system lost 15,000 jobs between 2008 and 2010, and a number of leading firms dissolved while others imposed layoffs and salary freezes, ceased recruiting, deferred associate start dates, and/or instituted structural changes in hiring and promotion practices (such as more contract and counsel positions, and longer tracks to partnership).[54]

One firm, Brobeck, Phleger & Harrison LLP (Brobeck) became the subject of sufficient public scrutiny to provide an illuminating case history of law firm leadership gone awry. At its height, Brobeck was one of the nation's most respected firms. It had over 1000 attorneys in offices across the nation, generated $68 million in annual profits, and provided partners yearly average earnings of $1.17 million.[55] It attempted to position itself as "*the* law firm for the Internet economy," and its clients included technology giants such as Apple, as well as leading businesses such as Wells Fargo, Bank of America, Gap, Clorox, and Chevron.[56]

To outsiders, the collapse of Brobeck in 2003 came as a surprise. Some attributed it to the recession.[57] Others saw it as a belated casualty of the high-tech boom-and-bust cycle.[58] However, interviews with former Brobeck employees suggested a more complex story reflecting fundamental differences over leadership. As one in-depth profile summarized the situation, some senior lawyers, including the firm's chair, Tower Snow, believed that the partners should take pay cuts during the downturn: "[D]eal-makers," he argued, "should share the wealth with colleagues."[59] By contrast, many of his colleagues believed that "[p]artners are owners and [major dips in their] income are disconcerting and undesirable."[60]

Snow joined Brobeck in 1995, having already built an impressive reputation as a securities litigator for high-tech firms. In 1998, he was unanimously elected chairman, and initially proved adept at managing what insiders described as an exceptionally competitive, combative, and Balkanized culture. He spearheaded an expansion into several cities, along with a multimillion-dollar advertisement blitz, and firm partners began earning on average

$400,000 more than other Bay Area partners. Not everyone, however, was pleased with the direction of the firm. Some felt non-tech clients were slighted, while others were uneasy with the firm's increasing focus on profits and growth.[61]

The issues came to a head as the economy worsened. Snow opposed layoffs from the start. He felt that they would undermine the "stand and fall together" culture he was trying to create and that the firm would need its currently underutilized talent when the economy rebounded. Moreover, it seemed "only fair that the people who had benefited the most from the boom should absorb the shock of the bust. A partner who earned hundreds of thousands of bucks a year instead of $1.17 million would still be rich. A laid-off secretary or associate was in danger of losing everything."[62] As he put it to colleagues, "Do you really want to fire 100 people to put $10,000 in your pocket, $5000 of which will go to Uncle Sam?"[63] Others disagreed and were annoyed by public statements that exposed internal disagreements and implicitly criticized partners' greed. In late 2001, after a year in which Snow had logged 4000 hours and had barely seen his family, he learned that one of his colleagues had circulated a no-confidence petition. He stepped down as chair.

His replacements, Richard S. Odom and Richard L. Parker, immediately began dismantling the firm's previous management team and many day-to-day operations fell to attorneys who were ill-equipped to handle them. Without strong central leadership, branch offices began running themselves and key partners began jumping ship with entire practice groups in tow. When the firm leadership heard that Snow and thirty colleagues were talking with British-based Clifford Chance, it summarily expelled him and cut off access to his office, e-mail, and voice mail. By the end of 2002, some seventy partners had left and the firm had trouble paying bills and funding its retirement accounts.[64] It then retained outside lawyers to assist in reducing debt and renegotiating leases. However, to avoid reducing partner income, the firm also began drawing down its line of credit.

The situation worsened when Citibank demanded repayment of the debt. Partners agreed to forgo salaries for the first quarter of 2003, and negotiations concerning a merger with another prominent firm took on new urgency. But then another group of partners defected, which caused landlords to rescind newly renegotiated leases, and the merger to fall through. At that point, Brobeck's most powerful partners decided to cut their potential losses and disband the firm. It subsequently filed for bankruptcy.[65]

NOTES AND QUESTIONS

1. As the preceding materials indicate, a key leadership strategy is aligning individual and organizational objectives and uniting stakeholders around a common vision. Could Snow, Odom, and Parker have done anything differently to achieve such unity and prevent Brobeck's dissolution? A 2010 survey of leaders of professional service firms (including law firms) found that the most important qualities involved interpersonal skills and emotional intelligence: ability to influence and build coalitions (42 percent); inspiration and passion (34 percent); vision (29 percent);

listening (24 percent); good communication (25 percent); business understanding (21 percent); ability to attract followers (21 percent); empathy (21 percent); integrity (17 percent); courage (16 percent); humility (16 percent); respect for others (12 percent). Only one quality, understanding of the business (21 percent), involved technical, analytical skill. Particularly in times of stress, a key capacity was the ability of leaders to engage colleagues around a vision that was emotionally compelling and attainable.[66] Such research is consistent with other published views of law firm managing partners, who consistently emphasize the importance of emotional intelligence and interpersonal skills.[67]

So too, in their recent study of professional service firms (including law firms), Harvard Business School professors Thomas De Long and John Garro and professional development consultant Robert Lees found that the qualities most essential to effective leadership were charting a direction; gaining commitment to that direction; following through on goals; and setting personal examples. One of their case histories of success involves the real estate practice group of Herbert Smith, a London-based law firm with 1100 attorneys in Europe and Asia. The group was underperforming in relation to the rest of the firm, largely due to changes in the real estate market. In response, its leaders united around a new focus on premium work for premium clients. Each attorney received a personalized development plan and candid 360-degree feedback. Within six years profits had dramatically increased and the group was recognized by a leading trade publication as "Real Estate Team of the Year."[68] Could similar strategies have worked at Brobeck? What would they have required?

Not all such restructuring efforts have happy endings. According to the Hildebrandt consulting group's analysis of some eighty law firm failures, a common contributing factor is an unwillingness to oust unproductive partners. More "collegial" approaches, such as reduced compensation or removal of equity status, "hardly ever work." They reportedly build frustration and trigger defection by high performers.[69] As one managing partner put it, "[W]e are the only industry that carries their wounded."[70] In an increasingly competitive market, some law firm leaders believe that this is a luxury that they can no longer afford. By contrast, others believe that a commitment to assisting partners who are victims of market swings or temporary personal problems is part of what distinguishes professional firms from businesses. An excessive focus on billable hours can erode collegiality and cooperation, and devalue other contributions to law firm performance, such as mentoring, recruitment, and pro bono service. What is your view?

2. When and how to conduct layoffs in the workforce has attracted increasing attention given recent financial conditions. Many experts note that the downsides of downsizing are often underestimated. Historically, the average economic recession lasts only about eleven months, and companies that must rehire shortly after cutbacks generally do worse than those that ride out the downturn, given the costs of recruitment and retraining, and the morale, stress, and defections that accompany layoffs.[71] When downsizing is necessary, mistakes to avoid include inadequate information, unfulfilled promises of consultation and assistance, or generous bonuses

to those responsible for the decision.[72] A more positive model comes from Jeffrey Pfeffer's description of the New Zealand Postal Service's transition to a market-like enterprise. It coupled layoffs with generous severance plans, ceremonies recognizing departing employees' service, and involvement of staff in determining who would go.[73] Other experts similarly advocate "downsizing with dignity." Such approaches demand honesty and fairness: realistic appraisals of the organization's economic circumstances and distribution of hardships in as even-handed a way as possible. Leaders should avoid "death by a thousand cuts," which triggers defection by the most marketable employees and demoralization and anxiety among the others.[74] Would these approaches be feasible for law firms under circumstances such as those in problem 2-2?

3. Leadership experts note that budget crises are often symptomatic of deeper problems involving productivity and clashes in organizational priorities. Short-term strategies such as additional borrowing, layoffs, and expenditure freezes may prove to be only temporary solutions to long-term difficulties. Such strategies may sustain profits and retain investors and creditors, but they do not increase productivity or efficiency, and they may paper over conflicts that will ultimately prove debilitating.[75] In firms with low-trust environments, the "best and the brightest lawyers [often] jump quickly to a less risky platform" rather than help stabilize a difficult situation.[76]

A case similar to Brobeck involved Wolf Block, a distinguished Philadelphia-based firm with 300 lawyers in nine offices. In 2009, it dissolved. The precipitating cause was the recession, particularly the downturn in the real estate market, which accounted for about 40 percent of the firm's revenues. Deeper problems reflected failures of leadership. For a decade, the firm was chaired by a troika that reportedly "ruled by fear" and secrecy.[77] Its approach led to hoarding of clients, defections of partners, and a failure to diversify into profitable specialties. A highly publicized sex discrimination lawsuit that the leaders chose to litigate rather than settle exposed embarrassing biases in promotion processes and compromised the firm's ability to attract and retain women.[78] The chair who replaced the troika was by all accounts a pleasant and talented attorney, but he was also indecisive and unwilling to make tough choices or pressure colleagues to do so.[79] When the firm faced difficulties in obtaining a necessary line of credit, many partners were reluctant to accept the loan out of fear that others would defect. The chair's equivocation about his own plans was the final straw.

What broader lessons about leadership do such case histories suggest? In a 2008 white paper, the Hildebrandt consulting firm analyzed factors contributing to the failure of eighty law firms. Problems fell into three main areas, all of which involved leadership failures. The first was inadequate financial performance, typically involving unproductive partners, excessive borrowing to fuel growth or sustain profits, and poor "financial hygiene," such as failing to control partners' discounts on fees. A second category of problems involved internal dynamics, including lack of realistic strategic focus, loss of trust, and poorly conceived compensation structures. A third group of difficulties involved external competitive pressures, and leaders' failure to respond to market trends and to manage partner expectations in light of those dynamics.[80]

Some experts see the recession in general and these failures in particular as occasions for the profession to rethink traditional structures. They recommend more flexibility in ownership and compensation structures, more involvement of the entire firm in designing cost-saving strategies, and more implementation of professional development programs that involve leaders in addressing concrete challenges.[81] What other alternatives are available to firms facing difficulties of the sort confronting Brobeck and Wolf Block?

MEDIA RESOURCES

Layoffs and plant closings are the subjects of many excellent media portraits.[82] The film *Up in the Air* features George Clooney as a consultant who makes his living by firing workers whose managers do not want to do it themselves. The film involves a difficult ethical issue when Clooney is asked about a termination that his subordinate orchestrated, in which the employee threatened suicide and later made good on her threat. An honest answer to the question could derail the subordinate's career. *The Company Men* chronicles the effect of downsizing on the lives of three executives at a fictional Boston corporation. *Roger and Me*, one of Michael Moore's first documentaries, is about the economic conditions that ravaged Detroit and the leaders who did not want to deal with the consequences. Season 3, episode 13 ("Shut the Door. Have a Seat.") of the television series *Mad Men* explores challenges facing the central characters as they orchestrate a secret defection from their advertising agency, which is being absorbed in a merger.

Other issues specific to the lawyer's role as a leader of leaders emerge in season 2, episode 2 ("In the Shadow of Two Gunmen, Part 2") of *The West Wing*, the television series featuring dilemmas facing the president and his White House staff. In a flashback scene, Sam Seaborn, who later becomes the administration's chief communications officer, is then an associate about to make partner in a prominent New York law firm. He is at a meeting to finalize the purchase agreement for some large ocean tankers. Just as the senior partner present announces that nothing is left to do but "to dot the tees," Sam suddenly interjects his advice: "Don't buy these ships. Buy other ships. Better ships." He then explains that spending $11 million more on safer tankers could prevent environmental disasters, such as the Exxon Valdez oil spill. This spectacularly ineffective (and entertaining) attempt at influence raises many of the questions that Heineman identifies: how lawyers could play a more constructive role in fostering socially responsible corporate conduct, and what, from business leaders' perspective, stands in the way.

D. LEARNING LEADERSHIP

1. THE STATE OF LEADERSHIP EDUCATION

As the introduction to this chapter noted, leadership education is a relatively recent phenomenon, and it has yet to secure widespread support and respect in many academic institutions. Law schools have been especially slow to embrace the need for formal training, which is particularly puzzling given the high proportion of their graduates who occupy leadership positions.[83] As Gregory Williams noted while president of the Association of American Law Schools, although schools happily take credit for launching the leadership careers of their prominent graduates, few have "focused attention on fostering leadership . . . curricula."[84] Lawyers' leadership responsibilities are a dominant theme in extracurricular programs, commencement speeches, and alumni awards, but the topic is missing in action in day-to-day teaching.[85]

The inadequate attention to leadership development is rooted in broader problems in legal education that are attracting increased concern. A recent Lexis Nexis survey on the state of the legal industry found that almost two-thirds of law students, and 90 percent of lawyers, felt that law school effectively teaches legal doctrine but not the practical skills necessary in the current economic climate.[86] Leaders of the bar have expressed growing discontent about the disconnect between academic preparation and the needs of practice.[87] So too, the consensus among experts, including authors of the recent Carnegie Foundation report *Educating Lawyers*, is that schools have not done enough to integrate issues of values into the core curriculum.[88] The need for more effective training in practical skills and ethical judgment is particularly pronounced at leadership levels. Large law firms, in-house counsel offices, government agencies, and public-interest organizations are run by individuals who generally have had no management training, and whose abilities as lawyers do not necessarily meet the demands of leadership. As managing partner Jeffrey Lutsky noted in an interview with the *Legal Intelligencer*, "[T]he historical model for law firms is to put [people] in a leadership position often not because of leadership skills but because of [rainmaking] . . . and hope that they don't drive into a ditch."[89] This inattention to leadership development raises particular concern in light of a recent statistical study by Laurie Bassi and Daniel McMurrer. They found that the most powerful predictor of large-firm profitability is "the quality of partners' leadership skills."[90] Similar points apply to leaders in the nonprofit sector. In noting the current demands of his job, the executive director of the public-interest Immigrant Legal Resources Center wondered: "Why didn't I go to business school?"[91]

Yet if he had gone to business school, he might have had similar frustrations. Harvard Business School professors Nitin Nohria and Rakesh Khurana, and Stanford Business School professor Jeffrey Pfeffer note that despite most MBA programs' announced mission to train leaders, the topic generally remains on the periphery of their research and teaching.[92] Surveys by the Aspen Institute consistently find that among the future leaders graduating from these programs, confidence in their ability to manage value conflicts actually falls during their time as students.[93] Only about two-fifths of surveyed students believed that schools were doing enough to enable them to manage value conflicts.[94]

QUESTIONS

1. What accounts for law schools' traditional lack of interest in leadership courses? Given the influence that the legal profession exercises, why isn't there more interest in training members not just to think like lawyers but also to think like leaders?

2. What might explain the disconnect between MBA programs' professed commitment and actual priorities concerning leadership education? What might increase students' capacity to manage value conflicts?

2. THE LEARNING PROCESS

How then can individuals learn to lead? There is no substitute for experience. It is one thing to read about the Charge of the Light Brigade and quite another to lead soldiers into battle. Diverse leadership experiences supply the foundation for effective exercises of power and influence. But experience alone is not sufficient. As Mark Twain famously observed, a cat that sits on a hot stove will not sit on a hot stove again, but it will not sit on a cold one either. What is needed is reflection on experience: a capacity to learn from mistakes and to build on such knowledge in future action. Research on high performers who demonstrate leadership potential early in their careers finds that they are particularly gifted "catalytic" learners; that is, they are able to identify and absorb ideas and translate them into practical strategies.[95]

How then does one learn to be a learner? Individuals vary, and they need to seek out the structures that are most effective for them. Do they learn best by reading, discussion, observation, coaching, or group interaction?[96] For many people, formal programs during or after their academic education can be valuable. At a minimum, they can enhance individuals' understanding of how to exercise influence and what cognitive biases, interpersonal responses, and organizational dynamics can sabotage effectiveness. Through exposure to leadership research, case studies, historical examples, role simulations, and guided analysis, individuals can prepare for dilemmas that they will face in practice.[97] Such settings can also provide a safe space for leaders and potential leaders to explore mistakes and the rationalizations that they have created for dysfunctional behaviors. However, for those with full-time employment, intensive educational programs can be expensive, and their lessons may not always be readily transferable to particular workplace contexts. For these individuals, many experts have stressed "self-development" strategies, such as tailored on-the-job assignments, coaching, and mentoring.[98] Whatever the setting, the fundamental objective is to promote guided reflection that helps individuals become more effective learners.

Part of that learning process involves leaders' reflection on their own strengths and weaknesses, and on the kinds of positions that will best match their talents and commitments. Many organizations and educational programs attempt to improve performance by focusing solely on deficiencies. Feedback becomes a predominately negative experience, which can discourage individuals from seeking it and erode self-confidence. Although constructive criticism is necessary for leadership development, it is not sufficient. Most individuals develop best by capitalizing on their strengths and pursuing their most fundamental goals and values.[99] That requires self-awareness and a plan for enhancing capabilities that are necessary to realize one's own aspirations.

3. OBSTACLES TO THE LEARNING PROCESS

Chris Argyris argues in the excerpt below that most organizations "not only have difficulty in addressing the learning dilemma, they aren't even aware that it exists."[100] Part of the reason is misfocused attention. As Harvard psychology professor Howard Gardner notes, too often individuals engage in "Monday morning quarterbacking" the substance of an erroneous decision, but fail to analyze the decision-making process, and the obstacles that prevent effective learning from mistakes.[101]

The first obstacle is the failure to acknowledge the need for continuous learning and to invite the criticism on which it depends. Leadership experts James Kouzes and Barry Posner put it bluntly: "[M]ost leaders don't want honest feedback, don't ask for honest feedback, and don't get much of it unless it's forced on them."[102] Of course, leaders are scarcely unique in this respect. But the understandable human tendency toward self-protection is particularly problematic for leaders, because of both the power they hold and the reluctance of subordinates to volunteer criticism. In Kouzes and Posner's survey of some 70,000 individuals, the statement that ranked the lowest in a list of thirty leadership behaviors was that the leader "asks for feedback on how his/her actions affect others' performance."[103] Only 40 percent of law firms offer associates the opportunity to evaluate their supervisor, and of those who engage in the process, only 5 percent report a change for the better.[104]

Yet, without such feedback, leaders may fail to identify problems in their own performance. Harvard economist John Kenneth Galbraith once noted that "[f]aced with the alternatives between changing one's mind and proving it unnecessary, just about everybody gets busy on the proof."[105] Defensiveness and denial are particularly apparent when individuals' own self-evaluations are at issue, and the cognitive biases discussed more extensively in Chapter 3 can reinforce this tendency. One common bias is the fundamental attribution error: people's tendency to attribute success to their own competence and character, and failure to external circumstances. A related problem stems from confirmation and assimilation biases. People tend to seek out evidence that confirms their preexisting, typically favorable vision of themselves, and avoid evidence that contradicts it. They also assimilate evidence in ways that favor their preexisting beliefs and self-image.[106] In one random sample of adult men, 70 percent rated themselves in the top quarter of the population in leadership capabilities, whereas 98 percent rated themselves above average.[107]

Other obstacles to effective learning are more specific to leadership positions. Often those who achieve such positions are individuals with high needs for approval. For those individuals, as one consultant notes, "the intention to *look* good displaces the intention to *be* good" and to pay attention to needs that do not translate into immediate recognition.[108] So too, the intense demands of many leadership positions can create a ready rationalization for not investing the effort necessary to change behavior; "I don't have time" is a common response to avoid opportunities for leadership programs or coaching.[109] Avoiding such opportunities can also help individuals evade their own responsibility for performance problems and to stay within their comfort zones.[110]

A further obstacle to effective learning is the assumption that leadership education is a "touchy-feely" process, unworthy of attention from intellectually sophisticated individuals. Yet as one prominent consultant puts it, "[T]he soft stuff is the hard stuff."[111] Effective leadership requires more than analytic skills, and high achievers in intellectual domains may not have developed corresponding interpersonal capabilities.

A final set of obstacles involves organizational failures. In one recent survey of the most profitable law firms, only a fifth had leadership development programs.[112] Although the figure is much higher in American corporations, with some estimates suggesting that 60 percent had programs, not all of them are well tailored to individual needs.[113] In business, law, and policy settings, overcommitted supervisors are often reluctant to invest the time in mentoring others, planning an appropriate sequence of developmental opportunities, or taking risks in giving inexperienced employees the new responsibilities that would best expand their competence.[114] As Morgan McCall puts it, "[D]eveloping leadership requires leadership," and it is not always forthcoming.[115]

4. LEARNING STRATEGIES

The first step in overcoming these obstacles to effective learning requires self-knowledge. Individuals must be reflective about what they want and what experiences and abilities will be necessary to achieve it.[116] Leaders and prospective leaders need a sense of their "ideal selves": what positions they aspire to hold, what qualities they are missing, and what is standing in their way.[117] One often unacknowledged obstacle is what psychologists call self-handicapping.[118] Individuals avoid making efforts that might fail and thus put their own self-esteem at risk. Refusing to compete or to prepare adequately for an interview, test, or other competitive selection process gives people an explanation for their lack of success other than that they were not good enough. In gauging their leadership objectives, individuals need to be honest about their tolerance for risk, failure, conflict, competition, pressure, and sweatshop schedules.

For those unaccustomed to self-scrutiny, formal educational programs may help by forcing them to think deeply about their values, passions, and priorities, and what personal changes and sacrifices they are prepared to make to realize their professional aspirations. At various stages of their careers, individuals should examine their current job and determine how much of their time goes to work they really enjoy and find meaningful. If the ratio is too low, individuals should think about how to move to a position that is a better match for their interests and talents.[119]

Individuals also need a plan for diagnosing their learning needs; formulating goals; identifying the resources, experiences, and capabilities that they will need to advance to their desired leadership roles; choosing learning strategies; and evaluating outcomes.[120] At the most general level, that plan should include a mix of methods: learning through doing, learning through analysis, and learning through social interaction.[121] Individuals need to develop a "nose for opportunity," and be proactive in seeking positions and "stretch assignments" that develop new skills.[122] For students, that means extracurricular commitments that give them leadership experience. For individuals starting their careers, that involves finding work or volunteer positions that give them opportunities to lead and to learn from their mistakes. For mid-career professionals and managers, that may require job rotation or unpaid leadership roles that broaden and develop their skills.[123] High levels of responsibility and pressure, coupled with adequate organizational coaching and support, often provide the best learning experiences.[124] Warren Bennis emphasizes the importance of "taking risks as a matter of course, with the knowledge that failure is as vital as it is inevitable . . . [and thinking through mistakes to] see where we went wrong, mentally revise what we're doing, and then act on the revisions. . . ."[125]

A key aspect of an effective learning process is feedback. As experts often emphasize, the "more elevated your position, the more important it is to solicit feedback," because candid criticism is unlikely to be volunteered by subordinates.[126] The feedback can come in varying forms in both educational and real-life settings: objective measures of behavior, observations by others, bottom-up 360-degree evaluations, and mentoring.[127] Enlisting trusted and respected mentors is critical and not always easy. Ideally, advisors should have honesty, knowledge of their advisee's work setting, and effective interpersonal and communication skills.[128] For individuals well integrated in certain demographic or workplace groups, effective mentoring often comes from someone outside these groups. As Chapter 8 notes, demand for mentors frequently outpaces supply, particularly for women and minorities. For individuals at early stages of their leadership development, the best strategy may be not to seek "perfect mentors," but rather to become "perfect protégés," so superiors will want to provide coaching.[129] That means being respectful of mentors' own needs and constraints, responding positively to advice, and finding ways to reciprocate or to express gratitude.

For individuals already holding top positions, the most useful advice may come from predecessors, from those who hold comparable positions in other settings, or from experts in the field. For example, Jack Welch, a widely admired CEO of General Electric (GE), credits a conversation with Peter Drucker as transformative. In discussing which of GE's various businesses were worth keeping, Drucker reportedly asked, "If you weren't already in the business today, would you go into it?" That question crystallized Welch's thinking and ultimately resulted in his famous strategy: be number one or two in an industry, or "fix, close, or sell."[130]

Similar examples come from the nonprofit sector. Ann Colby and William Damon studied morally exemplary leadership by individuals who had maintained ethical commitments and had made exceptional contributions in the face of continued frustration and hardship. One distinguishing characteristic of these individuals was their willingness to subject their views to challenge and criticism. They developed leadership skills by actively seeking advice from others who shared their fundamental moral goals but had a different perspective on how to realize them.[131]

Leaders also can benefit from formal networks and individualized coaching. Networks can connect individuals in similar positions who can be a source of advice, support, and innovative ideas. Professional coaching can supply the kind of expert assessment and candid evaluation that may be unavailable from other sources. An example comes from an executive coach profiled in the *New Yorker*, who told a client, "I can't help you make money. You're already making more than God. But do you want a funeral that no one attends? Because that's where this train is heading."[132]

Both public- and private-sector organizations need to help individuals develop leadership potential and to engage in their own succession planning. A growing trend is toward customized in-house programs and action learning — team-based experiential exercises involving issues of immediate relevance to the organization.[133] Successful initiatives generally require continuing reinforcement and feedback, as well as rewards for mentoring prospective leaders. As one *Harvard Business Review* study notes, in organizations where advancement depends partly on the

> ability to nurture leaders, even people who say that leadership cannot be developed somehow find ways to do it. . . . Just as we need more people to provide leadership in complex organizations that dominate our world today, we also need more people to develop the cultures that will create that leadership. Institutionalizing a leadership-centered culture is the ultimate act of leadership.[134]

To that end, some experts distinguish between developing leaders and developing leadership.[135] Efforts need to focus both on enhancing individual skills and on building organizational capacities for collaboration, adaptation, and innovation.

5. ORGANIZATIONAL LEARNING

Leaders need to focus not only on their own learning process but also on creating what Peter Senge termed "learning organizations." By his definition, these are institutions in which individuals are "continually learning how to learn together to expand their capacity to create the results they truly desire."[136] Other experts describe a learning organization as one "skilled in creating, acquiring and transferring knowledge, and at modifying its behavior to reflect new knowledge and insights."[137] Leaders can foster such learning environments by becoming "multipliers" of collective intelligence; they can optimize talent by extending opportunities and sharing credit, control, and ownership of organizational objectives.[138] Leaders can also support innovation along the lines described in Chapter 4. They can reward experimentation, demand better evaluation of development programs, and create networks for collaboration and information exchange.[139] Learning organizations can also make it safe for individuals to acknowledge mistakes. Warren Bennis and Burt Nanus offer the example of Tom Watkins, the legendary founder of IBM. During his leadership, a junior executive involved the company in a risky venture that proved financially disastrous. When Watson called the man into his office, he offered his resignation. Watson responded, "You can't be serious. We just spent $10 million educating you."[140]

These kinds of learning environments treat individual mistakes not simply as discrete events but as possible signals of broader organizational problems.

So, for example, many technology companies experience difficulty in leadership development because they reward people for being "the smartest techies in the room, not for nurturing the careers [of others]."[141] Organizations that are serious about mentoring can adjust their incentive structure. They can also seek feedback on their own performance through benchmarking: finding out how other high-performing organizations handle similar functions.[142]

Consider these approaches to individual and organizational learning in light of the readings that follow. What insights do they suggest about your own experience in learning to lead?

Chris Argyris, "Teaching Smart People How to Learn"

Harvard Business Review 69(3) (1991):99-109

Any company that aspires to succeed in [today's] tougher business environment . . . must first resolve a basic dilemma: success in the marketplace increasingly depends on learning, yet most people don't know how to learn. What's more, those members of the organization that many assume to be the best at learning are, in fact, not very good at it. I am talking about the well-educated, high-powered, high-commitment professionals who occupy key leadership positions in the modern corporation.

Most companies not only have tremendous difficulty addressing this learning dilemma; they aren't even aware that it exists. The reason: they misunderstand what learning is and how to bring it about.

As a result, they tend to make two mistakes in their efforts to become a learning organization.

First, most people define learning too narrowly as mere "problem solving," so they focus on identifying and correcting errors in the external environment. Solving problems is important. But if learning is to persist, managers and employees must also look inward. They need to reflect critically on their own behavior, identify the ways they often inadvertently contribute to the organization's problems, and then change how they act. In particular, they must learn how the very way they go about defining and solving problems can be a source of problems in its own right.

I have coined the terms "single loop" and "double loop" learning to capture this crucial distinction. To give a simple analogy: a thermostat that automatically turns on the heat whenever the temperature in a room drops below 68 degrees is a good example of single-loop learning. A thermostat that could ask, "Why am I set at 68 degrees?" and then explore whether or not some other temperature might more economically achieve the goal of heating the room would be engaging in double-loop learning.

Highly skilled professionals are frequently very good at single-loop learning. After all, they have spent much of their lives acquiring academic credentials, mastering one or a number of intellectual disciplines, and applying those disciplines to solve real-world problems. But ironically, this very fact helps explain why professionals are often so bad at double-loop learning.

Put simply, because many professionals are almost always successful at what they do, they rarely experience failure. And because they have rarely failed, they have never learned how to learn from failure. So whenever their single-loop learning strategies go wrong, they become defensive, screen out criticism, and put the "blame" on anyone and everyone but themselves. In short, their ability to learn shuts down precisely at the moment they need it the most.

The propensity among professionals to behave defensively helps shed light on the second mistake that companies make about learning. The common assumption is that getting people to learn is largely a matter of motivation. When people have the right attitudes and commitment, learning automatically follows. So companies focus on creating new organizational structures — compensation programs, performance reviews, corporate cultures, and the like — that are designed to create motivated and committed employees.

But effective double-loop learning is not simply a function of how people feel. It is a reflection of how they think — that is, the cognitive rules or reasoning they use to design and implement their actions. Think of these rules as a kind of "master program" stored in the brain, governing all behavior. Defensive reasoning can block learning even when the individual commitment to it is high, just as a computer program with hidden bugs can produce results exactly the opposite of what its designers had planned.

Companies can learn how to resolve the learning dilemma. What it takes is to make the ways managers and employees reason about their behavior a focus of organizational learning and continuous improvement programs. Teaching people how to reason about their behavior in new and more effective ways breaks down the defenses that block learning. . . .

Defensive Reasoning and the Doom Loop

When you observe people's behavior and try to come up with rules that would make sense of it, you discover a very different theory of action — what I call the individual's "theory-in-use." Put simply, people consistently act inconsistently, unaware of the contradiction between their espoused theory and their theory-in-use, between the way they think they are acting and the way they really act. What's more, most theories-in-use rest on the same set of governing values. There seems to be a universal human tendency to design one's actions consistently according to four basic values:

1. To remain in unilateral control;
2. To maximize "winning" and minimize "losing";
3. To suppress negative feelings; and
4. To be as "rational" as possible — by which people mean defining clear objectives and evaluating their behavior in terms of whether or not they have achieved them.

The purpose of all these values is to avoid embarrassment or threat, feeling vulnerable or incompetent. In this respect, the master program that most people use is profoundly defensive. Defensive reasoning encourages individuals to keep private the premises, inferences, and conclusions that shape their behavior and to avoid testing them in a truly independent, objective fashion.

Because the attributions that go into defensive reasoning are never really tested, it is a closed loop, remarkably impervious to conflicting points of view.

The inevitable response to the observation that somebody is reasoning defensively is yet more defensive reasoning. [In one representative team that we studied], whenever anyone pointed out the professionals' defensive behavior to them, their initial reaction was to look for the cause in somebody else — clients who were so sensitive that they would have been alienated if the consultants had criticized them or a manager so weak that he couldn't have taken it had the consultants raised their concerns with him. In other words, the case team members once again denied their own responsibility by externalizing the problem and putting it on someone else.

In such situations, the simple act of encouraging more open inquiry is often attacked by others as "intimidating." Those who do the attacking deal with their feelings about possibly being wrong by blaming the more open individual for arousing these feelings and upsetting them.

Needless to say, such a master program inevitably short-circuits learning. And for a number of reasons unique to their psychology, well-educated professionals are especially susceptible to this. . . . Behind this high aspiration for success is an equally high fear of failure and a propensity to feel shame and guilt when they do fail to meet their high standards. "You must avoid mistakes," said one. "I hate making them. Many of us fear failure, whether we admit it or not."

To the extent that these consultants have experienced success in their lives, they have not had to be concerned about failure and the attendant feelings of shame and guilt. But to exactly the same extent, they also have never developed the tolerance for feelings of failure or the skills to deal with these feelings. This in turn has led them not only to fear failure but also to fear the fear of failure itself. For they know that they will not cope with it superlatively — their usual level of aspiration.

The consultants use two intriguing metaphors to describe this phenomenon. They talk about the "doom loop" and "doom zoom." Often, consultants will perform well on the case team, but because they don't do the jobs perfectly or receive accolades from their managers, they go into a doom loop of despair. And they don't ease into the doom loop, they zoom into it.

As a result, many professionals have extremely "brittle" personalities. When suddenly faced with a situation they cannot immediately handle, they tend to fall apart. They cover up their distress in front of the client. They talk about it constantly with their fellow case team members. Interestingly, these conversations commonly take the form of bad-mouthing clients. . . .

Learning How to Reason Productively

. . . The key to any educational experience designed to teach senior managers how to reason productively is to connect the program to real business problems. The best demonstration of the usefulness of productive reasoning is for business managers to see how it can make a direct difference in their own performance and in that of the organization. This will not happen overnight. Managers need plenty of opportunity to practice the new skills. But once they grasp the powerful impact that productive reasoning can have on actual performance, they will have a strong incentive to reason productively not just in a training session but in all their work relationships.

One simple approach I have used to get this process started is to have participants produce a kind of rudimentary case study. The subject is a real business problem that the manager either wants to deal with or has tried unsuccessfully to address in the past. Writing the actual case usually takes less than an hour. But then the case becomes the focal point of an extended analysis.

For example, a CEO at a large organizational-development consulting company was preoccupied with the problems caused by the intense competition among the various business functions represented by his four direct reports. Not only was he tired of having the problems dumped in his lap, but he was also worried about the impact the inter-functional conflicts were having on the organization's flexibility. He had even calculated that the money being spent to iron out disagreements amounted to hundreds of thousands of dollars every year. And the more fights there were, the more defensive people became, which only increased the costs to the organization.

In a paragraph or so, the CEO described a meeting he intended to have with his direct reports to address the problem. Next, he divided the paper in half, and on the right-hand side of the page, he wrote a scenario for the meeting — much like the script for a movie or play — describing what he would say and how his subordinates would likely respond. On the left-hand side of the page, he wrote down any thoughts and feelings that he would be likely to have during the meeting but that he wouldn't express for fear they would derail the discussion.

But instead of holding the meeting, the CEO analyzed this scenario *with* his direct reports. The case became the catalyst for a discussion in which the CEO learned several things about the way he acted with his management team.

He discovered that his four direct reports often perceived his conversations as counterproductive. In the guise of being "diplomatic," he would pretend that a consensus about the problem existed, when in fact none existed. The unintended result: instead of feeling reassured, his subordinates felt wary and tried to figure out "what is he *really* getting at."

The CEO also realized that the way he dealt with the competitiveness among department heads was completely contradictory. On the one hand, he kept urging them to "think of the organization as a whole." On the other, he kept calling for actions — department budget cuts, for example — that placed them directly in competition with each other.

Finally, the CEO discovered that many of the tacit evaluations and attributions he had listed turned out to be wrong. Since he had never expressed these assumptions, he had never found out just how wrong they were. What's more, he learned that much of what he thought he was hiding came through to his subordinates anyway — but with the added message that the boss was covering up.

The CEO's colleagues also learned about their own ineffective behavior. They learned by examining their own behavior as they tried to help the CEO analyze his case. They also learned by writing and analyzing cases of their own. They began to see that they too tended to bypass and cover up the real issues and that the CEO was often aware of it but did not say so. They too made inaccurate attributions and evaluations that they did not express. Moreover, the belief that they had to hide important ideas and feelings from the CEO and from each other in order not to upset anyone turned out to be mistaken. In the context of the case discussions, the entire senior management team was quite willing to discuss what had always been undiscussable.

In effect, the case study exercise legitimizes talking about issues that people have never been able to address before. Such a discussion can be emotional — even painful. But for managers with the courage to persist, the payoff is great: management teams and entire organizations work more openly and more effectively and have greater options for behaving flexibly and adapting to particular situations. . . .

DAVID W. JOHNSON AND FRANK P. JOHNSON,
JOINING TOGETHER: GROUP THEORY AND GROUP SKILLS

(Allyn and Bacon, 2005), pp. 43-48

All humans need to become competent in taking action and simultaneously reflecting on their action to learn from it. Integrating thought with action requires that we plan our behavior, engage in it, and then reflect on how effective we were. When we learn a pattern of behavior that deals effectively with a recurrent situation, we tend to repeat it over and over until it functions automatically. Such habitual behavioral patterns are based on theories of action. An action theory is a theory as to what actions are needed to achieve a desired consequence in a given situation. All theories have an "if . . . then . . ." form. An action theory states that in a given situation if we do x, then y will result. Our theories of action are normative. They state what we ought to do if we wish to achieve certain results. Examples of action theories can be found in almost everything we do. If we smile and say hello, then others will return our smile and greeting. If we apologize, then the other person will excuse us. . . . All our behavior is based on theories that connect our actions with certain consequences. In essence, we build an action theory. As our behavior becomes habitual and automatic, our action theories become tacit — we are not able to put them into words. When our behavior becomes ineffective, we become aware of our action theories and modify them. . . .

An action is usually based on tacit knowledge — knowledge that we are not always able to put into words. Because most of our action theories function automatically, we are rarely conscious of our assumed connections between actions and their consequences. One of the purposes of [the discussion that follows] . . . is to help you become more conscious of the action theories that guide how you behave in small-group situations, test these theories against reality, and modify them to make them more effective. . . .

Many aspects of group dynamics can be learned only by experience. Hearing a lecture on resisting group pressure is not the same as actually experiencing group pressure. . . . Reading a description of leadership is not the same as leading the charge up San Juan Hill. It takes more than listening to explanations to learn group skills. Experiential learning may be defined as generating an action theory from your own experiences and then continually modifying it to improve your effectiveness. The purpose of experiential learning is to affect the learner in three ways: (1) the learner's cognitive structures are altered,

(2) the learner's attitudes are modified, and (3) the learner's repertoire of behavioral skills is expanded. These three elements are interconnected and change as a whole, not as separate parts. Working on any one part in the absence of the other two will be ineffective:

1. Information and knowledge can generate interest in changing, but will not bring about change. Knowing a rationale for change is not sufficient for motivating a person to change.
2. Firsthand experience alone will not generate valid knowledge. . . . Besides experience there must be a theoretical system that the expertise tests out and reflection on the meaning of the experience.
3. It takes more than engaging in a new behavior to result in permanent change. New skills may be practiced and mastered but will fade away unless action theories and attitudes also change.

To learn leadership skills, for example, the learner must develop a concept of what leadership is (knowledge), an action theory concerning what leadership behaviors will lead to effective group functioning, positive attitudes toward new leadership procedures, and perceptions that the new leadership actions are appropriate and that he or she is capable of performing them. Finally, the learner must develop the skills needed to perform the new leadership actions. . . . Experiential learning can be conceived of in a simplified way as a four-stage cycle: (1) take action on the basis of one's current action theory, (2) assess consequences and obtain feedback, (3) reflect on how effective actions were and reformulate and refine the action theory, and (4) implement the revised action theory by taking modified action. . . . This process of continuous improvement is repeated over and over again until expertise in the use of group skills is developed.

People will believe more in knowledge they have discovered themselves than in knowledge presented by others. [Kurt] Lewin was a great believer in experimental procedures whereby a person behaviorally validates or disproves a theory and [is involved in an] . . . active rather than a passive process. When a learner can take a theory, concept, or practice and "try it on for size," he or she will understand it more completely, integrate it more effectively with past learning, and retain it longer. . . . It takes more than firsthand experience to generate valid knowledge. Lewin used to state that thousands of years of human experience with falling bodies did not bring humans to a correct theory of gravity. Besides experience, there needs to be a theoretical system that the experience tests out and reflection on the meaning of the experience.

Behavior changes will be temporary unless the action theories and attitudes underlying them are changed. New behavioral skills may be practiced and mastered, but without changes in the person's action theories and attitudes, the new behavior patterns will fade away. . . . Changes in perceptions of oneself and one's social environment are necessary before changes in action theories, attitudes, and behavior will take place. Learners must perceive themselves as capable of doing the needed behaviors and must see the behaviors as being appropriate to the situation before they will engage in them. . . . The more supportive, accepting, and caring the social environment, the freer a person is to experiment with new behaviors, attitudes, and action theories.

As the need to justify oneself and protect oneself against rejection decreases, it becomes easier to experiment with new ways of behaving, thinking, and valuing.

PROBLEM 2-3

1. Think about a leadership mistake that you have made or observed. What was responsible? What lessons did you draw from the experience at the time? What insights would you draw now?
2. Think about a leadership dilemma that you or someone you know resolved effectively. What did you or that person do well? Ask someone else involved in the situation if their perception is the same. What lessons did you both take away from the experience?

NOTES AND QUESTIONS

1. Chris Argyris distinguishes between single-loop and double-loop learning. The first involves finding a solution to a problem; the second involves understanding your own contribution to that problem. Can you identify leadership experiences where it would have been better for you or for your leader to engage in double- rather than single-loop analysis? What got in the way? Construct a timeline in which you list your own greatest successes in leadership above the line, and your most significant failures below the line. Can you identify common patterns in the experiences in which you were most and least effective? What learning needs do they suggest?[143]
2. David and Frank Johnson describe a process of experiential learning that involves taking action, assessing its consequences, reflecting on how effective it was, and modifying future action. Construct such a process for yourself on a quality you would like to develop and spend the next week attempting to follow your plan. How successful were you? What did you learn from the experience?
3. In his article "Financial Leaders Go AWOL in the Meltdown," Harvard lecturer and former general counsel for General Electric Ben Heineman writes:

> In all good business organizations, facing failures honestly, looking at root causes, disciplining individuals and implementing systemic change to prevent recurrences is as important as planning for new products, markets or technologies.
>
> Yet a voracious reader of economic and business reports would have a hard time finding a financial industry statesman talking candidly about the errors and flawed judgment among managers or directors. Nor will you find a hint about how these private institutions should govern themselves in the future to avoid a recurrence of such widespread devastation.
>
> Instead, the chairman of a failed investment bank testifies on Capitol Hill that he is responsible — then blames everyone else. Financial CEOs at a session organized by the New York Stock Exchange call for more Wall Street tax breaks, repeal of the Sarbanes-Oxley Act, and limits on class-action lawsuits. . . . [Some suggest that acknowledgement of error appears too dangerous in a litigious society.] But retired leaders or sitting CEOs in institutions

singed by the crisis can surely find a way to discuss these issues without putting their heads in a noose.[144]

Do you agree? What might encourage more self-critical reflection among those responsible for the crisis?

END NOTES

1. Joseph S. Nye Jr., The Powers to Lead (New York: Oxford University Press, 2008), 19.

2. Nye, The Powers to Lead, 85.

3. Between 1995 and 2006, the rate at which CEOs were fired or pushed out grew by over 300 percent. Jeffrey Pfeffer, Power: Why Some Have It — and Others Don't (New York: Harper Collins, 2010), 199.

4. For an overview for public interest organizations, see Deborah L. Rhode, Public Interest Law: The Movement at Midlife, Stanford Law Review 60 (2008):2027.

5. Montgomery Van Wart, Dynamics of Leadership in Public Service: Theory and Practice (Armonk, NY: M.E. Sharpe, 2005), 186 (quoting David Sarnoff).

6. Scott L. Cummings, The Politics of Pro Bono, UCLA Law Review 52 (2004-2005):35; Rhode, Public Interest Law, 2032.

7. United States Bureau of the Census, 1988-2006 SUSB Totals for U.S. & States, available at http://www.cenus.gov/econ/susb/historical_data.htm.

8. Tough at the Top, The Economist, October 25, 2003.

9. John Gardner, On Leadership (New York: Free Press, 1990), 27.

10. Bob Johansen, Leaders Make the Future (San Francisco: Berrett-Koehler, 2009), 11.

11. Michael Fullan, Leading in a Culture of Change (San Francisco: Jossey-Bass, 2001), 2.

12. Elizabeth Vrato, Counselors (Philadelphia: Running Press, 2002), 51 (quoting Jamie Gorelick).

13. For lawyers, see Symposium: Perspectives on Lawyer Happiness, Syracuse Law Review 58 (2008).

14. In her remarks at an N.A.A.C.P. event, Sherrod talked about an incident twenty-four years earlier in which she acknowledged not helping rural white farmers with the same "full force" as black farmers, but then added that she learned she was wrong and that there was "no difference between us." The acknowledgement was not part of the clip initially released, and officials failed to check it before condemning her statement. Faster than a Speeding Blog, New York Times, July 22, 2010, A26. Andy Ostroy, What the Shirley Sherrod Saga Says about America, Huffingtonpost.com, September 30, 2010.

15. Manseur Javidan, Peter W. Dorfman, Jon Paul Howell, and Paul J. Hanges, Leadership and Cultural Context, in Nitin Nohria and Rakesh Khurana, eds., Handbook of Leadership Theory and Practice (Cambridge, MA: Harvard Business Press, 2010), 335, 366-368.

16. Nye, The Powers to Lead, 2.

17. Warren Bennis and James O'Toole, Don't Hire the Wrong CEO, Harvard Business Review (May-June 2000):174; Gill, Theory and Practice of Leadership, 20.

18. David Maister, The Trouble with Lawyers, The American Lawyer (April 2006):100. For discussion of lawyers' need for autonomy and the difficulties that poses for leadership, see Larry Richard and Susan Raridon Lambreth, What Does It Take to Develop Effective Law Firm Leaders?, March 2006, available at http://www.abanet.org/pm/lpt/articles/pmqa03061.shtm; Leadership Partners or Managing Partners, Law Office Management and Administration Report (October 2010):1, 5.

19. Montgomery Van Wart, Dynamics of Leadership in Public Service, 55-56.

20. Barbara C. Crosby, Leadership for the Common Good (San Francisco: Jossey-Bass, 2005), 161-162.

21. Jennifer A. Chatman and Jessica A. Kennedy, Psychological Perspectives on Leadership, in Nitin Nohria and Rakesh Khurana, eds., Handbook of Leadership Theory and Practice (Cambridge, MA: Harvard Business Press, 2010), 169, 174.

22. Robert Hogan and Robert B. Kaiser, What We Know about Leadership, Review of General Psychology 9 (2005):169, 176; Pfeffer, Power, 199-200.

23. Pfeffer, Power, 221-222. In the nonprofit sector, the problem is sufficiently common with founders of organizations that experts have coined the label "founders syndrome."

Leslie Crutchfeld and Heather McLead, Forces for Good: The Six Practices of High Impact Nonprofits, in Mathew Perry, ed., Nonprofit and Public Leadership (San Francisco: Jossey-Bass, 2008), 124, 140.

24. Manfred Kets de Vries and Elisabet Engellau, A Clinical Approach to the Dynamics of Leadership and Executive Transformation, in Nohria and Khurana, eds., Handbook of Leadership Theory and Practice, 183, 195; Terry Price, The Leadership Challenge, in Ciulla, ed., Ethics: The Heart of Leadership, 111-113; George R. Goethals, David W. Messick, and Scott T. Allison, The Uniqueness Bias: Studies of Constructive Social Comparison, in J. Suls and A. Wills, eds., Social Comparison: Contemporary Theory and Research (Hillsdale, NJ: Erlbaum, 1991), 149, 153-155. See also Roderick Kramer, The Harder They Fall, Harvard Business Review (October 2003):61.

25. James M. Kouzes and Barry Posner, A Leader's Legacy (San Francisco: Jossey-Bass, 2006), 128.

26. Noel M. Tichy and Warren G. Bennis, Judgment: How Winning Leaders Make Great Calls (New York: Portfolio, 2007), 80 (quoting George).

27. Jim Collins, Good to Great: Why Some Companies Make the Leap . . . and Others Don't (New York: Harper Business Press, 2001), 20-22, 38. See also James C. Collins and Jerry I. Porras, Built to Last: Successful Habits of Visionary Companies (New York: Collins Business Essentials, 1994).

28. Ronald A. Heifetz and Marty Linsky, Leadership on the Line: Staying Alive through the Dangers of Leading (Boston: Harvard Business School Publishing, 2002), 53.

29. See Chapter 1 and Scott W. Sprier, Mary H. Fontaine, and Ruth L. Malloy, Leadership Run Amok: The Destructive Potential of Overachievers, Harvard Business Review (June 2006):74-79

30. Liz Wiseman with Greg Mckeown, Multipliers (New York: HarperCollins, 2010), 100, 121.

31. Nye, The Powers to Lead, 82.

32. For the research, see Pfeffer, Power, 135, and Rhode and Kellerman's excerpt in Chapter 8. For bully broads, see Neela Banerjee, Some Bullies Seek Ways to Soften Up; Toughness has Risks for Women Executives, New York Times, August 10, 2001, C1.

33. Richard Nixon, Leaders (New York: Touchstone, 1982), 287-288.

34. Michael Lewis, The Man Who Crashed the World, Vanity Fair, August 2009, 136.

35. Lewis, The Man Who Crashed the World, 139.

36. Id. at 137.

37. Id.

38. Steven Berglas, Victims of Success, Leadership Excellence (March 2009):10.

39. Id. at 10, quoting Argyris.

40. Hamilton, Ethical Leadership, 383.

41. Id. at 363, quoting Jim Collins.

42. Id. at 385-386.

43. Jeffrey Pfeffer, Managing with Power (Boston: Harvard Business Press, 1992), 261.

44. Hal G. Rainey, Understanding and Managing Public Organizations (San Francisco: Jossey-Bass, 3d ed. 2003), 77; Hal G. Rainey, Robert W. Backoff, and Charles H. Levine, Comparing Public and Private Organizations, Public Administration Review (March-April 1976):233-242.

45. Montgomery Van Wart, Public-Sector Leadership Theory: An Assessment, in James L. Perry, The Jossey-Bass Reader on Nonprofit and Public Leadership (San Francisco: Jossey-Bass, 2010), 73, 90-91.

46. Pfeffer, Managing with Power, 79-80; Nancy C. Roberts and Raymond Trevor Bradley, Limits of Charisma, in Jay Conger and Rabinda N. Kanungo, eds., Charismatic Leadership: The Elusive Factor in Organizational Effectiveness (San Francisco: Jossey-Bass, 1988), 253-263.

47. Roberts and Bradley, Limits of Charisma, 268.

48. United States Bureau of Labor Statistics, Mass Layoffs—September 2010 (2010), 1, http://www.bls.gov/news.release/archives/mmls_10222010.pdf.

49. Bradford W. Hildebrandt and James W. Jones, The Anatomy of Large Firm Failures (Somerset, NJ: Hildebrandt, November 19, 2008), 3, available at http://www.hildebrandt.com/Hubbard.FileSystem/files/Publication/a018bee0-b710-493c-8f07-006057d169b8/Presentation/PublicationAttachment/7d0507dd-0ed4-4b0e-901f-01989cecbef9/Anatomy%20of%20Law%20Firm%20Failures.pdf.

50. David Maister, The Trouble with Lawyers, American Lawyer (April 2006):100; Larry Richard, Herding Cats: The Lawyer Personality Revealed, Personality and Practice, LAWPRO Magazine (Winter 2008):1, 3; Jeff Foster, Larry Richard, Lisa Rohrer, and Mark Sirkin, Understanding Lawyers: The Personality Traits of Successful Practitioners (Hildebrandt White Paper, 2010).

51. Maister, The Trouble with Lawyers, 100.

52. Ida Abbott, Taking the Lead, available at www.IdaAbbott.com.

53. Peter D. Zeughauser and Ron Beard, Rewarding Leadership, The American Lawyer (January 2008):60.

54. David Segal, Is Law School a Losing Game?, New York Times, January 8, 2011, B1; Eli Wald, Foreword: The Great Recession and the Legal Profession, Fordham Law Review 78 (2010):2051;

Nathan Koppel, Recession Batters Law Firms, Triggering Layoffs, Closings, Wall Street Journal, January 26, 2009, A1, A11; Joan Indiana Rigdon, Cost Effect, Washington Lawyer (April 2010):17.

55. Susan Kostal, SanFrancisco online, The Brobeck Mutiny (2003), available at http://www.sanfranmag.com/story/brobeck-mutiny.

56. Id.

57. Jonathan Glater, West Coast Law Firm Closing after Dot-Com Collapse, New York Times, January 31, 2003, C1.

58. Todd Wallack and Harriet Chang, Top S.F. Dot-Com Law Firm to Close: Brobeck, Phleger, and Harrison Grew with Tech Boom, San Francisco Chronicle, January 31, 2003, A1.

59. Kostal, The Brobeck Mutiny.

60. Id.

61. Id.

62. Id.

63. Id., quoting Snow.

64. Kostal, The Brobeck Mutiny.

65. Glater, West Coast Law Firm Closing after Dot-Com Collapse.

66. Maureen Broderick, The Art of Managing Professional Services (Philadelphia, PA: Wharton School Publishing, 2010), 267, excerpted in Maureen Broderick, Leading Gently, American Lawyer (December 2010):63,64.

67. Kenneth Van Winkle Jr., The Managing Partner in Today's World, in Managing A Law Firm (New York: Aspatore, Thomson Reuters, 2010), 46, 47; Abraham C. Reich and Mark L. Silow, Democracy, Transparency and Rotation: Keys to Running a Successful Law Firm, in Managing a Law Firm, supra, 71, 81.

68. Thomas DeLong, John Gabarro, and Robert J. Lees, When Professionals Have to Lead, excerpted in The American Lawyer (December 2007):125-129.

69. Hildebrandt, The Anatomy of Law Firm Failures, November 19, 2008, available at http://www.hildebrandt.com/The-Anatomy-of-Law-Firm-Failures.

70. John S. Smock, John W. Sterling, and Peter A. Giuliani, What Law Firm Leaders Are Saying, Of Counsel 28 (June 2009):5, 7.

71. Darrell Rigby, Look Before You Lay Off, Harvard Business Review (April 2002):3; Robert Sutton, Layoffs: Are They Ever the Answer?, in Doing Layoffs Right, Harvard Business Review Collection, June 11, 2009.

72. Lee Bolman and Terence E. Deal, Uncommon Journey (San Francisco: Jossey- Bass, 2001), 93-95; Anthony J. Nyerg and Charile O. Trevor, After Layoffs, Help Survivors Be More Effective, Harvard Business Review (June 2009):15 (describing costs in productivity from anticipation of layoffs and role of inadequate information); Leslie Gaines-Ross, Corporate Reputation (Hoboken, NJ: John Wiley & Sons 2008), 108 (describing AT&T's ill-timed grant of $10 million in stock options to its CEO following layoffs).

73. Pfeffer, The Real Keys to High Performance, in Leader to Leader 8 (Spring 1998), available at http://www.pfdf.org/knowledgecenter/journal.aspx?ArticleID=155.

74. Della Costa, The Ethical Imperative (Reading, MA: Addison Wesley, 1990), 274-275.

75. Pfeffer, The Real Keys to High Performance (quoting Richard Kovacevich); Ronald A. Heifetz and Marty Linsky, Leadership on the Line: Staying Alive through the Dangers of Leading (Boston: Harvard Business School Publishing, 2002), 59.

76. Koppel, Recession Batters Law Firms, A11 (quoting consultant Brennan).

77. Jason Fagone, Wrongful Death, Philadelphia Magazine (June 2009):2, 4, 6, available at http://www.phillymag.com/articles/wrongful_death.

78. Brian Baxter, Former Wolf Block Associate Who Sued Firm Speaks Out, American Lawyer Daily March 25, 2009; Deborah L. Rhode, What's Sex Got to Do with It?: Diversity in the Legal Profession, in Deborah L. Rhode and David Luban, eds., Legal Ethics Stories (New York: Foundation Press, 2006), 233.

79. Fagone, Wrongful Death. See also Gina Passarella, No Easy Answers in Wolf Block's Demise, Legal Intelligencer, March 25, 2009.

80. Hildebrandt, The Anatomy of Law Firm Failures.

81. Sarah Kellogg, Queasy Street, Washington Lawyer (June 2009):28, 30; Douglas B. Richardson and Douglas P. Coopersmith, Learning to Lead, American Lawyer (July 2008):57, 58.

82. For an overview of the layoff situation in 2009, see http://www.cbsnews.com/video/watch/?id=4754388n. For Jon Stewart's profile of Ford layoffs, see http://www.thedailyshow.com/watch/tue-january-24-2006/corddry-layoff-fever. For a CBS report on *Lemonade*, a film about layoffs and a silver lining, see http://www.cbsnews.com/video/watch/?id=6035912n.

83. For fuller exploration of the themes in this section, see Deborah L. Rhode, Lawyers and Leadership, The Professional Lawyer 20 (2010):1.

84. Gregory Williams, Teaching Leaders and Leadership, Association of American Law Schools Newsletter, April 1999.

85. Neil W. Hamilton, Ethical Leadership in Professional Life, University of St. Thomas Law Journal 62 (2009):362, 370.

86. Lexis Nexis, State of the Legal Industry Survey, Executive Summary, http://legalblogwatch .typepad.com/files.state-of-the-legal-industry-survey-executivesummary.pdf.

87. For a sampling of the criticisms, see Harry Edwards, The Growing Disjunction between Legal Education and the Legal Profession, Michigan Law Review 91 (1992):34; Thomas S. Ulen, The Impending Train Wreck in Current Legal Education: How We Might Teach Law as the Scientific Study of Social Governance, St. Thomas Law Journal 6 (2009):302; ABA Section on Legal Education and Admission to the Bar, Report of the Task Force on Law Schools and the Profession: Narrowing the Gap: An Educational Continuum (1997).

88. William Sullivan et al., Educating Lawyers: Preparation for the Profession of Law (Menlo Park, CA: Carnegie Foundation for the Advancement of Teaching, 2007), 87-89.

89. Gina Passarella, Leadership Programs Born from Lack of Born Leaders, The Legal Intelligencer, November 16, 2007, available at http://www.law.com/jsp/11f/PubArticleLLF.jsp?id= 1195120555535 (quoting Jeffrey Lutsky).

90. Laurie Bassi and Daniel McMurrer, Leadership and Large Firm Success: A Statistical Analysis, available at http://www.mcbassi.com/resources/documents/WhitePaper-LeadershipAndLaw FirmSuccess.pdf.

91. Rhode, Public Interest Law, 2046 (quoting Eric Cohen).

92. Nohria and Khurana, Advancing Leadership Theory and Practice, 5; Jeffrey Pfeffer, Leadership Development in Business Schools: An Agenda for Change, in Jordi Canals, ed., The Future of Leadership Development: The Role of Business Schools (New York: Palgrave Macmillan, 2011).

93. Pfeffer, Leadership Development; Kelley Holland, Is it Time to Retrain B-Schools?, New York Times, March 15, 2009, B2.

94. Aspen Institute, Where Will They Lead? 2008 MBA Student Attitudes about Business and Society (New York: Aspen Institute, 2008).

95. Douglas A. Ready, Jay A. Conger, and Linda A. Hill, Are You a High Potential?, Harvard Business Review (June 2010):78, 82.

96. Gill, Theory and Practice of Leadership, 275; Peter E. Drucker, Managing Oneself, Harvard Business Review (March-April 1999):68-69; Doug Lennick and Fred Kiehl, Moral Intelligence: Enhancing Business Performance and Leadership Success (Upper Saddle River, NJ: Wharton School Publishing, 2008), 239.

97. Nye, The Powers to Lead, 24; Jay A. Conger, Leadership Development Initiatives, in Nohria and Khurana, eds., Handbook of Leadership Theory and Practice, 712, 714.

98. Lisa A. Boyce, Stephen J. Zaccaro, and Michelle Zaanis Wisecarver, Propensity for Self-Development of Leadership Attributes: Understanding, Predicting, and Supporting Performance of Leader Self-Development, Leadership Quarterly 21 (2010):159.

99. Doug Lennick and Fred Kiehl, Moral Intelligence: Enhancing Business Performance and Leadership Success (Upper Saddle River, NJ: Wharton School Publishing, 2008), 245-248. For discussion of research showing performance improvement when people are told that they did a task well, see Thomas J. Peters and Robert H. Waterman, In Search of Excellence: Lessons from America's Best Run Corporations (New York: Harper and Row, 2004), 58-59.

100. Chris Argyris, Teaching Smart People How to Learn, Harvard Business Review (1991):2.

101. Howard Gardner, Changing Minds (Cambridge, MA: Harvard Business School Press, 2004), 110.

102. James M. Kouzes and Barry Z. Posner, A Leader's Legacy (San Francisco: Jossey-Bass, 2006), 28. See also Richards, Herding Cats, 3 (noting that lawyers score low on resiliency, which means that they tend to be defensive and resistant to negative feedback).

103. Kouzes and Posner, A Leader's Legacy, 28.

104. National Association for Law Placement Foundation (NALPF), How Associate Evaluations Measure Up: A National Study of Associate Performance Assessments (Washington, DC: NALPF, 2006), 74.

105. Robert Hargrove, Masterful Coaching (San Francisco: Jossey-Bass, 2008), 302 (quoting Galbraith).

106. For discussion of such biases, see Chapter 3 and Peters and Waterman, In Search of Excellence, 58.

107. David G. Myers, The Inflated Self: How Do I Love Me? Let Me Count the Ways, Psychology Today (May 1980):16.

108. Hargrove, Masterful Coaching, 124. See also Argyris, Teaching Smart People How to Learn, 2.

109. Hargrove, Masterful Coaching, 124.

110. Hargrove, Masterful Coaching, 124; Argyris, Teaching Smart People How to Learn.

111. Richard J. Leider, The Ultimate Leadership Task: Self-Leadership, in Frances Hesselbein, Marshall Goldsmith, and Richard Beckhard, eds., The Leader of the Future: New Visions, Strategies, and Practices for the Next Era (San Francisco: Jossey-Bass, 1996), 189.

112. Douglas B. Richardson and Douglas P. Coopersmith, Learning to Lead, American Lawyer (July 2008):57.

113. For estimates, see Pfeffer, Leadership Development. For inadequacies, see Morgan W. McCall Jr., The Experience Conundrum, in Nohria and Khurana, eds., Handbook of Leadership Theory and Practice, 679, 690-693.

114. McCall, The Experience Conundrum, 692-693; Ben W. Heineman Jr. and David B. Wilkins, The Lost Generation?, The American Lawyer, March 1, 2008, 85.

115. McCall, The Experience Conundrum, 699.

116. John Gardner, On Leadership (New York: Free Press, 1990), 117.

117. Lennick and Kiehl, Moral Intelligence, 239.

118. Pfeffer, Power, 13-14.

119. Leider, The Leader of the Future, 194-195.

120. Boyce, Zaccaro, and Wisecarver, Propensity for Self-Development of Leaders, 161.

121. Gill, Theory and Practice of Leadership, 281.

122. Ready, Conger, and Hill, Are You a High Potential, 82; Linda Hill, Developing the Star Performer, in Frances Hesselbein and Paul M. Cohen, eds., Leader to Leader (San Francisco: Jossey-Bass, 1999), 296; V.D. Day, Leadership Development: A Review in Context, Leadership Quarterly 11 (2001):581.

123. See Cohen, Drucker on Leadership, 139-140, 193; John P. Kotter, What Leaders Really Do, Harvard Business Review 68 (May-June 1990):103; Sheri-Lynne Leskiw and Parbudyal Singh, Leadership Development: Learning from Best Practices, Leadership and Organizational Development Journal 28 (2007):444, 450-454.

124. Morgan W. McCall Jr., The Experience Conundrum, in Nohria and Khurana, eds., Handbook of Leadership Theory and Practice, 679, 683-685.

125. Warren Bennis, On Becoming a Leader (Reading, MA: Addison-Wesley, 2002), 108-109.

126. Lennick and Kiehl, Moral Intelligence, 97.

127. Gill, Theory and Practice, 273-277; Day, Leadership Development, 594.

128. Day, Leadership Development; Gomez, The Leader as Learner, 283.

129. Hill, Developing the Star Performer, 299.

130. Noel M. Tichy and Warren G. Bennis, Judgment: How Leaders Make Great Calls (New York: Portfolio, Penguin, 2007), 26. For another example, see Gill, Theory and Practice of Leadership, 283.

131. Ann Colby and William Damon, Some Do Care (New York: The Free Press, 1992), 198-199.

132. Larissa MacFarquhar, The Better Boss, The New Yorker, April 22, 2002, 114. See also Gomez, The Leader as Learner, 280, 283.

133. Conger, Leadership Development Interventions, 714 (citing estimates that 75 percent of executive education dollars are spent on customized programs). For the trend to action learning, see Leskiw and Singh, Leadership Development, 154.

134. Kotter, What Leaders Really Do.

135. David V. Day, Leadership Development: A Review in Context, Leadership Quarterly 11 (2001):581, 582.

136. Peter Senge, The Fifth Discipline: The Art and Practice of the Learning Organization (New York: Doubleday, 1990), 3.

137. D.A. Gavin, Building a Learning Organization, Harvard Business Review (July-August 1993):78, 79.

138. Wiseman with McKeown, Multipliers, 20-22.

139. Sean T. Hannah and Paul B. Lester, A Multilevel Approach to Building and Leading Learning Organizations, Leadership Quarterly 20 (2009):34, 35; Gavin, Building a Learning Organization. For the inadequacy of leadership development evaluation, see Doris B. Collins and Elwood F. Holton III, The Effectiveness of Managerial Development Programs: A Meta-Analysis of Studies from 1982 to 2001, Human Resource Development Quarterly 15 (2004):217, 218.

140. Warren Bennis and Burt Nanus, On Leaders: Strategies for Taking Charge (New York: Harper and Row, 1985), quoted in Carol Tavris and Eliot Aronson, Mistakes Were Made (but not by me) (New York: HarperCollins, 2007), 225, n. 9.

141. Robert M. Fulmer and Byron Hanson, Do Techies Make Good Leaders?, Wall Street Journal, August 23, 2010, 23.

142. Montgomery Van Wart, Dynamics of Leadership in Public Service: Theory and Practice (Armonk, NY: M.E. Sharpe, 2005), 185-186.

143. See Barbara C. Crosby and John M. Bryson, Leadership for the Common Good (San Francisco: Jossey-Bass, 2005), 50.

144. Ben W. Heineman Jr., Financial Leaders Go AWOL in the Meltdown, Bloomberg.com, November 4, 2008, 1-2, available at http://www.law.harvard.edu/programs/plp/pdf/Financial_Leaders_Go_AWOL.pdf.

LEADERSHIP SKILLS

3

LEADERS AS DECISION MAKERS

"I'm the decider" was President George W. Bush's much parodied response to criticism about his deference to Defense Secretary Donald Rumsfeld's strategies concerning Iraq.[1] Whatever the adequacy of the response in that particular context, it does capture the centrality of decision making in the leadership role. This chapter focuses on what enables leaders to make effective judgments, and the cognitive biases and organizational dynamics that get in the way.

Decision making generally has two core objectives: quality and acceptability. Both are subject to external constraints, such as time and cost, and trade-offs are often necessary. For example, broad participation will often enhance the soundness and legitimacy of decisions, but it will typically require more time, effort, and expense. In many contexts, the optimal decision is out of reach due to the complexity of issues, the limitations of information, and the costs of obtaining it. Excessive information can also impair decision making. The brain can process only so many facts at any one time, and an overload may misdirect our focus. As Herbert Simon noted, "a wealth of information creates a poverty of attention."[2] Given these constraints, individuals fall back on heuristics — processes based on intuition, habit, or rules of thumb. These mental shortcuts may not seem "rational" from a purely logical point of view, but they are reasonable responses to the social environment of decision making.[3]

That environment is inevitably subject to cognitive biases and constraints, and one of leaders' most important tasks is to create processes that are most cost effective and least subject to distortion. In designing such decision-making processes, experts recommend that leaders take into account concerns such as:

- How important is the quality of the decision?
- How much information is necessary to make a reasonably good decision?
- Who else has such information and can be involved in the process?
- Do those individuals share the organization's objectives or have other personal concerns that might skew their judgment?
- How important is followers' commitment to the outcome, and how much is it likely to depend on their involvement in the process?
- What values apart from efficiency and effectiveness are at stake?
- What are the time and cost constraints?[4]

In addition to these concerns, leaders also need to consider the appropriate decision-making framework. Three approaches are common. The first, the "reasoned choice" framework, is the most typical. It takes a rational pragmatic approach to identifying objectives, analyzing options, and evaluating responses. However, in contexts where full information on these issues is impossible or too costly to obtain, an "incremental" strategy may be preferable. Under this framework, the decision maker takes small steps that can be assessed and adjusted in light of experience, thus avoiding major risks of failure.[5] A third possibility is a "mixed scanning model" in which decision makers first survey the external environment for major economic, technical, political, competitive, or related trends that require a response. They then examine the internal organizational environment for significant problems, such as declines in productivity or employee retention, or inadequate responses to stakeholder concerns. If any such warning signals are present, leaders should invest substantial effort in exploring solutions.[6] Otherwise, resorting to an incremental approach will be sufficient.

A key characteristic of effective leaders is their ability to analyze what issues are at stake in particular decisions and to design a process that will produce cost-effective responses. The readings that follow explore some of the challenges involved in that role.

A. THE DECISION-MAKING PROCESS AND COGNITIVE BIASES

Paul Brest and Linda Krieger begin their book on decision making by noting that many problems facing leaders and their advisors, including lawyers, "seldom conform to the boundaries that define and divide different disciplines." So, for example, "most clients expect their lawyers to integrate legal considerations with other aspects of their problem. . . . Reflecting this reality, an American Bar Association report on the ten 'fundamental lawyering skills' that new lawyers should acquire places 'problem solving' at the very top of the list—even before legal analysis."[7] Whatever their substantive backgrounds, those who wish to be successful in law, management, and policy need the kind of decision-making skills described in the excerpts below.

PAUL BREST AND LINDA HAMILTON KRIEGER, PROBLEM SOLVING,
DECISION MAKING, AND PROFESSIONAL JUDGMENT

(New York: Oxford University Press, 2010), pp. 3, 11-23, 241-252, and 257-265

Problem Solving & Decision Making Processes: Deliberation, Intuition, and Expertise

Deliberative Processes

An ideal deliberative model of decisionmaking consists of the following steps or elements:

1. State, or "frame," the problem to be solved;
2. Identify and prioritize the relevant values, interests, and objectives;

3. Identify and resolve major uncertainties concerning the cause of the problem;
4. Generate a range of plausible solutions or alternative courses of action;
5. Predict the consequences of the courses of action and assess their impact on the relevant interests or objectives;
6. Select the course of action that optimizes the interests or objectives to be served (i.e., make a decision);
7. Implement, observe, and learn from the outcome of the decision.

The process is recursive, beginning with the need to frame the problem in terms of the interests involved and to consider the interests in the context of the particular problem. After completing step 5, a decisionmaker would be wise to review the earlier steps, not just because he may have accidentally omitted something, but because the concreteness of positing solutions can reframe objectives and his conception of the overall problem.

Framing the problem. Problem solvers sometimes go about solving the wrong problem because they do not frame the issues adequately. They may mistake symptoms of a problem for the problem itself, or define the problem too narrowly, or define the problem in terms of a ready solution without taking account of the objectives they are actually trying to achieve. . . .

Identifying interests and objectives. The German philosopher Friedrich Nietzsche is reputed to have proposed, "To forget one's purpose is the commonest form of stupidity."

The best frame for a problem is the one that incorporates the broadest possible range of purposes, interests, objectives, and values implicated by the situation. . . .

Divergent and Convergent Thinking

The deliberative approach to problem solving combines elements of *divergent* and *convergent* thinking. Divergent thinking expands the range of perspectives, dimensions, and options relating to a problem. Convergent thinking eliminates possible alternatives through the application of critical analysis, thereby eventually reducing the number of available options. Divergent thinking conceives; convergent thinking critiques. Divergent thinking envisions; convergent thinking troubleshoots, fine tunes, selects, and implements. . . .

Intuitive Processes in Problem Solving and Decision Making

. . . Most of the time we solve problems without coming close to the conscious, step-by-step analysis of the deliberative approach. In fact, attempting to encounter even a small fraction of the problems we encounter in a full, deliberative manner would bring our activities to a screeching halt. Out of necessity, most of problem-solving is intuitive. In contrast with the deliberative model of decision making, intuitive decisions rely on a process "that somehow produces an answer, solution, or idea without the use of a conscious, logically defensible step-by-step process." Intuitive responses "are reached with little apparent effort, and typically without conscious awareness." . . .

The Role of Schemas and Scripts

. . . In a classic article entitled *On Perceptual Readiness*, cognitive psychologist Jerome Bruner observed that when we perceive a stimulus from our environment, our first task is to fit that information into some existing knowledge structure represented in memory. Perception is given meaning only when filtered through and incorporated into preexisting cognitive elements, such as schemas. . . . A schema imposes meaning on the inherently ambiguous information supplied by raw perception. Once a schema is activated, we implicitly expect incoming information to be consistent with its elements. Schematic processing is both inevitable and a pervasive source of errors of judgment. Our need to impose order on the world leads us to see patterns even where they do not exist, and schemas lie at the core of inaccurate stereotypes based on race, sex, and other factors.

A *script* is a schema consisting of a sequence of social interactions in which you are an actor or observer. Richard Nisbett and Lee Ross analogize a script to a cartoon strip, in which each scene depicts a basic social action; for example, a restaurant script might involve entering, ordering, eating, paying, and leaving. "The importance of scripts . . . lies in the speed and ease with which they make events (or secondhand accounts of events) readily comprehensible and predictable. Their potential cost . . . is the possibility of erroneous interpretations, inaccurate expectations and inflexible modes of response." . . .

The Role of Affect

The heart has its reasons that reason does not understand.

Blaise Pascal

Intuitive problem solving and decision making depends not only on the essentially mental processes of recognizing patterns, but on affect as well. . . . Without emotions, our decision-making processes would be overwhelmed by the burdens of cognition. . . . Emotions and reasoning exist in a delicate balance, however, and . . . emotions can sometimes overwhelm reasoning to our detriment. . . . Among other things, the skilled professional must be able to differentiate between her own emotions and those of clients and others. This capacity is a component of so-called *emotional intelligence*. . . .

The Interaction of Intuition and Deliberation

The Two-Systems Model of Cognition

. . . [F]ollowing the pathbreaking work of Amos Tversy and Daniel Kahneman, [pscychologists] have described [the two models of decision making] as a dual process or two-systems model of cognition. "System 1 quickly proposes intuitive answers to judgment problems as they arise, and System 2 monitors the quality of these proposals, which it may endorse, correct, or override. The judgments that are eventually expressed are *intuitive* if they retain the hypothesized initial proposal without much modification." . . .

The Limits of Deliberation: Bounded Rationality

Problem solving and decision making in professional contexts and in everyday life call for a mixture of intuition and deliberation—of System 1 and System 2 processes. The predominance of intuitive decision making is an inevitable aspect of the human condition of limited cognitive ability and time—what Herbert Simon has called the condition of *bounded rationality*. . . . [T]o use Simon's evocative neologism, we *satisfice*, opting for a reasonably good outcome—often the first that meets some threshold of satisfaction—rather than devoting excessive cognitive energy to seeking the very best. . . .

Biases in Perception and Memory—Introduction: Stages of Information Processing

. . . Cognitive psychologists have likened a person making a judgment to an "information processor" that proceeds through a number of stages from the availability of information to the generation of a response to that information. . . . Every moment of our lives, we are bombarded with vast amounts of *information*, of which we *attend* to only a small fraction. We *encode* the information, structuring, evaluating, and interpreting it and transforming into some sort of mental representation. You might think of *perception* . . . as overlapping attention and encoding. We *store* information in memory and, on occasion, *retrieve* it from memory (i.e., become aware of it) and *process* it with respect to particular objectives. Our *response* to processing may be a factual judgment or inference, an evaluative judgment or opinion, a choice among alternatives or decision, or a solution to a problem. [A wide range of] . . . biases and distortions . . . can affect these stages of information processing. . . .

Biases in Acquisition, Retention, and Retrieval

. . . Our memory does not store complete representations of what was perceived, but only fragments of our *interpretations* of the relevant facts or events. Recollection requires reconstructing one's interpretation, often using (more or less) logical inferences to fill in missing details. [Bias can occur in acquiring, retaining, and retreiving information.] . . .

Dolly Chugh and Max Bazerman describe what they call *bounded awareness*—the phenomenon where "individuals fail to see, seek, use, or share highly relevant, easily accessible, and readily perceivable information during the decision-making process." Because our cognitive power is limited, we can focus only on a small part of everything that goes on around us—often only on one thing at a time.

Much of our daily experience involves multitasking, but we aren't as good at multitasking as we would like to believe. Most of the time, we just don't notice things that are not in our mental field of vision. . . . Chugh and Bazerman characterize the misalignment of available information of which one is unaware with the information needed for a decision as a *focusing failure*. . . .

[People also] interpret the same ambiguous information in different ways. . . . At the worst, from all the events going on in the environment, we sometimes notice those that are significant from our egocentric postion, and fail to notice those that [aren't]. . . . [In one classic experiment,] participants who had previously identified themselves as pro-Arab, pro-Israeli, or neutral viewed extensive samples of media coverage of the massacre of Palestinians in Lebanese refugee camps by allies of Israel. . . . The pro-Arab participants saw the media as biased toward Israel; the pro-Israeli participants saw the news programs as biased against Israel. . . . [Researchers] concluded that "the pro-Arab and pro-Israeli participants 'saw' different news programs — that is, they disagreed about the very nature of the stimulus they had viewed." For example, the groups reported that a higher percentage of the references to Israel were, respectively, favorable or unfavorable. And each believed that the programs would lead an undecided or ambivalent viewer to favor the opposing position. . . .

[So too,] experiences after an event can distort one's recollection of the event. For example, people who read an inaccurate newspaper description of an event they personally witnessed are prone to incorporate the inaccuracies into their recollections. . . . Leading questions (which invite a particular answer) [and one's own intervening thoughts] can distort memory. . . . [To guard against such biases, one expert] suggests cultivating a *distinctiveness heuristic*, under which we demand recollections of distinctive details of an experience before we are willing to say we remember it. This would help prevent adding imagined facts to a recalled experience. . . .

Availability, Vividness and Inference

Richard Nisbett and Lee Ross note that "vivid information is more likely to be stored and remembered than pallid information," and thus more likely to be retrieved at some later date and to affect later inference. Factors that contribute to the vividness of information include:

- *Emotional interest.* Events in which we or people we know are involved have more emotional interest than those involving strangers.
- *Concreteness.* Even events involving strangers can be emotionally gripping if they are described in sufficient detail to prompt imagery. Compare "Jack was killed by a semi-trailer that rolled over his car and crushed his skull" to "Jack sustained fatal injuries in a car accident." . . . Statistics may be the least concrete form of information.
- *Direct experience.* First-hand information has more salience than the reports of others. By the same token, a face-to-face recommendation is likely to be more effective than the same recommendation in writing.

In addition to its availability, vivid information is more likely to recruit additional information from one's memory and people are more likely to rehearse, or mull over, vivid information, making it even more memorable.

The normative problem of using vividness, and availability more generally, as criteria for inference is that they are not always strongly correlated with their evidential value. This is illustrated by a number of experiments in which vividness caused participants to generalize from obviously biased samples. For example, Ruth Hamill, Timothy Wilson and Richard Nisbett showed participants a videotape interview of a prison guard, which depicted him as either humane or brutal. Some were told that the guard was typical, some that he was highly atypical. When later asked to generalize about prison guards, both groups of participants concluded that prison guards generally tended to be like the one they had seen in the interview [even participants who were told the portrayal was atypical]. . . .

Egocentrism: A Particular Memory Bias in Acquisition and/or Retrieval

... [P]eople's recollections and judgments tend to be clouded by an egocentric bias. When married couples estimate their proportionate contribution to household tasks, the sum exceeds 100 percent. So too of collaborators' estimates of their contributions to joint projects, such as this book. While the phenomenon may be partially explained by self-serving motives of having inflatedly positive views of oneself, it extends to negative behaviors as well. Spouses report *causing*, as well as resolving, most of the problems in their relationship, and people are prone to overestimate their own errors and unattractive behaviors.

One plausible explanation for the egocentric bias is that our own actions are more readily accessible to our memories than those of others. ... Even when an individual holds himself accountable for an outcome vis-à-vis others, the question remains open whether the outcome was due to internal factors such as skill or its absence, or to external factors, such as bad luck. In an analysis of newspaper accounts of sporting events, Richard Lau and Dan Russell found that players attributed good outcomes to their skill 75 percent of the time, but took responsibility for bad outcomes only 55 percent of the time. ... [E]ven sportswriters were more likely to provide internal attributions for their home teams' wins than for losses.

Egocentrism is often correlated with self-servingness. Among people working different amounts of time in a joint enterprise, those who work more believe they should be paid more, while those who work less believe that both parties should be paid equally. ...

Conclusion: Naïve Realism

... The biases in the acquisition and recollection of information outlined above are exacerbated by three related convictions that people have about their perceptions and judgments and [those] of other people. These are the elements of what Lee Ross has termed *naive realism*:

1. I see actions and events as they are in reality. My perceptions and reactions are not biased: rather, they are an unmediated reflection of the "real nature" of whatever it is I am responding to.
2. Other people, to the extent that they are willing and able to see things in a similarly objective fashion, will share my perceptions and reactions.
3. When others perceive some event or react to it differently from me, they (but not I) have been influenced by something other than the objective features of the events in question. Their divergent views probably result from an unwarranted ideological rigidity or a self-serving bias that I am not influenced by. The more extreme the view is in divergence from my own, the stronger their bias probably is.

Naïve realism can be especially pernicious in the context of disagreement or conflict. It has the practical implications that:

- Partisans tend to overestimate the number of others who agree with their views—the *false consensus* effect—or at least overestimate the number who would agree with them if apprised of the "real" facts;

partisans therefore assume that disinterested third parties would agree with them.

- Partisans tend to see viewpoints that differ from their own as highly revealing both of personal dispositions (for example, gullibility, aggressiveness, pessimism, or charitableness), and of various cognitive and motivational biases. In fact, differences in judgment often reflect differences in the way a given issue or object of judgment is perceived and construed rather than a difference in the perceivers' values or personality traits. . . .
- Partisans will be polarized and extreme in their view of others. Once they believe a person to be biased, they tend to discount his views entirely, and will underestimate areas of agreement and underestimate the prospects of finding "common ground" through discussion or negotiation.

We have seen that being asked to articulate the weaknesses of one's own position may counter perceptual biases in some situations. A broader hope . . . is that students and readers who understand[ ] those biases and the phenomena of naïve realism will be less likely to fall into their traps. But we should be among the first to admit that the hope does not rest on much of an empirical foundation.

PROBLEM 3-1[8]

You are general counsel for Sears. Yesterday, state and national media reported allegations by a former employee that Sears Auto Centers systematically defraud customers by selling them unnecessary car repairs. The employee told reporters that Sears uses a commission-based compensation system for its mechanics and requires them to meet mandatory repair-dollars-per-hour quotas. He also described high-stakes contests to encourage mechanics to exceed the quotas.

Sears's CEO asks you to meet in his office first thing tomorrow. He is livid and says that he wants the publicity squashed immediately, whatever the cost. In quickly preparing for the meeting, you learn that the employee's description of the compensation practices is essentially correct — though Sears abandoned the contests several years ago. You also learn that the employee left Sears after being accused of sexually harassing a fellow worker. The employee disputed this allegation, and the matter was settled with a confidential termination agreement, in which both he and the company agreed to refrain from making negative public statements about the other.

Treat this as a problem of decision making in which you:

- Frame the problem to be solved;
- Identify and prioritize the relevant values, interests and objectives;
- Identify and resolve major uncertainties concerning the cause of the problem;
- Generate a range of plausible courses of action and predict their consequences;
- Select the course of action that best serves the relevant objectives and values; and
- Establish criteria for evaluating the outcome of the decision.

NOTES AND QUESTIONS

1. Consider an example of flawed decision making that involved inadequate framing of the problem or distorted processing of information. What accounted for the failures and what strategies might have improved the analytic process?

2. Some evidence suggests that cognitive biases were apparent in the run-up to the BP oil spill disaster. In a press conference following the explosion, a reporter asked President Barack Obama whether he regretted his earlier support for increased oil drilling. Obama responded:

> I continue to believe what I said at that time, which was that domestic oil production is an important part of overall energy mix. . . . Where I was wrong was in my belief that the oil companies had their act together when it came to worst case scenarios. . . . Oil drilling has been going on in the Gulf, including deepwater, for quite some time. And the record of accidents like this we hadn't seen before. But it just takes one to have a wake-up call and recognize that claims that fail-safe procedures were in place . . . those assumptions were faulty.[9]

What cognitive biases and group dynamics may have contributed to those assumptions? Psychology professors David Messick and Max Bazerman note that leaders, like other decision makers, are prone to unrealistic optimism about the future, and tend to discount low-probability events and to exaggerate their ability to avert errors and risks.[10] The result may be insufficient worst-case planning by both private-sector decision makers and their government regulators.

In the case of BP, ample evidence was available prior to the disaster concerning the company's abysmal safety record and federal regulators' inadequate responses. Obama acknowledged in his press conference that "[f]or years, there has been a scandalously close relationship between oil companies and the agency that regulates them."[11] In the years preceding the spill, BP reportedly accounted for 97 percent of flagrant violations of environmental standards in the refining industry (760 offenses compared to 8 by the next highest offender).[12] Sanctions for these violations (including the largest fine ever administered by the Occupational Safety and Health Administration) were demonstrably ineffective. In its report on the disaster, the National Commission on the BP Deepwater Horizon Oil Spill and Offshore Drilling concluded that the blowout was not the result of "aberrational decisions . . . that could not have been anticipated or expected to recur again. Rather, the . . . missteps were rooted in systemic failures by industry management . . . and also by failures of government to provide effective regulatory oversight of offshore drilling." According to the Commission, the principal problem was a failure of management, reflected in insufficient review of last-minute changes in drilling procedures, inadequate safety testing requirements, and failures of communication between BP and its contractors Transocean and Halliburton concerning safety-related issues.[13] A broader problem was that regulators, particularly those in the Minerals Management Service (the branch of the Interior Department responsible for offshore drilling leases), lacked the resources and trained personnel necessary for oversight. These regulators largely ignored scientists' warnings about the inevitable and potentially catastrophic risks accompanying deepwater drilling, and frequently rubber-stamped permits and proposed changes in well design.[14] Commenting on the problem, Michael Odom, a Coast Guard lieutenant commander, noted: "The pace of technology has definitely outrun the regulators."[15] Although risk management procedures can undoubtedly be improved, is that an adequate solution? Or does an accurate framing of the problem point to broader, costlier reforms aimed at reducing dependence on oil and preventing agency capture by the industry to be regulated?

3. Another factor that complicates decision making in contexts such as the BP disaster is stress, which increases when both speed and precision are critical, and the stakes are substantial. Although moderate stress can be helpful in mobilizing energy, concentrating the mind, and eliminating distraction, intense stress generally impairs reasoning.[16] One of the best antidotes is a well-functioning team, which is why combat units and other dangerous occupations put such a high premium on group cohesion. To encourage effective team decision making, sharing information is critical, as is knowing when to stop the search for perfect information.[17] In some contexts, timeliness is essential, and the worst decision is indecision, because it offers no basis for learning whether the most plausible alternative was right or wrong. The United States Marine Corps' widely emulated response to these circumstances is the "70 percent solution." Leaders are told to act if they have 70 percent of the necessary information, have performed 70 percent of the analysis, and feel 70 percent confident in their decision.[18] Can you identify situations where this approach makes sense? Situations where it does not?

4. Cognitive psychologists have been much more effective in exposing biases than in identifying correctives. Simply describing the direction of bias or warning individuals about its effects is generally not sufficient. More productive approaches involve receiving intensive feedback, taking a disinterested outsider's perspective, or consulting such an outsider.[19] Other strategies involve changing the environment to reduce biases or to "nudge" individuals toward more rational choices. So, for example, Richard Thaler and Cass Sunstein's *Nudge* proposes ways of taking account of individuals' tendency to discount future risks by requiring them to opt out of policies that correct for that tendency.[20] Could any of these approaches have helped in the examples of bias you have observed, or in the problem set forth below?

5. Two other cognitive tendencies common among leaders are "action bias" and "motivated reasoning." Action bias leads them to look for ways to respond to risks and to discount the problems that their responses might entail. In England, the tendency in policy making settings is known as the "dangerous dog" effect, based on a clumsy legislative overreaction to several dog bite incidents.[21] Motivated reasoning involves the "rationalization of preferred opinions, our tendency to arrive, by seemingly purely rational reasoning, at the opinions that we prefer for other motives."[22] So, for example, government leaders may see expansion of their agency's influence

as serving the public interest, and may discount the downsides to such strategies without realizing the biases that underpin their evaluations. When these biases are combined with the tendency to overestimate one's own competence, the result may be the reinforcement of naïve realism.

PROBLEM 3-2

Henry Louis Gates Jr. is a professor at Harvard and one of the world's pre-eminent scholars of African American studies. In July 2009, on returning home around noon from a "14 hour flight and nursing a bronchial infection," Gates found the front door to his Cambridge home jammed.[23] Gates, who is 58 and walks with a cane because of a lifelong disability, asked for help in forcing the door open from his cabdriver, a dark-skinned Moroccan.[24]

A concerned neighbor who saw the men struggle with the door called the Cambridge police to report a possible burglary. In the preceding six months, the neighborhood had twenty-three break-ins, many of which had occurred during the day.[25] The first on the scene was Sergeant James M. Crowley, an officer with eleven years of experience, an adviser to the Cambridge police commissioner, an instructor on methods to avoid racial profiling, and a role model for younger officers. He had the reputation of being a "by-the-book" sergeant.[26] Crowley saw Gates in the foyer and asked him to step outside. Gates refused.

What happened next is a matter of dispute. According to Charles J. Ogletree, a Harvard law professor who represented Gates in the matter, Gates explained that the house belonged to him and showed Crowley his Massachusetts and Harvard identification cards.[27] When Crowley questioned the explanation, Gates grew frustrated and asked for the sergeant's name and badge number.

According to the police report, Gates initially refused to show identification. Crowley explained to Gates that he was investigating a possible break-in, and Gates exclaimed, "Why, because I'm a black man in America?" and accused Crowley of racism.[28] Crowley further noted in the police report that he was led to believe Gates lived in the home but was "quite surprised and confused" by Gates's behavior.[29]

As the encounter escalated, the Cambridge police unsuccessfully tried to reach Crowley on his radio at least three times. When they received no response, they sent six cars to the scene, which surprised Gates as he exited his home.[30] A video showed Gates responding belligerently as he was charged with disorderly conduct and led in handcuffs from the house.[31] Charges were subsequently dismissed. A joint statement by Gates's lawyer, the Cambridge Police Department, the City of Cambridge, and the county district attorney's office called the incident "regrettable and unfortunate" and emphasized that it "should not be viewed as one that demeans the character and reputation of Professor Gates or the character of the Cambridge Police Department."[32]

Six days after Gates's arrest, President Obama was asked about the incident at the close of a press conference on health care. He responded:

> Now, I don't know, not having been there and not seeing all the facts, what role race played in that, but I think it's fair to say, number one, any of us would be

pretty angry; number two, that the Cambridge police acted stupidly in arrest-ing somebody when there was already proof that they were in their own home; and, number three, what I think we know, separate and apart from this incident, is that there is a long history in this country of African-Americans and Latinos being stopped by law enforcement disproportionately. And that's just a fact.[33]

Obama's comments triggered widespread controversy. Critics claimed that he had prejudged the situation and had helped further "fuel the controversy" by charging the police with acting "stupidly."[34] According to Ben Heineman, a former GE General Counsel and leadership expert, Obama missed a "teaching moment."[35] By not stressing the need to make judgments based on facts rather than assumptions, he undercut his own position on racial profiling. He also diverted attention from the theme of his press conference — the urgency of health care reform.[36]

In the wake of public criticism, Obama made another statement to the press acknowledging that he "could have calibrated" his words more care-fully.[37] However he also stressed his conviction that the incident was "a sign of how race remains a factor in this society."[38] When the controversy persisted, Obama invited Gates and Crowley to the White House for a beer.

The gesture met with mixed reviews. Some commentators parodied the effort:

> President Obama today named this Thursday, Drink a Beer With Someone Who Arrested You Day. Explaining his decision, the President told reporters, "When tempers run a little high, there's one thing that always helps people think more rationally: beer." The President said he hoped that his proclama-tion would result in thousands of friendly get-togethers around the country between police officers and the innocent people they recently arrested.[39]

Considerable media attention focused on the types of beer chosen and whether Obama's beer selection (Bud Light) was "a safe political choice." After all, Jon Stewart noted, the parent company of that beer was Belgian. Wasn't this a moment to "buy American"?[40] David Letterman's Top Ten com-ments overheard at the meeting included, "Let's call Rush Limbaugh and take this party to the next level."[41]

The meeting generated relatively few substantive efforts to address the pro-blems that the incident exposed. In a public statement following the "beer summit," Crowley stated that he and Gates had "agreed to disagree" and "decided to look forward."[42] Gates reported that the meeting had helped them bridge their divide and "make a larger contribution to American society."[43]

1. What role might cognitive bias have played in the way that Gates, Crowley, and Obama each framed the incident? Was there evidence of:
   - Recognition primed decision making (use of schemas to size up a situation);
   - Bounded rationality (limitations of time and cognitive processes leading to reliance on intuitive rather than deliberative decision making);
   - Retention and retrieval biases (overreliance on vivid, personal, concrete information); or

- Naïve realism (assumptions that our view is neutral while others are biased)?

If they had been aware of these potential biases, might participants have responded differently?

2. How should the Cambridge Police Department have handled the incident?

3. Another factor that can impair decision making is what Zachery Shore labels "exposure anxiety": an unwillingness to appear weak or inadequate.[44] George Orwell's celebrated story "Shooting an Elephant" offers a case in point. There a British police officer serving in Burma during the mid-1920s receives word that an elephant had broken its chains, killed a coolie, and trampled property. The officer sets off with a rifle and townspeople follow. He finds the elephant grazing in a field, no longer causing danger. But the crowd, which has grown to two thousand, expects a show and he yields to the pressure. He fires several shots into the animal's brain and throat, but it refuses to die. Tormented by the animal's suffering, he sends for a smaller rifle and empties its contents. The tiny bullets have no apparent effect. Unable to endure the spectacle, the officer leaves before the elephant painfully expires. Orwell intended the story as an allegory for imperialism. However, as Shore notes in *Blunder*, the dynamic plays out in many contexts where leaders worry that failure to take decisive action will weaken their authority.[45] Could this concern help account for incidents in which police are reluctant to back down in the face of challenges to their judgment? How should President Obama have responded to press questions? Do you agree that his statement inappropriately "fueled the controversy"? Ben Heineman proposed the following alternative statement:

> I don't know the facts of this local police matter. But there is a potential question of racial profiling. Without passing judgment on Professor Gates' arrest, let me address that larger problem which, in my judgment, clearly continues to exist in America today.[46]

Is that what you would have said? Why or why not?

4. Was the beer summit an example of effective leadership? If not, what would you have done?

5. According to a *New Yorker* account of the incident, the takeaway for Obama was that "talking about race, especially extemporaneously, was just not worth it."[47] Would that be your assessment?

MEDIA RESOURCES

Ample media coverage is available on the Gates incident, including police videos of his arrest, Obama's initial statement, and participant interviews.[48] Many news programs replayed Obama's statement about the BP disaster, and commentary on the underlying regulatory and risk prevention failures. A video of a classic psychology experiment can be used to explore perceptual errors. In the video, viewers are asked to count the passes made by teams in white shirts and black shirts passing a basketball, and then asked what they saw. What they did not see is equally instructive.[49]

B. GROUP DECISION MAKING

Although our image of a leader's decision making tends to be a solitary individual "decider," that person's judgments are often the product of collective processes. The reasons are obvious. As Harvard Business School professor Harold Leavit suggested in his classic article "Suppose We Took Groups Seriously," decision making often benefits from the different information, values, skills, and perspectives that members bring to the table.[50] Subsequent theorists emphasized that group involvement in decision making could also increase the legitimacy of the process and enhance the commitment of members who would need to live with the outcomes. But as researchers also noted, group decision making took more time and could result in poor decisions if the members lacked sufficient expertise, if conflicts and power disparities were not well managed, and if tendencies to conformity were not well controlled. Social psychologist Irving Janis explored the latter problem. His widely discussed book and article in *Psychology Today* on "groupthink" described the ways that highly cohesive groups could suppress independent views and too quickly converge on ill-conceived decisions.[51]

1. THE PROBLEM OF GROUPTHINK

IRVING L. JANIS, "GROUPTHINK"

Psychology Today Magazine (1971), pp. 84-89

. . . There is evidence from a number of social-psychological studies that as the members of a group feel more accepted by the others, which is a central feature of increased group cohesiveness, they display less overt conformity to group norms. Thus we would expect that the more cohesive a group becomes, the less the members will feel constrained to censor what they say out of fear of being socially punished for antagonizing the leader or any of their fellow members.

In contrast, the groupthink type of conformity tends to increase as group cohesiveness increases. Groupthink involves nondeliberate suppression of critical thoughts as a result of internalization of the group's norms, which is quite different from deliberate suppression on the basis of external threats of social punishment. The more cohesive the group, the greater the inner compulsion on the part of each member to avoid creating disunity, which inclines him to believe in the soundness of whatever proposals are promoted by the leader or by a majority of the group's members.

In a cohesive group, the danger is not so much that each individual will fail to reveal his objections to what the others propose but that he will think the proposal is a good one, without attempting to carry out a careful, critical scrutiny of the pros and cons of the alternatives. When groupthink becomes dominant, there also is considerable suppression of deviant thoughts, but it takes the form of each person's deciding that his misgivings are not relevant and should be set aside, that the benefit of the doubt regarding any lingering uncertainties should be given to the group consensus.

Stress. I do not mean to imply that all cohesive groups necessarily suffer from groupthink. All ingroups may have a mild tendency toward groupthink, displaying one or another of the symptoms from time to time, but it need not be so dominant as to influence the quality of the group's final decision. Neither do I mean to imply that there is anything necessarily inefficient or harmful about group decisions in general. On the contrary, a group whose members have properly defined roles, with traditions concerning the procedures to follow in pursuing a critical inquiry, probably is capable of making better decisions than any individual group member working alone.

The problem is that the advantages of having decisions made by groups are often lost because of powerful psychological pressures that arise when the members work closely together, share the same set of values and, above all, face a crisis situation that puts everyone under intense stress.

The main principle of groupthink, which I offer in the spirit of Parkinson's Law, is this: *The more amiability and esprit de corps there is among the members of a policy-making ingroup, the greater the danger that independent critical thinking will be replaced by groupthink, which is likely to result in irrational and dehumanizing actions directed against outgroups.*

Symptoms. In my studies of high-level governmental decision-makers, both civilian and military, I have found eight main symptoms of groupthink.

(1) *Invulnerability.* Most or all of the members of the ingroup share an *illusion* of invulnerability that provides for them some degree of reassurance about obvious dangers and leads them to become over-optimistic and willing to take extraordinary risks. It also causes them to fail to respond to clear warnings of danger. . . .

(2) *Rationale.* As we see, victims of groupthink ignore warnings; they also collectively construct rationalizations in order to discount warnings and other forms of negative feedback that, taken seriously, might lead the group members to reconsider their assumptions each time they recommit themselves to past decisions. . . .

(3) *Morality.* Victims of groupthink believe unquestioningly in the inherent morality of their ingroup; this belief inclines the members to ignore the ethical or moral consequences of their decisions.

Evidence that this symptom is at work usually is of a negative kind — the things that are left unsaid in group meetings. . . .

(4) *Stereotypes.* Victims of groupthink hold stereotyped views of the leaders of enemy groups: they are so evil that genuine attempts at negotiating differences with them are unwarranted, or they are too weak or too stupid to deal effectively with whatever attempts the ingroup makes to defeat their purposes, no matter how risky the attempts are. . . .

(5) *Pressure.* Victims of groupthink apply direct pressure to any individual who momentarily expresses doubts about any of the group's shared illusions or who questions the validity of the arguments supporting a policy alternative favored by the majority. . . .

(6) *Self-censorship.* Victims of groupthink avoid deviating from what appears to be group consensus; they keep silent about their misgivings and even minimize to themselves the importance of their doubts. . . .

(7) *Unanimity.* Victims of groupthink share an *illusion* of unanimity within the group concerning almost all judgments expressed by members who speak in favor of the majority view. This symptom results partly from the preceding one, whose effects are augmented by the false assumption that any individual who remains silent during any part of the discussion is in full accord with what the others are saying. . . .

(8) *Mindguards.* Victims of groupthink sometimes appoint themselves as mindguards to protect the leader and fellow members from adverse information that might break the complacency they shared about the effectiveness and morality of past decisions. . . .

Remedies. . . . 1. The leader of a policy-forming group should assign the role of critical evaluator to each member, encouraging the group to give high priority to open airing of objections and doubts. This practice needs to be reinforced by the leader's acceptance of criticism of his own judgments in order to discourage members from soft-pedaling their disagreements and from allowing their striving for concurrence to inhibit critical thinking.

2. When the key members of a hierarchy assign a policy-planning mission to any group within their organization, they should adopt an impartial stance instead of stating preferences and expectations at the beginning. This will encourage open inquiry and impartial probing of a wide range of policy alternatives.

3. The organization routinely should set up several outside policy-planning and evaluation groups to work on the same policy question, each deliberating under a different leader. This can prevent the insulation of an ingroup.

4. At intervals before the group reaches a final consensus, the leader should require each member to discuss the group's deliberations with associates in his own unit of the organization — assuming that those associates can be trusted to adhere to the same security regulations that govern the policy-makers — and then to report back their reactions to the group.

5. The group should invite one or more outside experts to each meeting on a staggered basis and encourage the experts to challenge the views of the core members. . . .

9. After reaching a preliminary consensus about what seems to be the best policy, the group should hold a "second-chance" meeting at which every member expresses as vividly as he can all his residual doubts, and rethinks the entire issue before making a definitive choice.

2. STRENGTHS, LIMITATIONS, AND STRATEGIES FOR IMPROVEMENT OF GROUP DECISION MAKING

Groupthink is not the only way in cognitive and interpersonal dynamics that can compromise group decision. In the following excerpt, Paul Brest and Linda Krieger explore other biases as well as strategies to address them.

Paul Brest and Linda Hamilton Krieger, Problem Solving, Decision Making, and Professional Judgment

(New York: Oxford University Press, 2010), pp. 595-597, 604-608, 611, 614-618, and 623-629

Thinking about Group Decision Making

Three decades of research tell a more nuanced and complex story than many [accounts of collective decision making suggest]. . . . Groups can add value to a decision-making process, but they can also run it off the rails. Small groups often make better decisions than their average member would make alone, but they seldom outperform their best members. Small groups fall prey to virtually all of the cognitive biases that plague individual decision makers and sometimes actually amplify the effects of those biases. . . .

Aggregation without Group Process: The Wisdom of Crowds

In a phenomenon that James Surowiecki has termed the "wisdom of crowds," combining a sufficient number of diverse and independent judgments often yields a better outcome than the judgment of any isolated person, no matter how smart or well-informed he or she might be. The result requires that four conditions be met:

1. The "group" must reflect a *diversity* of skills, opinions, information, and perspectives.
2. Each member's judgments must be *independent* from the others. That is, an individual's knowledge and opinions cannot be influenced by the knowledge and opinions of other group members.
3. The members must make and report their "sincere" judgments rather than skewing them for strategic purposes.
4. The decision maker needs a mechanism for *aggregating* the individual judgments to turn large numbers of private judgments into a single one. . . .

The Common Knowledge Effect

[These conditions are not met in circumstances of groupthink, and where] . . . deliberations often focus on shared rather than unshared information. The so-called "common knowledge effect" biases group decision making in the direction supported by shared information. . . . [The strength of the common knowledge effect depends on several factors, including the verifiability of the unshared information, the number of members who have it, and contextual factors. For example,] time pressure increases reliance on common information, as does an increase in the decision's apparent importance and group members' sense of accountability for it. . . .

But, certain measures tend to reduce the common knowledge effect:

- *Framing* the task as a "problem to be solved," implying that it has a "correct" answer.
- *Publicly* assigning roles to different group members [and giving them] the responsibility to supply information on a particular decision-relevant topic.

- *Extending* the time for discussion, which results in the use of more unshared information.
- Increasing the number of options from which the group can choose, and explicitly listing those options.
- Providing an objective source of verification of unshared information. . . .

Group Polarization

. . . [P]eople generally want to be viewed well by others. In order to present themselves in a socially desirable light, they constantly monitor others' reactions to determine how to adjust their self-presentation. As group members see how others view the issue under discussion, they tend to present themselves to be congruent with the perceived emerging trend. Indeed, to be "distinct" from their peers in the socially valued direction they often go "one step further" in the direction of increasingly extreme positions. Seen in this way, group polarization can be understood as a type of bandwagon effect.

Second, people generally see themselves and like to be seen by others as moderate, and initially express positions that may be more moderate than their true beliefs. But after being exposed to others having their own viewpoints, people become disinhibited from expressing more extreme views and they become more confident of those views. Robert Baron and his colleagues demonstrated that discussion with like-minded people can move individuals to more extreme positions solely by virtue of this *social corroboration* effect.

A third account of polarization, *social identity*, concerns the relationship of the group to others outside the group. As group members begin interacting with each other, they collectively begin to identify the characteristics, behaviors, and norms that differentiate their group from other groups. To differentiate their group from others, members attribute more extremity to their own group than is objectively the case; they distinguish their group from others by accentuating the perceived distance between their group norm and the norms they attribute to out-groups. Group members then conform their own behaviors, norms, and self-conceptions to the group's. Polarization thus occurs through a process of contrast with other groups within a specific social context.

. . . Another cognitive account of group polarization understands group interaction as an exercise in *rationale construction* rather than information collection. This model posits that people bring to a discussion their ex ante preferences and that interaction calls upon them to explain these to other group members. As people explain their positions, they gain confidence in them, whether or not they are accurate. Indeed, as Chip Heath and Richard Gonzales have shown, interaction with others increases confidence in, but not accuracy of, judgments. A related causal theory draws on the *effects of repeated expression:* polarization occurs as people repeat their own arguments and are repeatedly exposed to particular arguments, evidence, or expressions of a conclusion by like-minded others.

Reducing the Tendency Toward Group Polarization

There has been very little research directly testing the effectiveness of particular interventions in reducing group polarization. However, some inferences can be drawn from research on the contextual factors that tend to reduce or exacerbate the effect:

- Polarization is moderated by heterogeneity of initial opinions within a deliberating group.
- As with groupthink, polarization is exacerbated where the group is an ideologically cohering, high-solidarity entity.
- Groups that work together over a sustained period of time, making numerous similar decisions, may get feedback on the quality of those decisions, which may moderate overconfidence and lead to more effective use of information in subsequent decision making.
- Polarization is moderated where a group is subject to external shocks (e.g. losing an election, being sued, experiencing a severe policy failure) or where the group must temper its preferences to preserve its prestige with external constituencies.
- Polarization can be reduced by increasing decision-making independence through mechanisms like the Delphi technique ([below]), and through norms and facilitation that encourage open-mindedness, the inclusion of minority perspectives, and evidence-based decision making.

Strategic Participation in Group Decision Making

Group members' concerns about their relations with others in the group play a significant role in the pathologies of group decision making. Individual group members may have interests that differ from those of their colleagues. So, for example, in a meeting to help a company's managers decide whether to settle or litigate an employment discrimination case, the lawyer may be concerned to maintain the impression that she is "on their side" even as she attempts to impress upon them the nature of the exposure to risk that they face. She may also want to convey a gender counter-stereotypical "toughness" that she hopes will instill confidence in her competence as a vigorous advocate.

Other participants in the decision-making process may have their own sets of competing processing goals. The manager who made the now-challenged decision may seek to save face, preventing his colleagues from concluding that he made a mistake or otherwise acted imprudently. Yet another group member may simply want to create a good impression and be viewed as a "team player." And all (or almost all) of the group members will be attempting to maintain a certain level of social harmony, both during and after the decision-making process.

In other words, the goal of making of a "good" decision is only one of the items on members' individual and collective agendas. The susceptibility of a group to decision-making errors will depend in substantial measure on these often hidden competing motivations.

The Susceptibility of Groups to Biases and Heuristics

Overconfidence. . . . . [I]ndividuals often are overconfident in the accuracy of their own judgment. It turns out that groups don't do better. . . . Group overconfidence may result from the group polarization effect. . . .

Confirmation bias. Small deliberating groups, no less than individuals, fall prey to the tendency to overweight information that confirms a prior position, theory, or attitude and to underweight information that would tend to disconfirm it. . . .

Improving Group Decision Making

Preventing Premature Convergence: Devil's Advocacy and Dialectical Inquiry

One of the most common structures for group-based strategic decision making is an "expert approach," where a group of individuals, selected for their presumed expertise, present and seek consensus for a single recommended course of action. This procedure invites premature convergence.

Devil's advocacy is one way to inhibit premature convergence. After a plan is proposed by an individual or subgroup, another individual or subgroup attempts to identify everything wrong with the plan. The larger group then uses this critique to improve or replace the original proposal. Problem-solving groups that use devil's advocacy have been shown to generate a wider range of alternative courses of action than do conventional deliberating groups. Janis cites President Kennedy's handling of the Cuban Missile Crisis as an example of successful use of devil's advocacy. During those critical days in October 1962, President Kennedy assigned his brother, Attorney General Robert F. Kennedy, the role of devil's advocate with the task of aggressively challenging the assumptions and analysis underlying any emerging consensus. Devil's advocacy is not without its limitations: for example, if group members view the devil's advocate as being insincere, they may ignore his critique.

In *dialectical inquiry*, the entire group plays the role of devil's advocate. After identifying and discussing an initial plan, the entire group develops a "counterplan." There follows a structured debate, in which those responsible for making an ultimate decision hear arguments for and against the plan and the counterplan, with the possibility that yet another plan may emerge. . . .

The Stepladder Technique

Many of the dysfunctions of small decision-making groups result from social processes that interfere with the group's ability to fully utilize the potential contribution of all of its members. The group may be dominated by particularly aggressive individuals who stifle input from others in the group. Some group members may engage in social loafing, depriving the group of their potential contribution. Social pressures and social conformity effects may cause group members to withhold valuable information, opinions, or perspectives.

In the 1990s, Steven Rogelberg and his colleagues developed a procedure known as the *stepladder technique* to minimize the impact of these negative dynamics on group deliberation. The stepladder technique structures the entry of individuals into a decision-making group so as to maximize their independence from other group members and highlight their uniquely held information, opinions, ideas, and perspectives.

Before entering the discussion, each member is presented with the group's task and sufficient time to think about it alone. After the first two members discuss the problem, new members join the group one at a time. When entering the group, each new member must present his or her preliminary solution to the problem before hearing what the other group members think. Then the group discusses the problem before another new member enters. No final decision is made until all group members have been incorporated into the group in this manner.

The stepladder technique tends to improve a group's decision performance. Stepladder groups outperformed both their average and best member more often than conventional deliberating groups.

Generating and Evaluating Alternatives with Nominal Groups: The Delphi Technique

As described [above], the members of a "nominal group" work alone to solve a problem and their individual solutions are then aggregated. In some situations, nominal groups are more effective than either individuals or interactive groups. For example, nominal groups tend to outperform face-to-face groups in brainstorming tasks, where the goal is to generate lots of ideas and eventually improve on them.

The *Delphi Technique* is a well-known form of nominal group brainstorming. A coordinator transmits questions to group members. Working alone, the members transmit their responses to the coordinator, who assembles the information and generates additional information requests. Suppose, for example, that a humanitarian relief NGO is deciding what precautions to take in a conflict-ridden country in which its workers are in physical danger, or whether to pull out altogether. The coordinator states the problem, and asks each participant to generate as many ideas as possible for dealing with the issue. The coordinator then asks for comments on their strengths and weaknesses, and asks for refinements and new ideas. The process continues, with eventual resolution either through the emergence of a consensus or through voting. . . .

The Effects of Accountability on Individual and Group Decision Making Performance

. . . Accountability has become a popular concept in business, politics, and elsewhere, but its effects are not always clearly understood. Received wisdom tells us that a decision maker's accountability to others improves the quality of the decision. Though this sometimes is true, accountability can also lead to poorer decision making. This section summarizes the literature on the effects of accountability.

All other things being equal, accountability is likely to reduce error and bias in contexts in which, for whatever reason, people tend to make mistakes that they could prevent with extra attention or effort. For example, the expectation that they will have to justify their decision leads people to think more carefully and logically, and not to be satisfied with using unarticulated criteria or unsubstantiated empirical judgments to arrive at answers. Moreover, accountability makes people more likely to identify their own sources of bias, because of the need to justify themselves to others who do not necessarily view the decision with the same biases.

But, . . . the benefits of accountability depend on a number of factors, such as:

- *Whether the views of the audience are known or unknown.* Decision makers who know the views of the audience to whom they are accountable tend to conform decisions to gain the audience's favor. . . . When the audience's views are unknown, decision makers tend to engage in *preemptive self-criticism,* anticipating how the decision would be viewed from various perspectives.
- *Whether one is accountable for the quality of the decision process or the decision's substantive outcome.* For example, a foundation could hold its program officers accountable for the success of their grants each year, or it could focus instead on whether the program officers were making thoughtful, informed outcome-focused decisions. Ultimately, the proof of a good process is in its outcomes; but this may take many years. A program officer who is held accountable only for outcomes may be afraid to take appropriate risks in making grants since, even if the risks are well-considered in terms of expected value, they could still fail and lead to a bad outcome. On the whole, accountability for the process tends to improve the decision's accuracy and calibration while accountability for outcome can reduce decision quality. . . . Accountability may actually lead to poorer decision making when a biased choice seems the easiest to justify. For example decision makers may anticipate less criticism of a decision if they choose the middle ground between two extreme values . . . or if they take into account all the information presented, including irrelevant information.

NOTES AND QUESTIONS

1. Can you identify circumstances in which you observed examples of group-think, or common-knowledge effects? What effort was, or should have been, made to counteract them?
2. As a general matter, researchers find that team performance improves when members have different expertise and perspectives, but declines when they have different goals and values. Consider the implications of this finding for conflict management issues discussed in Chapter 4 and diversity initiatives discussed in Chapter 8.
3. In a recent essay, Paul Brest highlights a number of biases that are particularly problematic in public-policy settings.[52] One involves confirmation bias that makes it difficult to separate political preferences from fact-finding. So, for example, a legislator worried about the political and economic consequences of restricting greenhouse gas emissions may tend to discount the risks of global warming that the restrictions seek to address. A second problem is the "cognitive myopia" that leads to undervaluing future costs and benefits. When considering social investments, policy leaders tend to find the immediate costs more concrete, salient, and thus analytically "available" than long-term consequences. The problem is compounded by accountability to current constituents, who exhibit the same biases.

A third difficulty arises from leaders' tendency to overvalue consistency and sunk costs. A representative case involves members of Congress who cited the dollars spent and lives lost in NASA's space shuttle program as a reason for its continued support.[53] Have you observed such tendencies in recent policy-making processes? Is the size of the deficit an example? How might such biases be overcome?

4. Some observers have argued that the Bush administration's decision to invade Iraq, and the faulty intelligence on which it was based, was an illustration of groupthink. In 2004, the Senate Intelligence Committee issued a report concluding that the intelligence community had seriously misjudged Iraq's military capabilities. One of the report's conclusions was that

> [t]he Intelligence Community (IC) suffered from a collective presumption that Iraq had an active and growing weapons of mass destruction (WMD) program [based on Iraq's prior deception and refusal to cooperate fully with UN inspectors]. This "group think" dynamic led Intelligence Community analysts, collectors, and managers to both interpret ambiguous evidence as conclusively indicative of a WMD program as well as ignore or minimize evidence that Iraq did not have active and expanding weapons of mass destruction programs. This presumption was so strong that formalized IC mechanisms established to challenge assumptions and group think [such as devil's advocacy] were not utilized. . . . IC personnel involved in the Iraq WMD issue demonstrated several aspects of group think: examining few alternatives, selective gathering of information, pressure to conform within the group or withhold criticism, and collective rationalization.[54]

Other commentators noted that confirmation biases may also have inclined the intelligence community to interpret evidence in a way consistent with the political convictions of administration leaders.[55]

If these accounts are correct, how could such misjudgments be prevented in the future? The report mentioned the need for the Intelligence Community to "make sure to question presumptions instead of rationalizing/explaining away lack of strong evidence with self-reinforcing premises."[56] How could this be achieved? What stands in the way?

A related problem is that the voters on whom we rely to check reckless political decisions are themselves subject to cognitive bias. Psychologists Carol Tavris and Elliot Aronson see a desire to reduce cognitive dissonance at work in the insistence of half of surveyed Republicans that weapons of mass destruction were found in Iraq, despite intensive news coverage to the contrary.[57] In some instances, individuals who are ideologically committed to a position will become even more entrenched in their views when presented with evidence exposing their error. Researchers found evidence of such "backfire" effects among conservatives who received the findings of the Duelfer Report, which documented the absence of stockpiles of such weapons or an active production program prior to the U.S. invasion.[58] What lessons should policy leaders draw from these examples?

5. Abraham Lincoln avoided some perils of groupthink by appointing a "team of rivals" in his cabinet, including his most formidable opponents.[59] President Obama has also seemed sensitive to the potential pitfalls in group decision making. In 2008, after appointing his national security team,

which included Hillary Clinton, he was asked about how he would ensure that the group would function as a team of rivals rather than a class of rivals. He responded:

> I assembled this team because I am a strong believer in strong personalities and strong opinions. I think this is how the best decisions are made. One of the dangers in a White House based on my reading of history is that you get wrapped up in group think and everybody agrees with everything and there is no dissenting view. So I am going to be welcoming a vigorous debate inside the White House.[60]

Subsequent news reports indicated that Obama had, in fact, developed a "culture of debate" on major foreign-policy decisions, such as expansion of the war in Afghanistan.[61] Although he has also been criticized for failing to build a sufficiently diverse team of advisors on domestic policy issues, his approach is generally viewed as more open to contention than that of his predecessor.[62] In an interview with Bob Woodward, George Bush described himself as a "gut player," someone who tends to "play by intuition" rather than extended debate.[63] What are the strengths and limitations of these different leadership approaches?

6. Some experts have attributed the investment community's misplaced faith in ever-rising real estate prices and in the market's self-policing capabilities to groupthink, overconfidence, and confirmation biases — a combination resulting in "contagious wishful thinking."[64] According to an article by David Leonhardt in the *New York Times*, federal regulators, along with other analysts, "got trapped in an echo chamber of conventional wisdom" about rising real estate prices.[65] Robert Schiller, author of *Irrational Exuberance*, described the pressure he felt in advising financial institutions to avoid "deviating too far from consensus." He didn't want to risk "ostracism," and feared criticism for "gratuitous alarmism" in his warnings about stock and housing market bubbles. In his view, another reason economists consistently underestimate the likelihood of bubbles is that they "aren't generally trained in psychology," and prefer to focus on the "rational" behaviors that "they understand well."[66] Other commentators suggested that some policy leaders' prior commitment to deregulation may also have led them to overlook subprime lending abuses calling for greater oversight.[67]

Malcolm Gladwell similarly faults overconfidence in financial markets and analogizes it to the complacency that has led to military disasters, such as Great Britain's infamous 1915 attempt to invade Gallipoli. Military analysts attribute this botched effort to leaders' failure to adapt when circumstances were not what they anticipated, a failure rooted in their confidence that they did not need to adapt. One commander, Sir Ian Hamilton, wrote in his diary: "Let me bring my lads face to face with Turks in the open field. We must beat them every time because British volunteer soldiers are superior individuals to . . . Syrians or Arabs. . . ."[68] Gladwell sees some of the same "cocksure" attitudes at work in the collapse of Bear Stearns and other financial institutions. Too many corporate leaders forgot that "in wars and Wall Street there is no such thing as absolute expertise, that every step taken toward mastery brings with it an increased risk of mastery's curse. . . . At the end [Bear Stearns's C.E.O. still] saw the world that he wanted to see," not the one that existed.[69]

George Soros also attributes part of the financial meltdown to cognitive biases, particularly the fallacy resulting from "positive feedback loops." When investors get false favorable results, such as escalating profits, from an incorrect market analysis, they engage in increasingly risky behavior.[70] Housing lenders, he believes, got caught in such a feedback loop. When they made loans easier to obtain, they saw an increase in demand, which stimulated further lending. By bundling and reselling these risky loans in less transparent financial instruments, they were able to protect themselves from immediate negative consequences. When the bubble burst, millions of homeowners with unaffordable mortgages paid the price, as did lending institutions and taxpayers who financed their bailouts.

Neuroscientists have also joined the search for underlying causes of such market meltdowns. Some research on brain activity during simulated financial bubbles finds a physiological craving for rewards that come from early returns on investment. Dopamine neurons fire rapidly and stimulate the brain nucleus, which increases individuals' excitement and encourages them to pour more money into the market. The rational centers of the brain then come up with all sorts of reasons why the market will not decline in order to sustain the heightened activity. This reasoning persists even after dopamine neurons cease firing shortly before the bubble bursts. Neuroscientists also find that high-risk activity is exacerbated by group competition. The desire to outsmart others encourages ever more speculative behavior.[71]

Consider the strategies for combating cognitive biases discussed below and the problems in regulating the financial market explored in Chapter 5. What initiatives might have helped to avert unduly risky behavior? What might have prompted more executives to follow the example of Alfred Sloan, former chair of General Motors, who once adjourned a board meeting shortly after it began? "Gentlemen," he observed, "I take it we are all in complete agreement on the decision here. . . . Then I propose we postpone further discussion of this matter until our next meeting to give ourselves time to develop disagreement and perhaps gain some understanding of what the decision is all about."[72] Consider commentator Ezra Klein's conclusion that everyone running or regulating financial institutions is human and therefore subject to a certain level of cognitive "idiocy." And because you cannot "idiot proof a system run by idiots," the best you can do is to design an oversight system that "anticipates [their] inevitable failure and limits the damage that it can do."[73]

3. A CASE STUDY: THE HEWLETT PACKARD PRETEXTING SCANDAL

DEBORAH L. RHODE AND DAVID LUBAN, LEGAL ETHICS

(New York: Foundation Press, 5th ed. 2009), pp. 431-434

In 2006, the Silicon Valley computer company, Hewlett-Packard, became embroiled in a highly publicized scandal. The problems arose from pretexting, the use of investigators to obtain confidential information through false pretenses. The case provides a highly illuminating portrayal of "how the good go bad"—how well intentioned lawyers and managers can become complicit in conduct widely viewed as unethical if not unlawful.

In 2005, leaks of confidential information accompanied the widely publicized firing of HP C.E.O. Carly Fiorina. Patricia Dunn, a member of the board of directors became its new chair and Mark Hurd became C.E.O. Neither had legal background; Dunn came from investment services and Hurd had headed a technology company. Among Dunn's first challenges was to address leaks that could only have come from board members or top executives. At the suggestion of an HP security manager, Dunn launched an investigation headed by a Boston-based private investigator, Ron DeLia, who had done work for HP in the past. In the late spring of 2005, DeLia sent a report to Dunn, which she forwarded to General Counsel Ann Baskins. In that report, and a subsequent June 15 telephone conference call, DeLia explained that investigators had obtained phone records through pretexting. Baskins expressed concerns about the legality of the process, and he responded that he was aware of no laws that made it illegal and no criminal prosecutions for such activities. Although the investigation failed to identify the leakers, HP leadership hoped that the process would deter future disclosures.

However, in January 2006, reporter Dawn Kawamoto ran a story on HP's long-term strategies. George Keyworth, a board member, later acknowledged having been the source. He did not believe he had disclosed any proprietary information and considered the story to be good press. Hewlett-Packard's leadership, by contrast, viewed the story with alarm, particularly because it addressed potential acquisitions. Baskins asked an HP employment lawyer, Ken Hunsaker, to head an investigation. Through pretexting, the investigation team obtained phone records of two HP employees, seven directors and nine reporters. It also created a fictional disgruntled HP employee who contacted Kawamoto by e-mail, and attached a file with tracking capability. Investigators hoped that she would forward the e-mail to her source for confirmation. Hurd, the C.E.O. authorized the process but later denied knowledge of the tracking aspect.

Around the same time, Baskins asked Hunsaker to explore the legality of pretexting. He put the question to Anthony Gentilucci, an HP security manager. Gentilucci responded that pretexting was common. In his view, although phone operators shouldn't give the information out and were in some sense "liable," the practice was "on the edge, but above board." Hunsaker's now infamous e-mail answer was "I should not have asked." Hunsaker also spent about an hour researching the issue on line. It is not clear what sources he consulted, but had he looked at the websites of the Federal Trade Commission or the Federal Communications Commission, he would have discovered that both considered the practice illegal.

In February, the issue arose again. Two HP security employees sent an e-mail to Hunsaker stating that pretexting "is very unethical at the least and probably illegal." So too, Baskins again asked Hunsaker about the legality of pretexting, and he again put the question to DeLia. This time DeLia consulted his outside counsel. That lawyer offered a quick judgment that pretexting was not illegal, based on research done by a summer associate the preceding year. DeLia then sent an e-mail to Hunsaker indicating that no state or federal laws prohibited pretexting but that there was "a risk of litigation."

In March, Hunsaker circulated a report connecting Keyworth to the leaks. In preparation for a meeting with Hurd, Baskins asked Hunsaker to talk to outside counsel about pretexting. . . . [In response, DeLia's] lawyer had a paralegal prepare a response. She told Gentilucci that she was unable to find any criminal charges to indicate that pretexting was illegal. In April, at Baskin's request, Hunsaker prepared a memo on the issues raised by pretexting. He noted his online research and his contacts with DeLia and his outside counsel. According to the memo, counsel's firm had conducted "extensive research" and found the practice "not unlawful." Mark Hurd then met with Keyworth privately and gave him an opportunity to acknowledge his leaks. Keyworth did not do so. As he later recalled the meeting, Hurd did not ask him about the reporter and Keyworth was not aware that her story was the focus of the investigation.

In May, a divided board asked Keyworth to resign. One of its most influential members, Tom Perkins, objected to the decision and resigned in protest. He also recalled objecting to the legality of pretexting. Dunn and other board members recalled no such objection and Dunn denied making any promise to keep the leaker's identity confidential. Larry Sonsini, HP's outside counsel then contacted Perkins about how to handle the resignation. Post-Enron reforms require that a company report board resignations to the SEC, and if the resignation stems from any disagreement with the company or the board, the reasons must also be disclosed. Perkins said his disagreement was with Dunn not the company, and the SEC report included no reasons.

Perkins subsequently consulted law professor Viet Dinh, who served with him on another board. Dinh raised concerns about pretexting that Perkins then conveyed to Sonsini. Sonsini responded that pretext calls were a "common investigatory method" and that "it appears, therefore, that the process was well done and within legal limits." Perkins relayed this to Dinh who then expressed doubts that the records could have been lawfully obtained. Perkins' dissatisfaction continued to escalate after receiving a notice from the phone company suggesting that his phone records were "hacked." He was also angry that the minutes of his final board meeting did not reflect the objections to pretexting that he recalled making. Perkins demanded that the minutes be amended, and that the company file a notice with the SEC since he now considered his dispute to be with the company. Baskins subsequently wrote to Perkins denying his requests, because the minutes had been approved and were accurate as drafted, and because he had earlier characterized the reasons for his resignation as personal. Perkins, represented by Dinh, then contacted the SEC, the California Attorney General, and the U.S. Attorney for the Northern District of California, which all launched investigations.

A national scandal erupted, fueled by Congressional hearings at which Dunn and Hurd testified and Baskins and Hunsaker invoked their 5th amendment privilege. Dunn, Baskins, Hunsaker, and Gentilucci were all forced to resign. The California Attorney General charged Dunn, Hunsaker, DeLia, and two private investigators with four felony counts: fraudulent wire communications, wrongful use of computer data, identity theft, and conspiracy. The counts were later reduced to misdemeanors. A state court dismissed the charges against Dunn, and then later against all other defendants based on evidence that they had performed community service. One investigator pleaded guilty to federal charges.

In his Congressional testimony, Hurd apologized for the "rogue" investigation and for authorizing the fake email. While denying knowledge of certain other pretexting activity that others had permitted, he acknowledged that failing to read a report that described it was not "my finest hour." Patricia Dunn stated: "I do not accept personal responsibility for what happened." She added: "I relied on the expertise of others in whom I had full confidence. I deeply regret that so many people, including me, were let down." Larry Sonsini maintained that his response to Perkins about the legality of pretexting was not a "legal opinion. It was conveying the truth of what I was told." Ann Baskins made no public statement. Her lawyer told *New Yorker* reporter James Stewart: "A general counsel has to be able to rely on her senior counsel's research and advice, particularly when she has hundreds of lawyers working for her worldwide." Hunsaker's lawyer assured Stewart that "There cannot be a violation without intent to violate the law and Kevin absolutely believed that the investigation was being done in a legal and proper way."

The financial and personal effects of the scandal varied considerably. HP reimbursed Perkins for $1.5 million in legal expenses and agreed to pay Keyworth's as well. Ann Baskins, in exchange for cooperating with HP's investigation and releasing the company from liability, received the right to exercise stock options worth over $3.7 million, with another million in options to vest immediately. Mark Hurd, who according to Dunn, had received the same legal advice that she had received, got a bonus of $8.6 million in 2007, along with options on over 500,000 shares of stock. HP stock rose to its highest value in over six years.

Both Congress and the California legislature subsequently passed legislation making pretexting a criminal offense.

A federal grand jury investigation into the HP scandal has remained open, but as of the fall of 2010 has resulted in only one prosecution. A Colorado investigator pled guilty to a conspiracy to illegally obtain telephone records. Ann Baskin lost her job but not her license to practice law. Wilson Sonsini lost its long-standing role as HP outside counsel.[74]

Eric Dezenhall and John Weber, Damage Control: Why Everything You Know about Crisis Management Is Wrong

(New York: Portfolio of Penguin Books, 2007), pp. 34-37

Hewlett-Packard: Overkill in Crisis Management

If ever there were a case of failing to differentiate between a nuisance, a problem, and a crisis, it was the bungled 2006 attempt by Hewlett-Packard's top brass to ferret out boardroom leaks by spying on their own board of directors, among others. In this notorious sin of excess, the cure became worse than the disease.

The scandal's climax came in the form of congressional hearings in which ten witnesses invoked their Fifth Amendment right against self-incrimination—sinister optics that helped turn a problem (a leaky board) into a crisis (Nixonian dirty tricks).

By most accounts, in late 2005 HP chairman Patricia Dunn set in motion a private investigation that resulted in, among other things, the collection of the private phone records of nine journalists, two HP employees, and seven HP board members. These records were gathered via the use of "pretexting." Pretexting is gathering information through misrepresentation—in the case of the HP scandal, pretending to be the person to whom those private phone records belonged. As Representative Joe Barton (R-TX) said at the congressional hearing, "Pretexting is pretending to be somebody you're not to get something you probably shouldn't have to use in a way that's probably wrong." These revelations came to light in early September 2006.

Dunn, who was indicted for fraud and conspiracy the following month, was not fundamentally wrong to be concerned about boardroom leaks. As CEO Mark Hurd said upon her resignation: "The intent of the investigation was proper and appropriate. The fact that we had leaks on the board needed to be resolved." The problem was that her team appeared to have been obsessed to the point of monomania.

Nor was Dunn wrong to entertain the use of private investigators, a practice that is indiscriminately branded as unethical in today's scandal climate. Some private investigations, dare we say, are good things. Without investigators, General Motors never would have learned that journalists at *Dateline NBC* had rigged a GM truck to explode in order to portray an alleged pattern of flammability. Indeed, our own experience has been that private investigations can identify and stop bad actors who have no God-given right to ignore the law in pursuit of their corporate quarry.

The problem with HP's actions was that they were undertaken without seasoned leadership, and whatever flimsy parameters were set apparently cascaded out of control and came to include tactics and targets that should have been off-limits. . . . There is such a thing as overresponding to a threat, which is what HP did when confronted by leaks. While as of this writing the facts of the case are still unfolding, one thing is certain: The operation that was put in place to plug the leaks did more damage to HP than the leaks ever did.

Excess also can reign when companies try to correct a misstep. The resignations of HP's general counsel, chief ethics officer, and a security manager weren't considered sufficient by some in the news media. Pundits were calling for a complete housecleaning at HP, unwisely believing that overkill was the answer. In reality, sometimes the best people to lead a company through a crisis are the ones who have already demonstrated strong leadership. Leaving a company in crisis without a leader would likely spin it even deeper into crisis. It should not be the objective of a company under siege to satisfy the bloodlust of the news media or business pundits, who are notorious for equating drastic gestures of self-flagellation with good crisis management.

"Tell it all," "Get it all out," went the extreme chants of the scandal's Greek chorus in the weeks before HP spoke publicly. One problem with these absolutes is that companies in crisis rarely know everything they need to know in order to make immediate and ideal decisions. That's why it's a crisis.

Another problem is that complete disclosures, while theoretically desirable, may be admissible in court and can place the company in legal jeopardy. If HP had begun speculating publicly about who did what, innocent people could have been smeared, forcing them to take legal action against the company. Moreover, HP didn't want to give fodder to prosecutors who were investigating the matter. Herein lies the tension between attorneys, who tend to counsel silence, and communicators, who tend to counsel openness. Who's right? Both are "right" within the context of their disciplines; however, each crisis has its own special set of considerations. It's up to the chief crisis officer (usually the CEO) to determine where on the silence-openness continuum public statements must fall.

On Friday, September 22, 2006, HP CEO Mark Hurd held a news conference (but took no questions) in which, for the first time since the affair broke in the press several weeks earlier, he commented at some length on the scandal and announced the resignation of chairman Dunn. Hurd also apologized to those who were spied upon and announced the appointment of former U.S. prosecutor Bart Schwartz to look into the investigative methods that were employed by the company in its attempt to plug leaks. . . .

Was Hurd's news conference held too late? In a perfect world, sure; but in the real world where a leader needs to know what he's talking about, it was the best of his bad options.

Hurd was criticized for not taking questions, but he was probably wise not to. When legal issues are at stake — especially when information is so limited — open-ended give-and-take with the news media is laden with mines. In the proverbial battle between lawyers and public relations people, the HP press conference was a thoughtful compromise between the two disciplines.

At the time of the congressional hearings on the scandal in 2006, HP's shares were up 25 percent. Key corporate units, such as HP's printing products, which had been faltering, have recovered under Hurd. Analysts rightly remain bullish on the stock despite the leak scandal, which, in the end, had nothing to do with the company's fundamental businesses.

NOTES AND QUESTIONS

1. How would you evaluate the conduct of the leaders involved in the pretexting scandal? What accounts for their conduct? What role might cognitive biases have played? If the problem that HP officers identified was "find the leak," was this an adequate frame? Should they also have asked, "Why is this problem a problem?" and tried to get the entire board invested in the solution? Did their authorization of deceptive investigative techniques reflect a bias that psychologists label escalation of commitment, known colloquially as the "boiled frog" problem? A frog dropped into a pot of boiling water will hop out; a frog in water with gradually increasing temperatures will calmly boil to death.[75] If this dynamic, along with other groupthink pathologies,

was present among the HP leadership, what might have been done to counteract them?

2. Bart Schwartz, the former federal prosecutor later hired to evaluate the company's conduct told a *New York Times* reporter that he was struck by the lack of consideration of ethical issues in the company's efforts to trace press leaks. "Doing it legally should not be the test; that is given. You have to ask what is appropriate and what is ethical."[76] What accounted for so many HP leaders' willingness to outsource ethics? What broader lessons does it suggest?

3. "Where were the lawyers?" asked one congressman in hearings on the HP scandal. "The red flags were waving all over the place," but "none of the lawyers stepped up to their responsibilities."[77] The same point has been raised about lawyers' complicity in other corporate scandals, and the search for explanations has led some commentators to build on identity theory and research. This framework demonstrates how individuals' role identification can encourage them to process information in ways that support their self-perception.[78] So, for example, a survey of several hundred in-house counsel found that those who identified themselves more as an employee than a lawyer were more likely to interpret an attorney's obligations in a hypothetical ethical dilemma in ways consistent with management's interests rather than with professional norms.[79] Could such dynamics have been at work in the HP scandal? What correctives might be effective?

4. Compare HP's strategy in delaying public statements regarding the scandal to Warren Buffett's response to rogue trading at Salomon Brothers, discussed in Chapter 5. Buffett made immediate and full disclosure of corporate misconduct, and cooperated fully with government investigators, even when it meant waiving the corporation's attorney-client privilege. Would such a strategy have been preferable for HP, or do you agree with Dezenhall and Weber's endorsement of Hurd's approach? What lessons does the HP case suggest about the role of those charged with ensuring ethical compliance? How would you structure such positions?

MEDIA RESOURCES

A Fox News report offered a groupthink explanation for the misdiagnosis of Iraq's military capabilities.[80] Hurd's congressional testimony is also available.[81] *Twelve Angry Men* is a classic film portrayal of one man's efforts to overcome groupthink among his fellow jurors. *Philadelphia* portrays the stereotypes and group dynamics that lead a law firm to fire an attorney (Tom Hanks) with AIDS. *Wall Street: Money Never Weeps*, a National Public Radio broadcast, includes illuminating interviews with financial services professionals who refused to believe that the Wall Street community was in any sense responsible for the recent economic crisis.[82]

C. COST-BENEFIT ANALYSIS

Some of leaders' most common decision-making challenges involve cost-benefit trade-offs. Problems arise when values and risks cannot be definitively quantified and compared. The materials that follow explore these challenges in representative legal, policy, and business settings.

PROBLEM 3-3[83]

You are the chief of staff for your state's governor. The state's Commission on Highway Safety has advised, based on good statistical evidence, that reducing the current highway speed limit of 70 miles per hour to 65 miles per hour would save about 120 lives annually by reducing the number and seriousness of highway accidents. Safety First, a nonprofit group representing victims of highway accidents, is pressing the governor to propose legislation to reduce the speed limit to 65 miles per hour. The proposal is opposed by groups representing commuters and truckers, who believe that the change, by increasing travel time, would result in significant inconvenience, frustration, and additional shipping expenses. The governor seeks your advice.

1. How would you analyze the trade-off between speed and lives?
2. What further information might you need to make a recommendation?
3. What arguments would you present if you were the lawyer for the truckers' association or the president of Safety First?
4. Suppose that the issue had been whether to increase the speed limit from 65 to 70 miles per hour. How might this affect your analysis of the trade-offs?

PAUL BREST AND LINDA HAMILTON KRIEGER, PROBLEM SOLVING, DECISION MAKING, AND PROFESSIONAL JUDGMENT

(New York: Oxford University Press, 2010), pp. 370-371, 373-374, 376-380, and 383-384

The problem [in much cost-benefit analysis] involves what Philip Tetlock and his colleagues call *constitutive incommensurability*—based on cultural values and norms:

> The guiding idea is that our commitments to other people forbid certain comparisons. To transgress these normative boundaries, to attach a monetary value to one's friendships or one's children or one's loyalty to one's country is to disqualify oneself from certain social roles, to demonstrate that one "just doesn't get it"—that one does not understand what it means to be a true friend or parent or citizen. . . .

For these among other reasons, the use of cost-benefit analysis to guide public or corporate policymaking has sometimes been criticized for requiring "immoral commodification" by placing a dollar value on life's unquantifiables—such as human life, health, or the existence of a wilderness area. [Jurors often impose punitive damages on corporate defendants who seem cold blooded in engaging in cost-benefit analysis.] In *Retaking Rationality*, Richard Revesz [responds]:

> This criticism confuses pricing with commodification. Pricing, a mechanism used to allocate society's resources, is the most effective way to aggregate information and allocate scarce resources to produce the most benefit. . . .

Commodification has to do with the social significance of pricing—the fear that assigning a price to the good things in life obscures their inherent worth.

To be sure, some decisions call for existential choices—for example, trade-offs between peace and justice—that far transcend the capacity of cost-benefit analysis. But as Robert Frank notes:

> Scarcity is a simple fact of the human condition. To have more of one good thing, we must settle for less of another. Claiming that different values are incommensurable simply hinders clear thinking about difficult tradeoffs. . . .

Policy makers (and others) use various strategies to avoid explicit tradeoffs between constitutively incommensurable values. When they cannot avoid a conscious or public tradeoff, they engage in buck-passing, procrastination, and obfuscation. And when responsibility for a decision cannot be avoided, they tend to "spread the alternatives," "playing down the strengths of the to-be-slighted value and playing up the strengths of the to-be selected value." . . .

From Expected Utility to Expected Return: Cost-Benefit Analysis

. . . Governments frequently require that regulatory decisions be subject to cost-benefit analysis [(CBA)]. For example, Executive Order 12866, signed by President Bill Clinton in 1993, requires federal agencies to "assess all costs and benefits of available regulatory alternatives, including the alternative of not regulating."

The most difficult and contested applications of CBA involve risk. . . . Even when risk is not a major factor, however, CBA can present difficulties in monetizing benefits and in making distributional decisions (for example, where the benefits flow partly to an individual beneficiary of a program and partly to taxpayers). And even when the calculation is reasonably clear, there may be reasons not to follow the logic of CBA: For better or worse, politics, ideology, and issues of fairness and rights may trump CBA. But CBA almost always provides a useful norm or reference point for decisionmaking. . . .

Quantifying Reduced Risks in Mortality

Some of the most divisive debates surrounding CBA concern the valuation of human life—an issue that arises in government regulatory efforts to reduce workplace, toxic, and other risks. . . . Currently, there exist three main methods for the assessment of human life: VSL (Value of a Statistical Life), VSLY (Value of Statistical Life-Years), and QALYs (Quality Adjusted Life Years). . . .

Value of a Statistical Life (VSL). Perhaps the most widely used method, VSL assigns a fixed monetary value to every human life in a certain population. It does not seek to estimate the *intrinsic* value of an individual human life, but is based on people's willingness to pay (WTP) to avoid an aggregation of many small health and safety risks in their lives. . . . VSL can be determined through WTP by using:

(1) people's *stated preferences* for how much they would pay to eliminate risks, or

(2) people's *revealed preferences*, analyzing decisions that people have already made about risk tradeoffs for goods and/or workplace risk reductions.

Utilizing both these techniques, the Environmental Protection Agency reviewed twenty-six peer-reviewed value-of-life studies from academic literature to arrive at a single VSL of $6.3 million for the United States (in year 2000 dollars). Subsequently, however, an [EPA] work group asserted that, since VSL values vary widely by social and economic status, race, population, and country, there "does not appear to be a universal VSL value that is applicable to all specific subpopulations." Furthermore, the work group recommended that VSL studies using stated and revealed preferences be analyzed separately, since they sometimes lead to significantly different estimates.

Citizens of a developing country, such as India, have a lower WTP and thus a lower VSL than an economically developed country, such as the United States. In fact, VSL evaluations conducted around the world range from $70,000 to $16.3 million. Nonetheless, some scholars advocate, on moral grounds, the use of a universal VSL for all peoples, regardless of their economic status or willingness to pay. On the other hand, others, including Cass Sunstein, assert that policymakers should establish specific, local VSLs for communities and countries. Sunstein argues that VSLs should be assessed within the population where regulations force the beneficiaries to bear the costs. If an inflated VSL is used, poorer citizens may be forced to "spend" their money to reduce a workplace risk when they would prefer to put that money to other uses.

Value of Statistical Life-Years (VSLY). VSL treats the lives of the very young and very old as equally valuable. Under the VSLY approach, benefits to individuals are assessed based on their estimated remaining years of life. VSLY values are derived from VSLs drawn from age-specific populations. Michael J. Moore and W. Kip Viscusi, proponents of this approach, note that "in the case of fatalities, a young person loses a much greater amount of lifetime utility than does an older person," and thus assert that it doesn't make sense to use the same value for an elderly person with a remaining five-year life expectancy as for a 25-year-old. Critics of VSLY term it the "senior death discount." . . . [T]he U.S. Office of Management and Budget has encouraged federal agencies to conduct analysis using both approaches.

Quality-Adjusted Life Years (QALYs). QALYs incorporate a coefficient that measures "quality of life" and can be used to assess the efficiency of health care policies and procedures. Consider an example by Dr. Fritz Allhoff:

> If treating a patient would lead to a life expectancy of 20 years with a high quality of life (e.g., hypertension, which only requires daily pills and rarely manifests negative symptoms), coverage for this patient's treatment should presumably have priority over treatment for a patient who would have a life expectancy of 20 years with a comparatively low quality of life (e.g., diabetes, which requires daily injections and often manifests symptoms such as neuropathy, blindness, etc.).

This "quality of life" coefficient ranges from 0 to1, valuing a healthy year of life at 1 and a year where one suffers under a disease or disability at some fraction of 1. The QALYs assigned to a particular reduction in mortality, then, are based on the expected number of years of life gained adjusted by their perceived quality of life. Proponents of this method argue that this system distributes finite resources as efficiently and fairly as possible.

The perceived quality-of-life coefficient, which has a large impact on the final assigned value, is typically determined through contingent valuation, asking "healthy people, ex ante, to evaluate various health states." But healthy individuals may fail to take *adaptation* into account and thus underestimate the quality of life of disabled persons, leading to disproportionately low QALY values. Additionally, as Revesz notes, the "empirical work comparing how willingness to pay relates to QALYs confirms there is no simple dollar-per-QALY conversion rate." . . .

Conclusion

Cost-benefit analysis depends on determining people's WTP for certain benefits. Yet individuals' WTP is essentially irrelevant to many important policy decisions, such as discrimination and abortion; as Cass Sunstein notes, these are appropriately resolved by citizens' preferences and values. . . . [But we believe] that if one is explicit about its inaccuracies, biases, and limitations, CBA can provide a "concrete sense of what actually is at stake." Consider James Hammit's March 2003 letter to the editor of the *New York Times*:

> The Office of Management and Budget's interest in applying cost-benefit analysis to homeland security measures is laudable. Even if precise quantification of the benefits to security and harms to civil liberties is impossible, analytic consideration of the trade-offs is wise.
>
> As John Graham, director of regulatory affairs at O.M.B., says, "Simply identifying some of these costs will help understand them and get people to think about alternatives that might reduce those costs."
>
> Cost-benefit analysis should have also been used to evaluate the potential war in Iraq. The benefits of ousting Saddam Hussein should be measured against the costs of casualties, waging war, reconstruction, retaliatory terrorism and increased anti-Americanism. Such analysis would prompt us "to think about alternatives that might reduce those costs."

NOTES AND QUESTIONS

1. As Brest and Krieger note, jurors have sometimes punished defendants for engaging in explicit cost-benefit analysis concerning the value of human life. A widely discussed example was the $176 million damage award (later reduced to $6.6 million) against Ford Motor Company for deaths resulting from a Pinto gas tank explosion. A company memo indicated that Ford had estimated the costs of improvements to the gas tank at $37 million ($11 per car), and determined that they exceeded the value of injuries averted and lives saved, estimated at $49.5 million ($67,000 per injury and $200,000 per life). The value of life figures came from federal studies on the costs to economy of lives lost in traffic accidents. Other

federal agencies at the time used figures ranging from $70,000 to $132 million.[84] Jury verdicts around the time averaged $950,000 for the death of a man in his thirties, and $85,000 for a woman over 65.[85] The Ford Pinto model had a much worse safety record for rear-end collisions than other subcompact models, but a better overall safety performance because a very small proportion of traffic fatalities are caused by rear-end fires.[86]

If you had held a leadership position at Ford, would you have engaged in similar cost-benefit calculations? If so, what figures would you have used for value of life? Would you have included other potential costs in the calculations, such as reputational injury? Is there an alternative approach to the decision that might have been preferable, such as analyzing whether the Pinto without the improvement would meet reasonable consumer expectations in light of industry standards? If so, how would you determine what is reasonable?

2. What follows from the wide disparity in measures of value of life for purposes of safety decisions? Brest and Krieger note the controversy over OMB's cost-benefit analysis concerning homeland security measures. What are the capabilities and limitations of such analysis in determining the merits of certain passenger screening techniques or warrantless phone taps?

3. Many cognitive biases affect the way people value life in cost-safety trade-offs. One example is the underinvestment in prevention. The public is often willing to spend vast sums to save identifiable victims, such as a baby trapped in a well, or coal workers trapped in a mine, but is unwilling to invest proportionate amounts in safety measures to prevent such tragedies.[87] A related dynamic is "psychosocial numbing: people value lives less as the number of lives at risk increases."[88] As Joseph Stalin famously put it, "[T]he death of a single Russian soldier is a tragedy. A million deaths is a statistic."[89]

Are these examples of irrational decision making that policy leaders should strive to overcome? Or do they reflect inevitable, and to some extent commendable, tendencies to empathize with individuals whom we can visualize, and whose suffering is most cognitively "available"?[90] Some research suggests that the most significant reason for people's disproportionate concern for identifiable victims is that a high proportion of those apparently at risk can be saved. But as researchers point out, that factor bears no obvious normative relevance in policy making, particularly since who is in the reference group of possible victims is often a matter of framing that can be manipulated.[91] Yet telling people about their bias in favor of identifiable victims does not entirely solve the problem because it causes them to spend less on behalf of those victims rather than to spend more to save statistical lives.[92] In one telling experiment, subjects made lower financial contributions to famine relief when they received information about both an individual victim and statistics about hunger in Africa. Simply thinking about large numbers appeared to dampen the emotional responses that encouraged altruism.[93]

What implications should policy leaders and heads of nonprofit organizations draw from such findings? What trade-offs would you make between identifiable and statistical victims? Would you limit the resources you would invest in saving identifiable victims? On what basis?

END NOTES

1. Peter Spiegel, Rumsfeld Links Generals' Flak to Resentment over Shake-Ups, Los Angeles Times, April 19, 2006, 14 (quoting Bush).

2. Jonah Lehrer, How We Decide (Boston: Houghton, Mifflin and Harcourt, 2009), 159 (quoting Simon and citing research).

3. Gerd Gigerenzer, Heuristics, in Gerd Gigerenzer and Christoph Engel, eds., Heuristics and the Law (Cambridge, MA: MIT Press, 2006), 17.

4. Montgomery Van Wart, Dynamics of Leadership in the Public Sector: Theory and Practice (Armonk, NY: M.E. Sharpe, 2005), 329-330.

5. Van Wart, Dynamics of Leadership, 259-260. For a landmark formulation, see Charles E. Lindbloom, The Science of Muddling Through, Public Administration Review 19 (1959):79.

6. Van Wart, Dynamics of Leadership, 260. For a classic description, see Amitai Etzioni, Mixed-Scanning: A "Third" Approach to Decision-Making, Public Administration Review 27 (1967):385.

7. Paul Brest and Linda Hamilton Krieger, Problem Solving, Decision Making, and Professional Judgment (New York: Oxford University Press, 2010), 3.

8. This problem draws on Paul Brest and Linda Hamilton Krieger, Problem Solving, Decision-making, and Professional Judgment (New York: Oxford University Press, 2010), 39; Deborah L. Rhode, Where Is the Leadership in Moral Leadership?, in Deborah L. Rhode, ed., Moral Leadership: The Theory and Practice of Power, Judgment, and Policy (San Francisco: Jossey Bass, 2006), 31.

9. Remarks by President Obama on the Gulf oil spill, May 27, 2010, Federal Information and News Dispatch.

10. David M. Messick and Max H. Bazerman, Ethical Leadership and the Psychology of Decision Making, Sloan Management Review 37 (1996):1, 4.

11. Remarks by President Obama, 2.

12. Frank Rich, Don't Get Mad, Mr. President, Get Even, New York Times, June 6, 2010, WK 10.

13. National Commission on the BP Deepwater Horizon Oil Spill and Offshore Drilling (Washington, DC: Government Printing Office, 2011), available at http:www.oilspillcommisssion.gov/.

14. See Michael T. Klare, The Oil Catastrophe, The Nation, June 14, 2010, 4, 6; Bryan Walsh, The Spreading Stain, Time Magazine, June 21, 2010, 56; National Commission on the BP Deepwater Horizon Oil Spill.

15. Ian Urbina, At Issue in Gulf: Who Was in Charge, New York Times, June 6, 2010, A1, 19 (quoting Odom).

16. Michael Useem, Decision Making as Leadership Foundation, in Nitin Nohria and Rakesh Khurana, eds., Handbook of Leadership Theory and Practice (Boston: Harvard Business School Publishing, 2010), 507.

17. Michael Useem, The Leadership Moment (New York: Times Business, 1998), 85-86; Useem, Decision Making, 514.

18. Useem, Decision Making, 514.

19. Katherine L. Milkman, Dolly Chugh, and Max H. Bazerman, How Can Decision Making Be Improved?, Perspectives on Psychological Science 4 (2009):379, 389-381.

20. Richard H. Thaler and Cass R. Sunstein, Nudge (New Haven, CT: Yale University Press, 2008).

21. Slavisa Tasic, Are Regulators Rational? (Bruno Leoni Institute Working Paper, available at http:brunoleonimedia.servingfreedom.net/mises2010/papers/IBL_mises2010_Tasic.pdf); Matt Ridely, Studying the Biases of Bureaucrats, Wall Street Journal, October 23, 2010, C4.

22. Tasic, Are Regulators Rational?; Ridely, Studying the Biases of Bureaucrats, Wall Street Journal, October 23, 2010, C4.

23. Don Van Natta Jr. and Abby Goodnough, 2 Cambridge Worlds Collide in Unlikely Meeting, New York Times, July 27, 2009, A13.

24. Id.

25. Id.

26. Id.

27. Abby Goodnough, Harvard Professor Jailed; Officer Is Accused of Bias, New York Times, July 21, 2009, A13.

28. Gates Police Report (2009), http://www.scribd.com/doc/17512830/Gates-Police-Report.

29. Goodnough, Harvard Professor Jailed; Officer is Accused of Bias, at A13.

30. Van Natta Jr. and Goodnough, 2 Cambridge Worlds, A13.

31. Good Morning America, Henry Louis Gates Jr.: I'm Outraged, http://www.youtube.com/watch?v = AeRK_0lc3yQ&feature = fvsr (last viewed December 5, 2009).

32. John Hechinger and Simmi Aujla, Police Drop Charges against Black Scholar, Wall Street Journal, July 22, 2009, A6.

33. Katharine Q. Seelye, Obama Wades into a Volatile Racial Issue, New York Times, July 23, 2009, http://www.nytimes.com/2009/07/23/us/23race.html.

34. Anahad O'Connor, Beer Summit Goes for a Second Round, New York Times, October 30, 2009, http://thecaucus.blogs.nytimes.com/2009/10/30/beer-summit-goes-for-a-second-round/?scp = 3&sq = obama%20%22acted%20stupidly%22%20blog&st = cse.

35. Ben W. Heineman Jr., A Due Process Teaching Moment — WASTED, The Atlantic, July 25, 2009, http://www.theatlantic.com/politics/archive/2009/07/a-due-process-teaching-moment-wasted/22124.

36. Heineman, A Due Process Teaching Moment.

37. Jeff Zeleny, Obama Expresses His Regrets on Gates Incident, The Caucus, The Politics and Government Blog of The Times, July 24, 2009, http://thecaucus.blogs.nytimes.com/2009/07/24/obama-expresses-his-regrets-on-gates-incident/?apage = 4.

38. Seelye, Obama Wades into a Volatile Racial Issue.

39. The Borowitz Report, Funny Times, September 2009, 5.

40. The Daily Show with John Stewart, July 30, 2009: White House Beer Simulation, http://www.thedailyshow.com/watch/thu-july-30-2009/white-house-beer-simulation (last viewed December 5, 2009).

41. Late Show with David Letterman, Top Ten Things Overheard at the White House Beer Summit, http://www.youtube.com/watch?v = U_AjybtHYXI (last viewed December 5, 2009).

42. Abby Goodnough, Gates Reflects on Beers at the White House, The Caucus, The Politics and Government Blog of The Times, July 31, 2009, http://thecaucus.blogs.nytimes.com/2009/07/31/gates-reflects-on-beers-at-the-white-house.

43. Id.

44. Zachery Shore, Blunder: Why Smart People Make Bad Decisions (New York: Bloomsbury, 2008), 14.

45. Id.

46. Heineman, A Due Process Teaching Moment.

47. Ken Auletta, Non-Stop News, New Yorker, June 25, 2010, 38.

48. Henry Gates's breaking story, available at http://www.youtube.com/watch?v = AGAiFoRZvX0; Gates's perspective, available at http://www.youtube.com/watch?v = CC3-Pjxksus; Crowley's statement, available at http://www.youtube.com/watch?v = nNztOdgXUlw.

49. See Daniel J. Simons and Christopher Chabris's Gorilla Basketball Experiment clip, http://viscog.beckman.illinois.edu/grafs/demos/15.html.

50. Harold Leavit, Suppose We Took Groups Seriously, in Eugene L. Cass and Frederick G. Zimmer, eds. Man and Work in Society (New York: VanNostrand Reinhold, 1975), 67-77.

51. Janis revised his 1972 book in an expanded 1982 version. Irving L Janis, Groupthink: Psychological Studies of Policy Decisions and Fiascos (Boston: Houghton Mifflin, 1982).

52. Paul Brest, Quis Custodiet Ipsos Custodes? Debiasing the Policy Makers Themselves, in Eldar Shafir, ed., The Behavioral Foundations of Policy (New York: Russell Sage Foundation and Princeton University Press, forthcoming).

53. The Space Shuttle: Old, Unsafe, and Costly, The Economist, August 28, 2003.

54. Report of the Select Committee on Intelligence on the U.S. Intelligence Community's Prewar Intelligence Assessments on Iraq, 108th Congress 2d. Session, Senate Report 106-301 (Washington, D.C.: Government Printing Office, July 9, 2004), 18.

55. Brest, Quis Custodiet Ipsos Custodes?

56. Report of the Select Committee, 22.

57. Carol Tavris and Eliott Aronson, Mistakes Were Made (but not by me) (New York: HarperCollins, 2007), 19.

58. Brendan Nyhan and Jason Reiffler, When Corrections Fail: The Persistence of Political Misperceptions, Political Behavior 32 (2010):303, 313-315, 323. For other research, see Joe Keohane, How Facts Backfire, Boston Globe, July 11, 2010.

59. Doris Kearns Goodwin, Team of Rivals (New York: Simon and Schuster, 2005).

60. Liz Wiseman with George McKeown, Multipliers

61. Id., quoting David Brooks.

62. Peter Wallsten and Jonathan Weisman, Pressure Builds on Obama to Shake Up Inner Circle, Wall Street Journal, November 2, 2010, A4.

63. Bob Woodward, State of Denial: Bush at War, Part III (New York: Simon and Schuster, 2007),11 (quoting Frontline interview with Bush).

64. See sources cited in Roland Benabou, Groupthink: Collective Delusions in Organizations and Markets, National Bureau of Economic Research Working Paper 14764 (March 2009), and sources cited in notes 62, 63, 65, and 66.

65. David Leonhardt, If Fed Missed This Bubble, Will It See a New One?, New York Times, January 6, 2010, A1.

66. Robert J. Shiller, Challenging the Crowd in Whispers, Not Shouts, New York Times, November 2, 2008, BU5. Shiller was a member of an economic advisory panel for the Federal Reserve Bank of New York.

67. For wishful thinking, see Benabou; for the commitment to deregulation, see Carol A. Needham, Listening to Cassandra: The Difficulty of Recognizing Risks and Taking Action, Fordham Law Review 78 (2010):2329.

68. Malcolm Gladwell, Cocksure, New Yorker, July 27, 2009, 25.

69. Id. at 28.

70. George Soros, Financial Markets: Lecture before the Central European University, October 27, 2009, available at http://www.soros.org/resources/multimedia/sorosceu_20091112/financialmarkets_transcript.

71. Jonah Lehrer, Microscopic Microeconomics, New York Times Magazine, October 31, 2010.

72. Leher, How We Decide, 218 (quoting Sloan).

73. Ezra Klein, Michael Lewis and the Idiots, Washington Post, April 7, 2010, http://voices.washingtonpost.com/ezra-klein/2010/04/michael_lewis_and_the_idiots.html.

74. Seth Hettena, Ready for the next Scandal, American Lawyer, October 2010, 17.

75. See the discussion in Deborah L. Rhode, Where Is the Leadership in Moral Leadership?, excerpted in Chapter 5.

76. Damon Darlin, Adviser Urges H.P. to Focus on Ethics over Legalities, New York Times, October 4, 2006, C3 (quoting Schwartz).

77. Hearing before the Subcommittee on Oversight and Investigations of the House Committee on Energy and Commerce, Hewlett-Packard's Pretexting Scandal, 109th Congress, 2006, 13.

78. Peter J. Burke et al. eds., Advances in Identity Theory and Research (New York: Kluwer Academic/Plenum, 2003); Sheldon Stryker and Peter J. Burke, The Past, Present, and Future of an Identity Theory, Social Psychological Quarterly 63 (2000):28; Cassandra Burke Robertson, Judgment, Identity and Independence, Connecticut Law Review 42 (2009):1, 14-20.

79. Hugh Gunz and Sally Gunz, Hired Professional to Hired Gun: An Identity Theory Approach to Understanding the Ethical Behavior of Professionals in Non-Professional Organizations, Human Relations 60 (2007):851, 882-886.

80. Liza Porteus, "Group Think" Led to Iraq WMD Assessment, FoxNews.com, July 11, 2004, http://www.foxnews.com/story/0,2933,125123,00.html.

81. Transcript of Mark Hurd's Oral Remarks before the House of Representatives Energy and Commerce Oversight and Investigations Subcommittee, September 28, 2006, available at http://i.i.com/cnwk.1d/pdf/ne/2006/hurd_remarks.pdf; video of entire HP hearing, http://www.c-spanvideo.org/program/id/164745.

82. The segment aired on This American Life, "Crybabies" (episode 415), WBEZ Chicago, September 24, 2010, http://www.thisamericanlife.org/radio-archives/episode/415/crybabies.

83. This problem is adapted from the Teacher's Manual for Paul Brest and Linda Krieger, Problem Solving, Decision Making, and Professional Judgment, http://brestandkrieger.pbworks.com.

84. For Ford's calculation and liability, see Deborah L. Rhode and David Luban, Legal Ethics (New York: Foundation Press, 5th ed. 2009), 394-395. For federal figures, see Marianne Lavelle, Placing a Price on Human Life, National Law Journal, October 10, 1988, 1, 28-29. The low figure came from proposed regulations on space heaters; the high estimate came from an FDA decision to ban DES pesticide in cattle feed.

85. Lavelle, Placing a Price, 28.

86. Gary T. Schwartz, The Myth of the Ford Pinto Case, Rutgers Law Review 43 (1990-1991):1032.

87. Karen E. Jenni and George Loewenstein, Explaining the Identifiable Victim Effect, Journal of Risk and Uncertainty 14 (1997):235. In 1987, people gave $700,000 in unsolicited funds to the family of Baby Jessica, who was trapped for 58 hours in a Texas well. See "Baby Jessica" 20 Years Later, Today, http://today.msnbc.com/id/19165433/?GTI = 1156.

88. James Friedrich et al., Psychophysical Numbing: When Lives Are Valued Less as the Lives at Risk Increase, Journal of Consumer Psychology 8 (1999):277, 285.

89. Richard Nisbett and Lee Ross, Human Inference: Strategies and Shortcomings of Social Judgment (Englewood Cliffs, NJ: Prentice Hall, 1980), 43 (quoting Stalin).

90. For a review of the availability bias, see Shelley E. Taylor, The Availability Bias in Social Perception and Interaction, in Daniel Kahneman, Paul Slovic, and Amos Tversky, eds., Judgment under Uncertainty: Heuristics and Biases (New York: Cambridge University Press, 1982), 190. For the social value of the identifiable victim response, see Douglas A. Kysar et al., Group Report: Are Heuristics a Problem or a Solution?, in Gigerenzer and Engel, eds., Heuristics and the Law, 135 (suggesting that the preference is socially "useful nonsense").

91. Jenni and Loewenstein, Explaining the Identifiable Victim Effect, 254.

92. Deborah A. Small, George Loewenstein, and Paul Slovic, Sympathy and Callousness: The Impact of Deliberative Thought on Donations to Identifiable and Statistical Victims, Organizational Behavior and Human Decision Processes 102 (2007):143.

93. Dan Ariely, The Upside of Irrationality (New York: Harper Collins, 2010), 248; Lehrer, How We Decide, 188.

CHAPTER 4

INFLUENCE

If, as Chapter 1 suggested, the core of leadership is influence, a key issue is how best to achieve it. What resources are available and what strategies are most effective? How do leaders influence followers? How do followers influence — or circumvent — leaders? How do those in positions of authority foster innovation and manage conflict? How do they communicate most persuasively?

A. FORMS OF INFLUENCE

As is clear from the readings below and the discussion of soft power in Chapter 1, the currency of influence can come in many forms. Strategies fall across a spectrum. Leaders compel, intimidate, pressure, negotiate, model, co-opt, and inspire. They exercise such influence at personal, group, and organizational levels, with varying degrees of success. Recent research identifies forms of influence that cluster under the following primary categories: authority, reciprocity, social influence, and association.

1. AUTHORITY

The most obvious source of influence stems from position: the power to reward and punish. This power does not need to be explicit to be effective. Colin Powell reportedly claimed that he never had to say "this is an order." Nor is leverage restricted to the obvious forms of benefits and sanctions, such as promotions, bonuses, dismissals, or discipline. Authority can arise from the credibility that attaches to a particular status. Prominent examples include the doctors who received undeserved deference from nurses in the study that psychologist Robert Cialdini discusses below, and the researchers in the famous obedience experiments by Stanley Milgram, reviewed in Chapter 6. These studies find that 95 percent of nurses were willing to administer a dangerous dose of an unauthorized drug, and that two-thirds of subjects were prepared to deliver ostensibly dangerous levels of electric shocks when a person in authority gave them orders to do so. Such results speak volumes about people's willingness to obey leaders even in the absence of hard power.

2. RECIPROCITY

One of the most effective forms of soft power is reciprocity, an impulse that sociobiologists argue is hardwired through evolution. A widely shared and deeply held sense of obligation to return favors has been highly adaptive for human survival because it encourages individuals to share food, care, defense, and other forms of assistance.[1] Sociologists and anthropologists have documented the pervasiveness of this impulse in virtually every society, and psychologists have identified its influence in a wide variety of contemporary exchanges. For example, in one famous experiment by Cornell professor Dennis Regan, subjects bought twice as many raffle tickets when an experimenter did them a small unsolicited favor — bringing them a bottle of Coke during a break. Unlike other subjects, who had received no favor and whose purchase of raffle tickets was affected by how much they liked the experimenter, those who had received the drink felt a sense of obligation to repay the favor and bought the same number of tickets irrespective of how they felt about the experimenter.[2] Behavioral economists note a similar dynamic at work in circumstances modeled in the game "Ultimatum." There, one person (the proposer) receives ten dollars and a partner (the responder) receives nothing. The proposer suggests how the money should be divided and the responder can accept or reject the division. If he or she rejects it, both players walk away with nothing. Although, in theory, responders would benefit by receiving any amount, in practice they refuse what seems unjust. Anticipating that reaction, proposers typically offer around five dollars.[3] In *Influence: The Psychology of Persuasion,* Cialdini explores how reciprocity functions in real-world settings. For example, marketers have substantially increased response rates to surveys or charitable appeals by enclosing a nominal payment or gift, and sellers achieve similar results through free samples.[4] The Hare Krishna religious sect perfected the use of reciprocity in personal solicitations by giving flowers or publications to passing strangers.[5]

Reciprocity is similarly critical in many leadership contexts. In politics, it underpins lobbying, campaign contributions, and legislative coalitions. Lyndon Johnson was legendary for his ability to trade favors when seeking support for policy initiatives.[6] The importance of "pay to play" in lobbying activities is well illustrated by a famous statement by Charles Keating, who served prison time for assisting fraudulent conduct by savings and loans institutions. When asked whether a connection existed between the $1.3 million he had contributed to the campaigns of five U.S. senators and their subsequent interventions on his behalf with federal regulators, he responded, "I certainly hope so."[7]

Reciprocity also influences leadership in international relations. Cialdini notes that many analysts puzzled over the decision of poverty-stricken Ethiopia to send financial aid to victims of a 1985 earthquake in Mexico City. The explanation was that Mexico had helped Ethiopia fifty years earlier when it was fighting invasion by fascist Italy.[8] The same impulse is at work in current American foreign relations. Many nations have received substantial economic and military aid in exchange for their assistance in the war against terrorism and other U.S. policy objectives.

More subtle forms of reciprocity also underpin relationships between leaders and followers. When subordinates help superiors look good or perform well, superiors often respond in kind, not only through pay and promotions but also with verbal recognition, mentoring, and personal support. Leaders and aspiring leaders can similarly build loyalty by sharing information, credit, and other forms of recognition. Robert Kennedy was famous for motivating lower-level Justice Department employees to "pla[y] over their heads" by getting them invitations to the White House, sending notes to those who worked on holidays, and calling to congratulate those who achieved some small victory.[9] In *The Seven Habits of Highly Effective People*, Steven Covey advises cultivating a "mentality of abundance" in allocating rewards and recognition.[10] Flattery, even when transparent, is often effective partly because it evokes norms of reciprocity. When people give us compliments, our natural inclination is to respond in kind and to look for corresponding ways to think well of them.[11]

Conversely, leadership failures often involve inadequate understanding of the importance of reciprocity and the limits of hard power. In *Changing Minds*, psychology professor Howard Gardner cites several examples leading to the forced resignation of Larry Summers as president of Harvard University. One involved well-publicized friction between Summers and Cornell West, a prominent member of Harvard's African-American Studies Department. In 2001, Summers initiated a meeting with West to discuss various concerns. According to West's account, these included too many classroom absences due to outside speaking obligations, and preparation of a hip-hop CD that was an "embarrassment," rather than publication of an "important" book that would "insure [his] place as a scholar."[12] West was insulted; he had never missed a class, his courses were popular, and he already was a recognized scholar. The meeting helped convince him to move to Princeton, and take several important members of the department with him. Gardner notes that Summers might have averted the disaster by starting on a different footing, by asking what West wanted to achieve, and what assistance Summers could provide. Summers should have recognized that his leverage over West was limited, that tenured faculty expect considerable autonomy, and that extending support was more likely to exert influence than demeaning or bullying tactics. It was Summers's responsibility to "keep the conversation open, upbeat, optimistic."[13] When interviewed five years later about the incident, West was no longer bitter: "I forgive the brother. He's just got deep problems with his social skills."[14]

3. SOCIAL INFLUENCE

As is clear from research summarized in Chapters 3 and 6, individuals are highly susceptible to social influence, which psychologists variously label "social proof" or "conformity." Some of the influence stems from self-doubt, and some from individuals' desire for social approval and inclusion. Particularly in contexts of imperfect information, individuals rely on the behaviors of others for cues or social proof about what is appropriate. The result in circumstances of collective decisions is often the kind of groupthink described in the previous chapter. But the dynamic also affects individuals' behavior even when they have reason for confidence in their own judgments. In Solomon Asch's famous experiment asking subjects which of several lines was the same length as another "standard" line, about four-fifths of the subjects gave at least one wrong answer in order to conform to incorrect answers given by other members of a group.[15] When asked later about their reasons, some subjects acknowledged that they knowingly gave a wrong answer just to go along with the group; others reported that they thought that they must somehow have been misunderstanding the nature of the task. The same dynamic is apparent in a famous *Candid Camera* scene in which a man in an elevator, surrounded by actors facing the wrong way, turns around as well.

4. ASSOCIATION

A final form of influence comes from association bias, which makes a message or messenger's influence depend on its relationship with events and individuals that evoke positive or negative reactions. The association principle can affect leaders' effectiveness in several ways. Positive spillover can come from endorsements by well-respected and well-connected individuals. So, for example, leaders who are seeking change within an organization or community can benefit from having such individuals become "early adopters" and speak in its favor; as experts note, "[I]nfluence is often best exerted horizontally rather than vertically."[16] Pleasant experiences at events can also have positive effects, which is why so many business dollars are spent on dining.

Negative spillover can be equally powerful. Leaders have to worry about both being damned by association and being shielded from information by others who are concerned about the same effect and do not want to be the bearer of ill tidings. In the excerpt below, Robert Cialdini describes a powerful example of association bias at work, as well as a chilling case study on the role of authority.

ROBERT B. CIALDINI, INFLUENCE: THE PSYCHOLOGY OF PERSUASION

(New York: Harper Collins, 2007), pp. 188-190 and 224-225

[Shakespeare captured the essence of the association bias] with one vivid line. "The nature of bad news," he said, "infects the teller." There is a natural human tendency to dislike a person who brings us unpleasant information, even when that person did not cause the bad news. The simple association with it is enough to stimulate our dislike. . . . [Consider the following example.]

Television weather forecasters make a good living talking about the weather, but when Mother Nature throws a curve ball, they duck for cover.

Conversations with several veteran prognosticators across the country this week turned up stories of them being whacked by old ladies with umbrellas, accosted by drunks in bars, pelted with snowballs and galoshes, threatened with death, and accused of trying to play God [or ruining a daughter's wedding].

"I had one guy call and tell me that if it snowed over Christmas, I wouldn't live to see New Year's," said Bob Gregory, who has been the forecaster at WTHR-TV in Indianapolis for nine years.

Most of the forecasters claimed they are accurate 80 percent to 90 percent of the time on one-day forecasts, but longer-range predictions get tricky. And most conceded they are simply reporting information supplied by computers and anonymous meteorologists from the National Weather Service or a private agency.

But it's the face on the television screen that people go after.

Tom Bonner, 35, who has been with KARK-TV in Little Rock, Ark., for 11 years, remembers the time a burly farmer from Lonoke, with too much to drink, walked up to him in a bar, poked a finger in his chest and said: "You're the one that sent that tornado and tore my house up. . . . I'm going to take your head off."

Bonner said he looked for the bouncer, couldn't spot him, and replied, "That's right about the tornado, and I'll tell you something else, I'll send another one if you don't back off." . . .

As for the positive associations, . . . [consider how marketers are] incessantly trying to connect themselves or their products with the things we like. Did you ever wonder what all those good-looking models are doing standing around in the automobile ads? What the advertiser hopes they are doing is lending their positive traits—beauty and desirability—to the cars. The advertiser is betting that we will respond to the product in the same ways we respond to the attractive models merely associated with it.

And they are right. In one study, men who saw a new-car ad that included a seductive young woman model rated the car as faster, more appealing, more expensive looking, and better designed than did men who viewed the same ad without the model. Yet when asked later, the men refused to believe that the presence of the young woman had influenced their judgments. [The association bias is why celebrities are paid to peddle even products wholly irrelevant to their role] (soft drinks, popcorn poppers, panty hose). The important thing for the advertiser is to establish the connection; it doesn't have to be a logical one, just a positive one. . . .

[Authority can also exert profound influence. Consider the following example.] A group of researchers, composed of doctors and nurses with connections to three Midwestern hospitals, became increasingly concerned with the extent of mechanical obedience to doctors' orders on the part of nurses. . . . To twenty-two separate nurses' stations on various surgical, medical, pediatric, and psychiatric wards, one of the researchers made an identical phone call in which he identified himself as a hospital physician and directed the answering nurse to give twenty milligrams of a drug (Astrogen) to a specific ward patient. There were four excellent reasons for a nurse's caution in response to this order: (1) The prescription was transmitted by phone, in direct violation of hospital policy. (2) The medication itself was unauthorized; Astrogen had not been cleared for use nor placed on the ward stock list. (3) The prescribed dosage was obviously and dangerously excessive. The medication containers clearly stated that the "maximum daily dose" was only ten milligrams, half of what had been ordered. (4) The directive was given by a man the nurse had never met, seen, or even talked with before on the phone. Yet, in 95 percent of the instances, the nurses went straightaway to the ward medicine cabinet, where they secured the ordered dosage of Astrogen and started for the patient's room to administer it. It was at this point that they were stopped by a secret observer, who revealed the nature of the experiment. . . .

The following excerpt focuses on the role of social proof in skewing behavior, and on strategies that can counteract it.

PAUL BREST AND LINDA HAMILTON KRIEGER, PROBLEM SOLVING, DECISIONMAKING, AND PROFESSIONAL JUDGMENT: A GUIDE FOR LAWYERS AND POLICYMAKERS

(New York: Oxford University Press, 2010), pp. 545-546, 554, and 556

Social Proof and Professional and Corporate Malfeasance

Many "ethical train wrecks" in law and business can be traced, at least in part, to social proof effects. Consider, for example, the ruin of in-house Enron lawyer Kristina Mordaunt, described by Kurt Eichenwald in his book, *Conspiracy of Fools*. In 2001, Ms. Mordaunt played a minor role in working out "LJM1," one of the shady partnerships (known in accountant-speak as a "special purpose entity") that had been used to manipulate Enron's apparent financial performance and enrich certain Enron executives. LJM1's status as a valid special purpose entity, which accorded it favorable accounting treatment, was highly questionable. But from Mordaunt's point of view, the relevant accounting rules were ambiguous, the deal had been approved by Enron financial officers and accountants, and the executives who had put it together were rising stars in one of the country's best-regarded corporations.

A short time after her work on LMJ1 was completed, Mordaunt was offhandedly asked by Enron Treasurer, Ben Glisan, Jr., whether she wanted to invest $10,000 in a similar special purpose entity, known by Enron insiders as "Southampton." She ended up investing only $5,800, but a few weeks later, when the Southampton deal wound down, she found in her bank account a return of over a million dollars. Weeks later, her career was ruined, and by the middle of 2002, prosecutors had filed a forfeiture action to seize her home and car.

It is easy — perhaps too easy — to conclude that Mordaunt was a knowing participant in a patently fraudulent scheme who got precisely what she deserved. But Eichenwald suggests an alternative explanation. Caught up in a web of mind-numbingly complex and ambiguous accounting rules, and watching apparently well-respected, successful high level executives participating in complex transactions like LJM1 and Southampton, Mordaunt could easily have concluded that the deals were legitimate, and that she was doing nothing wrong. The "proof" was all around her, in the actions of her superiors and colleagues.

The social proof phenomenon can explain lawyers' passive acquiescence in client misconduct in various legal contexts. For example, Donald C. Langevoort suggests that it can explain attorney inaction in the face of client fraud:

> [A]n attorney who is new to a situation, especially an inexperienced one, is particularly prone to rely on social learning as the basis for constructing a

schema. The fact that those more senior and more familiar with the situation are behaving as if there is no problem provides a strong cue. This, indeed, is one explanation for the reduced tendency of people in groups to act heroically, since responsibility is effectively diffused. To this, naturally, must be added the situational pressures on junior members of groups to conform to apparent norms. . . .

Defusing the Impulses toward Obedience

. . . Psychologists Philip Zimbardo and Michael Lieppe suggest [the following approaches to inoculating oneself against automatic obedience]:

- remain engaged with alternate systems of authority, such as a those deriving from one's religious, spiritual, political, or philosophical commitments;
- trust your intuition when you find yourself thinking, "something is wrong here";
- when in doubt, seek out a knowledgeable — but independent — person to give you an "obedience check";
- mentally rehearse disobedience strategies and techniques for various situations;
- be particularly vigilant when you notice people using euphemisms to describe harmful behaviors or the people they harm;
- don't expect not to suffer adverse consequences when refusing to obey an authority figure — rather, consider the worst case scenario and act on that possibility;
- chose [sic] carefully the organizations and situations in which you place yourself, because it's all too easy to overestimate your powers to resist.

NOTES AND QUESTIONS

1. Might other dynamics besides social proof have been at work in explaining Mordaunt's conduct? Recall the material on self-serving cognitive biases in Chapter 3. In *The Smartest Guys in the Room,* a documentary on Enron, interviews with former employees suggest that part of what accounted for some extremely stupid decisions by some very intelligent leaders was the enormous amount of money they stood to gain from discounting risks and cutting ethical corners. Consider how all these psychological factors worked in tandem with skewed organizational reward structures discussed in Chapter 5.
2. An increasing number of organizations are attempting to harness social proof in the service of progressive social change. For example, after a soap opera in Mexico City showed characters seeking adult literacy materials, a quarter million viewers did the same. A radio play in Tanzania had similar impact in changing AIDS prevention behavior among a quarter of the population in its broadcast area.[17] Can you identify similar efforts or opportunities in this country?

The currencies of influence come in many forms, and the following excerpt details the wide range of strategies available even to individuals who lack formal positions of authority. Consider how some of these currencies might have assisted you in a situation in which you failed to exercise as much influence as you hoped.

DAVID L. BRADFORD AND ALLAN COHEN, "INFLUENCE WITHOUT AUTHORITY"

Organizational Dynamics, American Management Association, Winter 1989, pp. 5-17

Currencies: The Source of Influence

If the basis of organizational influence depends on mutually satisfactory exchanges, then people are influential only insofar as they can offer something that others need. Thus power comes from the ability to meet others' needs.

A useful way to think of how the process of exchange actually works in organizations is to use the metaphor of "currencies." This metaphor provides a powerful way to conceptualize what is important to the influencer and the person to be influenced. Just as many types of currencies are traded in the world financial market, many types are "traded" in organizational life. Too often people think only of money or promotion and status. Those "currencies," however, usually are available only to a manager in dealing with his or her employees. Peers who want to influence colleagues or employees who want to influence their supervisors often feel helpless. They need to recognize that many types of payments exist, broadening the range of what can be exchanged.

Some major currencies that are commonly valued and traded in organizations are listed in Exhibit 1. Although not exhaustive, the list makes evident that a person does not have to be at the top of an organization or have hands on the formal levers of power to command multiple resources that others may value.

Part of the usefulness of currencies comes from their flexibility. For example, there are many ways to express gratitude and to give assistance. A manager who most values the currency of appreciation could be paid through verbal thanks, praise, a public statement at a meeting, informal comments to his peers, and/or a note to her boss. However, the same note of thanks seen by one person as a sign of appreciation may be seen by another person as an attempt to brownnose or by a third person as a cheap way to try to repay extensive favors and service. Thus currencies have value not in some abstract sense but as defined by the receiver.

Although we have stressed the interactive nature of exchange, "payments" do not always have to be made by the other person. They can be self-generated to fit beliefs about being virtuous, benevolent, or committed to the organization's welfare. Someone may respond to another person's request because it reinforces cherished values, a sense of identity, or feelings of self-worth. The exchange is interpersonally stimulated because the one who wants influence has set up conditions that allow this kind of self-payment to occur by asking for cooperation to accomplish organizational goals. However, the person who responds because "it is the right thing to do" and who feels good about being the "kind of person who does not act out of narrow self-interest" is printing currency (virtue) that is self-satisfying.

Of course, the five categories of currencies listed in Exhibit 1 are not mutually exclusive. When the demand from the other person is high, people are likely to pay in several currencies across several categories. They may, for example, stress the organizational value of their request, promise to return the favor at a later time, imply that it will increase the other's prestige in the organization, and express their appreciation. . . .

Exhibit 1
Commonly Traded Organizational Currencies

Inspiration-Related Currencies

Vision	Being involved in a task that has larger significance for the unit, organization, customers, or society
Excellence	Having a chance to do important things really well
Moral/Ethical Correctness	Doing what is "right" by a higher standard than efficiency

Task-Related Currencies

Resources	Lending or giving money, budget increases, personnel, space, and so forth
Assistance	Helping with existing projects or undertaking unwanted tasks
Cooperation	Giving task support, providing quicker response time, approving a project, or aiding implementation

Position-Related Currencies

Advancement	Giving a task or assignment that can aid in promotion
Recognition	Acknowledging effort, accomplishment, or abilities
Visibility	Providing the chance to be known by higher-ups or significant others in the organization
Reputation	Enhancing the way a person is seen
Importance/Insiderness	Offering a sense of importance, of "belonging"
Network/Contacts	Providing opportunities for linking with others

Relationship-Based Currencies

Acceptance/Inclusion	Providing closeness and friendship
Personal Support	Giving personal and emotional backing
Understanding	Listening to others' concerns and issues

Personal-Related Currencies

Self-Concept	Affirming one's values, self-esteem, and identity
Challenge/Learning	Sharing tasks that increase skills and abilities
Ownership/Involvement	Letting others have ownership and influence
Gratitude	Expressing appreciation or indebtedness

The Process of Exchange

To make the exchange process effective, the influencer needs to (1) think about the person to be influenced as a potential ally, not an adversary; (2) know the world of the potential ally, including the pressures as well as the person's needs and goals; (3) be aware of key goals and available resources that may be valued by the potential ally; and (4) understand the exchange transaction itself so that win-win outcomes are achieved. . . . Unfortunately, people desiring influence are not always aware of precisely what they want. . . . They fail to think through which aspects are more important and which can be jettisoned if necessary. . . .

All of the preceding discussion needs to be conditioned by one important variable: the nature of the relationship between both parties. The greater the extent to which the influencer has worked with the potential ally and created trust, the easier the exchange process will be. Each party will know the other's desired currencies and situational pressures, and each will have developed a mutually productive interaction style. With trust, less energy will be spent on figuring out the intentions of the ally, and there will be less suspicion about when and how the payback will occur.

A poor relationship (based on previous interactions, on the reputation each party has in the organization, and/or on stereotypes and animosities between the functions or departments that each party represents) will impede an otherwise easy exchange. Distrust of the goodwill, veracity, or reliability of the influencer can lead to the demand for "no credit; cash up front," which constrains the flexibility of both parties. . . .

Few transactions within organizations are one-time deals. (Who knows when the other person may be needed again or even who may be working for him or her in the future?) Thus in most exchange situations two outcomes matter: success in achieving task goals and success in improving the relationship so that the next interaction will be even more productive. Too often, people who want to be influential focus only on the task and act as if there is no tomorrow. Although both task accomplishment and an improved relationship cannot always be realized at the same time, on some occasions the latter can be more important than the former. Winning the battle but losing the war is an expensive outcome. . . .

PROBLEM 4-1

Break into pairs. Construct a situation in which one of you attempts to persuade the other to alter some workplace behavior. Reverse roles. Which strategies were most and least effective? What might you do differently?

NOTES

Research suggests that the effectiveness of various forms of influence depends on three conditions. First, the individuals whom a leader seeks to influence must believe that their efforts can bring the desired results—that they have the necessary ability, training, resources, clarity about assignment, and so forth. Second, they have to believe that there will be an accurate linkage between performance and rewards or sanctions — for example, that shirking will be detected or that they, not just their supervisor, will reap the benefits of a job well done. Third, they have to fear or value the sanctions or rewards that are likely to follow. In some job settings, particularly those in the public and nonprofit sectors, additional compensation may be a less effective motivator than other factors such as job security or flexibility, recognition, challenge, and a sense of contributing to a meaningful cause.[18] Even in some private-sector contexts, money may not be the most important source of influence. One survey of some 7,000 workers in technology companies found that fair pay ranked fourth on the list of reasons why workers stayed in their jobs. Other factors in the order ranked were the challenge of the work, workplace relationships, opportunities for growth and development, recognition and respect, involvement in work that is meaningful and that makes a difference, pride in the organization, and job benefits.[19]

Some reward systems backfire because they are based on results that can be manipulated by dysfunctional behaviors or because workers perceive them as arbitrary. This dynamic, famously described as the "folly of rewarding A while hoping for B," explains why focusing only on productivity (hours billed, widgets made) can lead to problems of quality and efficiency.[20] The development of "surgical report cards," which rate doctors and hospitals on outcomes, led them to cherry-pick patients and to refuse those who may have needed operations most but whose prognosis made a high grade for their doctors less likely.[21] Introducing fines for parents who were late to pick up their children at daycare were also counterproductive because they replaced a sense of moral obligation with a cost-benefit calculation.[22] Employee of the month programs have led to similarly unwelcome by-products. In some research, half of those interviewed felt they were more deserving than recipients, and a number of the recipients themselves experienced "losing while winning." A commemorative plaque did not compensate them for the weeks of ridicule and resentment from their co-workers.[23] Such research underscores the importance of knowing, not simply assuming, what factors will be most influential in a given context.[24]

Although situational knowledge is crucial, social science research also suggests some general lessons on influence that can guide leaders' strategies. One is that sanctions are more difficult than rewards to use effectively. Disincentives can lead to poorer performance by undermining confidence and self-esteem, and by provoking resentment, sabotage, manipulation, and litigation.[25] Experts emphasize the need to investigate thoroughly before resorting to negative sanctions, and to use them sequentially, beginning with coaching and warnings, before escalation to more serious penalties or dismissals. A second research finding is that extrinsic rewards are typically less effective than intrinsic motivation in promoting high performance, particularly in matters involving creativity and ethics.[26] For example, a survey of art institute students found that those who were most successful by external measures (recognition, income) some twenty years into their careers were not those who had been most interested in such rewards, but rather those with inner drives to achievement.[27] Other large-scale studies find that the factors most likely to produce high job satisfaction involve factors intrinsic to the work itself, including the sense of achievement, contribution, and opportunity for recognition that it creates. Factors most likely to contribute to dissatisfaction involved extrinsic factors: workplace policies and conditions, salary, job security, and relationships.[28] In summarizing this research, an influential *Harvard Business Review* article noted that "kick in the pants" responses to job motivation problems were frequently ineffective. A better strategy typically involved job enrichment, which might provide greater opportunities for control and credit.[29]

QUESTIONS

1. What rewards and sanctions have been most effective in influencing your workplace performance? Did organizations where you have worked make use of the best strategies for affecting your behavior? If not, why not?
2. Consider the factors that most influenced followers in the excerpts below. Can you draw any general insights from these examples?

MEDIA RESOURCES

Descriptions of the Asch experiments and Cialdini's research are readily available, as are the elevator scenes from *Candid Camera*.[30] For an illustration of the association principle, season 36, episode 4 of *Saturday Night Live*, which aired on October 23, 2010, shortly before the midterm elections, opened with a parody of Harry Reid distancing himself from President Obama in a joint appearance, and Obama responding in kind. Materials on Enron and other more recent financial scandals in addition to *The Smartest Guys in the Room* are described in Chapters 5 and 7. *The Young Victoria*, which chronicles the early life of Great Britain's Queen Victoria, offers telling portrayals of her responses to influence—both resistance to bullying and vulnerability to flattery. In one scene that raises issues of ethics as well as tactics, Lord Melbourne is currying her favor at a court dinner by portraying her father (whom she never knew) as a kind and gifted leader. One of Melbourne's political rivals, observing the scene with distaste, notes his own inability to revise reality—the father was one of the most brutal officers he had ever seen.

B. FOLLOWERS

1. THE IMPORTANCE OF FOLLOWERS

Although leadership is widely recognized as involving a relationship, the study of leadership has largely neglected followers. This is beginning to change, partly in recognition of their importance in influencing outcomes. Warren Bennis points out that "followers do the heavy lifting of any successful enterprise. No matter who is memorialized as founder, no nation or organization is built without the collective effort of a group of able, energetic, unsung followers."[31] Even achievements for which we credit leaders often involve collegial efforts. Michelangelo worked with sixteen others to paint the ceiling of the Sistine Chapel.[32] Leaders need followers and, as John Gardner noted, "[L]eadership is conferred by followers."[33] In the book excerpted below,

Barbara Kellerman, of Harvard's Center for Public Leadership, similarly reminds us how much followers matter, even when they do nothing.[34]

Moreover, their power is increasing in response to the decline of command-and-control managerial styles and the rise of technologies that facilitate ground-up communication and organization. The result is to blur the boundaries of leader and follower. Followers may lack authority, but they do not necessarily lack power. In some respects, all leaders are followers; to retain their influence, those in positions of authority have no choice but to "track, to follow their followers if only to be sure that they stay in line."[35] Leaders have long recognized as much. In the possibly apocryphal words of the French revolutionary leader Comte de Mirabeau, "There goes the mob, and I must follow them, for I am their leader."[36] Expressions such as "leading from behind" acknowledge the way that informal power structures may trump formal lines of authority.[37] So too, as international research by James Kouzes and Barry Posner makes clear, "the best leaders turn their followers into leaders, realizing that the journey ahead requires many guides."[38] Given the relationship between leaders and followers, some commentators reject the dichotomy and even its terminology. For John Gardner, "the connotations of the 'follower' suggest too much passivity and dependence to make it a fit term for those who are at the other end of the dialogue with leaders."[39]

Yet while all leaders may in some sense be followers, the converse is not necessarily true. Rather, as Kellerman notes, although in some circumstances it may be possible for followers to "lead up," such initiatives from the bottom will not always be tolerated.[40] Hierarchies are real, and subordinates may be at the mercy of those in positions of authority. For that reason, the common trend in leadership studies is to maintain the distinction between leaders and followers, while recognizing the fluidity of boundaries and the complexity of power dynamics that do not run in only one direction. Most of us most of the time "lead from the middle, attracting and persuading both upward and downward" to influence superiors and subordinates.[41] Our effectiveness depends on understanding the conditions of these leader-follower relationships.

In exploring such relationships, it is helpful to clarify what defines and also what differentiates followers. Most experts label someone a follower based on rank and responses. The category includes individuals who hold less formal authority than leaders and who generally defer to those holding leadership roles. Yet within that category are many different kinds and degrees of compliance. In *The Courageous Follower*, Ira Chaleff draws distinctions based on the amount of support and challenge that followers supply.[42] Some military leaders differentiate between those who will always "get it done" because they want the job above them, those who are "on the team" but lack the same degree of motivation, and those who are "least conformist" but sometimes the "most productive" because they argue about what should be done.[43] Other theorists explore differences in forms of resistance: strikes, whistle-blowing, sabotage, manipulation, and reduced effort.[44] Kellerman's typology of followers turns on their degree of engagement. She differentiates among isolates, bystanders, participants, activists, and diehards.

Why do followers follow? Common explanations include rewards and punishment; desires for stability, safety, security, and community; admiration, identification, and respect; and appeals to values and a vision of the future.[45] Barbara Kellerman explores those reasons, as well as some potential downsides of deference. As you read the excerpt below, think about the types of followers that you have observed in organizations and social movements. What accounts for the different levels of support, resistance, and engagement that you have observed? If, as a British government report on the public sector asserted, "responsible followers prevent irresponsible leaders," what can encourage subordinates to assume that role?[46]

BARBARA KELLERMAN, FOLLOWERSHIP: HOW FOLLOWERS ARE CREATING CHANGE AND CHANGING LEADERS

(Boston: Harvard Business Press, 2008), pp. 53-56, 57-59, 61, 65-68, 84-87, and 89-93

Why We Follow — Individual Benefits

Freud was first. He was the first to provide us with a psychological explanation of why followers follow their leaders. . . . Here, in part, was his answer:

> Why the great man should rise to significance at all we have no doubt whatsoever. We know that the great majority of people have a strong need for authority which they can admire, to which they can submit, and which dominates and sometimes even ill-treats them. We have learned from the psychology of the individual whence comes this need of the masses. It is the longing for the father that lives in each of us from his childhood days.

The book *Moses and Monotheism* [also] . . . suggested that in all power relationships there are elements of admiration and envy on the one hand, and fear and loathing on the other. . . .

. . . [T]hese "human desires" are strongest in times of uncertainty, especially in times of crisis. For example, if an election for mayor had been held in New York City on September 10, 2001, it is not at all clear that Rudolph Giuliani would have won. A poll taken earlier in the year showed that only 32 percent of New Yorkers approved of him as mayor, and his standing among African American voters was "so low as to be virtually unmeasurable." But after the attacks on the World Trade Center, the situation changed dramatically: Giuliani became a hero. In good part this was because he performed admirably under impossibly difficult circumstances. In greater part this was because in that moment, a moment of crisis, his followers needed nothing so much as a leader to whom they could turn for comfort and guidance. Nine days after the towers fell, an editorial about Giuliani in the *New York Times* read in part: "He moves about the stricken city like a god. People want to be in his presence. They want to touch him. They want to praise him. . . . He is not only respected, but revered. And not only revered, but loved."

. . . Clearly, our needs and wants as individuals are met by our playing the part of follower, at least most of the time. We go along because we consciously or unconsciously determine it in our interest to do so. Here are only three of the reasons why: (1) leaders provide individuals with safety, security, and a sense of order; (2) leaders provide individuals with a group, a community, to which they can belong; and (3) leaders provide individuals with someone who does the collective work. Of course, some of the time, followers comply only involuntarily. Some of the time, their leader compels them to comply.

. . . [So too,] *followers follow not only because it is in their interest to conform to their leaders, but also because it is in their interest to conform to their fellow followers.* Followers provide each other with crucial reference points. . . . Followers also follow other followers for some of the same reasons they follow their leaders. That is, followers go along with other followers because they (1) lend stability and security, (2) provide order and meaning, and (3) constitute the group to which they want to belong. . . .

Why We Follow — Group Benefits

Freud was first here too. He was the first to provide us with a sophisticated psychological understanding of why *individuals* follow leaders. And he was the first to provide us with a sophisticated psychological understanding of why *groups* follow leaders. . . . Freud believed that we behave differently — worse — as members of groups than we do as individuals. In groups our "unconscious instinctual impulses" trump what turns out to be the fragile veneer of civilization. "By the mere fact that he forms part of an organized group," Freud wrote, "a man descends several rungs in the ladder of civilization. Isolated, he may be a cultivated individual; in a crowd he is a barbarian — that is, a creature acting by instinct," capable of committing acts in "utter contradiction with his character and habits." Therefore, like Thomas Hobbes, Freud concluded that groups need leaders, strong leaders, because without them they will revert to being "barbarian."

This, though, presented Freud with a dilemma. On the one hand, groups need leaders to, among other things, protect us from ourselves. But on the other hand, bad leaders can direct groups toward danger and destruction. Finally, Freud concluded, we have no choice: bad leaders are a risk we assume, if only because by nature we have what he called "an extreme passion for authority." Put another way, well before the worst of the twentieth-century dictators — Stalin, Hitler, Mao — Freud declared that we actually want "to be governed by unrestricted force."

As we have seen, Robert Michels also addressed the question of what benefits we derive from leaders. It turns out these benefits are bestowed not only on individuals but also on groups. Why the "iron law of oligarchy"? Because, as one observer put it, "Thirty people can sit around a campfire and arrive at a consensual decision; thirty million people cannot." Michels went even a step further. It is, he argued, "the incompetence of the masses" that makes leaders absolutely indispensable. Thus is the common good served by having the few (the leaders) assume responsibility for the many (the followers).

Since Freud and Michels, another leadership function has emerged, one also excluded from the standard leadership literature. It comes to us from the study of social movements and demonstrates that some people need leaders for the purpose of what in the late 1960s and early 1970s was called *consciousness-raising*. That is, some followers need leaders to show them the world has possibilities beyond anything they had previously conceived. [In addition,] . . . (1) leaders provide groups with a structure; (2) leaders provide groups with a goal; and (3) leaders provide groups with instruments of goal achievement. . . .

Follower-Leader Relations

. . . In his book *Domination and the Arts of Resistance,* James C. Scott makes this point: people who resist, who speak "truth to power," are rare, really rare. Scott does not claim that speaking truth to power is impossible, that subordinates can never speak freely and frankly to their superiors. But he does argue that when there is a high degree of control by the latter over the former, resistance is unlikely to be open. It's just too dangerous. What, then, is the alternative? Does this mean there is no resistance at all? Or do followers find other ways of opposing leaders who give them no way to say their piece?

Scott argues that what you see is *not* necessarily what you get. . . . Hidden transcripts tell us what is being said privately, behind closed doors. And they manifest themselves in secret acts of rebellion, such as sabotage, poaching, pilfering, and tax evasion. In short, hidden transcripts are "written" by the powerless in order to resist the powerful, without risking their lives in the process.

Scott's message is far-reaching in its consequences, for these private forms of resistance pave the way for public resistance later on. . . . [I]f it succeeds, its capacity to beat back oppression "is potentially awesome."

At the other end of the spectrum from totalitarian leadership is, of course, democratic leadership, leadership in keeping with a social contract, in which power between leaders and followers is shared. . . . The terms *transactional* and *transformational leadership,* as described by groundbreaking political scientist James MacGregor Burns, generally presume both democratic leadership and democratic followership. That is, they presume followers who know where their interests are, and who are ready, willing, and able to act accordingly. According to Burns, transactional leadership is based on an economic model in which leaders and followers have an exchange of some kind, from which both parties stand to benefit. Transforming leadership, in turn, "occurs when one or more persons *engage* with others in such a way that leaders and followers raise one another to higher levels of motivation and morality." Clearly, Burns intended for the two types of leadership to be quite different. But the differences notwithstanding, transactional and transformational leadership are in the most important way similar: they take into account not only the needs and wants of leaders but those of followers as well. . . .

Contexts and Characteristics

The ways in which followers and leaders relate depend on the contexts within which they are embedded. This in any case we know: context is critical. As the great sociologist George Homans put it, "The relationship between superior and subordinate is to some degree the same in every group." But, he added, "It varies greatly in intensity from group to group according to various circumstances, including the relationship of the group to its environment, the ability of the subordinate to escape from authority, and the extent to which the superior is chosen by the members of the group." . . .

Present Types

. . . Like the few who tilled this soil before me, I came to conclude that followers are different one from the other, and that they can and should be divided into at least a few different groups. . . .

I settled finally on a typology based on a single, simple metric. It aligns followers along only one—the all-important one—axis. It is *level of engagement*. That is, I divide all followers into five different types, according to where they fall along a continuum that ranges from feeling and doing absolutely nothing on the one end to being passionately committed and deeply involved on the other. The five types are:

- Isolate
- Bystander
- Participant
- Activist
- Diehard

Isolates

Isolates are completely detached. They do not care about their leaders, or know anything about them, or respond to them in any way. Their alienation is, nevertheless, of consequence. By default—by knowing nothing and doing nothing—Isolates strengthen still further leaders who already have the upper hand.

Consider the case of the American voter or, more precisely, the case of Americans who are eligible to vote but never do. . . . Some 15 million Americans reported that they did not vote in 2004 because they "were not interested in the election or were not involved in politics." . . . Since the subject here is followership, I should point out that the disenchantment that underlies each of these excuses is less with government as it is broadly conceived than it is with public officials, with leaders. "The vast majority of Americans find the playing field of politics to be tilted. Fifty-six percent agree that politics is a means for the already powerful to maintain advantage; just one third believe that politics is a way for the powerless to acquire equal footing." . . . Australia provides [an alternate] model: registered voters who do not go to the polls must either provide a reason for not voting or pay a modest fine that increases each time there is another offense. The result is a turnout rate of more than 95 percent. The fine is obviously a disincentive to stay home and not vote. But the system is about more than penalizing political truants. It instills the idea that voting is a social obligation and that it elevates the political dialogue. . . .

However, the problem of the Isolate is scarcely confined to the political realm. We know full well that the workplace similarly has a considerable contingent of subordinates who are totally detached, there to do what they must to get by and no more. Isolates in the workplace are uninformed, uninterested, and unmotivated. They have no relationship with their leaders or managers. They are alienated from the system, from the group or organization that constitutes the whole. Finally, they are silent because they are detached — and because they are silent, they are ignored. Isolates have a problem. Isolates *are* a problem.

Bystanders, Participants, Activists, and Diehards

The four other types of followers are all in some way engaged. They are engaged with their leaders, and with other followers, and with the group or organization in which they are embedded. Recall that they each presume subordinate rank, and they are ordered according to the level of their engagement.

- *Bystanders observe but do not participate. They make a deliberate decision to stand aside, to disengage from their leaders and from whatever is the group dynamic. This withdrawal is, in effect, a declaration of neutrality that amounts to tacit support for whoever and whatever constitutes the status quo.*
- *Participants are in some way engaged. They clearly favor their leaders and the groups and organizations of which they are members — or they are clearly opposed. In either case, they care enough to put their money where their mouths are — that is, to invest some of what they have (time, for example) to try to have an impact.*
- *Activists feel strongly about their leaders and they act accordingly. They are eager, energetic, and engaged. Because they are heavily invested in people and process, they work hard either on behalf of their leaders or to undermine and even unseat them.*
- *Diehards are as their name implies — prepared to die if necessary for their cause, whether an individual, or an idea, or both. Diehards are deeply devoted to their leaders; or, in contrast, they are ready to remove them from positions of power, authority, and influence by any means necessary. In either case, Diehards are defined by their dedication, including their willingness to risk life and limb. Being a Diehard is all-consuming. It is who you are. It determines what you do.*

. . . My primary point is this: we are followers. Followers are us. This does not, of course, mean that all of us follow all of the time — sometimes we lead. But all of us follow some of the time. It's the human condition.

NOTES AND QUESTIONS

1. What makes followers effective? Researchers suggest that ideal followers are informed, engaged, independent, and innovative.[47] In effect, they need a "courageous conscience."[48] As Bennis notes, the "tools of great followership are not so different from those of leadership."[49] Yet such qualities are not always what supervisors or organizational structures foster. As is clear from the examples in Chapters 6 and 7, and problem 4-2 below, peer pressure and institutional reward structures can produce dysfunctional patterns of conformity. Leaders unconsciously compound the problem when they discourage dissent and reward ingratiation. Followers' flattery can then become toxic; it reinforces leaders' narcissism and distances them from discomfiting realities.[50]

2. Under what circumstances should followers assume the responsibility that Mary Gentile describes as "giving voice to values"?[51] The issue gained significant attention following the murder of Kitty Genovese in New York City's Kew Garden, in view of apartment residents who failed to call the police. Under what some philosophers subsequently labeled the "Kew Garden principles," individuals' responsibility to act depends on the significance of the need, their proximity, their capability, and the alternatives to their intervention. So, for example, ethical obligations are greatest when followers have the ability to prevent serious injury and are the parties of "last resort."[52]

3. What leadership behaviors can reinforce followers' sense of moral responsibility and encourage a culture of candor rather than conformity? The first step is recognition of the challenge. The art of leadership is not as Dwight Eisenhower once reportedly described it: "[G]etting someone else to do something you want done because he wants to do it."[53] Effective leadership also requires inviting constructive questions about what you want done and creating channels for internal dissent and whistle-blowing. Leaders often find that the more they listen to followers, the more followers listen to them, and that trust is the most important factor affecting follower satisfaction and performance.[54] Common strategies for improving relationships with followers include: offering opportunities for 360-degree feedback and sharing information; providing positive recognition and reinforcement for constructive criticism; creating a climate of transparency, responsiveness, accountability, and mutual respect; and involving individuals in key decisions that will affect their performance.[55]

What stands in the way of creating those conditions for effective followers? One difficulty is that leaders come to "believe their own press" and lose sight of the advice that cartoonist Hank Ketchum once offered: "Flattery is like chewing gum. Enjoy it but don't swallow it."[56] Leaders' tendency to micromanage or desire to retain control can also sap followers' initiative and commitment. As one senior executive in a Fortune 500 company put it, "[W]e can't afford loose cannons around here," to which another executive responded, "When was the last time you saw a cannon of any kind around here?"[57] Recall the strategies for avoiding group think discussed in Chapter 3. What organizational structures and practices might prevent overly conformist cultures such as those involved in problem 4-2 below?

4. If the problems that followers observe pose significant risk to the organization and/or third parties, what steps can they take to increase the effectiveness and lessen the risks of whistle-blowing? Research suggests that somewhere between a half to two-thirds of whistle-blowers lose their jobs, and that the risks of retaliation are almost the same for internal as external disclosures.[58] Even when dissenters do not go outside the organization, they remind colleagues "that there is an outside," which can have disruptive, discomfiting, and destabilizing effects.[59] Assertions of wrongdoing make "everyone wonder whose actions will next come under unwanted scrutiny with unforeseeable results. . . . Even those who welcome the consequences of betrayal mistrust the betrayer."[60]

Yet the benefits, both personal and societal, from whistle-blowing can be substantial. Some individuals become heroes; others avoid guilt and experience the satisfaction of living up to their own best sense of themselves. As one whistle-blower in the Department of Energy explained her decision to expose risks at a nuclear reactor site: "I just couldn't stop imagining what would happen if children jumped over the fence and played in the radioactive dust." When asked why colleagues did not feel the same way, she responded: "They just didn't think about it. No one wanted to talk about it. Site protection wasn't our responsibility."[61]

Studies of whistle-blowers and other "change agents" within organizations suggest several strategies for success: identify whether concerns are widely shared, enlist allies, create a written record, appeal to shared values, explore possibilities for internal influence, and seek "small wins."[62] Incremental victories can be important in creating ripple effects and building confidence that change is possible.

5. In "Tempered Radicals," her research on successful agents of organizational change, Stanford professor Debra Meyerson explores these strategies through representative cases. One involves Barb Waugh, a personnel director at Hewlett Packard and member of its Gay and Lesbian Employee Network. When the company's executive team initially decided not to offer domestic partner benefits, she considered resigning in protest. Instead, she began soliciting stories of how homophobia had harmed HP's productivity. She wrote up the most compelling accounts as a reader's theater piece, performed by thirteen employees. A Greek chorus in the background read out the names of HP competitors who offered such benefits. The script was e-mailed widely and the piece was performed some sixty times at HP sites across the globe, including one attended by the CEO and his executive staff. Within six months, the company reversed its decision and became the first Fortune 50 corporation to offer domestic partner benefits.[63] Have you observed comparable examples?

Not every story has such a happy ending. Consider situations such as those described in the problems below. What lessons do they suggest about how best to give "voice to values"?

PROBLEM 4-2[64]

1. Think about a situation in which you were asked to do something contrary to your values. How did you respond? How satisfied are you with what you did and what happened as a result? What might have made it easier for you to gain a successful resolution of the issue?[65]

2. Consider the dilemma of an employee that Gentile describes in *Giving Voice to Values*: "Jeff Salett was about to assume a promotion to corporate controller in a major industrial products firm when he was asked to adjust financial restructuring charges to present a more positive financial picture of the firm's performance." Although he did not want to alienate allies he would need in his new position, neither did he want his first act to be a distortion of the company's performance. If he started down that path, Salett believed that "it would never get easier" to do the right thing. He now has a meeting scheduled with the CEO to discuss the situation. What would you advise Salett to do? What factors would be relevant to your advice?[66]

PROBLEM 4-3

Suppose that you are an associate in the Wall Street law firm Donovan Leisure, under the circumstances that Steven Brill describes in the excerpt below. For the past two years you have worked principally for one senior partner on a large antitrust suit brought by Berkey Photo against your client, Eastman Kodak. One of the major issues in the suit concerns whether Kodak's acquisitions of early competitors or its superior product innovations were the primary cause of its dominant market position. In connection with that issue, Kodak has retained a highly regarded Yale economics professor to study the photography industry in the hope that he will develop an expert opinion that Kodak's innovations, rather than its acquisitions, enabled it to attain dominance. Ultimately, the professor does develop such a theory. However, in one early letter to the senior partner, the expert indicates that he is unable to explain how Kodak's early acquisitions could be irrelevant to its present market position.

Your firm has not provided this letter and certain documents reviewed by the economist in response to Berkey's demand in pretrial discovery proceedings for all such documents and for "interim reports" prepared by the economist. The partner in charge of the case has executed an affidavit under oath stating that he inadvertently destroyed the documents, believing them to be duplicates of material still available. The partner also privately maintains that he does not consider the economist's correspondence to be a "report" within the meaning of the discovery demand.

You find the interpretation contrived, and try unsuccessfully to convince the partner that the expert's preliminary expression of doubt is precisely the sort of interim statement that Berkey is seeking for cross-examination purposes. At the very least, you believe the trial court should be asked to rule on that question. You also know that the documents have not been destroyed, although they reveal nothing of substantive value to Berkey. You greatly respect the senior partner and are at a loss to explain his behavior. What is your response?

Suppose that Steven Brill's account of the Berkey-Kodak litigation excerpted below is essentially correct. Assume that you are a member of the firm's management committee. You have worked with the attorneys whose conduct is now open to question and, prior to this incident, you had respect for all those involved. What action do you believe the firm should take with regard to those individuals?

STEVEN BRILL, "WHEN A LAWYER LIES"

Esquire 23-24 (December 19, 1979)

Eighteen months ago, Joseph Fortenberry, Harvard College . . . and Yale Law [graduate], was on the perfect big-time lawyer's career path. At thirty-three, he had a federal court of appeals clerkship under his belt and was a senior associate at the New York law firm of Donovan Leisure Newton & Irvine working on the all-important antitrust case that Kodak was defending against Berkey Photo.

His prospects for being made partner at the prestige firm the following year were excellent: He was regarded not only as brilliant but also as engaging and enjoyable to work with; Kodak was the firm's biggest case (occupying twenty lawyers full time, with gross billings of some $4 million a year); and he was working hand in hand with Mahon Perkins Jr., one of the firm's most respected partners.

Then . . . [one] morning, in the middle of one of hundreds of depositions . . . that he had sat through for months, Joe Fortenberry's career unraveled.

Alvin Stein, the lawyer for Berkey Photo, was questioning a Kodak "expert witness," Yale economics professor Merton Peck, about files and other materials the professor had received from Kodak in order to prepare his testimony. In such suits, each side is allowed to obtain — or "discover" — almost any documents that the other side has used to prepare and bolster its case. Such materials can often be used to attack the credibility of witnesses.

Peck told Berkey lawyer Stein that he had shipped all the materials back to Perkins of Donovan Leisure earlier that year. What happened then, to the documents, Stein asked Perkins. I threw them out as soon as I got them, the Donovan Leisure partner replied.

Perkins was lying. He'd saved all the documents in a suitcase, frequently taking them back and forth between his office at the firm and a special office he'd leased near the federal courthouse for the trial. And Joe Fortenberry, sitting at Perkins's side during this deposition, knew his boss was lying. He'd worked with the suitcase full of documents, and at least once he'd carried it between Perkins's two offices. Two weeks later, Perkins submitted a sworn statement to the court confirming that he'd destroyed the documents. . . .

Perkins's perjury came to light when Stein, at the end of the Kodak-Berkey trial, asked Peck about any reports he had submitted prior to the trial to Kodak's lawyers. This led back to more probing questions about the materials Peck had used to prepare his testimony. Then — in what has since become a much-reported, pinstriped soap opera — on the Sunday night before the last week of trial, a frightened Perkins broke down and confessed to Kodak lead lawyer John Doar that he'd never destroyed the documents but had actually hid them in a cupboard in his office. Perkins told the judge the next day, then resigned from the firm; Stein used Donovan Leisure's withholding of documents to help convince the jury of Kodak's bad faith and guilt; Kodak lost the case in a spectacular $113 million verdict (since reduced to $87 million); Kodak dropped Donovan Leisure; and Perkins was convicted of contempt of court for his perjury and sentenced to a month in prison.

But what about Joe Fortenberry?

The rules by which the bar disciplines lawyers — the Code of Professional Responsibility — require that "a lawyer who receives information clearly establishing that . . . a person other than his client has perpetrated a fraud upon the tribunal shall promptly reveal the fraud to the tribunal." Moreover, the code requires that a lawyer who knows that another lawyer has engaged in dishonesty, deceit, or misrepresentation must report the offending lawyer to proper prosecutorial authorities.

In short, Fortenberry was obligated to speak up when Perkins lied. Instead, he said nothing to anyone. To be sure, Perkins, perhaps thinking he was helping Fortenberry, told the federal prosecutors who later investigated the case that Fortenberry had whispered in his ear and reminded him of the existence of the documents when Perkins told Stein he'd destroyed them. Fortenberry denies this. What's undisputed, and more relevant, is that Fortenberry never said a word about Perkins's lie to the judge, as he was obligated to, or even to any other Donovan Leisure partner.

Throw the book at him, right? Wrong. Law firms teach young associates that they are apprentices to the partners, not whistle blowers. The partners, after all, are supposed to be the ones with the experience and standing to make decisions about right and wrong. Fortenberry had worked for Perkins for more than six months. In an environment like Donovan Leisure, this means that he respected the fifty-nine-year-old "Perk," as his admiring partners called him, for the well-liked senior litigator that he was. It also means that he was intimidated by Perkins and, of course, that he knew Perkins was his ticket to partnership when the firm partners would decide in the following year which of the associates at Fortenberry's level would be offered that golden prize. "What happened to Joe" says a close associate "was that he saw Perk lie and really couldn't believe it. And he just had no idea what to do. I mean, he knew Perkins was lying, but he kept thinking that there must be a reason. Besides, what do you do? The guy was his boss and a great guy!" . . .

Donovan Leisure senior partner Murphy says that "the firm is trying to create an atmosphere in which associates in positions like Fortenberry's will feel free to take the story of one partner acting improperly to another partner." But Perkins's impropriety—a clear, deliberate lie—is an easy call. What about an associate who thinks his partner is filing a frivolous motion or is bilking his client? "You know, when you come to work at a big firm you do give up independence," Murphy concedes. "And a young lawyer's ideas about what is frivolous, for example, can't always be accepted, though we do encourage them to tell the partners they're working for what they think."

And what about firms other than Donovan Leisure that haven't been clubbed by a Perkins disaster into thinking about "open doors" and the like? I asked eight different associates, ages twenty-seven to thirty-two, at major firms around the country what they'd do in Fortenberry's situation. None said that they'd speak up to the judge in the case as their Code of Professional Responsibility requires; only four suggested that there was another partner at the firm they'd feel free to go to if their boss did something like that; and one told a story of watching a partner bill a client (a major utility) for three times the hours worked and, not knowing what to do, doing nothing.

Judge Marvin E. Frankel, the trial judge in the Kodak-Berkey case, was highly critical of Donovan Leisure's conduct during the trial and so outraged by Perkins's lie that he personally called it to the attention of the federal prosecutors. Frankel has since left the bench and become a partner at the midtown firm of Proskauer Rose Goetz & Mendelsohn. An associate there told me last week he'd "have no idea" what to do in a Perkins situation. "There isn't any way for an associate to handle that problem," Frankel concedes. Yet, unexplainably, the once-outraged judge shifts the direct responsibility from the individual law firm, where it belongs, to the organized bar generally: "All firms, including this one, should push the bar association to evolve procedures so that an associate doesn't have to be a hero to do what's ethical."

Every year more and more of the best brains in our society go from law school to firms like Donovan Leisure. And every year these firms get larger — and more competitive. Without some real effort from those at the top, this is an environment that is destined to make automatons out of those who get by and tragedies out of those, like Fortenberry, who have the bad luck to get tripped up.

NOTES

Following the trial, Judge Frankel made clear his own dissatisfaction with Donavan Leisure's performance, including its lawyers' failure to let him determine whether Berkey Photo's counsel should see the expert's letter, and their failure to press Perkins about his explanation of the missing documents. To Frankel, this conduct reflected a "single-minded interest in winning, winning, winning" that he found inappropriate and "upsetting."[67]

The result was upsetting to others as well. Kodak eventually paid Berkey Photo $6.75 million to settle the case. Donovan Leisure paid Kodak $675,000 to prevent a malpractice claim for failure to turn over documents.[68] John Doar, who was widely criticized by Donovan Leisure colleagues for his arrogant and ineffective supervision of the Kodak litigation, resigned from the firm. Fortenberry's career reeled off track. According to an account in the *American Lawyer*,

> [t]he firm had actually passed him over two months before the Perkins matter ever came to light, partners there say. It later concealed its decision so as to enhance Fortenberry's chances of getting another job, keeping him working so that prospective employers would not see his immediate dismissal from the firm and conclude that Fortenberry was indeed implicated in Perkins's wrongdoing. Even so, Fortenberry was not hired by any private law firm to which he applied for a job.[69]

Ironically, of all the major players, Perkins ultimately came out the best. Although he served twenty-seven days in jail for contempt of court, he was never disbarred. Subsequently, he traveled extensively, taught English in Japan, and served as president of his local orchestra. One of his former partners described him as "happier, I believe, than he had been as a practicing lawyer."[70]

In his midsixties, Perkins began working as a volunteer at the Center for Constitutional Rights, a prominent public-interest law firm. "Intellectually, the work here is every bit as satisfying as what I did before," he told a *New York Times* reporter. "And politically, I derive a lot more satisfaction than I did at Donovan Leisure. I'm helping in causes I believe in very deeply. This wasn't a very good way to have gotten out, but at this point, I'm very happy not to be there, and very happy to be here."[71]

QUESTIONS

1. Contemporary research leaves no doubt about the pressures for conformity by junior lawyers, particularly in large firms, where they spend most of their early career under the supervision of senior attorneys. The need to secure interesting work and favorable evaluations makes subordinates captives to

the judgments of supervisors. In that culture, it is often difficult for associates "to question the ethics of a particular practice or decision."[72] What implications can be drawn from the Berkey-Kodak case for the leadership of law firms? Most large firms now have a designated counsel to provide advice on professional responsibility issues.[73] However, little research is available on the effectiveness of these individuals in circumstances such as those confronting Fortenberry. Not all procedures guarantee the confidentiality, credibility, and objectivity that experts believe is necessary.[74] What structural protections might have encouraged Fortenberry to disclose Perkins's conduct to other partners in the firm at a point when the affidavit could have been withdrawn, the letter disclosed, and scandal averted?

2. What would you have done in Fortenberry's position? Should law firm associates be subject to formal or informal sanctions for failure to disclose a clear violation of legal or ethical rules? If you were the hiring partner at another firm, would Fortenberry's conduct in the Berkey-Kodak case keep you from offering him a job if he was otherwise qualified?

3. Does Perkins's subsequent career affect your view about whether he should have been disbarred?

4. After the Berkey-Kodak case, the American Bar Association adopted the Model Rules of Professional Conduct, which includes requirements beyond those that Brill's article noted. Rule 5.1(a) makes partners in a law firm responsible for ensuring policies that give "reasonable assurance that all lawyers in the firm conform to the rules of professional conduct." Should firm leaders be subject to disciplinary liability based on this rule under circumstances such as Berkey-Kodak? Would it be preferable to hold the firm liable?[75]

5. Another Rule, 5.2, provides that a lawyer is bound by professional rules "notwithstanding that the lawyer acted at the direction of another person." However, "a subordinate lawyer does not violate the rules of professional conduct if that lawyer acts in accordance with a supervisory lawyer's reasonable resolution of an arguable question of professional duty." Would that rule help an associate in Fortenberry's situation?

Does the rule strike the right balance between competing values? Some law professors claim that it is neither necessary nor appropriate. In their view, lawyers do not need its protections because even in states without the rule, discipline is virtually never imposed for "reasonable resolutions of an arguable question of professional duty."[76] From the standpoint of encouraging ethical debate, critics see the rule as counterproductive because it gives junior lawyers "little incentive to even consider tough ethical issues, let alone raise them.[77] By contrast, defenders claim that the rule encourages subordinate lawyers to "test supervisors' ethically questionable decisions or directives" because that is the only way they can be sure a resolution is "reasonable" and a shield against disciplinary liability.[78] What is your view?

6. If you were the head of a large private corporation or government agency, what rules would you support for employees who observe misconduct by their supervisor? Under what, if any circumstances, would you dismiss or sanction employees for not reporting unethical or illegal conduct?

MEDIA RESOURCES

For the general topic of followers, a documentary on Eichmann and footage showing rallies of the Third Reich or recent parades by the North Korean army offer chilling reminders of the costs of conformity.[79] Clips from the television series *The Office* show different follower styles, including Stanley, the Isolate, and Dwight, the Diehard.[80] *30 Rock* offers a parody of Tina Fey receiving a Followership award.[81] Other interesting portraits include a Chinese activist in the Tiananmen Square protest, and a Kamikaze pilot during World War II.[82] A chilling account of a high school teacher who created a cult is based on a real experience.[83] For discussion of whistle-blowing, *The Insider* chronicles the story of an executive willing to violate a confidential non-disclosure agreement in order to expose tobacco industry abuses on *60 Minutes*. A particularly compelling episode features a meeting between journalists and CBS corporate representatives (including a lawyer) who want to censor the story. Some more nuanced portraits of the follower's role appear in *The Remains of the Day*, discussed in Chapter 12, in which a butler played by Anthony Hopkins faces ethical conflicts with his employer, a Nazi sympathizer in the pre–World War II era.

2. ADAPTIVE LEADERSHIP

Ronald A. Heifetz, Leadership without Easy Answers

(Cambridge, MA: Belknap Press of Harvard University Press, 1994), pp. 88-100

Tacoma

On July 12, 1983, the head of the U.S. Environmental Protection Agency (EPA), William Ruckelshaus, took unprecedented action in a case involving a copper plant owned by the American Smelting and Refining Company (Asarco) near Tacoma, Washington. The Asarco plant was the only one in the nation to use copper ore with a high content of arsenic, and arsenic had been found to cause cancer. As authorized by Amendments to the Clean Air Act of 1970, Ruckelshaus was expected to decide what to do about the plant; in particular, he had to determine what constituted an "ample margin of safety" in the plant's operation to protect public health.

This was both a technically and politically difficult question. In the years since the 1970 Clean Air Act Amendments had been written, scientists were discovering that many hazardous wastes lacked a clear threshold of safety. Even a minuscule amount of "nonthreshold chemicals" could produce adverse effects. As Ruckelshaus put it in his June 1983 address to the National Academy of Sciences, "We must assume that life now takes place in a minefield of risks from hundreds, perhaps thousands, of substances. No more can we tell the public: You are home free with an adequate margin of safety."

The Asarco plant had long been regarded as one of the major polluters in the Northwestern United States, but it had also provided employment to generations of people since its opening in 1890. By 1983, nearly one hundred years later, the plant employed about 575 workers in the town of Ruston with a payroll of $23 million. It contributed significantly to the local economy through its purchases of $12 million worth of supplies, and it provided $13 million of revenue to auxiliary businesses in addition to paying $3 million in state and local taxes. If Asarco were to close the plant, the state of Washington would have to pay as much as $5.5 million in unemployment benefits. Closing the plant would be a devastating blow to a region where several major industries had not yet recovered from recession.

    ... The Asarco company itself was well aware of the pollution problem. Under pressure from the regional air pollution authority, Asarco had spent about $40 million since 1970 in equipment and practices to reduce emissions. In the late 1970s they had agreed to install, by 1984, secondary converter hoods at a cost of roughly $4 million to bring emissions down further. Indeed, the hoods were considered the best available technology to reduce pollution at a smelter like Asarco's. Going further would require one of three options: develop a new technology to reduce emissions; ship in low arsenic ore at high cost; or convert the entire plant to electric smelting, a different process altogether, at a projected cost of $150 million.

    According to the company, any of these three options would force the closing of the plant. World copper prices had crashed between 1980 and 1982 from $1.45 per pound to 60 cents per pound. To break even, the Asarco plant required 82 cents per pound, which meant that at current prices it was losing money already.

    The battle, like many environmental battles, was pitched between jobs and health. According to the EPA, installing the converter hoods as planned would reduce the risk of arsenic related cancer from four persons a year to one. Would this be acceptable? Did an "ample margin of safety" to protect public health require more? Should regulations demand zero emissions? Or was the livelihood generated by the plant worth the added risk of one case of cancer per year?

    Complicating these questions was the fact that the emissions, and thus the risks of cancer, were spread out over a twelve mile area that involved people even at a distance from the plant and its jobs. For example, Vashon Island lay two miles offshore, but because of prevailing winds it became, as one resident put it, "the dumping grounds for these pollutants without any benefits such as jobs or Asarco tax payments." Many islanders were afraid of the high levels of arsenic found in the urine samples of their children and in the soil from their local gardens. Should they bear the side-effects of Asarco? People in the city of Tacoma were in the same predicament. Receiving tons of air pollution a year from the plant, and few tax benefits, one member of the Tacoma city council said it was as if "somebody [were] standing on the other side of the city line with a thirty-ought-six [rifle] and firing it into Tacoma."

    Who should decide? By habit and statute, Ruckelshaus and the EPA were supposed to decide. The company and many of its workers looked to the EPA to confirm the acceptability of the actions they were about to take by spending $4 million on converter hoods. They were using the best available technology to reduce emissions from their plant. They looked to the EPA to resist taking action that would push them economically over the brink. Yet many area residents, along with environmental activists, looked to the EPA to provide "an ample margin of safety," and were quite willing to push the plant to the edge, if not over it, to reduce emissions significantly further.

Remarkably, Ruckelshaus, on July 12, 1983, refused publicly and dramatically to decide on his own. Going way beyond the perfunctory public hearings mandated by statute to accompany national rulemaking, Ruckelshaus proposed to engage the community at large in facing the problem. He announced the EPA's intention to solicit actively the views and wishes of the people that would be most affected by the EPA ruling. "For me to sit here in Washington and tell the people of Tacoma what is an acceptable risk would be at best arrogant and at worst inexcusable." As he later told the *Los Angeles Times*: "My view is that these are the kinds of tough, balancing questions that we're involved in here in this country in trying to regulate all kinds of hazardous substances. I don't like these questions either, but the societal issue is what risks are we willing to take and for what benefits?" Ruckelshaus even quoted Thomas Jefferson to back up his unprecedented stand: "If we think (the people) not enlightened enough to exercise their control with a wholesome discretion, the remedy is not to take it from them, but to inform their discretion." . . .

Few people reacted positively. The press framed the issue starkly: "What Cost a Life? EPA Asks Tacoma" (*Los Angeles Times*), "Smelter Workers Have Choice: Keep their Jobs or their Health" (*Chicago Tribune*). *The New York Times* ran an editorial that branded "Mr. Ruckelshaus as Caesar . . . who would ask the amphitheater crowd to signal with thumbs up or down whether a defeated gladiator should live or die." For Ruckelshaus to "impose such an impossible choice on Tacomans was . . . inexcusable." The head of the local chapter of the Sierra Club said, "It is up to the EPA to protect public health, not to ask the public what it is willing to sacrifice not to die from cancer." In the community's opinion as well, Ruckelshaus was neglecting his duties. Local citizens called it "copping out." "We elected people to run our government; we don't expect them to turn around and ask us to run it for them."

Ruckelshaus fought back in various encounters with the press. In a letter to *The New York Times,* he wrote, "Your Caesar analogy is seriously flawed. The Roman Caesars asked the crowd for thumbs up or down before sparing or condemning the gladiator. In Tacoma, the ones being asked for their reaction are at risk themselves. No one ever asked the gladiator his opinion, which may be the principal difference between Rome and the EPA." "Listen," he told the *Los Angeles Times,* "I know people don't like these kinds of decisions. Welcome to the world of regulation. People have demanded to be involved and now I have involved them and they say: 'Don't ask that question.' What's the alternative? Don't involve them?"

Resistance to Ruckelshaus also ran high within the EPA itself. Never before had the agency pushed problems back into the laps of a community. Like most government officials, managers within the EPA took seriously their charge to solve problems on behalf of the public. Indeed, public involvement seemed so messy a process compared with rational and expert decisionmaking that even the public hearings demanded by law were seen more as a formality to be suffered than an essential component of the problem-solving process. As a regional staff member described, "At headquarters [in Washington, D.C.] they thought we were a bunch of bozos out here in the region. They could not understand why we were scrambling and bending over backwards to organize the workshops and put out easily digestible information for the public."

As one might expect, the three public workshops held that August were controversial and packed with people, including a large number of smelter workers, union representatives, local citizen organizations, and environmental groups. The first workshop was held on Vashon Island, and the last two in Tacoma itself. The format was the same for all three, and all were covered by local and national television. After a formal presentation by the EPA staff, with graphs and charts to illustrate the technical facts regarding arsenic emission, dispersion, and the risk of illness, the audience was divided into smaller groups to facilitate individual responses. The EPA staff distributed several handouts with fact sheets, illustrations of how hooding helped control emissions, and excerpts from Ruckelshaus's National Academy of Sciences speech which outlined his philosophy (and Jefferson's) of public education. They then circulated among the groups to answer questions and record the comments of participants.

Many of the comments had little to do with verifiable facts. Hired by the EPA to observe, the dean of the School of Public Health at the University of Washington remarked on how "the personal nature of the complaints and questions made a striking counterpoint to the presentations of meteorological models and health effect extrapolations." People asked whether or not they could eat food from their Vashon Island gardens, how much soil should they remove to make it safe, how would their pets be affected. One woman asked, "Will my child die of cancer?"

The workshops had both immediate and subtle effects. Immediately, the EPA and the public learned some lessons. As one analyst for the EPA described, "We . . . got educated. The questions raised at the workshops sent some people back to the drawing board." Several public groups asked the EPA to postpone the formal hearings, scheduled for late August, to allow them more time to prepare testimony. In the meantime, the public held more workshops on its own under the sponsorship of the city of Tacoma and the Steel-worker's Union. Many more questions were raised, and not only questions about pollution and health, but about other options as well, like diversifying the local economy. Yet the EPA was still taking the heat. Some comments bordered on the openly hostile, "I have seen studies which show that stress is the main source of cancer; the EPA is one main cause of stress."

By the time of the hearings in November, the EPA had clarified several scientific questions raised by the public's involvement. Significantly, its computer model estimating the amount of arsenic emissions had been wrong. Yet the corrected model still predicted a risk of one additional cancer death per year from arsenic, even after placement of the new hooding devices.

The workshops and hearings surprised the staff at the EPA. As Ruckelshaus put it, local citizens had shown that they were "capable of understanding [the problem of the smelter] in its complexities and dealing with it and coming back to us with rather sensible suggestions." In fact, "the public — the non-technical, unschooled public — came back with some very good suggestions as to how they could reduce the emissions of arsenic in the plant [and still keep it open]."

Perhaps of greater import, local people began to see the situation in a new light. Rather than view it solely as a conflict between jobs and health, many people began to see a new possibility: the diversification of the local economy. Although no one knew whether or not the plant would have to close in the near future, many could see that remaining so dependent on this one struggling industry was a bad idea.

No one, including Ruckelshaus, saw the new possibility at the start. The idea of diversification, although obvious in retrospect, had not been part of anyone's mindset. The EPA, industry, labor, environmentalists, and local officials had been thinking in more narrow terms of emissions, health risks, and jobs. It took the noisy and conflictive process of public workshops, debates in the press, and the mobilization of neighborhoods to generate new ideas.

One year later, in June 1984, although Ruckelshaus had not yet come to a decision, Asarco announced that it would close the Tacoma plant the following year. Precipitated primarily by depressed copper prices and shortages of high-arsenic copper ore, Asarco nevertheless spread the blame for the shutdown to federal, state, and local environmental agencies for requiring it to install converter hoods costing $3 million by the end of that year. Furthermore, Asarco claimed that the EPA would require a great deal more investment in the future. Although this was not true, since Ruckelshaus had not yet made a final ruling, somebody would have to take the heat, and the EPA was the obvious lightning rod. As one worker told reporters, "I'll tell you something, it's the EPA's fault!"

Yet the community, however distressed, was also better prepared than it might have been. By the time the announcement came in 1984, the new goal had already been set: finding new jobs for the workers and attracting new industry to the region. When the plant closed in 1985, Tacoma and Ruston already had begun the task of diversifying its economy. People had come to the early workshops displaying buttons labeled either "Jobs" or "Health." By the final workshops, people were sporting buttons that said "BOTH."

In retrospect, nearly ten years later, Colin Conant, Executive Director of the Private Industry Council for Tacoma, looked back on the efforts of the Dislocated Workers Project for those laid off by Asarco:

> We created a model for re-training the workforce, and the community got behind it. We got many many people involved on advisory committees: the labor union, United Way, the Private Industry Council, Asarco, the Economic Development Board, employees, and the State Employment Security Department. People might do it that way now, but back then nobody was. The support made a big difference in how well people adjusted. It could have been much more psychologically disruptive. There were far fewer casualties than there might have been without so many people and organizations backing us up. Since Asarco's closing, there have been several more closings in the area and we basically applied the same model. We learned a lot from how we did it then.

In addition to helping the workers adapt, the Asarco effort also served as a model in later years for resolving other environmental disputes in the Tacoma area. . . .

Implications

Ruckelshaus recognized that the Asarco situation represented an adaptive challenge rather than a technical problem. Consequently, he resisted pressures from within the EPA and from the public to provide an authoritative solution. Instead, he chose to engage people in facing the challenge. By doing so, he placed an unusual problem in the laps of his own agency. The EPA had no real experience in orchestrating public deliberation. Public hearings routinely had been pro forma, with presentations of technical arguments by interested parties and little more. Hearings tended to focus on narrowly defined issues, without much creativity in exploring new possibilities like diversifying a local economy. Parties did not talk to one another; they presented testimony to a panel of EPA administrators and experts.

The EPA had never seen itself in the role of orchestrating public thinking on problems. In the public workshops in Tacoma, it quickly found itself "over its head" in problems about which its technical expertise meant little. What could pollution experts say about the value of jobs versus the value of health, or ways to cope with a risk-filled life, or paths to economic diversification?

Bearing the brunt of managing the tasks of informing and involving the public, the regional EPA office exhausted itself in the undertaking. Roughly thirty people devoted full time for four months to this one case. Was it worth it? According to one official, the whole "process proved terrifically costly and time-consuming." And in the end, the decision was still the EPA's to make.

Yet there were at least three significant benefits. First, within the EPA itself, the staff at headquarters began to appreciate what it meant to be on the frontlines. Because the regional staff had frequent contact with area groups, they knew better how to engage with the public. On arriving in Tacoma, staff from Washington, D.C., had quickly found themselves out of touch with the real-world import of scientific findings at the local level. As one regional staff member put it, "When they arrived in Tacoma and found themselves face-to-face with a well-informed and often angry public, they began to appreciate our problem a little better." Now, information relevant to public policymaking would flow up from the frontlines rather than just down from headquarters. That made policymaking better. Routine procedures to involve the community began to change. In following years, the EPA began to act as a frequent sponsor and forum for negotiation among stakeholders to resolve environmental disputes. Furthermore, the agency began routinely to make use of the central distinction Ruckelshaus had made in Tacoma—between the science of assessing risk and the problem of managing the public implications of living with risk. The focus on risk management broadened the mission of the EPA, giving a larger context to its previously narrow scientific orientation.

Second, the Tacoma experiment in public deliberation restored the credibility of the EPA, which in 1983 had just come out of two years mired in public scandal. . . . As a member of the Washington Environmental Council put it, the EPA's cooperation and openness went "a long way toward restoring trust and confidence in the agency here in the region." Even previous skeptics of public deliberation later praised the effort. Ruth Weiner of the Sierra Club, who had criticized Ruckelshaus earlier for "copping out," stated at the conclusion of her public testimony that the Clean Air Act "requires public involvement." "Moreover," she said, "in becoming involved, the public begins to appreciate the difficulty attendant on making regulatory decision, the ease with which EPA can be made a scapegoat because the agency's blunders are so readily magnified, and the inadequacy of simply identifying 'heroes' and 'villains' in environmental protection. It may have been hard work and a headache for all of us, but the public involvement is most certainly worth it."

Third, and perhaps most significantly, the communities of Tacoma and Ruston began seeing the need to adapt. Certain facts were now being faced. Asarco's use of outdated technology in its Ruston plant made it only sporadically competitive in the world copper market. The town's reliance on a single industry placed it in a precarious position of dependence. In addition, some people were paying the price of the plant in terms of health, yet without benefit from jobs or tax revenues.

With the advantage of hindsight, we can see these benefits of public engagement. However, when Ruckelshaus broke precedent by involving the public in solving its problem, he met resistance from every quarter: industry, environmental interests, labor, the press, and within the EPA itself. With problems as tough as jobs, health, and economic diversification, it is no wonder that everyone expects authority to make the decision. That seems our inclination — to look to someone or some agency to take the heat in choosing what to do. Ordinarily, these expectations act as constraints on people in authority, inhibiting them from exercising leadership. Yet Ruckelshaus cut against the grain when he insisted that the public realize that the job of regulating pollutants was not simply a technical matter of setting safe thresholds of emission. Trade-offs would have to be made that involved value conflicts not amenable to scientific analysis. And if those trade-offs between jobs and health were to be faced, then perhaps new adaptations might be achieved in the face of loss.

Ruckelshaus insisted that these problems represented challenges to business-as-usual. At the very least, public attitudes toward living with risk had to change. Otherwise, agencies like the EPA would continue to be called upon to do the impossible, to provide fixes for what could not be fixed by fiat from above. Hard choices were necessary, requiring people to clarify and change their values. The EPA could stimulate those changes but it could not make them. . . .

NOTES AND QUESTIONS

1. According to Heifetz, "Ruckelshaus recognized that the Asarco situation represented an adaptive challenge rather than a technical solution." What about the case made that characterization appropriate? Would the same kind of participatory process be appropriate for any situation requiring a trade-off between health and economic stability? If not, what distinguished the Asarco situation? Could you imagine some variation of Ruckelshaus's approach guiding the Obama administration's decision about whether to allow offshore drilling in the wake of the 2010 British Petroleum oil well disaster?

2. Heifetz describes three primary benefits from the way Ruckelshaus proceeded: it improved the decision-making process at EPA, it restored the public credibility of the agency, and it forced the community to diversify its economy. Do you think the leaders of Asarco would come to the same assessment? Are their perspectives important in evaluating the outcome?
3. What if Asarco had not decided to close the plant and Ruckelshaus had been forced to make a decision? Suppose that his view was different from that of the community. How would you weigh the risks and benefits of involving stakeholders if you are not prepared to defer to their decision?

3. FOSTERING INNOVATION AND MANAGING CHANGE

Former army chief of staff Eric Shinseki observed that "[i]f you don't like change, you're going to like irrelevance even less."[84] Any successful organization or movement needs to adapt to social, political, economic, and technological developments. Any effective leader needs to create the conditions for such adaptation. Estimates suggest that most companies need moderate change at least once a year and major changes every four to five years.[85] In the private sector, those that do not adapt do not survive. The average life expectancy of companies in the developed world is about twelve years, and half fail before their first decade.[86] In the public sector, the insulation from competition may somewhat lessen the pressures for change, but organizations that lose touch with stakeholders' needs will eventually pay the price in diminished legitimacy and inadequate political and financial support.[87]

Change comes in many forms, but much of the literature on leadership stresses innovation, defined as adaptation of an idea to a new setting.[88] Unlike invention or creativity, which refers to the development of something new, and may involve only individual effort and unsuccessful implementation, innovation requires collective practices that produce change.[89] The importance of innovation varies by context. In Jim Collins's research on "great" companies — those with sustained high economic performance — only about half made innovation a core value.[90] But whether or not they excel at innovation, successful organizations must at least create conditions for adaptation. Leaders need not themselves be the source of innovative ideas, but they do need to foster a culture that anticipates change and that positions their organizations accordingly. Collins notes that Thomas Edison's greatest innovation was not the light bulb, but the concept of a research and development lab.[91] Innovation is particularly critical in contexts of rapidly evolving technologies or shifting stakeholder expectations. As Peter Drucker famously observed, the "best way to predict the future is to create it," and "[w]hat brought you here won't get you there."[92]

Change occurs on a continuum, ranging in speed and scope. At one end of the spectrum lies incremental evolution of norms and practices; at the other end lies sudden and dramatic progress.[93] The impetus for such innovation varies. A crisis frequently dramatizes the need for change and creates the sense of urgency that makes it possible. A slow erosion of market power or public support can also propel organizations into action, as can regulatory reforms or recurrent problems that have yielded only temporary solutions.[94]

Technological innovations can also make clear the need for organizational innovation; the rise in Internet usage is an obvious example.

Experts identify three stages in which leaders can guide change.[95] The initial phase requires overcoming inertia and creating a compelling vision for the future.[96] To this end, leaders must first identify the obstacles to change in their own organizations. In some contexts, the problem lies in inadequate investment in research and development. Other organizations suffer from the "curse of homogeneity": too many insiders are drinking the same Kool-Aid, or have too much personal investment in outdated strategies.[97] To counteract these tendencies, leaders can identify looming problems or opportunities, and build coalitions to propose appropriate responses. Getting buy-in from key participants at an early stage can help minimize opposition later.[98] Reaching people on an emotional level through direct experience, compelling stories, and visual images can often create the urgency that inspires action. Researchers on influence and innovation offer multiple examples. Sending American auto workers to a Japanese plant with 40 percent higher productivity broke through their denial and enlisted them as agents for change.[99] Asking senior medical care executives to investigate examples of fatal but preventable mistakes at their own hospitals gave them a sense of the human tragedies that are often masked by data spreadsheets; the result was a new commitment to specific remedial actions.[100] Requiring employees to listen to a recording of an angry business customer describing unresponsive sales personnel taught them to become better listeners. A visually compelling strategy came from an executive who could not get his division presidents to see the waste created by non-uniform purchasing procedures, which he estimated was costing about $200 million a year. To dramatize the problem, he had an intern collect samples of one product—factory gloves—used in every division. The leader then displayed the 424 different gloves on a table, with prices varying from $5 to $17 for essentially the same item. After inviting all the division presidents to view the display, he turned it into a traveling road show. That exhibit, coupled with benchmarking research showing how other competitors handled the issue, created the necessary impetus for reform.[101]

A second stage involves developing a strategy for implementing change and enlisting others in its support. That requires effectively communicating the mission, removing obstacles to its realization, encouraging innovation, and promoting short-term visible improvements that can lay foundations for broader transformations.[102] Theorists such as Harvard professor Rosabeth Moss Kanter describe the need to support three levels of a pyramid. At the base should be a large number of incremental strategies that suggest promising directions. In the middle should be a portfolio of plausible early stage ventures or prototypes. At the top should be "a few big bets about the future."[103] To foster creative ideas at the base, some organizations give employees unstructured time or special rewards for innovation. In settings where such ideas are especially critical, enabling employees to "fail early, fail often" without penalty may be necessary to encourage risk.[104] Other common strategies for change include fostering friendly rivalry among divisions or branches; streamlining approval processes; engaging in benchmarking through comparative analysis of other successful projects; and establishing contests, team projects, and other support structures for creative problem solving.[105] Some professional service firms have created innovative brainstorming sessions or centers for clients and employees, and online resources to jump-start innovation programs in branch offices.[106]

Where people are the problem, leaders can seek ways to address their concerns or to work around resisters. The typical reasons why people oppose change are its threats to their status, power, autonomy, competence, comfort, and job security.[107] Leaders can help allay such concerns by proactively helping employees adapt, retool, or find other assignments or positions.[108]

A third stage involves assessing and consolidating change. Here, the key is identifying the right time and metrics to evaluate progress. Premature assessment can stifle innovation. "Pulling up the radishes" to see how they are growing defeats the enterprise.[109] But at some point, the test of a good idea is whether it can be implemented effectively. Leaders ultimately will be judged less by their broad visions than by their actual accomplishments. In this final stage of change, leaders need to institutionalize what works, create systems and reward structures that reinforce progress, and look for ways to continue reinvigorating the process.[110]

In *Switch,* psychologists Chip Heath and Dan Heath analogize the process of leading change to riding an elephant. The rider holds the reins, but if the elephant does not want to go, they are both stuck. To make progress, the rider needs to know the direction, motivate the elephant, and clear the path of obstacles.[111] If you wanted to change some aspect of your environment, what strategies might this metaphor suggest?

PROBLEM 4-4

1. Consider an example of organizational change with which you are familiar. What factors prompted the organization to act? What role did its leaders play? How successful were they? What resistance did they confront? What might you have done differently?
2. Consider an example of an organization that failed to innovate. A case in point is Blockbuster Video. Its basic business model, which required customers to go to stores to rent movies and pay late fees for tardy returns, became unsustainable when Netflix developed a rival mail order system with no such fees. It took Blockbuster six years to market a competing system, and it did so only after failed efforts to expand store sales of other film-related merchandise, such as T-shirts, toys, and books. The delay proved deadly. In 2002, Blockbuster had 8000 stores and a market value of $3 billion. In 2010, it was broke. When it filed for bankruptcy, Netflix had profits of $9 million.[112] What do you think accounts for this failure to adapt to market changes? What broader lessons does this example, or similar business failures, suggest?
3. Meet with other members in your class in groups of four to brainstorm about solutions to a problem at your institution. Each member should write down three proposed solutions to share with the group. After everyone has reported their ideas, the group should discuss them in order, modify any proposals in light of the discussion, and then vote for their top three

choices. The group should then compare the top three ideas and either reach consensus on one or begin a new round of brainstorming. After a solution has been identified, members should evaluate the process and the result.

4. FEEDBACK

One of the key ways that leaders can build effective relationships with followers is through constructive feedback. Candid dialogue is particularly critical when individuals are not performing in ways consistent with organizational needs and expectations. To address such performance difficulties, leaders should consider underlying causes.

- Awareness: do individuals know how others perceive their work and how they are falling short?
- Competence: do individuals have the right skills, experience, and knowledge?
- Barriers: do individuals have adequate responsibility, authority, and support?
- Motivation: do individuals want to do what is necessary, do they see a need to do it, and do they believe they will be rewarded for doing it?

In providing feedback around such issues, leaders need to structure candid dialogue that involves active listening and mutual problem solving.[113] Best practices for feedback include

- making sure that the person in need of coaching is ready to hear it, and that there is sufficient time and privacy for honest conversation;
- providing support and encouragement as well as criticism, and identifying positive as well as negative behaviors;
- presenting specific and recent examples, and giving the other person full opportunity to respond, explain, and correct any misperceptions; and
- developing a joint action plan, which includes ways of helping the other person improve.[114]

C. CONFLICT MANAGEMENT

A related way in which leaders exercise influence is through resolving, or at least managing, conflict. They play multiple roles: negotiating and mediating disputes, advising disputants, and structuring processes for dispute resolution. These roles are significant in terms of the time they require and the impact they have on performance. Estimates suggest that business leaders spend between 15 and 40 percent of their time dealing with conflicts.[115] For lawyers holding leadership positions, the percentage may be even higher. Not only do they face problems in their own workplaces, they also represent clients involved in disputes. Policy leaders similarly confront conflict in multiple settings involving subordinates, peers, and other stakeholders.

Failure to handle conflict effectively carries substantial costs. Unresolved workplace disputes can lead to stress, mental health difficulties, turnover, absenteeism, lack of cooperation and communication, litigation, retaliation, sabotage, and sometimes even violence. Fear of conflict can inhibit constructive criticism. Mishandled legal disputes can cost millions, ruin reputations, and derail careers. In cases of international conflict or civil war, the human costs are staggering.

Yet, when managed effectively, conflict can be a source of necessary communication and change. It can provide the catalyst for innovation and challenges to received wisdom. There is truth in the quip that when two people always agree, "one of them is unnecessary."[116] Conflict can also signal problems in relationships or organizational practices that need attention. In short, conflict can be a source of leaders' best ideas as well as worst failures.[117]

The following overview explores conflict resolution skills that are necessary for any leadership position. For those interested in the topic, it also provides references to more in-depth treatment of negotiation, mediation, international relations, interpersonal dynamics, alternative dispute resolution, and related topics. The point here is not to offer an exhaustive summary, but rather to offer basic foundations for dealing with recurrent leadership challenges.

1. THE DYNAMICS OF CONFLICT

Definitions of conflict vary. Some experts include any situation involving "apparently incompatible interests, goals, principles, or feelings."[118] Others define it as a struggle over values, resources, status, and power.[119] In some settings, it makes sense to distinguish between conflicts involving relationships and those involving tasks or issues. Of the disputes common in workplaces, employees express most frustration with those raising relational issues, such as conflicting work styles or personalities.[120] Many circumstances hold potential for conflict, but whether it develops depends on factors including the importance of issues at stake, the costs of fighting for them, the resources available, and the likelihood of success.

The causes of conflict obviously vary, but certain patterns are common. Often a history of unresolved differences and repressed animosity will flare up in response to some precipitating event or change in conditions. Even relatively trivial incidents can become hot buttons for dispute when invested with deeper meaning.

The stakes in conflict can include values (such as priorities and ethical commitments), interests (such as money, status, or control) and underlying needs (such as security, recognition, or meaning).[121] Root causes frequently involve objective circumstances, such as insufficient resources; incompatible interests; power disparities; and differences in race, ethnicity, religion, and culture. Subjective perceptions matter as well, particularly when fueled by incomplete information, miscommunication, and cognitive biases.[122] For example, a history of acrimony may result in attribution errors; parties may assign malicious motives to opponents' actions, rather than consider more benign explanations. Selective perception can then kick in to confirm prior assumptions in order to reduce cognitive dissonance.[123] People also tend to define fairness in terms of distributional principles (such as equality, need, merit, and precedent) that favor their own self-interest.[124] And they often engage in "reactive devaluation": their perception of the attractiveness of a proposal or concession diminishes if it comes from an opponent.[125] Recall the study described in Chapter 3, in which the researcher took peace proposals developed by Israeli negotiators and mislabeled them as Palestinian proposals, and mislabeled Palestinian proposals as Israeli proposals. When he asked Israeli citizens to evaluate the suggestions, they preferred those misattributed to Israelis.[126]

Once conflicts escalate, they are unlikely to be resolved as long as underlying causes remain unaddressed. Tensions may ebb and flow, but a cycle of resistance and retaliation will continue, sometimes resulting in intractable disputes that parties pursue as ends in themselves.

2. RESPONSES TO CONFLICT

Responses to conflict fall into certain common categories. Experts use somewhat different labels, but generally identify avoidance, contention, coercion, appeasement, compromise, and collaboration. No single approach is categorically preferable, and research on relative effectiveness is mixed.[127] On the whole, however, experts agree on certain general points.

Avoidance is many people's preferred response, and with reason.[128] Open confrontation risks unpleasantness, stress, and retaliation, and may seem pointless if the adversary has substantially greater power and a history of unresponsiveness. Leaders' desire for approval can also keep them from using their influence to broach difficult issues.[129] Yet, as a general matter, research suggests that avoidance should be avoided. Unresolved problems are likely to fester, impair productivity, and lead to more costly confrontations later. Of course, under some circumstances, flight may be preferable to fight. Delayed response makes sense if it gives parties time to let their emotions cool and the adrenaline rush subside so they can carefully consider their reaction.[130] Temporary disengagement can be useful to prevent hostilities that will be difficult to remedy later, but it should not substitute for mutual problem solving under less volatile circumstances.

More direct responses to conflict involve contention or coercion. Openly vying for victory or imposing a solution authoritatively can seem satisfying to the winning party in the short run, but it is often counterproductive in the long term. In some instances, quick decisive action may be justifiable, and a prudent means of deterring further hostile acts. But outcomes that leave losers' fundamental needs or immediate interests unmet are likely to prove unstable, and to provoke resentment, resistance, or recurring confrontations. Competitive and coercive approaches also short-circuit opportunities for more creative, mutually acceptable solutions.

The same is true of appeasement. Parties who yield not because they believe the outcome is reasonable, but because they perceive no viable alternative, may nurse grievances that will erupt in more destructive fashion later. Moreover, capitulation may encourage even more oppressive behavior from a victorious bully. As experts note, "[T]he leader who always appeases is like someone who feeds crocodiles hoping that they'll eat him last."[131]

An often preferable option is compromise. Splitting differences may be productive particularly in contexts involving zero-sum trade-offs, in which no party can be made better-off without the other party suffering. But that approach risks leaving both sides dissatisfied, and it may fail to promote fair resolutions if the baseline for division is highly unequal.[132]

The alternative most experts promote is collaboration, or what some label integrative problem solving. Under this approach, parties work together to identify win-win outcomes that build on shared concerns and mutual respect.[133] Although this process has obvious advantages when it is successful, it tends to be time consuming, and may not work if parties' differences are too great.

Cultural as well as situational differences will inform the choice of responses. Groups vary in their tolerance for open disagreement and expression of emotion, and their preferences in negotiating styles and outcomes. Asian societies, for example, tend to be relatively restrained and accommodating, and to ascribe high value to harmonious relationships.[134] Yet individuals carry multiple identities—national, religious, racial, gender, occupational, and so forth. Stereotyping on the basis of any single attribute is bound to be misleading.[135] Leaders' responses to conflict thus need to be sensitive to diversity without making crude generalizations based on demographic characteristics.

3. STRATEGIES

Leaders play multiple roles in conflict management. They negotiate, mediate, facilitate, and advise concerning specific disputes, and they create organizational structures designed to prevent, resolve, or creatively use conflict. Each of these roles presents distinct challenges but also calls for certain common skills and strategies.

The first requirement is knowledge, both of self and others. In seeking to resolve conflicts in which they are personally involved, leaders need to be aware of their own "hot buttons," their underlying interests and needs, and their "best alternative to a negotiated agreement" (BATNA).[136] So for example, individuals who feel themselves losing control due to anger or anxiety can ask for a break, begin writing down constructive points that they wish to discuss later, or "freeze frames" by mentally imagining a pleasant situation or one in which they felt calm and self-confident.[137] An effective resolution often depends on learning as much as possible about the goals and concerns of everyone involved in the conflict. Seeking information from multiple sources is often critical, as is active or empathic listening. Common techniques involve listening without interrupting; restating points to be sure that the other parties' meaning is understood; paying attention to body language and what is unsaid as well as said; avoiding accusations, blame, moral judgment, or inflammatory rhetoric; probing for underlying reasons and concerns; and brainstorming about creative solutions.[138] It is often helpful for leaders to identify the effects that the other person's behavior is having, and how those might be inconsistent with that person's goals.[139] Once parties have identified a solution, they need to agree on specific steps for implementation, which may include strategies for avoiding problems in the future.

In their landmark negotiation primer, *Getting to Yes,* Roger Fisher and William Ury similarly suggest focusing on interests, not on positions; insisting on objective criteria for assessing those interests; and inventing options for mutual gain.[140] Although the book also suggested the need to "separate the people from the problem," Fisher has subsequently acknowledged that "[i]n some cases the people are the problem; negotiating a good relationship with them may be more important than the substantive outcome of any one negotiation."[141]

To that end, other experts advise that leaders be willing to reach out to restore productive communication. An apology that is genuine and does not make unwarranted concessions of fault can often be a first step in building trust and empathy. In short, the overarching goal should be to reframe the conflict as an opportunity for collaborative problem solving and to create the conditions that will enable such a resolution to occur.

That same approach is useful for leaders who are mediating conflict among others or facilitating its resolution through advice and coaching. This role typically involves

- establishing credibility and rapport by expressing concern for all parties and maintaining impartiality;
- insisting that parties remain civil, respectful, and committed to creating a productive working environment;
- helping parties identify shared values and objectives, and express underlying needs and concerns;
- providing a disinterested reliable source of information; and
- assisting the parties develop solutions and agree on a plan for action that is specific and avoids "toothless" promises (such as a willingness to seek input in the future).[142]

Research on resolving contested issues in group settings emphasizes creating common goals; maximizing information; multiplying proposed solutions; focusing the discussion on facts; ensuring that no significant issues are "undiscussable"; maintaining a balanced power structure; injecting humor; asking people to look at multiple sides of the same question; and resolving issues without forcing consensus.[143]

Leaders can also play a crucial role in creating "conflict competent" organizations. That requires creating cultures that value civility and constructive disagreement; provide multiple channels for dispute resolution; and offer support, training, and mediation for those involved in conflict.[144] Research makes clear that people's sense of the fairness of dispute resolution processes is even more important than substantive outcomes in promoting overall satisfaction and confidence, so leaders should be sure that organizational structures are meeting participants' expectations of equity and legitimacy.[145]

In *Leading through Conflict,* Mark Gerzon describes an example of rethinking organizational structures for handling friction in a global insurance company. Headquartered in the United States, the company had rapidly growing European and Asian divisions that came into conflict with American divisions over salary differentials, lack of follow-through for each others' multinational clients, and more subtle cultural tensions.[146] At prior meetings involving thirty senior executives of regional divisions, the practice had been to float ideas for new strategies and adopt those that received the most support. The result was that executives would spend countless hours giving examples about what someone else was doing wrong and needed to change. With the help of an international consulting group, the leader structured the meeting differently. Each executive was placed on a team charged with taking responsibility for the company's problems and proposing solutions. The point was to force them out of their self-interested positions and make them wrestle with the big picture.

Consider circumstances in which you have faced similar conflicts. Would such a strategy have been effective? If not, what other approaches might have worked better?

PROBLEM 4-5

1. How would you evaluate your own strengths and weaknesses concerning conflict management?[147] Make a list of areas in which you could improve. If you have hot buttons, how could you better address them? Think of two recent situations in which you have experienced significant conflict. How well did you manage them? What could you have done differently? To aid your analysis, make a list of all the strategies that you pursued and all the barriers that you confronted. Make another list of all the thoughts and feelings that you did not express. Think about why you did not voice those concerns and whether a fuller discussion would have yielded a better resolution. Identify approaches that might be effective in similar future situations.
2. Structure a conversation with someone with whom you have a significant disagreement. Actively listen to his or her views and try to understand the situation from your partner's point of view. Challenge yourself to gain new insights and information, and to avoid passing judgment. Ask your partner to listen to your responses and give you feedback on what was most and least persuasive.
3. Investigate a conflict that has generated significant public attention. What were its underlying causes and dynamics? What barriers to resolution did opposing sides face? How well did leaders handle the situation? What might you have done differently?

MEDIA RESOURCES

Masterful examples of conflict resolution, influence, and leader-follower behavior appear in *Invictus*, a film based on Nelson Mandela's early years as president of South Africa and his strategies to help the country overcome the bitter legacy of apartheid. As Chapter 12 notes, one of the first tests of his strategies comes when the new black commander of the presidential bodyguards objects to Mandela's order to include white officers. These individuals were part of the previous administration's law enforcement structure, which had brutalized blacks. Mandela insists that white guards be among his protectors. "Reconciliation and forgiveness begin here," he tells the commander.

"Forgiveness liberates the soul." The film's main focus is the unlikely relationship between Mandela and François Pienaar, captain of the nation's largely white rugby team. As the story begins, the team, the Springboks, are revered by whites, reviled by blacks, and ridiculed by the sporting world for their lackluster performance. The newly black-controlled rugby association wants to change the team's name, a gesture that Mandela believes will inflame the white community. In a crucial scene, he prevents the change. He then enlists Pienaar in an effort to alter the team's image and performance in time for the 1995 Rugby World Cup finals, scheduled to be held in South Africa. With Mandela's coaching, Pienaar himself becomes a leader and an increasingly effective coach. He takes the team to Robben Island to tour the prison where Mandela was imprisoned for twenty-nine years, and has them provide workshops for impoverished black youths. As followers on the team come to see their symbolic role in the nation's reconciliation, their performance rises to the occasion.

Other examples of influence come from *The Young Victoria*. One scene shows her resolving a dispute over the composition of her ladies-in-waiting. Although she revels in a peremptory exercise of power, she quickly comes to regret the political fallout that it engenders.

D. COMMUNICATION

1. STRATEGIES

One of the critical ways that leaders exercise influence is through communication. In both public and private settings, leaders try to persuade followers, allies, adversaries, and the broader public. Although not everyone is equally skilled in all forums, any aspiring leader needs to master certain basic techniques of effective communication. The excerpts below set forth key principles, beginning with those applicable to oral presentations.

DEBORAH L. RHODE, "PUBLIC PRESENTATIONS"

(Unpublished speech, Stanford, California, 2010)

Knowledge is power in leadership as in life, and public presentations are no exception. The first step in preparation is to know your objectives, your audience, your occasion, and your substance.

Speakers often have multiple agendas and multiple constituencies that can pull in different directions. For example, politicians need to consider whether a particular speech is primarily intended to mobilize their base, persuade uncommitted voters, attract favorable media coverage, shore up their legacy, or send a message to other national and international leaders. Is a presentation to employees or potential clients designed mainly to convey information, build a relationship, sell an idea, or motivate change? What speakers most hope to accomplish needs to guide their style and substance. The importance of such choices is captured in Roman historian Cato's famous observation: "When Cicero spoke, people marveled. When Caesar spoke, people marched."

Obvious though the need for clarity of purpose may seem, even seasoned speakers can lose sight of their main objective. Robert Reich, former Secretary of Labor in the Clinton administration wryly recalls his own foibles in preparing for his Senate confirmation hearing. When asked in practice sessions about any significant — and therefore potentially divisive — issue, his tendency as a professor of public policy was to elaborate his views. This was a mistake. As senior administration officials explained, "You have to respond to [Senators'] questions. You don't have to answer them. You *shouldn't* answer them. You're not expected to answer them." The main point of confirmation hearings, from Senators' point of view, was to give them, not the nominee, an opportunity to look learned and wise. The point from the nominee's point of view was to gain support, which called for dodging controversy while exuding deference. An ideal answer was something like, "Senator, you know far more about that issue than I do and I look forward to hearing your views in the months to come."[148] So too, professionals seeking jobs or pitching clients need to recall that their primary objective is to win support, not to score points by showing how much smarter they are than those asking questions. Throughout their presentations, speakers need to stay on message and avoid being thrown by minor distractions or technological malfunctions. Bill Gates famously experienced a computer shutdown during his public launch of Windows 98.[149] If it can happen to him, it can happen to anyone, so speakers should plan accordingly and have a backup strategy.

Knowledge of the audience is equally critical. How likely are members to be informed on the subject under discussion or sympathetic to the speakers' goals and objectives? How engaged or distracted will they be? Will they have read materials sent out in advance? Will they expect handouts, PowerPoints, or opportunities for interaction? What kind of arguments and evidence will be most persuasive? Humor tailored to the occasion can be highly effective. At a point in Clinton's presidency after his wife had taken enormous criticism for her role in health care reform and the Whitewater real estate scandal, the president opened his Gridiron speech before Washington journalists and politicians by expressing regret. "The First Lady is sorry she can't be with you tonight," he told them. "If you believe that, 'I've got some land in Arkansas I'd like to sell you.'"[150] Ronald Reagan scored a telling victory in his debates with presidential candidate Walter Mondale when he responded to a question about his age by stating, "I refuse to make age an issue in this election. I will not exploit, for political purposes, my opponent's youth and inexperience."[151]

Finding ways to establish credibility or connect with audience members, collectively or individually, is always helpful. If the introduction has not established the speaker's credibility, that is his or her first task, and the relevant credentials aren't always titles. Successful communicators have an art of finding or fabricating commonalities: a similar job, a family member who was from the area, a longstanding interest in a local product, athletic team, or landmark. It helps to make verbal or visual contact with as many members of the audience as possible, both before, during, and after the presentation. It is also important to gauge the audience's interest in the speaker's own experience. Overly self-referential material can leave captive audience members feeling like the P.G. Wodehouse character, who complains: "The Agee woman told us for three quarters of an hour how she came to write her beastly book when a simple apology was all that was required."[152]

Leaders also need to know their forum and to adapt their style accordingly. It is always crucial to convey energy and enthusiasm, but strategies for doing so need to vary. For example, television is a notoriously cool medium, and calls for low-key conversational styles, not the flamboyant oratorical flourishes that are effective before large crowds. Body language and appearance are equally important. Some research finds that content is less important than voice and nonverbal expression as a factor in evaluations of performance.[153] Eye contact, a smile, and a manner that demonstrates self-confidence and engagement can be critical, as is eliminating "verbal graffiti" ("ah," "um," "so").[154] Clothes and grooming can also matter, particularly for women, who face more intense scrutiny and more severe consequences for falling short.[155] First impressions are highly durable, and whether a speaker meets the audience's expectations is generally part of what is relevant.[156] If leaders don't know how to look the part, what else don't they know?

It is almost always a mistake to "speak from the heart," even if that is what the occasion seems to demand. Effective speakers prepare. They at least think about what they might say, even if they abandon or adapt their message in light of the circumstances. If the presentation needs to look unrehearsed, that often requires rehearsal. Speaking without notes is always impressive but doing it effectively generally requires preparation. Even the ablest speakers recognize as much. Winston Churchill practiced in his bath, and when a startled valet once came rushing to the door, Churchill explained: "I was not speaking to you Norman, I was addressing the House of Commons."[157]

Finally, the speaker needs to know the subject. That means not just substantive knowledge, but what part of that knowledge is most important and accessible in the format available. Many otherwise impressive presentations suffer from one fact too many, or maybe more than one. For main points, communication experts suggest a rule of three. The goal is to provide enough to support the main theme but not so much as to dwarf the audience's normal attention span. A compelling start and close are crucial, and they are particularly effective if tied together in a way that completes the circle and enhances coherence. A successful opening is often a story, an amusing quotation, or a surprising, counterintuitive claim that will attract audience interest. Humorist and screenwriter Nora Ephron makes the point with a story about her first day of a high school journalism course. The class was asked to write the lead for an article in the school newspaper about an upcoming conference. The entire faculty was to participate in an all-day program the following week in the state capitol, led by speakers including then California governor Pat Brown and the world renowned anthropologist Margaret Mead. Ephron recalled that she and most of her classmates produced opening sentences explaining "who, what, where, and when." No one spotted the lead that their teacher suggested: "There will be no school next Thursday."[158]

Communication research suggests a number of guiding principles about what makes for an effective presentation. Speakers should show emotion, emphasize stories not statistics, propose solutions, and appeal to common concerns and values. Effective means of accomplishing that end rely on metaphor, symbols, repetition, and terms of inclusion (we and our not them and they).[159] Even highly educated audiences, such as Stanford business students, are more likely to remember facts and figures presented through stories than through statistics, whether presented verbally or graphically.[160] In *Made to Stick*, Chip and Dan Heath offer a framework for communicating messages that will be retained: they should be simple, unexpected, concrete, credible, emotional, and tell a story [SUCCESs].[161] An example that makes their messages stick comes from a campaign by the Center for Science in the Public Interest. Its challenge was to reduce consumption of popcorn popped in coconut oil. Movie theatres used the oil because it provided an appealing texture and aroma, but it also was extremely high in saturated fats; one typical popcorn carton had almost twice the U.S. Department of Agriculture's recommended average for the entire day. Center staff recognized that a campaign based on that fact would "have zero appeal. It's dry, it's academic, who cares?"[162] Instead they staged a press conference with the following message: "A medium-sized 'butter' popcorn at a typical neighborhood movie theatre contains more artery-clogging fat than a bacon and egg breakfast, a Big Mac and fries for lunch, and a steak dinner with all the trimmings—combined." The conference included a buffet table with all the fatty foods mentioned. The press had a field day. Typical headlines read: "Popcorn Gets an R Rating," "Lights, Action, Cholesterol," "Theatre Popcorn is a Double Feature of Fat."[163]

Effective communication often relies on such dramatic communication strategies. Gandhi perfected methods of nonviolent protest including prayer, fasting, and marches against heavily armed opponents to highlight differences between colonial brutality and peaceful Indian resistance.[164] Nelson Mandela, at his inauguration as South Africa's first post-apartheid president, had one of his former white prison guards sit in the front row, thus underscoring his faith in racial reconciliation.[165] Margaret Thatcher won election as Britain's first female prime minister using clever visual campaign ads, such as a poster picturing a long queue outside a British unemployment office and a caption reading: "Labour isn't working."[166]

The growing influence of the mass media and Internet have amplified the importance of such graphic presentations. "An Inconvenient Truth," Al Gore's documentary on global warming, brought public consciousness to new levels by showing footage of ice caps melting, polar bears stranded, and mockups of the potential environmental disasters of uncurbed temperature changes. Earth Island Institute's video of dolphins killed by tuna nets helped achieve customer boycotts, federal legislation, and corporate pledges to alter fishing methods.[167] PowerPoint now makes such visual material available to any speaker, but too few take full advantage of the possibilities. Many make the mistake of simply presenting text, often in dense, list-like formats rather than relying on visually compelling images.[168] Such death-by-PowerPoint presentations leave many audiences if not half asleep then otherwise engaged—checking their messages or catching up on other work. The problem is compounded when speakers misjudge the length of their material, yet insist on getting through the entire slide collection either by speeding up or spilling over their allotted time. This leaves many audiences feeling about PowerPoint as Samuel Johnson did about Milton's *Paradise Lost*: "No one ever wished it longer."

Avoiding these mistakes and crafting truly effective presentations can be time consuming, so one final form of knowledge is knowing how and when to delegate the drafting task. To take an obvious example, American presidents can ill afford to labor over what White House insiders label "Rose Garden rubbish." But they can issue clear instructions, along the lines of one of Dwight Eisenhower's directives: "tell them to go to hell but put it so they won't be offended."[169] There are, however, limits to what can be outsourced. Assistants can help in finding the right visuals and offering research and feedback, but at least for important occasions, speakers need to be sure that the material they are presenting reflects their own voice, vision, and values.

In the excerpt below, Heath and Heath summarize their strategies for effective communication that apply not only to oral presentations but also to many advocacy efforts.

Chip Heath and Dan Heath, Made to Stick: Why Some Ideas Survive and Others Die

(New York: Random House, 2007), pp. 242-247

The Speakers and the Stickers

Each year in the second session of Chip's "Making Ideas Stick" class at Stanford, the students participate in an exercise, a kind of testable credential to show what kinds of messages stick and don't stick. The students are given some data from a government source on crime patterns in the United States. Half of them are asked to make a one-minute persuasive speech to convince their peers that nonviolent crime is a serious problem in this country. The other half are asked to take the position that it's not particularly serious.

Stanford students, as you'd expect, are smart. They also tend to be quick thinkers and good communicators. No one in the room ever gives a poor speech.

The students divide into small groups and each one gives a one-minute speech while the others listen. After each speech, the listeners rate the speaker: How impressive was the delivery? How persuasive?

What happens, invariably, is that the most polished speakers get the highest ratings. Students who are poised, smooth, and charismatic are rated at the top of the class. No surprise, right? Good speakers score well in speaking contexts.

The surprise comes next. The exercise appears to be over; in fact, Chip often plays a brief Monty Python clip to kill a few minutes and distract the students. Then, abruptly, he asks them to pull out a sheet of paper and write down, for each speaker they heard, every single idea that they remember.

The students are flabbergasted at how little they remember. Keep in mind that only ten minutes have elapsed since the speeches were given. Nor was there a huge volume of information to begin with—at most, they've heard eight one-minute speeches. And yet the students are lucky to recall one or two ideas from each speaker's presentation. Many draw a complete blank on some speeches—unable to remember a single concept.

In the average one-minute speech, the typical student uses 2.5 statistics. Only one student in ten tells a story. Those are the speaking statistics. The "remembering" statistics, on the other hand, are almost a mirror image: When students are asked to recall the speeches, 63 percent remember the stories. Only 5 percent remember any individual statistic.

Furthermore, almost no correlation emerges between "speaking talent" and the ability to make ideas stick. The people who were captivating speakers typically do no better than others in making their ideas stick. Foreign students—whose less-polished English often leaves them at the bottom of the speaking-skills rankings—are suddenly on a par with native speakers. The stars of stickiness are the students who made their case by telling stories, or by tapping into emotion, or by stressing a single point rather than ten. There is no question that a ringer—a student who came into the exercise having read this book—would squash the other students. A community college student for whom English is a second language could easily out-perform unwitting Stanford graduate students.

Why can't these smart, talented speakers make their ideas stick? A few of the villains discussed in this book are implicated. The first villain is the natural tendency to bury the lead—to get lost in a sea of information. One of the worst things about knowing a lot, or having access to a lot of information, is that we're tempted to share it all. High school teachers will tell you that when students write research papers they feel obligated to include every unearthed fact, as though the value were in the quantity of data amassed rather than its purpose or clarity. Stripping out information, in order to focus on the core, is not instinctual.

The second villain is the tendency to focus on the presentation rather than on the message. Public speakers naturally want to appear composed, charismatic, and motivational. And, certainly, charisma will help a properly designed message stick better. But all the charisma in the world won't save a dense, unfocused speech, as some Stanford students learn the hard way.

More Villains

. . . To beat decision paralysis, communicators have to do the hard work of finding the core. Lawyers must stress one or two points in their closing arguments, not ten. A teacher's lesson plans may contain fifty concepts to share with her students, but in order to be effective that teacher must devote most of her efforts to making the most critical two or three stick. Managers must share proverbs—"Names, names, and names," or "THE low-fare airline"—that help employees wring decisions out of ambiguous situations.

The archvillain of sticky ideas, as you know by now, is the Curse of Knowledge. The Stanford students didn't face the Curse of Knowledge because the data on crime were brand-new to them—they were more akin to reporters trying to avoid burying the lead on a news story than to experts who have forgotten what it's like not to know something.

The Curse of Knowledge is a worthy adversary, because in some sense it's inevitable. Getting a message across has two stages: the Answer stage and the Telling Others stage. In the Answer stage, you use your expertise to arrive at the idea you want to share. Doctors study for a decade to be capable of giving the Answer. Business managers may deliberate for months to arrive at the Answer.

Here's the rub: The same factors that worked to your advantage in the Answer stage will backfire on you during the Telling Others stage. To get the Answer, you need expertise, but you can't dissociate expertise from the Curse of Knowledge. You know things that others don't know, and you can't remember what it was like not to know those things. So when you get around to sharing the Answer, you'll tend to communicate *as if your audience were you.*

You'll stress the scads of statistics that were pivotal in arriving at the Answer—and, like the Stanford students, you'll find that no one remembers them afterward. You'll share the punch line—the over-arching truth that emerged from months of study and analysis—and, like the CEO who stresses "maximizing shareholder value" to his frontline employees, no one will have a clue how your punch line relates to the day-to-day work.

There is a curious disconnect between the amount of time we invest in training people how to arrive at the Answer and the amount of time we invest in training them how to Tell Others. It's easy to graduate from medical school or an MBA program without ever taking a class in communication.... Business managers seem to believe that, once they've clicked through a Power-Point presentation showcasing their conclusions, they've successfully communicated their ideas. What they've done is share data. If they're good speakers, they may even have created an enhanced sense, among their employees and peers, that they are "decisive" or "managerial" or "motivational." But, like the Stanford students, the surprise will come when they realize that nothing they've said had impact. They've shared data, but they haven't created ideas that are useful and lasting. Nothing stuck.

Making an Idea Stick: The Communication Framework

For an idea to stick, for it to be useful and lasting, it's got to make the audience:

1. Pay attention
2. Understand and remember it
3. Agree/Believe
4. Care
5. Be able to act on it

... The SUCCESS checklist is a substitute for the framework above, and its advantage is that it's more tangible and less subject to the Curse of Knowledge. In fact, if you think back across the chapters you've read, you'll notice that the framework matches up nicely:

1. Pay attention: UNEXPECTED
2. Understand and remember it: CONCRETE
3. Agree/Believe: CREDIBLE
4. Care: EMOTIONAL
5. Be able to act on it: STORY ...

PROBLEM 4-6

1. Select a policy issue about which you feel strongly. Prepare a five-minute speech attempting to convince someone not familiar with the topic of the merits of your position. Have another member of the class later recall your points and evaluate your effort.
2. Prepare a forty-five-second "elevator pitch" that summarizes the key points of your argument.
3. Prepare a visual display that dramatizes your position.
4. Analyze one of the publications summarized below, or a political speech that you have found particularly persuasive. What made it effective?
5. Write a two-page rebuttal to any of the speeches excerpted or listed in the media resources below, incorporating the insights summarized above. Ask someone else in the class to identify what he or she found most or least persuasive.

2. EXAMPLES

The following documents represent two of the most influential publications in the American struggle for human rights and social justice. Although issued a century apart, the Declaration of Sentiments and Letter from a Birmingham Jail sound similar themes, build on similar values, and employ similar rhetorical techniques to persuade a skeptical public.

Elizabeth Cady Stanton drafted the Declaration of Sentiments for ratification at the 1848 Seneca Falls Convention, the nation's first women's rights conference. The immediate impetus for the convention was the exclusion of Stanton and fellow abolitionist Lucretia Mott from the floor of an earlier antislavery conference in London. Women were relegated to the balcony, and the experience of marginalization there and in other American abolitionist activities underscored the need to extend the principles underlying those activities on behalf of women. Modeled on the Declaration of Independence, the Declaration of Sentiments asserted that rights to life, liberty, and the pursuit of happiness belonged equally to both sexes.

Martin Luther King Jr. issued his Letter from a Birmingham Jail in 1963, following his arrest for peaceably marching to protest racial segregation. His march violated a city ordinance prohibiting parades without a permit and a court injunction against the demonstration. During his eight-day imprisonment, King read a public statement by eight of Alabama's most prominent white religious leaders. They questioned why King and his followers did not pursue elective action instead of protests and boycotts in seeking of social justice. King's response, although addressed to these ministers, was in fact not sent to them but circulated to the national press, where it received widespread coverage.[170] His argument became the basis for *Why We Can't Wait*, a book chronicling the early civil rights campaign.

As you read these excerpts, consider the extent to which their messages are "made to stick." What rhetorical techniques are most effective?

Elizabeth Cady Stanton, Declaration of Sentiments

(1848), available at http://ecssba.rutgers.edu/docs/seneca.html (accessed 2/3/11)

When, in the course of human events, it becomes necessary for one portion of the family of man to assume among the people of the earth a position different from that which they have hitherto occupied, but one to which the laws of nature and of nature's God entitle them, a decent respect to the opinions of mankind requires that they should declare the causes that impel them to such a course.

We hold these truths to be self-evident: that all men and women are created equal; that they are endowed by their Creator with certain inalienable rights; that among these are life, liberty, and the pursuit of happiness; that to secure these rights governments are instituted, deriving their just powers from the consent of the governed. Whenever any form of Government becomes destructive of these ends, it is the right of those who suffer from it to refuse allegiance to it, and to insist upon the institution of a new government, laying its foundation on such principles, and organizing its powers in such form as to them shall seem most likely to effect their safety and happiness. . . . The history of mankind is a history of repeated injuries and usurpations on the part of man toward woman, having in direct object the establishment of an absolute tyranny over her. To prove this, let facts be submitted to a candid world.

He has never permitted her to exercise her inalienable right to the elective franchise.

He has compelled her to submit to laws, in the formation of which she had no voice.

He has withheld from her rights which are given to the most ignorant and degraded men — both natives and foreigners. . . .

He has taken from her all right in property, even to the wages she earns.

He has monopolized nearly all the profitable employments, and from those she is permitted to follow, she receives but a scanty remuneration.

He closes against her all the avenues to wealth and distinction, which he considers most honorable to himself. As a teacher of theology, medicine, or law, she is not known.

He has denied her the facilities for obtaining a thorough education — all colleges being closed against her. . . .

He has created a false public sentiment, by giving to the world a different code of morals for men and women, by which moral delinquencies which exclude women from society, are not only tolerated but deemed of little account in man. . . .

Therefore,

Resolved, That such laws as conflict, in any way, with the true and substantial happiness of woman, are contrary to the great precept of nature, and of no validity; for this is superior in obligation to any other.

Resolved, That all laws which prevent woman from occupying such a station in society as her conscience shall dictate, or which place her in a position inferior to that of man, are contrary to the great precept of nature, and therefore of no force or authority.

Resolved, That woman is man's equal—was intended to be so by the Creator, and the highest good of the race demands that she should be recognized as such.

Resolved, That the women of this country ought to be enlightened in regard to the laws under which they live, that they may no longer publish their degradation, by declaring themselves satisfied with their present position, nor their ignorance, by asserting that they have all the rights they want. . . .

Resolved, That the same amount of virtue, delicacy, and refinement of behavior, that is required of woman in the social state, should also be required of man, and the same transgressions should be visited with equal severity on both man and woman.

Resolved, That it is the duty of the women of this country to secure to themselves their sacred right to the elective franchise. . . .

Resolved, That the speedy success of our cause depends upon the zealous and untiring efforts of both men and women, for the overthrow of the monopoly of the pulpit, and for the securing to woman an equal participation with men in the various trades, professions and commerce.

NOTES AND QUESTIONS

1. Why do you suppose that Seneca Falls leaders chose to model their Declaration of Sentiments on the Declaration of Independence? Was it an effective way to gain legitimacy and credibility? What other considerations might have been at work? Are the grievances in the Declaration of Sentiments comparable to those that colonists invoked? Are they persuasively presented?
2. No other publication or speech by leaders of the contemporary women's movement has had comparable influence. Why not? What would a current version of the Declaration of Sentiments look like in this country or in another nation where women's rights are not yet recognized?
3. The nineteenth-century women's rights movement had leaders of extraordinary courage and vision, but they were not without their own set of prejudices. Like many other leaders of the women's suffrage movement, Stanton supported the franchise only for educated voters. She joined with Susan B. Anthony in arguing that enfranchising white women would be a bulwark against rule by "brutish ignorant Negro men and unlettered and unwashed immigrants."[171] The Declaration of Sentiments anticipates this argument when referring to the injustice of denying women the rights given to "the most ignorant and degraded men—both natives and foreigners." As a political strategy, such racist appeals were often effective at that time, but they also compromised the principles of equal justice that activists invoked. The same was true of suffrage activities that excluded, marginalized, or segregated women of color. How might you have attempted to persuade early feminists that these strategies were a mistake?

   Do similar issues of race, ethnicity, and class play out in current gender politics? How have leaders such as Barack Obama and Hillary Clinton attempted to bridge the divisions?

4. Consider the way in which Martin Luther King Jr. handles the issue of racism among his audience. What are his most effective persuasive strategies?

MARTIN LUTHER KING JR., "LETTER FROM A BIRMINGHAM JAIL"

April 16, 1963, available at http://mlk-kpp01.stanford.edu/index.php/resources/article/annotated_letter_from_birmingham/ (accessed 2/3/11)

My Dear Fellow Clergymen:

While confined here in the Birmingham city jail, I came across your recent statement calling my present activities "unwise and untimely." Seldom do I pause to answer criticism of my work and ideas. If I sought to answer all the criticisms that cross my desk . . . I would have no time for constructive work. But since I feel that you are men of genuine good will and that your criticisms are sincerely set forth, I want to try to answer your statement in what I hope will be patient and reasonable terms.

I think I should indicate why I am here in Birmingham, since you have been influenced by the view which argues against "outsiders coming in." I have the honor of serving as president of the Southern Christian Leadership Conference, an organization operating in every southern state, with headquarters in Atlanta, Georgia. We have some eighty five affiliated organizations across the South, and one of them is the Alabama Christian Movement for Human Rights. . . . I, along with several members of my staff, am here because I was invited here [by this affiliate]. . . .

But more basically, I am in Birmingham because injustice is here. Just as the prophets of the eighth century B.C. left their villages and carried their "thus saith the Lord" far beyond the boundaries of their home towns, and just as the Apostle Paul left his village of Tarsus and carried the gospel of Jesus Christ to the far corners of the Greco Roman world, so am I compelled to carry the gospel of freedom beyond my own home town. Like Paul, I must constantly respond to the Macedonian call for aid.

Moreover, I am cognizant of the interrelatedness of all communities and states. I cannot sit idly by in Atlanta and not be concerned about what happens in Birmingham. Injustice anywhere is a threat to justice everywhere. We are caught in an inescapable network of mutuality, tied in a single garment of destiny. Whatever affects one directly, affects all indirectly. Never again can we afford to live with the narrow, provincial "outside agitator" idea. Anyone who lives inside the United States can never be considered an outsider anywhere within its bounds.

You deplore the demonstrations taking place in Birmingham. But your statement, I am sorry to say, fails to express a similar concern for the conditions that brought about the demonstrations. I am sure that none of you would want to rest content with the superficial kind of social analysis that deals merely with effects and does not grapple with underlying causes. It is unfortunate that demonstrations are taking place in Birmingham, but it is even more unfortunate that the city's white power structure left the Negro community with no alternative. . . .

Birmingham is probably the most thoroughly segregated city in the United States. Its ugly record of brutality is widely known. Negroes have experienced grossly unjust treatment in the courts. There have been more unsolved bombings of Negro homes and churches in Birmingham than in any other city in the nation. These are the hard, brutal facts of the case. On the basis of these conditions, Negro leaders sought to negotiate with the city fathers. But the latter consistently refused to engage in good faith negotiation.

Then, last September, came the opportunity to talk with leaders of Birmingham's economic community. In the course of the negotiations, certain promises were made by the merchants — for example, to remove the stores' humiliating racial signs. On the basis of these promises, the Reverend Fred Shuttlesworth and the leaders of the Alabama Christian Movement for Human Rights agreed to a moratorium on all demonstrations. As the weeks and months went by, we realized that we were the victims of a broken promise. A few signs, briefly removed, returned; the others remained. As in so many past experiences, our hopes had been blasted, and the shadow of deep disappointment settled upon us. We had no alternative except to prepare for direct action, whereby we would present our very bodies as a means of laying our case before the conscience of the local and the national community. Mindful of the difficulties involved, we decided to undertake a process of self purification. We began a series of workshops on nonviolence, and we repeatedly asked ourselves: "Are you able to accept blows without retaliating?" "Are you able to endure the ordeal of jail?" We decided to schedule our direct action program for the Easter season, realizing that except for Christmas, this is the main shopping period of the year. Knowing that a strong economic-withdrawal program would be the by product of direct action, we felt that this would be the best time to bring pressure to bear on the merchants for the needed change.

[We then postponed the protest twice to avoid clouding issues in the mayoral election and runoff.] Having aided in this community need, we felt that our direct action program could be delayed no longer.

You may well ask: "Why direct action? Why sit ins, marches and so forth? Isn't negotiation a better path?" You are quite right in calling for negotiation. Indeed, this is the very purpose of direct action. Nonviolent direct action seeks to create such a crisis and foster such a tension that a community which has constantly refused to negotiate is forced to confront the issue. It seeks so to dramatize the issue that it can no longer be ignored. . . . My friends, I must say to you that we have not made a single gain in civil rights without determined legal and nonviolent pressure. Lamentably, it is an historical fact that privileged groups seldom give up their privileges voluntarily. Individuals may see the moral light and voluntarily give up their unjust posture; but, as Reinhold Niebuhr has reminded us, groups tend to be more immoral than individuals.

We know through painful experience that freedom is never voluntarily given by the oppressor; it must be demanded by the oppressed. Frankly, I have yet to engage in a direct action campaign that was "well timed" in the view of those who have not suffered unduly from the disease of segregation. For years now I have heard the word "Wait!" It rings in the ear of every Negro with piercing familiarity. This "Wait" has almost always meant "Never."

We must come to see, with one of our distinguished jurists, that "justice too long delayed is justice denied."

We have waited for more than 340 years for our constitutional and God given rights. The nations of Asia and Africa are moving with jetlike speed toward gaining political independence, but we still creep at horse and buggy pace toward gaining a cup of coffee at a lunch counter. Perhaps it is easy for those who have never felt the stinging darts of segregation to say, "Wait." But when you have seen vicious mobs lynch your mothers and fathers at will and drown your sisters and brothers at whim; when you have seen hate filled policemen curse, kick and even kill your black brothers and sisters; when you see the vast majority of your twenty million Negro brothers smothering in an airtight cage of poverty in the midst of an affluent society; when you suddenly find your tongue twisted and your speech stammering as you seek to explain to your six year old daughter why she can't go to the public amusement park that has just been advertised on television, and see tears welling up in her eyes when she is told that Funtown is closed to colored children, and see ominous clouds of inferiority beginning to form in her little mental sky, and see her beginning to distort her personality by developing an unconscious bitterness toward white people; when you have to concoct an answer for a five year old son who is asking: "Daddy, why do white people treat colored people so mean?"; when you take a cross county drive and find it necessary to sleep night after night in the uncomfortable corners of your automobile because no motel will accept you; when you are humiliated day in and day out by nagging signs reading "white" and "colored"; when your first name becomes "nigger," your middle name becomes "boy" (however old you are) and your last name becomes "John," and your wife and mother are never given the respected title "Mrs."; when you are harried by day and haunted by night by the fact that you are a Negro, living constantly at tiptoe stance, never quite knowing what to expect next, and are plagued with inner fears and outer resentments; when you are forever fighting a degenerating sense of "nobodiness" — then you will understand why we find it difficult to wait. There comes a time when the cup of endurance runs over, and men are no longer willing to be plunged into the abyss of despair. I hope, sirs, you can understand our legitimate and unavoidable impatience. You express a great deal of anxiety over our willingness to break laws. This is certainly a legitimate concern. Since we so diligently urge people to obey the Supreme Court's decision of 1954 outlawing segregation in the public schools, at first glance it may seem rather paradoxical for us consciously to break laws. One may well ask: "How can you advocate breaking some laws and obeying others?" The answer lies in the fact that there are two types of laws: just and unjust. I would be the first to advocate obeying just laws. One has not only a legal but a moral responsibility to obey just laws. Conversely, one has a moral responsibility to disobey unjust laws. I would agree with St. Augustine that "an unjust law is no law at all."

Now, what is the difference between the two? How does one determine whether a law is just or unjust? A just law is a man made code that squares with the moral law or the law of God. An unjust law is a code that is out of harmony with the moral law. To put it in the terms of St. Thomas Aquinas: An unjust law is a human law that is not rooted in eternal law and natural law. . . .

Let me give another explanation. A law is unjust if it is inflicted on a minority that, as a result of being denied the right to vote, had no part in enacting or devising the law. Who can say that the legislature of Alabama which set up that state's segregation laws was democratically elected? Throughout Alabama all sorts of devious methods are used to prevent Negroes from becoming registered voters, and there are some counties in which, even though Negroes constitute a majority of the population, not a single Negro is registered. Can any law enacted under such circumstances be considered democratically structured?

Sometimes a law is just on its face and unjust in its application. For instance, I have been arrested on a charge of parading without a permit. Now, there is nothing wrong in having an ordinance which requires a permit for a parade. But such an ordinance becomes unjust when it is used to maintain segregation and to deny citizens the First-Amendment privilege of peaceful assembly and protest. . . .

Of course, there is nothing new about this kind of civil disobedience. . . . To a degree, academic freedom is a reality today because Socrates practiced civil disobedience. In our own nation, the Boston Tea Party represented a massive act of civil disobedience. We should never forget that everything Adolf Hitler did in Germany was "legal" and everything the Hungarian freedom fighters did in Hungary was "illegal." It was "illegal" to aid and comfort a Jew in Hitler's Germany. . . .

I must make two honest confessions to you, my Christian and Jewish brothers. First, I must confess that over the past few years I have been gravely disappointed with the white moderate. I have almost reached the regrettable conclusion that the Negro's great stumbling block in his stride toward freedom is not the White Citizen's Counciler or the Ku Klux Klanner, but the white moderate, who is more devoted to "order" than to justice; who prefers a negative peace which is the absence of tension to a positive peace which is the presence of justice; who constantly says: "I agree with you in the goal you seek, but I cannot agree with your methods of direct action"; who paternalistically believes he can set the timetable for another man's freedom; who lives by a mythical concept of time and who constantly advises the Negro to wait for a "more convenient season." Shallow understanding from people of good will is more frustrating than absolute misunderstanding from people of ill will. Lukewarm acceptance is much more bewildering than outright rejection. . . .

It is true that the police have exercised a degree of discipline in handling the demonstrators. In this sense they have conducted themselves rather "nonviolently" in public. But for what purpose? To preserve the evil system of segregation. Over the past few years I have consistently preached that nonviolence demands that the means we use must be as pure as the ends we seek. I have tried to make clear that it is wrong to use immoral means to attain moral ends. But now I must affirm that it is just as wrong, or perhaps even more so, to use moral means to preserve immoral ends. . . . [Southern police have too often] used the moral means of nonviolence to maintain the immoral end of racial injustice. As T. S. Eliot has said: "The last temptation is the greatest treason: To do the right deed for the wrong reason."

I wish you had commended the Negro sit inners and demonstrators of Birmingham for their sublime courage, their willingness to suffer and their amazing discipline in the midst of great provocation. One day the South will recognize its real heroes. They will be the James Merediths, with the noble sense of purpose that enables them to face jeering and hostile mobs, and with the agonizing loneliness that characterizes the life of the pioneer. They will be old, oppressed, battered Negro women, symbolized in a seventy two year old woman in Montgomery, Alabama, who rose up with a sense of dignity and with her people decided not to ride segregated buses, and who responded with ungrammatical profundity to one who inquired about her weariness: "My feets is tired, but my soul is at rest." They will be the young high school and college students, the young ministers of the gospel and a host of their elders, courageously and nonviolently sitting in at lunch counters and willingly going to jail for conscience' sake. One day the South will know that when these disinherited children of God sat down at lunch counters, they were in reality standing up for what is best in the American dream and for the most sacred values in our Judaeo Christian heritage, thereby bringing our nation back to those great wells of democracy which were dug deep by the founding fathers in their formulation of the Constitution and the Declaration of Independence.

Never before have I written so long a letter. I'm afraid it is much too long to take your precious time. I can assure you that it would have been much shorter if I had been writing from a comfortable desk, but what else can one do when he is alone in a narrow jail cell, other than write long letters, think long thoughts and pray long prayers?

If I have said anything in this letter that overstates the truth and indicates an unreasonable impatience, I beg you to forgive me. If I have said anything that understates the truth and indicates my having a patience that allows me to settle for anything less than brotherhood, I beg God to forgive me.

I hope this letter finds you strong in the faith. I also hope that circumstances will soon make it possible for me to meet each of you, not as an integrationist or a civil-rights leader but as a fellow clergyman and a Christian brother. Let us all hope that the dark clouds of racial prejudice will soon pass away and the deep fog of misunderstanding will be lifted from our fear drenched communities, and in some not too distant tomorrow the radiant stars of love and brotherhood will shine over our great nation with all their scintillating beauty.

Yours for the cause of Peace and Brotherhood,
Martin Luther King, Jr.

NOTES AND QUESTIONS

1. What did you find most and least effective about this letter? Was it "much too long"? If so, what would you have advised him to cut?

2. King's Letter, excerpted in the *New York Post,* was highly influential and echoed strategies apparent in other influential speeches on racism and racial identity. In his famous 1964 address on the Washington mall, King again appealed to values in the nation's founding documents: "I still have a dream . . . deeply rooted in the American dream. I have a dream that one day this nation will rise up and live out the true meaning of its creed: that all

men are created equal."[172] Barack Obama's references to race during his presidential campaign often employed rhetorical techniques described earlier — vivid narrative tied to expressions of hope and appeals to common values. When he announced his candidacy from Springfield, Illinois, his location and rhetoric evoked Abraham Lincoln's calls for a "more perfect union." Subsequent speeches invoked Martin Luther King Jr.'s references to the moral arc of the universe "bending toward justice."[173] Obama's address before the 2004 Democratic National Convention referred to his father's childhood herding goats in Kenya and maintained that "my story is part of the larger American story . . . and that in no other country on earth is my story even possible.[174] In his inaugural address, he made similar references to the "meaning of our liberty and our creed, why men and women and children of every race and every faith can join in celebration across this magnificent mall. And why a man whose father less than 60 years ago might not have been served at a local restaurant can now stand before you to take a most sacred oath."[175] His campaign slogan, often credited as one of the most memorable of American presidents, epitomized messages of hope and inclusion: "Yes we can."[176]

Obama is credited with being a " 'shape shifter,' with an remarkable ability to come across differently to disparate constituencies" and to adjust his rhetorical style to church basements, huge stadiums, backyard barbeques, and elite policy forums.[177] Bill Clinton had similar skills:

> He seemed to sense what audiences needed and deliver to them — trimming his pitch here, emphasizing different priorities, there, always aiming to please. This was one of his most effective, and maddening, qualities in private meetings as well. He always grabbed on to some points of agreement, while steering the conversation away from the larger points of disagreement, leaving his seducee with the distinct impression that they were in total harmony on just about everything.[178]

Yet Obama and other democratic politicians have also been faulted for not continuing to find the right framing strategies after their election. George Lakoff, one of the nation's leading experts on linguistics and political rhetoric, criticized Obama's early health care messages as a "policy-speak disaster." Is his criticism convincing? If you were Obama's chief advisor, how would you respond?

George Lakoff, "The Policy-Speak Disaster for Health Care"

Truthout, Aug. 20, 2009

Policy Speak is the principle that: *If you just tell people the policy facts, they will reason to the right conclusion and support the policy wholeheartedly.*

Policy speak is the policy behind the president's new Reality Check web site. To my knowledge, the Reality Check web site has not had a reality check. That is, the administration has not hired a first-class cognitive psychologist to take subjects who have been convinced by right-wing myths and lies, have them read the Reality Check web site, and see if the Reality Check web site has changed their minds a couple of days or a week later. I have my doubts, but do the test. . . . Truth matters. But it can only be comprehended when it is framed effectively and heard constantly. . . .

Policy Speak is supposed to be reasoned, objective discourse. [Yet] . . . [t]he scientific research in neuroscience and cognitive science has shown that most reason is unconscious. . . . Emotion is necessary for rational thought; if you cannot feel emotion, you will not know what to want or how anyone else would react to your actions. Rational decisions depend on emotion. Empathy with others has a physical basis, and as much as self-interest, empathy lies behind reason. . . .

Ideas are constituted by brain structures called "frames" and "metaphors," and reason uses them. Frames form systems called worldviews. All language is defined relative to such frames and metaphors. There are very different conservative and progressive worldviews, and different words can activate different worldviews [and different circuits in the brain]. . . .

Whenever brain circuitry is activated, the synapses get stronger and the circuits are easier to activate again. Conservative language will activate conservative frames, which will activate and strengthen the conservative worldview. Conservative tacticians may not know about brain research, but they know about marketing, and marketing theorists use that brain research. That is why conservatives place such importance on language choice, from the classic "socialized medicine," to Luntz's "government takeover" [of health care] to Palin's "death panels." When repeated over and over, the words evoke a conservative worldview [and hold emotional appeal]. . . .

Conservative language will activate and strengthen conservative worldviews—even when negated! I titled a book "Don't Think of an Elephant!" to make this point. . . . I've heard President Obama say, "We don't want a government takeover," which activates the idea of a government takeover. Mediamatters.org's major story, as I write this, is: "The media have debunked the death panels—more than 40 times." It then gives a list of 40 cases of debunking, each one of which uses the term "death panels." And you wonder, after so many debunkings, why it is still believed! Each "debunking" reinforced the idea. The first rule of effective communication is stating the positive in your own terms, not quoting the other side's language with a negation. . . . As I was writing this, I received the viral email written by David Axelrod, which he refers to as "probably one of the longest emails I've ever sent." It is indeed long. It is accurate. It lays out the president's list of needed reforms. It answers the myths. It appeals to people who would personally benefit from the president's plan. . . . And it is written in Policy Speak. It has 24 points—three sets of eight.

Ask yourself which is more memorable: "Government takeover," "socialized medicine" and "death panels"—or Axelrod's 24 points? Did the administration do a reality check on the 24 points? That is, did they have one of our superb cognitive psychologists test subjects who were convinced of the right-wing framing, have them read the 24 points and test them a couple days or a week later on whether Axelrod's 24 points had convinced them? Policy Speak folks don't tend to think of such things. . . . I respect Axelrod deeply. But the strategist who ran the best-framed campaign I've ever seen is giving in to Policy

Speak. . . . In the Obama campaign, honest, effective framing was used with great success. But in the Obama administration, something has changed. It needs to change back.

NOTES AND QUESTIONS

1. Social critic Amitai Etzioni similarly claims that progressive leaders lack accessible and inspiring narratives. They too often produce "platformlike statements" without mobilizing power; they lack a clear concise explanation of why we are in difficulty and what will get us out. The need is not just for new rhetoric but for a more compelling narrative.[179] In the run-up to the 2010 midterm elections, long-time political analyst George Packer summarized similar criticism by congressional representatives and staff. They viewed efforts by Obama and his advisors to have sophisticated conversations on issues such as foreclosure as "tone deaf." "You can't say to people whose homes are in foreclosure, who are losing their businesses, 'It's a complicated situation.' The President is having a very eloquent one-sided conversation. The country doesn't want to have the conversation he wants to have."[180] House Democratic Congressman Barney Frank agreed that Obama's "technocratic style" had been ineffective and that he would have been better-off with a more "adversarial approach" toward pharmaceutical firms, insurance companies, and banks.[181]

   Do you agree? Packer noted that the public "wants many things these days, some of them contradictory. It wants the government to stop piling up debt and it also wants the government to spend aggressively on jobs, education, and health care."[182] Is there a way that the administration can better convey an unpopular message — that difficult trade-offs are inevitable? When should leaders force followers to have a conversation they do not want to have?

2. Lawyers often face similar challenges when clients are not interested in legal complexities or risk analysis and just want the lawyer to get the deal done or make the problem go away. What communication strategies might be helpful in packaging unwelcome messages?

3. Take a recent controversial policy issue and compare how leaders from different political perspectives frame their arguments. What techniques are most effective? How do they respond to opposition claims? How would you?

MEDIA RESOURCES

Many examples of inspiring leadership rhetoric are available in films and documentaries, as well as political speeches and debates. Famous scenes of rallying the troops before battle provide classic illustrations: Henry IV on the eve of the Battle of Agincourt, Queen Elizabeth sending troops into France, and Julius Caesar asking for support in his march on Rome.[183] Examples of successful and unsuccessful lawyers' speeches at meetings with clients in class actions appear in *Erin Brockovich* and *A Civil Action*. Interviews with professors

Steven Pinker and Jonathan Haidt offer insights on political rhetoric and values.[184] Excerpts from civil rights leaders including King are described in Chapter 9, on social movements.

Examples of successful and unsuccessful persuasive strategies appear in the 1987 Iran-Contra Congressional Hearings. The testimony of Lieutenant Colonel Oliver North is particularly illuminating in the way it reclaims the moral high ground of the hearing. When Committee lawyers attempted to pin North down on the details of document destruction, he reframed the issue in terms of national security. He shredded material not because it was politically "embarrassing" but because lives were at stake. When questioned about illegal arms deals, he accepted full responsibility for his actions, declined to throw anyone else under the bus, and insisted that he had done what was right. He would have offered the Iranians "a free trip to Disneyland" if necessary to save the hostages. A useful class exercise is to watch part of his testimony without sound and observe the way his body language and appearance (full dress uniform) reinforce his sincerity, self-confidence, and appeal to higher principles. It is also instructive to ask students to role-play the lawyers and attempt to develop better strategies for challenging his credibility and apparent indifference to the rule of law.

END NOTES

1. Robert B. Cialdini, Influence: The Psychology of Persuasion (New York: Harper Collins, 2007); Lionel Tiger and Richard Fox, The Imperial Animal (New York: Holt, Reinhart and Winston, 1971); Alvin W. Gouldner, The Norm of Reciprocity: A Preliminary Statement, American Sociological Review 25 (1960):161.

2. Dennis T. Regan, Effects of a Favor and Liking Compliance, Journal of Social Psychology 7 (1971):267.

3. Jonah Lehrer, How We Decide (New York: Bloomsbury, 2009), 181-182.

4. Cialdini, Influence, 30.

5. Id. at 22-23.

6. Id. at 27; see also A Tutorial from Lyndon B. Johnson, Don't Let Dead Cats Stand on Your Porch, New York Times, September 20, 2009, wk rev. 5.

7. Cialdini, Influence, 26 (quoting Keating).

8. Id. at 19.

9. Victor S. Navasky, Kennedy Justice (New York: Atheneum, 1971), 347, 355, 359, 444.

10. Steven R. Covey, The Seven Habits of Highly Effective People (New York: Simon and Schuster, 1990), 289-290.

11. Jeffrey Pfeffer, Power: Why Some People Have It and Others Don't (New York: Harper Collins, 2010), 33.

12. Ryan Lizza, Inside the Crisis: Larry Summers and the White House Economic Team, New Yorker, October 12, 2009, available at http://www.newyorker.com/reporting/2009/10/12/091012fa_lizza (quoting West). For Gardner's account, see Howard Gardner, Changing Minds (Cambridge, MA: Harvard Business Press, 2004), 155-159.

13. Gardner, Changing Minds, 159.

14. Lizza, Inside the Crisis (quoting West).

15. Solomon E. Asch, Effects of Group Pressure upon the Modification and Distortion of Judgment, in Harold S. Guietzkow, ed., Groups, Leadership, and Men (Pittsburgh, PA: Carnegie Press, 1951).

16. Robert Cialdini, Harnessing the Science of Persuasion, Harvard Business Review (October 2001):76. For early adopters, see Kerry Patterson, Joseph Grenny, David Maxfield, Ron McMillan, and Al Switlzer, Influencers: The Power to Change Anything (New York: McGraw Hill, 2008), 148-150. See also Jay Conger, The Necessary Art of Persuasion, Harvard Business Review 76(3) (May-June 1998):88.

17. Kerry Patterson et al., Influencer: The Power to Change Anything (New York: McGraw-Hill, 2008).

18. For the motivations of government employees, see Hal G. Rainey, Understanding and Managing Public Organizations (San Francisco: Jossey-Bass, 2003), 233.

19. Robert E. Quinn, Sue R. Faerman, Michael P. Thompson, Michael R. McGrath, and Lynda S. St. Clair, Becoming a Master Manager (Hoboken, NJ: John Wiley & Sons, 5th ed. 2010), 219.

20. Patterson et al., Influencer, 209; Steve Kerr, On the Folly of Rewarding A While Hoping for B, Academy of Management Executive 9 (1995):7 (describing incentive structure that led some American troops in Vietnam to search and escape rather than search and destroy).

21. Barry Schwartz and Kenneth Sharpe, Practical Wisdom (New York: Penguin, 2010), 183; Sandeep Jauhar, The Pitfalls of Linking Doctors' Pay to Performance, New York Times, September 9, 2008, F5, F7.

22. Schwartz and Sharpe, Practical Wisdom, 190-191; Uri Gneezy and Aldo Rustichini, A Fine Is a Price, Journal of Legal Studies 29 (2000):1.

23. Patterson et al., Influencer, 196 (quoting Demetri Martin).

24. Montgomery Van Wart, Dynamics of Leadership in Public Service: Theory and Practice (Armonk, NY: M.E. Sharpe, 2005), 210.

25. Van Wart, Dynamics of Leadership, 209-213.

26. Daniel H. Pink, Drive: The Surprising Truth about What Motivates Us (New York: Penguin, 2009), 45-46, 59.

27. Id. at 46.

28. Frederick Herzberg, One More Time: How Do You Motivate Employees, Harvard Business Review (September-October 1987):6, 8-9.

29. Id. at 6-12.

30. For Robert Cialdini on the importance of reciprocity, see http://www.youtube.com/watch?v=tkyGOAWoYxA. For elevators and conformity, see http://www.youtube.com/watch?v=sicoCkUZ-dkd.

31. Warren Bennis, Introduction, in Ronald E. Riggio, Ira Chaleff, and Jean Lipman-Blumen, eds., The Art of Followership: How Great Followers Create Great Leaders and Organizations (San Francisco: Jossey-Bass, 2008), xxiv, xxvi.

32. Warren Bennis, The Secrets of Great Groups, Leader to Leader, 1997, available at http://www.consultpivotal.com/great_groups.html.

33. John Gardner, On Leadership (New York: Free Press, 1990), 24.

34. Barbara Kellerman, Followership: How Followers are Creating Change and Changing Leaders (Cambridge, MA: Harvard Business Press, 2008), 23.

35. Kellerman, Followership, 8.

36. Robert Nye, Power and Leadership, in Nitin Nohria and Rakesh Khurana, eds., Handbook of Leadership Theory and Practice (Boston: Harvard Business Press, 2010), 305, 312 (quoting de Mirabeau).

37. Nannerl O. Keohane, Thinking about Leadership (Princeton, NJ: Princeton University Press, 2010), 30.

38. James M. Kouzes and Barry Z. Posner, A Leader's Legacy (San Francisco: Jossey-Bass, 2006), 91.

39. John Gardner, The Nature of Leadership: Introductory Considerations (Washington, D.C.: The Independent Sector, 1986), 5-6.

40. Kellerman, Followership, 10.

41. Nye, Power and Leadership, 312.

42. Ira Chaleff, The Courageous Follower: Standing up to and for Our Leaders (San Francisco: Berrett-Koehler Publishers, 2003).

43. A Military General's Leadership Lessons, Interview with Lieutenant General Russell Honore, Gallup Management Journal, January 8, 2009, http://gmj.gallup.com/content/113629/military-generals-leadership-lessons.aspx.

44. David Collinson, Conformist, Resistant, and Disguised Selves: A Post-Structuralist Approach to Identity and Workplace Followership, in Riggio, Chaleff, and Lipman-Blumen, eds., The Art of Followership (San Francisco: Jossey-Bass, 2008), 309, 314.

45. Kellerman, Followership, 55-59.

46. Roger Gill, The Theory and Practice of Leadership (Thousand Oaks, CA: Sage, 2006), 12 (quoting Strengthening Leadership).

47. Gill, The Theory and Practice of Leadership, 12; Roger Kelly, Rethinking Followership, in Riggio, Chaleff, and Lipman-Blumen, eds., The Art of Followership, 13, 15. See generally Roger E. Kelly, The Power of Followership (New York: Doubleday, 1992).

48. Kelly, Rethinking Followership, 13, 15. See also Roger E. Kelly, In Praise of Followers, Harvard Business Review (November-December 1988):142, 146 (noting the importance of "initiative, self control, commitment, talent, honesty, credibility, and courage").

49. Bennis, Introduction, xxvi.

50. Lynn R. Offerman, When Followers Become Toxic, Harvard Business Review (January 2004):55, 57, 59; John B. Howell and Mark Mendez, Three Perspectives on Followership, in Riggio, Chaleff, and Lipman-Blumen, eds., The Art of Followership, 25, 35.

51. Mary Gentile, Giving Voice to Values (New Haven, CT: Yale University Press, 2010).

52. Gentile, Giving Voice to Values, 181.

53. James W. Robinson, Jack Welch and Leadership (New York: Forum, 2001), 154.

54. Gill, Theory and Practice of Leadership, 140.

55. William A. Cohen, Drucker on Leadership (San Francisco: Jossey-Bass, 2010), 219; Gill, Theory and Practice of Leadership, 216; Bruce J. Avolio and Rebecca J. Richard, The Rise of Authentic Followership, in Riggio, Chaleff, and Lipman-Blumen, eds., The Art of Followership, 325, 329-335.

56. Offerman, When Followers Become Toxic, 59 (quoting Ketchum).

57. Gill, Theory and Practice of Leadership, 222.

58. C. Fred Alford, Whistleblowing as Responsible Followership, in Riggio, Chaleff, and Lipman-Blumen, eds., The Art of Followership, 309, 314.

59. Alford, Whistleblowing as Responsible Followership, 238.

60. Robert Jackall, Whistleblowing and Its Quandaries, Georgetown Journal of Legal Ethics 20 (2007):1133, 1134-1136.

61. Alford, Whistleblowing, 240.

62. Roberta Ann Johnson, Whistleblowing: When It Works and Why (Boulder, CO: Lynne Rienner, 2003); Alford, Whistleblowing, 241-242; Debra E. Meyerson, Tempered Radicals: How Everyday Leaders Inspire Change at Work (Boston: Harvard Business School Press, 2003).

63. Debra E. Meyerson, The Tempered Radicals, Stanford Social Innovation Review (Fall 2004):23.

64. This problem draws from Deborah L. Rhode and David Luban, Legal Ethics (New York: Foundation Press, 5th ed. 2009), 438-439.

65. Gentile, Giving Voice to Values, 52.

66. Id. at 165.

67. Trial Transcript at 16,742, January 21, 1978.

68. Stephen Wermiel, Lawyers' Public Image Is Dreadful, Spurring Concern by Attorneys, Wall Street Journal, October 11, 1983, 1.

69. James B. Stewart Jr., Kodak and Donovan Leisure: The Untold Story, The American Lawyer, January 1983, 24, 62.

70. Id.

71. David Margolick, The Long Road Back for a Disgraced Patrician, New York Times, January 19, 1990, B6.

72. Christine Parker et al., The Ethical Infrastructure of Legal Practice in Larger Law Firms: Values, Policy and Behavior, University of New South Wales Law Journal 31 (2008):158; Kimberly Kirkland, Ethics in Large Law Firms: The Principles of Pragmatism, University of Memphis Law Review 35 (2005):631, 637.

73. Ward Bower, Altman Weil Inc., Report to Legal Management: Major Law Firms Embrace General Counsel Concept (2004) (finding that two-thirds of responding firms in a survey of the United States' 200 largest firms had designated counsel to provide ethics advice).

74. Elizabeth Chambliss, The Nirvana Fallacy in Law Firm Regulation Debates, Fordham Urban Law Journal 33 (2005):119, 128-129.

75. New York is one of the few states that permits firms to be subject to discipline, but such organizational sanctions are rare. For discussion, see Rhode and Luban, Legal Ethics, 1001-1002.

76. Andrew Perlman, The Silliest Rule of Professional Conduct: Model Rule 5.2(b), The Professional Lawyer 19 (2009):14.

77. Carol M. Rice, The Superior Orders Defense in Legal Ethics: Sending the Wrong Message to Young Lawyers, Wake Forest Law Review 32 (1997):887, 889.

78. Douglas R. Richmond, Academic Silliness about Model Rule 5.2(b), The Professional Lawyer 19 (2009):15, 20.

79. Hitler's speeches are also available on http//:www.youtube.com/watch?v=eghdxlsbky.

80. For Stanley, the Isolate, see http://www.youtube.com/watch?v=ZmXPeSzlc6A. For Dwight, the Diehard, see http://www.hulu.com/watch/109986/the-office-recyclops.

81. Season 2, episode 4—Rosemary's Baby. http://www.netflix.com/WiPlayer?movieid=70108660&trkid=438381.

82. The Tiananmen Square protester is available at http://www.youtube.com/watch?v=9-nXT8lSnPQ&feature=related, http://www.youtube.com/watch?v=M5sNN9HvTgY&NR=1&feature=fvwp. The Kamikaze pilot is available at http://www.youtube.com/watch?v=v-Kia79GyWU& and http://www.youtube.com/watch?v=imtQEMU9BEg&.

83. Cults: The Wave, Part 1: http://www.youtube.com/watch?v=BVRXXbU-z7U, Part 2: http://www.youtube.com/watch?v=GXi71XBdh1o.

84. Eric K. Shinseki, quoted in Deputy Secretary Paul Wolfowitz Interview with Peter Boyer of the New Yorker, June 18, 2002, http://www.defenselink.mil/transcripts.aspx?transcriptid=3527.

85. John P. Kotter and Leonard A. Schlesinger, Choosing Strategies for Change, Harvard Business Review (March-April 1979):106. Since that account, the pace of change has undoubtedly accelerated.

86. Arie de Geus, Beware: Innovation Kills!, in Frances Hesselbein, Iain Somerville, and Marshall Goldsmith, eds., Leading for Innovation (San Francisco: Jossey-Bass, 2002), 226.

87. Hal G. Raines, Understanding and Managing Public Organizations (San Francisco: Jossey-Bass, 2003), 16-18 (discussing public opinion).

88. Montgomery van Wart, Dynamics of Leadership in Public Service: Theory and Practice (Armonk, NY: M.E. Sharpe, 2005), 40; Sanford Borins, Loose Cannons and Rule Breakers, or Enterprising Leaders: Some Evidence about Innovative Public Managers, Public Administration Review 60 (November-December 2000):498, 499.

89. Mark Gerzon, Leading through Conflict (Boston, MA: Harvard Business Press, 2006), 208.

90. Jim Collins, The Ultimate Creation, in Leading for Innovation, 131.

91. Id. at 134.

92. William H. Cohen, Drucker on Leadership (San Francisco: Jossey-Bass, 2010), 1; Neil M. Tichy and Warren G. Bennis, Judgment (New York: Portfolio, Penguin, 2002), 58 (quoting Drucker).

93. Debra E. Meyerson, Radical Change, The Quiet Way, Harvard Business Review (October 2001):92, 94.

94. Van Wart, Dynamics of Leadership, 40; Borins, Loose Cannons, 503.

95. Stephen P. Robbins and Timothy A. Judge, Organizational Behavior (Upper Saddle River, NJ: Pearson Prentice Hall, 13th ed. 2009), 625-626; John P. Kotter, Making Change Happen, in Francis Hesselbein and Paul M. Cohen, eds., Leader to Leader (San Francisco: Jossey-Bass, 1999), 69, 70-71.

96. Peter M. Senge, The Practice of Innovation, in Hesselbein and Coehn, eds., Leader to Leader, 55, 60.

97. Peter Firestein, Crisis of Character: Corporate Reputation in an Age of Skepticism (New York: Union Square Press, 2009), 128, 133.

98. Robbins and Judge, Organizational Behavior, 623-624; Kotter and Schlesinger, Choosing Strategies for Change, 109; Gerzon, Leading through Conflict, 209.

99. Patterson et al., Influencer, 51.

100. Patterson et al., Influencer, 68-69, 102.

101. John P. Kotter and Dan S. Cohen, The Heart of Change (Boston: Harvard Business School Press, 2002), 18, 30-31.

102. Kotter, Making Change Happen, 70.

103. Rosabeth Moss Kanter, Creating the Culture for Innovation (Cambridge, MA: Goodmeasure, Inc., 2000), 6, reprinted in Frances Hesselbein, Marshall Goldsmith, and Iain Somerville, eds., Leading for Innovation: And Organizing for Results (San Francisco: Jossey-Bass, 2002), 82.

104. Jeffrey Pfeffer, To Build a Culture of Innovation, Avoid Conventional Management Wisdom, in Hesselbein, Goldsmith, and Summerfield, eds., Leading for Innovation, 101 (quoting David Kelly).

105. Van Wart, Dynamics of Leadership, 54; Kanter, Creating the Culture for Innovation, 4.

106. Maureen Broderick, The Art of Managing Professional Services (Upper Saddle River, NJ: Wharton, 2011), 105-107.

107. Robbins and Judge, Organizational Behavior, 623; Kotter and Schlesinger, Choosing Strategies for Change, 107; Larina Kase, The Confident Leader (New York: McGraw-Hill, 2009), 11.

108. Barbara C. Crosby and John M. Bryson, Implementing and Evaluating New Policies, Programs, and Plans, in Barbara C. Crosby and John M. Bryson, Leadership for the Common Good (San Francisco: Jossey-Bass, 2005), 335.

109. Senge, The Practice of Innovation, 65 (quoting O'Brien).

110. Kotter, Making Change Happen, 71.

111. Chip Heath and Dan Heath, Switch (New York: Broadway, 2010), 16-20.

112. Stephen Gandel-Dallas, How Blockbuster Failed at Failing, Time (October 11, 2010):38-40.

113. See Douglas Stone, Bruce Patton, and Sheila Heen, Difficult Conversations: How to Discuss What Matters Most (New York: Penguin Books, 1998); Cynthia M. Phoel, Feedback That Works, Harvard Management Update 11 (2006):3.

114. For a similar list, see Quinn et al., Becoming a Master Manager, 62.

115. Studies by the Leadership Development Institute and the Center for Creative Leadership estimate between 20 to 40 percent. Craig E. Runde and Tim A. Flanagan, Becoming a Conflict

Competent Leader (San Francisco: Jossey-Bass, 2007), 12. Other research estimates that the average executive spends the equivalent of seven weeks a year (roughly 15 percent of his or her time) dealing with workplace disputes. Gerzon, Leading through Conflict, 34.

116. Robert E. Quinn, Sue R. Faerman, Michael P. Thompson, Michael R. McGrath, and Lynda S. St. Clair, Becoming a Master Manager (Hoboken, NJ: John Wiley & Sons, 5th ed. 2011), 89 (quoting William Wrigley).

117. Barbara A. Nagle Lechman, Conflict and Resolution (New York: Aspen Publishers, 2008), 4; Runde and Flanagan, Becoming a Conflict Competent Leader, 115.

118. Runde and Flanagan, Becoming a Conflict Competent Leader, 21.

119. Ho-Wan Joeng, Understanding Conflict and Conflict Analysis (Thousand Oaks, CA: Sage Publications, 2008), 5.

120. Quinn et al., Becoming a Master Manager, 89.

121. Kenneth R. Melchin and Cherryl A Picard, Transforming Conflict through Insight (Toronto: University of Toronto Press, 2008), 36-38.

122. See Joeng, Understanding Conflict and Conflict Analysis, 8-13; Lechman, Conflict and Resolution, 8; Runde and Flanagan, Becoming a Conflict Competent Leader, 28-35.

123. See Jeong, Understanding Conflict, 74; Runde and Flanagan, Becoming a Conflict Competent Leader, 49; and Chapter 4.

124. Richard Birke and Craig R. Fox, Psychological Principles in Negotiating Civil Settlements, Harvard Negotiation Law Review 4 (1999):34-35.

125. Robert Mnookin, Why Negotiations Fail: An Exploration of Barriers to the Resolution of Conflict, Ohio State Journal on Dispute Resolution 8 (1993):235, 246.

126. Carol Tavris and Eliot Aronsen, Mistakes Were Made (but not by me) (New York: Harcourt, 2007), 42.

127. Connie Green, Leader Member Exchange and the Use of Moderating Conflict Management Styles, International Journal of Conflict Management 19 (2008):92.

128. Jeong, Understanding Conflict, 30; Lechman, Conflict and Resolution, 21-22.

129. David L. Bradford and Allan R. Cohen, Power Talk: A Hands-on Guide to Supportive Confrontation, in Alla R. Cohen and David L. Bradford, eds., Power Up: Transforming Organizations through Shared Leadership (New York: Wiley and Sons, 1998), 321, 323, 345.

130. Runde and Flanagan, Becoming a Conflict Competent Leader, 117, 161.

131. Manfred Kets de Vries and Elizabeth Engellau, A Clinical Approach to the Dynamics of Leadership and Executive Transformation, in Nohria and Khurana, eds., Handbook of Leadership Theory and Practice, 183, 199.

132. Gary Goodpaster, A Primer on Competitive Bargaining, Journal of Dispute Resolution (1996):327.

133. Green, Leader Member Exchange, 96; Jeong, Understanding Conflict, 40; Runde and Flanagan, Becoming a Conflict Competent Leader, 44.

134. Runde and Flanagan, Becoming a Conflict Competent Leader, 45; Jeswald W. Salacuse, Ten Ways That Culture Affects Negotiating Style: Some Survey Results, Negotiation Journal 14 (1998):221; Deborah A. Prentice and Dale T. Miller eds., Cultural Divides: Understanding and Overcoming Group Conflict (New York: Russell Sage, 2001). See also discussion in Chapter 2.

135. Kevin Avruch, Culture as Context, Culture as Communication: Considerations for Humanitarian Negotiators, Harvard Negotiation Law Review 9 (2004):391, 392-398.

136. For discussion of BATNAs and negotiation strategy generally, see William Ury and Roger Fisher, Getting to Yes (New York: Penguin, 2d ed. 1991).

137. Robert S. Adler, Benson Rosen, and Elliot M. Silverstein, Emotions in Negotiation: How to Manage Fear and Anger, Negotiation Journal 142 (1998):161.

138. Melchin and Picard, Transforming Conflict through Insight, 79; Lechman, Conflict and Resolution, 28 (noting that experts estimate that less than 10 percent of communication comes from substantive content; the rest comes from facial gesture, tone, and so forth).

139. Bradford and Cohen, Power Talk: A Hands-on Guide to Supportive Confrontation, 331.

140. Fisher and Ury, Getting to Yes, ix.

141. James J. White, The Pros and Cons of 'Getting to Yes,' Journal of Legal Education 34 (1984):115, 123 (comments of Roger Fisher).

142. Melchin and Piccard, Transforming Conflict, 79-80; Van Wart, Dynamics of Leadership in Public Service, 222; Bradford and Cohen, Power Talk, 340 (discussing toothless promises). See also Gerzon, Leading through Conflict, 50, 136 (suggesting open-ended questions, such as "What would it take to increase your trust?").

143. Kathleen M. Eisenhardt, Jean L. Kahwajy, and L.J. Bourgeois, How Management Teams Can Have a Good Fight, Harvard Business Review (July-August 1997):2; Robert Hargrove, Masterful Coaching (New York: Pfeiffer, 3d ed. 2008), 235-245.

144. Runde and Flanagan, Becoming a Conflict Competent Leader, 171; Van Wart, Dynamics of Leadership, 221-224.

145. Tom R. Tyler, Why People Obey the Law (Princeton, NJ: Princeton University Press, 2006); Tom R. Tyler, ed., Readings in Procedural Justice (Burlington, VT: Ashgate, 2005).

146. Mark Gerzon, Leading through Conflict (Boston: Harvard Business School Press, 2006), 69.

147. For an example of a self-rating questionnaire, see Steven L. Wilson and Michael S. Waldman, Assessing the Putnam-Wilson Organizational Communication Conflict Instrument (OCCI), Management Communication Quarterly 1 (February 1988):382-384.

148. Robert Reich, Locked in the Cabinet, excerpted in the New Yorker, April 21, 1997, 43.

149. Timothy J. Koegel, The Exceptional Presenter (Austin, TX: Greenleaf Book Group, 2007), 37.

150. Hillary Clinton, Living History (New York: Simon and Schuster, 2003), 187.

151. Koegel, The Exceptional Presenter, 109.

152. P.G. Woodehouse, The Girl in Blue (New York: Simon and Schuster, 1971), 100-101.

153. Koegel, The Exceptional Presenter, 14.

154. Koegel, The Exceptional Presenter, 91-93.

155. Deborah L. Rhode, The Beauty Bias (New York: Oxford, 2010), 30-31.

156. For the importance of first impressions, see Jeffrey Pfeffer, Power: Why Some People Have It and Others Don't (New York: Harper Collins, 2010), 148-149.

157. William Manchester, The Last Lion, Winston Spencer Churchill 1874-1932 (New York: Dell, 1983), quoted in John W. Gardner, On Leadership (New York: Free Press 1990), 51.

158. Heath and Heath, Made to Stick, 75.

159. Roger Gill, Theory and Practice of Leadership (Thousand Oaks, CA: Sage Publications, 2006), 260-262. D. Armstrong, Managing by Storying Around: A New Method of Leadership (New York: Doubleday, 1992).

160. Patterson et al., Influencer, 60 (describing experiment in which students were asked to recall information several weeks later).

161. Chip Heath and Dan Heath, Made to Stick: Why Some Ideas Survive and Others Die (New York: Random House, 2007), 16-18.

162. Id. at 6-7 (quoting Abe Silverman).

163. Heath and Heath, Made to Stick, 6-7.

164. Gardner, Changing Minds 85, 101

165. Id. at 86.

166. Id. at 76.

167. Sarah A. Soule, Contention and Corporate Social Responsibility (New York: Cambridge University Press, 2009).

168. See C. Atkinson, Beyond Bullet Points: Using Microsoft PowerPoint to Create Presentations That Inform, Motivate, and Inspire (Redmond, WA: Microsoft Press, 2007).

169. William Safire, Prolegemon, in William Safire and Leonard Safire, eds., Leadership (New York: Simon and Schuster, 1990), 19 (quoting Eisenhower).

170. S. Jonathan Bass, Blessed Are the Peacemakers: Martin Luther King, Jr., Eight White Religious Leaders, and the Letter from Birmingham Jail (Baton Rouge: Louisiana State University Press, 2001); Foster Hailey, Dr. King Arrested at Birmingham, New York Times, April 13, 1963, 1.

171. Philip Foner, Frederick Douglas on Women's Rights (Westport, CT: Greenwood Press, 1976), 30 (quoting Anthony). For racism within the women's movement, see Deborah L. Rhode, Justice and Gender (Cambridge, MA: Harvard University Press, 1989), 16.

172. Martin Luther King Jr., I Have a Dream, August 28, 1963, Martin Luther King Papers, King Library, Stanford University, available at http://mk-kpp01.stanford.edu/kingweb/publications/speeches/addressatmarchonWashington.pdf. For discussion of this speech and the Birmingham letter, see Mark Vail, The Integrative Rhetoric of Martin Luther King Jr.'s, 'I Have a Dream Speech, Rhetoric and Public Affairs 9 (2006):51.

173. Eric J. Sundquist, We Dreamed a Dream; Ralph Ellison, Martin Luther King, Jr., and Barack Obama, Daedelus (Winter 2011):114.

174. Barack Obama, Candidate for U.S. Senate in Illinois, Keynote Address at the Democratic National Convention (July 27, 2004) (transcript available at http://www.washingtonpost.com/ac2/wp-dyn/A19751-2004Jul27?language=printer).

175. Barack Obama, Inaugural Address, January 20, 2009, available at http://www.presidency.ucsb.edu/ws/index.php?pid=44&st=&st1=.

176. Hillel Italie, Critics Assess Obama's Speeches, Capital Culture, January 26, 2010.

177. Frank Rich, It's a Bird, It's a Plane, It's Obama, New York Times, April 4, 2010, WK 9.

178. Joe Klein, The Natural (New York: Doubleday, 2002), 40, 79

179. Amitai Etzioni, Needed: A Progressive Story, The Nation, May 24, 2010, 22-23.

180. George Packer, Obama's Last Year, New Yorker, March 15, 2010, 46 (quoting aide).

181. Id. at 49 (quoting Frank).

182. Packer, Obama's Last Year, 49.

183. Julius Caesar's speech to his army from HBO's Rome is available at http://www.youtube.com/watch?v=5PeN1k9AAMg

184. For Pinker, see http://www.youtube.com/watch?v=DS4xVcko9qw. For Haidt, see http://www.youtube.com/watch?v=vs41JrnGaxc.

PART III

ETHICS IN LEADERSHIP

5

MORAL LEADERSHIP

In principle, the need for moral leadership is never in dispute. But in practice, controversy arises over what exactly it requires and how it can be achieved. Conflicts arise between means and ends, and between personal principles, political priorities, and organizational interests. Leaders face challenges not only in resolving their own ethical dilemmas but also in creating cultures that sustain moral values. The materials that follow explore these challenges and begin by setting them in historical context.

A. HISTORICAL FRAMEWORKS

Niccolò Machiavelli is a much maligned and much misunderstood thinker. His insights about political life are often reduced to simplistic sound bites, and his name carries pejorative connotations. Shakespeare referred to the "murderous Machiavel," and he was denounced as the "enemy of mankind" even by leaders such as Frederick the Great, who followed his advice.[1] Yet understood in context, Machiavelli offered a much more nuanced view of the role of leaders than is commonly acknowledged. Halfway through *The Prince*, he reminds readers of his goal: "Since my intention is to say something that will prove of practical use to the inquirer, I have thought it proper to represent things as they are in real truth, rather than as they are imagined."[2] Five centuries since its publication, the book remains one of the most realistic descriptions of the dilemmas of leadership.[3]

Machiavelli was very much a product of his times, but the problems he identified and the trade-offs he advocated have relevance for our own era. His insights can assist advisors as well as decision makers. Like Machiavelli, many lawyers, managers, and public officials are in the position of counseling leaders on how to make the best of bad situations and how to balance their own moral principles with the practical realities of governance.

To understand *The Prince*, it is necessary also to understand its historical context. Niccolò Machiavelli was born in Florence, Italy, in 1469. Although his family was not wealthy, his father was intimate with the city's leading scholars, and Machiavelli received an extensive humanist education steeped in the classics, Latin, rhetoric, ancient history and moral philosophy.[4] He lived in a climate of significant political instability. The Italian peninsula was fractured into several warring city states and was vulnerable to outside invasion by aggressive European monarchies and the Ottoman Empire. Florence was plagued by competing factions among the richest families and social unrest among the lower classes. Machiavelli saw the Florentine government change hands three times during his lifetime as a result of bloody internal coups and invasions by French and papal troops.[5] In 1494, Savonarola, a Dominican friar, began a reign in which he plunged the city into four years of religious fanaticism, until he was charged with heresy, excommunicated, tortured, and burned at the stake.[6] Machiavelli received his first government appointment when Savonarola was excommunicated and the officials associated with him were expelled. At age 29, Machiavelli became head of the Second Chancery, which required him to help manage Florence's territories and to travel on diplomatic missions. After fourteen years of service, he lost his position when Florence's republic fell in 1512. Papal troops invaded and reinstated the Medici family during a series of wars between Pope Julius II, Venice, Spain, and France. At first suspected of conspiracy against the new regime, Machiavelli was tortured, imprisoned, and fined.[7]

Machiavelli wrote *The Prince* in an effort to gain favor with the new Medici government. He dedicated the work to Lorenzo de Medici, and hoped to win a political appointment by displaying his considerable "knowledge of the actions of great men, learned by me from long experience with modern things and a continuous reading of ancient ones."[8] The book is structured as a straightforward presentation of different forms of governance using classical and contemporary leaders as illustrative models of successes and failures. Ironically, although Machiavelli was highly critical of "unarmed prophets" such as Savonarola, he himself was "armed with only a pen when he became the prophet of a new understanding of politics."[9]

The work is famous for its recognition of the role of chance, and infamous for its conclusion that morality is situational and that rulers must do whatever is necessary to maintain the state, however incompatible with conventional moral principles. One of Machiavelli's core arguments is that a leader can be only as good as circumstances allow and that many individuals of great ability and integrity can be "ruined by fortune." Although often reviled for his elevation of prudence over principle, Machiavelli believed that the cruelties he advocated were morally justified to maintain social order and to prevent greater, more widespread brutality. Without a functioning state or a strong leader, "disorders . . . continue, from which come killings or robberies; for these customarily hurt a whole community."[10] Individuals could not survive outside society, and society could not survive if led by those who put private morality first. A "virtuous" leader who fails to create "security and well-being" is unworthy of praise.[11] In effect, Machiavelli distinguished between public and private morality and argued that the "greatest good that one could do and the most gratifying to God is that which one does for one's country."[12] Contrary to popular views, Machiavelli did not lack a moral compass. It was rather, as he put it in a letter to a contemporary, he loved his country more than his soul.[13]

In the following excerpts from *The Prince*, Machiavelli elaborates on the qualities of successful leadership.

Niccolò Machiavelli, The Prince (1532)

Harvey C. Mansfield, trans. (Chicago: University of Chicago Press, 2d ed. 1998)

Chapter VIII: Of Those Who Have Attained a Principality through Crimes

Yet one cannot call it virtue to kill one's citizens, betray one's friends, to be without faith, without mercy, without religion; these modes can enable one to acquire empire, but not glory. . . . [The test is whether] cruelties [are] badly used or well used. Those can be called well used (if it is permissible to speak well of evil) that are done at a stroke, out of the necessity to secure oneself, and then are not persisted in but are turned to as much utility for the subjects as one can. Those cruelties are badly used which, though few in the beginning, rather grow with time than are eliminated. Those who observe the first mode can have some remedy for their state with God and with men . . . ; as for the others it is impossible for them to maintain themselves.

Hence it should be noted that in taking hold of a state, he who seizes it should review all the offenses necessary for him to commit, and do them all at a stroke, so as not to have to renew them every day and, by not renewing them, to secure men and gain them to himself with benefits. Whoever does otherwise, either through timidity or through bad counsel, is always under necessity to hold a knife in his hand; nor can one ever found himself on his subjects if, because of fresh and continued injuries, they cannot be secure against him. For injuries must be done all together, so that, being tasted less, they offend less; and benefits should be done little by little so that they may be tasted better. And above all, a prince should live with his subjects so that no single accident whether bad or good has to make him change; for when necessities come in adverse times you will not be in time for evil, and the good that you do does not help you, because it is judged to be forced on you, and cannot bring you any gratitude. . . .

Chapter XV: Of Those Things for Which Men and Especially Princes Are Praised or Blamed

. . . For a man who wants to make a profession of good in all regards must come to ruin among so many who are not good. Hence it is necessary to a prince, if he wants to maintain himself, to learn to be able not to be good, and to use this and not use it according to necessity. . . .

Chapter XVII: Of Cruelty and Mercy, and Whether It Is Better to Be Loved Than Feared, or the Contrary

Descending next to the other qualities cited before, I say that each prince should desire to be held merciful and not cruel; nonetheless he should take care not to use this mercy badly. . . . A prince, therefore, so as to keep his subjects united and faithful, should not care about the infamy of cruelty, because with very few examples he will be more merciful than those who for the sake of too much mercy allow disorders to continue, from which come killings or robberies; for these customarily hurt a whole community, but the executions that come from the prince hurt one particular person. . . .

[D]ispute arises whether it is better to be loved than feared, or the reverse. The response is that one would want to be both the one and the other; but because it is difficult to put them together, it is much safer to be feared than loved, if one has to lack one of the two. For one can say this generally of men: that they are ungrateful, fickle, pretenders and dissemblers, evaders of danger, eager for gain. While you do them good, they are yours, offering you their blood, property, lives, and children, as I said above, when the need for them is far away; but, when it is close to you, they revolt. And that prince who has founded himself entirely on their words, stripped of other preparation, is ruined; for friendships that are acquired at a price and not with greatness and nobility of spirit are brought, but they are not owned and when the time comes they cannot be spent. And men have less hesitation to offend one who makes himself loved than one who makes himself feared; for love is held by a chain of obligation, which, because men are wicked, is broken at every opportunity for their own utility, but fear is held by a dread of punishment that never forsakes you.

The prince should nonetheless make himself feared in such a mode that if he does not acquire love, he escapes hatred, because being feared and not being hated can go together very well. This he will do if he abstains from the property of his citizens and his subjects, and from their women; and if he also needs to proceed against someone's life, he must do it when there is suitable justification and manifest cause for it. But above all, he must abstain from the property of others, because men forget the death of a father more quickly than the loss of a patrimony. Furthermore, causes for taking away property are never lacking, and he who begins to live by rapine always finds cause to seize others' property; and, on the contrary, causes for taking life are rarer and disappear more quickly. . . .

I conclude, then, returning to being feared and loved, that since men love at their convenience and fear at the convenience of the prince, a wise prince should found himself on what is his, not on what is someone else's; he should only contrive to avoid hatred, as was said.

Chapter XVIII: In What Mode Faith Should Be Kept by Princes

How praiseworthy it is for a prince to keep his faith, and to live with honesty and not by astuteness, everyone understands. Nonetheless one sees by experience in our times that the princes who have done great things are those who have taken little account of faith and have known how to get around men's brains with their astuteness; and in the end they have overcome those who have founded themselves on loyalty.

Thus, you must know that there are two kinds of combat: one with laws, the other with force. The first is proper to man, the second to beasts; but because the first is often not enough, one must have recourse to the second. Therefore it is necessary for a prince to know well how to use the beast and the man. . . . [S]ince a prince is compelled of necessity to know well how to use the beast, he should pick the fox and the lion, because the lion does not defend itself from snares and the fox does not defend itself from wolves. So one needs to be a fox to recognize snares and a lion to frighten the wolves. Those who stay simply with the lion do not understand this. A prudent lord, therefore, cannot observe faith, nor should he, when such observance turns against him, and the causes that made him promise have been eliminated. And if all men were good, this teaching would not be good; but because they are wicked and do not observe faith with you, you do not always have to observe it with them. Nor does a prince ever lack legitimate causes to color his failure to observe faith. One could give infinite modern examples of this, and show how many peace treaties and promises have been rendered invalid and vain through the infidelity of princes; and the one who has known best how to use the fox has come out the best. But it is necessary to know well how to color this nature, and to be a great pretender and dissembler; and men are so simple and so obedient to present necessities that he who deceives will always find someone who will let himself be deceived. . . .

Thus, it is not necessary for a prince to have all the . . . [virtues] in fact, but it is indeed necessary to appear to have them. Nay, I dare say this, that by having them and always observing them, they are harmful; and by appearing to have them, they are useful as it is to appear merciful, faithful, humane, honest, and religious, and to be so; but to remain with a spirit built so that, if you need not to be those things, you are able and know how to change to the contrary. This has to be understood: that a prince, and especially a new prince, cannot observe all those things for which men are held to be good, since he is often under a necessity, to maintain his state, of acting against faith, against charity, against humanity, against religion. And so he needs to have a spirit disposed to change as the winds of fortune and variations of things command him, and as I said above, not depart from good, when possible, but know how to enter into evil, when forced by necessity.

A prince should thus take great care that nothing escape his mouth that is not full of the above-mentioned five qualities and that, to see him and hear him, he should appear all mercy, all faith, all honesty, all humanity, all religion. And nothing is more necessary to appear to have than this last quality. Men in general judge more by their eyes than by their hands, because seeing is given to everyone, touching to few. Everyone sees how you appear, few touch what you are; and these few dare not to oppose the opinion of many who have the majesty of the state to defend them; and in the actions of all men, and especially of princes, where there is not court to appeal to, one looks to the end. So let a prince win and maintain his state: the means will always be judged honorable, and will be praised by everyone. For the vulgar are taken in by the appearance and outcome of a thing, and in the world there is no one but the vulgar; the few have a place there when the many have somewhere to lean on.

NOTES AND QUESTIONS

1. Machiavelli is scarcely alone among political leaders and theorists in viewing the stability and security of the state as the preeminent responsibility of the ruler. From their perspective, the rule of law and conventional moral values must sometimes be subordinated to national security because without such security, there can be no law or protection of values. In effect, desperate times require desperate remedies.[14] Yet what is distinctive about Machiavelli is that he saw such measures not as extraordinary interventions to preserve a system in which they would be unnecessary, but as ordinary

demands of political life. Does his account adequately frame the issue and give due regard to the competing interests at issue? Many actions might add somewhat to security, but they would compromise other core commitments (e.g., assassination, indefinite detention of suspected terrorists, or assistance to despotic regimes). How should the trade-offs be made? Consider President Truman's decision whether to drop the atomic bomb on Japanese cities.[15] What considerations should be most relevant in making such decisions?

2. Machiavelli argues that it is "much safer to be feared than loved." Is this true of leaders generally? Does it depend on how much hard power a leader has and the nature of compliance being sought? Recall Roderick Kramer's article "Great Intimidators," and Daniel Goleman's work on emotional intelligence discussed in Chapter 2. Does Machiavelli offer insights about fear that are relevant for leadership today? How often will rulers who are ruthless and intimidating enough to be effective in the circumstances that Machiavelli envisioned also be sufficiently disinterested to put the interests of the public above their own?

3. As the renowned British philosopher Isaiah Berlin noted, Machiavelli's "psychology seems excessively primitive. He scarcely seems to allow for the bare possibility of sustained and genuine altruism."[16] Nor does his vision of followers seem plausible in light of what we now know about the importance of intrinsic motivation and the limits of hard power. How might a more complicated understanding of human psychology affect his analysis?

4. Machiavelli argues that it is "useful to appear to be merciful, faithful, humane, honest, and religious," but also to "know how to change to the contrary." He discounts concerns about hypocrisy on the theory that "men are so simple and so obedient" that they will let themselves be deceived. Is that true today? If not, what follows? Would it be better for leaders to be less hypocritical and more honest about the moral trade-offs that they face? Or, as theorists such as Ruth Grant argue, "because society requires morality but men are not always moral, hypocrisy is inevitable. Hypocrisy only occurs where . . . people need to be thought of as good and to think of themselves as good. Where there is political hypocrisy, there is a public moral standard and a significant moral impulse."[17] Are there ways other than hypocrisy for leaders to honor that moral impulse even when they fall short of its demands? Chapter 7 explores that issue in connection with personal scandals. Michael Walzer takes up that question as it plays out for political leaders.

B. DIRTY HANDS

Michael Walzer, "Political Action: The Problem of Dirty Hands"

Philosophy & Public Affairs, 2(2) (Winter 1973):160-180

[Are there moral dilemmas in which a man] must choose between two courses of action both of which it would be wrong for him to undertake[?] . . .

In modern times the dilemma appears most often as the problem of "dirty hands," and it is typically stated by the Communist leader Hoerderer in Sartre's play of that name: "I have dirty hands right up to the elbows. I've plunged them in filth and blood. Do you think you can govern innocently?" My own answer is no, I don't think I could govern innocently; nor do most of us believe that those who govern us are innocent — as I shall argue below — even the best of them. But this does not mean that it isn't possible to do the right thing while governing. It means that a particular act of government (in a political party or in the state) may be exactly the right thing to do in utilitarian terms and yet leave the man who does it guilty of a moral wrong. The innocent man, afterwards, is no longer innocent. If on the other hand he remains innocent, chooses, that is, the "absolutist" [position], . . . he not only fails to do the right thing (in utilitarian terms), he may also fail to measure up to the duties of his office (which imposes on him a considerable responsibility for consequences and outcomes). Most often, of course, political leaders accept the utilitarian calculation; they try to measure up. One might offer a number of sardonic comments on this fact, the most obvious being that by the calculations they usually make they demonstrate the great virtues of the "absolutist" position. Nevertheless, we would not want to be governed by men who consistently adopted that position. . . .

Let me begin, then, with a piece of conventional wisdom to the effect that politicians are a good deal worse, morally worse, than the rest of us (it is the wisdom of the rest of us). Without either endorsing it or pretending to disbelieve it, I am going to expound this convention. For it suggests that the dilemma of dirty hands is a central feature of political life, that it arises not merely as an occasional crisis in the career of this or that unlucky politician but systematically and frequently.

Why is the politician singled out? Isn't he like the other entrepreneurs in an open society, who hustle, lie, intrigue, wear masks, smile and are villains? He is not, no doubt for many reasons, three of which I need to consider. First of all, the politician claims to play a different part than other entrepreneurs. He doesn't merely cater to our interests; he acts on our behalf, even in our name. He has purposes in mind, causes and projects that require the support and redound to the benefit, not of each of us individually, but of all of us together. He hustles, lies, and intrigues *for us* — or so he claims. Perhaps he is right, or at least sincere, but we suspect that he acts for himself also. Indeed, he cannot serve us without serving himself, for success brings him power and glory, the greatest rewards that men can win from their fellows. The competition for these two is fierce; the risks are often great, but the temptations are greater. We imagine ourselves succumbing. Why should our representatives act differently? Even if they would like to act differently, they probably can not: for other men are all too ready to hustle and lie for power and glory, and it is the others who set the terms of the competition. Hustling and lying are necessary because power and glory are so desirable — that is, so widely desired. And so the men who act for us and in our name are necessarily hustlers and liars.

Politicians are also thought to be worse than the rest of us because they rule over us, and the pleasures of ruling are much greater than the pleasures of being ruled. The successful politician becomes the visible architect of our restraint. He taxes us, licenses us, forbids and permits us, directs us to this or that distant goal — all for our greater good. Moreover, he takes chances for our greater good that put us, or some of us, in danger. . . . There are undoubtedly times when it is good or necessary to direct the affairs of other people and to put them in danger. But we are a little frightened of the man who seeks, ordinarily and every day, the power to do so. And the fear is reasonable enough. The politician has, or pretends to have, a kind of confidence in his own judgment that the rest of us know to be presumptuous in any man. . . .

No one succeeds in politics without getting his hands dirty. This is conventional wisdom again, and again I don't mean to insist that it is true without qualification. I repeat it only to disclose the moral dilemma inherent in the convention. For sometimes it is right to try to succeed, and then it must also be right to get one's hands dirty. But one's hands get dirty from doing what it is wrong to do. And how can it be wrong to do what is right? Or, how can we get our hands dirty by doing what we ought to do? . . .

It will be best to turn quickly to some examples. I have chosen two, one relating to the struggle for power and one to its exercise. . . . [L]et us imagine a politician . . . [who] wants to do good only by doing good, or at least he is certain that he can stop short of the most corrupting and brutal uses of political power. . . . In order to win the election the candidate must make a deal with a dishonest ward boss, involving the granting of contracts for school construction over the next four years. Should he make the deal? Well, at least he shouldn't be surprised by the offer, most of us would probably say (a conventional piece of sarcasm). And he should accept it or not, depending on exactly what is at stake in the election. But that is not the candidate's view. He is extremely reluctant even to consider the deal, puts off his aides when they remind him of it, refuses to calculate its possible effects upon the campaign. Now, if he is acting this way because the very thought of bargaining with that particular ward boss makes him feel unclean, his reluctance isn't very interesting. His feelings by themselves are not important. But he may also have reasons for his reluctance. He may know, for example, that some of his supporters support him precisely because they believe he is a good man, and this means to them a man who won't make such deals. Or he may doubt his own motives for considering the deal, wondering whether it is the political campaign or his own candidacy that makes the bargain at all tempting. Or he may believe that if he makes deals of this sort now he may not be able later on to achieve those ends that make the campaign worthwhile, and he may not feel entitled to take such risks with a future that is not only his own future. Or he may simply think that the deal is dishonest and therefore wrong, corrupting not only himself but all those human relations in which he is involved.

Because he has scruples of this sort, we know him to be a good man. But we view the campaign in a certain light, estimate its importance in a certain way, and hope that he will overcome his scruples and make the deal. It is important to stress that we don't want just *anyone* to make the deal; we want *him* to make it, precisely because he has scruples about it. We know he is doing right when he makes the deal because he knows he is doing wrong. I don't mean merely that he will feel badly or even very badly after he makes the deal. If he is the good man I am imagining him to be, he will feel guilty, that is, he will believe himself to be guilty. That is what it means to have dirty hands.

All this may become clearer if we look at a more dramatic example, for we are, perhaps, a little blasé about political deals and disinclined to worry much about the man who makes one. So consider a politician who has seized upon a national crisis—a prolonged colonial war—to reach for power. He and his friends win office pledged to decolonization and peace; they are honestly committed to both, though not without some sense of the advantages of the commitment. In any case, they have no responsibility for the war; they have steadfastly opposed it. Immediately, the politician goes off to the colonial capital to open negotiations with the rebels. But the capital is in the grip of a terrorist campaign, and the first decision the new leader faces is this—he is asked to authorize the torture of a captured rebel leader who knows or probably knows the location of a number of bombs hidden in apartment buildings around the city, set to go off within the next twenty-four hours. He orders the man tortured, convinced that he must do so for the sake of the people who might otherwise die in the explosions—even though he believes that torture is wrong, indeed abominable, not just sometimes, but always. He had expressed this belief often and angrily during his own campaign; the rest of us took it as a sign of his goodness. How should we regard him now? (How should he regard himself?)

Once again, it does not seem enough to say that he should feel very badly. But why not? Why shouldn't he have feelings like those of St. Augustine's melancholy soldier, who understood both that his war was just and that killing, even in a just war, is a terrible thing to do? The difference is that Augustine did not believe that it was wrong to kill in a just war; it was just sad, or the sort of thing a good man would be saddened by. But he might have thought it wrong to torture in a just war, and later Catholic theorists have certainly thought it wrong. Moreover, the politician I am imagining thinks it wrong, as do many of us who supported him. Surely we have a right to expect more than melancholy from him now. When he ordered the prisoner tortured, he committed a moral crime and he accepted a moral burden. Now he is a guilty man. His willingness to acknowledge and bear (and perhaps to repent and do penance for) his guilt is evidence, and it is the only evidence he can offer us, both that he is not too good for politics and that he is good enough. Here is the moral politician: it is by his dirty hands that we know him. If he were a moral man and nothing else, his hands would not be dirty; if he were a politician and nothing else, he would pretend that they were clean. . . .

[There are three ways to try to escape this dilemma.] First, it might be said that every political choice ought to be made solely in terms of its particular and immediate circumstances—in terms, that is, of the reasonable alternatives, available knowledge, likely consequences, and so on. Then the good man will face difficult choices (when his knowledge of options and outcomes is radically uncertain), but it cannot happen that he will face a moral dilemma. . . . Even when he lies and tortures, his hands will be clean, for he has done what he should do as best he can, standing alone in a moment of time, forced to choose.

This is in some ways an attractive description of moral decision-making, but it is also a very improbable one. For while any one of us may stand alone, and so on, when we make this or that decision, we are not isolated or solitary in our moral lives. Moral life is a social phenomenon, and it is constituted at least in part by rules, the knowing of which (and perhaps the making of which) we share with our fellows. The experience of coming up against these rules, challenging their prohibitions, and explaining ourselves to other men and women is so common and so obviously important that no account of moral decision-making can possibly fail to come to grips with it. Hence the second utilitarian argument: such rules do indeed exist, but they are not really prohibitions of wrongful actions (though they do, perhaps for pedagogic reasons, have that form). They are moral guidelines, summaries of previous calculations. They ease our choices in ordinary cases, for we can simply follow their injunctions and do what has been found useful in the past; in exceptional cases they serve as signals warning us against doing too quickly or without the most careful calculations what has not been found useful in the past. But they do no more than that; they have no other purpose, and so it cannot be the case that it is or even might be a crime to override them. Nor is it necessary to feel guilty when one does so. Once again, if it is right to break the rule in some hard case, after conscientiously worrying about it, the man who acts (especially if he knows that many of his fellows would simply worry rather than act) may properly feel pride in his achievement.

But this view, it seems to me, captures the reality of our moral life no better than the last. It may well be right to say that moral rules ought to have the character of guidelines, but it seems that in fact they do not. Or at least, we defend ourselves when we break the rules as if they had some status entirely independent of their previous utility (and we rarely feel proud of ourselves). . . .

When rules are overridden, we do not talk or act as if they had been set aside, canceled, or annulled. They still stand and have this much effect at least: that we know we have done something wrong even if what we have done was also the best thing to do on the whole in the circumstances. Or at least we feel that way, and this feeling is itself a crucial feature of our moral life. Hence the third utilitarian argument, which recognizes the usefulness of guilt and seeks to explain it. There are, it appears, good reasons for "overvaluing" as well as for overriding the rules. For the consequences might be very bad indeed if the rules were overridden every time the moral calculation seemed to go against them. It is probably best if most men do not calculate too nicely, but simply follow the rules; they are less likely to make mistakes that way, all in all. And so a good man (or at least an ordinary good man) will respect the rules rather more than he would if he thought them merely guidelines, and he will feel guilty when he overrides them. Indeed, if he did not feel guilty, "he would not be such a good man." It is by his feelings that we know him. Because of those feelings he will never be in a hurry to override the rules, but will wait until there is no choice, acting only to avoid consequences that are both imminent and almost certainly disastrous.

The obvious difficulty with this argument is that the feeling whose usefulness is being explained is most unlikely to be felt by someone who is convinced only of its usefulness. He breaks a utilitarian rule (guideline), let us say, for good utilitarian reasons: but can he then feel guilty, also for good utilitarian reasons, when he has no reason for believing that he is guilty? . . . I do not want to exclude the possibility of a kind of superstitious anxiety, the possibility, that is, that some men will continue to feel guilty even after they have been taught, and have agreed, that they cannot possibly *be* guilty. It is best to say only that the more fully they accept the utilitarian account, the less likely they are to feel that (useful) feeling. . . .

. . . The first tradition [of thinking about dirty hands] is best represented by Machiavelli, the first man, so far as I know, to state the paradox that I am examining. The good man who aims to found or reform a republic must, Machiavelli tells us, do terrible things to reach his goal. . . . Sometimes, however, "when the act accuses, the result excuses." This sentence from *The Discourses* is often taken to mean that the politician's deceit and cruelty are justified by the good results he brings about. But if they were justified, it wouldn't be necessary to learn what Machiavelli claims to teach: how not to be good. It would only be necessary to learn how to be good in a new, more difficult, perhaps roundabout way. That is not Machiavelli's argument. His political judgments are indeed consequentialist in character, but not his moral judgments. We know whether cruelty is used well or badly by its effects over time. But that it is bad to use cruelty we know in some other way. The deceitful and cruel politician is excused (if he succeeds) only in the sense that the rest of us come to agree that the results were "worth it" or, more likely, that we simply forget his crimes when we praise his success.

It is important to stress Machiavelli's own commitment to the existence of moral standards. His paradox depends upon that commitment as it depends upon the general stability of the standards — which he upholds in his consistent use of words like good and bad. If he wants the standards to be disregarded by good men more often than they are, he has nothing with which to replace them and no other way of recognizing the good men except by their allegiance to those same standards. It is exceedingly rare, he writes, that a good man is willing to employ bad means to become prince. Machiavelli's purpose is to persuade such a person to make the attempt, and he holds out the supreme political rewards, power and glory, to the man who does so and succeeds. The good man is not rewarded (or excused), however, merely for his willingness to get his hands dirty. He must do bad things well. There is no reward for doing bad things badly, though they are done with the best of intentions. And so political action necessarily involves taking a risk. But it should be clear that what is risked is not personal goodness — *that is thrown away* — but power and glory. If the politician succeeds, he is a hero; eternal praise is the supreme reward for not being good.

What the penalties are for not being good, Machiavelli doesn't say, and it is probably for this reason above all that his moral sensitivity has so often been questioned. He is suspect not because he tells political actors they must get their hands dirty, but because he does not specify the state of mind appropriate to a man with dirty hands. A Machiavellian hero has no inwardness. What he thinks of himself we don't know. I would guess, along with most other readers of Machiavelli, that he basks in his glory. But then it is difficult to account for the strength of his original reluctance to learn how not to be good. In any case, he is the sort of man who is unlikely to keep a diary and so we cannot find out what he thinks. Yet we do want to know; above all, we want a record of his anguish. That is, a sign of our own conscientiousness and of the impact on us of the second tradition of thought that I want to examine, in which personal anguish sometimes seems the only acceptable excuse for political crimes.

The second tradition is best represented, I think, by Max Weber, who outlines its essential features with great power at the very end of his essay "Politics as a Vocation." For Weber, the good man with dirty hands is a hero still, but he is a tragic hero. In part, his tragedy is that though politics is his vocation, he has not been called by God and so cannot be justified by Him. Weber's hero is alone in a world that seems to belong to Satan, and his vocation is entirely his own choice. He still wants what Christian magistrates have always wanted, both to do good in the world and to save his soul, but now these two ends have come into sharp contradiction. They are contradictory because of the necessity for violence in a world where God has not instituted the sword. The politician takes the sword himself, and only by doing so does he measure up to his vocation. With full consciousness of what he is doing, he does bad in order to do good, and surrenders his soul. He "lets himself in," Weber says, "for the diabolic forces lurking in all violence." Perhaps Machiavelli also meant to suggest that his hero surrenders salvation in exchange for glory, but he does not explicitly say so. Weber is absolutely clear: "the genius or demon of politics lives in an inner tension with the god of love . . . [which] can at any time lead to an irreconcilable conflict." His politician views this conflict when it comes with a tough realism, never pretends that it might be solved by compromise, chooses politics once again, and turns decisively away from love. . . .

Weber attempts to resolve the problem of dirty hands entirely within the confines of the individual conscience, but I am inclined to think that this is neither possible nor desirable. The self-awareness of the tragic hero is obviously of great value. We want the politician to have an inner life at least something like that which Weber describes. But sometimes the hero's suffering needs to be socially expressed (for like punishment, it confirms and reinforces our sense that certain acts are wrong). And equally important, it sometimes needs to be socially limited. We don't want to be ruled by men who have lost their souls. A politician with dirty hands needs a soul, and it is best for us all if he has some hope of personal salvation, however that is conceived. It is not the case that when he does bad in order to do good he surrenders himself forever to the demon of politics. He commits a determinate crime, and he must pay a determinate penalty. When he has done so, his hands will be clean again, or as clean as human hands can ever be. So the Catholic Church has always taught, and this teaching is central to the third tradition that I want to examine.

Once again I will take a . . . lapsed representative of the tradition and consider Albert Camus' The Just Assassins. The heroes of this play are terrorists at work in nineteenth-century Russia. The dirt on their hands is human blood. And yet Camus' admiration for them, he tells us, is complete. We consent to being criminals, one of them says, but there is nothing with which anyone can reproach us. Here is the dilemma of dirty hands in a new form. The heroes are innocent criminals, just assassins, because, having killed, they are prepared to *die — and will die.* Only their execution, by the same despotic authorities they are attacking, will complete the action in which they are engaged: dying, they need make no excuses. That is the end of their guilt and pain. The execution is not so much punishment as self-punishment and expiation. On the scaffold they wash their hands clean and, unlike the suffering servant, they die happy. . . .

[J]ust assassination, I want to suggest, is like civil disobedience. In both men violate a set of rules, go beyond a moral or legal limit, in order to do what they believe they should do. At the same time, they acknowledge their responsibility for the violation by accepting punishment or doing penance. But there is also a difference between the two, which has to do with the difference between law and morality. In most cases of civil disobedience the laws of the state are broken for moral reasons, and the state provides the punishment. In most cases of dirty hands moral rules are broken for reasons of state, and no one provides the punishment. There is rarely a Czarist executioner waiting in the wings for politicians with dirty hands, even the most deserving among them. Moral rules are not usually enforced against the sort of actor I am considering, largely because he acts in an official capacity. . . . I am nevertheless inclined to think Camus' view the most attractive of the three, if only because it requires us at least to imagine a punishment or a penance that fits the crime and so to examine closely the nature of the crime. . . . Without the executioner, however, there is no one to set the stakes or maintain the values except ourselves, and probably no way to do either except through philosophic reiteration and political activity.

"We shall not abolish lying by refusing to tell lies," says Hoerderer, "but by using every means at hand to abolish social classes." I suspect we shall not abolish lying at all, but we might see to it that fewer lies were told if we contrived to deny power and glory to the greatest liars — except, of course, in the case of those lucky few whose extraordinary achievements make us forget the lies they told. If Hoerderer succeeds in abolishing social classes, perhaps he will join the lucky few. Meanwhile, he lies, manipulates, and kills, and we must make sure he pays the price. We won't be able to do that, however, without getting our own hands dirty, and then we must find some way of paying the price ourselves.

NOTES AND QUESTIONS

1. Walzer takes his title from Sartre's play, *Dirty Hands*, and quotes the communist leader who acknowledges, "I have dirty hands right up to the elbows. Do you think you can govern innocently?" Walzer, like Machiavelli, answers no, but he also believes, unlike Machiavelli, that the ruler should suffer anguish when he departs from moral principles. Machiavelli is known for the principle that when the act accuses, the result excuses. But according to Walzer, that cannot mean that wrongful acts are justified by good ends; if that were true, then the acts would not be wrongful, and Machiavelli would not need to provide instruction in how not to be good. The dilemma of political governance as Walzer presents it is one in which a leader must choose between two wrongs. Do you agree? How should the politician deal with the dishonest ward boss? Is moral anguish sufficient absolution?

Do all politicians who sacrifice moral conviction to win votes or campaign contributions dirty their hands? Or is Walzer talking about a different kind of dirt?

2. Are there parallels to dirty hands in corporate and professional life? Practices such as child labor, corrupt payments to foreign governments, and environmental damage have often been justified as the lesser of two evils, and necessary to prevent dire economic consequences. Are these fair analogies? What examples have you observed in legal or managerial contexts? Were they effectively resolved?

3. George Bernard Shaw captured the dirty hands dilemma in commenting on a Labour Party colleague who lost his seat in Parliament after refusing to compromise on an issue:

> When I think of my own unfortunate character, smirched with compromise, rotted with opportunism, mildewed by expediency . . . I do think Joe might have put up with just a speck or two on those white robes of his for the sake of the millions of poor devils who cannot afford any character at all because they have no friend in Parliament. Oh, these moral dandies, these spiritual toffs, these superior persons. Who is Joe anyhow, that he should not risk his soul occasionally like the rest of us?[18]

Some trade-offs between moral means and moral ends appear particularly necessary in government, because success is often "measured by a historian's yardstick" and undue insistence on principle can prevent compromises that are in society's long-term interests.[19]

As Richard Nixon put it:

> [A] leader has to deal with people and nations as they are, not as they should be. As a result, the qualities required for leadership are not necessarily those that we would want our children to emulate — unless we wanted them to be leaders. . . . Guile, vanity, dissembling — in other circumstances these might be unattractive habits, but to the leader they can be essential. . . . Roosevelt talked of keeping America out of war while maneuvering to bring it into war.[20]

Although dilemmas of dirty hands do not yield categorical solutions, many theorists agree that they should be subject to moral reasoning of the sort that Walzer supplies. British philosopher Bernard Williams suggests that conflating Plato's question "how can the good rule?" and Machiavelli's question "how to rule the world as it is?" leads to cynicism unless one adjusts the definitions: "[T]he good need not be pure, so long as they retain some active sense of moral costs and moral limits and [the culture] has some genuinely settled expectations of civic respectability."[21]

How helpful are such formulations in resolving concrete cases? One common criticism of utilitarian analysis in these contexts is that the costs and benefits may be contested, uncertain, indeterminate, and incommensurable. Decision makers' own stake in the outcome may also skew their evaluation of long-term consequences. Consider those difficulties in the following problem. What are their implications for resolving dirty-hands dilemmas more generally?

PROBLEM 5-1

In *Democracy*, Henry Adams's celebrated nineteenth-century novel, the narrative centers on Madeleine Lee, an idealistic Washington socialite who is courted by Ratcliffe, a highly successful Illinois senator in the post–Civil War era. Senator Ratcliffe takes an unabashedly Machiavellian view of politics, particularly when rationalizing his own involvement in two election scandals. About the first scandal he says:

> In the worst days of the war there was almost a certainty that my State would be carried by the peace party, by fraud. . . . Had Illinois been lost then, we should certainly have lost the Presidential election, and with it probably the Union. At any rate, I believed the fate of the war to depend on the result. I was then Governor, and upon me the responsibility rested.

To secure victory, Ratcliffe and his fellow party members stuffed the ballot boxes. He was "not proud of the transaction, but [he] would do it again, and worse than that, if [he] thought it would save this country from disunion."[22]

The second incident, according to Ratcliffe's account, occurred during a hotly contested postwar presidential election:

> [Party leaders believed] that the result of the election would be almost as important to the nation as the result of the war itself. Our defeat meant that the government must pass into the bloodstained hands of rebels, men whose designs were more than doubtful and who could not, even if their designs had been good, restrain the violence of their followers. In consequence we strained every nerve. Money was freely spent, even to an amount much in excess of our resources. How it was employed, I will not say. I do not even know for I held myself aloof from these details, which fell to the National Central Committee of which I was not a member. The great point was that a very large sum had been borrowed on pledged securities, and must be repaid. . . . [Party leaders subsequently] came to me and told me that I much abandon my opposition to the Steamship Subsidy. They made no open avowal of their reasons, and I did not press for one. Their declaration, as the responsible heads of the organization, that certain action on my part was essential to the interests of the party, satisfied me. I did not consider myself at liberty to persist in a mere private opinion in regard to a measure about which I recognized the extreme likelihood of my being in error. I accordingly reported the bill, and voted for it, as did a large majority of the party. . . .
>
> I do not take to undertake to defend this affair. It is the act of my public life that I most regret — not the doing, but the necessity of doing. . . . [T]here are conflicting duties in all the transactions of life, except the simplest. However we may act, do what we may, we must violate some moral obligation. All that can be asked of us is that we should guide ourselves by what we think the highest. At the time this affair occurred . . . I owed duties to my constituents, to the government to the people. I might interpret these duties narrowly or broadly. I might say: Perish the government, perish the Union, perish this people, rather than that I should soil my hands! Or I might say, as I did, and as I would say again: Be my fate what it may, this glorious Union, the last hope of suffering humanity shall be preserved.[23]

At other points in the novel, Ratcliffe elaborates the view that underpinned his decisions:

> No representative government can long be much better or much worse than the society it represents. . . . Only fools and theorists imagine that our society can be handled with gloves or long poles. One must make one's self a part of it. If virtue won't answer our purpose, we must use vice, or our opponents will put us out of office, and this was as true in [George] Washington's day as it is now, and always will be. . . . In politics we cannot keep our hands clean. I have done many things in my political career that are not defensible. To act with entire honesty and self-respect, one should live in a pure atmosphere, and the atmosphere of politics is impure.[24]

1. Would Machiavelli have agreed with Ratcliffe's reasoning and decisions? Would Walzer? Do you? Does trading votes for money pose the same ethical issue as stuffing the ballot box if the ends are the same? Does it matter whether the opposition is also guilty? How different is Ratcliffe's argument from the one that Abraham Lincoln advanced for suspending certain constitutional rights (such as habeas corpus) during wartime? "My oath to preserve the constitution . . . imposed upon on me the duty of preserving by every indispensable means, that government—that nation—of which that constitution was the organic law. . . . I felt that measures otherwise unconstitutional, might become lawful, by becoming indispensable to the preservation . . . of the nation."[25]
2. Lee is unpersuaded by Ratcliffe's explanation. He "rightly judged that there must be some moral defect in his last remarks, although he could not see it," so he takes a different tact, and appeals to her to marry him and join his efforts to reform politics. She is even less convinced.

> [Only later, on reflection] did she fairly grasp the absurdity of Ratcliffe's wish that in the face of such a story as this, she should still have vanity enough to undertake the reform of politics. And with his aid too! The audacity of the man would have seemed sublime if she had felt sure that he knew the difference between good and evil, between a lie and the truth; but the more she saw of him, the surer she was that his courage was mere moral paralysis, and that he talked about virtue and vice as a man who is colorblind talks about red and green; he did not see them as she saw them; if left to chose for himself he would have nothing to guide him. Was it politics that had caused this atrophy of the moral senses by disuse?[26]

Is this a vindication of Walzer's desire that politicians retain the capacity for anguish because we "don't want to be ruled by men who have lost their souls"? Or is Adams suggesting that some moral callousness is a necessary consequence of dealing with a system that sometimes requires dirty hands? If so, is he right? What would follow from that conclusion?

3. Lee, like other characters in the novel, comes to view Ratcliffe's political agenda as motivated by his own ambition, rather than by some higher vision of the public interest. This is what some commentators have described as "Machiavellism without Machiavelli."[27] Does motive matter under Machiavelli's framework or only results? What is your view?

MEDIA RESOURCES

Dirty-hands dilemmas are common in many contemporary media portraits of war, national security, law enforcement, and politics.[28] Several of the films described in Chapter 12 involve such dilemmas—for example, *A Man for All Seasons, All the King's Men*, and *Primary Colors. Frost/Nixon*, a dramatization of David Frost's interview of Richard Nixon, includes a gripping exchange on Watergate. The television series *24* features a number of episodes in which Jack Bauer is willing to dirty his hands for what he perceives as national security reasons.[29] *The American President*, starring Michael Douglas, centers on a leader trying to rise above politics as usual. His televised press conference raises key questions about the difference between what he calls "keeping my job" and "doing my job."

Another particularly powerful example comes from season 3, episode 21 of the series *West Wing*, in which President Bartlet debates whether to authorize an assassination of a foreign diplomat. The diplomat, a secretary of defense from a fictional Middle East nation, Qumar, had scheduled a visit to the United States before the Bartlet administration learned of the extent of his involvement in terrorist activities. He cannot be tried when he visits because of diplomatic immunity. However, a plane accident could be faked over the Caribbean on his return, which would presumably save many lives and avert a major security threat to the United States. The president's chief of staff, Leo McGarry, has no doubt that the assassination is necessary. When Bartlet protests that it's "just wrong; it's absolutely wrong," McGarry responds, "But you have to do it anyway." "Why?" asks Bartlet. "Because you won," McGarry answers. What further complicates the analysis, both for Bartlet and for viewers assessing his conduct, is how the decision might affect his own reputation and political career. At one point in his discussion with McGarry, Bartlet expresses concern that Qumar would realize the accident was staged. In that case, it could trigger a war and put Bartlet's own reelection in further jeopardy. That too would have national security consequences, particularly given Bartlet's assessment of his opponent's inadequate foreign policy capabilities. The episode can spark discussion of what factors should most influence such decisions and what members of the class would have done in those circumstances. Related issues arise in the discussion of torture in Chapter 6.

C. HOW THE GOOD GO BAD: ETHICAL MISCONDUCT AND INSTITUTIONAL RESPONSES

1. INTRODUCTION

What accounts for the gap between ethical aspiration and achievement in contemporary settings? Discussion begins with an overview of what constitutes moral leadership, what gets in the way, and what strategies at the individual, organizational, and societal level could promote it.

Deborah L. Rhode, "Introduction: Where Is the Leadership in Moral Leadership?"

Deborah L. Rhode, ed., Moral Leadership: The Theory and Practice of Power, Judgment, and Policy (San Francisco: Jossey-Bass, 2007), pp. 1-45 and 53

Moral leadership has always been with us, but only recently has the concept attracted systematic attention. Political philosophers dating from the early Greeks and theologians dating from the Middle Ages occasionally discussed virtue in the context of leadership. However, not until the later half of the twentieth century did leadership or business ethics emerge as distinct fields of study, and attention to their overlap has been intermittent and incomplete. In the United States, it took a succession of scandals to launch moral leadership as an area of research in its own right. Price fixing in the 1950s, defense contracting in the 1960s, Watergate and securities fraud in the 1970s, savings and loans and political abuses in the 1980s, and massive moral meltdowns in the corporate sector in the late 1990s and early 2000s underscored the need for greater attention to ethics. . . .

[Still], the subdiscipline of moral leadership remains an academic backwater. One recent survey of some eighteen hundred articles in psychology, business, religion, philosophy, anthropology, sociology, and political science found only a handful that addressed leadership ethics in any depth. Few of those articles, or the books recently released on this topic, are informed by relevant research outside their field. Publications written by and for managers have typically been at best superficial and at worst misleading, littered with vacuous platitudes and self-serving anecdotes. Many of the all-purpose prescriptions marketed in the popular press are at odds with the limited scholarship that is available. . . .

To assist inquiry along these lines, this Introduction surveys the state of moral leadership literature. It aims to identify what we know, and what we only think we know, about the role of ethics in key decision-making positions. The focus is primarily on leadership in business contexts, because that is where most work has been done and where the need in practice appears greatest. However, the overview that follows also draws on research from related fields and offers insights applicable to other organizational contexts. . . .

Moral Leadership Defined

Ethics and Effectiveness

. . . [T]here is surprisingly little systematic analysis of a key issue: whether all leadership has a moral dimension. To borrow Machiavelli's classic formulation, can one be a "good" leader in terms of effectiveness without being a "good" leader in terms of morality? The limited leadership commentary that focuses on this question stakes out a range of views. . . .

An increasingly common position, encountered in both scholarly and popular literature, is that the essence of effective leadership is ethical leadership. The first prominent theorist to take this view was historian James McGregor Burns. In his 1978 account, Leadership, Burns . . . [advocated] transformational leadership, [in which] leaders and followers "raise one another to higher levels of motivation and morality," beyond "everyday wants and needs." They aspire to reach more "principled levels of judgment" in pursuit of end values such as liberty, justice, and self-fulfillment. Similarly, John Gardner, in *The Moral Aspect of Leadership,* argued that leaders should "serve the basic needs of their constituents," defend "fundamental moral principles," seek the "fulfillment of human possibilities," and improve the communities of which they are a part. To Gardner, like other contemporary commentators, men such as Hitler and Stalin can be considered rulers but not leaders.

Many scholars see this definition as too limiting. Some argue that effective leadership requires morality in means, although not necessarily in ends. Underlying this distinction is the assumption that widely shared principles are available for judging process but no comparable consensus exists for judging objectives. According to this view, leadership cannot be coercive or authoritarian, but it can seek ends that most people would regard as morally unjustified.

Yet this distinction is inconsistent with conventional understandings and not particularly helpful for most purposes. As Bennis notes, "People in top positions [can often be] doing the wrong thing well." "Like it or not," others point out, Hitler, Stalin, and Saddam Hussein were animated by a moral vision and were extremely effective in inspiring others in its pursuit. In her recent account, *Bad Leadership,* Barbara Kellerman similarly suggests that it is unproductive to exclude from definitions of leadership those whose means or ends are abhorrent but nonetheless effective, and therefore instructive. As she puts it, "How can we stop what we don't study?"

Values-Based Leadership

... [A related problem is that] even commentators who see an ethical dimension to values leadership often discuss it in only the most perfunctory and platitudinous terms. Publications aimed at managerial audiences frequently just list a few key qualities that have "stood the test of time," such as integrity, honesty, fairness, compassion, and respect, without acknowledging any complexity or potential conflict in their exercise. Other commentators simply add "moral" as an all-purpose adjective in the mix of desirable characteristics: leaders should have "moral imagination," "moral courage," "moral excellence," and, of course, a "moral compass." ...

Part of the problem is that few of the publications marketed to leaders make any concessions to complexity. Only rarely does a note of realism creep in, typically by way of acknowledgment that reconciling priorities may be difficult or that most people, including leaders, act from mixed motives, not all of them disinterested. But rarer still are any real insights about how to strike the appropriate balance among competing concerns. When examples are given, they generally appear as stylized, often self-serving morality plays in which virtue is its own reward and dishonesty does not pay. The party line is that violating "timeless values" is always wrong, "pure and simple." In this uncomplicated leadership landscape, the "right thing for business and the right thing ethically have become one and the same."

Would that it were true. But ... [recent research] ... paints a much more complicated portrait than the mainstream commentary conveys.

The discussion that follows focuses on this process of moral leadership, using the term in its colloquial sense of exercising influence in ways that are ethical in means and ends. In essence, the point is that . . . effective leadership requires a moral dimension too often missing or marginal in American business and professional organizations.

The Historical Backdrop and Current Need for Moral Leadership

Although the need for moral leadership is longstanding, only in the past half-century has that need given rise to formal ethics initiatives. And despite a recent flurry of efforts, fundamental challenges remain.

The Emergence of Ethics Initiatives

A few corporations began adopting internal codes of conduct early in the twentieth century, but it was not until a sequence of scandals, starting in the 1960s, that interest in business ethics and corporate social responsibility gained significant attention. By the mid-1980s, repeated exposés of fraud and corruption among American defense contractors led to the creation of the Defense Industry Initiative; its participants established ethical compliance programs that eventually became models for other corporate sectors. During the 1970s and 1980s, the need for such programs became increasingly apparent, given recurrent waves of securities fraud, insider trading, international bribery, antitrust violations, environmental hazards, unsafe products, and related abuses. One representative survey of America's largest corporations in the early 1990s found that two-thirds had been involved in illegal activities over the preceding decade. In 1991, the U.S. Sentencing Commission responded to such patterns by substantially increasing fines for organizational crimes, but permitting reduced penalties if the defendant had adopted "effective programs for preventing and detecting" wrongful behavior. This initiative, together with the enormous legal expenses and reputational damage that often accompanied criminal and civil liability proceedings, intensified pressure for reforms. By the turn of the twenty-first century, about 75 to 80 percent of surveyed companies and 90 percent of large corporations had ethical codes, up from 15 percent in the late 1960s. About half of all businesses provided formal ethics training. A third also had ethics officers, and the percentage increased to over half among *Fortune* 500 companies after another spate of Wall Street scandals in the early twenty-first century. . . .

Business Ethics: Competing Perspectives on the Problem

. . . [Public perceptions of business ethics suggest considerable room for improvement.] In a Gallup poll on . . . confidence in some twenty major institutions . . . , Americans rated "big business" second to last. Only about a fifth expressed high levels of confidence. . . . In other . . . polls, close to half of Americans said they had "not much trust" or "no trust" in large U.S. companies, and almost three-quarters believed that wrongdoing was widespread. Only 10 percent thought that current rules designed to promote responsible and ethical corporate behavior were working "pretty well"; almost half thought they needed "major changes" or a "complete overhaul."

... Other empirical research also suggests too wide a gap between professed commitments to ethical integrity and actual workplace practices. For example, one recent survey of executive members of the American Management Association found that about a third believed that their company's public statements on ethics sometimes conflicted with internal messages and realities. Over a third indicated that although their company would follow the law, it would not always do what would be perceived as ethical. In another study involving responses to hypothetical fact situations based on Securities and Exchange Commission cases, almost half of top executives expressed a willingness to make fraudulent financial statements under at least some circumstances. The consequences of such attitudes are not just hypothetical. Business and professional leaders' involvement in recent corporate misconduct contributed to losses in shareholder value estimated as high as $7 trillion.

Societal Interests and the Limits of Regulation

Shareholders' economic interests are only part of society's enormous stake in the moral leadership of business and professional organizations. These organizations shape the quality of our lives across multiple dimensions, including health, safety, jobs, savings, consumer products, and the environment. As leading economic and legal theorists have long noted, neither market forces nor regulatory strategies are a full substitute for ethical commitments that leaders can help institutionalize in organizational cultures. Amartya Sen and Kenneth Arrow have both underscored the dependence of markets on shared moral expectations and behaviors. Economic institutions depend on mutual confidence in the honesty and fair dealing of multiple parties. Yet market forces provide inadequate protection against free riders: those who seek to benefit from general norms of integrity without observing them personally. Market processes also provide insufficient correctives for information barriers and social externalities. If, for example, consumers lack cost-effective ways to assess the quality of goods, services, and investment opportunities, sellers may lack adequate incentives to meet socially desirable standards. . . .

Legal regulation is a necessary but not sufficient response. Legislatures and government agencies often have inadequate information or political leverage to impose socially optimal standards. Industry organizations frequently exercise more influence over regulatory processes than unorganized or uninformed stakeholders do.

Oversight agencies may also be uninformed or understaffed, or captured by special interests. Enforcement may be too costly or penalty levels that are politically acceptable may be too low to achieve deterrence. Where regulation falls short, the health and financial consequences can be irreversible. The problem is particularly acute in countries that lack the economic or governmental strength to constrain powerful global corporations. . . .

In this world of imperfectly functioning markets and regulatory processes, the public interest in self-restraint by socially responsible corporate leaders is obvious. What is less obvious is the extent to which corporations' own interests point in similar directions and what can be done to insure a closer alignment.

Doing Good and Doing Well: When Does Ethics Pay?

"Ethics pays" is the mantra of most moral leadership literature, particularly the publications written by and for managers. *If Aristotle Ran General Motors* offers a representative sample of reassuring homilies: a "climate of goodness will always pay," "you can't put a simple price on trust," and "unethical conduct is self-defeating or even self-destructive over the long run." A dispassionate review of global business practices might suggest that Aristotle would need to be running more than GM for this all to be true. But no matter; in most of this commentary, a few spectacularly expensive examples of moral myopia will do: companies that make "billion-dollar errors in judgment" by marketing unsafe products, fiddling with the numbers in securities filings, or failing to report or discipline rogue employees. The moral of the story is always that if "values are lost, everything is lost."

Even more hard-headed leadership advice is often tempered with lip-service to the cost-effectiveness of integrity and reminders that profits are not an end in themselves. "The top companies make meaning, not just money," Peters and Waterman assure us. . . .

Corporate Social Responsibility, Ethical Conduct, and Financial Performance

A wide range of studies have attempted to address the "value" of values. [They confront significant methodological challenges, including the absence of consistent definitions or metrics of social responsibility and the impossibility of drawing causal inferences from correlations between social and financial performance. However, most research findings suggest some positive relationship between ethics and financial results. For example, . . .] employees who view their organization as supporting fair and ethical conduct and its leadership as caring about ethical issues observe less unethical behavior and perform better along a range of dimensions; they are more willing to share information and knowledge and "go the extra mile" in meeting job requirements. Employees also show more concern for the customer when employers show more concern for them, and workers who feel justly treated respond in kind; they are less likely to engage in petty dishonesty such as pilfering, fudging on hours and expenses, or misusing business opportunities. The financial payoffs are obvious: employee satisfaction improves customer satisfaction and retention; enhances workplace trust, cooperation, and innovation; and saves substantial costs resulting from misconduct and surveillance designed to prevent it.

Such findings are consistent with well-documented principles of individual behavior and group dynamics. People care deeply about "organizational justice" and perform better when they believe that their workplace is treating them with dignity and respect and ensuring basic rights and equitable reward structures. Workers also respond to cues from peers and leaders. Virtue begets virtue, and observing moral behavior by others promotes similar conduct. Employers reap the rewards in higher morale, recruitment, and retention. . . .

Ethical Reputation and Financial Value

A reputation for ethical conduct by leaders and organizations also has financial value. Most obvious, it can attract customers, employees, and investors and can build good relationships with government regulators. . . . The reputational penalty from engaging in criminal or unethical conduct can be substantial and can dramatically affect market share and stock value. According to some research, most of the decline in shareholder value following allegations or proof of illegal behavior reflects damage to reputation, not prospective fines or liability damages. A substantial body of research also suggests that the goodwill accumulated by doing good can buffer a company during periods of difficulty resulting from scandals, product or environmental hazards, or downsizing.

A celebrated case in point is Johnson & Johnson's decision to recall Tylenol after an incident of product tampering. It was a socially responsible decision that was highly risky in financial terms; pulling the capsules cost more than $100 million, and many experts at the time believed that it would doom one of the company's most profitable products. But Johnson & Johnson's reputation for integrity, reinforced by the recall decision, maintained public confidence, and the product bounced back with new safety features and no long-term damage. Examples of unhappy endings also abound. A notorious example of a public relations disaster that could have been averted was Royal Dutch Shell's decision to sink an obsolete oil rig with potentially radioactive residues in the North Sea despite strong environmental protests. The adverse publicity and consumer boycotts took a huge financial toll.

When Ethics Doesn't Pay: The Case for Values

Such examples are not uncommon. Business ethics textbooks offer countless variations on the same theme. But the reasons that the examples are so abundant also point out the problems with "ethics pays" as an all-purpose prescription for leadership dilemmas. As Harvard professor Lynn Sharp Paine puts it, a more accurate guide would be "ethics counts." Whether doing good results in doing well depends on the institutional and social context. The "financial case for values," Paine notes, is strongest when certain conditions are met:

- Legal and regulatory systems are effective in enforcing ethical norms.
- Individuals have choices in employment, investment, and consumption and are well informed concerning those choices.
- The public expects organizations to operate within an ethical framework.

Berkeley professor David Vogel [makes a similar point, and notes that it is] . . . naive and misleading to suggest that [a "market for virtue" is] always in place. It is also self-defeating. To make the case for "values" turn solely on instrumental considerations is to reinforce patterns of reasoning that undermine ethical commitments. We respect moral conduct most when it occurs despite, not because of, self-interest. . . .

Ultimately what defines moral behavior is a commitment to do right whether or not it is personally beneficial. What defines moral leadership is adherence to fundamental principles even when they carry a cost. Our challenge as a society is to find ways of minimizing these costs and reinforcing such leadership. That, in turn, will require a clearer understanding of the dynamics of moral conduct. . . .

Individual and Contextual Dimensions of Moral Conduct

Moral Character and Moral Decision Making

Moral and religious philosophers since Aristotle have generally assumed the existence of fixed character traits that are largely responsible for ethical and unethical behavior. Much of the widely read work on moral leadership shares that assumption. A recurrent theme is that "character is the defining feature of authentic leadership" and that most recent problems are a "function of flawed integrity and flawed character." The perception that personality traits are consistent, deeply rooted, and responsible for ethical conduct reinforces our sense of predictability and control. It is also consistent with a widely documented cognitive bias that psychologists label the "fundamental attribution error": our tendency to overvalue the importance of individual character and undervalue the role of situational factors in shaping behavior. Yet social science research makes clear that many such assumptions about personality traits are a "figment of our aspirations." As discussion below indicates, moral conduct is highly situational and heavily influenced by peer pressures and reward structures.

Although the importance of personal qualities should not be overstated, neither should their role be overlooked. Individuals vary in their approach toward ethical issues in ways that matter for understanding leadership. In his influential analysis of moral development, psychologist James Rest identified four "components of ethical decision making":

- Moral awareness: recognition that a situation raises ethical issues
- Moral reasoning: determining what course of action is ethically sound
- Moral intent: identifying which values should take priority in the decision
- Moral behaviors: acting on ethical decisions

Moral Awareness and Ethical Culture

Moral awareness, the first element, reflects both personal and situational factors. One involves the moral intensity of the issue at stake. Intensity is, in turn, affected by both social consensus about the ethical status of the acts in question and the social proximity of their consequences. When issues arise in workplace contexts, it is the degree of consensus in these settings that has the greatest influence on moral awareness. Organizations that place overwhelming priority on bottom-line concerns encourage individuals to "put their moral values on hold." Such workplace cultures may help account for the large numbers of surveyed managers and professionals who claim never to have faced a moral conflict.

A second influence on moral awareness involves the "feeling of nearness (social, cultural, psychological, or physical)" that the decision maker has for victims or beneficiaries of the act in question. Individuals' capacity for empathy and their sense of human or group solidarity positively affect ethical sensitivity, which encourages altruistic action and receptiveness to principles of justice, equality, and fairness. Conversely, people's capacity to distance, devalue, or dehumanize victims leads to moral disengagement and denial of moral responsibility. These capabilities are themselves influenced by child-hood socialization, religious and political commitments, direct exposure to injustice, and educational approaches that build awareness of others' needs.

A wide array of quantitative and qualitative research also demonstrates the effect of workplace cultures on ethical sensitivity. Two widely reported case studies are Sunbeam under the leadership of "Chainsaw" Al Dunlop and Enron under the direction of Kenneth Lay, Andrew Fastow, and Jeffrey Skilling. Dun-lop was notorious for moral myopia in defining the company's vision and moral callousness in carrying it out. In his view, the notion of ethical respon-sibility to stakeholders such as employees, customers, suppliers, or local community residents was "total rubbish. It's the shareholders who own the company." Consistent with that view, Dunlop subjected subordinates to abu-sive working conditions, punishing schedules, and unrealistically demanding performance expectations; "either they hit the numbers or another person would be found to do it for them." This bottom-line mentality did not ulti-mately serve the bottom line. Sunbeam ended up in bankruptcy, and Dunlop ended up settling a civil lawsuit by paying a $500,000 fine and agreeing never to serve again as an officer or director of a major corporation. So too, Enron's plummet from the nation's seventh largest corporation to a bankrupt shell has been partly attributed to its relentless focus on "profits at all costs." The message conveyed by corporate leaders was that accounting and ethics rules were niceties made to be stretched, circumvented, and suspended when necessary. Those who advanced were those able to "stay focused" on corporate objectives "unburdened by moral anxiety."

Moral Reasoning, Situational Incentives, and Cognitive Biases

Rest's second key element in moral leadership is moral reasoning. Individ-uals vary in their analysis of moral issues, although here again, context plays an important role. . . .

Most evidence suggests that individuals have a relatively poor grasp of their own reasoning processes and use different, typically lower, levels of reasoning in business contexts than in other aspects of their lives. As one manager put it in Robert Jackall's famous case study, *Moral Mazes,* "What's right in the corporation is not what is right in a man's home or his church." Abundant evidence indicates that this view is pervasive, that organizational reward structures affect the judgments of leaders, and that their decisions have a corresponding impact on subordinates.

One powerful influence involves compensation. In a culture where money buys not just goods and services but also power and status, economic rewards can skew decision-making processes in predictable ways. For top managers, stock options are an increasingly important factor. They account for about 60 percent of the pay of chief executives at the largest corporations and can give rise to large fortunes. This incentive structure may encourage leaders to seek short-term increases in stock prices even when that involves cutting eth-ical corners and damaging the corporation's performance over the long term.

. . . Other forms of self-interest can similarly skew ethical decision making. Psychologists have documented a variety of cognitive biases that contribute to moral myopia. Those who obtain leadership positions often have a high confidence in their own capacities and judgment. That can readily lead to arrogance, overoptimism, and an escalation of commitment to choices that turn out to be wrong either factually or morally. As a result, individuals may ignore or suppress dissent, overestimate their ability to rectify adverse consequences, and cover up mistakes by denying, withholding, or sometimes destroying information. A related bias involves cognitive dissonance; individuals tend to suppress or reconstrue information that casts doubt on a prior belief or action. Such biases may lead individuals to discount or devalue evidence of the harms of their conduct or the extent of their own responsibility.

In-group biases similarly can result in unconscious discrimination or in ostracism of inconvenient and unwelcome views. Those dynamics in turn generate perceptions of unfairness and encourage team loyalty at the expense of moral candor and socially responsible decision making.

Moral Intent, Moral Conduct, and Situational Pressures

Yet individuals' moral reasoning processes, however affected by these cognitive biases, are only part of what explains moral conduct. Indeed, most research finds only a modest correlation between ethical reasoning and behavior. It is not enough for people to make a sound moral judgment. They must also have "moral intent" — the motivation to give priority to moral values — as well as the ability to follow through and act on that intent. Moral motivations are in part a reflection of the centrality of moral concerns to individuals' identity and self-esteem. Much depends on how they weigh these concerns in relation to other needs for power, status, money, peer approval, and so forth. So too, what psychologists label "ego strength" will help determine whether individuals are able to put their moral values into action. Factors include the person's ability to work around impediments, cope with frustration, and remain focused on moral objectives.

A variety of situational pressures can affect that ability. Some of the best documented involve time and [obedience to authority, discussed in Chapter 6.] . . .

Moral Behavior: Diffusion of Responsibility, Socialization, and Peer Pressure

Studies on behavior in group settings similarly underscore the malleability of moral conduct. This research typically finds that individuals are more likely to engage in unethical conduct when acting with others. Three dynamics often work to "protect people from their own conscience": diffusion of responsibility, socialization to expedient norms, and peer pressure.

. . . [D]isplacement of responsibility may help account for the passivity of many corporate boards during periods of massive misconduct. In the cases noted earlier involving Al Dunlop, Dennis Kozlowski, and Andrew Fastow, directors approved grossly excessive compensation and failed to heed warning signals of financial and ethical difficulties. Indeed, Enron's board even twice suspended conflict-of-interest rules to allow Fastow to profit at the corporation's expense. Part of the problem, as a former Enron prosecutor notes, is that directors generally lack individual accountability for collective decision making; their reputations rarely suffer and insurance typically insulates them from personal liability.

A famous simulation by Wharton professor Scott Armstrong illustrates the pathologies that too often play out in real life. The experiment asked fifty-seven groups of executives and business students to assume the role of an imaginary pharmaceutical company's board of directors. Each group received a fact pattern indicating that one of their company's most profitable drugs was causing an estimated fourteen to twenty-two "unnecessary" deaths a year and would likely be banned by regulators in the company's home country. The drug accounted for some 12 percent of the company's sales and a larger percentage of its profits. A competitor offered an alternative medication with the same benefits at the same price but without the serious side effects. More than 80 percent of the boards decided to continue marketing the product both domestically and overseas and to take legal and political action to prevent a ban. Some of the remaining 20 percent that would not fight the prohibition would continue marketing until it went into effect. None of the boards decided to recall the drug. By contrast, when a different group of individuals with similar business backgrounds was asked for their personal views on the same hypothetical situation, 97 percent believed that continuing to market the product was socially irresponsible.

Other group dynamics apart from diffusion of responsibility also help explain the gaps between personal principles and practices. Socialization and peer pressure play important roles in signaling what ethical norms are appropriate and in penalizing those who fail to comply. Under circumstances where bending the rules has payoffs for the group, at least in the short term, members may feel substantial pressure to put their moral convictions on hold. That is especially likely when organizations place heavy emphasis on loyalty and offer substantial rewards to "team players." Strategies of disengagement such as euphemistic labeling, reattribution of blame, and denigration of victims then enable individuals to deny problematic aspects of their collective conduct.

The cognitive biases described previously also conspire in this process. For example, once individuals yield to group pressure when the moral cost seems small, the commitment bias and the desire to reduce cognitive dissonance may kick in and entrap them in more serious misconduct. The result is what is known as "the boiled frog" problem: a frog thrown into boiling water will jump out of the pot; a frog placed in tepid water that gradually becomes hotter and hotter will calmly boil to death.

In "The Inner Ring," C. S. Lewis describes the process by which people's need to belong to a favored circle undermines moral commitments:

> Just at the moment when you are most anxious not to appear crude, or naif, or a prig — the hint will come. It will be the hint of something which is not quite in accordance with the rules of fair play: something which the public, the ignorant, romantic public would never understand . . . but something, says your new friend, which "we" — and at the word "we" you try not to blush for mere pleasure — something "we always do." And you will be drawn in, if you are drawn in, not by desire for gain or ease, but simply because at that moment you cannot bear to be thrust back again into the cold outer world. . . . And then, if

you are drawn in, next week it will be something a little further from the rules, and next year something further still. . . . It may end in a crash, a scandal, and penal servitude; it may end in millions [and] a peerage. . . . But you will be a scoundrel.

Organizational Structure, Climate, and Reward Systems

Other characteristics of organizations can be similarly corrosive and add a further dimension to the personal frameworks that theorists like Rest propose. One such characteristic involves the fragmentation of information. The size and structure of bureaucratic institutions and the complexity of the issues involved may work against informed ethical judgments. In many of the recent scandals, as well as earlier financial, health, safety, and environmental disasters, a large number of the upper-level participants were not well informed. Lawyers, accountants, financial analysts, board members, and even officers often lacked knowledge about matters raising both moral and legal concerns. In some instances, the reason may have been willful blindness: keeping one's eyes demurely averted is a handy skill, particularly when the alternative might be civil or criminal liability. In other cases, the problem has had more to do with organizational structures and practices. Work has been allocated in ways that prevented key players from seeing the full picture, and channels for expressing concerns have been inadequate. Shooting the messenger was the standard response to unwelcome tidings in cases like Enron, and ultimately, it was not just the messenger who paid the price.

Additional aspects of the organizational culture play a critical role. As earlier discussion indicated, a key factor is ethical climate: the moral meanings that employees place on workplace policies and practices. Organizations signal their priorities in multiple ways: the content and enforcement of ethical standards; the criteria for hiring, promotion, and compensation; the fairness and respect with which they treat employees; and the social responsibility they demonstrate toward other stakeholders. . . .

. . . [For example, o]ne surveyed company that invested significant resources in its "world-class" ethics compliance program had leaders who failed to take it seriously. As a disillusioned senior manager noted, at their monthly two-hour meetings with the chief operating officer, "we spend 5 minutes on compliance and 115 minutes on profitability. So, you tell me — what matters here?"

In the moral meltdowns recently on display, a range of factors contributed to the unethical climates. However, the scandals generally shared one fundamental characteristic: the elevation of decision makers' short-term interests over moral values. In this respect, Enron was a "perfect storm." The corporation's hypercompetitive, profits-at-any-cost culture and reward structure had a predictably pathological impact on ethical commitments. Under the company's "rank and yank" evaluation system, employees who rated the lowest in financial performance were publicly demoted, passed over, or let go. Board directors who signed off on huge compensation packages for top managers were rewarded in kind. They all received highly generous option-based payments for service. Some who headed allied businesses got lucrative contracts with Enron; others who worked for nonprofit institutions got six-figure charitable donations. Many of the "independent" professionals—lawyers, auditors, and financial analysts—who blessed ethically problematic transactions were part of organizations with similarly skewed incentives. The leadership of Enron's outside law and accounting firms generally placed such a high priority on maintaining lucrative client business that they could not avoid complicity in client misconduct. Precisely how much complicity is unclear and likely to remain so, given the massive destruction of potential evidence and the protections of confidentiality for many key decisions. But what is abundantly clear about Enron and other major scandals is that many participants in leadership roles failed to exercise appropriate moral oversight and create a climate that would encourage it. Yet these were not, for the most part, individuals who appeared demonstrably immoral. Rather, they were caught in corrosive cultures and seemed indifferent or insensitive to the ethical consequences of their activities. . . . Designing correctives for such ethical indifference is one of the central leadership challenges of our era. Addressing that challenge will require strategies on two levels. We need to enable those in positions of power to exercise moral leadership more effectively. And we need to increase the willingness of leaders to make moral leadership a priority.

Strategies of Moral Leadership

. . . [Significant progress will require] solidly grounded strategic analyses, packaged in forms accessible to those in leadership positions. At a minimum, such analyses should address the role of ethical codes and compliance programs, the importance of integrating ethical concerns and stakeholder responsibilities into all organizational functions, and the necessity for visible moral commitment at the top. That commitment must include adherence not only to legal requirements, but also to widely accepted principles of social responsibility. In contexts where there is no consensus about ethically appropriate conduct, leaders should strive for a decision-making process that is transparent and responsive to competing stakeholder interests.

Ethical Codes and Compliance Programs

The vast majority of large organizations have ethical codes and compliance programs. In principle, their rationale is clear. Codes of conduct can clarify rules and expectations, establish consistent standards, and project a responsible public image. If widely accepted and enforced, codified rules can also reinforce ethical commitments, deter ethical misconduct, promote trust, reduce the organization's risks of liability, and prevent free riders (those who benefit from others' adherence to moral norms without observing them personally).

In practice, however, the value of codes is subject to debate. [Vagueness and lack of enforcement are common problems.] . . . In many organizations, ethical codes and compliance structures are viewed primarily as window dressing—public relations gestures or formalities needed to satisfy the federal sentencing guidelines. . . . "Good optics" was how one manager discussed Enron's ethical code, and shortly after the company's collapse, copies of the document were selling on eBay, advertised as "never been read."

. . . An increasing array of research is also available that can guide program design and suggest best practice standards. One key finding is that employees should have opportunities for involvement in the development of codes, training, and evaluation structures. . . .

Most organizations also need to do a far better job of providing adequate power, status, and resources for compliance officers and of evaluating the performance of their ethics programs. How often are ethical issues raised? How well does the organization follow up on reports of misconduct? How effectively does it protect whistle-blowers from retaliation? How do employees perceive the program? Do they feel able to deliver bad news or make confidential reports without reprisals? These are all key factors in predicting ethical conduct, and too few organizations have made serious attempts to assess them. More systematic strategies of program evaluation are necessary, such as surveys of employees and stakeholders, exit interviews, focus groups, and independent audits.

Establishing an effective ethics and compliance structure is a demanding task. The common practice of offloading responsibility to an outside consultant or underfunded midlevel manager is a setup for failure. Efforts to institutionalize ethics can succeed only if they are integral to the workplace culture and taken seriously by those at leadership levels.

Integrating Ethics

A true commitment to moral leadership requires the integration of ethical concerns into all organizational activities. In business and professional contexts, that means factoring moral considerations into day-to-day functions, including planning, resource allocation, hiring, promotion, compensation, performance evaluations, auditing, communications, public relations, and philanthropy. Responsibilities to stakeholders need to figure in strategic decision making at more than a rhetorical level. To that end, assessments of organizational performance need to reflect values in addition to profits.

. . . Yet obvious though this seems, many leaders appear oblivious to how it plays out in practice; neither the formal nor informal reward structures of many organizations pay serious attention to the ethics of upper-level personnel or of the units that they supervise. Performance evaluations that focus only on short-term, bottom-line outcomes are particularly likely to skew moral decision making. Most of the scandals discussed earlier were partly attributable to reward structures that encouraged pushing the ethical edge and failed to sanction conduct on the fringes of fraud. . . .

The Ethical Commitment of Leaders

One consistent finding of research on organizational culture is the significance of leaders' own ethical commitments. That commitment is critical in several respects. First, leaders set a moral tone and a moral example by their own behavior. Employees take cues about appropriate behavior from those in supervisory positions. Whether workers believe that leaders care about principles as much as profits significantly affects the frequency of ethical conduct. . . . Hypocrisy may be the bow that vice pays to virtue, but it is a singularly unsuccessful leadership strategy.

. . . At a less obvious level, leaders face a host of issues where the moral course of action is by no means self-evident. Values may be in conflict, facts may be contested or incomplete, and realistic options may be limited. Yet while there may be no unarguably right answers, some will be more right than others: that is, more informed by available evidence, more consistent with widely accepted principles, and more responsive to all the interests at issue. A defining feature of moral leadership is a willingness to ask uncomfortable questions: Not just, "Is it legal?" but, "Is it fair?" "Is it honest?" "Does it advance societal interests or pose unreasonable risks?" "How would it feel to defend the decision on the evening news?"

Not only do leaders need to ask those questions of themselves, they also need to invite unwelcome answers from others. To counter the self-serving biases and organizational pressures noted earlier, individuals in positions of power should actively solicit diverse perspectives and dissenting views. That will require more protection for whistle-blowers and more channels for disagreement over ethical issues. Studies of whistle-blowing consistently find that those who seek to expose legal or ethical violations typically encounter harassment, ostracism, and retaliation; some become permanent pariahs in their fields. The costs do not appear significantly lower for those who report the misconduct to supervisors rather than to external agencies or the media. And all too often, disclosures go largely unheeded or produce no lasting change. In commenting on the odds of vindication, one whistle-blower wryly predicted, "If you have God, the law, the press, and the facts on your side, you have a 50-50 chance of [victory]." Fear of reprisals, along with lack of confidence that reports would be productive, are the major reasons that employees give for not disclosing abuses or airing ethical concerns. Many doubt that anonymous or confidential disclosures would remain so or that paper protections against job retaliation would prove effective.

Those who are seriously committed to moral leadership need to create more safe spaces for both reports of misconduct and moral disagreements generally. The problem in too many organizations, as one expert puts it, is "not only does no one want to listen but no one wants to talk about not listening." It is of course true that some dissenters are unbalanced or vindictive employees who air unmerited claims or self-serving grievances. But creating adequate internal channels even for these reports is the best way to prevent the far greater costs of external whistle-blowing. And even those whose motives are tainted may have valid concerns. A widely publicized case in point is the disgruntled Texaco employee who leaked tapes of racist slurs and plans for document destruction in order to protect his own job during restructuring. Whatever the costs of coping with unjustified internal dissent, the price of suppression is likely to be greater. Candid dialogue on ethical issues is essential for informed decision making. Every leader's internal moral compass needs to be checked against external reference points. Recognizing ways in which they might be wrong is crucial in determining what is likely to be right.

Promoting Moral Leadership

A final set of strategies should focus on promoting moral leadership. As a society, we need to do more to reward and reinforce exemplary leaders. And as educators, we need to make moral leadership a more central curricular and research priority. . . .

A wide range of public policy initiatives is necessary to build commitment to and capacity for moral leadership. Among the most promising directions of reform are those that involve increasing information about performance, strengthening rewards and sanctions, and enhancing capacities for monitoring those incentive structures.

One set of strategies should seek to increase the information available both to leaders of organizations and to the government regulators and stakeholder constituencies that can hold those leaders accountable. . . . [Another approach] is for government agencies, industry associations, and public interest organizations to establish more voluntary codes or best practice standards, along with more ways of encouraging and monitoring compliance. . . .

Governments and industry organizations could also do more to increase information by expanding reporting requirements. One central obstacle to monitoring corporate legal compliance and social responsibility is the lack of standardized public data. Mandatory reporting on these measures could assist stakeholders and public interest organizations in assessing organizational performance and in enabling leaders to benchmark their own progress. Governments and stock exchanges could also improve the quality of information provided by requiring more independent auditing.

Expanded safeguards for whistle-blowing, both internally and externally, could be equally useful. The current patchwork of federal and state law leaves far too many workers unprotected from retaliation. . . .

A second cluster of strategies should focus on increasing the rewards and punishments for leadership behavior and organizational performance. Greater recognition for exemplary conduct is essential, such as awards, rankings, and media coverage. Harnessing the purchasing power of socially concerned consumers should be a key priority. . . .

An equally obvious strategy is to increase the sanctions for illegal and unethical conduct. Recent increases in white-collar criminal prosecutions and civil liability proceedings against those who abuse their leadership positions are a promising development. However, most state and federal regulatory agencies are still woefully understaffed and underfunded, and much socially irresponsible but not clearly illegal behavior falls through the cracks. More enforcement resources and more creative use of penalties would help to reinforce desirable conduct and the leadership necessary to achieve it. Many experts believe that strategies focused on shaming offenders and improving internal compliance structures are preferable to the modest fines that courts and regulators often impose. Finally, the government could require corporate leaders to engage in more systematic self-evaluation of their companies' ethical performance. Such evaluations could include surveys of employees and stakeholders, as well as reviews of legal compliance and internal complaint records. Requirements for self-assessment could be incorporated in licensing and regulatory standards or imposed in response to legal violations. The results of these evaluations could then be made available to stakeholders, courts, and government agencies and could become the basis for designing more effective internal and external regulatory structures. Corporate leaders are now drowning in data about their organizations' financial performance. They need comparable information about their ethical records and more prodding to collect it. . . .

[Conclusion]

. . . Those who occupy leadership positions in the research community have unique opportunities and corresponding obligations to underscore the importance of moral values in leadership roles. As a profession and a society, we cannot afford to treat issues of ethical responsibility as someone else's responsibility. If we are seriously committed to promoting moral leadership, we need to make good on that commitment in our own research priorities.

PROBLEM 5-2

Break up into groups. Take an issue involving competing values on which contemporary organizations need ethical policies, such as employees' occasional use of work time and computers for personal matters. Assign roles (such as representatives of workers, management, and legal affairs) and make recommendations for a code of conduct and enforcement structure.

QUESTIONS

1. What do we mean by moral leadership? Does it imply morality in means, ends, or both?
2. How do we judge the morality of ends? The preceding essay assumes that we want more values-driven leadership. Is that always true? Pol Pot believed he was purifying Cambodian society. Muslim fundamentalists who train suicide bombers are inspired by a moral vision. If such examples suggest that we want leaders who share *our* values, what follows from that fact? Consider Walter Lippman's definition of the public interest: "[W]hat men would choose they saw clearly, thought rationally, acted disinterestedly and benevolently."[30] Is that a helpful starting point, or a standard too vague to apply?
3. If moral leadership is necessary because market forces and government regulation provide imperfect checks on misconduct, what supplies the necessary motivation for such leadership? Is it simply character? What happens when it is in short supply?
4. José Lutzenberger, the celebrated Brazilian environmentalist, recalls his motivation for becoming an activist. He was working as a chemical engineer marketing pesticides for a large multinational corporation. One day, when he was visiting the apple orchards of a buyer, he inquired about health concerns that were beginning to surface. "I asked him if he wasn't afraid and he replied with the utmost frankness that he wasn't worried because he wasn't the one who was going to eat the apples." Shocked by the realization that he was the one "selling the poison," Lutzenberg quit his job and started an environmental group.[31] Was that his only option? If the orchard owner grew and sold his produce only in countries with regulatory and legal systems incapable of holding him accountable for health risks, is there anything that might have encouraged him to exercise moral leadership?

5. If, as Berkeley Business School professor David Vogel reminds us, "ethics costs," how should leaders decide when they are worth the price?[32] As Rhode's excerpt notes, "Chainsaw Al Dunlop" was widely criticized for his moral callousness in firing workers and closing divisions that failed to "hit their numbers." But although this strategy proved disastrous for Sunbeam, it served shareholders well in other contexts where Dunlop had held leadership positions. Was Dunlop "morally myopic," or was he just focused on one value: maximizing owners' financial returns in order to promote organizational growth and productivity? How should the interests of shareholders be balanced against those of other stakeholders? How should that decision be made?

6. The 2010 Toyota vehicle recall offers a case study in misplaced leadership priorities. Although the company had built its reputation on reliability, management's desire to become the leader in global automotive sales led to an increasing focus on quantity over quality.[33] The "Toyota Way," with its commitment to "continuous improvement," is famous for giving workers the power to halt production and to suggest correctives for problems that they identify.[34] But particularly in recent years, that communication style failed to extend to top executives, who reportedly became insular, overconfident, and dismissive of evidence suggesting quality control issues.[35] When complaints about acceleration began surfacing, the company was slow to respond, and slower still in disclosing information to the National Highway Safety Administration and launching a recall.[36] The delays led to a record fine, congressional hearings, class action lawsuits, and plummeting sales figures.

   What broader lessons does Toyota's experience suggest? One *Economist* commentator quotes the advice of Anne Mulcahy, former CEO of Xerox: "First, get the cow out of the ditch. Second, find out how the cow got into the ditch. Third, make sure you do whatever it takes so that cow doesn't go into the ditch again."[37] By virtually all accounts, Toyota bungled its rescue of the cow. However, it appears to have learned from that experience in subsequent recalls. Its broader challenge will be getting to the root of the quality control problems and the organizational culture that prevented them from being adequately addressed. What steps would you advise its leaders to take?

   To prevent tunnel vision at the top, commentators have proposed a range of strategies, such as proactive efforts to solicit concerns from ground level workers, and engagement with outside critics and experts.[38] In reflecting on Monsanto's disastrous handling of European concerns over genetically modified crops, its then CEO Robert Shapiro observes: "Because we thought it was our job to persuade, too often we failed to listen."[39] To promote responsiveness, some companies have set up external advisory groups or monitoring structures along the lines discussed in Chapter 10's review of corporate social responsibility initiatives. One model is the respected panel that British Petroleum established to make recommendations on safety and security issues in connection with a pipeline along the Caspian Sea.[40] Should Toyota pursue such strategies? How would you assess their costs and benefits?

7. In *Giving Voice to Values,* Mary Gentile describes four common rationalizations given for morally problematic practices:
   - "Everyone does this so it's really standard practice";
   - This action "doesn't really hurt anyone";
   - "This is not my responsibility";
   - "I know this isn't quite fair . . . but I don't want to hurt my . . . team/boss/company."[41]

   Have you encountered these arguments? How would you respond?
8. Have you experienced the pull of "the inner ring" that C.S. Lewis described? What enables individuals to resist such pressures?

2. LEADERSHIP FAILURES IN THE FINANCIAL MARKETS

PROBLEM 5-3[42]

"Rogue traders" are experts in financial markets who make unauthorized purchases or sales of securities or commodities. The practice is long-standing; one of the most celebrated American scandals dates to the 1880s. But the issue has gained increasing attention, both because of the scale and persistence of misconduct despite efforts at internal control. In recent decades, rogue traders have sometimes made over a billion dollars in illicit trades before discovery.[43]

What drives the misconduct is readily apparent. In the financial world, money is the measure of success. As anthropologist Clifford Geertz notes, particularly in contexts "where the amounts of money are great, much more is at stake than material gain: namely esteem, honor, dignity, respect—in a word . . . status."[44] What prevents organizations from dealing adequately with the misconduct is less obvious, and provides a window into more general leadership issues: what can cause so many extremely smart people to make such disastrous judgments?

In 1991, the Securities and Exchange Commission (SEC) initiated widely publicized proceedings against the CEO, top officers, and general counsel of Salomon Inc., one of Wall Street's leading investment companies. The action arose from the firm's failure to discipline and disclose securities law violations by Paul Mozer, the head of the Government Trading Desk of Salomon Brothers, the firm's main subsidiary. To settle the case, the firm ended up paying some $290 million in fines, the second-largest ever penalty for a financial institution. It also lost major clients and over $4 billion in trades during a brief suspension. Its stock price plummeted, and a year after the scandal, its share of the underwriting market had dropped from 8 to 2 percent. According to Deryck C. Maughan, the CEO who assumed the position after the SEC charges, the events constituted a "billion-dollar error of judgment."[45] How that error occurred provides an illuminating case history of failed leadership.

The culture at Salomon was highly competitive. Conventional wisdom was that although the CEO John Gutfreund may have sometimes "talked about values . . . his conduct often sent a contrary message. He ordered his staff to arrive each morning ready to 'bite the ass of a bear.'"[46] He was known for getting rid of individuals and divisions without warning if they failed to meet his bottom-line expectations.

Paul Mozer was a thirty-four-year-old trader whose aggressive style fit the Salomon culture. He was very rich but from his vantage point, not rich enough. Although he had made over $4 million in 1989 and 1990, he compared his compensation to an arbitrage trader whose bonuses yielded six times that amount.[47] His own income would turn on his ability to dominate the government securities market. That challenge was complicated by Treasury rules limiting traders at auctions of government securities to bids not exceeding 35 percent of the value of bonds being sold. In February 1991, Mozer slightly exceeded the limit by placing a false bid on behalf of S.G. Warburg, one of his customers, in addition to Salomon's own bid. The violation might not have come to light but for the fact that Warburg, without Mozer's knowledge, also had placed its own bid at the auction. This caused Treasury staff to ask for an explanation. Mozer initially claimed that his bid should have been in the name of a Warburg-affiliated management company, and constituted an inadvertent error. He then unsuccessfully tried to convince that company and a personal acquaintance at Warburg to ignore the government's request for information. In April, when it became clear that Warburg would disclose what it knew, Mozer informed his supervisor, Salomon vice president John Meriwether. Although Mozer claimed that this had been his only transgression, other incidents during his decade at Salomon Brothers suggested some cause for concern. He had been a highly aggressive trader, and had created ill will with Treasury officials by publicly denouncing the 35 percent limit.[48] In a recent incident, he had exploded when Salomon Brothers' chief auditor requested a routine review.

Over Mozer's objections, Meriwether notified Salomon president Thomas Strauss, and they then discussed the matter with general counsel Donald Feurstein and CEO John Gutfreund. Without further investigation, the group accepted Mozer's characterization of the bid as an isolated incident. However, Feurstein believed that the conduct was "probably criminal" and the group agreed it should be reported to the New York Federal Reserve Bank.[49] A subsequent SEC report described the decision making as follows:

> [E]ach of the four executives who attended meetings . . . placed the responsibility for investigating Mozer's conduct and placing limits on his activities on someone else. Meriwether stated that he believed that once he had taken the matter of Mozer's conduct to Strauss and Strauss had brought Feuerstein and Gutfruend into the process, he had no further responsibility to take action with respect to the false bid unless instructed to do so by one of those individuals. Meriwether stated that he also believed that, though he had the authority to recommend that action be taken to discipline Mozer or limit his activities, he had no authority to take such action unilaterally. Strauss stated that he believed that Meriwether, who was Mozer's direct supervisor, and Feuerstein, who was responsible for the legal and compliance activities of the firm, would take whatever steps were necessary or required as a result of Mozer's disclosure. Feuerstein stated that he believed that, once a report to the government was made, the government would instruct Salomon about how to investigate the matter. Gutfreund stated that he believed that the other executives would take whatever steps were necessary to properly handle the matter. According to the executives, there was no discussion among them about any action that would be taken to investigate Mozer's conduct or to place limitations on his activities.

After that discussion, Meriwether admonished Mozer and told him that the firm would report his conduct to the government. Gutfreund and Strauss agreed to raise the issue with Gerald Corrigan, head of the Federal Reserve Bank in New York. However, their busy travel schedules made the meeting hard to arrange. Although Gutfreund expected to run into Corrigan at another event where he could arrange a discussion, that opportunity never arose and the issue fell through the cracks. Some speculated that Gutfreund was concerned that a public disclosure might have triggered fines, lawsuits, and adverse publicity, which could have jeopardized his already precarious leadership position.[50] According to one insider, Gutfreund "went to sleep hoping it would just go away."[51]

It did not. Three months later, in May 2001, Mozer again submitted an illegal bid, and effectively cornered the market at that auction. Traders who had been shut out complained to the SEC, which launched a confidential investigation. The public attention caused Salomon to launch its own internal investigation, which revealed that Mozer had exceeded the limit on three other occasions and that several other unauthorized bids had occurred since the Treasury imposed a 35 percent ceiling.[52] However, not until August did Gutfreund notify the SEC and issue a press release acknowledging the misconduct; and that release did not disclose management's prior awareness of the incident. A week later, Salomon Brothers issued another release acknowledging that the company had known about at least one illegal trade since April, but that due to a "lack of sufficient attention," its determination to report the matter "was not implemented promptly." An earlier draft of the release, which had incensed Salomon's board, had attributed the inaction to the "press of other business."[53]

This revelation set off a flood of efforts to unload Salomon stock, and trading was temporarily suspended. When Corrigan threatened "drastic action" by the Federal Reserve Bank unless the firm took immediate dramatic steps, Gutfreund, Strauss, and Meriwether resigned.[54] The board fired Mozer and three others implicated in the scandal. Gutfreund convinced Warren Buffet to take over as interim chair and CEO. Gutfreund had previously recruited Buffet to be a major investor, board member, and advisor. Ironically enough, part of what had originally attracted Buffet to the company had been Gutfreund's "principled" work for another client in which Buffet's company was heavily invested.[55] Although Gutfreund's mishandling of the false bid nearly torpedoed Salomon, his enlistment of Buffet may have saved it.

Buffet faced both external and internal challenges. His external efforts involved convincing the Treasury Department not to suspend the firm's privileges to bid at Treasury auctions, the Federal Reserve not to terminate the firm's status as a primary dealer, and the SEC not to bring criminal actions against the firm. The Treasury and Federal Reserve actions would likely have triggered Salomon's collapse, and might also have caused a major panic on Wall Street. Key factors in government officials' decisions included Buffet's own reputation and his willingness to cooperate fully with regulators. Over objection of counsel, he waived the attorney-client privilege concerning Salomon's internal reports of wrongdoing. He also assured the SEC that if anyone failed to provide information requested, the Commission staff could call him personally and they would "have a new person to deal with in twenty minutes."[56]

Buffet also took internal steps to change Salomon's culture and to restore public confidence. To that end, he issued a series of memos and letters underscoring the firm's commitment to integrity. In one he stated,

> I don't think we can do any better than go back to J.P. Morgan, "First class business in a first class way." . . . If you lose money for the firm by bad decisions as I've done plenty of times for Berkshire, I will be very understanding. If you lose reputation for the firm, I will be ruthless. . . . We want people basically to get rich around here but we want them to get rich *through* the firm not *off* the firm.[57]

He designated himself "chief compliance officer," and informed all officers that they were "expected to report, instantaneously and directly to [him], any legal violation or moral failure on behalf of any employee of Salomon." He exempted parking tickets and listed his personal telephone number.[58] Under the leadership of Buffet and Maughan, the firm also instituted other compliance mechanisms designed to prevent concealment of illegal acts and increase legal oversight. In addition, Salomon altered its compensation structure to reduce incentives for risky behavior and to give employees a greater stake in the firm's performance; for example, income was tied to departmental performance, and an increasing percentage of salary came in the form of restricted stock that could not be sold for five years.[59]

In an open letter to shareholders, published as an advertisement in the *New York Times, Wall Street Journal, Financial Times,* and *Washington Post,* Buffet emphasized the new compliance and compensation structures. He also quoted his directive to employees indicating that they should be guided

> by a test that goes beyond rules; contemplating any business act, an employee should ask himself whether he would be willing to see it immediately described by an informed and critical reporter on the front page of his local paper, there to be read by his spouse, children and friends. At Salomon, we simply want no part of any activities that pass legal tests but that we as citizens would find offensive. . . . Good profits simply are not inconsistent with good behavior.

Although acknowledging that some employees might leave as a result of the changes, he maintained, "In the end we must have people to match our principles not the reverse."[60]

Buffett was right about responses within the firm. Salomon initially witnessed a mass exodus of talent. Many Wall Street insiders, including lawyers, condemned Buffet for "pandering to the regulators" and showing so little compassion to former officers, who were cut off without medical benefits and reimbursement of legal fees.[61] But his actions had the intended effect within the financial market. Major investors soon returned and earnings rebounded. Summing up the situation for a *Fortune* profile, Buffet concluded: "All's well that ends."[62]

For those responsible for the scandal, however, the end was anything but happy. Their experience reflected an insight that Gutfreund had once expressed but seemingly failed to internalize in the Mozer affair: the government bond market is a "world where mistakes are not charitably dealt with."[63] The SEC brought civil charges against Salomon officers under Section 15(b)(4)(E) of the 1934 Securities Exchange Act. That section authorizes the Commission to impose sanctions against a broker dealer who "failed reasonably to supervise, with a view to preventing violations [of federal securities laws], another person who commits such a violation, if such person is subject to his supervision." A settlement of those charges banned Gutfreund for life from serving as a chair or CEO of a securities firm and imposed a $100,000 fine. He also lost his Salomon stock options and retirement benefits. Thomas Strauss received a $75,000 fine and a six-month suspension from securities work. John Meriwether received a $50,000 fine and a three-month suspension from trading. Paul Mozer pleaded guilty to criminal charges of lying to the Federal Reserve Bank through his false February auction bid. He served four months in prison and was banned from the securities industry for life.

General Counsel Donald Feurstein was not a direct supervisor of the trader and had made no false representations, so he escaped liability. However, the Commission also viewed the proceeding as an

> appropriate opportunity to amplify our views on the supervisory responsibilities of legal and compliance officers in Feuerstein's position. . . . Once a person in Feuerstein's position becomes involved in formulating management's response to the problem, he or she is obligated to take affirmative steps to insure that appropriate action is taken to address the misconduct. For example, such a person could direct or monitor an investigation of the conduct at issue, make appropriate recommendations for limiting the activities of the employee, or for the institution of appropriate procedures, reasonably designed to prevent and detect future misconduct, and verify that his or her recommendations, or acceptable alternatives, are implemented. If such a person takes appropriate steps but management fails to act and that person knows or has reason to know of that failure, he or she should consider what additional steps are appropriate to address the matter. These steps may include disclosure of the matter to the entity's board of directors, resignation from the firm, or disclosure to regulatory authorities.

In a footnote, the Commission added, "[o]f course, in the case of an attorney, the applicable [ethical rules] . . . may bear upon what course of conduct that individual may properly pursue."

1. Did the conduct of any of the major players in the Salomon saga reflect the cognitive biases discussed in Chapter 3? Was Paul Mozer's confidence in his capacity to outsmart the regulators a reflection of uniqueness bias? Was his continuation of the unauthorized trading an example of escalation of commitment? When Salomon leaders accepted Mozer's characterization of his March trade as an "isolated incident," were they reducing cognitive dissonance?[64] What other factors might have been at work, and what correctives might have been useful?

2. What accounts for the failure of Salomon Brothers officers to respond more forcefully to reports of Mozer's illegal bids? Note that the SEC's statements of fact, including its description of the April meeting, are negotiated with the principals involved. Do you think that description is accurate? Does it

seem like a neutral third party's account, or a rationalization by the principals after the fact? In either case, does it reflect the pathology that Hannah Arendt described as "rule by Nobody"? To Arendt, this form of bureaucracy was the most dangerous of all, "since there is no one left who could even be asked to answer for what is being done."[65]

3. Law professor Kimberly Krawiec argues that rogue trading persists because leaders and sometimes shareholders benefit from the extremely competitive, high-risk institutional cultures that produce it. In order to sustain short-term profits, management often supports internal compliance structures that may satisfy regulators and investors, but that are in fact insufficient to detect and deter unauthorized conduct.[66] How might Warren Buffett respond? How would you? If Krawiec is correct, what other strategies are necessary? How important are changes in compensation structures, government oversight, and the "tone at the top"?

4. According to prominent Wall Street lawyers Dennis Block and Jonathan Hoff, the Commission's statement about attorneys' responsibilities in Salomon raised several concerns. In their view, the Commission offered inadequate guidelines for misconduct less clear than that facing Feuerstein:

> [It provided] little guidance as to the kinds of steps which should be taken: what level of investigation, restrictions or disciplinary action is required and what new obligations do the firm, line management and legal/compliance officers undertake if the wrongdoing is not terminated? . . . [H]olding [lawyers] accountable may create a reluctance on the part of capable professionals to assume or retain significant compliance authority; dampen the legal/compliance staff's motivation [to intervene; and] . . . dilute the emphasis on responsibility of the line manager, who in most firms is the only person who can, in fact, have significant impact on practices.[67]

Moreover, the Commission's suggestion that legal/compliance personnel should consider resigning if management is uncooperative appears at odds with the desire to see these individuals gain influence within their organizations. In the words of one industry spokesman, to target lawyers and compliance personnel who are on the same side as the SEC "seems to me from a regulatory policy point of view to be shooting at your own troops."[68]

Some of the ambiguities were resolved by the bar's subsequent adoption and amendment of Rule 1.13 of the Model Rules of Professional Conduct and the Congress' enactment of the Sarbanes-Oxley Act of 2002. Rule 1.13 provides that if a lawyer knows of illegal conduct likely to result in substantial injury to an organization, the lawyer must report the matter to a higher authority, and if necessary to its highest authority, typically the board of directors, unless the lawyer reasonably believes that it is not necessary in the best interest of the organization. If no adequate response is forthcoming, the lawyer may resign or reveal the information in order to prevent substantial injury to the organization. If the matter involves a material violation of the law by a client who issues securities, the lawyer also has internal reporting obligations under the Sarbanes-Oxley Act.[69]

If Rule 1.13 had been in effect, and Feurstein had followed it, would the outcome for Salomon necessarily have been different? Note that Feurstein apparently did not believe that the firm was obligated to disclose the unlawful bid. Could he also reasonably have taken the view that Meriwether's admonishment of Mozer was a sufficient response to an "incidental mistake"? How would you have handled the situation? Should lawyers in leadership positions such as Feurstein's be enlisted as "gatekeepers" of regulatory policy?[70] If that would make management less willing to trust them with potentially implicating information, would it be worth the price? How would you know? Who should decide?

MEDIA RESOURCES

Corporate misconduct has generated a wide variety of media portraits. Particularly instructive documentaries include *Inside Job*, which chronicles the recent financial crisis, and *The Smartest Guys in the Room*, which documents the rise and fall of Enron. *The Corporation*, a provocative British production, analogizes large businesses to psychopaths—both are single-minded and remorseless in pursuit of goals that put others at risk. A chronicle of whistleblowing traces Wendell Porter's experience with CIGNA.[71] Among popular films, *The Informant, Michael Clayton, Duplicity*, and *The Firm* all have scenes that dramatize the personal ambitions and organizational pathologies that produce corporate misconduct.

The BBC series *Yes Minister* also offers satirical treatment of the corrosive relationship between corporate interests and government officials. One episode, "The Moral Dimension," portrays a cabinet minister and his staff negotiating a trade deal in an Arab country. Several ethical issues arise: the Minister arranges to have liquor secretly available at an embassy function in violation of religious and cultural norms; one of his undersecretaries allows a gift from the country to be undervalued so the Minister's wife can keep it; and the Minister learns of bribes paid to secure the deal. When he self-righteously announces his intent to launch a full inquiry into the bribes, which would implicate his staff, his permanent undersecretary threatens to make a clean breast of the liquor on similar moral principles. Subsequent press inquiries into the gift force the Minister to lie about his intent to give it away, and the recognition of his own moral compromises on that issue as well as the liquor ends any thoughts of disclosing the bribe. What makes the portrayal especially effective for leadership purposes is its exposure of how small indiscretions can create a climate that perpetuates serious corruption.

WILLIAM A. SAHLMAN, MANAGEMENT AND THE FINANCIAL CRISIS
(WE HAVE MET THE ENEMY AND HE IS US . . .)

Harvard Business School Working Paper 10-033, Oct. 28, 2009,
pp. 1-2 and 4 (forthcoming in Economics, Management,
and Financial Markets (Addleton Academic Publishers))

The current model of corporate governance in the United States and abroad is badly broken and has been for many years. The financial crisis has revealed the degree to which there are problems. Neither managers nor boards of directors foresaw or prevented the massive value destruction that took place at companies like AIG, Bear Stearns, Fannie Mae, General Motors or General Electric. Nor did external private monitors like the media, securities analysts, credit analysts or ratings agencies raise sufficient warnings about building dangers. Certainly, public agencies like the Federal Reserve, FDIC and the Securities and Exchange Commission did little to preclude the financial conflagration.

The assertion that systematic failures of corporate governance caused the economic crisis is perhaps controversial. Some argue that lack of adequate regulation combined with excessive corporate greed was sufficient to cause the problems. If regulation had been more stringent, or executives less greedy, the crisis would have been averted.

Yet, I wonder what corporate manager would with hindsight have wanted what has happened to happen. Everyone, including those who behaved unethically and those who were consumed by greed (some overlap), ended up getting battered. Surely, independent of the existence of a strong and competent regulatory regime, sensible actors would have self-policed. Even greedy executives would not have wanted to see their companies disappear or their net worths vaporize.

Given the nearly universal harm inflicted by the crisis, one has to wonder why managers and boards of directors engaged in such risky behaviors and failed to protect themselves, their companies, and any other constituencies, from employees to communities. Even if their only stated objective was to "maximize shareholder wealth," they failed beyond all reasonable measures.

So, what went wrong? What should managers have done to protect their company (and the world)? What should boards of directors have done? What should regulators have done? What should investors have done? An interesting and parallel question is: What could they have done?

I believe that there are ways to improve how our global economic system operates but there are no magic bullets. Every aspect of the system needs change—from government accounting to corporate board roles and structure—and changes to any single element of the system will fail unless all elements are changed. The most important and most difficult changes are those required of corporate managers. Managers bear a disproportionate share of the responsibility for what transpired and therefore for what must change.

Sadly, there seem to be few new lessons from the crisis. What happened recently has happened before though perhaps not at the same scale. There were some unique contextual factors that created and sustained a larger and more pervasive than average financial bubble, but the underlying managerial failures were no different than in previous episodes of financial excess. Managers made dangerous and foolish decisions, consumers and investors engaged in risky behavior, and regulators were ineffective. Greed played a role but the bigger problem was incompetence. . . .

In studying the financial crisis as it unfolded over the past couple of years, it seems clear that many organizations suffered from a lethal combination of powerful, sometimes misguided incentives; inadequate control and risk management systems; misleading accounting; and low quality human capital in terms of integrity and/or competence, all wrapped in a culture that failed to provide a sensible guide for managerial behavior. . . .

NOTES

The first decade of the twenty-first century will surely rank as a historic low point of leadership in the United States financial market. First came a series of massive frauds, such as Enron and WorldCom. Then, after a brief wave of reforms, followed a series of Ponzi schemes, predatory lending practices, deceptive financial transactions, and reckless investment behavior leading to the worst recession since the 1930s. During both phases, inadequate leadership in corporate, professional, and regulatory circles played a significant role. In a speech supporting overhaul of the financial regulatory system, President Obama noted that the financial crisis "was born of a failure of responsibility—from Wall Street all the way to Washington—that brought down many of the world's largest financial firms and nearly dragged our economy into a second Great Depression."[72] Although responsibility for the debacle is still being apportioned, a few leadership lessons seem clear.

The first is that legal compliance is a necessary but not sufficient benchmark of moral leadership. As President Obama famously noted, "[H]ere's the dirty little secret, though. Most of the stuff that got us into trouble was perfectly legal."[73] Part of the reason was that financial institutions had successfully lobbied for lax regulatory structures that had left gaps in coverage and had exempted major banks from specified debt/equity rules. The result was over-reliance on high-risk investments and exploitation of loopholes. For example, the A.I.G. insurance firm issued several hundred billion dollars of credit default swaps from an unregulated non-insurance subsidiary based in London.[74] Even where regulations were in place, they often left considerable room to maneuver, and the same was true of accounting standards applicable to complex transactions.[75] As legal ethics expert Steven Gillers points out, "[L]aw, after all, is only a language and language is pretty pliable. In the hands of a creative, motivated lawyer, with a demanding client, the language of the law can have astonishing elasticity."[76]

A second leadership lesson is that there will be plenty of such motivated professionals and demanding clients in contexts of misaligned incentive systems and strong competitive and peer pressures. Investment banking and residential mortgages are two such contexts. In both, compensation generally has been tied to short-term financial performance—deals completed and loan agreements signed.[77] The longer-term consequences of risky transactions have been someone else's problem—most recently, American taxpayers, who subsidized bailouts. In the early 2000s, subprime mortgages were particularly lucrative because borrowers paid higher rates than those applicable under prime mortgages due to increased risk. The subprime loans then could be sold to investment banks, which in turn repackaged them for sale as less transparent collateralized debt obligations, all before repayment problems developed. Accordingly, leaders in residential mortgage companies established commission structures that led employees to accept high-risk borrowers and to steer other customers toward subprime loans. Many lending officers, who were paid by the loan (at higher rates for higher risks), treated underwriting guidelines as "obstacles to overcome"; these employees failed to verify income or coached borrowers on what to say to qualify for rates they could ill afford.

Although leaders of financial institutions were not unaware of risks, they generally took a "Y.B.G. and I.B.G" perspective: "You'll be gone and I'll be gone" before the problems arose.[78] When the housing market bubble finally crashed, these "liar loans" resulted in high rates of defaults and foreclosures for borrowers, and insolvency for institutions holding too much of this collateralized debt.[79]

Competitive and peer pressures compounded the problem. Any company that scaled back lending or investing in mortgage-backed securities was likely to fall behind in short-term profitability and market share. So even when leaders recognized the longer-term risks, it was difficult not to keep "running with the herd."[80] In home-lending institutions and investment banks, executives who questioned assumptions about ever-rising real estate prices were ostracized, told that they "worr[ied] too much," or forced out.[81] Many simply repressed their doubts, reinforcing the kind of myopic groupthink discussed in Chapter 3. As Laurence Siegel of the Ford Foundation put it, "You can be wrong and with the crowd, which isn't actually so bad. . . . Or you can be wrong and alone and then you really look like an idiot."[82] A notorious example of that mindset at work came from Charles Prince, CEO of Citigroup. In 2007, just as the collapse was beginning, interviewers for the *Financial Times* asked whether the banks were getting over their heads with collateralized debt obligations. He responded: "When the music stops in terms of liquidity, things will get complicated, but as long as the music is playing, you've got to get up and dance. We're still dancing."[83] When the music stopped it was too late. According to Columbia law professor John Coffee, Prince, like other leaders, saw the risks, "but the fear of falling even slightly behind the competition [was] . . . more compelling. Collectively, other banks behaved the same and the result was a break-neck race over the cliff of financial solvency."[84]

Many lenders had help along the way, partly due to the similar competitive pressures and misaligned incentives for professionals who should have been involved in oversight roles. John Dunbar, co-author of a report on the financial meltdown for the Center for Public Integrity put the point rhetorically: "These big banks were lousy with lawyers, so where . . . were all the lawyers as the system was crashing right in front of them?"[85] Others raised questions about attorneys' complicity in fraudulent documents that forced many large lenders to suspend foreclosure proceedings.[86] Given the confidentiality protections of the attorney-client privilege, lawyers' degree of involvement may be difficult to determine. But the structural underpinnings of the problem seem clear. As Coffee notes, in-house counsel generally have leverage to prevent irresponsible behavior but lack the independence to play that gatekeeping function, while outside lawyers have independence but lack leverage — they can too readily be replaced by attorneys willing to suspend judgment.[87] Yale law professor Robert Gordon agrees. Given escalating competition in the legal market, clients "feel enabled to shop around for law firms that will give advice they want to hear."[88] Leaders of bond-rating agencies fell victim to similar pressures since they were paid by those subject to ratings and dissatisfied clients could shop elsewhere.[89]

Government officials, for their part, also failed to exercise effective leadership. Although the reasons are complex, at least some of the problem may be rooted in analogous pressures. In the United States' balkanized regulatory structure, different agencies regulate each class of financial institution with different levels of intensity and are often funded by those institutions. Organizations could sometimes design themselves to fall within the jurisdiction of the least demanding oversight bodies; national banks had four options from which to choose. Regulators who worried about keeping their jobs and budgets also had to worry about not alienating their targets with overly intrusive scrutiny.[90] In one famous incident of pandering, heads of several regulatory agencies appeared at a press conference to announce their efforts to ease regulations by cutting through red tape. Leaders from the Federal Reserve Board and the FDIC showed up with garden shears; the head of the Office of Thrift Supervision, already known for offering the lightest regulatory touch, brought a chainsaw.[91] The corrosive effects of this structure appeared clearly in Senate hearings tracing OTS' repeated failures to halt fraudulent lending practices by Washington Mutual. The bank accounted for 12 to 15 percent of OTS' budget, and for four years, the agency had failed to bring enforcement actions despite audits finding that between 58 and 83 percent of loans revealed evidence of fraud. Summarizing the conclusions of extensive testimony and a joint report by the Treasury and FDIC inspector generals, Senator Carl Levin described OTS as a "spectator, chronicling the bank's frauds rather than preventing them."[92]

So too, in the relentlessly optimistic market climate preceding the collapse, major oversight agencies came under political and industry pressure not to exercise the full extent of their regulatory authority. So, for example, the SEC left credit default swaps largely unmonitored, and the Federal Reserve Board declined to respond to complaints of abusive lending practices.[93] Given their inadequate enforcement resources and their administration's general deregulatory stance, some authorities appeared reluctant to take on "prominent Wall Street insiders," such as Bernie Madoff and Bear Stearns.[94]

Other factors were of course at work. As Chapter 3 indicates, cognitive biases may have led both public and private decision makers to discount crucial information that ran counter to prior assumptions and principles. Indeed, even Alan Greenspan, former Federal Reserve Board chair, conceded as much. In hearings before the House of Representatives Committee on Government Oversight and Reform, Chair Henry Waxman asked Greenspan whether his "ideology" concerning deregulation "pushed you to make decisions that you wish you had not made." Greenspan responded, "Yes, I've found a flaw. . . . I've been very distressed by that fact."[95]

The difficulties of rational decision making were further compounded by the sheer complexity of many of the transactions and market models at issue. As President Obama explained,

> part of what led to this crisis was firms . . . who were making huge and risky bets, using derivatives and other complicated financial instruments, in ways that defied accountability, or even common sense. In fact, many practices were so opaque, so confusing, so complex that people inside the firms didn't understand them, much less those who were charged with overseeing them. They

weren't fully aware of the massive bets that were being placed. That's what led Warren Buffet to describe derivatives that were bought and sold with little oversight as "financial weapons of mass destruction."[96]

Lawyers, board members, executives, and regulators who signed off on particular practices often lacked the time, information, and expertise to appreciate their full legal and financial implications. That problem, repeatedly documented in reports on the financial crisis, is captured by Calvin Trillin in a satirical *New York Times* op-ed. The root cause of the crisis, according to Trillin's fictionalized inside source, was that "smart guys had started working on Wall Street." Big money had lured geniuses from M.I.T. and CalTech to calculate arbitrage odds and begin "securitizing things that didn't even exist in the first place." They were managed and regulated by individuals who "couldn't [do] the math" and didn't have the "foggiest notion" of what was at risk.[97] More nuanced treatments attribute the problem not simply to technical incompetence but to the sheer magnitude of the challenge. As Sahlman notes, "The SEC faces an almost impossible task considering the enormity of its scope, the complexity of the economic and regulatory issues, and the relative inexperience of most of its staff."[98]

None of these problems has easy solutions, and the structure of necessary reforms will be a matter of extended debate for years to come. For present purposes, what bears emphasis is both the necessity and limits of structural responses. Improving regulatory structures is obviously critical to prevent races to the bottom. Yet, as many commentators have noted, it is "ludicrous to imagine that government could ever come up with regulations comprehensive enough to protect against systemic risk while allowing the economy to function."[99] There will always be a need for moral leadership. Although it may be unrealistic to expect most individuals to withstand the intense pressures and incentives that gave rise to the recent crisis, it is not unreasonable to expect both private and public sector leaders to become more actively engaged in designing institutional correctives. As Chapter 1 indicated, one of the key characteristics of effective leadership is the ability to transcend personal and short-term interests in pursuit of broader goals.

QUESTIONS

1. What does the recent economic crisis suggest about how to encourage more effective leadership in financial markets? What reforms seem most critical?
2. Sahlman advocates the use of external monitors who would take an in-depth look at major financial services firms, and make recommendations that could inform both organizational decision making and regulatory policy. If such an approach makes sense, how might it be achieved?
3. In his speech on Wall Street reform, President Obama criticized firms' salary and bonus structures for "creat[ing] perverse incentives to take reckless risks that contributed to the crisis. It's what helped lead to a relentless focus on the next quarter, to the detriment of its next year or its next decade."[100] How can investment companies foster a culture that includes a willingness to forgo short-term payoffs in order to avoid more serious long-term risks?

MEDIA RESOURCES

Congressional hearings on the Toyota acceleration problem and various aspects of the financial crisis are available. Scenes particularly worth reviewing are those in which Wall Street leaders attempt to deflect responsibility. Commentary by prominent business leaders also speak to these issues. Examples include Warren Buffet's congressional testimony concerning the Salomon scandal, as well as his appearance with Bill Gates at a 2009 Columbia Business School panel on leadership.[101] The corrosive effects of short-term profit orientations are portrayed in somewhat stylized form in both movie versions of *Wall Street*. The documentary *Inside Job* portrays the causes of the financial crisis of 2008 as a combination of "warped values and groupthink" within business, government, and academia.[102]

END NOTES

1. Isaiah Berlin, The Question of Machiavelli, New York Review of Books, November 4, 1971 (quoting Frederick the Great), available at http://www.nybooks.com/articles/10391.
2. Niccolò Machiavelli, The Prince (New York: Penguin Books, 1999 ed.), 49.
3. For the scope of his influence, see Silvia Fiore, Niccolo Machiavelli: An Annotated Bibliography of Modern Criticism and Scholarship (New York: Greenwood Press, 1990); Joseph Femia, Machiavelli Revisited (Cardiff: University of Wales Press, 2004).
4. Quentin Skinner, Machiavelli (New York: Hill and Wang, 1981), 3-4.
5. Christopher Duggan, A Concise History of Italy (Cambridge, UK: Cambridge University Press, 1994), 46, 50-51, 57-59.
6. Carol Bresnahan Menning, Florence in the Renaissance, in Paul F. Grendler, ed., 2 Encyclopedia of the Renaissance (New York: Scribner's, 1999), 377-379.
7. Skinner, Machiavelli, 3, 6, 19-20.
8. Niccolò Machiavelli, The Prince 3 (Harvey C. Mansfield trans., University of Chicago Press, 2d ed. 1998) (1532).
9. Anthony Grafton, Introduction, Machiavelli, The Prince (New York: Penguin, 1999), xxvii.
10. Id. at 65-66.
11. Id. at 62.
12. Michael A. Ledeen, Machiavelli on Modern Leadership (New York: St. Martin's Press, 1999), 117 (quoting Machiavelli).
13. Berlin, The Question of Machiavelli, citing a letter to Guicciardini.
14. For a review, see Berlin, The Question of Machiavelli.
15. For overviews of the decision to use nuclear weapons, their devastating consequences for the populations affected, and their legitimacy in terms of theories of just wars, see Ronald Takaki, Hiroshima: Why America Dropped the Atomic Bomb (New York: Little Brown & Co., 1995); John Hersey, Hiroshima (New York: Alfred Knopf, 1998); Michael Walzer, Just and Unjust Wars: A Moral Argument with Historical Illustrations (New York: Basic Books, 1977).
16. Berlin, The Question of Machiavelli.
17. Ruth Grant, Hypocrisy and Integrity (Chicago: University of Chicago Press, 1997), 53.
18. Bernard Shaw, quoted in John Rohr, Ethics for Bureaucrats (New York: Marcel Decker, 1978), 8-9; and Stephen K. Bailey, Ethics and the Politician (Santa Barbara, CA: Center for the Study of Democratic Institutions, 1960), 6.
19. Stuart Hampshire, Public and Private Morality, in Stuart Hampshire et al., eds., Public and Private Morality (New York: Cambridge University Press, 1978), 50.
20. Richard M. Nixon, Leaders (New York: Warner, 1982), 324.
21. Bernard Williams, Politics and Moral Character, in Public and Private Morality, 69.
22. Henry Adams, Democracy (New York: Harmony, 1981), 72-73.
23. Id. at 233-234.
24. Id. at 49, 94, 204.
25. Abraham Lincoln, Letter to Albert G. Hodges (April 4, 1864), in Don Fehrenbacher, ed., Selected Speeches and Writings: Abraham Lincoln (New York: Library of America, 1992), 419, 419-420. See Dennis J. Hutchinson, Lincoln the Dictator, South Dakota Law Review 55, n. 65

(2010):284, 298. Richard Nixon quotes the passage in his book Leaders: Profiles and Reminisces of Men Who Have Shaped the Modern World (New York: Grand Central Publishing, 1982), 326.

26. Adams, Democracy, 232-233.

27. Leeden, Machiavelli on Modern Leadership, 139.

28. The television series *24* includes many examples. A famous film depiction of political corruption is *All the Kings' Men*, based on Robert Penn Warren's fictionalized portrait of Huey Long's rise to power in Louisiana. For a discussion of *All the Kings' Men*, see Chapter 12. *Buddy* is a contemporary documentary about trade-offs for the mayor of Providence, Rhode Island.

29. For a scene in which Bauer breaks into the armory at CTU, see http://www.hulu.com/watch/120787m/24-500-pm—-600-pm?c=2331:2507.

30. Virginia Held, The Public Interest and Individual Interests (New York: Basic Books, 1970), 205 (quoting Lippman).

31. Larry Rohter, Jose Lutzenberger, Brazilian Environmentalist, Dies at 75, New York Times, May 16, 2002.

32. David Vogel, The Market for Virtue (Washington, D.C.: The Brookings Institution, 2006), 165.

33. Bill Saporito, Behind the Troubles at Toyota, Time.com, February 11, 2010, http://www.time.com/time/business/article/0,8599,1963595,00.html; Bill Saporito, Toyota's Flawed Focus on Quantity over Quality, Time.com, February 4, 2010, http://www.time.com/time/business/article/0,8599,1958991,00.html; Alan Ohnsman, Jeff Green, and Kae Inoue, The Humbling of Toyota, Bloomberg Business Week, March 11, 2010, http://www.businessweek.com/magazine/content/10_12/b4171032583967.htm.

34. For the Toyota culture, see Inculcating Culture: The Toyota Way, The Economist, January 19, 2006.

35. Saporito, Behind the Troubles at Toyota; Jeff Kingston, A Crisis Made in Japan, Wall Street Journal, February 6, 7, 2010, W1. The quality control problems predated the 2010 scandal. See A Wobble on the Road to the Top, The Economist, November 8, 2007, http://www.economist.com/node/10097827/print.

36. James Kanter, Micheline Maynard, and Hiroko Tabuchi, Toyota Has Pattern of Slow Response on Safety Issues, New York Times, February 7, 2010, A1; Kate Linebaugh, Dionne Swearcey, and Norithiko Shirouzu, Secretive Culture Led Toyota Astray, Wall Street Journal, February 10, 2010, A1.

37. Schumpeter: Getting the Cow out of the Ditch, The Economist, February 11, 2010, http://www.economist.com/node/15496136 (quoting Mulcahy).

38. Linda Klebe Trevino, Out of Touch: The CEO's Role in Corporate Misbehavior, Brooklyn Law Review 70 (2005):1195, 1209; Peter Firestein, Crisis of Character: Building Corporate Reputation in the Age of Skepticism (New York: Union Square Press, 2009), 24-29.

39. Firestein, Crisis of Character.

40. Id. at 194.

41. Mary Gentile, Giving Voice to Values (New Haven, CT: Yale University Press, 2010), 179.

42. This problem is based on facts set forth in *In re Gutfreund*, Sec. Exch. Release No. 34-31554 (Dec. 3, 1992); Deborah L. Rhode, Professional Regulation: Ethics by the Pervasive Method (New York: Aspen Law and Business, 2d ed. 1998), 579-582; Patrick Moreton and Dwight Crane, Salomon and the Treasury Securities Auction (including 1992 update) (Cambridge, MA: Harvard Business School, 1992); Lynn Sharp Paine, Salomon Brothers B (Harvard Business School, May 2005); Statement of Salomon Inc., submitted by Warren Buffet, in testimony before the Securities Subcommittee on Banking, Housing and Urban Affairs, U.S. Senate, September 10, 1991; Michael Useem, The Leadership Moment (New York: Random House, 1998), 178-207; Carol J. Loomis, Warren Buffett's Wild Ride at Salomon, Fortune, October 27, 1997, available at http://chinese-school.netfirms.com/Warren-Buffett-Salomon.html; Linda Grant, Taming the Bond Buccaneers at Salomon Brothers, Los Angeles Times, February 16, 1992, available at http://articles.latimes.com/1992-02-16/magazine/tm-4654_1_salomon-brothers.

43. Kimberly D. Krawiec, Accounting for Greed: Unraveling the Rogue Trader Mystery, Oregon Law Review 79 (2000):301.

44. Clifford Geertz, The Interpretation of Culture (New York: Basic Books, 1973), 433 (quoted in Krawiec, Accounting for Greed, 310, n. 36).

45. Useem, Leadership Moment (quoting Maughan).

46. Grant, Taming the Bond Buccaneers. For the Salomon culture generally, see Michael Lewis, Liar's Poker (New York: Norton, 1989), 63-67, 69-70, 73, 75-76, 81-83.

47. Useem, Leadership Moment, 186.

48. Id. at 183 (quoting Mozer).

49. Loomis, Warren Buffet's Wild Ride.

50. Grant, Taming the Bond Bucaneers. According to insiders, some of the firm's top executives favored a change in leadership and Gutfreund had temporarily appeased them with inflated pay that might not be sustainable if a scandal broke. Id.

51. Useem, Leadership Moment, 197.

52. Paine, Salomon Brothers B, 1.

53. Loomis, Warren Buffet's Wild Ride (quoting release).

54. Grant, Taming the Bond Buccaneers (quoting Corrigan).

55. Loomis, Warren Buffet's Wild Ride.

56. Useem, Leadership Moment, 205-206 (quoting Buffett).

57. Id. at 192 (quoting Buffet Memo, Aug 26, 1991).

58. Useem, Leadership Moment, 191.

59. Paine, Salomon Brothers B, 3.

60. Id. at 2, (quoting ad from October 31, 2001).

61. Grant, Taming the Bond Buccaneers.

62. Loomis, Warren Buffet's Wild Ride (quoting Buffet). For the financial turnaround, see Paine, Salomon Brothers B.

63. Sarah Bartlett, A Career Skids to a Halt for "King of Wall Street," New York Times, Aug. 17, 1991, 33 (quoting Buffet).

64. For discussion of these problems of cognitive bias in the context of rogue trading, see Krawiec, Accounting for Greed, 316-318.

65. Hannah Arendt, On Violence (New York: Harcourt Brace & Co., 1970), 38-39.

66. Krawiec, Accounting for Greed; Kimberly D. Krawiec, Organizational Misconduct: Beyond the Principal-Agent Model, Florida State Law Review 32 (2005):571, 602-610. Kimberly Krawiec, Cosmetic Compliance and the Failure of Negotiated Governance, Washington University Law Review 81 (2003):487, 492-493.

67. Dennis J. Block and Jonathan M. Hoff, "Mergers and Acquisitions: Liability Extended to Legal and Compliance Officers," New York Law Journal, Mar. 18, 1993, 10, 11 (citations omitted).

68. Id.

69. See 17 Code of Federal Regulations, Part 205 (2003). For discussion of lawyers obligations under Sarbanes-Oxley, see Deborah L. Rhode and David Luban, Legal Ethics (New York: Foundation Press, 5th ed., 2008), 416-423.

70. Renier H. Kraakman, Gatekeepers: The Anatomy of a Third-Party Enforcement Strategy, Journal of Law Economics & Organization 1 (1986):53.

71. http://www.youtube.com/watch?v=ST5rimNAZN0 (4 mins).

72. Remarks by the President on Wall Street Reform, Cooper Union, New York, NY, White House Office of the Press Secretary, April 22, 2010, available at http://www.whitehouse.gov/the-press-office/remarks-president-wall-street-reform.

73. The Tonight Show with Jay Leno, March 19, 2009, available at http://www.whitehouse.gov/the-press-office/interview-president-jay-leno-tonight-show-3-19-09.

74. John C. Coffee Jr., What Went Wrong? A Tragedy in Three Acts, University of St. Thomas Law Journal 6 (2009):403, 417.

75. The complexities are especially great in transactions involving pools of securities with contingent payoffs and liabilities. William A. Sahlman, Management and the Financial Crisis, Harvard Business School Working Paper 10-033 (October 2009).

76. Sarah Kellogg, Financial Crisis 2008: Where Were the Lawyers?, Washington Lawyer, January 2010, 26 (quoting Steven Gillers).

77. Coffee, What Went Wrong, 417; David Hechler, Risky Business: Did Compliance Programs Fail the Test during the Financial Meltdown?, Corporate Counsel, April 1, 2009, available at http://www.law.com/jsp/cc/PubArticleCC.jsp?id=1202429141994.

78. Thomas Friedman, Why How Matters, New York Times, October 15, 2008, A35.

79. David Hechler, Risky Business (quoting Tim Mazur).

80. Steven Pearlstein, A Perfect Storm? No, A Failure of Leadership, Washington Post, December 10, 2008, D01; Paul Krugman, Executives Gone Wild, New York Times Book Review, February 8, 2004, 9.

81. Adam Michaelson, The Foreclosure of America (New York: Berkeley, 2009), 205, 260-261; Steve Fishman, Burning Down His House, New York Times Magazine, December 8, 2008; Barbara Ehrenreich, Bright Sided: How the Relentless Promotion of Positive Thinking Has Undermined America (New York: Henry Holt, 2009), 188-189.

82. Krugman, Executives Gone Wild, 9 (quoting Siegel).

83. Nichiyo Nakamoto and David Wighton, Bullish Citigroup Is "Still Dancing" to the Beat of the Buy-Out Boom, Financial Times, July 10, 2007.

84. Coffee, What Went Wrong, 417.

85. Sarah Kellogg, Financial Crisis 2008: Where Were the Lawyers?, Washington Lawyer, January 2010, 22 (quoting Dunbar).

86. Stephanie Armour and Thomas Frank, Ex-Worker: Law Firm Ran "Foreclosure Mill," U.S.A. Today, October 19, 2010, 3B.

87. John Coffee, Gatekeepers: The Professions and Corporate Governance (New York: Oxford University Press, 2006), 15, 104, 195.

88. Kellogg, Financial Crisis, 26 (quoting Gordon).

89. Roger Lowenstein, Triple-A Failure, New York Times Magazine, April 27, 2008, 27, available at http://www.nytimes.com/2008/04/27/magazine/27Credit-t.html?pagewanted=print.

90. For the ability of institutions to shop around, see Coffee, What Went Wrong, 417. For the pressure on agencies, such as OTS, see National Public Radio, All Things Considered, Who Fell Asleep on the Job?, June 5, 2009; Sahlman, Management and the Financial Crisis, 18.

91. NPR, All Things Considered, Who Fell Asleep on the Job?, June 5, 2009.

92. Opening Statement of Senator Carl Levin before the U.S. Senate Permanent Subcommittee on Investigations on Wall Street and the Financial Crisis: The Role of Bank Regulators, April 16, 2010, http://levin.senate.gov/senate/investigations/index.html.

93. Jill Fish, Top Cop or Regulatory Flop? The SEC at 75, Virginia Law Review 95 (2009):785, 807; Carol A. Needham, Listening to Cassandra: The Difficulty of Recognizing Risks and Taking Action, Fordham Law Review 78 (2010):2329, 2331-2345; Martin Neil Baily, Robert E. Litan, and Matthew S. Johnson, The Origins of the Financial Crisis (Washington, D.C.: Brookings Institution, 2008), 41.

94. See Associated Press, Congress Plans to Investigate Madoff Scheme, Law.com, December 18, 2008 (quoting Coffee); sources cited in Fish, Top Cop, 811; United States Securities and Exchange Commission (SEC) Office of Inspector General, Report OIG-509, Investigation of Failure of the SEC to Uncover Bernard Madoff's Ponzi Scheme, September 3, 2009, 10 (faulting inexperience of investigators); SEC, Office of Inspector General, SEC's Oversight of Bear Stearns and Related Entities: Broker-Dealer Risk Assessment Program, Report 446-B, September 25, 2008 (describing oversight failures); Jesse Westbrook, Cox Quits at SEC, Leaves Shapiro to Restore Clout, Bloomberg.com, January 21, 2009 (discussing leadership failures).

95. Edmund L. Andrews, Greenspan Concedes Error on Regulation, New York Times, October 24, 2008, B1.

96. Remarks by the President on Wall Street Reform, Cooper Union, New York, NY, White House Office of the Press Secretary, April 22, 2010, available at http://www.whitehouse.gov/the-press-office/remarks-president-wall-street-reform.

97. Calvin Trillin, Wall Street Smarts, New York Times, October 14, 2009, A31.

98. Sahlman, Management and the Financial Crisis, 32.

99. Id. at 30.

100. Remarks by the President on Wall Street Reform, Cooper Union, New York, NY, White House Office of the Press Secretary, April 22, 2010, available at http://www.whitehouse.gov/the-press-office/remarks-president-wall-street-reform.

101. For Buffett, see http://www.youtube.com/watch?v=OOR_9L_D2Yk. For Buffet and Gates, see http://www.youtube.com/watch?v=tgbZzgyHZgI&feature=related.

102. A.O. Scott, Movie Review: Inside Job: Who Maimed the Economy and How, New York Times, October 8, 2010, C1.

6

AUTHORITY AND ACCOUNTABILITY

How individuals exercise and respond to authority is central to leadership relationships. Those holding upper-level positions are on the giving and receiving end of various forms of hard and soft power. This chapter explores the structure of authority, the dynamics of obedience, and the strategies for resistance. It provides case histories and psychological accounts of leaders who both gave and followed orders in ways that compromised legal or ethical standards. Attention centers on the situational pressures, cultural norms, personal ambitions, and regulatory frameworks that permit abuse, and on appropriate policy responses.

A. FOLLOWING ORDERS

Following World War II, increased attention focused on how obedience to authority led to the suspension or erosion of moral judgment. One of the most probing accounts was philosopher Hannah Arendt's review of the trial of Adolf Eichmann, one of the high-level Nazi officials charged with crimes against humanity for helping to orchestrate the genocide of millions of European Jews. Her profile of his life and his rationalizations provides a chilling description of what she termed "the banality of evil."

HANNAH ARENDT, EICHMANN IN JERUSALEM: A REPORT ON THE BANALITY OF EVIL

(New York: Penguin Books, 1994), 22, 25-26, 135, and 276-279

First of all, the indictment for murder was wrong: "With the killing of Jews I had nothing to do. I never killed a Jew, or a non-Jew, for that matter — I never killed any human being. I never gave an order to kill either a Jew or a non-Jew; I just did not do it," or, as he was later to qualify this statement, "It so happened . . . that I had not once to do it" — for he left no doubt that he would have killed his own father if he had received an order to that effect.

. . .

Throughout the trial, Eichmann tried to clarify, mostly without success, this second point in his plea of "not guilty in the sense of the indictment." The indictment implied not only that he had acted on purpose, which he did not deny, but out of base motives and in full knowledge of the criminal nature of his deeds.

. . .

his was obviously also no case of insane hatred of Jews, of fanatical anti-Semitism or indoctrination of any kind. He "personally" never had anything whatever against Jews; on the contrary, he had plenty of "private reasons" for not being a Jew hater.

. . .

So Eichmann's opportunities for feeling like Pontius Pilate were many, and as the months and the years went by, he lost the need to feel anything at all. This was the way things were, this was the new law of the land, based on the Führer's order; whatever he did he did, as far as he could see, as a law-abiding citizen. He did his *duty*, as he told the police and the court over and over again; he not only obeyed *orders*, he also obeyed the *law*.

. . .

The trouble with Eichmann was precisely that so many were like him, and that the many were neither perverted nor sadistic, that they were, and still are, terribly and terrifyingly normal. From the viewpoint of our legal institutions and of our moral standards of judgment, this normality was much more ter-rifying than all the atrocities put together, for it implied — as had been said at Nuremberg over and over again by the defendants and their counsels — that this new type of criminal, who is in actual fact *hostis generis humani*, commits his crimes under circumstances that make it well-nigh impossible for him to know or to feel that he is doing wrong.

. . .

Because he had been implicated and had played a central role in an enter-prise whose open purpose was to eliminate forever certain "races" from the surface of the earth, he had to be eliminated. And if it is true that "justice must not only be done but must be seen to be done," then the justice of what was done in Jerusalem would have emerged to be seen by all if the judges had dared to address their defendant in something like the following terms:

> "You admitted that the crime committed against the Jewish people during the war was the greatest crime in recorded history, and you admitted your role in it. But you said you had never acted from base motives, that you had never had any inclination to kill anybody, that you had never hated Jews, and still that you could not have acted otherwise and that you did not feel guilty. We find this difficult, though not altogether impossible, to believe;
>
> . . .
>
> You also said that your role in the Final Solution was an accident and that almost anybody could have taken your place, so that potentially almost all Germans are equally guilty. What you meant to say was that where all, or almost all, are guilty, nobody is. This is an indeed quite common conclusion, but one we are not willing to grant you.
>
> . . .

In other words, guilt and innocence before the law are of an objective nature, and even if eighty million Germans had done as you did, this would not have been an excuse for you.

"Luckily, we don't have to go that far. You yourself claimed not the actuality but only the potentiality of equal guilt on the part of all who lived in a state whose main political purpose had become the commission of unheard-of crimes. And no matter through what accidents of exterior or interior circumstances you were pushed onto the road of becoming a criminal, there is an abyss between the actuality of what you did and the potentiality of what others might have done. We are concerned here only with what you did, and not with the possible noncriminal nature of your inner life and of your motives or with the criminal potentialities of those around you. You told your story in terms of a hard-luck story, and, knowing the circumstances, we are, up to a point, willing to grant you that under more favorable circumstances it is highly unlikely that you would ever have come before us or before any other criminal court. Let us assume, for the sake of argument, that it was nothing more than misfortune that made you a willing instrument in the organization of mass murder; there still remains the fact that you have carried out, and therefore actively supported, a policy of mass murder. For politics is not like the nursery; in politics obedience and support are the same. And just as you supported and carried out a policy of not wanting to share the earth with the Jewish people and the people of a number of other nations—as though you and your superiors had any right to determine who should and who should not inhabit the world—we find that no one, that is, no member of the human race, can be expected to want to share the earth with you. This is the reason, and the only reason, you must hang."

QUESTION

If you had been Eichmann or his lawyer, how would you have responded to the judicial statement that Arendt proposes? One question that her account raises is why leaders in Eichmann's position felt that they had no choice but to "follow orders." Stanford psychologist Philip Zimbardo, author of the excerpt below, is one of the world's leading experts on the potentially corrosive influences of authority and the responses they require.

PHILIP G. ZIMBARDO, "THE PSYCHOLOGY OF POWER: TO THE PERSON?
TO THE SITUATION? TO THE SYSTEM?"

Deborah L. Rhode, ed., Moral Leadership: The Theory and Practice of Power, Judgment, and Policy (San Francisco: Jossey-Bass, 2006), pp. 129-157

. . . The same human mind that creates the most beautiful works of art and extraordinary marvels of technology is equally responsible for the perversion of its own perfection. This most dynamic organ in the universe has been a seemingly endless source for creating ever more vile torture chambers and instruments of horror: the concentration camps of the Third Reich, the "bestial machinery" of Japanese soldiers in their rape of Nanking, and the recent demonstration of "creative evil" of 9/11 by turning commercial airlines into weapons of mass destruction. How can the unimaginable become so readily imagined?

My concern centers around how normal individuals can be recruited, induced, and seduced into behaving in ways that could be classified as evil and the role of leaders in that process. In contrast to the traditional approach of trying to identify "evil people" to account for the evil in our midst, I will focus on the central conditions that underpin the transformation of good, or average, people into perpetrators of evil.

Locating Evil within Particular People: The Rush to Judgment

"Who is responsible for evil in the world, given that there is an all-powerful, omniscient God who is also all-Good?" That conundrum began the intellectual scaffolding of the Inquisition in the sixteenth and seventeenth centuries in Europe. As revealed in *Malleus Maleficarum,* the handbook of the German Inquisitors from the Roman Catholic church, the inquiry concluded that the devil was the source of all evil. However, these theologians argued that the devil works his evil through intermediaries, lesser demons, and, of course, human witches. Therefore, the hunt for evil focused on those marginalized people who looked or acted differently from ordinary people, who might, under rigorous examination or torture, be exposed as witches and then put to death. . . .

Paradoxically, this early effort of the Inquisition to understand the origins of evil and develop responses to evil instead created new forms of evil. It exemplifies the risk of simplifying complex problems by blaming individual perpetrators.

The same risk emerged following World War II, when a team of psychologists sought to make sense of the Holocaust and the broad appeal of national fascism and Hitler. Their focus was on the authoritarian personality: a set of traits underlying the fascist mentality. However, what they overlooked was the host of processes operating at political, economic, societal, and historical levels of analysis that influenced so many millions of individuals to revere their dictator and hate Jews.

This tendency to explain observed behavior by reference to dispositions, while ignoring or minimizing the impact of situational variables, is what Stanford psychologist Lee Ross has called the fundamental attribution error. We are all subject to this dual bias of overemphasizing dispositional analyses and underemphasizing situational explanations. We succumb to this effect because so much of our education, training, and law enforcement are geared toward a focus on individual orientations. . . . Thus, it is individuals who receive praise, fame, and wealth for achievement and are honored for their uniqueness, but it is also individuals who are blamed for the ills of society. Our legal, medical, educational, and religious systems are all founded on principles of individualism.

Dispositional analyses always include strategies for behavior modification to assist deviant individuals, by education or therapy, or to exclude them from society by imprisonment, exile, or execution. Locating evil within selected individuals or groups has the virtue of rendering society blameless. The focus on people as causes for evil then exonerates social structures and political decision making for contributing to underlying conditions that foster evil: poverty, racism, sexism, and elitism.

Most of us take comfort in the illusion that there is an impermeable boundary separating the evil (them) from the good (us). That view leaves us with less interest in understanding the motivations and circumstances that contributed to evil behavior. But in fact, as is clear from the Russian novelist Alexander Solzhenitsyn, a victim of persecution by the Soviet KGB, that the line between good and evil lies in the center of every human heart.

It has been my mission as a psychologist to understand better how virtually anyone could be recruited to engage in evil deeds that deprive other human beings of their lives, dignity, and humanity. . . .

Blind Obedience to Authority: The Milgram Investigations

Stanley Milgram developed an ingenious research procedure to demonstrate the extent to which situational forces could overwhelm individual will to resist. He shocked the world with his unexpected finding of extremely high rates of compliance to the demands of an authority figure to deliver apparently dangerous electric shocks to an innocent victim. He found that about 67 percent of research participants went all the way up to the top shock level of 450 volts in attempting to "help" another person learn appropriate behaviors. Milgram's study revealed that ordinary American citizens could so easily be led to engage in "electrocuting a nice stranger" as the Nazis had been led to murder Jews.

After this initial demonstration with Yale College students, Milgram went on to conduct eighteen experimental variations on more than a thousand subjects from a variety of backgrounds, ages, and educational levels. In each of these studies, he varied one social psychological variable and observed its impact on the extent of obedience by a subject to shock the "learner-victim," who pretended to be suffering. The data told the story of the extreme pliability of human nature. Almost everyone could be totally obedient, or almost everyone could resist authority pressures; it depended on situational differences. Milgram was able to demonstrate that compliance rates could soar to 90 percent of people who delivered the maximum 450 volts to the learner-victim, or could be reduced to less than 10 percent of total obedience by introducing one variable into the compliance recipe[—another participant who resisted].

Want maximum obedience? Provide social models of compliance by having participants observe peers behaving obediently. Want people to resist authority pressures? Provide social models of peers who rebelled. Interestingly, almost no one shocked the learner-victim when he actually asked to be shocked. They refused authority pressure when the target seemed to be a masochist. In each of the other variations on this diverse range of ordinary Connecticut citizens, low, medium, or high levels of compliant obedience could be readily elicited as if one were simply turning a human nature dial.

What is the expected rate of such obedience in the Milgram setting according to experts on human nature? When forty psychiatrists were given the basic description of this experiment, their average estimate of the number of United States citizens who would give the full 450 volts was only 1 percent. Only sadists would engage in such behavior, they believed. These experts on human behavior were totally wrong because they ignored situational determinants. Their training in psychiatry had led them to overly rely on dispositional explanations. This is a strong instance of the operation of the fundamental attribution error in action.

Ten Steps to Creating Evil Traps for Good People

What were the procedures in this research paradigm that seduces many ordinary citizens to engage in such apparently abusive behavior? These procedures parallel compliance strategies used in many real-world settings by "influence professionals" such as salespeople, cult recruiters, and national leaders.

These are the influences that will lead ordinary people to do things they originally believe they would not:

1. Offering an ideology that justifies any means to achieve a seemingly desirable goal. In clinical experiments like Milgram's, the rationale is helping people improve their memories. For nations, it is often a "threat to national security" that justifies going to war or suppressing dissident political opposition. . . . As research by Susan Fiske and her colleagues indicates, that reasoning contributes to ordinary people's willingness to torture enemy prisoners in contexts like Abu Ghraib prison.
2. Arranging some form of contractual obligation, verbal or written.
3. Giving participants meaningful roles to play (teacher, student) that carry with them previously learned positive values and response scripts.
4. Presenting basic rules to be followed that seem to make sense prior to their actual use, but then can be arbitrarily used to justify mindless compliance. Make the rules vague, and change them as necessary.
5. Altering the semantics of the act, the actor, and the action (from hurting victims to helping learners); replace reality with desirable rhetoric.
6. Creating opportunities for diffusion of responsibility or suggesting that others will be responsible or that the actor will not be held liable.
7. Starting the path toward the ultimate evil act with a small, insignificant first step (only 15 volts in the Milgram experiment).
8. Gradually increasing steps on the pathway to abuse, so that they appear no different from prior actions. Increases of only 30 volts presented no noticeable difference in harm to the Milgram participants.
9. Changing the nature of the influence authority from initially "just" and reasonable to "unjust" and demanding, which elicits confusion but continued obedience.
10. Making the exit costs high by allowing the usual forms of verbal dissent (that make people feel good about themselves), while insisting on behavioral compliance ("I know you are not that kind of person; just keep doing as I tell you").

Such procedures can prepare people psychologically to do the unthinkable.

On Being Anonymous: Deindividuation and Destructiveness

. . . [One of my most important experiments] involved having young women deliver a series of painful electric shocks to each of two other young women whom they could see and hear in a one-way mirror before them. Half the subjects were randomly assigned to a condition of anonymity, or deindividuation, and half to one of uniqueness, or individuation. The four college student subjects in each deindividuation cluster were treated as members of a group, not as individuals; their appearances were concealed by hoods, and their names were replaced by numbers. The comparison group consisted of individuals who wore name tags and were made to feel unique. . . . The results were clear: women in the deindividuation condition delivered twice as much shock to both victims as did the women in the individuated comparison condition. Moreover, they shocked both victims, the one previously rated as pleasant and the other unpleasant victim, more over the course of the twenty trials, while the individuated subjects shocked the pleasant woman less over time than they did the unpleasant one. One important conclusion flows from this research and its various replications and extensions, some using military personnel from the Belgian army: anything that makes people feel anonymous reduces a sense of accountability and increases their propensity to evil under situations inviting violence. . . .

Moral Disengagement and Dehumanization

Psychologist Al Bandura has developed a model of moral disengagement that specifies the conditions under which anyone can be led to act immorally, even those who usually ascribe to high levels of morality. The model outlines a set of cognitive mechanisms that alter a person's (1) perception of the reprehensible conduct (engaging in moral justifications, making palliative comparisons, using euphemistic labeling); (2) sense of the detrimental effects of that conduct (minimizing, ignoring, or misconstruing the consequences); (3) sense of responsibility for the link between reprehensible conduct and its detrimental effects (displacing or diffusing responsibility); and (4) view of victims (dehumanizing or blaming them).

Bandura and his colleagues designed a powerful experiment that is an elegantly simple demonstration of the power of dehumanizing labels. It reveals how easy it is to induce normal, intelligent individuals to accept a dehumanizing label of other people and then to act aggressively based on that classification. A group of four participants were led to believe they were overhearing a research assistant tell the experimenter that the students from another college were present to start the study in which they were to deliver electric shocks of varying intensity (allegedly as part of a group problem-solving study). In one of the three randomly assigned conditions, the subjects overheard the assistant say to the experimenter that the other students seemed "nice." In second condition, they heard that the other students seemed like "animals." In a third variation, the assistant did not label the students.

This situational manipulation clearly affected behavior. Experimental subjects gave the most shock to those labeled "animals," and their shock level increased over the ten trials. Those labeled "nice" were given the least shock, and the unlabeled group fell between these extremes. Thus, a single word, *animals*, was sufficient to induce intelligent college students to treat others as if they deserved to be harmed.

What is also of interest is the progressive nature of abuse. On the first trial, there is no difference across the three experimental situations in the level of shock administered, but with each successive opportunity, the shock levels diverge. Those shocking so-called animals shocked them more and more over time, a result comparable to the escalating shock level of the deindividuated female students in my earlier study. That increase in aggression over time, with practice or with experience, illustrates a self-reinforcing effect of abuse. Perhaps its appeal is not so much in inflicting pain to others as in the sense of power and control in such a situation of dominance.

A more positive finding was that individuals receive more respectful treatment if someone in authority labels them positively. Those perceived as "nice" were least harmed. There is an important message here about the power of words, to be used for good or evil.

Suspension of the Usual Cognitive Controls Guiding Moral Action

Part of what is necessary to get good people to engage in evil is to minimize or reorient normal cognitive control processes. That process suspends conscience, self-awareness, sense of personal responsibility, obligation, commitment, liability, morality, and analyses in terms of costs and benefits of given actions. The two general strategies for accomplishing this objective are reducing cues of social accountability of the actor (no one knows who I am or cares to) and reducing concerns for self-evaluation. The first strategy minimizes concerns for social evaluation and social approval by making the actor feel anonymous. It works in an environment that masks identity and diffuses personal responsibility across others in the situation. The second strategy stops self-monitoring by relying on tactics that alter one's state of consciousness (such as by drugs, strong emotions, or hyperintense activity) and projecting responsibility outward onto others.

The Hostile Imagination Created by Faces of the Enemy

The importance of situational influences is also apparent in the ways that nations prepare soldiers to engage in wars and prepare citizens to support the risks of going to war, especially a war of aggression. This difficult transformation is accomplished by a special form of cognitive conditioning. Images of the "enemy" are created to prepare the minds of soldiers and citizens to hate those who fit the category. This mental conditioning is the military's most potent weapon. . . . The enemy is aggressor; faceless; rapist; godless; barbarian; greedy; criminal; torturer; death; a dehumanized animal, or just an abstraction. Alternatively, there is a vision of the enemy as worthy, combatant, a powerful opponent to be crushed in "mortal combat" — as in the video game of the same name.

Can Ordinary Old Men Become Murderers Overnight?

One of the clearest illustrations of the transformation of ordinary people into agents of mass atrocities comes from the chronicle of Nazi genocides [over 11 months] by British historian Christopher Browning. . . . In just four months they had shot to death at point-blank range at least thirty-eight thousand Jews and deported another forty-five thousand to the concentration camp at Treblinka. Initially their commander acknowledged that this was a difficult mission and any individual could refuse to execute these men, women, and children. Records indicate that at first, about half the German police reservists refused and let others engage in the mass murder. But over time, social modeling processes took their toll, as did guilt-induced persuasion by those who had been doing the shooting. By the end of their journey, up to 90 percent of the men in Battalion 101 were involved in the shootings, even proudly taking close-up photographs of their killings. Like the guards at Abu Ghraib Prison, these policemen put themselves in their "trophy photos" as proud exterminators of the Jewish menace.

Browning makes clear that there was no special selection of these men. They were as ordinary as can be imagined — until they were put into a situation in which they had official permission and encouragement to act sadistically against those labeled as the "enemy." He also compares the underlying mechanism operating in that far-off land at that distant time to both the psychological processes at work in the Milgram research and the Stanford Prison Experiment discussed below. . . .

The Stanford Prison Experiment: Institutional and Systemic Power to Corrupt

My own 1971 prison experiment synthesized many of the processes and variables outlined earlier: anonymity of place and person, dehumanization of victims, and a setting with differentials in control and power. This experiment was designed to extend over a two-week period . . . [but] had to be terminated after only six days because of the pathology we were witnessing. Normal students were behaving sadistically in their role of guards, inflicting humiliation, pain, and suffering. Some guards even reported they were enjoying doing so. Others had "emotional breakdowns" and stress disorders so extreme that five of them had to be excused within that first week. Those who adapted better to the situation were prisoners who mindlessly followed orders, became blindly obedient to authority, and allowed the guards to dehumanize and degrade them. . . .

The Evil of Inaction

British statesman Edmund Burke aptly observed, "The only thing necessary for evil to triumph is for good men to do nothing." Our usual take on evil focuses on violent, destructive actions, but non-action can also become a form of evil, when assistance, dissent, or disobedience are called for. . . . A counter to this dispositional analysis came in the form of a series of classic studies by Bibb Latane and John Darley on bystander intervention. One key finding was that people are less likely to help when they are in a group, when they perceive others are available who could help, than when those people are alone. The presence of others diffuses the sense of personal responsibility of any individual.

A powerful demonstration of the failure to help strangers in distress was staged by John Darley and Dan Batson. Imagine you are a theology student on your way to deliver the sermon of the Good Samaritan in order to have it videotaped for a psychology study on effective communication. Further imagine that as you are heading from the Psychology Department to the videotaping center, you pass a stranger huddled in an alley in dire distress. . . .

The researchers randomly assigned students of the Princeton Theological Seminary to three conditions that varied how much time they had to get to the Communication Department to tape their Good Samaritan speeches. The conclusion: don't be a victim in distress when people are late and in a hurry, because 90 percent of them are likely to pass you by. The more time the seminarians believed they had, the more likely they were to stop and help. So the situational variable of time press accounted for the major variance in helping, without any need to resort to dispositional explanations about theology students being callous, cynical, or indifferent. . . .

In situations of evil, there are almost always those who know what is going on and do not intervene to help. There were "good" guards in the Stanford Prison Experiment who did no harm to the prisoners, but they never once opposed the demeaning deeds of the bad guards. In the recent Abu Ghraib Prison abuse case, it is clear that many people knew of the abuse, even doctors and nurses, but never intervened to prevent it. . . .

Understanding What Went Wrong in Abu Ghraib Prison

The situational influences of evil came to the fore in recent trials of American prison guards at Abu Ghraib. In October 2004, I testified via closed circuit television to the military trial judge in Baghdad in defense of one of the guards, Sergeant Ivan Frederick. . . .

With regard to disposition, this soldier was totally and unequivocally normal on all measures assessed by an army clinical psychologist (and independently validated by a civilian expert in assessment). There was no evidence of any psychopathology or sadistic tendencies. Rather, Frederick matches our stereotypes of the All-American man. He is a patriotic son of a West Virginia coal miner. He hunts, fishes, plays Softball, attends Baptist church services regularly, and has a strong marriage to an African American woman. As a reserve soldier, he had a blameless record as a guard in a low-security, small-town civilian prison with one hundred inmates. He was proud to serve in Iraq and initially worked with children in a small village where he was starting to learn Arabic.

The situational conditions, the behavioral context, involved working conditions that bordered on the inhumane for both guards and prisoners. The processes operating in that prison were directly comparable to those in the Stanford Prison Experiment: deindividuation, dehumanization, moral disengagement, social modeling, pressures for conformity, passive bystanders, power differentials, use of enforced nakedness, and sexually humiliating tactics. The worst abuses in both settings took place on the night shift. The working conditions for Frederick included twelve-hour night shifts (4:00 P.M. to 4:00 A.M.), seven days a week, for forty days with not a day off, then fourteen days after one day off. Exhaustion and stress were exacerbated by chaotic conditions: unsanitary and filthy surroundings that smelled like a putrid sewer, with limited water for showering. Frequent electrical blackouts created dangerous opportunities for prisoner attacks. This young man with no mission-specific training was put in charge of more than three hundred prisoners initially; that number soon swelled to more than a thousand. He was also in charge of twelve army reserve guards and sixty Iraqi police, who often smuggled contraband to the inmates. He rarely left the prison. When off duty, he slept in a cell in a different part of prison. He missed breakfasts and stopped exercising or socializing. Tier 1-A became his total reference setting.

This of itself would qualify anyone for total job burnout. But guards were also under the stress of frequent insurgency attacks. Five U.S. soldiers and twenty prisoners were killed, and many others were wounded by almost daily shelling during Frederick's service. Finally, there were abusive acts by the prisoners themselves. Seven had rioted in another part of the prison and were sent to Tier 1-A for "safe keeping." Four others had raped a fellow boy prisoner. Five separate military investigations concerning Abu Ghraib acknowledge its horrendous conditions. They also acknowledge "failures of leadership, lack of leadership, indifferent leadership, and conflicting leadership demands." What is clear from these independent investigations is a total absence of accountability and oversight and an encouragement of stress interrogation.

The military judge took none of these conditions into account when he issued his sentence. Frederick received the maximum penalty: imprisonment for eight years, a dishonorable discharge, and loss of twenty-two years of army reserve retirement funds. This verdict represents yet another failure of leadership. It ignores the systemic conditions encouraging abuse and absolves the military and political officials responsible.

Promoting Civic Virtue, Moral Engagement, and Human Goodness

There are no simple solutions for the evils addressed here; if there were, they would already have been enacted by those far wiser than I. But the past half-century of psychological research provides some insight about what might be done at the individual and situational levels. . . .

Some of the same social-psychological forces that fostered the abuses described could also be harnessed for positive ends. We could, for example, construct an eleven-step plan for promoting civic virtue that parallels the ten steps toward evil outlined earlier:

1. Openly acknowledge errors in judgments. This reduces the need to justify mistakes and continue immoral action. It undercuts the motivation to reduce dissonance by reaffirming a bad decision.
2. Encourage mindfulness. People need reminders not to live their lives on automatic pilot, but to reflect on the situation and consider its ethical implications before acting.
3. Promote a sense of personal responsibility and accountability for all of one's actions. People need a better understanding of how conditions of diffused responsibility disguise their own individual role in the outcomes of their actions.
4. Discourage minor transgressions. Small acts — cheating, gossiping, lying, teasing, and bullying — provide the first steps toward escalating abuses.

5. Distinguish between just and unjust authority. The fact that individuals occupy a position of authority, as in the Milgram experiment, does not entitle them to obedience in unethical actions.
6. Support critical thinking. People need to be encouraged to demand evidence and moral justifications and to evaluate their credibility.
7. Reward moral behavior. More recognition needs to be available for those who do the right thing under difficult situations, such as whistle-blowers in public and private sector positions.
8. Respect human diversity. Appreciating difference is key to reducing in-group biases and prejudices.
9. Change social conditions that promote anonymity. Making people feel special and accountable can promote socially desirable actions and reinforce individuals' sense of self-worth.
10. Challenge pressures for conformity. Individuals need strategies for resisting group influences and maintaining their own moral compass.
11. Refuse to sacrifice crucial freedoms for elusive promises of security. These sacrifices are often the first step toward fascism, and the price is often prohibitive.

NOTES AND QUESTIONS

One irony of the Stanford and Milgram experiments is that they have not only made enormous contributions to our understanding of moral behavior, they have also been subject to widespread criticism on moral grounds. Since the experiments were conducted, ethical oversight of research has become more rigorous. In the United States, any institution that receives federal funds must establish an institutional review board (IRB) to approve research involving human subjects. Criteria for approval, set forth in federal regulations, include whether the risks to subjects have been reduced to those necessary to achieve valid research objectives; whether those risks are outweighed by benefits to the participants or society generally; and whether the subjects have given informed consent that includes their right to withdraw at any time.[1]

If you were the chair of an IRB, would you approve research modeled on the Stanford prison or Milgram shock experiments? What changes if any would you require? Would it affect your view if, as Zimbardo claims, all of his participants returned to "normal" after extensive debriefing and most claimed that participation in the experiment was a valuable experience, although none would volunteer again?[2]

PROBLEM 6-1

Abuse of detainees held at the Abu Ghraib prison in Iraq received worldwide attention in 2004 through pictures and articles chronicling the degradation. Prisoners were subject to beatings, death threats, sleep deprivation, stress positions, forced nudity, forced masturbation, and sex with dogs or other prisoners. Some observers such as Senator James Inhofe discounted the abuse by demonizing the prisoners as "murderers" and "terrorists." Military experts, however, including Brigadier General Janis Karpinski, the commanding officer at the prison, estimated that about 90 percent of the detainees were innocent.[3]

The United States Department of Defense removed seventeen members of the military from duty in response to abuses. Eleven soldiers were convicted in courts martial. Most received relatively light sentences: several months in prison, financial penalties, demotions, and dishonorable discharges. Sergeant Ivan Frederick, however, for whom Philip Zimbardo gave testimony, received an eight-year prison sentence for abuses that included forcing three prisoners to masturbate and punching one so hard that he needed resuscitation. No officers were convicted. Brigadier General Karpinski was demoted to the rank of colonel, despite her claims that she had no knowledge of the abuse and that enhanced interrogation had been authorized by superiors and performed by subcontractors. Thomas Pappas, commander of the military brigade in charge of the prison, was reprimanded, relieved of his command, demoted, and fined $8000.

In testimony before the Senate Armed Services Committee, then Secretary of Defense Donald Rumsfeld stated:

> These events occurred on my watch. As secretary of defense, I am accountable for them. I take full responsibility. It is my obligation to evaluate what happened to make sure those who have committed wrongdoing are brought to justice and to make changes as needed to see that it doesn't happen again. . . . To those Iraqis who were mistreated by members of the U.S. armed forces, I offer my deepest apology. It was un-American. It was inconsistent with the values of our nation.[4]

Rumsfeld also denounced those who had illegally distributed photos to the media and he declined to call the abuse "torture."[5] Although he offered to resign, he added, "What was going on in the midnight shift in Abu Ghraib prison halfway across the world is something that clearly someone in Washington, DC, can't manage or deal with. And so I have no regrets. . . . We've made a lot of corrections to make sure that those kinds of things [that] happened either don't happen again or are immediately found out and limited and contained."[6] His offers to resign were rejected by President Bush, who also denounced the incidents as un-American.[7]

The Final Report of the Independent Panel to Review DOD Detention Operations specifically found that no senior U.S. military or political leaders "were directly involved in the incidents at Abu Ghraib."[8] Discussion of the leaders involved in decisions to allow "enhanced interrogation" of terrorist suspects appears in Part C below.

1. If you had been the president or the secretary of defense in 2004, how would you have responded to the abuses at Abu Ghraib?
2. Was the allocation of responsibility for the Abu Ghraib abuses appropriate: lengthy prison sentences for those who perpetrated the abuses, and no criminal or civil liability for those who allowed the conditions that made it possible? A *New York Times* editorial claimed that "each new revelation

[concerning the prison] makes it more clear that the inhumanity of Abu Ghraib grew out of a morally dubious culture" fostered by the administration.[9] If that is true, what follows in terms of appropriate sanctions and preventive conduct?

3. Philip Zimbardo would clearly take issue with Rumsfeld's claim that the Abu Ghraib abuse was "un-American." Would you? If the thrust of Zimbardo's argument is that many "normal" Americans would behave like the Abu Ghraib guards under similar stressful circumstances, does that lessen the gravity of the offenses committed? Consider that issue in light of Hannah Arendt's discussion of Third Reich officers in the reading above.

MEDIA RESOURCES

A narrated video on the original version of the Milgram experiment is available, as are replications with comparable results.[10] One of the most interesting variations sought to ensure that participants believed that the shocks were real. The experiment used a puppy rather than a person as the subject of the "learning" exercise. Each participant watched the puppy first barking, then jumping up and down, and finally howling in pain from the shocks. Participants were horrified. They paced back and forth, hyperventilated, and gestured with their hands to show the puppy where to stand. Many openly wept. Yet the majority of them, twenty out of twenty-six, continued the shocks up to the maximum voltage. Contrary to gender stereotypes that women are more caring and empathetic than men, none of the six who refused to continue were female. All thirteen women who participated in the experiment obeyed until the end.[11] Another variation divided the teacher's role into two parts: a person who transmitted the order to shock and the person who administered it. Obedience among the transmitters was substantially greater than among the administrators, which underscores the role of distance from victims in moral meltdowns.[12] One of the most recent versions of the Milgram experiment occurred at Santa Clara University, with modifications to secure IRB approval. The revised experiment involved lower voltage and clear instructions that the participants could drop out at any time.[13] The Stanford prison experiment also has generated an extensive video record.[14]

Images of the Abu Ghraib abuses and interviews with guards are also available.[15] A Canadian Broadcasting Company documentary includes discussion with a soldier and Pentagon official who deny responsibility, a soldier who decided to report abuse, and John Yoo, a White House lawyer who defended enhanced interrogation methods.[16]

B. MORAL MELTDOWNS

In the following essays, David Luban, John Dean, and Peter Irons describe forces that have led to certain widely publicized "moral meltdowns." Recall the cognitive biases described in Chapter 3. To what extent are they at work in the examples described? What other factors may have been at work?

David Luban, "Making Sense of Moral Meltdowns"

Deborah L. Rhode, ed., Moral Leadership: The Theory and Practice of Power, Judgment, and Policy (San Francisco: Jossey-Bass, 2007), pp. 57-75

. . . My aim in this chapter is to explore why executive and professional leadership goes sour. The examination proceeds along four principal dimensions: ethical, cultural, economic, and psychological.

The Ethical Dimension: Adversarial Ethics

At its simplest, what we seem to have witnessed in Enron, WorldCom, Global Crossing, Arthur Andersen, Merrill Lynch, and the other high-profile cases of the past few years is an epidemic of dishonesty, self-dealing, cheating, and even outright theft — an incredible failure to honor the most basic rules of Sunday school morality by executives and professionals who people trusted to know better than that and to do better than that. . . .

What conclusions we should draw from pandemic business scandals is likely to depend on one's overall outlook on business regulation. Those who think that our economy works best when executives have lots of power and discretion to make innovative, high-risk decisions are likely to favor tough enforcement over new regulation. According to their view, the fraudulent executives are bad apples in a basically sweet barrel. Whatever we do, let us make sure we do not kill the apple tree with a regulatory chainsaw. Others argue that the problem is not a few bad apples but a system that allows gross conflicts of interest and cries out for regulation. Their view is that the rottenness goes a lot deeper into the barrel than the notorious bad apples on top. With a system that makes self-dealing so easy and so profitable, it is no wonder that basic honesty goes out the window.

I take a different outlook from both of these. My proposition is that most of the people who brought us these scandals have ethical belief systems that are not much different from yours and mine. I suspect that if you asked them whether they think lying and cheating are okay, they would answer with an indignant no, and if you gave them a lie detector test when they said it, the needle would not budge. I do not pretend to see into people's brains, but I would be willing to bet that virtually none of the architects of these scandals — not the executives, not the accountants, not the lawyers — really thinks he or she did anything wrong. In that case, you might be asking what planet these people come from, but the answer, of course, is that we are standing on it. In their basic moral outlook, most will not turn out to be that much different from anyone else.

The fact is that everyday morality does not have settled principles for hypercompetitive, highly adversarial settings. For example, when the other side fights dirty, can you fight dirty too? On this issue, most people's moral intuitions are conflicted. Even Sunday school sends a double message. On the one hand, we say that two wrongs do not make a right and tell ourselves to turn the other cheek. On the other hand, we say that turnabout is fair play, we say an eye for an eye, we say you have to fight fire with fire. . . . I am not suggesting that "everyone does it" is a legitimate moral excuse. Rather, I am suggesting that there are very few consensus moral rules for highly adversarial, competitive settings. That implies a lot of moral uncertainty and ambiguity in a culture as addicted to competition as ours is.

The Cultural Dimension: America's Love Affair with Winners

This takes me to the second point: the cultural obstacles to dealing with Enron-type ethical meltdowns. The fact is that our culture loves the Fastows and Skillings of the world as long as they succeed. . . . The employees, managers, accountants, and attorneys who work for the winners are no exception.

More than that, I think it is undeniable that American culture has always had a soft spot in its heart for bad boys who break rules to get results, as long as they do it in style. . . .

Having a soft spot for bad boy winners seems harmless enough, but the flip side is a little uglier. As a culture, we have little patience with losers. If they did something wrong, we do not cut them the same slack we do for winners. Even if they were blameless, we are unlikely to find them all that appealing. In a fascinating series of experiments, the social psychologist Melvin Lerner discovered that the worse someone is treated, the more likely observers are to rate the victim as an unattractive, flawed person. Lerner explains this phenomenon as an unconscious attempt to ward off the scary thought that if unfair stuff can happen to her, it can happen to me. We unconsciously disparage the victim in order to find a distinction, some distinction, between her and us in order to reassure ourselves that *we* will not get victimized next. I find this explanation entirely plausible. Whatever the explanation, though, the experiment provides powerful evidence that we do not tend to find losers beautiful.

I think everyone instinctively understands this, and the implications for business ethics are disturbing. Given the choice between breaking rules and winning or being a law-abiding loser, you are far more likely to win friends and influence people if you break the rules — especially if you can portray the rules as red tape crying out to be cut. No wonder that Enron executives took the most aggressive accounting positions they possibly could. Pushing rules as hard as you can in order to be a winner is exactly what our culture prizes. . . .

The accountants' and lawyers' job is to keep the flamboyant bad boys out of trouble. The problem is that when a successful client is flying high, as high as Enron flew, no one wants to be the doomsayer who puts on the brakes. A hundred years ago, Elihu Root, one of the founders of Cravath, Swaine & Moore, said, "The client never wants to be told he can't do what he wants to do; he wants to be told how to do it, and it is the lawyer's business to tell him how." The same ethos permeates large accounting firms. The culture's love affair with bad boy businessmen creates a behavioral echo among the employees whose job is to hold them in check but who may see their real job as guarding the CEO's back.

The Economic Dimension: The Feudal and Socialist Character of American Capitalism

. . . [The third major challenge to reform] is the economic fact that a capitalist economy always produces losers. . . . It does not matter how smart executives are or how fast on their feet. The world around them is faster.

Inevitably they set their quarterly targets based on inadequate or obsolete information. And sometimes reality catches up with them. The economy goes south just when they have placed their bets on a few more golden quarters of going north.

The problem is that a manager who has set an impossible target has usually put his boss and employees on the line as well. Robert Jackall, who authored one of the best studies ever on the moral world of corporate managers, points out that corporate hierarchies are almost feudal in structure. Ask a contemporary corporate manager what his job is, and he is likely to answer, "I work for Joe Smith." He answers the question by naming his boss, not by offering an impersonal description of his job. . . . Like the vassalages of medieval Europe, American corporate hierarchies are networks of personal patron-client relations. Managers offer perks and protection in return for loyalty and performance. A manager extracts targets and promises from subordinates and on the basis of those numbers makes promises to his own boss, who does the same with her own boss. When one of those promises fails, it runs the risk of taking down not just yourself but the people above and below you as well. In an odd way, executives fighting desperately to hide their losses and stay in business act in part out of a warped sense of fiduciary obligation to other people in the company. The moral pressure to meet your numbers, combined with self-interest, is overwhelming. . . .

What do you do when you cannot keep your promises and meet your targets? You have four choices. One is to pin the blame on someone else. Claiming you did not know what others were doing is the simplest way, but more subtle methods exist as well. For example, Jackall discovered a system of "milking" factories in the chemical giant he studied. A manager struggling to meet his numbers shortchanges essential maintenance on the equipment. Eventually the equipment breaks down in a very expensive way, but by that time the manager has been promoted, and the meltdown happens on someone else's watch. Top management had little interest in tracking accountability, because in Jackall's company, everyone knew that the boss got to the top the same way.

If you cannot pin the blame on someone else, a second option is to arrange things so the losses fall on your customers, your shareholders, your employees — anywhere but yourself. . . . Option three, Enron's main strategy, is to smear on the cosmetics, cover up the losses as long as possible, and hope for a miracle turnaround to pull you from the fire. Rational managers should know better than to rely on miracles. But look at the character traits that make for successful entrepreneurs: boundless optimism, big egos, a taste for risk, unwillingness to take no for an answer. Exactly these traits predispose high-flying CEOs to bet the farm on one last roll of the dice and assume that Lady Luck will smile on them. Surely the economy will rebound and get you out of your troubles. Only sometimes it does not.

These are the three dishonest strategies: blame someone else, shaft someone else, or cover up and hope against hope. The fourth strategy is to accept that you have lost, take your lumps, and move on. . . . What we now see is that the failures that drive executives to cheat and cover up are built into the very nature of a corporation, which is a planned economy that cannot avoid placing high-risk bets. Put these three factors together, and you have a recipe for scandals. The conclusion seems unavoidable: the crooks, like the poor, will always be with us.

The Psychological Dimension: Cognitive Dissonance and Moral Compass

But none of this explains our original puzzle of why the crooks continue to think they are not crooks. Here social psychology offers an answer. The basic reason is cognitive dissonance. Whenever our conduct and principles clash with each other in a way that threatens our self-image as an upstanding person, the result is a kind of inner tension — dissonance. And dissonance theory tells us that wired into us is a fundamental drive to reduce dissonance. How do you accomplish that? Obviously, you cannot change your past conduct. Instead, you change your beliefs. That is what fifty years of research have taught. In situation after situation, literally hundreds of experiments reveal that when our conduct clashes with our prior beliefs, our beliefs swing into conformity with our conduct, without our noticing that this is going on. . . .

How can this happen? The answer, as any psychiatrist will tell you, is that we do not automatically know our own beliefs. Instead, we figure them out by examining our own behavior. . . . If I covered up losses with smoke-and-mirrors accounting, I must think that smoke-and-mirrors does not really count as a cover-up. And what if this contradicts what I have always been taught and always thought I believed in the past? I tell myself that only a fanatic refuses to learn from experience — and I am no fanatic.

One surprising result follows. Most of us are inclined to think that the big problem in the ethics scandals is lack of integrity on the part of the principals. But if integrity means doing what you think is right, these men and women had integrity to burn. They got it the cheap way: once they did things, they believed those things were right. Integrity does not help very much when you are in the grips of self-deception.

The problem is not simply that we unconsciously adjust our moral beliefs so they inevitably make us look good. Psychologists have also shown that our judgment is deeply affected by the people around us. Show a group of people two lines, and if eleven of them say that the shorter line is longer, the twelfth is likely to see it that way as well.

The same thing is true with moral judgment, and that is the special problem that organizational settings create: you are always in the room with eleven other people. In the 1960s, a young woman named Kitty Genovese was assaulted and murdered in Queens, New York, as dozens of people in their apartments witnessed the assault. Not a single person called the police. The media were filled with dismay at this sign of social indifference. But two social psychologists had a different explanation: they conjectured that groups of people are usually less likely to help out in emergencies than single individuals are. To test their hypothesis, they had subjects fill out questionnaires in a room. While a subject worked on the questionnaire, a staged emergency happened — either the sound of crashing equipment and screams from the next room or smoke billowing into the room where the subject was sitting. The results were remarkable: when subjects were by themselves, most responded quickly to the emergency. But when another person sat next to them and failed to respond, they mimicked the other person and did nothing themselves. Evidently we respond to unusual situations by first checking to see how other people respond. And just as we take cues from the other person, he or she takes cues from us. . . .

The Kitty Genovese effect goes a long way toward explaining why no one blew the whistle on the corporate scandals: insiders simply took their cues from each other. They saw everyone else acting as though everything was perfectly all right, and they acted that way themselves, each reinforcing the others' passivity. . . . The desire to fit in with those around us helps explain how [managers,] . . . lawyers and accountants become fatally implicated in corporate wrongdoing. In large organizations, decisions get parceled out among many people, and every piece of work is the product of many hands. Information filters in piecemeal, a little at a time. As a result, decisive moral moments are not obvious. They are not really moments at all. They do not scream out, "You've reached the crossroads!" Changes come gradually, like walking in a very large circle. Not only that, the consequences of decisions are often nearly unfathomable. And working in teams, it is seldom obvious whose responsibility any choice ultimately is. It may be everyone's or nobody's at all. The ground is fertile for the Kitty Genovese effect. . . .

Suppose, for example, that a chief financial officer calls in an in-house lawyer, and a consultant, and an accountant, and says that he would like to structure some deals that will help push accounting losses off the books. (Think Andrew Fastow.) The lawyer may not know off the top of her head whether there is a legal way to do it, but that is what she gets paid to figure out. The last thing the lawyer thinks about is that an ethical rule forbids her from counseling or assisting in a client fraud. The conversation is about business goals, not about fraud (such an ugly word!). The lawyer, accountant, and consultant accept the business goal of making business losses vanish from the balance sheets, and reason backward to whatever complicated structure it will take to achieve it. So what if the law requires a proper business purpose other than sanitizing an annual statement? The whole lawyering problem is figuring out some way to package the client's goal as a proper business purpose, although that might require drifting into the gray zone at the margin of the law. Transparency avoidance feels to the lawyer, accountant, and consultant like little more than a formalistic game, not much different from tax avoidance.

The trouble is that transparency is what the law requires, and transparency avoidance bears an uncanny resemblance to fraud. . . . In a corporate culture, the incredible plasticity of conscience that social psychology reveals creates perhaps the biggest challenge to reformers. If you cannot trust your own conscience to tell you the difference between right and wrong, how are you supposed to do what is right? Remember what we have learned so far: the stakes in business are high, the corporate culture puts out powerful cues, the wider culture reinforces them, and no settled guidelines about morality in competitive settings push hard in the opposite direction. It should hardly astonish us that the result is ethical self-deception on a grand scale.

It may sound as though I am saying dishonesty is a social disease that is nobody's fault. That is not my intention at all. The goal is to understand, not to make excuses. In fact, I am not a great believer in the idea that to understand all is to forgive all. People make their choices under constraints, including psychological ones, but in the end, all sane adults are still accountable for the choices they make. We should never forget that not everyone gives in to social pressures. If my conscience lets me down, the fact remains that it is *my* conscience, not the company's conscience and not society's conscience.

Lessons for Leaders?

. . . What advice can I offer to managers, accountants, and lawyers in corporate settings? Is it really true that forces you are barely aware of can disconnect your conscience as thoroughly as the Stanford prison guards or the administrators of electric shocks? If the answer is yes, then how can anyone deal with forces they are barely aware of?

I have three suggestions. First, all the experimental studies suggest that cognitive dissonance disconnects the wires of conscience slowly and one step at a time. . . . For that reason, it becomes critically important to give ourselves some kind of warning. Set yourself some telltale sign—something that you know is wrong. Write down on a piece of paper, "I will never backdate a document." Or "I will never let a coworker get blamed for something that was my fault." Or "I will never paper a deal that I don't understand." Or "I will never do anything that I couldn't describe to my dad while looking him in the eye." Pick your telltale sign carefully, and the moment the alarm rings, evacuate the building.

Second, we may take a cue from Stanley Milgram's electric shock experiments. When Milgram debriefed his compliantly murderous subjects afterward, he asked them whose fault the shocks were: the scientist who ordered the shocks, the victim who provoked them by getting wrong answers on a test, or the subject who administered them. Not too surprisingly, the compliant subjects usually blamed the other two (while the defiant subjects, who refused to follow murderous orders, took on themselves primary responsibility for their conduct). My advice, then, is to notice when you are blaming someone else. Right or wrong, the very fact that you are blaming it on the CFO or the accountant is a telltale sign that your own conscience is on the road to perdition.

Finally, I suggest that a certain amount of self-doubt and self-skepticism is not such a bad thing. Moral meltdowns happen when the reactor overheats. There is a kind of euphoria that comes from working on big cases, big deals, for high-energy businesses and high-powered clients. Intoxicating though it may be, it is a bad idea to trust euphoria. My version of Socrates' "know yourself!" is "doubt yourself!" This is hard advice in a nation that admires self-confident, don't-look-back leaders. "Doubt yourself!" sounds like a recipe for neurosis. But without some healthy skepticism, the temptation to take your cues from the client-executive with the most hubris may be unavoidable. Icarus makes a terrible role model.

John W. Dean III, Blind Ambition

(New York: Simon and Schuster, 1976), 32-35, 38-39, 47-48,
52-55, 58-59, and 62-63

THE TESTS STARTED that first day at the White House. After a brief examination of my meager quarters, I had sat down at my desk. I didn't have anything to do, but then my secretary brought me a sealed envelope with a small red tag. I asked her what it was. She had not opened it; it was stamped "CONFIDEN-TIAL," and the red tag meant "priority." Someone had been planning work for the new counsel. The cover memorandum was a printed form, with striking blue and red instructions filled in . . . :

SUBJECT: Request that you rebut the recent attack on the Vice-President.

An attached "confidential memorandum" said that a new muckraking magazine called *Scanlan's Monthly* had published a bogus memo linking Vice-President Agnew with a top-secret plan to cancel the 1972 election and to repeal the entire Bill of Rights. Agnew had publicly denounced the memo as "completely false" and "ridiculous," and the editors of *Scanlan's* had replied: "The Vice President's denial is as clumsy as it is fraudulent. The document came directly from Mr. Agnew's office and he knows it." My instructions were clear: "It was noted that this is a vicious attack and possibly a suit should be filed or a federal investigation ordered to follow up on it."

"Noted" by whom? Since the memorandum was signed by John Brown, a member of Haldeman's staff, I called him to find out. The "noter" was the President, I was told; he had scrawled my orders in the margin of his daily news summary. No one had to explain why the President's name was not used. He was always to be kept one step removed, insulated, to preserve his "deniability."

So this is my baptism, I thought. I was astounded that the president would be so angrily concerned about a funny article in a fledgling magazine. It did not square with my picture of his being absorbed in diplomacy, wars and high matters of state. Was it possible that we *had* a secret plan to cancel the election and the Bill of Rights? I was embarrassed by the thought. Now I cannot look back on this episode without laughing, but then I was not at all loose about it. It was the President of the United States talking. Maybe he was right.

On the due date, I wrote my first memorandum to the President, explaining the hazards of a lawsuit and the wisdom of waiting to see what an FBI investigation produced. I thought the affair had been put to rest. Not so. Back came another action memorandum from the staff secretary. The President agreed with my conclusions, but he wasn't yet content. "It was requested," said the memorandum, "that as part of this inquiry you should have the Internal Revenue Service conduct a field investigation on the tax front."

This was the "old Nixon" at work, heavy-handed, after somebody. I began to fret. How could anything be at once so troubling and so absurd? The President was asking me to do something I thought was dangerous, unnecessary and wrong. I did nothing for several days, but the deadline was hard upon me. I couldn't simply respond, "Dean opposes this request because it is wrong and possibly illegal." I had to find some practical reason for doing the right thing or I would be gone. I called Bud Krogh several times, but he was out. Then I thought of my recent acquaintance, Murray Chotiner, and arranged to meet him.

"I need some counsel, Murray."

"You're the lawyer. You're the one who is supposed to give counsel around here," he said with a chuckle.

"I'm still trying to find the water fountains in this place," I said. "Murray, seriously, I need some advice. The President wants me to turn the IRS loose on a shit-ass magazine called *Scanlan's Monthly* because it printed a bogus memo from the Vice-President's office about canceling the 'seventy-two election and repealing the Bill of Rights."

Murray laughed. "Hell, Agnew's got a great idea. I hope he has a good plan worked out. It would save us a lot of trouble if we dispensed with the 'seventy-two campaign." Murray wasn't taking my visit as seriously as I was. We joked about Agnew for a few minutes before I could get him to focus on my problem, and he had the answer. "If the President wants you to turn the IRS loose, then you turn the IRS loose. It's that simple, John."

"I really don't think it's necessary, Murray. The President's already got Mitchell investigating it. The FBI, I guess."

"I'll tell you this, if Richard Nixon thinks it's necessary you'd better think it's necessary. If you don't, he'll find someone who does."

I was not convinced and said so, but nicely. "Okay, but let me ask you this, Murray. You're a lawyer. Isn't it illegal and therefore crazy to use IRS to attack someone the President doesn't like?"

"Not so," he snorted. He stopped and retrieved the calm he rarely lost. "John, the President is the head of the executive branch of this damn government. If he wants his tax collectors to check into the affairs of anyone, it's his prerogative. I don't see anything illegal about it. It's the way the game is played. Do you think for a second that Lyndon Johnson was above using the IRS to harass those guys who were giving him a hard time on the war? No sir. Nor was Lyndon above using IRS against some good Republicans like Richard Nixon. I'll tell you he damn near ruined a few."

Murray was testy, or maybe defensive — I couldn't decide. It was clear that he didn't want to discuss the matter further. I thanked him and left. If I was going to play ball in Richard Nixon's league, I would have to get over my squeamishness. I am not sure what I would have done if John J. Caulfield had not walked into my office.

Jack Caulfield . . . had moved up the ranks of the New York police force, from a street beat to detective, arriving at the White House after an assignment as candidate Nixon's personal bodyguard in 1968. Bob Haldeman had assigned him to me without telling me why. Caulfield explained that he was White House liaison with the Secret Service and the local police, but his principal assignment was to investigate Senator Edward M. Kennedy's conduct in the Chappaquiddick accident for John Ehrlichman.

Jack was a bountiful source of information. He knew what everybody was doing. He could tell you how to get a refrigerator or parking privileges and who was sleeping with whose secretary. And he wanted to help me find my bearings. He seemed a natural person to turn to with my IRS orders, and I decided to show him the memos. "How would you handle this assignment?" I asked.

"This isn't any problem. I'll take care of it for you with a phone call," he answered confidently. He returned the next day to report that a tax inquiry would be fruitless because the magazine was only six months old and its owners had yet to file their first return. Being resourceful, however, he had asked the IRS to look into the owners themselves. "You can tell the President everything is taken care of," he assured me. . . .

I summarized the tax situation in my report. "The fact that *Scanlan's* is a new entity does not make the tax inquiry very promising," I concluded. "Accordingly, I have also requested that the inquiry be extended to the principal organizers and promoters of the publication." Thus, within a month of coming to the White House, I had crossed an ethical line. I had no choice, as I saw it. The fact that I had not carried out the assignment myself eased my conscience slightly. I had no idea how Jack had done it so easily, nor did I ask, and I never found out what became of the IRS inquiry. . . .

I [now] had learned to expect anything in special assignments. But I also focused on my regular duties and was adjusting my instincts to what I saw daily in the White House. . . . We put in long grueling hours, and word soon got around that the counsel's office was eager to tackle anyone and everyone's problems and do it discreetly. We gave advice on the divorce laws to staff members whose marriages had been ruined, and we answered questions about immigration law for the Filipino stewards who worked in the mess. Although our work was technical and legal, we discovered that we could use it to get a foothold in substantive areas. If we were alert in conflict-of-interest reviews and investigations, we would have a small say in Presidential appointments. As with any law firm, our influence depended largely on our reputation, and our reputation was good. We cultivated it with care.

Haldeman's assignments always received priority, of course, and he fired questions at us regularly. A Presidential fact-finding committee had returned from Vietnam with two captured Chinese rifles for the President, and the Treasury Department wanted to disallow the gifts because they had been illegally imported. What could we do? After a crash study of the relevant law, we had no trouble persuading Treasury to classify the rifles as legal "war trophies" for the Commander in Chief. A corporation, said Haldeman, had upset the President by marketing a replica of the Presidential seal. Could anything be done? A few statutes cited on White House stationery made the company desist. Congress wanted the General Accounting Office to audit the White House budgets in which the redecorating expenses had been buried. Haldeman wanted to know if the audit could be blocked legally. We let the auditors in but assured Haldeman we could stall them for four years. . . .

Back in Washington, I was visited by Bud Krogh. . . . As part of his mandate to stop leaks, he wanted to harass the Brookings Institution in any way he could, and he was checking in with me. . . . He seemed almost apologetic, and I sensed he was slightly embarrassed at being chosen to head an intelligence operation that should logically have been mine. It was an uneasy conversation, with much nonverbal communication, and Bud was finally moved to offer an explanation: "John, I guess there are some people around here who think you have some little old lady in you."

Bud knows about the Brookings break-in, I thought. I was upset that they thought of me as a little old lady, but I tried not to let on. Later, as if to prove myself again, I had Caulfield obtain the tax records of Brookings from IRS as Bud had requested and sent them to him with a covering memo, noting that

Brookings received many government contracts we might cut off. I also told him there were Nixon loyalists on the Brookings board whom we might use clandestinely. A week later I sent Bud another terse and self-serving memo, offering to help "turn off the spigot" of funds to Brookings, but he never called on me. . . .

[In 1972 an antitrust settlement with ITT] exploded in the Administration's face when Jack Anderson published a memo purportedly written by ITT lobbyist Dita Beard, in which she baldly told her boss that the antitrust suit against ITT would be dropped in return for a $400,000 contribution of ITT cash and services to the GOP convention in San Diego. The next day Anderson lobbed another bombshell: he charged that Kleindienst, who had just been appointed Attorney General (Mitchell having left to head the Committee to Reelect the President), had lied "outright" about the settlement of the ITT case. Impulsively, Kleindienst demanded that his confirmation hearings be reopened so that he could clear his name.

As usual, John Ehrlichman took charge at the White House. On March 8, 1972, I was invited to his office for my first of many meetings on the Kleindienst-ITT matter, along with Chuck Colson, public relations pros and Congressional-liaison men. . . . "Kleindienst is a damn fool," Colson said instantly. "Jim Eastland tried to talk him out of going back to the Hill, but Kleindienst charged off after his honor like Sir Galahad. We wouldn't be in this mess if he wasn't so stupid." . . . From the beginning, Colson's extraordinary efforts centered upon his conviction that the Dita Beard memo was a forgery. If he could prove it, he would expose the Democrats as hucksters. . . . Since J. Edgar Hoover did not like Colson, I was sent to enlist the director's cooperation; a delicate mission. . . .

"Mr. Hoover, we, the White House that is, Mr. Ehrlichman and others" — I wanted to get my authority established — "have good reason to believe the so-called Dita Beard memorandum is a phony, and we'd like to have your lab test it because we are sure that your test will confirm that it is forgery." . . .

"I understand exactly, Mr. Dean, what you need," the director said with emphasis, "and I'm delighted to be of service. Jack Anderson is the lowest form of human being to walk the earth. He's a muckraker who lies, steals, and let me tell you this, Mr. Dean, he'll go lower than dog shit for a story." The director turned his red leather chair to face me as I sat in a matching-color chair beside his desk. This was not the Edgar Hoover I had expected.

"Lower than dog shit," he went on. "Mr. Dean, let me tell you a story. My housekeeper puts papers down in the hall, every night, for my dogs, and every morning she picks up the paper and puts it in the trashcans in the back of the house. Well, one day Anderson and his boys came out to my house to fish in my trashcans for a story. To look at my *trash*, can you believe that? Anyway, they fished all through that trash and all the way to the bottom, underneath the dog shit, to see what they could find. So when you're talking about Anderson I know you're talking about a man that'll go lower than dog shit to find his stories. Isn't that something, Mr. Dean?" he asked, shaking the fleshy jowls of his face.

I strained to hold back a chuckle, not sure if I was supposed to laugh or not. The story was funny, but he was not joking. I finally nodded and said, "It certainly is some story, Mr. Hoover, some story indeed." . . .

[However the FBI lab found that] the Dita Beard memo was legitimate. . . . Colson carried the FBI's draft letter to the President's office, and when he returned he said he had never before seen the President so furious. The President penned a note to his friend Edgar, asking him to "cooperate," then gave it to Ehrlichman with instructions to turn Hoover around. Ehrlichman could not budge the director an inch. When the President was told, he mused, "I don't understand Edgar sometimes. He hates Anderson." . . .

A fresh wave of anti-Hoover sentiment lapped through the Administration. Had he deliberately doctored the lab reports after discovering the work of ITT's experts? . . . Colson wanted to fire Hoover. The idea was, as always, discarded. There was a question on Hoover in each secret poll of public opinion conducted by the White House, and he always ranked extremely high. This piece of political realism, more than fear of blackmail, probably guaranteed Hoover his job until he died, unexpectedly, a few months later. . . .

Looking back, I wonder that I failed to see the signs of worse to come. At the time, I was relieved to have passed. The ITT scandal at last melted to the back pages of the papers, and Kleindienst was confirmed. . . .

"Well, Johnny," [a colleague] said as we walked slowly back from lunch one day in mid-May, "I read back in January where Jeane Dixon predicted Nixon would have a serious scandal this year but would survive it. It's amazing, she was right. We've had it, and the President was untouched." I agreed.

We were all wrong, of course. The machinery had long been cranking through the White House toward a scandal that would grind down the President himself. And I was part of the machinery. . . .

NOTES AND QUESTIONS

1. *Blind Ambition* is a case study of the moral meltdowns that Zimbardo's and Luban's essays describe. To what extent was John Dean's misconduct a function of character weaknesses, that is, blind ambition? To what extent was it attributable to situational pressures that might have resulted in similar conduct by many governmental officials? Under psychologist James Rest's framework described in the Rhode excerpt in Chapter 5, which of Dean's ethical lapses reflected inadequate moral awareness or moral reasoning, and which involved inadequate moral intent and disposition? Does it matter for purposes of preventing future scandals like Watergate?

2. Dean describes a number of dynamics that are common contributors to individual and organizational misconduct:
   - *Diffusion and displacement of responsibility*
     - Murray Chotiner tells Dean that if "Richard Nixon thinks it's necessary, you better think it's necessary. If you don't, he'll find someone who does."
     - After requesting Jack Caufield to have the IRS investigate political opponents, Dean notes: "The fact that I had not carried out the assignment myself eased my conscience slightly. I had no idea how Jack had done it so easily, nor did I ask. . . ."
   - *Willful ignorance*
     - Dean notes: "I never found out what became of the IRS inquiry."

- *Peer pressure*
  - Bud Krogh warns Dean: "[T]here are some people around here who think you have some little old lady in you."
  - Dean notes: "If I was going to play ball in Richard Nixon's league, I would have to get over my squeamishness."
- *Euphemistic descriptions*
  - "Squeamishness" is how Dean describes his sense of ethics.
- *Social Proof*
  - "It's how the game is played" is how Murray Chotiner describes the use of IRS tax investigations to harass political opponents.
- *Demonization of opponents and rationalization of retaliation*
  - J. Edgar Hoover's description of columnist Jack Anderson as the "lowest form of human being to walk the earth."
  - Murray Chotiner's assertion that Lyndon Johnson "damn near ruined a few" good Republicans through his use of IRS investigations.

In this morally toxic setting, how would you have responded if you had been in Dean's position? Would you have been willing to stall the IRS audit or pull the Brookings contracts? Do these cross the moral trip wires that Luban advises setting? Is there anything Dean could have done differently, short of resignation?

3. Jeb Stuart Magruder, Nixon's special assistant who was involved in authorizing the Watergate burglary, describes another cognitive bias that affected decision making. The plan was proposed by G. Gordon Liddy, Magruder's general counsel, after the Committee to Reelect the President rejected more extreme ideas — such as mugging squads that would rough up anti-Nixon demonstrators, or "high class" prostitutes, who would seduce and blackmail leading Democratic politicians. Committee members, who included Attorney General John Mitchell, felt that they "needed" Liddy and were "reluctant to send him away with nothing." Yet, according to Magruder, if Liddy had come to them at the outset with the idea to break into the Democratic National Headquarters at the Watergate and install wiretaps, committee members would have "reject[ed] the idea out of hand."[17]

4. Darryl Zanuck, the legendary Hollywood studio head, was famous for saying "Don't say yes until I've finished talking." Corporate and political leaders accustomed to getting their way may have little patience for legal technicalities or for the messengers who invoke them. What strategies are available to advisors who want to do right without losing their jobs? What were the options for the government lawyers in the problem below?

PROBLEM 6-2[18]

Peter Irons's *Justice at War* (1983) provides another case history of the ethical dilemmas that can confront government officials, including lawyers. His account chronicles dilemmas for individuals defending the detention and relocation of Japanese Americans during World War II.

One such dilemma involved Edward Ennis, the director of the Alien Enemy Control Unit in the Justice Department. He had primary responsibility for presenting the Department's position supporting internment in

Hirabayashi v. United States, 320 U.S. 81 (1943), and *Korematsu v. United States*, 323 U.S. 214 (1944). Ennis had opposed the policy but was prepared to defend it. However, during the course of his work on *Hirabayashi*, he discovered a crucial internal memorandum by staffers in the Office of Naval Intelligence. That memo, by the military unit most knowledgeable on the issue, reached conclusions that directly undercut the rationale for the military's wholesale evacuation. In particular, the memo concluded that the "Japanese Problem" had been magnified out of proportion, that the small number of Japanese Americans who posed potential threats were in custody or were already known and subject to apprehension, and that case-by-case determinations of dangerousness were preferable to a categorical evacuation.

Ennis believed that this report should be called to the Supreme Court's attention, and he so advised the Solicitor General, Charles Fahy, the lawyer in charge of defending the government's position in any case that comes before the United States Supreme Court.

> Appealing to Fahy's sense of rectitude and his responsibility as Solicitor-General, Ennis argued that "in view of the fact that the Department of Justice is now representing the Army in the Supreme Court of the United States and is arguing that a partial, selective evacuation was impracticable, we must consider most carefully what our obligation to the Court is in view of the fact that the responsible Intelligence agency regarded a selective evacuation as not only sufficient but preferable." Ennis further noted that "one of the most difficult questions" in the Hirabayashi case is raised by the fact that the Army did not evacuate people after any hearing or any individual determination of dangerousness, but evacuated the entire racial group." . . . "[T]he Government is forced to argue that individual selective evacuation would have been impractical and insufficient when we have positive knowledge that the only Intelligence agency responsible for advising General DeWitt gave him advice directly to the contrary." Ennis phrased his final plea to Fahy in terms that waved a warning flag before the Solicitor General: "I think we should consider very carefully whether we do not have a duty to advise the Court of the existence of the [internal] memorandum and of the fact that this represents the view of the Office of Naval Intelligence. It occurs to me that any other course of conduct might approximate the suppression of evidence."[19]

Ennis's position did not prevail. Rather, Arnold Raum, the author of the brief for the government in *Hirabayashi*, maintained that

> [t]he rationale behind [military] orders was "not the loyalty or disloyalty of individuals but the danger from the residence of the class as such within a vital military area." Such a judgment about the "danger" posed by Japanese Americans as a group, however, necessarily required as the "rational basis" demanded by the due process clause some reasonable estimation of loyalty within the group. In searching for such rationality, Raum retreated to speculation and supposition. Japanese Americans had been "treated as a group," he wrote, because some of them were "thought" to be dangerous. Raum did not identify those who harbored these thoughts, nor did he explain why it would be a "virtually impossible task" to determine loyalty on the basis of hearings. . . . Rebuffed in his attempt to alert the Supreme Court . . . , Ennis gave up for the time his objection to Fahy's "suppression of evidence." As a

loyal government lawyer, Ennis swallowed his doubts and added his name to the Hirabayashi brief along with those of Fahy [and] Raum.[20]

A similar problem arose a year later in preparing the government's brief in *Korematsu*. Ennis had cause to be skeptical of certain assertions in the military's final report justifying the evacuation. At his request, the attorney general authorized an FBI and FCC investigation of allegations regarding Japanese espionage efforts (including radio signaling) on the West Coast. Both agencies concluded that some assertions in a report justifying evacuation were false. It also appeared that the errors were known to General DeWitt, who had authorized the report and supported the evacuation.

Ennis and one of his staff members, John Burling, who was working on the *Korematsu* brief, were determined to avoid reliance on the final report in presenting the government's case. They added a footnote acknowledging that certain evidence, particularly about espionage, was "in conflict with information in possession of the Department of Justice." Accordingly, the government was not asking the Court to "take judicial notice" of those facts set out in the DeWitt report. This attempt to "wave the red flag" met opposition with the Solicitor General and the Assistant Attorney General. He substituted a footnote that eliminated any reference to the espionage allegations in the report. Instead, the footnote stated:

> "We have specifically recited in this brief the facts relating to the justification for the evacuation, of which we ask the Court to take judicial notice; and we rely upon the Final Report only to the extent that it relates to such facts." . . . Semantic ambiguity had replaced forthright repudiation. The final page of the brief, urging that the Supreme Court affirm Korematsu's conviction, included the names of Edward Ennis and John Burling. Institutional loyalty had prevailed over personal conscience.[21]

In subsequent interviews reflecting on these incidents,

> Ennis offered an explanation of why he and John Burling (who died in 1959) had swallowed their doubts and continued to work on the internment cases. . . . I really believe we didn't [quit] . . . because we didn't want to put it in the hands of Justice Department lawyers who were gung-ho for the Army's position. I think we felt that we'd just stay with it and do the best that we could, which wasn't a hell of a lot." Ennis also confessed . . . that "when I look back on it now I don't know why I didn't resign."
>
> Ennis had in fact talked of resigning [in protest of the evacuation order]. . . . There seems little doubt that his resignation at that point would not have affected Roosevelt's decision. . . . It seems more likely, however, that had Ennis and Burling resigned in October 1944, in protest at Solicitor General Fahy's capitulation to McCloy over the disputed footnote in the Korematsu brief, such a dramatic step might well have changed the outcome of that crucial case.[22]

1. How would you have handled the problems confronting Ennis and Burling in the wartime evacuation cases? Does preparing a brief from the Solicitor General's office carry special responsibilities to present a full and fair record?

Consider the view of former Solicitor General Archibald Cox, who maintained that the office would maximize its credibility if it was willing to take a "somewhat disinterested and wholly candid position even when it means surrendering a victory."[23]

On the one hand, it is clear that the record was inadequate to support the military's justification for the evacuation. A fuller factual record might have led to a better Supreme Court decision. Concealment ultimately damaged the credibility of all concerned — the Court, the army, the government's lawyers. Given the enormous human costs for Japanese Americans, should government lawyers have taken special care to ensure the integrity of military and judicial decision making?

On the other hand, how would you assess the costs of provoking a confrontation with high-level army officials during wartime and eroding their trust in government attorneys? Are you persuaded by Ennis's argument that he wanted to prevent the case from falling into the hands of more "gung-ho" pro-military lawyers? Consider Bernard Williams's observation that the rationale of "working from within" has kept many "queasy people tied to many appalling ventures for remarkably long periods."[24] Is this an example?

2. For lawyers, the difficulties of making such moral judgments are further complicated by questions of role. Where trade-offs between ethical principles and political expediency appear necessary, who should decide what balance to strike? In legal practice generally, bar ethical rules provide that lawyers "shall abide by a client's decisions concerning the objectives of representation . . . and shall consult with clients as to the means by which they are to be pursued."[25] Who is the client of the government lawyer? If, as many commentators insist, it is the public generally, and not any particular government agency or decision maker, how is the public's interest to be determined?

University of Chicago law professor Geoffrey Miller notes:

> Despite its surface plausibility, the notion that government attorneys represent some transcendental "public interest" is, I believe, incoherent. It is commonplace that there are as many ideas of the "public interest" as there are people who think about the subject. . . . If attorneys could freely sabotage the actions of their agencies out of a subjective sense of the public interest, the result would be a disorganized, inefficient bureaucracy, and a public distrustful of its own government. More fundamentally, the idea that government attorneys serve some higher purpose fails to place the attorney within a structure of democratic government.[26]

Miller concludes that although government attorneys should not assist clearly illegal conduct, neither should they substitute their judgment for that of a political process that is generally accepted as legitimate.

Many practitioners take a similar view. As one study concluded, "most Justice Department lawyers continue to believe that most agencies, most of the time, are entitled to their day in court and to have the best said in their behalf that the legal imagination can devise — the more so because the agencies are captive clients who cannot seek representation elsewhere." On this analysis, a government lawyer who attempts to further the public interest is "not a lawyer representing a client but a lawyer representing herself."[27]

By contrast, other lawyers argue that government counsel have obligations as public servants to "pursue justice" and to avoid assisting an action that they believe is unconstitutional. From this perspective, "where the client is the Government itself, he who represents this vague entity often becomes its conscience, bearing a heavier responsibility than usually encountered by . . . lawyers."[28] What is your view? If you had been Ennis, how would you have defined your responsibilities? What situational pressures might have influenced your view?

3. In his memoir *Decision Points*, former president George Bush gives an example of an effective threat of resignation. At issue was the 2004 renewal of the Terrorist Surveillance Program. Objections from Justice Department lawyers to one aspect of the program had stalled reauthorization. On the eve of the program's expiration, Bush sent officials to the hospital where Attorney General John Ashcroft was recovering from emergency gall bladder surgery. When he refused to sign the reauthorization order, Bush did so in his place. The Acting Attorney General and FBI director then threatened to resign. Bush recalled the last time a presidential order had triggered such high-level resignations. In the infamous "Saturday night massacre," President Richard Nixon's insistence on firing Watergate Special Prosecutor Archibald Cox triggered resignations of his Attorney General and Assistant Attorney General and calls for his own resignation. Bush decided to avoid a confrontation and modified the program to meet Justice Department concerns.[29] What broader lessons do these examples suggest about successful resignations?

4. At the end of his essay on moral meltdowns, Luban suggests several lessons for leaders: draw lines in the sand, accept personal responsibility for your actions, and retain the capacity for self-doubt. Another possibility is the mental exercise colloquially known as the "60 Minutes" or "New York Times" test: how would this decision look on prime-time television or the front page of an international newspaper as presented by a skeptical reporter? Would any of those strategies have been helpful for Dean and Ennis? What might have helped you in situations posing analogous moral dilemmas?

5. Another issue raised by the Japanese internment cases involves the distribution of ethical responsibility between leaders and their subordinates. For example, Rule 5.2 of the American Bar Association's Model Rules of Professional Conduct provides that lawyers are bound by ethical rules when they act at another's direction, but that they do not violate those rules if they act in accordance with a supervisory lawyer's "reasonable resolution of an arguable question of professional duty." How helpful is this rule on the facts of the *Korematsu* case, or on the problem on torture set forth below? Does it resolve lawyers' moral responsibility as well as their disciplinary liability?

C. ACCOUNTABILITY

Torture is one of the most long-standing morally troubling leadership issues that has resurfaced with new force during the "war on terror." The materials that follow explore the issues it poses for government officials, including lawyers, who have been instrumental in shaping American policy.

PHILIP BOBBIT, TERROR AND CONSENT: THE WARS FOR THE TWENTY-FIRST CENTURY

(New York: Alfred A. Knopf, 2008), 361-366, 369-370, 373, 376, 387-388, 390-392

[On] the awful subject of torture . . . I am anxious to make one overriding point: the moral rules that govern the official of a state of consent impose a "duty of consequentialism" — that is, any contemplated course of action must be measured in terms of the foreseeable costs and benefits that are its result and not against any absolute or categorical rule, including those regarding intentions. That is, what is achieved in such contexts is at least as important as how this is done.

Let me deal at once with the notorious hypothetical of the "ticking bomb." The . . . hypothetical is usually posed like this: Imagine that interrogators learn that a terrorist in custody knows where a bomb has been planted. In order "to overcome an obdurate will not to disclose [this] information and to overcome the fear of the person under interrogation that harm will befall him from his own organization, if he does reveal" the location of the bomb, it is proposed that sufficient dissuasion be applied to prevent the terrorist from refusing to provide the needed information. Threats, harsh words, unpleasant behavior escalating to beatings and other violence, are suggested, and the question is asked: At which of these methods would one cavil?

The right answer — the only answer available to the official of the state of consent who has taken up the responsibility of protecting the safety of the public whose endorsement has put him in this position of authority — is that whatever methods are most effective must be employed. Indeed, Judge Richard Posner has argued, "If the stakes are high enough [even] torture is permissible. No one who doubts that should be in a position of responsibility." It is an easy question.

But look closely at the assumptions the hypothetical enfolds. We are to assume (1) that we have a person in custody, (2) that the person is a terrorist who (3) actually knows the location of a bomb that (4) is about to go off, and that (5) under torture he will accurately disclose the location of the bomb, that (6) cannot be determined by any other means. In such a situation, only a self-absorbed monster would say, sweetly, "Oh no, I mustn't (even if I wish I could), sorry," thus deliberately sentencing unnumbered innocents to death and dismemberment in order to protect the manifestly guilty.

The real difficulty does not lie in such a situation, as we shall see, but rather with cases whose contours are not so carefully shaped so as to provide such perfect information. Suppose the person we have in custody is a roommate — someone otherwise unimplicated who can lead us to the terrorist but who refuses to give this information. Suppose that person is suspected of terrorist activity, but there is substantial doubt about his involvement. Suppose his pleas that he really doesn't know the location of the bomb are plausible. Suppose there is no bomb—yet—but the person knows of plans to acquire such weapons. Suppose he is so averse to pain that he will say anything that he believes will appease his captors and in his fear provides the most plausible, but not the most accurate, information. Suppose an inhibition-reducing drug, coupled with a friendly and trusted interrogator, is a more effective means than violence, or that data cross-correlation, sensors that detect explosives, or other methods are more effective. Suppose that all these suppositions are in fact true or, more likely, suppose that we don't really know which ones are true.

This is not to assume that coercive interrogations and even torture are necessarily ineffective, a claim that will be discussed below. It is rather that their potential effectiveness depends upon a great many factors and that the "ticking bomb" hypothetical tends to focus our attention away from those contextual factors.

The preliminary claim I wish to make is simply that anyone with the responsibility for protecting others must discharge that responsibility with an eye firmly on the consequences—that is, the relationship between means and ends must govern the decision. If, for the public official whose role has been authorized by the consent of the governed, anything else trumps this relationship, he or she should resign. A pacifist should not be asked (or allowed) to be a general. . . .

The origin of the "duty of consequentialism" lies in the constitutional makeup of the state of consent. That is because the officials of a state of consent are bound to behave, in their official capacity, in a way that maximizes the "ends" or goals of the persons in whose name they govern. It is this delegation that imposes the duty of evaluating means in terms of the ends they serve, and that displaces the deontological or a priori moral rules that are so much a part of personal life. . . .

If the customary institutions of a state of consent have forbidden the torture and the cruel and degrading treatment of prisoners, then the conscientious official has little choice but to obey. He cannot substitute his personal moral imperatives as if he were acting as a nongovernmental agent. So what does he do when the "ticking bomb" case actually does arise? He disobeys the treaty, the statute, the regulation, and saves the city, of course. It is the right thing to do, not because of his private morality (which might in any case vary from official to official), but rather because the consequentialist calculus of obeying the law is so clear and so absolutely negative. This was, it will be recalled, Lincoln's position when he suspended habeas corpus during the American Civil War—in direct contradiction of a specific provision of the U.S. Constitution—in order to arrest some 13,000 persons under martial law. Defending his decision in a message to Congress on July 4, 1861, he wrote:

> To state the question more directly, are all the laws, but one, to go unexecuted and the government itself go to pieces, lest that one be violated? Even in such a case, would not the official oath be broken, if the government should be overthrown, when it was believed that disregarding the single law, would tend to preserve it?

This is plainly a consequentialist argument, but look carefully at how it sorts out ends and means. The objective sought (the end) that justifies the violation of law (the means) is in fact the preservation of the rule of law, which is shall we say "dented" by the very means that avoid a catastrophic collision. . . .

The Prevailing Law

Following the exposure of German and Japanese practices in World War II, the U.N. General Assembly adopted in 1948 the Universal Declaration of Human Rights, which contains an absolute ban on torture in order to eliminate, according to the drafters, "methods of torture and cruel punishment which were practiced in the recent past by the Nazis and fascists." Article 5 of the declaration provides: "No one shall be subjected to torture or to cruel, inhuman or degrading treatment or punishment."

This ban has been incorporated into the International Covenant on Civil and Political Rights (ICCPR) and into the Convention Against Torture or Other Cruel, Inhuman or Degrading Treatment or Punishment (the Torture Convention), which provides in Article 2 that "No exceptional circumstances whatsoever, whether a state of war or a threat of war, internal political instability or any other public emergency, may be invoked as a justification of torture." . . .

It may be, as Sanford Levinson has argued, that the very categorical nature of these prohibitions against torture has tempted states — including the U.K. and the U.S. — to write definitions of torture that are rather narrow. Indeed, because the U.S. administration at one time appeared to have interpreted away the restraints created by conventions to which it is a signatory, partly on the basis of Senate reservations made at the time of U.S. consent to these conventions, the U.S. Congress in 2005 adopted the McCain amendment, which provides: "No individual in the custody or under the physical control of the United States Government, regardless of nationality or physical location, shall be subject to cruel, inhuman, or degrading treatment or punishment."

[The distinction between torture and cruel and degrading treatment] . . . has been recognized by the European Court of Human Rights, the Israeli Supreme Court, and the U.S. Department of State. The importance of this distinction, since both are unlawful, is that the U.S. Supreme Court has recognized a "necessity" exception with respect to cruel and degrading treatment. This takes us a long way toward the recognition of certain otherwise unlawful methods that was at the core of the Bush administration's efforts to legitimate coercive interrogation techniques.

Ends and Means

There are three basic objectives (ends) sought by states when they employ torture. They can be categorized as evidentiary, political, and informational.

Evidentiary

. . . At present, there is no move in either the American or British jurisdictions to use information gained by torture conducted by their officials as evidence in court. And this in turn has led to rather absurd efforts to prosecute persons believed to be lethal terrorists on other, trivial grounds so as to continue their detention. . . .

Political

Torture is undertaken for political purposes when the object is less to coerce than to intimidate. This may be aimed at the victim himself, if he is subsequently released, or his family and associates, or even an entire society. Rather than hiding its hideous acts, if torture is employed for political ends, then it must be advertised. Although there is an ancient history of such practices, in the current day nothing is quite so exemplary as the practice of human beheadings by al Qaeda and its franchisees. . . . [An example was the video posted in 2004 of a Philadelphia businessman, Nicholas Berg, who was kidnapped while working on an Iraq construction project. He was pictured screaming in agony as his captors] appeared to saw through his neck, shouting, "God is great!" . . .

Informational

The infliction of pain and the fear of pain can also be used simply to extract information. It is in this context that the subject of torture was raised after 2001, when the urgency of preventing another 9/11 attack suggested to many that harsher methods of interrogation were necessary in order to thwart terrorist plots.

"Terrorists" was the term used by the Nazis in France for the Free French partisans known as the Resistance. Jean Moulin was called "the martyr of the Resistance" because following his capture by the Gestapo he was tortured so violently that he died on the way to a German prison. . . . [O]thers claim that [the torturers of Nicholas Berg], too, are resisters to an unlawful occupation. These complexities demand that we be able to tell the difference, and explain the difference, between those who wish to impose terror through an occupation and those occupiers who come to dispel terror and are risking their lives to do so.

It is of course tempting to shun this difficult task and simply to say that the use of violence in interrogation, for any purpose, is always impermissible; that it is the means, and not the ends, that must guide our judgment. This move is made immeasurably easier by making the assumption that torture simply never works. Persons in pain and afraid are unlikely to give correct information in their eagerness to appease their tormenters. Consider then this account, however, told to Bruce Hoffman by a Sri Lankan army officer charged with fighting the Tamil Tigers:

> [His] unit had apprehended three terrorists who, it suspected, had recently planted somewhere in the city a bomb that was then ticking away, the minutes counting down to catastrophe. The three men were brought before [him]. He asked them where the bomb was. The terrorists—highly dedicated and steeled to resist interrogation—remained silent. [He] asked the question again, advising them that if they did not tell him what he wanted to know, he would kill them. They were unmoved. So [he] took his pistol from his gun belt, pointed it at the forehead of one of them, and shot him dead. The other two, he said, talked immediately; the bomb, which had been placed in a crowded railway

station and set to explode during the evening rush hour, was found and defused, and countless lives were saved.

If we put this in the context that the Tamil insurgency had already claimed the lives of more than 60,000 people and that it was arrayed against a democratically elected government whose president, candidate for president, and the Indian prime minister Rajiv Gandhi it had murdered, one is hard-pressed not to conclude that the putative victims of an atrocity deserve more care than the would-be perpetrators.

Ends do matter. As we shall see, however, only when they are related to means can we derive usable rules.

Means

The problem is made more realistic by assuming that, in some circumstances, torture and assassination are effective—an assumption as to which there is some debate. Nevertheless, it must be obvious that at least in some situations this will prove to be the case and that these are the situations for which we require an answer, not a blithe assuming away of the problem. Because these activities are conducted in the dark, there is little adequate data to confirm an assumption either way. Occasionally, there are reports in open sources such as the case of an Al Qaeda terrorist, Jamal Beghal. He was arrested in the Dubai airport in October 2001. His lawyer subsequently charged that he had been "tossed into a darkened cell, handcuffed to a chair, blindfolded and beaten and that his family was threatened." It is not unreasonable to conclude that these measures had some effect: after some weeks in captivity, he suddenly decided to cooperate and "out poured a wealth of information" that thwarted a planned bombing of the U.S. embassy in Paris and could have prevented the 2001 bombing of the World Trade Center in New York had it come earlier.

I will discuss four alternatives prescribing what means of coercive interrogation are permissible. These are (1) an absolute ban; (2) a qualified ban, perhaps permitting some forms of cruel and degrading treatment but banning torture; (3) a ban with exceptions, perhaps permitting torture and any lesser means in certain certifiable circumstances; (4) rendition to a lawful authority, permitting some forms of coercive interrogation, including even torture, depending on the willingness of the State transparently to acknowledge its role.

Absolute Ban

The first thing to recognize about an absolute ban is that it will not prevent all torture any more than an absolute ban on smoking in elevators means that every cigar is extinguished by every solitary passenger. Even draconian penalties like stoning to death have not stopped adultery in Saudi Arabia; nor has capital punishment in America stopped capital crimes. . . . Indeed, the most important moral lesson of the "ticking bomb" problem is that no rule can entirely govern our conscience. That is the lesson of free will, which makes the conscience and thus morality itself possible. Free will makes alternative worlds possible, and one of these must always be a future in which a crime is committed rather than a law obeyed.

This means that an "absolute ban" is actually more like a lottery: it leaves to chance when torture occurs by refusing to specify the precise exculpatory circumstances. On the other hand, an absolute ban can be enforced with greater consistency and, if the penalties are significant, can bring about the highest level of deterrence. Indeed, an absolute ban has to be tightly enforced, or it loses its point. . . .

"No torture" rules sound fine, but the world in which they are to be applied can present situations in which such rules should not be followed. Is the "absolute ban" the right rule for the real world? In such a world, an order by the president to torture a captive would be an unlawful order, regardless of even the most extreme circumstances, and therefore it is highly unpredictable whether it would be obeyed.

Qualified Ban

This reflects an effort to capture in law and regulations those truly exceptional situations in which there is a political consensus that highly coercive methods, even torture, should be tried. Perhaps the most imaginative of these proposals is the suggestion by Alan Dershowitz, that courts—perhaps special courts—be authorized to issue "torture warrants." Studying practices in Israel—which is "the only country at the end of the twentieth century officially to sanction the intentional infliction of pain and suffering during interrogation"—Dershowitz concluded that the "ticking bomb" scenario had led officials to an increasing use of torture and highly coercive means of interrogation in cases quite remote from the assumptions of the scenario.

In 1987, the Landau Commission in Israel authorized the use of "moderate physical pressure" in ticking-bomb situations. A practice initially justified as rare and exceptional, taken only when necessary to save lives, gradually became standard procedure. Soon, some 80 to 90 percent of Palestinian security detainees were being tortured. . . .

Dershowitz argued that judicial oversight would curtail or eliminate these practices in a way that "don't ask, don't tell" rules and paper prohibitions had failed to do; he believed that requiring a warrant of some kind as "a precondition to the infliction of any type of torture under any circumstances" would accomplish this. When torture was taken out of the clandestine area of government activity and exposed to visibility and accountability, Dershowitz held, torture would drastically decline. In such circumstances, the "ticking bomb" hypothetical might actually serve as a limiting, rather than expanding, engine because a judicial warrant could be granted in this, but in no other, situation.

Notable objections have been made to this proposal: . . . that even with respect to warrants, the affidavits supporting them, the requests for them, and the judges' decisions granting them are all likely to be secret, which does little for transparency; that, because warrants are issued in ex parte proceedings before judges or magistrates chosen by the applicant, they are an ineffective check on executive discretion. What makes them effective in the ordinary criminal context is the use of materials gained by warrant in subsequent trials. That presumably is unlikely to be a significant motivation in a war against terror, particularly if enemy agents can be indefinitely detained without the usual trial proceedings. Finally, if torture is written into law—even if only for extreme situations — its use is bound to become routine, as interrogators test the limits of the law.

Ban with Exceptions

This proposal probably comes closest to the customary way in which such matters are usually dealt with in the democracies. In *Leon v. Wainwright* the Eleventh Circuit considered the following facts. Two kidnappers seized a taxi driver and held him for ransom. One of them was apprehended while collecting the ransom. The court found that

> [w]hen he refused to tell them the location, he was set upon by several of the officers . . . they threatened and physically abused him by twisting his arm and choking him until he revealed where [the cab driver] was being held. . . . This was . . . a group of concerned officers acting in a reasonable manner to obtain information they needed in order to protect another individual from bodily harm or death. [The acts of torture] were motivated by the immediate necessity to find the victim and save his life.

Sanford Levinson, who more than anyone courageously broke the silence of the academy on this subject, has concluded that such extraordinary methods must always be forbidden by law. This view need not make terrorists of those who protect us in the most perilous cases, however, because the last word rests with the juries and publics that are unlikely to condemn those persons who have acted wisely out of pity and not irresponsibly out of cruelty. Levinson holds that it is better wholly to outlaw such activities by the military and the police knowing that, on occasion, they may breach the law out of necessity. This is an appealing approach because it attempts to preserve our values in the face of anguishing choices. . . .

This approach relies upon a necessity defense to the purportedly "absolute" ban. Of course, the officers couldn't know for certain that the courts would exonerate them, any more than the intelligence officers who torture a terrorist to locate a ticking bomb are certain they will not be prosecuted. But it can be assumed that no jury is likely to convict the men who saved their city, especially if the alleged offense is committed against a person attempting mass murder.

The principal virtues of such uncertainty are three-fold. First, it allows us to state that we have an absolute ban on torture (in principle), not unlike the absolute prohibition against congressional action that abridges the freedom of speech, which in its application makes room for laws against disclosing classified documents, colluding to fix prices, and libel. Second, it depends upon the "bracketing" of the calculus of necessity, forcing the agent who must decide whether to disobey the law, to determine if torture would really save sufficient lives to justify its terrible imposition. As Henry Shue put one variation on this:

> An act of torture ought to remain illegal so that anyone who sincerely believes such an act to be the least available evil is placed in the position of needing to justify his or her act morally in order to defend himself or herself legally. . . . Anyone who thinks an act of torture is justified should have no alternative but to convince a group of peers in a public trial that all necessary conditions for a morally permissible act were indeed satisfied. . . . If the situation approximates those in the imaginary examples in which torture seems

possible to justify [such as the "ticking bomb" scenario], a judge can surely be expected to suspend the sentence.

Third, it avoids the real cost of giving potential adversaries and terrorists extensive knowledge about what to expect when they are captured. As with nuclear deterrence, governments have been unwilling to spell out exact limits to the action they would regard as tolerable in extremis.

This proposal has widespread support among civil libertarians, philosophers, and jurists who "want nonlethal torture to be used if it could prevent thousands of deaths, but [do] not want torture to be officially recognized by our legal system." "It is better," wrote Judge Richard Posner, "to stick with our perhaps overly strict rules, trusting executive officials to break them when the stakes are high enough to enable the officials to obtain political absolution for their illegal conduct."

Nevertheless, this approach is not without its flaws. Far from prompting the rigorous analysis that its proponents imagine, because it is essentially a customary approach it relies upon our intuitive sense of our values, which is specific to every particular culture. The reason to debate an issue openly and write our conclusions into law is to overcome the many different attitudes that prevail in the military, among lawyers, in religious circles, and so on. . . .

At what point does custom become law, whatever the actual provisions of the law? . . . [I]f the answer is "sometimes," then how can we expect conscientious men and women to obey the law — whatever it may be — the law being so uncertain?

None of these approaches seems fully satisfactory. Absolute bans on torture, absolutely enforced, are essentially lotteries, and while they are admirably conscientious about the rights of prisoners, they are studiedly indifferent to the fate of the terrorist's victims. Qualified bans are legalistic, political attempts to manage torture. They are, nevertheless, inconsistent with international law, import a judicial process into warfare, and as currently proposed, are probably unconstitutional on the grounds that they authorize punishment without a jury's determination of guilt. Bans on torture that depend upon exceptional behavior can call on the legitimating ethos of society because they are "customary" approaches. In the U.S. and the U.K., we rarely depend on legal rules to compel the behavior of the Good Samaritan, or heroic intervention in an emergency, or the self-sacrifice and deference that hold a society together. We depend instead on custom. Yet for that very reason, such an approach can be highly unreliable, especially in a complex society that holds many cultures within it. An approach that depends upon guessing how a court would calculate the necessity of breaking the law is a pretty uncertain one. To save a million lives, anyone ought to be willing to brutalize a terrorist in the midst of his fevered attempt to become a mass murderer. But what about five lives, when the person to be tortured may or may not have the crucial information — or may or may not be a terrorist?

Implications of an Ends and Means Analysis

. . . What is the overall objective of the state of consent in the Wars against Terror? It is to protect the lives and human rights of our own people or of others for whom we have accepted responsibility without becoming a state of terror, that is, while continuing to protect the rights of consent and conscience. From this premise alone we can infer that we can never torture persons for political ends. If the state of consent engages in acts that intimidate its own population it poisons any consent it may thereafter win, and thus sacrifices its legitimacy. Torture and coercive interrogation can never be used to achieve the "political" ends discussed above. . . .

If we bear in mind, however, that it is warfare — not crime — that is the arena of the Wars against Terror, then we ought to conclude that (except possibly for war crimes) states of consent can never use torture to gain evidence for prosecution and trial. The aims of warfare are prospective, not retrospective. We are not engaged in a war in order to punish our enemies, but to prevent them from imposing on us a political end of their own. A state of consent cannot bring torture to bear in order to gather evidence for a prosecution without importing the means of warfare into its own, domestic institutions — without, that is, becoming a state of terror and losing the war itself.

There remains, then, the goal of getting information through violence.

If we recognize that this "end" is also a "means" to another "end" — winning the Wars against Terror — then perhaps we can shape the proper means that serve those goals.

The use of violence in the Wars against Terror is justified by our claims of self-defense. Having been attacked, we have the right to defend our societies. . . . In the Wars against Terror, violence can be used when a state of consent is threatened with violence by the agents of states or inchoate would-be states of terror. . . . The argument from *self-defense*, however, permits [only measures against the suspected terrorist, not a terrorist's child or an] . . . innocent bystander who may have crucial information but declines to give it up. . . . There must be some independent authority whose incentives are not so wholly driven by the desire to maximize the amount of information gathered, who is trustworthy enough not to disclose the secrets of operations and intelligence sources, and who is sophisticated enough to be able to accurately assess the claims of the interrogator. Moreover, such authority must be accorded legal status under international law.

What is needed is not a judge so much as a jury — that is, not an official who represents the government seeking information but a group of persons chosen from a pool of responsible people who represent, not the government, but the society in whose name the government is acting. Their identities can be secret in order to avoid reprisal, but they should be chosen randomly from the largest number that is practicable. Unless they can be persuaded that the detainee is in fact a terrorist with valuable information, he cannot be coercively interrogated. Unless they can be persuaded that he has lied — unless, that is, his claims cannot be persuasively disconfirmed — any coercive methods beyond the mildest cannot be used. Such procedures, it apparently needs to be added, must be created pursuant to statutory action by legislative bodies, and whatever they authorize must be clearly distinguished from the infliction of pain that is tantamount to torture under existing law. I have in mind coercive methods such as sleep deprivation, isolation, and the administration of drugs. Where there is no pain, there is no torture. The terrifying prospect of pain is a kind of terror itself, and thus once a state of consent is believed to practice torture as a matter of course, then—even if some progress is made in a War against Terror by such practices—that state will have suffered a considerable blow in the Wars against Terror. To reiterate: it is terror that we are fighting, not simply terrorists. . . .

Summary

There must be an absolute ban on torture and coercive interrogations of any kind for political or evidentiary purposes. There ought to be an absolute ban on torture or coercive interrogations for the purpose of collecting tactical information, with the acceptance that this ban will be violated in the "ticking bomb" circumstances: the prosecutions that must follow will allow juries to consider the mitigating question of whether a reasonable person, motivated by a sincere desire to protect others, would have violated the law. There cannot be a ban on the collection of strategic information—information from terrorist leaders and senior managers—by whatever means are absolutely necessary short of torture when that information is likely to preclude future attacks, when it is disconfirmable by interrogators (and thus the means used are actually no more violent than is necessary), and when a nongovernmental committee has decided the government has met its burden of proof in establishing these matters. Such terrorists-at-war are in the same position as ordinary soldiers who can be compelled by violence to surrender their arms and cease hostile action. For the terrorist-at-war, in an information age, that means surrendering information. . . .

Bruce Hoffman and others have argued that it was the use of terror against captives in Algiers in 1957 that outraged public opinion in France while alienating the Muslim community in North Africa, swelling the ranks of the FLN and increasing its popularity even while French forces relying on information gained from torture were breaking the back of the revolt. The French army's tactical success in the Battle of Algiers led, in other words, to the strategic defeat of the overall endeavor. So it will be with the wars against global, networked terror if we do not openly and transparently confront these issues, writing laws that reflect a democratic debate, and applying those laws sensitively in those rare contexts when an heroic official risks prosecution to save the rest of us. Otherwise, when the dreadful truth emerges, domestic opinion will abandon its government's war efforts in disgust. . . .

Whatever the outcome of such a debate, we cannot lose sight of the distinction between our ends and those of terrorists, partly because to do so will disable us from using necessary violence to protect the innocent and partly because we might otherwise forget precisely what we are fighting for in the effort to ensure that we win.

NOTES AND QUESTIONS

1. In *Unspeakable Acts, Ordinary People*, John Conroy notes that "throughout the world torturers are rarely punished, and when they are, the punishment rarely corresponds to the severity of the crime."[30] One reason for this,

according to Conroy, is that torturers are generally not sadists who are easy to condemn. Rather, they often view themselves as servants of the state, engaged in a just war. To reduce cognitive dissonance, they often engage in the kind of euphemistic recharacterizations of the issue described in Chapters 3 and 5. So, as psychologists Carol Tavris and Elliot Aronson note, one strategy "is to say that if we do it, it isn't torture. 'We do not torture,' said George Bush, when he was confronted with evidence that we do. 'We use an alternative set of procedures.'"—that is, "enhanced interrogation."[31] Another reason for the inadequacy of sanctions is that government leaders are often reluctant to expose their own administration's complicity in abuse. Is the United States an exception? Consider that issue in light of the materials below on Justice Department officials who gave advice on interrogation policy in the war on terror.

2. Federal judge and law professor Richard Posner argues that even if torture is "always wrong, there is such a thing as a lesser wrong committed to avoid a greater one."[32] "If the stakes are high enough," Posner claims, "torture is permissible. No one who doubts that this is the case should be in a position of responsibility."[33] Do you agree?

3. Law professor David Luban acknowledges that the "ticking time bomb" scenario is not "completely unreal." One example he cites is a 1995 airline bomb and assassination attempt that was thwarted by Philippine police, who tortured a Pakistani conspirator. Other commentators have identified further examples.[34] However, as Luban notes, the difficulty in formulating policy based on the ticking-bomb hypothetical is that it "cheats its way around [real-world] difficulties by stipulating that the bomb is there and that officials know it and know they have the man who planted it."[35] But in all but the rarest circumstances, interrogators are dealing in probabilities. There may be a plot, the prisoner may know enough to prevent it, and may break under torture. Then the questions are, how likely do those circumstances need to be? How many lives need to be at stake? What techniques should be permissible? Should we torture the prisoner's wife or children? "Do you really want to make the torture decision by running the numbers?" Luban asks. And if only the numbers matter, he notes, "then torturing loved ones is almost a no brainer if you think it will work." A further problem with the ticking-bomb hypothetical is that it assumes a "single, ad hoc decision . . . in a desperate emergency. But . . . the real world is a world of policies, guidelines, and directives. It is a world of practices. . . ." That world requires addressing issues such as whether we want a "professional cadre of trained torturers" or federal grants for research on torture techniques. For Luban, the question then becomes: "Do we really want to create a torture culture and the kind of people who inhabit it?"[36]

Is that question rhetorical? Even Posner warns against creating rules that legitimize torture in specified circumstances. "Having been regularized, the practice will become regular. Better to leave in place the formal and customary prohibitions, but with the understanding that they will not be enforced in extreme circumstances."[37] But is that solution open to the problems of uncertainty and inconsistency that Bobbitt raises? Is there a better alternative?

4. In 2009, the CIA released three documents on the intelligence that had been gained from detainees. A 2004 report by its inspector general and memos from 2004 and 2005 failed to show that "enhanced interrogation techniques" (such as waterboarding) that many consider torture prevented a single imminent terrorist act.[38] Does that affect your assessment of the conduct of any of the lawyers involved in government decisions on the issue? Suppose there had been a successful example of prevention. Would that change your view? Consider Justice Holmes's classic dissent in a case involving illegal wiretaps. It should not, in his view, matter whether the wiretaps yielded important evidence:

> In a government of laws, existence of the government will be imperiled if it fails to observe the law scrupulously. Our Government is the potent, the omnipresent teacher. For good or for ill, it teaches the whole people by its example. Crime is contagious. If the Government becomes a lawbreaker, it breeds contempt for law; it invites every man to become a law unto himself; it invites anarchy.[39]

Do the same arguments apply to torture, and to governments that determine when violation of international conventions on torture are justified? How would Bobbitt respond? How would you?

5. To what extent should public opinion matter? Recent polls find that Americans are closely divided on how to handle terrorism suspects. One 2009 survey indicated that 58 percent of Americans believed that the government "should not use torture as part of the U.S. campaign against terrorism, no matter what the circumstances."[40] Another poll the same year found that 53 percent believed that torture is sometimes justifiable to gain important information from terror suspects.[41] Do you think the public is considering the ticking time bomb scenario when they answer that question? Should they? Does it matter in formulating government policy?

6. Whose opinion matters most? For example, the American public strongly opposes prosecuting terrorism suspects in civilian courts. The international community, however, is deeply suspicious of any verdicts reached in military proceedings that have fewer procedural protections and less transparency than criminal trials.[42] Attorney General Eric Holder has been caught in the middle. As Elisa Massimino, the president of Human Rights First, notes, "Politically, these issues are poisonous. . . . You can't finesse it."[43] Holder himself believes that trying 9/11 terrorism suspects in civilian courts conveys an important moral message: "Values matter in this fight. We need to give those who might follow these mad men a good sense of what America is and what America can be. We are militarily strong, but we are morally stronger."[44] Critics, however, believe that Holder was trying to "protect his own image" at the expense of "protecting the President from political fallout."[45] That fallout was sufficiently substantial to force Holder to back down from his initial decision to try 9/11 defendants in Manhattan.

If you were in Holder's position, what factors would be most important in your decision? Whose image should he be most concerned with protecting?

PROBLEM 6-3[46]

Consider the leadership roles of government officials who either authorized enhanced interrogation tactics or advised those who did. When public servants occupy pivotal positions in governmental decision making, they are often thought to have a special responsibility to the public as well as to the administration or agency that they serve.[47] The materials that follow explore this responsibility in several contexts related to the war on terror.

The first involves a 2002 meeting at Guantanamo Naval Base to discuss the use of enhanced interrogation techniques on detainees. Two of the ten participants listed in the meeting minutes were lawyers: one, Lieutenant Colonel Diane Beaver, was Staff Judge Advocate to the task force commander at Guantanamo; the other, Jonathan Fredman, was assistant general counsel to the CIA and chief counsel to the CIA's counterterrorism center. The other participants were military and intelligence officers.[48] Nine days after this meeting, LTC Beaver provided a legal memorandum that approved more than a dozen aggressive interrogation techniques, including stress positions, sleep deprivation, intimidation through the use of military dogs, forced nudity, and the "wet towel" form of waterboarding, a technique of simulated drowning.[49] Many of these techniques were used on detainees in Guantanamo and Abu Ghraib Prison in Iraq. According to minutes taken at the meeting, LTC Beaver first acknowledged that "we may need to curb the harsher operations while ICRC [the International Committee of the Red Cross] is around. It is better not to expose them to any controversial techniques." When informed that sleep deprivation was being reported at Bagram, LTC Beaver responded: "True, but officially it is not happening. It is not being reported officially. The ICRC is a serious concern. They will be in and out, scrutinizing our operations, unless they are displeased and decide to protest and leave. This would draw a lot of negative attention. . . ."

The following exchange occurred.

Fredman: The DOJ has provided much guidance on this issue. The CIA is not held to the same rules as the military. In the past when the ICRC has made a big deal about certain detainees, the DOD has "moved" them away from the attention of ICRC. Upon questioning from the ICRC about their whereabouts, the DOD's response has repeatedly been that the detainee merited no status under the Geneva Convention. The CIA has employed aggressive techniques against less than a handful of suspects since 9/11. Under the Torture Convention, torture has been prohibited under international law, but the language of the statutes is written vaguely. Severe mental and physical pain is prohibited. The mental part is explained as poorly as the physical. Severe physical pain described as anything causing permanent physical damage to major organs or body parts. Mental torture described as anything leading to permanent, profound damage to the senses or personality. It is basically subject to perception. If the detainee dies you're doing it wrong. . . . Any of the techniques that lie on the harshest end of the spectrum must be performed by a highly trained individual. Medical personnel should be present to treat any possible accidents. The CIA operates without military intervention. When the CIA has wanted to use more aggressive techniques in the past, the FBI has pulled their personnel from theatre. In those rare instances, aggressive techniques have proven very helpful.

LTC
Beaver: We will need documentation to protect us.

Fredman: Yes, if someone dies while aggressive techniques are being used, regardless of cause of death, the backlash of attention would be severely detrimental. Everything must be approved and documented.

When told that law enforcement agency personnel would not participate in harsh techniques, LTC Beaver responded: "There is no legal reason why LEA personnel cannot participate in these operations. . . . [The] LEA choice not to participate in these types of interrogations is more ethical and moral as opposed to legal." Fredman then added: "The videotaping of even totally legal techniques will look 'ugly.'" However he also noted that the United States had signed only the clause in the international Torture Convention prohibiting torture, not the clause prohibiting "cruel, inhumane and degrading treatment" because case law under the Eighth Amendment to the United States Constitution already had interpreted and enforced those prohibitions. Fredmen continued:

> This gives us more license to use more controversial techniques. [One involves the "wet towel" strategy.] . . . If a well-trained individual is used to perform this technique it can feel like you're drowning. The lymphatic system will react as if you're suffocating, but your body will not cease to function. It is very effective to identify phobias and use them (i.e., insects, snakes, claustrophobia). . . . The threat of death is also subject to scrutiny, and should be handled on a case by case basis. Mock executions don't work as well as friendly approaches, like letting someone write a letter home, or providing them with an extra book.

This memo drew internal criticism at the Department of Defense, including this e-mail from Mark Fallon, the deputy commander of DOD's Criminal Investigation Task Force:

> This looks like the kinds of stuff Congressional hearings are made of. Quotes from LTC Beaver regarding things that are not being reported give the appearance of impropriety. Other comments like "It is basically subject to perception. If the detainee dies you're doing it wrong" and "Any of the techniques that lie on the harshest end of the spectrum must be performed by a highly trained individual. Medical personnel should be present to treat any possible accidents" seem to stretch beyond the bounds of legal propriety. Talk of "wet towel treatment" which results in the lymphatic gland reacting as if you are suffocating, would in my opinion shock the conscience of any legal body looking at using the results of the interrogations or possibly even the interrogators. Someone needs to be considering how history will look back at this.[50]

A second context posing similar issues involved lawyers in the Department of Justice's Office of Legal Counsel (OLC) who participated in drafting what have become known as the "torture memos." They became public shortly after the revelation in 2004 of prisoner torture and humiliation at Abu Ghraib. OLC, which provides legal advice to the executive branch, has a distinguished staff, which has included Supreme Court justices, law professors, and high-ranking officials. OLC opinions are generally taken as authoritative statements of the law governing the executive branch of the federal government.[51] The OLC publishes some of its opinions, but others, including the torture memos, are intended to remain secret. The best known memo was signed by then OLC head Jay S. Bybee (now a federal court of appeals judge), but was written by another OLC lawyer, Berkeley law professor John Yoo.[52] It analyzes federal statutes making torture a crime, which implement the United States' commitment under the international Convention Against Torture (CAT). CAT requires signatories to criminalize torture, defined as government agents' intentional infliction of severe mental or physical pain or suffering. CAT also requires signatories to "undertake to prevent" cruel, inhuman, and degrading treatment which does not rise to the level of torture. The United States banned such treatment in 2005. Two other OLC memos concluded that the Geneva Conventions do not protect either Al Qaeda members or members of the Taliban. These conclusions were relevant in the war against terror because the Geneva Conventions prohibit not only torture but also "outrages against personal dignity, including humiliating and degrading treatment" of captives. Although the State Department's legal advisor and many legal experts strongly criticized the OLC analysis, in 2002 President Bush adopted its conclusions.[53]

Federal law prohibiting torture defines it as "severe physical or mental pain or suffering." In interpreting that prohibition, the Bybee-Yoo memo looked to a definition of "severe pain" in legislation entitling patients to Medicare benefits for emergency medical conditions. Based on that legislation, the memo concluded that the pain

> amounting to torture must be equivalent in intensity to the pain accompanying serious physical injury, such as organ failure, impairment of bodily function, or even death. For purely mental pain or suffering to amount to torture under Section 2340, it must result in significant psychological harm of significant duration, e.g., lasting for months or even years. . . . A defendant must specifically intend to cause prolonged mental harm for the defendant to have committed torture.

The memo also concluded that

> even if an interrogation method arguably were to violate [federal law on torture, it] would be unconstitutional if it impermissibly encroached on the President's constitutional power to conduct a military campaign. As Commander-in-Chief, the President has the constitutional authority to order interrogations of enemy combatants to gain intelligence information concerning the military plans of the enemy. . . . [Those who engaged in such interrogation could also raise] a defense of necessity. . . . [or self-defense]. Clearly, any harm that might occur during an interrogation would pale in significance compared

to the harm avoided by preventing such an attack, which could take hundreds or thousands of lives.

A third context involving leadership issues involved how to respond in the wake of public criticism that the Bybee-Yoo memo attracted. Although a few law professors pronounced it "standard lawyerly fare," almost all other experts were highly critical.[54] In their view, the lack of public scrutiny or adversarial safeguards for OLC decisions imposed a special responsibility on the office's lawyers to act as "honest brokers," not "hired guns."[55]

Eventually, OLC itself took the highly unusual step of withdrawing the Bybee-Yoo memo, and replacing it with an alternative memo, authored by acting OLC head Daniel Levin. Levin's memo analyzed cases under the Torture Victim's Protection Act and concluded:

> The inclusion of the words "or suffering" in the phrase "severe physical pain or suffering" suggests that the statutory category of physical torture is not limited to "severe physical pain." . . . We conclude that under some circumstances "physical suffering" may be of sufficient intensity and duration to meet the statutory definition of torture even if it does not involve "severe physical pain." To constitute such torture, "*severe* physical suffering" would have to be a condition of some extended duration or persistence as well as intensity.[56]

Levin's memo also attracted criticism, in part because its requirement that suffering must be of extended duration might exclude waterboarding, in which subjects generally break in a matter of minutes. Levin had himself waterboarded while writing the memo, raising questions about whether his experience was relevant.[57]

Controversy also centered on whether the lawyers who wrote or approved the torture memos should be subject to any disciplinary action. The Department of Justice's Office of Professional Responsibility (OPR) launched an investigation, the District of Columbia and Pennsylvania Bar associations received disciplinary complaints, and a detainee subject to enhanced interrogation sued Yoo in federal court for violation of his civil rights.[58] A Spanish court also opened a criminal investigation against Bybee and Yoo under the universal jurisdiction provision of the Convention on Torture. None of these actions have resulted in sanctions, although both court cases remain pending.

In 2010, the Department of Justice released both the report by the OPR and a decision by David Margolis, Aassociate Deputy Attorney General, rejecting its conclusion. The OPR found that Bybee and Yoo had committed misconduct by failing "to exercise independent legal judgment and render thorough, objective, and candid legal advice" as required by bar ethical rules.[59] Under OPR rules, attorneys engage in professional misconduct when they "intentionally violate or act in reckless disregard of a known unambiguous obligation imposed by law, rule of professional conduct, or Department regulation or policy." According to an OLC memo defining best practices, the office's role is to provide "candid, independent and principled advice — even when that advice may be inconsistent with the desires of policy makers." In general, opinions should strive for a "balanced presentation of arguments on each side of an issue. . . . OLC's interest is simply to provide the correct answer on the law, taking into account all reasonable counterarguments. . . ."[60] The report also noted that OLC lawyers must abide by professional rules of conduct. Under the District of Columbia's Rule 1.1, a lawyer must provide "competent representation, [which] requires the legal knowledge, skill, thoroughness, and preparation reasonably necessary for the representation." Under Rule 2.1, a lawyer must provide "independent professional judgment" and "candid advice."

In the view of OPR, the Bybee-Yoo memo fell short in several respects. It took its definition of torture from the use of "severe pain" in a medical benefits statute rather than from directly applicable precedents, failed to consider adverse authority, and misstated supporting authority.[61] Bybee was faulted for inadequate supervision and failure to consider relevant material, such as the military's determination that waterboarding constituted torture. Yoo's conduct was considered intentional, based both on the extent of his errors and on evidence that the CIA officials who had asked for the opinion were not interested in objective analysis, but rather in language that would protect interrogators from subsequent prosecution.[62] Accordingly, the OPR concluded that Yoo and Bybee should be referred to appropriate bar disciplinary agencies.

By contrast, Margolis determined that although both lawyers had exercised "poor judgment," they had not violated rules of professional conduct. The "memos contained some significant flaws," and constituted "an unfortunate chapter" in the history of the office, but in Margolis's view, they did not rise to the level of reckless or intentional misconduct.[63] The Department's inability to produce e-mails from around this period made it difficult to know the state of mind of the participants, but the record failed to show that Yoo's conclusion was the result of pressure from administration officials. Rather it appeared that "loyalty to his own ideology and convictions clouded his view of his obligation to his client and led him to author opinions that reflected his own extreme, albeit sincerely held, views of executive power."[64]

This conclusion met with mixed reviews. Supporters applauded the decision not to use disciplinary sanctions to resolve policy disagreements. Critics, including the *New York Times*' editorial board, viewed "poor judgment" as an "absurdly dismissive" way to characterize facilitation of torture.[65] Some saw the result less as a vindication of Yoo and Bybee than as an indictment of bar disciplinary standards and structures. According to many commentators, the case underscored the need for a "credible" oversight mechanism, "independent of the very department implicated" in the matter."[66]

QUESTIONS

1. What would you have done if you were a participant in the 2002 meeting discussing enhanced interrogation? What would you have done in Mark Fallon's position after learning of the substance of that meeting? Might you have leaked the minutes?

2. Those who formulated U.S. interrogation policy emphasize that at the time the torture memos were written, government leaders had great concern about a possible Al Qaeda attack on or around the anniversary of 9/11. According to General Richard Myers, who then chaired the Joint Chiefs

of Staff, "There was a sense of urgency that in my forty years of military experience hadn't existed in other contingencies. [We had a] real fear that one of the detainees might know when the next attack would happen, and that [we] would miss vital information."[67] Margolis's report also made reference to the security context in which the memos were drafted. Should such considerations influence legal conclusions about what constitutes torture? Or is it precisely in times of stress that government leaders should be most careful not to stretch the law to reach expedient results?

3. If you had been in Margolis's position, would you have reached the same conclusions? What are the best arguments for and against sanctions?

4. Some commentators believed that Yoo's interpretation of the law on torture may have been skewed by the identity bias discussed in Chapter 3. Because he was heavily involved in policy decisions governing the war on terror, his political allegiances may have colored his legal judgments. [68] If that is true, what is the appropriate response? If you were a bar leader, how would you assess the standards for assessing OLC lawyers? Note that its rules require "intentional" or "reckless" violations of clear duties, while bar disciplinary rules make any violation a basis for sanctions. What accounts for the restricted liability of government lawyers? Is it justifiable?

5. If you were the Attorney General, how would you respond to criticism of the OLC oversight process? Are there strategies, apart from criminal, civil, or disciplinary liability that might make government officials more accountable for their decisions? For example, should Congress require that all or certain specified OLC opinions be public, as some commentators and legislators have recommended? An unsuccessful proposed "OLC Reporting Act" would have obligated the Attorney General to report to Congress in a timely fashion any OLC opinions that expanded executive power at the expense of Congress or the courts.[69] If you were in Congress, would you support such legislation? Would Yoo and Bybee have been likely to draft their opinion the same way if that act had been in force?

6. In his 2010 memoir *Decision Points*, former President Bush justified his actions as follows:

> CIA experts drew up a list of enhanced interrogation techniques. . . . At my direction, Department of Justice and CIA lawyers conducted a careful legal review. The enhanced interrogation program complied with the Constitution and all applicable laws, including those that ban torture. There were two I felt went too far, even if they were legal. I directed the CIA not to use them. Another technique was waterboarding, a process of simulated drowning. No doubt the procedure was tough, but medical experts assured the CIA that it did no lasting harm. . . . Had I not authorized waterboarding on senior al Qaeda leaders, I would have to accept a greater risk that the country would be attacked. In the wake of 9/11, that was a risk I was unwilling to take. . . . The new techniques proved highly effective. Zubaydah revealed large amounts of information on al Qaeda structure and operations. . . . Khalid Sheikh Mohammed [provided information that revealed terrorist plots and the location of key operatives].[70]

In an interview following the book's publication, Matt Lauer asked Bush: "Why is waterboarding legal in your opinion?" Bush responded: "Because the lawyer said it was legal. He said it did not fall within the Anti-Torture Act. I'm not a lawyer, but you gotta trust the judgment of people around you and I do." When Lauer then asked whether it would be "okay for a foreign country to waterboard an American citizen," Bush replied, "all I ask is that people read the book."[71]

Many commentators raised concerns with these defenses. One criticism was that Bush's legal team had offered an opinion that was inconsistent with the consensus of the expert international community. Another was that he had vastly overstated the value of intelligence obtained through enhanced interrogation and understated the pervasiveness of its use. Investigative journalists, and one of the interrogators involved, agreed that no actionable intelligence was gained from Zubaydah's treatment and that his false confessions sent CIA and FBI investigators "scurrying in pursuit of phantoms." [72] Although Khalid Sheikh Mohammed had provided some useful information, none of it was shown to have thwarted well-developed plots or to have saved lives. Nor did the record in either case indicate that the information could not have been obtained through accepted interrogation methods.[73] Critics also noted that the techniques Bush authorized were not reserved to a few senior terrorist leaders, but were employed on countless detainees in Afghanistan, Iraq, and Guantanamo Bay.

What is your view? What would you have done in Bush's place? Does his reliance on lawyers affect your views of the gravity of conduct by Yoo and Bybee?

7. Are there other strategies that the United States government could pursue apart from sanctioning lawyers or those who relied on their advice? For example, law professor David Cole proposes that an independent commission could review conduct related to torture and enhanced interrogation, and recommend appropriate actions, including formal apologies and compensation to victims. The Canadian government took such action concerning a citizen who had been erroneously classified as a potential terrorist and sent to Syria, where he was tortured. He received $10 million in reparations.[74]

8. In 2010, various media sources revealed that President Obama had approved the targeted killing of an American citizen, the radical Muslim cleric Anwar al-Awlaki, who has been linked to Al Qaeda terrorist plots against the United States.[75] Such authorized killings are rare, but not unprecedented. As a general principle, international law permits the use of lethal force against individuals and groups that pose an imminent threat to the country. In the aftermath of 9/11, Congress approved the use of military force against Al Qaeda, and its leaders on the military's target list are considered national enemies and not subject to prohibitions on political assassination. Some commentators have questioned whether al-Awlaki, reportedly hiding in Yemen, stands on the same footing as an enemy combatant on a the battlefield, and whether such targeted killings should be subject to some oversight.[76] Yale law professor Stephen Carter notes that the law of war applies to both sides, and asks how the American public would react if the Taliban launched a predator attack on the White House.[77] What is your view? If it

would be unlawful to torture suspected terrorists, should it be lawful to assassinate them? Under what circumstances?

MEDIA RESOURCES

Many interviews with John Yoo are available, including one on the Daily Show with Jon Stewart from January 11, 2010, as are documentaries on the War against Terror.[78] Among the best are Frontline's *Cheney's War* and *Reckoning with Torture*, a documentary by the ACLU and PEN American Center, which features actors reading from official memos, e-mails, and speeches, as well as interviews with victims of torture. A *60 Minutes* interview with George Tenet includes a representative explanation of the administration's interrogation policy.[79] An interesting comparison of views on interrogation comes from former President Clinton's 2008 interview with Tim Russert on *Meet the Press*, former President Bush's 2010 NBC interview with Matt Lauer, and President Obama's public statement repudiating torture.[80] An illuminating portrayal of waterboarding shows a conservative talk show host, Erich "Mancow" Muller, recanting his views about the severity of the tactic.[81] Torture, rendition, and related practices also figure in many television plots, including segments of *24* and *The Wire*, and films such as *The Kingdom*, *Rendition*, and *Syriana*. The film *A Few Good Men* also includes a relevant scene in which a hardened military officer upbraids an idealistic army lawyer for his inability to understand military necessities.

END NOTES

1. 45 Code of Federal Regulations 46, http://ohsr.od.nih.gov/guidelines/45cfr46.html.
2. Philip Zimbardo, The Lucifer Effect (New York: Random House, 2007), 238-239.
3. Senator Inhofe made his comments on May 11, 2004, during the Senate Armed Services Committee hearings regarding prison abuses. For estimates of innocence rates, see Jen Banbury, "Rummy's Scapegoat," Salon.com, Nov. 10, 2005, http://dir.salon.com/story/books/int/2005/11/10/karpinski/index.html; and Report of the International Committee of the Red Cross on the Treatment by the Coalition Forces of Prisoners of War and Other Protected Persons by the Geneva Conventions in Iraq, #1, Treatment During Arrest (February 2004).
4. Testimony as Prepared by Secretary of Defense Donald H. Rumsfeld, The Senate and House Armed Services Committees, Friday, May 07, 2004, available at http://www.defense.gov/speeches/speech.aspx?speechid=118.
5. Adam Hochschild, What's in a Word? Torture, New York Times, May 23, 2004, 11.
6. "Rumsfeld Twice Offered to Resign," BBC News, news.bbc.co.uk, February 4, 2005, http://news.bbc.co.uk/2/hi/americas/4235045.stm.
7. Id.
8. Final Report of the Independent Panel to Review DoD Detention Operations, August 2004, at 43, available at http://www.defense.gov/news/Aug2004/d20040824finalreport.pdf.
9. The Roots of Abu Ghraib, New York Times, June 9, 2004, A24.
10. http://www.videosift.com/video/The-Original-Milgram-Experiment-1961.
11. See Charles Sheridan and Richard King, available at http://brianpuccio.net/keywords/charles_sheridan; http://freerepublic.com/focus/f-news/1889008/posts.
12. This variation is described in Wesley Kilham and Leon Mann, Level of Destructive Obedience as a Function of Transmitter and Executant Roles in the Milgram Obedience Paradigm, Journal of Personality and Social Psychology 29(5) (1974):696-702.
13. Available at http://www.psychologicalscience.org/observer/getArticle.cfm?id=2264.
14. Zimbardo's presentation on the Lucifer effect is available at http://www.youtube.com/watch?v=BYre8SlOO_k&feature=related; http://www.slate.com/id/2100419; http://www.prisonexp.

org/links.htm#iraq; http://www.bbcprisonstudy.org/; http://www.prisonexp.org/pdf/ap1998.pdf; http://www.prisonexp.org/pdf/blass.pdf. For video links aside from Zimbardo's presentation, see http://video.google.com/videoplay?docid=677084988379129606#; http://www.thedailyshow.com/watch/thu-march-29-2007/philip-zimbardo?videoId=84518.

15. For images, see Images: http://www.antiwar.com/news/?articleid=2444; http://www.afterdowningstreet.org/sites/afterdowningstreet.org/files/images/abu2.jpg; http://traceyricksfoster.files.wordpress.com/2009/05/abu-ghraib.jpg; http://blog.reidreport.com/uploaded_images/abu-ghraib-leash-715453.jpg; http://dancull.files.wordpress.com/2009/07/abu-ghraib21.jpg; http://filipspagnoli.files.wordpress.com/2009/07/abu-ghraib-torture.jpg. For an interview with the guard, see http://video.google.com/videoplay?docid=-5511717742437253654&ei=aFBnS_vTO5eyrAPZzuzkAw&q=abu+ghraib+prison&hl=en#.

16. Part I: http://www.youtube.com/watch?v=LZ_Vxoyu8zY(Yoo interview); Part III: http://www.youtube.com/watch?v=gnsC1Lt9H9E&NR=1(soldier who denies responsibility);16. Part IV: http://www.youtube.com/watch?v=T4EfL3_etuI&feature=related (soldiers discussing responsibility to report and lack of leadership, and Pentagon official denying responsibility).

17. Jeb Stuart Magruder, An American Life: One Man's Road to Watergate (New York: Atheneum, 1974), 214.

18. This problem is adapted from Deborah L. Rhode, Professional Responsibility: Ethics by the Pervasive Method (New York: Aspen Publishers, 2d ed. 1998), 483-488.

19. Peter Irons, Justice at War (Berkeley: University of California Press, 1993), 204.

20. Id. at 205-206.

21. Id. at 290-291.

22. Id. at 350-351.

23. Lincoln Kaplan, The Tenth Justice: The Solicitor General and the Rule of Law (New York: Knopf, 1987), 10.

24. Bernard Williams, Politics and Moral Character, in Stuart Hampshire, ed., Public and Private Morality (New York: Cambridge University Press, 1978), 58.

25. American Bar Association, Model Rules of Professional Conduct Rule 1.2 (Chicago: American Bar Association, 2008).

26. Geoffrey P. Miller, Government Lawyers' Ethics in a System of Checks and Balances, University of Chicago Law Review 54 (1987):1293, 1294-1295.

27. William Josephson and Russell Pearce, To Whom Does the Government Lawyer Owe the Duty of Loyalty When Clients Are in Conflict?, Howard Law Journal 29 (1986):539, 565.

28. Judge Charles Fahy, Special Ethical Problems of Counsel for the Government, Federal Bar Journal 33 (1974):331, 333-334; Jack B. Weinstein and Gay A. Crosthweit, Some Reflections on Conflicts between Government Attorneys and Clients, Touro Law Review 1 (1985):1. See also Catharine J. Lanctot, The Duty of Zealous Advocacy and the Ethics of the Federal Government Lawyer: The Three Hardest Questions, Southern California Law Review 64 (1991):951.

29. George Bush, Decision Points (New York: Crown Publishers, 2010), 172-173.

30. John Conroy, Unspeakable Acts, Ordinary People (New York: Knopf, 2000), 25-26. See also Sanford Levinson, Contemplating Torture: An Introduction, in Sanford Levinson, ed., Torture: A Collection (New York: Oxford, 2004), 36.

31. Carol Tavris and Eliot Aronson, Mistakes Were Made (but not by me), (New York: Harcourt, 2008), 202-203.

32. Richard Posner, Torture, Terrorism, and Interrogation, in Levinson, ed., Torture, 294.

33. Richard Posner, The Best Offense, The New Republic, September 2, 2002, 28, 30.

34. Stephen L. Carter, The Violence of Peace: America's Wars in the Age of Obama (New York: Beast Books, 2011), 43-44 (discussing French resistance fighters tortured by Nazis, and United States CIA officer tortured by Ethiopians).

35. David Luban, Liberalism, Torture and the Ticking Bomb, Virginia Law Review 91 (2005): 1425, 1442-1444.

36. Id. at 1445-1446.

37. Posner, The Best Offense, 30.

38. Ali Soufan, What Torture Never Taught Us, New York Times, September 7, 2009, at WK 9.

39. Olmstead v. United States, 277 U.S. 438, 485 (1927) (Holmes, J., dissenting).

40. Washington Post—ABC News Poll, Washington Post, January 13-16, 2009, available at http://www.washingtonpost.com/wp-srv/politics/documents/postpllo011709.html.

41. Dahlia Lithwick, Torture Bored, Slate, February 22, 2010.

42. Jane Mayer, The Trial, New Yorker, February 15 and 22, 2010, 57, 60.

43. Id. at 60 (quoting Massimino).

44. Id. at 62 (quoting Holder).

45. Id. at 57 (quoting anonymous source).

46. Some of the following material is adapted from Deborah L. Rhode and David Luban, Legal Ethics (New York: Foundation Press, 5th ed. 2009), 542-562.

47. For discussion of the heightened public-interest obligations of government lawyers, see, e.g., Steven K. Berenson, Public Lawyers, Private Values: Can, Should, and Will Government Lawyers Serve the Public Interest?, Boston College Law Review 41 (2000):789.

48. This document was released during Senate hearings on detainee abuse in June 2008, and is available at http://levin.senate.gov/newsroom/supporting/2008/Documents.SASC.061708.pdf, Tab 7.

49. Legal Brief on Proposed Counter-Resistance Strategies from Diane Beaver to Gen. James T. Hill, Oct. 11, 2002, in Karen J. Greenberg and Joshua L. Dratel, eds., The Torture Papers: The Road to Abu Ghraib (New York: Cambridge University Press, 2005), 229. The techniques are listed in id. at 227-228.

50. Memo from Mark Fallon to Sam McCahon, October 28, 2002.

51. Some dispute centers on whether they are binding as a matter of law or custom. Randolph D. Moss, Executive Branch Legal Interpretation: A Perspective from the Office of Legal Counsel, Administrative Law Review 52 (2000):1303, 1318-1320.

52. Memorandum from Jay S. Bybee to Alberto Gonzalez (August 1, 2002).

53. The OLC memos and President Bush's order are reproduced in Greenberg and Dratel, The Torture Papers, 38-79, 81-117, 134-135. The State Department's critique is Memo from William Howard Taft IV to John Yoo, January 11, 2002, available at http://www.cartoonbank.com/newyorker/slideshows/01TaftMemo.pdf. For critiques of government policy, see David Cole, The Torture Memos: Rationalizing the Unthinkable (New York: The New Press, 2009).

54. Eric Posner and Adrian Vermeule, A "Torture" Memo and Its Tortuous Critics, Wall Street Journal, July 6, 2004, A22; David Luban, The Torture Lawyers of Washington, in David Luban, Legal Ethics and Human Dignity (New York: Cambridge University Press, 2007); Robert K. Vischer, Legal Advice as Moral Perspective, Georgetown Journal of Legal Ethics 19 (2006):225; Jeremy Waldron, Torture and the Common Law: Jurisprudence for the White House, Columbia Law Review 105 (2005):1681; W. Bradley Wendell, Legal Ethics and the Separation of Law and Morals, Cornell Law Review 67 (2005):91; Ruth Wedgwood and R. James Woolsey, Law and Torture, Wall Street Journal, June 28, 2004, A10.

55. David Cole, Introductory Commentary, in Cole, ed., The Torture Memos, 13.

56. Memorandum from Daniel Levin to James B. Comey (December 30, 2004, available at news.findlaw.com/cnn/docs/terrorism/dojtorture123004mem.pdf.

57. Jan Crawford Greenburg and Ariane deVogue, Bush Administration Blocked Waterboarding Critic, ABC News, November 2, 2007, available at http://abcnews.go.com/WN/DOJ/story?id=3814076&page=1.

58. Press Release, Disbar Torture Lawyers, Disciplinary Complaint against Torture Memo Lawyers, Nov. 30, 2009, http://www.legalethicsforum.com/blog/2009/11/disciplinary-complaint-against-torture-memo-lawyers.html; Padilla v. Yoo, 633 F. Supp. 1005 (U.S.D. 2009) (partly denying motion to dismiss).

59. Investigation into the Office of Legal Counsel's Memoranda concerning Issues Relating to the Central Intelligence Agency's Use of Enhanced Interrogation Techniques on Suspected Terrorists (July 29, 2009).

60. Steven G. Bradbury, Principle Deputy Assistant Attorney General, Memorandum for Attorneys of the Office Re: Best Practices for OLC Opinions, May 16, 2005, quoted in OPR Report, 15.

61. OPR Report, 228.

62. Id. at 226-237.

63. David Margolis, Memorandum for the Attorney General of Decision regarding the Objections to the Findings of Professional Misconduct in the Office of Professional Responsibility's Report of Investigation, January 5, 2010.

64. Margolis, Memo, 67.

65. The Torture Lawyers, The New York Times, February 25, 2010, A26.

66. Stephen Gillers, Letter to the Editor, New York Times, March 4, 2010, A26; David Cole, Torture Lawyers on Trial, The Nation, March 1, 2010, 7.

67. Philippe Sands, The Torture Team: Rumsfeld's Memo and the Betrayal of American Values (New York: Palgrave Macmillan, 2008), 88.

68. Cassandra Burke Robinson, Judgment, Identity, and Independence, Connecticut Law Review 42 (2009):1, 27-29.

69. S. 3501, 110th Cong. (2008). Text of bill available at http://www.fas.org/irp/congress/2008_rpt/srpt110-528.html. Other commentators have proposed that all OLC opinions be public. See Norman Spaulding, Professional Independence in the Office of the Attorney General, Stanford Law Review 60 (2008):1931, 1978.

70. Bush, Decision Points, 169-170.

71. NBC News Special, Decision Points, interview of George W. Bush by Matt Lauer, November 8, 2010, available at http://www.msnbc.msn.com/id/40076644/ns/politicsw-decision_points.

72. Dan Froomkin, The Two Most Essential, Abhorrent, Intolerable Lies of George W. Bush's Memoir, Huffington Post, November 22, 2010, http://www.huffingtonpost.com/2010/11/22/the-two-most-esssential-a_n_786219.html (quoting Washington Post and citing other sources); Ali Soufan, My Tortured Decision, op-ed. New York Times, April 22, 2009.

73. Froomkin, The Two Lies, quoting sources; Soufan, My Tortured Decision.

74. Cole, Introductory Commentary, 3940.

75. Scott Shane, U.S. Approves Targeted Killing of Radical Muslim Cleric Tied to Domestic Terror Suspects, April 7, 2010, 12.

76. License to Kill, The Nation, May 3, 2010, 4-5.

77. Carter, The Violence of Peace, discussed in James Taub, The War Presidents, New York Times Book Review, January 30, 2011, 20.

78. For John Yoo interviews, see http://www.thedailyshow.com/watch/thu-january-7-2010/daily-show — exclusive — -john-yoo-extended-interview-pt — 1; http://fora.tv/2006/10/29/Uncommon_Knowledge_Richard_Epstein_John_Yoo; http://www.pbs.org/wgbh/pages/frontline/torture/interviews/yoo.html. For documentaries on the War on Terror, see http://www.pbs.org/wgbh/pages/frontline/bushswar/view/main.html; http://www.pbs.org/wgbh/pages/frontline/darkside/view; http://www.taxitothedarkside.com/taxi; http://arabsandterrorism.com; http://video.google.com/videoplay?docid=-210088912352527308#. For George Tenet on *60 Minutes*, see http://www.cbsnews.com/video/watch/?id=2739654n&tag=related;photovideo.

79. http://www.cbsnews.com/video/watch/?id=2739654n&tag=related;photovideo.

80. For Bill Clinton's analysis of torture, see http://www.youtube.com/watch?v=CvoFmvc-V1ug&feature=relatedh. For an earlier claim by Bush that the United States does not engage in torture, see http://www.youtube.com/watch?v=g6LtL9lCTRA. For Obama's statement, see http://www.youtube.com/watch?v=XM5FKawx1No.

81. http://www.youtube.com/watch?v=qUkj9pjx3H0.

CHAPTER 7

SCANDAL: PRIVATE LIVES, PUBLIC RESPONSIBILITIES, AND CRISIS MANAGEMENT

Scandals, notes Professor Laura Kipnis, will always be with us, "sniffing at the back door, nosing around for cracks in the façade." Because the "human personality is helpless against itself, we will always see leaders "orchestrating their own downfalls, crashing headlong into their own inner furies."[1] And we, the public, the "collective superego" cannot resist the spectacle. Nor can we sometimes help but "relish the pleasure of knocking the excessively privileged . . . down a notch or two" when they violate norms that inconveniently constrain our own behavior.[2]

However, what is distinctive about the modern era are the social, economic, and technological forces that have increased the visibility of scandals. Growing competition among media is one factor. As sociology professor Ari Adut notes in *On Scandal*, "[T]he proliferation of the media sources and the establishment of the round-the-clock cable news cycle have stoked the demand for scandal and facilitated its publicization process. The effects of the citizen-journalism of YouTube, which allows almost anyone to put any kind of compromising images about elites into the public domain, are obvious. . . ."[3] The rise in watchdog groups that trade in publicity, and communications strategists that specialize in spin, has brought heightened transparency to leadership missteps. Technology has also provided more ways to obtain information and more ways of making it instantly accessible. Those in positions of power are increasingly vulnerable to exposure for their own frailties, as well as increasingly responsible for messes not of their own making. According to recent studies, chief executive officers believe that reputational loss is the second-greatest hazard they confront (after business interruption).[4] Some experts suggest that close to two-thirds of a company's worth is tied to reputation.[5]

This chapter explores the dynamics of scandal. What enmeshes leaders in political, financial, and sexual misconduct? Under what circumstances does their private conduct become a subject of legitimate public concern? How important is hypocrisy, and how important should it be? What are the most effective ways of managing reputational crises? How can leaders prevent their own or their organization's mistakes from mushrooming into public relations disasters?

A. HYPOCRISY

Hypocrisy is at the foundation of many leadership scandals. This should come as no surprise. If, as conventional usage suggests, hypocrisy means assuming a false appearance of virtue, or failing to practice what one preaches, it is endemic to public life. As Somerset Maugham once quipped, hypocrisy is unlike other vices like gluttony or adultery, which can be "practiced at spare moments. It is a whole time job."[6] Leaders are subject to normal human frailties, exposed to the temptations of power, and expected to rise above both. Psychologists have identified two cognitive biases that contribute to hypocrisy at leadership levels. One is people's tendency to see themselves as unique and superior to others, particularly concerning moral conduct.[7] This uniqueness bias is exacerbated by conditions of power. Leaders live in what consultant Eric Dezenhall labeled a "mental aquarium," an environment of admiration that leads to an inflated sense of self-confidence and self-importance.[8] A second cognitive bias encourages individuals to view their own transgressions as less objectionable than identical actions by others.[9] Placing individuals in positions of power again increases the likelihood of such hypocrisy.[10] Although social disapproval normally helps check self-interest, feelings of power tend to reduce sensitivity to that constraint.[11]

Yet, while no one doubts the pervasiveness of hypocrisy, commentators are divided on its significance and on the value of pointing it out. In sorting through these arguments, it is often useful to distinguish between individual and institutional hypocrisy. Leaders can be criticized either for failing to live up to their own principles, or for failing to keep an organization or institution from living up to its principles. So for example, Thomas Jefferson can be faulted for violating his professed commitment to liberty and equality because he owned slaves, or for designing a constitutional system that proclaimed adherence to those principles but ignored their meaning for African Americans.[12]

Some commentators view hypocrisy in politics as a special case, and one in which criticism on that ground is often unrealistic and unproductive. Political theorists Judith Shklar and Ruth Grant both argue that conventional definitions presuppose hypermoralistic, "overinclusive" standards: "[T]o define hypocrisy as [failing to] practice what one preaches . . . allows no distinction between hypocrisy and moral weakness. To profess principles that one has no intention of following is hypocrisy: to be unable to live up to our best expectations of ourselves is human nature."[13] Grant argues further that political hypocrisy is sometimes appropriate in democratic regimes in which compromise and coalitions are necessary, and people need to persuade others through rational argument rather than force. "The frank exposure of self-interested motivations is often a threat to that process."[14] Hypocrisy, she notes, "only occurs where people try to appear better than they are. . . . Where there is political hypocrisy, there is a . . . significant moral impulse."[15] That can be a positive influence in politics:

> Some sorts of hypocrisy . . . sustain the public conditions for political integrity. Every act of hypocrisy involves a pretense of virtue, which necessarily includes public acknowledgement of moral standards for political action, and sometimes, that public statement is the best that can be done. Moreover, even the pretense can serve as a genuine constraint. . . . In sum, the paradoxical truth is that there will be more genuine virtue and integrity in politics where there is a judicious appreciation of the role of political hypocrisy than where there is a strident and wholesale condemnation of it.[16]

Shklar similarly claims that politics can ill afford "honesty that humiliates" and a "stiff-necked sincerity that refuses compromise." She also worries that a focus on personal motives diverts attention from the substance of the conduct at issue.[17] Other commentators express concern that this focus will "drive our best hypocrites out of public life." Many talented leaders, who are basically "decent and well meaning" have also made some "significant missteps they would rather not read about in the morning paper."[18] By the same token, journalists end up in an "appallingly wasteful" diversion of scarce resources by duplicating each others' efforts to "sniff out the latest scandal."[19]

Yet exposure of hypocrisy can also serve legitimate functions. Political scientist Peter Furia argues that "when the very leaders who advocate morally demanding principles are unable to live up to them," it sparks a useful debate about the "practicability" of those principles.[20] Concerns about hypocrisy can also discourage overreaching, unprincipled, or self-righteous conduct that undermines the legitimacy of those in power. Accordingly, political theorist Suzanne Dovia argues that we need a contextual approach to hypocrisy, which evaluates the reasons why leaders have violated professed principles, and the consequences of their actions.[21]

Consider those arguments in light of the readings that follow. When do debates about leaders' hypocrisy serve a useful function? In contexts in which they are counterproductive, how should leaders respond?

JUDITH N. SHKLAR, ORDINARY VICES

(Cambridge, MA: The Belknap Press of Harvard University Press, 1984), pp. 47-48 and 77-78

Hypocrisy has always been odious. What is less obvious is just what hypocrisy is and why it should be so intensely resented. The *Oxford English Dictionary* is always helpful. Originally hypocrisy meant acting a part on the stage. For practical purposes the definition that counts is: "assuming a false appearance of virtue or goodness, with dissimulation of real character or inclination, especially in respect of religious life or belief." . . . The moral hypocrite . . . pretends that his motives and intentions and character are irreproachable when he knows that they are blameworthy. Then there are complacency and self-satisfaction, the hypocrisies of the wealthy and powerful. . . . Whatever is in their interest somehow is always also for the public good, in this best of all possible social worlds. There is, finally, a cluster of attitudes which taken together we call insincerity and inauthenticity. These need not express themselves in conduct that injures others directly, but they are said to deform one's personality. . . .

[Charges of hypocrisy are pervasive in political life because it] is not diffi-cult to show that politicians are often more interested in power than in any of the causes they so ardently proclaim. It is, therefore, easier to dispose of an opponent's character by exposing his hypocrisy than to show that his polit-ical convictions are wrong. . . . The paradox of liberal democracy is that it encourages hypocrisy because the politics of persuasion require, as any reader of Aristotle's *Rhetoric* knows, a certain amount of dissimulation on the part of all speakers. On the other hand, the structure of open political competition exaggerates the importance and the prevalence of hypocrisy because it is the vice of which all parties can and do accuse each other. It is not at all clear that zealous candor would serve liberal politics particularly well. Nevertheless, the distance between the demand for sincerity and the actualities of politics can become a great distraction, especially in time of social stress. . . .

[W]e assume that our public roles carry greater moral responsibilities than our private ones. We expect to behave better as citizens and public officials than as actors in the private sphere. The whole concern about corruption in government turns on that, and it does yield immense hypocrisy; but pretended virtue may curtail graft and similar vices as well. It is, far more significantly, no longer acceptable in the United States to make racist and anti-Semitic remarks in public [even though they appear in private.] . . . Would any egalitarian pre-fer more public frankness? Should our public conduct really mirror our private, inner selves? Often our public manners are better than our personal laxities. That "sugary grin" is, in any case, not a serious issue. On the contrary, it is a very necessary pretense, a witness to our moral efforts no less than to our failures.

Indeed, one might well argue that liberal democracy cannot afford public sincerity. Honesties that humiliate and a stiff-necked refusal to compromise would ruin democratic civility in a political society in which people have many serious differences of belief and interest. . . .

DAVID RUNCIMAN, POLITICAL HYPOCRISY: THE MASK OF POWER,
FROM HOBBES TO ORWELL AND BEYOND

(Princeton, NJ: Princeton University Press, 2008), pp. 222-226

Hypocrisy and the Environment

. . . Early in 2007 newspapers on both sides of the Atlantic were full of either deeply critical or sympathetically agonised articles about whether [Al] Gore's personal hypocrisy mattered, once it was discovered that the energy needs of his private home produced a carbon footprint many times the size of others in his neighborhood. Clearly, for any possible Gore candidature this was bad politics—blatant hypocrisy of this sort always gives your enemies a stick to beat you with. On the other hand, it is not clear that this kind of hypocrisy is the obstacle it sometimes appears, because there seems to be quite wide acceptance that some personal hypocrisy of this kind (not always practicing in the private sphere what you preach in public) is unavoidable in those who seek political power: they are like us, but they are not like us, and in some aspect of their lives the gap will show.

This kind of mismatch between public pronouncements and private practice is the hypocrisy we tend to hear most about, because it is the easiest to find, and the easiest to exploit to provoke a reaction. In many settings, and above all in the more censorious branches of the media (particularly online), not practicing what you preach is what hypocrisy has come to mean. . . . But the reaction to this sort of hypocrisy is often short-lived, and frequently surprisingly tolerant. . . . [V]oters seem far more censorious about public inconsistencies — "flip-flopping" in the jargon — than they do about private lapses from the highest public standards. So perhaps the more serious charge of hypocrisy to which a politician like Gore is vulnerable is that he didn't do much about global warming when he was in office. . . .

There is [moreover,] a big difference between those who do not live up to the standards they ask of others, and those who make a parade of their own ability to set an example. An environmental campaigner who travels the world by jet to spread the message that air travel is a significant cause of global warming is compromised, but such compromises may constitute the only efficient way to spread the message. Such a case is far removed from that of a politician like the British Conservative leader David Cameron, who has gone to great lengths to "green" his own personal lifestyle, and to make political capital out of that fact. When it emerged that Cameron's much publicised bicycle rides to the House of Commons involved the use of a car to ferry his personal belongings behind him, he revealed himself to be a second-order hypocrite. Second-order hypocrisy, because it makes a mockery of the whole business of public enactment, is corrosive in ways that first-order hypocrisy is not.

But even this is in a sense trivial. Far more significant than the question of whether individual politicians are hypocrites on environmental issues is the question of whether the most advanced democracies can cope with the charge of hypocrisy that is likely to be leveled against them by the rest of the world, regardless of the immediate twists and turns of their electoral politics. If global warming is as bad as most scientists fear, it will require sacrifices of everyone. But it will be easy to portray the demand by developed nations like the United States or Britain for equivalent sacrifices by developing nations that have yet to enjoy the full benefits of economic growth as a kind of hypocrisy. How then will democratic politicians in the most advanced countries be able to persuade their own electorates of the sacrifices needed if the burdens of those sacrifices are not more widely shared? It will be relatively easy for democratic politicians in the West to portray politicians elsewhere in the world (particularly in China) as hypocrites if they expect the West to take a lead in adopting growth-restricting measures while the Chinese economy continues to grow apace. But it will be relatively easy for Chinese politicians to portray democratic politicians as hypocrites if they expect the rest of the world to follow their lead without taking account of the unequal states of development of the various economies. Equal sacrifices are hard to justify in an unequal world. But unequal sacrifices will be hard to justify in the democratic world. And there lies the problem.

. . . [A]t the heart of this issue lies a dilemma that the prevalence of hypocrisy poses for all forms of modern politics. Some hypocrisy seems unavoidable when it comes to environmental politics — in relation both to personal conduct, and to the behavior of different regimes that will seek to hold each other to standards that they cannot readily meet themselves — and it would be a mistake to imagine that hypocrisy must cease before any real progress can be made. Equally, however, it would be a mistake to be too sanguine about hypocrisy in this context, given its capacity to generate political conflict, and to spill over into the most destructive forms of self-deception. So we must try to distinguish between different kinds of hypocrisy, and to decide which ones are worth worrying about.

It will not be easy — nothing about political hypocrisy ever is. But a sense of historical perspective can help. Liberal societies have always attracted accusations of hypocrisy from the outside, because of their failure to live up to their own standards. But . . . liberal politics, and liberal political theory, have the advantage that they are able to probe the gaps between political appearance and political reality. . . . [It is only,] as Hobbes says, when hypocrisy deprives us of our ability to see what is at stake in our political life, [that] it still has the capacity to ruin everything for everyone.

NOTES AND QUESTIONS

1. Runciman draws a distinction between "first order hypocrisy," the practice of "concealing vice as virtue," and "second order hypocrisy," the practice of "concealing the truth about this practice." It is the latter conduct that he finds troubling: "[W]e may need to hide the truth about ourselves in order to get by in this world, but we oughtn't to hide the truth from ourselves that this is what we are doing."[22] Is that a useful distinction? Think of examples of political hypocrisy that you find most offensive. Were they first order or second order? How much do you think it matters to the public?

2. Consider John Edwards's much-mocked $400 haircuts during the 2008 presidential campaign. Following a YouTube video of him fussing with hair and makeup, to the tune of "I Feel Pretty," Edwards reimbursed his campaign $800 for two Beverly Hills salon visits while insisting that he did not know how much they cost.[23] His gesture did little to quiet critics. As Maureen Dowd noted in the *New York Times*, "[S]omeone who aspires to talk credibly about [poverty and] the two Americas can't lavish on his locks what working families may spend on electricity in a year. You can't sell earnestness while indulging in decadence."[24] As Dowd also noted, Edwards at the time was living in a 28,000-square-foot North Carolina mansion with a basketball court, squash court, and swimming pool. Did that also undermine his ability to speak credibly about poverty? High-profile politicians and their families are routinely coached to give up preferences that seem too upscale. John Kerry's windsurfing did not poll well. Does that suggest a public ambivalence about authenticity? Voters demand that candidates look like "one of us" and then are disappointed when the pretense is revealed. Is that public

response productive? Do charges of hypocrisy serve to discourage wealthy leaders from running for office or from taking politically progressive positions?

3. For leaders, is the issue hypocrisy, symbolism, or some combination? Consider the criticism of First Lady Michelle Obama for heading to a five-star European beach resort with a cavalcade of taxpayer-subsidized staff and security agents, even as most of the country was "pinching pennies" and "sliding into a double-dip depression" and the president was "campaigning against the excesses of the rich." If Obama had wanted an ocean vacation, why not the Gulf coast, where she and her daughters could have "cleaned a few pelicans"?[25] Jay Leno quipped that Obama had a new book out: "Spain on $75,000 a day."[26] Is such criticism fair? When asked to comment on the expenditure, part of which was financed by taxpayers, White House advisor David Axelrod responded that "[f]olks in the public eye are also human" and should not have to defer all the opportunities that come with office.[27] Is that an adequate response? To what extent should prominent leaders' families be subject to public accountability? When John Kerry was charged with hypocrisy for owning two SUVs while preaching conservation, he responded that they belonged "not to me personally but to my family." Was that a sufficient defense?[28]

4. How would you evaluate the claims of hypocrisy leveled against leaders whose personal conduct is inconsistent with their pubic positions on immigration? For example, Meg Whitman, in her race for California governor, ran on a platform advocating tough sanctions for those who hire illegal immigrants. In the wake of public disclosures that she had employed an undocumented woman as her housekeeper for nearly a decade, she summarily fired the woman. Although Whitman claimed she was unaware of the woman's status, she and her husband had received correspondence from the Social Security Administration advising them of a problem.[29] Political commentator Lou Dobbs, who has been highly critical of employers who hire undocumented workers, has similarly faced charges that he has long retained such workers as gardeners and as stable hands for his daughter's show horses.[30]

5. To what extent are corporate leaders vulnerable to similar criticisms? Consider Tony Hayward, CEO of British Petroleum, whose participation in a European yachting race during the Gulf Coast oil spill disaster hastened his removal from office. In later defending his action, Hayward stated: "I hadn't seen my son for three months. I was on the boat for six hours. . . . I'm not certain I'd do anything different."[31] Consider also the decision of Lloyd Blankfein, Goldman Sachs's CEO, to accept a $9 million bonus in 2009 after the company nearly imploded, and $12.6 million in 2010 despite plummeting profits.[32] Humorist Calvin Trillin wrote a poem mocking the 2009 decision, with a title borrowed from a *New York Times* headline: "Goldman Chief's $9 Million Seen by Some as Show of Restraint." One stanza ran as follows:

> But nine is surely not enough
> For living well. Things could get rough. . . .

You know (you once got sixty-eight)
That nine cannot buy real estate
That's big enough or has a view
That wouldn't just embarrass you. . . .
The yacht nine million dollars buys
Is not a yacht of any size. . . .
Here's millions more. Just nod and sign.
I'd rather show restraint. Nine's fine.[33]

Is it fine? Was Trillin's caricature fair? Does that matter?

B. WHEN DOES THE PERSONAL BECOME POLITICAL?

A related set of questions involves the relevance of individuals' personal conduct in evaluating their fitness for leadership positions. The following excerpt explores that issue in the context of political and judicial office. Although written two decades ago, the analysis remains relevant and the examples can be readily updated. To what extent does it matter whether leadership candidates used drugs, embellished their résumés, evaded the draft, solicited prostitutes, or engaged in extramarital affairs?

DEBORAH L. RHODE, "MORAL CHARACTER: THE PERSONAL
AND THE POLITICAL"

10 Loyola University of Chicago Law Journal (1988-1989),
pp. 3-6 and 13-16

Those who support broad inquiries into moral character [for those in leadership] . . . positions generally make two claims. The first is that [individuals such as politicians and judges] occupy positions of public trust. To safeguard the interests of society in general and those of . . . litigants, and constituents in particular, it is critical to screen out candidates who are likely to abuse their positions. Given the difficulties of ousting incumbents or of rectifying the injury they cause, some preliminary inquiry into honesty, integrity, and moral judgment seems advisable to prevent harm before it occurs. Character cannot always be compartmentalized and the qualities that individuals display in their personal lives may spill over to professional relationships.

A second rationale for character inquiry involves issues of image. Those charged with making, administering, or upholding the law should not have defiled it. In order to maintain respect for legal and governmental processes, individuals holding positions of public responsibility should behave responsibly in their personal as well as their professional lives.

Of course, as subsequent discussion will suggest, there are important differences in our expectations for different offices and in our processes for moral inquiry. The degree of probity we demand in Supreme Court nominees is not what we accept in county commissioners. . . . Nevertheless, our rationales for character inquiry in all of these contexts are quite similar and they are vulnerable on several grounds.

A threshold difficulty involves the marginal relevance of much of the information that emerges from inquiries by . . . political journalists. Underlying these inquiries is the assumption that character reflects consistent personality traits, and that individuals who exhibit dishonesty or disrespect for law in one context will do so in another. Yet a vast array of social science research suggests that this assumption is, to a large extent, a "figment of our aspirations." Contextual factors play a critical role in shaping moral behavior and little correlation is apparent between seemingly similar character traits, such as lying and cheating. Even slight changes in situational variables can substantially affect tendencies toward deceit. For example, studies of students indicate that it is impossible to predict cheaters in French from cheaters in math.

If we cannot reliably make those sorts of predictions, it is hard to defend the far more attenuated inferences that underlie character assessments in . . . political campaigns. It is doubtful that any systematic study would confirm a frequent reaction to the Gary Hart affair, which was that anyone who would lie to his wife would find it easier to lie to voters with "whom he has a less intimate relationship." Whatever else one may say about infidelity in marriage, history does not disclose it to be a particularly accurate predictor of infidelity to constituents. Compare, for example, Richard Nixon and Franklin Delano Roosevelt. It is equally implausible to expect a close connection between performance in office and much of the other character information that emerged during recent judicial and political investigations. Such information included [presidential candidate] Bruce Babbitt's use of marijuana in college; [evangelical leader] Pat Robertson's efforts to disguise the illegitimacy of his son's birth decades ago; [vice presidential candidate] Dan Quayle's fraternity antics; [and Supreme Court nominee] Robert Bork's choices in home video rentals. . . .

The costs of this form of "character" inquiry are not born by candidates and their families alone. Society also suffers when its choices for leadership narrow to those willing to put their entire life histories on public display. Under the watchful eye of reporters scrambling for a scoop, most biographies will reveal something that is frayed around the ethical edges. Our nation has a limited supply of saints, and it is unclear how many will be willing and able to withstand our lengthening journalistic gauntlets.

Even more troubling is the risk that this kind of character scrutiny will deflect attention from more serious issues. As it is, the public's attention span is limited, and stories about sex are inevitably more sexy than those about farm price supports. Even after San Antonio's highly regarded mayor, Henry Cisneros, had withdrawn his candidacy for elective office, new revelations of his adultery eclipsed discussion of his administration's performance. Front page coverage focused on whether Dan Quayle whispered sweet nothings in the ear of then lobbyist and later *Playboy* model, Paula Parkinson. Of far less interest was Quayle's undistinguished Senate performance, his questionable Congressional campaign tactics, and his subordination of political responsibilities to personal interests. Similarly, a number of facts about

[Supreme Court nominee] Douglas Ginsburg's professional conduct raised serious ethical questions, including his affidavits concerning prior trial experience and his insensitivity to potential conflicts of interest while an official in the Justice Department. But it was marijuana use that captured public attention and prompted a series of true confessions by political candidates about their student smoking behavior. At the same time media leaders were dismissing such revelations as gratuitous, a national opinion poll reported that over a quarter of surveyed American would refuse to vote for a presidential candidate who had used marijuana in college.

Judging from recent allocations of media attention, not enough observers shared the view of one irate television talk show listener who informed [presidential candidate] Gary Hart that she was "sick of hearing about [his] sleeping habits." What bothered her was *not* hearing about his 1.4 million dollars in unpaid campaign debts. Yet that issue, as well as much of the other "character" evidence available from a fifteen year career in public service, received a tiny fraction of the attention devoted to Hart's marital infidelity. His "Monkey Business" in Bimini made page one; his tax proposals made page twenty-two. . . .

Once we license a general inquiry into candidates' personal lives, the risk is that a Gresham's law of journalism will prevail. All it takes is one reporter with a peephole perspective. As soon as a scandal breaks in any major media outlet, it becomes difficult for other members of the press to remain above the fray. The kind of "let the public decide" philosophy that currently guides character investigation encourages the media to pander to our worst instincts. To make national press conferences into open forums on adultery demeans not only candidates but ourselves. . . .

Such considerations have led some commentators to an alternative approach toward character issues, one which seeks to distinguish between the personal and the political, the private and the professional. In effect, this position is that those interested in public office or legal practice should not be subject to scrutiny for conduct that is not directly related to professional performance. Although the proper scope for character investigation may blur at the boundaries, matters such as marital infidelity or marijuana use at private gatherings should remain off limits. . . .

One example involves "womanizing," the charge leveled at Gary Hart. Underlying that allegation were two sets of objections: one went to the substance of his sexual activities, the other to the manner in which he conducted them. Although it is not clear that the two issues can be ultimately separated, both call into question the public/private boundary that some commentators have sought to establish.

Leaving aside, for the moment, the issue of the media's own conduct in investigating Hart's activities, the information that emerged was relevant to his candidacy in two respects. The first has to do with qualities of honesty and judgment that became apparent in the way Hart publicly responded to personal inquiries. Rather than refusing to discuss charges of extra-marital relationships, Hart flatly denied them and indeed challenged reporters to verify his claim. Yet once having painted a picture of marital rectitude, Hart found it difficult to sustain for even a few months, a fact that inevitably raised doubts about his judgment and self-control. Moreover, in the face of mounting evidence about his frequent contacts with model Donna Rice, Hart's denial that they had any "personal relationship" seemed inadequate to the occasion. As a *New York Times* editorial wryly inquired, "would 'political' or 'business' relationship better describe it?" However, we as individuals judge Hart's underlying conduct, his inability to predict how the public in general would assess that conduct suggests a troubling degree of moral myopia.

The lack of discretion with which Hart conducted his personal life at a critical juncture in his career raises broader concerns. In some respects, the point is reminiscent of a perhaps apocryphal but nonetheless telling anecdote about a former president of U.S. Steel. When forced to resign after his liaison with actress Lillian Russell became public, the president objected to his board of directors that he was being penalized for doing publicly what many of them did behind closed doors. To which the response was, "that's what doors are for."

But to take a harder case, suppose that Hart had been more discrete and utterly candid about his personal life and insisted that it had no bearing on his fitness for public office. In a recent interview, Yale Law School Dean Guido Calabresi maintained that while he could not approve of the conduct culminating in the Rice affair, his advice to Hart would have been to say:

> I have a problem. I have a weakness for beautiful women. It's not something I'm proud of. It's not something that's good. It's a weakness. It's made strains on my marriage. If I were to tell you I would never do that kind of thing again, that would be foolish. You never know. If that is so much of a problem for you that you cannot vote for me on it, so be it. That is what I am.

Yet to present Hart's conduct in those terms risks trivializing its significance. A habitual weakness for casual affairs is not like a weakness for chocolate. Womanizing degrades and "objectifies" women in general and can be hurtful and humiliating to one woman in particular. It signifies a lack of respect for an individual with whom one has an intimate relationship and ongoing responsibility. In an age in which divorce is publicly acceptable, an individual's choice to remain married, while repeatedly violating the commitments it is thought to entail, raises questions of his or her character. For positions involving moral leadership, those questions are relevant.

That is not to imply that such concerns should be conclusive. How a candidate treats another person in private life is not, of course, more critical than how he or she treats their concerns in a political capacity. What makes for personal goodness is not always synonymous with what makes for the common good. For the reasons indicated earlier, it would be a mistake to assume that private conduct will accurately predict public performance. Rather, my point is that when an important aspect of an important job involves expressing moral values, it makes sense to consider whether a particular individual can credibly speak for the standards we seek most to maintain. . . . In general, we expect individuals who play prominent roles in shaping or administering the law to abide by its mandates. Whatever our tolerance for hypocrisy in other contexts, we would prefer that our [judicial and governmental] leaders not — as the proverb has it — preach water and drink wine.

Again, this does not suggest that any legal violation is conclusive. Context matters. . . . [Not all] activity that arouses "gossip" warrants investigation. Public respect for the administration of justice is not necessarily enhanced by selective application of adultery or sodomy prohibitions. But neither do we want Supreme Court Justices who use illegal drugs or prominent SEC officials who batter their wives. The reason has nothing to do with attenuated inferences about professional competence. Some individuals with a weakness for marijuana might also have a flair for constitutional jurisprudence. Most of the country, however, would prefer that they exercise their talent in positions carrying less symbolic freight. . . .

NOTES AND QUESTIONS

1. As a presidential candidate, Bill Clinton engaged in a mea culpa somewhat along the lines that Calebresi suggested. During the New Hampshire primary campaign, former nightclub singer Gennifer Flowers went public with allegations that she and Clinton had engaged in a twelve-year affair and that he had assisted her search for a state job. With his wife by his side, Clinton appeared on *60 Minutes* and acknowledged having caused "pain in my marriage." He also claimed that he had already said more on the subject than any politician ever had, that he would "say no more," and that the "American people understood what [he] meant."[34] Six years later, in a deposition in Paula Jones's lawsuit for sex harassment, Clinton acknowledged having had an affair with Flowers.[35] What can we learn from that incident?

2. In the run-up to the impeachment of Clinton for lying about sex, *Hustler* magazine publisher Larry Flynt offered money for any information that would expose sexual hypocrisy by members of Congress. One victim was House Speaker Designate Robert Livingston. After calling for Clinton's resignation based on his relationship with White House intern Monica Lewinsky, Livingston faced disclosure of his own extramarital affairs, including one with a staff member and another with a lobbyist. Livingston initially denounced the attack, calling Flynt a "bottom feeder." Flynt responded, "Well, that's right. But look what I found when I got down there." In subsequently resigning his seat, Livingston explained that "I must set the example I hope President Clinton will follow."[36] In later reflecting on the resignation, Henry Hyde, chair of the House Judiciary Committee investigating Clinton, stated, "I wished [Livingston] had stuck it out. . . . I'd have liked to see an honest show of hands of members who had the same experience [of marital infidelity]. I felt it was an unnecessary waste of a good member."[37] Hyde himself had been targeted by *Salon* magazine based on an affair that he had with a hairdresser some thirty years earlier. How would you evaluate the conduct of those involved in these revelations?

3. In 2006, Congressman Mark Foley resigned after disclosures that he had sent sexually suggestive e-mails to adolescent male congressional pages. Foley had been chair of the House Caucus on Missing and Exploited Children, and had characterized Clinton's affair with Lewinsky as "vile." He added, "It's more sad than anything else, to see someone with such potential throw it all

down the drain because of a sexual addiction."[38] How relevant was Foley's hypocrisy? Could he have survived if that had not been a factor and he had pledged to undergo treatment?

4. In suggesting that South Carolina governor Mark Sanford was unfit for office because of lies about an extramarital affair, former cabinet member and conservative commentator William Bennett maintained that "[a] cheat in private is going to be a cheat in public. Someone who lies in private is going to lie in public and you can't trust someone who does that."[39] Do you agree? How would you respond to the evidence in Rhode's article suggesting that consistent character traits are a "figment of our aspirations"? Do comparisons between presidents who were models of marital fidelity (Richard Nixon, Ronald Reagan, Jimmy Carter, and George W. Bush) and those who were not (Franklin Delano Roosevelt, John F. Kennedy, and Bill Clinton) suggest close correlations between honesty about sex and honesty about public affairs or performance in office? Note that some evidence even suggests that presidents rated most highly by historians have also been willing to "bend the truth" in order to secure policy objectives.[40] If true, what implications follow? Under what circumstances does politicians' personal conduct become a matter of public concern?

C. THE PARADOX OF POWER: THE CORROSION OF JUDGMENT

Leadership scandals invite public attention not only because they offer the perverse pleasure of seeing the mighty fallen but also because they often present such a curious paradox. How can leaders who seem so smart in other aspects of their lives be so clueless in the matters that often cost them their positions? Why do such ambitious individuals risk so much for what seem relatively inconsequential rewards? Social scientists label this the paradox of power and suggest that much of the explanation lies in the cognitive biases and structural conditions noted earlier: leaders' tendencies to see themselves as unique and invulnerable, and to have those perceptions reinforced by the perks and deference that accompany powerful positions.[41] In the following excerpt, Stanford Business School professor Roderick Kramer explores these dynamics among corporate executives, and identifies some strategies for leaders who otherwise might find themselves tottering toward an abyss.

RODERICK KRAMER, "THE HARDER THEY FALL"

Harvard Business Review 81(10) (Oct. 2003):58-66

The past decade may well be remembered as the era of the bold, high-flying, "sky's the limit" leader. Throughout the 1990s, our society seemed to have a fetish for aggressive chiefs like Enron's Kenneth Lay, Tyco's Dennis Kozlowski, and WorldCom's Bernard Ebbers. These corner-office titans graced the covers of business magazines, and the public seemed fascinated with their willingness to flout the rules and break from the corporate herd with incredible daring and flair. But like Icarus, they flew too high. Scandal set in, and these once feted and envied leaders found themselves falling hard and fast. Other admired leaders — not just in business but also in politics, religion, and the media — are finding themselves in a similar free fall. One moment they are masters of their domain. The next they are on the pavement looking up, wondering where it all went wrong.

At first glance, the Lays, Kozlowskis, and Ebberses of the world are unlikely candidates for such swift and ignoble falls. In their brilliant and rapid ascents, "star" leaders repeatedly demonstrate the intelligence, resourcefulness, and drive to go the distance. They prove adept at overcoming whatever obstacles they encounter along the way. And they display a dazzling ability to woo investors, enchant employees, and charm the media with their charisma, grandiose visions, and seemingly unlimited strategic acumen. Yet just when they appear to have it all, these A-list performers demonstrate uncharacteristic lapses in professional judgment or personal conduct. . . .

[This article explores] what I like to call the *genius-to-folly syndrome* — a swift and steady rise by a brilliant, hard-driving, politically adept individual followed by surprising stints of miscalculation or recklessness. Why do so many individuals seem to fall prey to stunning bouts of folly once they seize power? Attributing it to personal failings or lack of moral fiber seems too glib — after all, wouldn't the flaws have emerged earlier in the leaders' careers? As a psychologist and consultant to many businesses, I've spent most of my career researching the process of getting to the top. . . . I've found that there is something about the pursuit of power that often changes people in profound ways. Indeed, to get to the apex of their profession, individuals are often forced to jettison certain attitudes and behaviors — the same attitudes and behaviors they need for survival once they get to the top. During the high-tech boom, we saw risk-taking and rule-breaking as markers of good leadership. As a result, we often ended up with leaders who lacked the prudence, sense of proportion, and self-restraint needed to cope with the trappings of power.

Winner Wants All

In any attractive professional domain — be it Silicon Valley, Washington, or Hollywood — there are lots of extremely smart and ambitious individuals vying for just a few top slots. Moving up the ranks can be like competing in a high-stakes tournament: As you make it through successive rounds, the pool of worthy candidates narrows, the margin for error is much smaller, and the competition intensifies. This winnowing process means just a handful of people will attain prominence or success. In some contests — such as those for CEO of a major corporation, head of a mainstream motion picture studio, dean of an elite law school, or president of the United States — there can be only one winner.

Researchers Robert Frank and Philip Cook have characterized such tournaments as "winner-take-all markets" — a very few star performers generate most of the value and *end* up enjoying the lion's share of the spoils. I interviewed leaders from the worlds of business, politics, and entertainment and found that the intense competition in these winner-take-all markets creates players who suffer from a "winner-wants-all" mind-set. These elite performers expect everything—but often end up with nothing.

There are many explanations for this. For a start, because there are so many talented, determined people competing for just one top slot, the players in winner-take-all markets must be extraordinarily aggressive about taking risks . . . [and] willing to act quickly on those impulses—often before there is time for adequate reflection. "It's a very steep climb in [Hollywood]—and a fast one. You have to seize every handhold that appears and learn to take advantage of it instantly," one former film studio executive told me. "If you lean back on your ropes to look up and ponder the risks, the moment may be gone." Indeed, the most ambitious and competitive players in winner-take-all markets often perceive that introspection is antithetical to success. As a result, these individuals develop a dangerous aversion to moderation.

Rules Are for Fools

Another conspicuous feature of the winner-wants-all mind-set has to do with individuals' attitudes about the rules of the game. Many players in winner-take-all markets believe that getting ahead means doing things differently from ordinary people—for instance, finding a back door to success that others have not been smart enough to spot.

Consider the case of legendary African-American entrepreneur Reginald Lewis. At the time of his death at age 50 from a brain tumor, Lewis had earned a spot on *Forbes's* list of the 400 wealthiest Americans, with a net worth estimated at around $400 million. More than 2,000 people attended his funeral, including former presidents Ronald Reagan and Bill Clinton as well as U.S. Secretary of State Colin Powell and entertainer Bill Cosby. Lewis not only orchestrated one of the biggest leveraged buyouts of his era, he also gave away millions, including $3 million to Harvard Law School. In his eulogy for Lewis, Cosby said, "We are all dealt a hand to play in this game of life, and believe me, Reg Lewis played the hell out of his hand."

But Lewis started life with a weak hand. The cards didn't get better until he came up with some new rules to play by. As an undergraduate at Virginia State, Lewis decided that a degree from Harvard Law School was just what he needed to get started on the path to prominence. But given his relatively undistinguished background, it was far from clear that he would be admitted to Harvard. Then he learned about a new Rockefeller Foundation–funded program at the law school that was aimed at minority students. Lewis devised a strategy to get into the program. In his own words, "First, have a tremendous final year in college. Second, know the objectives of the program. Third, break your ass over the summer, eliminate all distractions. Prove that you can compete. Do the job." These were the standards Lewis had set for himself, and he excelled, impressing everyone he met with his enthusiasm, intelligence, self-confidence, ambition, and hard work.

Unfortunately, there was a fly in the ointment. In setting up the summer program, Harvard had established a strict prohibition against using it as an entree into the law school. Undaunted by what seemed like yet another closed door, Lewis tirelessly started knocking on other doors, pitching himself as the ideal candidate for Harvard Law to anyone who would listen. Ultimately, it paid off. Lewis received a personal invitation to meet with the school's dean of admissions. And whatever was said during that meeting, it worked. Lewis became a member of the first-year class without even having filled out an application. He was reputedly the first person in the 148-year-history of Harvard Law ever admitted *before* he had applied.

People like Lewis are not the exception in high-stakes games; they are often the ones who win. Consider the case of David Geffen, cofounder of Dream-Works and currently worth an estimated $3.8 billion. When Geffen managed to wangle an entry-level job in the mail room at the William Morris Agency early in his career, he learned to his dismay that all employees had to provide proof of a college degree before they could advance. Geffen hadn't graduated from college. But unwilling to be held back by the facts, he dissembled on his application form that he had graduated from UCLA. When he learned that his employer would do a routine check on his credentials, Geffen got to work early every morning to intercept the incoming mail. When the letter from UCLA finally arrived, Geffen trashed it and replaced it with a forged letter indicating that he had indeed graduated from the university.

Lewis and Geffen broke the rules—and were deemed resourceful and enterprising by their bosses and peers, rather than immoral or criminal. Indeed, many players in winner-take-all markets believe that breaking the rules is not only necessary for getting ahead, it is virtually an act of creativity. "The rules are meant to be broken," one major automotive executive told me. "If you aren't willing to test the limits of what's acceptable and what works . . . you'll never make it to that next level of performance or attainment." An executive from the petroleum industry echoed that sentiment: "If you're too afraid of stepping over the foul line, you'll never figure out how close to it you can get."

Unfortunately, this disdain for the rules puts risk-taking leaders on a very slippery slope. They may consider themselves exempt from the rules that govern other people's behavior. Even more dangerous, leaders who want it all and who break the rules to get it often develop contempt for those who *do* play by the rules. Those who follow the letter of the law are seen as timid and unimaginative conformists who "just don't get it." As one advertising executive put it, "Frankly, it's hard to respect individuals who plod along by just following the rules." A highly successful Hollywood agent told me several years ago— and the quote seems ironic today—"If you want to follow all the rules, become an accountant. You'll be happier and live longer." It doesn't take too much imagination to see how, taken to the extreme, such attitudes foster the sort of can-do—yet ultimately dysfunctional—corporate cultures we observed in troubled companies such as Enron, Tyco, and WorldCom.

A Hefty Price Tag

Big-time success usually comes only after enormous sacrifice, and leaders who've made Faustian bargains on the way up are acutely aware of just how much they've invested to reach their goal. In my interviews, many people recounted in vivid detail the painful tradeoffs they had made. Consider a woman I'll call Carolyn Sears, a successful, 56-year-old executive vice president for a large multinational firm. In her mid-30s, Sears walked away from a marriage that no longer seemed right, abandoning her two-year-old daughter in the process. "It was impossible at [my company] to be on the promotion track and the mommy track at the same time. So I gave custody of my daughter to my husband and moved out," Sears says. "It was one of the most painful things I've ever done, but I just was not willing at that time to let all of this *Ozzie and Harriet* stuff slow me down or hold me back."

To the individual with a winner-wants-all mind-set, such sacrifices are the price of admission to the top. But making those sacrifices renders the leader extremely vulnerable to the heady effects of power's rewards. Leaders who've "made it" suddenly have to start coping with lavish expense accounts, travel in corporate jets, and a plethora of other compensations. Beyond these are innumerable social perks. Leaders find that their presence is desired at glamorous social gatherings. Influential foundations and boards court them. The media seek out their views. Other people, including the rich and famous, treat these newly arrived leaders as equally important members of the in crowd. And as Henry Kissinger once pointed out, "Power is the ultimate aphrodisiac." . . .

But as enjoyable as they can be, the trappings of power only serve to feed the dangerous illusions people already have about themselves. Decades of psychological research on self-enhancing illusions suggest that most people have highly (and overly) positive views of their abilities. Most people, for example, believe they are better-than-average drivers, lovers, and leaders. Without the steadying influence of a robust personal life and a network of friends who can help you maintain a healthy perspective, easy access to corporate jets and unlimited expense accounts turns those unrealistic beliefs into certain knowledge, resulting in a potentially fatal overconfidence. "Looking back on it, my judgment was often terribly wrong," said one young entrepreneur who had burned through more than $20 million trying to launch a Web-based business. "Unfortunately, I was never in doubt."

The sacrifices an individual makes on the way to the top not only make it harder to cope with the rewards when they do come, they also make the person greedier for more of the same. Indeed, getting more becomes "just deserts" for having paid such a high price for success. According to one report, former Tyco CEO Dennis Kozlowski spent millions on art and elaborate home furnishings. He allegedly charged to his company purchases of a $15,000 umbrella stand, a $17,000 traveling toilette box, a $5,900 set of bed sheets, and a $2,200 wastebasket. However easy it may be for leaders to rationalize such an exaggerated sense of entitlement, they create trouble for themselves when their indulgences become too out of sync with what other people believe is right or fair. While followers will experience obvious pleasure in seeing their beloved leaders work their way up the ranks, they will also get equal satisfaction out of seeing them brought down a notch. This malicious gloating over another's misfortune is such a universal feeling that there are words for it in both German *(schadenfreude)* and Chinese *(xing zai le huo)*.

The Sins of Omission

It's not only what new leaders *do* when they get to the top that gets them into trouble; it's also what they *don't* do. They get distracted by all the temptations — and often abandon the practices that helped them capture the crown. They may spend less time, for example, conscientiously monitoring their environments. They may pay less attention to what others around them are thinking or doing—especially their critics and potential enemies.

Of course, like everyone else, leaders like to have the positive images they have of themselves reflected back. But then, leaders are in a unique position: Their followers are keen to praise and defend the person on whom their livelihood depends. Most executives don't question this ingratiating behavior as much as they should. After all, even if they recognize their subordinates' ingratiation as slightly exaggerated, leaders like to think there is at least a kernel of truth to the nice things other people are saying about them. Thus, despite their best intentions, leaders may find that every mirror held up to them says, in effect, you *are* the fairest of them all.

One might think that reality would splash a little cold water now and then on leaders' splendid illusions. At the very least, one would expect some high-ranked lieutenant or trusted adviser to sound the alarm. In fact, this rarely happens because close subordinates are often more deferential to leaders than lower-ranked employees are. The people who most closely surround a leader often occupy a precarious perch, and they often don't want to risk their place by being labeled a disloyal doubter or naysayer. Thus, paradoxically, at the same time that people serving the leader are paying such close attention to every wrinkle on the leader's brow, they also tend to look the other way whenever he or she does something unseemly. "I can remember being in meetings where people's faces were absolutely impassive when the CEO said something truly stupid," one financial services executive told me. "But I have to confess, my face was just as impassive as everyone else's."

How to Have It All

A lauded leader can indeed succumb to recklessness once power has been achieved. But not all executives lose their footing. The behaviors and values of the leaders I interviewed who got to the top and managed to stay there are quite similar. They had different personalities and management styles, but they all seemed to retain a remarkable sense of proportion and displayed a high degree of self-awareness. When I asked them how they had been able to remain effective for so long, I learned that each had developed a certain combination of psychological and behavioral habits that helped them stay grounded.

Keep your life simple. "It helps to remain *awfully* ordinary," one CEO told me. . . . Such normal behavior may seem lackluster, but it helps leaders stay in touch with themselves and with other ordinary people, including their customers and employees. Indeed, if high-flying leaders hope to stay on top, they would do well to nurture their humility. It helps people view their accomplishments, and their foibles, with detachment. It also helps people to see adversity through a healthy lens. The best way of developing humility is to remind ourselves of what really matters in life. Take it from Warren Buffett. When asked how he learned to handle his enormous power and wealth, he said, "I live now the way I lived 30 years ago."

Hang a lantern on your foibles. Few leaders manage to reach the top and remain there very long without suffering from some occasional blunders.

We all have shortcomings, and they always interfere to some extent. The natural tendency with flaws and imperfections is to deny them or cover them up. But what we really need to do is to shine a light on our weaknesses to understand them better. What's more, acknowledging our shortcomings or mistakes helps to prevent others from punishing us too much for those failures. After the Bay of Pigs, for example, President Kennedy accepted full responsibility for the disastrous operation, and his popularity soared higher than ever. Kennedy was also famous for using humor to shine a light on his flaws. Responding to charges that his father was using personal funds to help his son win the 1960 presidential election, Kennedy quipped, "I just received the following wire from my generous daddy: 'Dear Jack, don't buy a single vote more than is necessary. I'll be damned if I'm going to pay for a landslide.'" Humor is an especially effective tool for acknowledging our flaws because it communicates vulnerability while, at the same time, indicates we are in control.

Float trial balloons. All the leaders I've studied who have thrived in power engage in a great deal of reality testing. They check and recheck the information they receive, they review their assumptions about that information, and they do it often. . . . Floating trial balloons helps leaders uncover the truth and prepares them for the unexpected — especially when mindful scrutinization of the business environment becomes a natural part of a leader's routine. One CFO at a large company noted, "We try to do a full sweep with our radar on a regular basis. I don't see how you can do your job as a leader responsibly in today's business environment without worrying about everything."

Sweat the small stuff. Some self-help books exhort people not to sweat the small stuff, and in many arenas of life, that's sound advice. But when it comes to running a film studio, a country, or a company, leaders *do* need to sweat the small stuff. They need to worry about what might be ahead so they can anticipate what might go wrong. In business particularly, sweating the small stuff is important because leaders often stumble on the little things. Indeed, sometimes it's only a small misstep that takes you from the fast track to total derailment. Perhaps the most famous practitioner of "sweating the small stuff" is former Intel CEO Andrew Grove, who explained it this way: "I believe in the value of paranoia. I worry about products getting screwed up, and I worry about products getting introduced prematurely. I worry about factories not performing well, and I worry about having too many factories. I worry about hiring the right people, and I worry about morale slacking off. And, of course, I worry about competitors. I worry about other people figuring out how to do what we do better or cheaper and displacing us with our customers."

Reflect more, not less. Successful leaders strive to become more reflective. That's paradoxical given that today's business culture celebrates action over hesitancy. Americans in particular admire leaders who break new ground, transform industries, and smash glass ceilings. Given this overemphasis on *doing*, perhaps it's not surprising that many of the fallen leaders I studied appeared to have a strikingly impoverished sense of self. Though they often know how to read others brilliantly, they remain curiously oblivious to many of their own tendencies that expose them to risk. When Bill Clinton was interrogated about his relationship with Monica Lewinsky, for example, he made the startling disclosure that he assumed all along that Monica would tell some of her friends about what was going on. Perhaps he should have spent a little more time reflecting about which friends — and with what consequences. John Reed, former CEO of Citibank, may harbor a similar regret. In 1999, his company entered into a merger with Travelers Group to form the behemoth Citigroup. Reed and Travelers' Sanford Weill were to lead the venture as co-CEOs — but there was only room for one at the top. Reed quickly found himself outmaneuvered and eventually ousted by the bold and resourceful Weill.

. . . Decades of research in the behavioral sciences suggests that people aren't good at predicting how they will be influenced by strong situations. My own research reinforces that idea. The process of getting to the top almost always changes people in ways they don't anticipate or appreciate. That lack of self-awareness seems to be part of the human condition, and if my work with MBA students is any indication, we shouldn't expect it to change anytime soon.

Each year, to encourage my students to become more mindful of the effects that success and power might have on their behavior as future business leaders, I ask them to write their obituaries. I encourage them to be as realistic as possible. Given the high caliber of these students, it is hardly surprising that most imagine their lives copiously filled with significant achievements. They expect to become CEOs, philanthropists, best-selling authors, and the like. The personal lives they accord themselves are no less spectacular. They describe large, happy families, wonderful vacations at summer and winter retreats, and a full complement of personal accomplishments. But when I ask the students to estimate how the process of attaining those achievements will change them, they rather uniformly report "very little" or "not at all." They don't expect, for example, their core values to change. Strikingly, they anticipate having to make few, if any, trade-offs in the pursuit of professional and personal success. Miraculously, they argue, they will manage to have it all.

When I ask respondents to explain why they think the process of experiencing great success will not change them in any fundamental way, they typically say something along the lines of, "Because I know what kind of person I am." These nascent leaders believe their personal characters and core values will buffer them from any temptation or travail that might be thrown at them on their paths to power. It is as if in finding success they will become merely bigger and better versions of what they are now. They can't even imagine that they could ever fall from grace. And that, of course, guarantees that some of them will. . . .

Recognizing the Symptoms of Reckless Leadership

When I talk to business executives and government leaders about the genius-to-folly syndrome, one of the questions I am asked most frequently is: "How will I know I'm in danger of falling?" There is no universal set of early warning signs, but there are some useful questions leaders can routinely ask themselves to find out how close to the precipice they really are. Just as shrewd leaders use accounting audits to see how financially healthy their organizations are, so too can they use *personal leader audits* to find out how robust their leadership is and to assess whether they are drifting toward disaster. These audits can help leaders reflect on the consequences of their actions. The questions might include the following:

Are you spending most of your time plugging holes and papering over cracks? In organizations headed for disaster, the leader has lost sight of the big picture. Instead, her attention is often myopically focused on staving off imminent disaster. Substantive problems are swept under the rug or pushed out of mind as she spends every waking moment obsessively focused on putting the best spin on the latest bad news, cleverly hiding any corporate blemishes. This frenetic sleight of hand is usually accompanied by the leader's rationalization that she is simply buying time and will get to the big fixes later. If you relentlessly find yourself hoping tomorrow will be a better day, maybe you should change what you are doing right now. How do you respond to those annoying, dissenting voices in your organization? In almost every instance of leadership folly I've studied, one or more individuals in the organization recognized trouble was brewing and earnestly tried to alert the CEO to the dangers. Instead of applause, however, they got tomatoes. As a result, these good corporate citizens swallowed their whistles instead of blowing them. Even worse, many fled from what they viewed as a sinking ship. Leaders should think long and hard about how they—and those closest to them—really respond to the bearers of bad news.

Who can you really trust to tell you the emperor has no clothes? It's great to have a chorus of loyal aides and advisers who march to your orders. But you also need someone to let you know when the team is marching toward an abyss. Bill Gates—a man who clearly knows his own mind and who has all the brainpower one could ask for—has Steve Ballmer to bounce ideas off of and to provide those much-needed reality checks. "We trusted each other from the beginning in a very deep way," Gates says. Having a doubting Thomas (or Ballmer) is especially important because those leaders most prone to recklessness and folly are often too adept at creating an organizational world that reflects their own optimistic values and forward-charging inclinations. It's critical for such leaders to have someone who can speak up and give them an honest assessment of the situation. Not having such a person on your staff—or in your life—is one of the first signs that you may be getting dangerously isolated and insulated.

Do you have illusions of grandeur? In the humorous film *Defending Your Life*, Albert Brooks's character finds himself forced to witness and defend the many misdeeds of his life, including his acts of hubris, selfishness, and cowardice. Ideally, none of us will ever have to answer for our actions in such a demanding court. However, in the personal audit it definitely helps to ask yourself, "Has my behavior changed since I became chief?" Have you grown so important that virtually everyone you know cowers before you or defers to your every whim and demand? Are you sometimes wrong but never in doubt? Be honest. If you can answer yes to any of these queries, you are in danger of becoming grandiose.

Are you too greedy for your own good? It's difficult for most of us to think of ourselves as greedy. We all know how hard we've worked to get to the top. Yet if there is one hallmark of the winner-wants-all mind-set, it's the acquisitive instinct gone wild. The relentless, competitive quest for more power and status becomes an end in itself. The real problem begins when the appetite to acquire more comes to dominate every decision. Suddenly, we not only want it all. We actually feel entitled to it all. This can happen all too easily given the human propensity to take for granted things that were previously benchmarks of progress or success. The alert leader tries to combat his greediness by giving something back to society.

Is this a good time to pause, consider doing something different, or even do nothing at all? This is a simple question to ask, but one of the hardest to answer — especially in moments when we seem in full control of our destiny, and there isn't a cloud in the sky. Many of the fallen leaders I've studied stumbled just when the waters seemed calmest. So sometimes slowing the pace or even calling a time-out to reassess your path may be the best strategy of all. . . .

NOTES AND QUESTIONS

1. Have you ever observed symptoms of reckless leadership in yourself or others? What were the causes? What responses were, or would have been, most effective?
2. Consider one of the leadership scandals described in the preceding materials or in recent news coverage. What factors contributed to the misconduct? Could they have been averted through interventions of the sort that Kramer describes?
3. Consistent with Kramer's analysis, other research suggests that the narcissism of CEOs correlates with greater risk taking and more volatile economic performance by their organizations (more big wins and losses).[42] What implications does that hold for improving leader performance?
4. Social scientists often suggest that the best response to the paradox of power is transparency: an active board of directors, government regulators, or consumer watchdogs who remind leaders that they are being monitored. In effect, the corner office needs windows.[43] If that is true, what might promote such oversight? Are scandals sometimes necessary to prevent further scandals?

D. CRISIS MANAGEMENT: APOLOGIES AND CORRECTIVE ACTION

Leaders confront crises of reputation based on their own conduct, their organization's conduct, or some combination. Whatever the context, the most fundamental challenges are similar. A case in point involves Mike Brown, the director of FEMA, the federal agency responsible for disaster relief efforts following hurricane Katrina. Expressing widely shared views, one commentator noted that Brown had handled the situation "perfectly, except for understanding what was happening and actually doing something about it."[44] The quip captures the essential tasks of crisis management: gaining a full appreciation of the causes and consequences of the situation and formulating a response that will both address the immediate problem and prevent a recurrence.

Although the need for full information is obvious, it is often difficult or impossible to assemble before the pressures for action become overwhelming. During the BP oil spill, when Today show host Matt Lauer suggested to President Obama that he needed to "kick some butt," Obama responded that he was doing his best to find "whose ass to kick."[45] How to respond in situations of uncertainty is one of the challenges of leadership that Dezenhall and Weber discuss in the excerpt below.

Once a crisis develops, leaders have four main options in terms of public statements: (1) a denial of wrongdoing, (2) a refusal to comment, (3) an expression of sympathy or regret (often termed a partial apology or non-apology apology), or (4) a full apology accepting responsibility. Each strategy has its advantages and limitations.

Denials take multiple forms. Leaders may claim that:

- No wrongful act occurred ("I did not have sex with that woman");
- "Mistakes were made" but not by me or my organization (I didn't know, a subsidiary or supplier is accountable for defects, customers were negligent);
- The acts were attributable to a rogue employee or a few bad apples, and were not typical of the organization.[46]

In some instances, those accused of wrongdoing may also attempt to reclaim the moral high ground by accusing their accusers of improper tactics or motivations. Richard Nixon, in his famous "Checkers speech," saved his spot on the vice presidential ticket by painting himself as the innocent victim of a political vendetta. After denying that he had misused a special campaign fund, he detailed his modest financial status and acknowledged having accepted only one gift from a Republican contributor—a cocker spaniel named Checkers that he refused to return because his daughters loved the dog so much.[47]

If they are credible, denials are typically the most effective response in a scandal, particularly if the conduct involves integrity.[48] Part of the reason is that when evaluating ethical behavior, people tend to weigh negative acts more heavily than positive acts, so any statement that suggests moral culpability will be hard to remedy.[49] So too, if the conduct could create legal liability, investors are likely to respond negatively to anything other than a denial.[50] However, if the facts are not strong enough to support a denial, or at least to create reasonable doubts, a refusal to acknowledge responsibility is counterproductive. When wrongdoing seems clearly to have occurred, the public expects conciliatory statements and corrective action. Excuses or denials under these circumstances fuel anger because they compound the misconduct and suggest the likelihood of future abuses.[51]

In the face of conflicting or unfavorable information, a *New Yorker* cartoon captures the relevant trade-off. It pictures a corporate meeting in which the chair says, "Let's never forget that the public's desire for transparency has to be balanced by our need for concealment."[52] Refusals to comment are a common strategy for striking that balance when leaders believe that evidence of culpability is unlikely to surface; the risks of creating potential liability for themselves or others are too great; more time is necessary to gain information; or the issues are so personal that full disclosure seems unwarranted.

However, in terms of public relations, the evidence available suggests that silence is usually the least effective option. It is less reassuring than denial, because it fails to disclaim guilt, or than apology, because it fails to signal remorse and promise corrective action.[53] If the goal is to convince others to withhold judgment, silence seldom succeeds, particularly when it is coupled with other evidence of culpability. A representative example involved Merrill Lynch's recommendation of stocks that analysts characterized in e-mails as "dogs," "trash," and "piece of s—." The purpose of the endorsements was to retain banking business from issuers of these stocks. To settle charges, the firm paid a $100 million fine without admitting misconduct. But as then New York Attorney General Eliot Spitzer pointedly noted, "You don't pay a $100 million fine if you didn't do anything wrong."[54]

Partial apologies that express sympathy without acknowledging responsibility also present trade-offs, but have higher upside potential. As common sense suggests and psychological research confirms, they are never as effective as full apologies in suggesting that the speaker is "aware of the social norms that have been violated" and therefore likely to "avoid the offense in future interactions."[55] Ritualistic apologies can also backfire. Those who utter frequent statements of regret may end up appearing weaker, less confident, and less sincere than those who do not apologize at all.[56] Yet, in some settings, expressions of sympathy are better than any alternative. If litigation is likely, acknowledging any responsibility is risky: "[E]very word used to persuade the public is a word that may be used to persuade a judge."[57] But some conciliatory statement may be necessary to avoid making the leaders or their organizations appear callous and unresponsive. Carefully crafted statements can reduce hostility, restore respect, and thus help to avoid or resolve disputes and international conflict.[58]

Full apologies are, however, more effective in defusing anger, rebuilding relationships, and encouraging confidence that the misconduct will not recur.[59] In politics, apologies by leaders have often served a largely symbolic role; they have expressed collective expiation for wrongdoing ranging from the internment of Japanese Americans to abusive practices by the Internal Revenue Service.[60] In contexts involving legal liability, apologies have reduced financial demands and the chance of lawsuits.[61] To encourage expeditious settlements, about two-thirds of states have statutes that limit or prevent the use of apologies as evidence of wrongdoing in subsequent litigation.[62] Even in cases that go to trial, apologies that accept responsibility can help mitigate guilt, and are much more likely to have a positive influence than those that simply express sympathy and remorse.[63]

The most effective apologies are ones in which leaders

- promptly acknowledge responsibility;
- are specific about the wrongs inflicted;
- convey sincere emotions;
- ask for forgiveness;

- promise not to repeat the conduct; and
- indicate a desire to do what is necessary to put things right.[64]

Apologies that fall short of this ideal can still serve their intended objective. For example, in describing his own strategy for handling questions about youthful indiscretions while later campaigning for president, George W. Bush relied on advice from his pastor: "[Don't] talk about the details of [your] transgressions, but talk about what [you] have learned."[65]

Leaders can often amplify the persuasiveness of apologies through symbolic gestures. Holy Roman Emperor Henry IV set the gold standard in 1077 when apologizing to Pope Gregory VII for church-state conflicts by standing barefoot in the snow for three days.[66] Japanese leaders have perfected the contemporary equivalent. A rich literature is available to advise them on the art of the apology, complete with photographs comparing the angles of leaders' bows and tips on wardrobe. Suits in "sedate, calming colors" like black or navy are recommended.[67] So are other symbols of abasement. On the anniversary of a death of a woman killed by a Mitsubishi truck, the company held a public day of atonement involving a minute of silence, a pledge to safety, a lowering of flags to half mast, and a suspension of advertising.[68]

As that example suggests, leaders need to be aware of cultural differences in what constitutes an adequate apology. One well-documented illustration of what does and does not work comes from a 2001 accident in which an American submarine sunk a Japanese fishing boat. Apologies from the president, secretary of state, secretary of defense, and two admirals proved inadequate to the task. Victims' families expected a personal acknowledgement of grief and wrongdoing from the commander of the vessel, and his original impersonal letter of apology to the Japanese people fell short.[69] Putting the matter right ultimately entailed a 2000-page report by a naval court of inquiry, the commander's forced resignation, his tearful delivery of an apology to a Japanese consulate, his subsequent visit to victims' graves, and the United States' $60 million effort to raise the sunken ship to recover the bodies.[70]

Even in more conventional corporate settings, American leaders have begun to pay greater attention to the symbolic dimensions of apologies. In the aftermath of the highly publicized Ford Explorer rollover problems, company officials filmed their bedside apologies to a victim paralyzed from the neck down.[71] Many CEOs have internalized Woody Allen's quip that 90 percent of life is showing up. Those who have not end up paying a price. American experts lambasted Toyota CEO Akio Toyoda for failing to "get on a plane" and manage the 2010 accelerator pedal recall problem, which earned him a new nickname, "no show Akio."[72]

Even more important are what leaders promise, and deliver, in long-term correctives. Particularly in the corporate context, as CEO apologies have become more common, they have also become less effective. According to a survey of global business executives, more important strategies are fully disclosing what happened and specifying appropriate remedies.[73] In the wake of the Explorer recall, Ford reformed its policies on reporting a possible defect, and ran advertisements pledging that in the future, "When we know it, so will the world."[74] After widespread public criticism, the Red Cross reversed its initial decision to reserve half the funds it had raised for 9/11 relief efforts. Not only did its leaders publicly apologize, they offered to return any donation at the donor's request, and hired George Mitchell, a highly respected former senator and international mediator, to supervise a full and immediate distribution of the funds.[75] So too, in the aftermath of a highly publicized plagiarism scandal, the *New York Times* fired its editor, formed a task force to recommend preventative strategies, and followed up one and two years later to determine the effectiveness of those correctives.[76] It has also become increasingly common for organizations to engage critics or outside experts in the reform process, as did Tyco when retaining a Wharton School professor of corporate governance to help redesign its oversight policies.[77]

Many experts further recommend that organizations conduct reputation audits.[78] Monitoring Internet postings can catch problems before they go viral, and random surveys of consumers, employees, customers, and investors can serve as early warnings systems. Despite (and in some sense because of) their position, leaders are often insulated from negative information.[79] Subordinates may see too little to gain and too much to lose from being the bearer of unwelcome tidings. As earlier chapters suggested, leaders need to be proactive about soliciting candid information and protective of anyone who supplies it.

They should also take the opportunities that scandals sometimes supply to address fundamental problems in organizational culture. "Never waste a good crisis," was the advice that Harvard professor William George offered to Toyota following its accelerator pedal recall. This was a "unique opportunity to make fundamental changes required to restore Toyota quality."[80] Similarly, Barack Obama characterized the BP oil spill as the "most painful and powerful reminder yet that the time to embrace a clean energy future is now."[81] Boeing Aircraft's CEO James McNerney also used a scandal involving government contracting to convey the need for broader cultural change. One of his first efforts after assuming the leadership was to address top management with a PowerPoint presentation displaying two numerical sequences on large video screens. "These are not ZIP codes," he noted. They were the prison numbers of the Boeing executive and Air Force procurement officer convicted in the scandal.[82] That was a message "made to stick."[83]

PROBLEM 7-1

Consider the following apologies. Which seem most and least effective? Why?

Public Safety and Product Defects

- "I am very, very sorry that this accident occurred, very sorry. . . . And I do believe that it's right to investigate it fully and draw the right conclusion. . . . This is a complex accident, caused by an unprecedented combination of failures." Tony Hayward, CEO British Petroleum, apologizing for an explosion killing eleven people and causing a massive oil spill.[84]

- "We're sorry for the massive disruption it's caused to their lives. There's no one who wants this things over more than I do. I'd like my life back." Tony Hayward, CEO British Petroleum.[85]
- "Our lawyers tell us it's not our fault, but it sure feels like our fault and we'll do anything we can to fix it." BP executive, following oil spill off San Diego.[86]
- "I myself, as well as Toyota, am not perfect. At times, we do find defects. But in such situations we always stop, strive to understand the problem, and make changes to improve further. . . . It has taken us too long to come to grips with a rare but serious set of safety issues, despite all of our good faith efforts." Jim Lentz, president and COO of Toyota Motor Sales, at U.S. Congressional Testimony concerning accelerator pedals.[87]
- "I come before you to apologize to you, the American people — especially to the families who have lost loved ones in these terrible rollover accidents. I also come to accept full and personal responsibility on behalf of Bridgestone/Firestone." Masatoshi Ono, CEO Bridgestone/Firestone, at a congressional testimony in 2000 concerning tire malfunctions in Ford Explorers.[88]
- "What Intel continues to believe is technically an extremely minor problem has taken on a life of its own. Although Intel firmly stands behind the quality of the current version of the Pentium processor, we recognize that many users have concerns. We want to resolve these concerns." Intel executives.[89]

Politics

- "Mistakes were quite possibly made by the administrations in which I served." Henry Kissinger, responding to charges that he committed war crimes in his role as Secretary of State overseeing actions in Vietnam, Cambodia, and South America in the 1970s.[90]
- "This administration intends to be candid about its errors; for as a wise man once said: 'An error does not become a mistake until you refuse to correct it. . . . [The final responsibility for the failure of the Bay of Pigs invasion was] mine and mine alone." President John F. Kennedy.[91]
- "On a few occasions I have misspoken about my [military service] and I regret that and I take full responsibility. . . . I have made mistakes and I am sorry. I truly regret offending anyone." Richard Blumenthal, Connecticut Attorney General, who fabricated military service in Vietnam during his Senate campaign.[92]
- "If it gave the impression that my military record was larger than it was I apologize. I simply misremembered it wrong." Illinois Senate candidate Mark Kirk, after revelations that he inflated his military service record.[93]
- "Bear in mind that this is a freewheeling anything-goes Internet radio show that is broadcast from a pub. It's like a political version of Saturday Night Live. Since my intended humorous context was lost in translation, I apologize. I still believe Ms. Haley is pretending to be someone she is not, much as Obama did, but I apologize to both for an unintended slur." Jake Knotts, South Carolina state senator, running for governor, after a statement concerning his primary opponent, Nikki Haley, who was

raised as a Sikh: "We already got one raghead in the White House. We don't need another in the governor's mansion."[94]

Financial Management

- "This is a painful decision for me to make after five years at H.P., but I believe it would difficult for me to continue as an effective leader. . . . As the investigation progressed, I realized that there have been instances in which I did not live up to the standards and principles of trust, respect and integrity that I have espoused at H.P." Mark Hurd, resigning as CEO of Hewlett-Packard, after revelations of a conflict of interest involving a female H-P contractor and fraudulent expense accounts totaling up to $20,000.[95]
- "Let me start by saying I'm sorry. I'm sorry that the financial crisis has had such a devastating impact for our country. I'm sorry about the millions of people, average Americans, who lost their homes. And I'm sorry that our management teams, starting with me, like so many others could not see the unprecedented market collapse that lay before us." Charles O. Prince III, former chair and CEO of Citigroup.[96]

Sex

- "It is true, as many in your country have pointed out, that the problem of child abuse is peculiar neither to Ireland nor to the church. Nevertheless the task you now face is to address the problem of abuse that has occurred within the Irish Catholic community, and to do so with courage and determination. No one imagines that this painful situation will be resolved swiftly. Real progress has been made, yet much more remains to be done. Perseverance and prayer are needed, with great trust in the healing power of God's grace. At the same time, I must also express my conviction that, in order to recover from this grievous wound, the Church in Ireland must first acknowledge before the Lord and before others the serious sins committed against defenceless children. Such an acknowledgement, accompanied by sincere sorrow for the damage caused to these victims and their families, must lead to a concerted effort to ensure the protection of children from similar crimes in the future." Pope Benedict XVI, Pastoral Letter of the Holy Father to the Catholics of Ireland, March 19, 2010.[97]

NOTES AND QUESTIONS

1. Which of these apologies might be evidence of civil or criminal liability? In his deposition in a class action lawsuit against Firestone, CEO Ono claimed that his congressional testimony did not constitute an admission of guilt. Rather, it was "a sympathy expressed for those individuals who operated vehicles using our products and got into accidents. . . . So it's not . . . an issue of a defect."[98] How do you think Ono's statements played among the American public? What about potential jurors? Ono resigned the day after his deposition, citing health reasons. In the wake of a

congressional investigation, product recall, and multiple lawsuits, Bridge-stone forecast that its 2000 profits would fall over 80 percent.

Subsequent independent investigations suggested that vehicle rollovers were attributable to a combination of faulty tire and vehicle design, as well as poor consumer care.[99] If you had been in Ono's position, and that was the information you had available at the time of the congressional hearings and depositions, what would you have said?

2. Hurd's resignation came after Jodie Fisher, a former reality TV actress and H-P contractor, claimed that he had sexually harassed her in connection with marketing events she had planned for the company. H-P's investigation revealed no basis for the claims and no evidence of a sexual relationship. It did, however, find that Hurd had violated the company's Standards of Business Conduct in submitting false expense reports, including instances where his accuser had received compensation for no business purpose. Hurd settled the claims for an undisclosed amount and received a severance package estimated at $45 to $50 million(including stock options and a $12 million immediate cash payout).

Hurd's conduct met with widespread astonishment. Ben Heineman, former GE General Counsel, captured common reactions: "I am staring at the headlines and asking, like so many others and on so many recent occasions, '[W]hat was he thinking?' "[100] Why didn't Hurd just pay for the items himself? Why didn't he take the chance she offered to settle the claim privately without it reaching the company?

The board's decision initially met with mixed reactions. *New York Times* business columnist Joe Nocera doubted that expense misstatements were, or should have been, the real reason for Hurd's resignation. "If everyone who ever fudged an expense report or flirted with an outside contractor were fired, there wouldn't be many people left in the American workforce."[101] Columbia Law School professor John Coffee noted, "If all you're concerned about is an expense account, there are other sanctions. You could have taken away his bonus for the year. Most companies would not have treated a peccadillo with this severity, particularly when it inflicts such a penalty on shareholders."[102] By contrast, others wondered how meaningful denial of a bonus would have been to someone whose take-home pay the previous year totaled about $24 million. Could Hurd have credibly enforced H-P's standards after his own violations? According to Ben Heineman, "for a CEO seeking to lead a company through word and deed—including a commitment to honest accounts . . . —the corporate death penalty that follows from violating such a standard cannot be stayed because Hurd is of great value to the company. As one of the HP investigators said, 'It had to do with integrity. . . .'"[103]

Oracle CEO Larry Ellison weighed in on the side of leniency. He lambasted the H-P board for "cowardly corporate political correctness."[104] Within a month, his company hired Hurd as Ellison's co-president. That prompted H-P to sue him for "inevitable disclosure" of trade secrets, and ultimately to settle the case for $8 million.[105]

Two months after the scandal broke, a *Wall Street Journal* investigative report revealed further details about Hurd's conduct. Fisher's letter seeking compensation claimed that Hurd had told her about a plan to acquire Electronic Data Systems Corp. before the acquisition became public. H-P investigators also revealed inconsistencies between what Hurd told the board and what the record showed. For example, Hurd initially claimed that he did not know Fisher well and was unaware of her prior career in adult movies. However, investigation revealed that he had visited Web pages showing her in pornographic scenes and that he had dined with her privately on many occasions, including several that involved no H-P event. The circumstances of her hiring also raised concerns. Normally, a CEO would not twice personally interview a person with no relevant experience for a minor position.[106]

Why do you suppose that H-P did not reveal these details of its investigative report at the time it terminated Hurd? Rather, the General Counsel simply cited his "profound lack of judgment," and the company gave him a generous severance package.[107]

Suppose that Hurd had been forthcoming with the board about his relationship with Fisher, and had offered to repay the expenses and settle her claims privately. If you had been General Counsel, would you have recommended that he be allowed to retain his position? Consider the research summarized in Chapter 5, suggesting a link between leaders' ethics and employee conduct?[108] If you had been on the board, how would you have balanced Hurd's ability to generate short-term profit increases averaging 18 percent a year, which doubled stock prices, against his ethical lapses in this case and in the pretexting scandal discussed in Chapter 3?[109] How would you have recommended handling publicity surrounding the event? What considerations would affect your decision? What advice might damage control experts Dezenhall and Weber have provided in light of the views expressed below?

Eric Dezenhall and John Weber, Damage Control: Why Everything You Know about Crisis Management Is Wrong

(New York: Portfolio of Penguin Group, 2008), pp. 79-92

Damage Control Means More than Having to Say You're Sorry

When they invented "I'm sorry," honor was lost.

Greek proverb

The most common question a crisis manager gets at a barbecue: "Why don't your clients just fess up and apologize?" The question is often smugly followed by, "If Nixon had just admitted 'I screwed up' and said he was sorry, the whole thing would have blown over. . . ."

Wrong. Instead of resigning and rising off into the heavens on Marine One in anticipation of a pardon, Nixon would probably have been tried in a court of law, convicted, and dragged down Pennsylvania Avenue chained to a pickup truck.

The scandal-plagued refuse to apologize because they don't think they're guilty. Sometimes they're not. Guilty or innocent, a protective enzyme kicks in that creates a barrier between one's actions and one's self-perception. No matter how wicked an individual or institution is, what's universal is the desire to be loved and respected independent of one's actions.

But a more strategic reason clients in crisis don't "fess up" is because it's often a very bad idea.

Crises have legal implications. Despite pretrial cries for Martha Stewart to apologize for her involvement in her alleged insider trading scandal, she couldn't, because in a court of law, an apology may be interpreted by a judge and jury as an admission of guilt. One cannot, after all, apologize for what one did not do. This logic applies to civil litigation as much as it does to criminal trials, which is why we see so few corporate apologies.

The tension between legal and public relations considerations should be adjudicated by the answer to one question: Would you rather be loved or acquitted? If the latter is the answer, silence is golden — especially for corporations, which are almost always seen as being guilty, not to mention irredeemable.

The apology has its practical origins in ancient Greek culture. When Plato issued his "Apologia" on behalf of Socrates, he was offering a defense, not suggesting Socrates was sorry for anything.

The mission of the apology shifted with the rise of Christianity, where winning God's love and forgiveness became the goal. In order for one to restore one's self to God's grace, one needed to convey remorse and sustain a punishment of some kind in order to demonstrate that a valuable lesson had been learned. Reparations then needed to be made to the injured parties, to God. In Catholicism particularly, confessions occur privately with a cleric, so it's possible that one can return to God's good graces without a media advisor.

Not so in the court of public opinion. Public apologies can come, at a very high price, such as when former New Jersey governor James McGreevey announced in 2004 that he was gay and then resigned when allegations surfaced that he had appointed a purported love interest to a government job. The good news was that the story quickly evaporated. The bad news was that McGreevey was out of a job.

The Transactional Apology

In crisis management, an apology is a transaction whereby the accused humbles himself in exchange for mercy. It is offered as a gesture marking the end of the play, the final encore permitting the audience to go home, the turning of the proverbial page so that a new chapter can begin. It most certainly does not necessarily equate with repentance or sorrow.

The contemporary apology is cheap. Everybody's doing it, from presidents to deranged ear-chomping prizefighters. The apology is the tactic du jour of the public relations industry because it is seen as a way for the mighty to show human qualities. The apology often stops short of confession, employing weasel words that give the apologizer immunity from the consequences of the original sin.

The key question is "Do apologies *work* as a crisis management technique?" An apology "works" when a transaction occurs whereby something small is surrendered (pride) but something of value — such as one's freedom — is preserved. Transactional apologies can be effective, but there's a catch: The *carrot* of apology works best when accompanied by the *stick* of personal exposure for the adversary. . . .

Why Three Apologies Don't Add Up to Forgiveness

On January 14, 2005, Harvard University president Lawrence Summers spoke at a conference on women in science. He was under the impression that his remarks would be off the record. This was his first mistake. His second was choosing as his subject speculation on how biological differences between men and women might account for why women aren't more successful in math and science. Outrage broke out on campus.

In a letter posted on Harvard's Web site several days later, Summers wrote, "I deeply regret the impact of my comments and apologize for having not weighed them more carefully. . . . I was wrong to have spoken in a way that was an unintended signal of discouragement to talented girls and women." Summers apologized three different times.

He wasn't forgiven.

Pointing out biological differences has a certain Third Reich whiff about it. Saying, for example, that blacks predominate in athletics is perceived as a backhanded way of saying (wink, wink), "they" aren't as smart scholastically. Saying that women are weaker in math and science validates the stereotype that women are emotional (read: not rational).

Despite his contrition, Summers didn't fare as well with women in his ordeal as his former boss, President Clinton, did during his.

Professor Harvey Mansfield believed that Summers received bad advice from Kennedy School of Government professor and political advisor David Gergen: "He said if you apologize, you'll make yourself look weak and vulnerable, and women will feel sympathetic. . . . He took that advice and, of course, the women despised him for looking weak, just as men would have done. So his backpedaling was a big mistake and hasn't been successful. . . ."

Indeed, one of the great mirages of crisis management is the notion that an apology will lead to catharsis, the sense of relief associated with absolution. The problem is that human affairs are not static, they are dynamic, with an ever-shifting cast of characters and agendas vying for dominance.

In Summers's case, his apology served to validate, not neutralize, the hard nugget that lay at the core of an acute cultural conflict. In an age where agendas have multiple media in which to play out at lightning speed, Summers's original sin became a political football, forever in play.

Simple mistakes often are forgiven with an apology. Ideological shibboleths related to gender and race are not. Women in academia didn't find enough else to like about Summers and his policies to stand by him in his hour of need. Digging himself more deeply into his position wasn't a great option either, since he had already offended progressives in 2002 in a dispute with black studies professor Cornel West that drove the charismatic scholar out of Harvard to Princeton. Summers had no great options, but one thing became clear: There isn't always a correlation between apology and forgiveness. Summers announced his resignation in February 2006.

Different Outcomes for a Similar Offense

Senator Trent Lott learned about the limits of apology the hard way. Why was Senator Robert Byrd (D-WV) swiftly forgiven after he apologized for his use of the word "nigger," while Lott, who used no such language, was stripped of his Senate majority leader position after a veritable apology road show for praising Strom Thurmond's political career?

The answer lies not so much in what was said as in who said it.

On March 4, 2001, Senator Byrd was speaking with Fox News's Tony Snow about improvements in race relations. During the interview, presumably in an effort to communicate that there are bad apples in all races and creeds, Byrd said:

> There are white niggers. I've seen a lot of white niggers in my time; I'm going to use that word. . . . We just need to work together to make our country a better country, and I'd just as soon quit talking about it so much.

Byrd's use of the "n-word" understandably sparked shock and outrage after the program, and Byrd quickly apologized, saying, "I apologize for the characterization I used on this program. The phrase dates back to my boyhood and has no place in today's society."

After a few frenzied days of gossip and editorializing, the subject evaporated from the news.

Senator Trent Lott's (R-MS) misadventures along racial fault lines had a very different ending. It happened in December 2002 at Strom Thurmond's 100th birthday party, when Lott said, "I want to say this about my state: When Strom Thurmond ran for president, we voted for him. We're proud of it. And if the rest of the country had followed our lead, we wouldn't have had all these problems over all these years." Thurmond's earlier career, of which Lott professed to be so fond, was anchored firmly in racial segregation.

Lott's formal apology characterized his comments: "A poor choice of words conveyed to some the impression that I embraced the discarded policies of the past. Nothing could be further from the truth, and I apologize to anyone who was offended by my statement."

Some pundits claimed that Lott hadn't apologized correctly, that he had apologized only for his statement versus the larger ideology it conveyed. No sale: No matter how he worded his apology, Lott was toast.

What accounts for the difference between how Byrd and Lott were treated? Essentially this: baggage, or lack thereof. By the time in his career that Byrd made his unfortunate remarks, he had a decades-long history of racially progressive politics in his portfolio. His comment, therefore, was viewed as being aberrant. One prominent African-American columnist even editorialized that it was hard to hold Byrd accountable for his language when so many black people referred to each other using the vulgar term.

Apologies tend to work better when the behavior in question is viewed as aberrant versus revelatory. Lott, unlike Byrd, had never shed his segregation-era narrative. In fact, notions of Lott's alleged bias were validated when the press reported that he had made almost identical remarks twenty-two years before, when Thurmond had spoken at a campaign rally for Ronald Reagan: "You know, if we had elected this man [Thurmond] thirty years ago, we wouldn't be in the mess we are today."

The *Wall Street Journal* summarized Lott's abandonment by his own party: "Lott played right into the hands of opponents who are eager to paint the Republican Party's Southern ascendance as nothing more than old-fashioned bigotry."

Bottom line: Byrd had a job; Lott was out of a leadership position for four years — a political lifetime — until deft inside maneuvering and a very different political climate allowed him to return as senate minority whip in late 2006. . . .

In Western culture, it's understandable that we tie apology to forgiveness. This is especially tempting since the public relations industry, in a desperate attempt to win the respect of the broader culture, preaches this line so zealously. Hard evidence from the PR war zones, however, suggests that apologies work best when the violation is either aberrant or isolated. As for defusing more chronic offenses, one is more likely to be forgiven if instead of using kid gloves, one takes out the brass knuckles.

Apology Scorecard

The following are famous apologists, the allegation at issue, the damage-control action taken, and the net outcome:

President George W. Bush, 2005. Abuse of prisoners at Abu Ghraib prison in Iraq by U.S. military. Bush apologized for troops' misbehavior. Apology rejected by Arab world, but intensity of media interest dissipated with trials of abusers.

New Jersey governor James McGreevey, 2004. Appointed alleged gay lover to high office. Admitted homosexuality, apologized, and resigned. Several days of intense media coverage, interest faded, no prosecution; McGreevey returned to private life. . . .

Domestic diva Martha Stewart, 2003-2005. Convicted of lying to investigators during insider trading scandal. Denied allegations, but actively cultivated her commercial base in communications and never apologized. Convicted, went to prison, emerged with base intact, company recovered.

Catholic Church. Covered up history of molestation by priests. Stonewalled, but Vatican eventually apologized. Numerous lawsuits against the Church remain.

Coca-Cola, 1999. Tainted product made dozens ill in Europe: Coke said to be slow to respond to Belgian reports of sick schoolchildren. Recalled products in Europe, apologized to consumers. Outrage lingered overseas; Coke CEO dismissed months later.

NOTES AND QUESTIONS

1. In a follow-up article, Dezenhall elaborated on ways that leaders often get crisis management wrong. One common myth is that they need to "get out in front of the story" by telling their side. In fact, Dezenhall argues, when you do not have a good side, sometimes the "less bad" solution is to just take

the hit. Tiger Woods would not have been better-off calling a press conference to "rattle through a list of lady friends declaring, 'Tiffany, yes; Trixy, no; Amber, don't remember. . . . ' "

2. Equally implausible are the assumptions that a crisis is primarily a communications problem and that public displays of corporate social responsibility can help. As Dezenhall notes, the people whose lives were obliterated by the BP oil spill "don't want a more artfully crafted apology; they want their lives and their ecosystem back. . . . Perhaps if BP had diverted some of its PR resources to safety in recent years, they wouldn't be in this mess."[110] Consider the parody running under the title "Experts Propose Plugging Oil Leak with BP Executives":

> "We've tried containment domes, rubber tires, and even golf balls," said William Cathermeyer of the National Oil Leakage Institute, a leading consultancy in the field of oil leaks. "Now it's time to shove some BP executives down there and hope for the best."
>
> "Submerging the oil company executives thousands of feet below the ocean's surface could be a 'win-win' situation," Mr. Cathermeyer said.
>
> "Best case scenario, they plug the leak," he said. "And at the very least, they'll shut the f—up."[111]

What should Woods and BP have done once their respective crises unfolded?

PROBLEM 7-2

You are chair of the governing board of Harvard University at the time that President Larry Summers made remarks on gender inequality at a conference of the National Bureau of Economic Research on Diversifying the Science and Engineering Workforce. Summers had agreed to participate as long as he could speak "unofficially," and could make some "attempts at provocation."[112] His attempts succeeded well beyond expectations. In accounting for women's underrepresentation in science and engineering, Summers maintained that the least important factor was gender "socialization" and discrimination. A more important factor was women's allegedly lower, biologically based aptitude for math and science at the "high end" of the performance range. In support of his hypothesis, Summers referred specifically to only one study. It had found half as many female as male twelfth graders who scored in the top 5 percent of mathematics and science aptitude tests. He also found it telling that his two-and-a-half-year-old twin daughters, when given trucks, concluded that the "daddy truck is carrying the baby truck." And, in full embrace of his provocateur role, Summers analogized the underrepresentation of women in math and engineering to the underrepresentation of white men in the National Basketball Association, and of Jews in farming.[113]

Summers's remarks attracted international coverage and widespread condemnation, both because of the substance of his claims and the leadership position from which he spoke. In an open letter to Summers following his remarks, Harvard's Standing Committee on Women noted: "The president of a university never speaks entirely as an individual, especially when that institution is Harvard."[114]

Members of the board generally share that view. They also believe that Summers's assertions about women's intellectual capabilities were particularly ill timed, given his administration's record on diversity. Over the past four years of his presidency, women's representation in tenured positions in the arts and sciences had dropped from 37 to 11 percent.[115] Even the *New York Times'* editorial page was moved to question whether Summers, in light of this record, was the "perfect person to free-associate on why women have trouble getting tenure."[116]

Not all agree. Some of Harvard's most liberal and prominent professors, including Alan Dershowitz and Richard Freeman, have applauded Summers for departing from the usual presidential "pablum" and "babble."[117] According to Dershowitz, "if we have a problem with presidents in major universities in the United States today, . . . it's not that they're being too provocative, it's that it's the opposite." They are "too worried about tipping the boat, too worried about alienating anybody. . . . [More of them] should become intellectual leaders and provocateurs on their campus."[118]

Summers's initial attempts at a public apology have done little to quell dispute. Opponents view his comments as illustrative of an intellectual arrogance and insensitivity that already has undermined his legitimacy. Leaders of the faculty senate have introduced a no-confidence resolution. How should the Board respond? How should they advise Summers and the university's Public Relations office to respond? What factors would be relevant to your analysis?

NOTES AND QUESTIONS

1. In commenting on the incident, Professor Stanley Fish suggested that if Summers truly believed that he was free to speak "unofficially" at a prominent conference, then he was "clueless in academe."[119] Do you agree? Should university presidents ever speak publicly on controversial public issues apart from those affecting higher education in general or their institution in particular?

2. Should analogous constraints apply to leaders in other public- and private-sector positions? Could the CEO of a major engineering firm make similar statements in explaining why so few women reached management levels? Is society better off if major public figures restrict themselves to "pablum" on controversial issues? Are their organizations? Is it fair for stakeholders to pay the price if a leader's stance results in consumer boycotts or donor backlash?

E. POLITICS

Ari Adut, On Scandal, Moral Disturbances
in Society, Politics, and Art

(New York: Cambridge University Press, 2008),
pp. 73-77, 80-81, 107-114, and 123-128

Political Scandal

A scandal is political to the extent that it affects the exercise of political power. Such events are almost always about high-status politicians, whose real or alleged transgressions pollute themselves and those they represent: their offices, parties, associates as well as the values they are supposed to stand for. The trust vested in these entities is thereby vitiated and the political process disrupted. The most common offenses that might give rise to political scandals are various uses of public office for private financial gain, abuse of power, and treason. Yet other transgressions, like sexual misconduct by politicians, can occasion political scandals as well by blotting the public persona of the offender as well as the office they represent. . . .

There is thus no sharp break between scandal and politics as usual. Rather we are presented with a continuum, at the one end of which we will find picayune, unexceptional bickering about morals and policy and on the other events such as Watergate with seismic effects. . . .

Nevertheless, political scandals seem to be on the rise in many Western democracies. Not all federal prosecutions generate full-fledged scandals in the United States, but it is difficult not to be impressed by their high incidence in the recent decades. . . . Corruption scandal waves have also engulfed European countries such as France, Italy, and Spain. What would affect the frequency of scandals in a political system? The objectivist paradigm perceives political scandal as the manifestation of corruption and puts the blame on the growing dependence of politicians on money and on the languishing internal controls on their comportment. Draconian measures along with more transparency are proposed. The constructivist perspective, in contrast, points the finger to media and elite activism. Some have decried the emergence of an "attack journalism" in the United States during the sixties and seventies, but journalists are not the only actors who can create scandals. Scholars have pointed to collusions among publicity-hungry prosecutors, belligerent investigative bodies of Congress, and the scoop-oriented press. Regardless of their differences, both objectivist and constructivists bemoan that political scandals erode public trust in government.

Since it conflates political scandal with political wrongdoing, the objectivist account is problematic. A lot of corruption goes unpublicized; arguments about its rise or decline are difficult to substantiate. By the same token, a rise in the frequency of political scandals does not necessarily reflect a corresponding growth in misconduct. Much of what was kept private and abided before (such as illegal party finance in Italy and France and sexual misconduct in the United States) now risks getting publicized and punished. Moreover, many scandals involve charges that do not get legally confirmed. . . .

Nevertheless, it cannot be denied that the proliferation of the media sources and . . . heightening competitive pressures on journalists . . . [leads] pundits to rely heavily on scandal and controversy in news coverage. . . . Nevertheless, since transgression is not equivalent to scandal, we also need to consider two additional elements that affect political scandal frequency: (1) incentives and capability to engage in moral attacks against high-status political actors and (2) vulnerability to such attacks. . . .

The Presidency after Watergate

. . . [T]he 1980s and 1990s [continued] to yield high levels of executive branch scandal activity, which affected the presidency in varying degrees.

More than 100 administration officials were accused of criminal or ethical misconduct during the two terms of the Reagan's presidency. Attorney General Edwin Meese [resigned and] . . . many staffers, including two national security advisors, were convicted with a host of charges including conspiracy and lying to Congress [in connection with the Iran Contra affair.] . . .

The Clinton years were remarkably rocky. . . . [In addition to his impeachment for lies regarding a sexual affair with Monica Lewinsky,] the president found himself ensnared in (1) Whitewater, which revolved around allegations of real estate fraud; (2) Cattlegate, which involved the first lady's cattle futures that earned questionably high returns; (3) Travelgate, in which the administration was battered for firing the members of the White House travel office; (4) Filegate, which broke with the charges that the White House had improperly obtained FBI files on more than 900 individuals, some of them prominent Republicans; (5) the Paula Jones sexual harassment case, in which the president was the defendant; and (6) the campaign finance scandal, during which the White House was accused of receiving illegal donations from foreign operatives and Asian-American donors. . . . Despite the general assumption of guilt in most of these affairs and despite the fact that the presidency itself did not inspire much confidence, the public ratings of Clinton's job performance, mainly thanks to the healthy economy, stayed high. Scandals could easily break against him and disrupt governance, but Clinton had the gumption, luck, and popular accommodation to fight them.

Imperial Tendencies in the 2000s

. . . An important question that arises out of [this] analysis is whether the low trust in the presidency and the multiplication of presidential scandals reveal a legitimacy crisis in the American political system. I don't think so. Degradation of their institutional authority makes life more difficult for presidents and renders governing harder. And a certain level of trust in public institutions is a public good. But the profanation of the presidency, which is always a question of degree, has some positive effects as well. The inviolability that sheathed Kennedy's Camelot had symbolic benefits for the public, but it also enabled a great deal of reckless behavior by the president, which could have easily resulted in a major calamity. If the American public had been more cynical about the presidency earlier on in the 1960s, Vietnam might have been averted—or at least fought differently. . . .

[A]s allegations about presidents become more and more a routine element of political life, their impact tends to decline. There is in fact a trade-off, a negative relationship between the intensity and the frequency of political scandals. One reason why there are more scandals is because they are less intense [and] . . . the anticipated collective costs [are lower].

PROBLEM 7-3

Van Jones is a globally recognized leader of the environmental justice community. From his base in San Francisco, he has launched several not-for-profit organizations, including the Ella Baker Center for Human Rights and Green For All. His influential book *The Green Collar Economy* advocates strategies for simultaneously reducing socioeconomic inequality and environmental degradation.[120] In 2007, Jones helped secure passage of the "Green Jobs Act." In 2008, President Obama appointed him as a Special Advisor for Green Jobs, Enterprise and Innovation and member of the White House Council for Environmental Quality (CEQ).[121] As special advisor for Green Jobs, Jones's responsibilities were to "advance the administration's climate and energy initiatives, with a special focus on improving vulnerable communities."[122]

Before joining the Obama Administration, Jones had been affiliated with a number of left-wing organizations, and had made statements that subsequently attracted widespread criticism. In the early 1990s, Jones was involved with an anticapitalist, antiwar organization, Standing Together to Organize a Revolutionary Movement (STORM) that sought "solidarity among all oppressed peoples" through "militant action."[123] In 2004, he signed a petition suggesting that President George W. Bush had knowingly allowed the terrorist attacks of 9/11 to occur in order to advance the administration's military objectives in the Middle East.[124] In 2005, following the acquittal of white police officers accused of beating Rodney King, Jones was quoted in an Oakland newspaper as saying: "By August, I was a Communist."[125] In a 2009 appearance before the Berkeley Energy & Resources Collaborative (BERC) event, a member of the audience asked why Republicans were more successful than Democrats in achieving legislative objectives; Jones replied, "They're assholes."[126]

After that last statement, leaders of the conservative news media began publicizing his prior comments and affiliations with "radical protest movements" and calling for his resignation.[127] Some also vowed "to dig deeper into the past of other policy 'czars' to raise questions about the President's judgment and policies."[128] For example, Fox News host Glenn Beck posted a request on Twitter asking readers to "find everything you can" on other liberal Obama appointees, such as Cass Sunstein and Carol Browner.[129] Many observers speculated that Glenn Beck's campaign to oust Jones was partly driven by his former affiliation with the Color of Change organization, which had launched a campaign pressuring advertisers to stop sponsoring Beck's television program.[130]

In response to the public outcry, Jones issued a series of statements expressing regret and attempting to put his conduct in context. An administration source said that Jones had not carefully reviewed the language of the 9/11 petition, and Jones added that "the petition does not reflect [his] views now or ever."[131] When these statements did little to halt the criticism, Jones resigned. In a statement accompanying his resignation, Jones maintained: "On the eve of historic fights for health care and clean energy, opponents of reform have mounted a vicious smear campaign against me. . . . They are using lies and distortions to distract and divide. . . . I cannot in good conscience ask my colleagues to expend precious time and energy defending or explaining my past. We need all hands on deck, fighting for our future."[132] Nancy Stutly, chair of the White House Council on Environmental Quality, accepted his resignation without comment.[133]

The fairness of Jones' treatment has been subject to debate. Howard Dean, the former chairman of the Democratic National Committee, claimed that Jones was being unjustly "penalized for not realizing what the petition he signed in 2004 was." The incident was not reflective of Jones's capabilities;

as Dean noted, "This guy's a Yale-educated lawyer . . . and best-selling author about his specialty."[134] By contrast, Jerry Taylor, a senior fellow with the Libertarian Cato Institute, saw scrutiny of Jones as "standard operating procedure," not as some "right wing conspiracy."[135] Ron Bonjean, former director of communications to Speaker of the House Dennis Hastert and press secretary to Senate Majority Leader Trent Lott, argued that Obama had created a "boomerang effect" by appointing so many advisers who were not subject to the Senate confirmation process. As a result, "there could be plenty of past controversial positions taken by these czars that are just waiting to be found and explode like ticking time bombs."[136]

1. If you had been in Jones's position, how would you have responded to the criticism? What information about your political past would you have volunteered to administration officials prior to your appointment?
2. If you had been one of President Obama's chief advisors, how would you have suggested that the administration respond to the criticisms? Is there anything that the White House could or should have done to prevent the scandal? Should Jones's past statements and political affiliations have been fully vetted before his appointment? Should any of them have been disqualifying? Was his resignation necessary? Should the administration have made any statement concerning his resignation?
3. A year after his resignation, Jones wrote a *New York Times* op-ed under the caption "Shirley Sherrod and Me." It suggested that they both had been victims of the media's "rush to judgment." In his case, the rush had occurred before he had made clear that he had never authorized STORM to post his name as a supporter on its website. In Sherrod's case, as Chapter 2 noted, she was fired for comments about race that were taken out of context. According to Jones,

> [l]ife inside the Beltway has become a combination of speed chess and Mortal Kombat; one wrong move can mean political death. In the era of YouTube, Twitter, and 24-hour cable news, nobody is safe. . . . The result is that people at all levels of government are becoming overly cautious, unwilling to venture new opinions or even live regular lives for fear of seeing even the most innocuous comment or photograph used against them. . . .
>
> [T]he breakthrough will come not when we are better able to spot the lies. It will come when we are better able to handle the truth about people. We are complex beings; no one is all good or all bad. And people do evolve . . . — just look at Senator Robert Byrd, who died this month and who entered politics as a segregationist and left as a statesman. . . . When it comes to politics in the age of Facebook, the killer app to stop the "gotcha" bullies won't be a technological one — it will be a wiser, more forgiving culture.[137]

Do you agree? If so, what could political and media leaders do to bring us closer to the world Jones envisions?

PROBLEM 7-4

ACORN, the Association of Community Organizations for Reform Now, was once America's largest organization of low-income people of color.[138]

Founded in 1970, it has employed as many as 400,000 member families to conduct voter registration and to assist economic development and organizing efforts in poor communities.[139] The organization has long been a target of conservatives. Under the administration of George W. Bush, the Justice Department fired New Mexico U.S. Attorney David Iglesias, who refused to pursue what he believed were unfounded fraud prosecutions against ACORN workers.[140]

In 2009, Veritas Visuals, a conservative activist group, orchestrated a sting operation against ACORN offices in five cities. It took videos of several workers explaining how to establish a brothel staffed by underage Salvadoran girls, avoid detection, and cheat on taxes.[141] ACORN's CEO, Bertha Lewis, denounced the employees' actions as "stupid" and "indefensible."[142] She immediately terminated those employees, suspended all walk-in interviews, and established new procedures for staff.[143] However, that was not sufficient to avert Congress from cutting off federal funding for ACORN programs.[144] It was also insufficient to prevent the Census Bureau and Internal Revenue Service from terminating relationships with ACORN, which had formerly helped collect census information and provide free tax preparation services.[145]

Lewis condemned the sting as "reminiscent of the McCarthy era," a reference to the hearings orchestrated by Joseph McCarthy in the 1950s to root out supposed communist sympathizers.[146] She also maintained that it was inappropriate to cut off funding for the organization based on conduct by a "few bad apples."[147] As she pointed out, the acts of five employees, though indefensible, were not illegal, because no paperwork was actually filed.[148] And ACORN took appropriate action, including making a report to the local police department when the misconduct came to light.[149]

Others responded that 40 percent of the ACORN employees approached had agreed to the scam and that, unlike most of McCarthy's charges, those against ACORN had a factual basis.[150] Eric Cantor, a Representative from Virginia, noted that "ACORN has violated serious federal laws, and . . . the House voted to ensure that taxpayer dollars would no longer be used to fund this corrupt organization. . . ."[151]

Some liberal groups urged Congress to wait for an independent inquiry to be completed before punishing ACORN. In their view, "the organization's work, in helping low-income families get health care, stave off foreclosure, and find jobs, is critical in this recession particularly."[152] Commentators also pointed out that a denial of funds is not the customary sanction for fraud by a federal contractor. Since 1995, the 1000 largest government contractors have been implicated in 676 cases of misconduct and have paid $26 billion to settle claims of fraud, waste, and abuses without jeopardizing their ability to provide future services.[153]

1. What is your view? If you had been in a leadership role at Veritas Visuals, would you have authorized the sting? What factors would have been relevant to your analysis? In thirty-eight states, surreptitious recordings are legal.[154] Should they be? Is it relevant that similar sting operations targeted other progressive groups, or that the leaders of the sting effort were subsequently found guilty of entering Louisiana Senator Mary Landrieu's office

under false pretenses and sued for violating California's Invasion of Privacy Act?[155]

2. If you had been Bertha Lewis, how would you have responded?

3. If you had been a Democratic member of Congress, how would you have voted on the funding cutoff? Why?

4. Six months after the sting, ACORN announced it was closing its state affiliate and field offices, as a consequence of reduced funding. Although the national organization has not dissolved, some former leaders are "looking forward to replacing ACORN with something that's an effective advocate for low- and moderate-income members."[156] Critics such as Representative Darrell Issa claim that "ACORN isn't folding; they're just trying to play dead to escape accountability for their wrongdoing. The core of [the] organization, despite the name changes and rhetoric, is still being run by the same bad actors, using the same bank accounts, and enjoying support from the same political figures."[157] If you were the leader of ACORN or one of its former affiliates, what strategies would you pursue?

5. In 2011, Live Action, an anti-abortion organization, staged at least a dozen sting operations at Planned Parenthood clinics. The group's president had previously worked with the activist behind the ACORN sting in undercover operations targeting family planning services. After its 2011 efforts, Live Action released edited footage of an interview with one New Jersey manager. She is advising a couple posing as a pimp and prostitute how to obtain medical care for underage sex workers. Planned Parenthood leaders promptly denounced the advice, fired the employee, and noted that all the targeted clinics had reported potential sex trafficking to law enforcement officials. The leaders also expressed concern about the hoax to Attorney General Eric Holder.[158] Holder and the New Jersey Attorney General then came under pressure from groups on both ends of the political spectrum. Anti-abortion activists called for a broad investigation of Planned Parenthood offices, which received public funding. Pro-choice groups called for a broad investigation of such sting operations, and limitations on their tactics. If you had been in the position of these attorney generals, how would you have proceeded?

NOTES AND QUESTIONS

1. In 2010, the U.S. House of Representatives censured Charles Rangel based on findings of its ethics committee that the congressman had committed eleven violations of House Ethics Rules. The violations included failing to pay income tax and sending letters on Congressional stationary seeking donations to New York City College's Charles B. Rangel Public Service Center. The letters targeted individuals and entities with interests that could be affected by legislation before the House Ways and Means Committee, which Rangel chaired. The committee also found that Rangel used House resources, including staff and supplies, to support these fund-raising efforts.[159] While these charges were pending, a *New York Times* investigation revealed about a dozen current or former lawmakers who had been similarly honored by academic institutions through donations from companies that

had business before Congress.[160] In some instances, the legislators personally solicited contributions or appeared at events to thank donors. Some of the amounts were quite substantial, and in excess of amounts that would be permissible as direct campaign contributions. For example, defense contractor Northrop Grumman donated $1 million to help establish the Trent Lott National Center at the University of Mississippi, and pharmaceutical company Amgen donated $5 million to the Edward Kennedy Institute while Kennedy was pushing legislation that would better protect companies, including Amgen, from competition from generic brands.

The House Ethics Committee concluded that Rangel's conduct was more egregious than that of others because he had used government stationery and staff to solicit contributions from entities with major concerns before his committee. According to a *New York Times* account, in one case the committee helped preserve tax loopholes worth millions of dollars for an oil-drilling company that had pledged $1 million.[161] Senator Mitch McConnell, who had sought funds for the McConnell Center for Political Leadership at the University of Louisville, went further in defending his own conduct. He told Fox News commentators that his situation was "totally different" from Rangel's. "This is a scholarship program for young people in Kentucky. They benefited from it, not me. It's a pure charitable activity."[162] Could Rangel make the same argument? Is it convincing? Is his conduct qualitatively different from that of other Congressional leaders?

2. Norman Ornstein, an expert in campaign finance at the American Enterprise Institute, argues that "[t]he simple fact is these things should not be named after people when they are in office. We all know what is going on here; the donors are trying to influence the lawmakers."[163] But isn't that also true of many donations to political campaigns? What makes this practice seem more offensive? Is it just the lack of transparency or the absence of limits on amounts?

3. Harvard government professor Dennis Thompson argues that congressional ethics rules serve three functions that are relevant to leaders' credibility: independence (making sure decisions are on the merits); fairness (playing by the rules); and accountability (maintaining public confidence).[164] What approach to donations honoring lawmakers would best serve these objectives?

4. If you had been president of City College of New York or the University of Louisville, would you have supported creation of centers honoring current congressional leaders? Once the centers were in place, how would you respond to public criticism? Under what, if any circumstances, should academic leaders reject "tainted money"?

5. Just as politicians sometimes use their positions to honor themselves, they also use them to honor campaign supporters. A notorious example was the 2006 "cash for peerages" scandal in Great Britain. The scandal surfaced after allegations that four businessmen had been nominated for lords after making substantial loans to the British Labour Party.[165] Some commentators expressed surprise that anyone was surprised by the news. As one noted, despite a law against the sale of titles,

[p]aying or brownnosing your way into the House of Lords has been going on for ages. All of the mainstream parties have nominated their donors, especially the generous ones, for peerages or knighthoods. The newspaper proprietor Lord Northcliffe . . . once declared, "When I want a peerage, I shall buy it like an honest man." . . . Privately, [then Prime Minister] Lloyd George told a colleague: "You and I know that the sale of honours is the cleanest way of raising money for a political party. The worst of it is that you cannot defend it in public."[166]

Is this British practice any more offensive than the common American tradition of handing out ambassador positions to large donors? What, if anything, makes the peerage sales a "scandal" rather than politics as usual?

MEDIA RESOURCES

All the scandals noted above received widespread television coverage. Clips are available of the ACORN workers, of Shirley Sherrod's edited speech, of Rangel's press statements, and of Fox News's coverage of Van Jones.[167] Jon Stewart offered critical accounts of many of these incidents, with especially biting coverage of Rangel and Hayward.[168] Radio interviews are available with Brenda Lewis of ACORN and with David Runciman on political hypocrisy.[169] Nixon's Checkers speech, Gloria Allred's press conference with Whitman's housekeeper Nicky Diaz Santillan, and Tony Hayward's and Mark Hurd's public statements all vividly illustrate the challenges of crisis management. *The Contender* features Joan Allen playing a politician whose chance to become the first female vice president is at risk because of her unwillingness to respond to accusations of misconduct.

F. MONEY

Money plays a prominent, or at least walk-on, role in most leadership scandals. The following materials explore two common contexts in which it figures in a leader's downfall. In the first case, the problem comes from paying too much attention to money—from letting it become the preeminent measure of personal status and well-being. In the second case, the difficulties arise from not paying enough attention to money—from skating too close to the line in accounting matters and not considering how certain personal and institutional expenditures would look to those footing the bill.

BRYAN BURROUGH, "MARC DREIER'S CRIME OF DESTINY"

Vanity Fair, November 2009

. . . Marc Dreier [is] 59 years old, and his life is over. . . . Dreier was once a hotshot New York litigator with multi-millionaire clients. Then he stole $380 million from a bunch of hedge funds, got caught, and was arrested in Toronto under bizarre circumstances, having attempted to impersonate a Canadian pension-fund lawyer as part of a scheme to sell bogus securities to the big American hedge fund Fortress Investment Group. . . .

Maybe you remember the Dreier case. . . . If he's remembered today, it's probably for the details of his arrest, the sheer audacity of impersonating that Toronto attorney inside the man's own offices.

The Canadian incident turned out to be the tip of one very dirty iceberg. Re-arrested upon his return to La Guardia Airport, Dreier was revealed to have defrauded more than a dozen hedge funds, not counting the $45 million or so he stole from his own clients' escrow accounts. His 270-lawyer Park Avenue firm, Dreier L.L.P., imploded practically overnight. He was indicted, thrown in a jail cell, then allowed to spend several months under house arrest at his 58th Street apartment. In June, [2009,] . . . he pleaded guilty to all charges. A judge sentenced him to 20 years in prison. . . .

Dreier's downfall left half the New York bar scratching their heads. Here was a lawyer who seemingly had every toy a middle-aged American man could want: not one but two waterfront homes in the Hamptons, condominiums in the Caribbean, a 120-foot yacht moored in St. Martin, a $200,000 Aston Martin, an oceanside condominium in Santa Monica, plus his own Los Angeles sushi restaurant, not to mention a collection of modern art that included works by Warhol, Hockney, Picasso, Matisse, and Lichtenstein.

There were all kinds of theories, though, most assuming that Dreier had resorted to theft to cover losses at his firm, or perhaps to support his outsize lifestyle. . . . They were all wrong. What no one understood is . . . that [t]his wasn't the case of a man who had everything going bad, [as] Dreier makes clear. What no one understood is that everything Dreier owned — the cars, the mansions, the yacht, the sushi restaurant, even the law firm itself — was made possible by his crimes. This was a man who went bad to have everything.

I Confess

. . . "Obviously, people who knew me are puzzled by what I did," Dreier says, "and I hope talking to you helps begin to explain it. I obviously am sincerely, deeply remorseful and sorry about what I did, and hopefully an interview can convey to people I hurt how remorseful I am. That's the truth. I am deeply sorry. And the frustrating thing is not to be able to say that." He wants the world to see he is not some comic-book villain, he says, that he was once a decent man who found himself swept up in a culture that rewards material gains. All he ever wanted, Dreier says, was to be viewed as a success, and when he wasn't, he began to steal to get the things he craved.

"Even a good person can lose their way," he goes on. "This is not just a story about someone who engaged in a significant crime, but the less dramatic point, you know, is people who are following a certain path, who go to the right schools, who do the right things. . . . You can still lose your way. In a terrible way. As I did."

. . . "I [grew] up experiencing a lot of success, even in elementary school," Dreier says. "I had always been a leader. Things just came easy to me. People expected I would achieve real success in my life."

He got into Yale, earned a degree in 1972, and went on to Harvard Law School, where he graduated in the middle of his class in 1975. He was hired as a litigation associate at the white-shoe Manhattan firm of Rosenman & Colin, where he fell under the supervision of its litigation chief, Max Freund, who was also the firm's co-chairman. . . . As they had since he was a child, people predicted great things.

In 1985, to no one's surprise, [Dreier] made partner. . . . But if Dreier's career was thriving, Rosenman wasn't. . . . Older lawyers jealously guarded their clients, frustrating their younger colleagues, many of whom, especially the litigators, began to grow restless. Some attorneys began to leave. . . .

Dreier, for one, found making partner didn't bring him the money or the responsibility he felt he deserved. "Life didn't change as much as I would've wanted it to change," he says. "I was disappointed the position didn't mean everything I had hoped for. I guess you would say I didn't get either the financial success or the recognition I would've liked."

Just as Dreier's eye began to roam, he received a job offer from Fulbright & Jaworski, the massive Houston firm, which was opening a New York office. Dreier leapt at the chance to head Fulbright's New York litigation section. The move meant more money and more recognition, and Dreier hoped he would be representing Fulbright's big Texas clients in their courtroom battles. Instead, as at Rosenman, he found older lawyers not willing to let go of their clients. For the most part, Dreier and his group were obliged to find their own clients, which was difficult. . . .

[After an ugly dispute with Fullbright's management committee and an unsuccessful stint at a small firm, Dreier decided to strike out on his own.] Dreier rented a small office suite in Rockefeller Center and hired a few associates. Shortly after, in 1996, he agreed to partner with a friend of his brother-in-law's, Neil Baritz, who practiced in Boca Raton, Florida. Their new firm, Dreier & Baritz, muddled along for several years with little distinction; Dreier argued a string of cases for various small businesses, and for a time he felt content. "I was much happier," Dreier says. "I loved being my own boss. For the first time I felt like I was doing something meaningful."

Running his own firm, however, presented a host of new challenges, chiefly the pressure of luring clients. That meant entertaining, and Dreier quickly realized that prospective clients judged him in large part not on his legal talent but on the trappings of his success. He moved his family into a duplex on 76th Street, then into a far larger apartment on 58th Street, which he rented because he couldn't afford to buy it. He spent nearly $1 million on renovations, then thousands more buying art and furnishings. In 1998 he moved his offices to 499 Park Avenue, designed by I. M. Pei.

"I needed to give people the idea I was doing very well," he says. "That was the first step in a pattern toward living above my means." His new surroundings, in fact, soon drove Dreier into debt. The only way to get out, he realized, was to expand his firm and its revenues. . . .

By 2000, after two full years, the expanded firm was having "modest success," Dreier says. "We were paying the bills." Dreier turned 50 that year, a point when many men assess their lives. As he took stock, Dreier began to realize he hadn't fulfilled the potential so many had seen in him. Friends from Harvard were heading giant firms and bringing in multi-million-dollar judgments. It was depressing that, after all those years as a golden boy, Dreier was still mired in a small firm, still hustling to pay his bills. It was then that 9/11 hit, bringing on the dark days when Dreier's world began to collapse. . . .

"I had a very emotional response to [9/11]," he says. "I remember feeling an emptiness I couldn't shake in the last quarter of '01, feeling emotionally drained and looking to find myself." . . . "I was very distraught," he says. "I was very disappointed in my life. I felt my career and my marriage were over. I was 52 and [I felt] maybe life was passing me by. . . . I felt like I was a failure." His feelings of despair were deepened by his keen, lifelong sense of entitlement, a hard-core belief that he was destined to achieve great things.

And now, suddenly, he realized he hadn't. . . . "I thought I was too smart, I was too confident," he says finally. "You can lose your way a little bit. It was all my fault. I didn't have a therapist, a wife, or a friend. I didn't have anyone I could talk to. I don't do that. I kept everything inside." . . .

For months he brooded over the wreckage of his life [and eventually] . . . came to two conclusions. He would buy himself a big house on the beach. And he would get the money by dramatically expanding his firm, now renamed Dreier L.L.P. Dreier knows how ridiculous this sounds, that his criminal behavior can be traced to his yearning for a better beach house.

. . . He returned to his Park Avenue office that fall determined to lure teams of all-star lawyers to Dreier L.L.P. Each would get a guaranteed salary, plus a bonus based on performance. But unlike other major U.S. firms, Dreier L.L.P. would not be a partnership. Dreier himself would own it all.

The plan looked promising on paper, but in practice there was one major problem. "It required a lot of cash," Dreier admits. Each lawyer had to be paid up front, and as more came on board Dreier was obliged to lease an entire new floor of offices, complete with furniture and computers. Every penny had to come from his own pocket — money, needless to say, that he simply didn't have. . . .

Easy Money

. . . Dreier says he can't remember the moment he actually began considering fraud. But he acknowledges the decision was made easier by a long track record of what he calls "cutting corners." As he acknowledges, "Yeah, I took advantage of expense accounts, statements on tax returns, that kind of thing. You know, I discovered once you cross a gray line it's much easier to cross a black line." And once he did begin thinking about fraud, he rationalized it as a onetime event that was necessary to fuel his expansion plans. "I thought I could do what I had to do, and get out of it relatively quickly," he explains. "How much did I struggle with the ethical issue? I'd like to say I have a clear recollection of going through some great ethical analysis and agonizing over it. But I don't believe I did. I should have. I just don't remember that kind of angst. I don't." . . .

[Dreier created a fictitious real estate development company and borrowed $20 million. Further fraudulent loans eventually totaled $200 million, and the firm grew to 175 lawyers. But during the 2008 audit crunch, hedge funds wanted out. One of the hedge fund's auditors discovered a forged financial statement, and one of Dreier's partners discovered funds missing from a firm escrow account. In a desperate effort to replace the necessary cash, Dreier staged an elaborate hoax requiring him to impersonate an executive of a former client, the Ontario Teachers' Pension Plan. The investor was suspicious and his efforts led to Dreier's arrest.]

There's a Moral to Draw

... [Dreier] didn't bother with denials for long. He would admit everything: four long years of fraud, 80 or more bogus notes, 13 hedge funds and four private investors, $380 million — everything. His glorious new life, the firm, the "Dreier Model" — it had all been built on lies. Within days, attorneys began resigning [and] . . . Dreier L.L.P. simply imploded. . . .

"I expect to spend most of the rest of my life in prison," he tells me. "I hope I don't die there. . . ." [S]ome of his final words were instructive. "Many people," he observed, "are caught up in the notion that success in life is measured in professional and financial achievements and material acquisitions, and it's hard to step back from that and see the fallacy. You have to try and measure your life by the moments in your day. I see people my children's age first coming into finance, the working world, as having to make basic choices about how to define happiness and success. Obviously, I made the wrong choices."

"But they don't have to."

NOTES AND QUESTIONS

1. The dynamics that Drier describes are common in many Ponzi schemes, most recently in Bernie Madoff's well-documented scam. Such practices have been less common in law firms because those with substantial assets typically are owned by multiple equity partners, who exercise some collective oversight of financial practices. However, in Dreier's firm, with only one equity partner, non-equity practice leaders never saw the firm's books until after his arrest.[170] Does that suggest that the Model Rules of Professional Conduct should ban single-person equity partnerships or require them to meet special financial accountability standards?

2. Such reforms would not, of course, prevent all such scandals. South Florida lawyer Scott Rothstein managed to perpetrate a scheme similar to Dreier's by consolidating control and paying his two other name partners sufficiently well to avert unwelcome inquiries. Before Rothstein's arrest in 2009, his firm had defrauded investors of nearly $1.6 billion based on shares that they had purchased in non-existent case settlements.[171] Through lavish expenditures and political and philanthropic contributions, Rothstein had cultivated an image of accomplishment. Oversight by colleagues had been limited by his highly secretive management practices, including an office separated from the rest of the firm by a bulletproof glass door and guarded by a uniformed security officer.[172] In such cases, money plays a corrosive role not just for leaders but also for followers, who are reluctant to voice concerns about practices that seem exceptionally profitable. Often subordinates, and sometimes investors, suspect that ethical corners are being cut; they just assume that they will not be the victims. What, if anything, can be done to counteract such dynamics and ensure greater transparency in financial governance?

MEDIA RESOURCES

A video tour of Rothstein's office and a profile of Marc Dreier are both available on YouTube.[173] A discussion of the massive accounting scandal that bankrupted the Crazy Eddie retail business provides insights into what motivates such fraud, and what missteps reveal it.[174] In a World Business forum address, former CEO and Harvard lecturer Bill George talks about the need for authentic leadership in the context of the recent financial crisis.[175] Accounts of Bernard Madoff's scandal also provide a window on the dynamics of massive meltdowns.[176]

PROBLEM 7-5

In 1990, national attention focused on alleged financial abuses at Stanford University in connection with government research grants. At issue were certain "indirect costs" chargeable to federally subsidized research. These costs reflected a specified percentage of overhead expenses, including administrative, library, and faculty support, that make such research possible. To calculate the appropriate amount, the university conducts studies to determine how much of a given function relates to research as opposed to instruction. Normally the proportion is approximately 30 percent, and at the end of the year, the government audits the total costs of grants to make sure that they conform to the studies. For convenience in accounting, all the expenditures for a given function become part of a single cost pool. So, for example, auditors do not review all library purchases of books and allocate the "cost of Huckleberry Finn to instruction and . . . the *Journal of Neurophysiology* to research."[177] Rather, the government assumes that 30 percent of all library costs will be attributable to research. Then the university negotiates an indirect cost surcharge for each grant to compensate the university for its research support. In 1990, the figure at Stanford was 73 percent. Many faculty members then, as now, have been unhappy about such rates, because the higher they run, the less competitive their grant proposals appear in comparison with those from other institutions with lower indirect costs.

In the 1990s, some disgruntled Stanford faculty members complained about indirect costs to Paul Biddle, a representative of the Office of Naval Research. He began looking into the university's accounting practices, which led to further inquiries by a congressional subcommittee. These inquiries revealed that certain charges were, or appeared to be, improperly allocated to cost pools. One well-publicized example involved depreciation on a yacht that had been given to the university's athletic department and was awaiting resale. Stanford's original computer coding error in allocating yacht expenses fueled anger by some subcommittee members, including its chair, Congressman John Dingle.

Just before subcommittee hearings on the indirect cost issue, the producer of ABC's *20/20* asked for Stanford's cooperation on a program they planned to run. The network had covered other subcommittee inquiries and the producer reportedly expected this one to be the "savings and loan story of the nineties."[178] Donald Kennedy, president of Stanford at the time, recounts the circumstances in his book, *Academic Duty*.[179] According to Kennedy,

> [We did not] expect objective treatment but we cooperated, knowing that a refusal would be subject to adverse interpretation. We even agreed to let ABC photograph inside the president's residence . . . [because] particular items in the house (furniture, flowers for official entertaining and the like) had been placed in one of the cost pools that were given special attention in the program. [In the subsequent hearings], the committee members focused on the so-called sensitive items. The chairman's opening statement referred to the following purchases for Hoover House, a National Historic Landmark that is the site of all official university entertaining: "a pair of George II lead urns at $12,000"; "$7,000 for sheets for Dr. Kennedy's bed"; "cedar lining for closets"; "a $1,600 shower curtain"; and "a $1,200 early-nineteenth-century Italian fruitwood commode."
>
> Because expenses of the president's office and the official residence are legitimate parts of the indirect cost pool for "general administration," these items had been included in accounts along with secretarial salaries, maintenance, and the like. OMB Circular A-21 provides for studies to determine what portion of such administrative expenses is attributable to research, and this determination is made for the pool as a whole. Twenty-three percent of each item in the pool is in fact charged as indirect cost, even though, of course, some items are more directly related to research than others. According to the government's own rules, these were legitimate, recoverable costs — and indeed the Defense Contract Audit Agency had actually reviewed and approved some of them. In the media, however, the story was that the taxpayers had bought flowers for the president's house and paid for the furniture. We removed these costs because we decided that however allowable they might be technically, they were simply inappropriate.
>
> The problem, of course, lay in the concept of pool accounting. Under that principle, expenses that most citizens would quickly conclude should be eligible for full government reimbursement as research costs are treated the same as ones that sound outrageously irrelevant to research. . . . On average, 23 percent of all the expenditures were shown by statistical studies to be research-related, and as a matter of auditing simplification they all carry the same reimbursement.
>
> The revelations were damaging, and made more so by the way in which the "sensitive items" were misrepresented. For example, there was no $1,600 shower curtain and no $7,000 bed sheets. The government's auditors failed to recognize that vendors often lump purchases. The shower curtain was one minor item in a bill for a large amount of upholstery and drapery work, and the sheets item was actually an extensive one-time re-placement of all the house's table linens. The urns were expensive, but the chairman had somehow mistakenly put the decimal point one place to the right, transforming a $1,200 purchase into a $12,000 purchase. As for the fruitwood commode — actually a cherry chest of drawers — the chairman could not resist a wry reminder of the costly toilet seat made famous in his earlier hearings on defense contractors. By innuendo and creative imprecision, he made his contempt for the university clear.
>
> The political climate in which the university had to sail for the next months was thus established not by the major issues surrounding indirect cost policy but by the carefully crafted public impression that at Stanford we were living high at public expense.[180]

As a result of the hearings, the government cut the university's 73 percent indirect cost rate, initially to 55 percent, and after litigation, to 63 percent. According to Stanford's calculations, the actual costs attributable to sponsored research in fact justified a rate close to 80 percent, and the shortfall caused severe budget problems. Other universities also experienced substantial cutbacks in indirect cost recoveries, and blamed Stanford for the consequences. Between 2000 and 2002, the problems generated some 1200 articles and cost the university an estimated $25 million in auditing expenses.[181] Kennedy felt that he was becoming a lightning rod for criticism, and announced his resignation. In commenting on lessons learned from the experience, he writes:

> We let the important matter of how public research funds are accounted for slip into a swamp of obscurity. By failing in our duty to explain what we were doing and why, we left ourselves open to a painful trial-by-media. Long before there was any interest in indirect cost accounting, we should have recognized that the agreements between the universities and the government were so arcane and so private that they were bound to raise troubling questions. Pool accounting, mixing as it does reimbursable and nonreimbursable items and relying on statistics to get the right outcome, is an invitation to public misunderstanding.[182]

Kennedy also suggested that the university may not have been sufficiently sensitive to faculty's concerns about their competitive position in obtaining government research grants. He does not, however, identify specific decisions that he would have made differently.

1. What might you have done differently as university president to head off the crisis?
2. Would you have made the same decision about the *20/20* program "Your Tax Dollars at Work"? If so, is there anything you would have done to try to avert the negative fallout from its broadcast?
3. In discussing costs attributable to the president's home, ABC correspondent Stone Phillips explained that Stanford is allowed to charge the government for a part of the house's upkeep but notes that the expenses must be reasonable. He then asked Kennedy about $2,600 for cedar-lined closets. Kennedy responded: "These closets are part of this structure, which we're maintaining in perpetuity. Part of the activity that goes on in this structure supports research and under the government's rules, investments that maintain that structure and its capacity are allowable." Biddle then followed up: "There's no way that a cedar-lined closet can help anyone do research. Even the people who are the researchers here at the university are shocked by that." Phillips went on to note that "when details of the Hoover House expense became public, Stanford suddenly withdrew them." Kennedy responded: "Sure, we're admitting there's a problem. We're getting adverse publicity. People are raising questions. We want those questions to be the right ones."

   Were Phillips's questions the right ones? Would you have given any different answers?
4. Another focus of attention by *20/20* reporters was a reception that the Stanford Board of Trustees gave for 600 guests and identified in accompanying

documents as "for the wedding of President Kennedy." When asked about the expenses, Kennedy noted that the reception was "some time after our wedding," that "large numbers of . . . Stanford faculty" were invited, and that he didn't know "how the costs were actually charged." Phillips did know. The government paid "about four grand" of the $20,000 tab. And he added, "Most people pay for their own wedding receptions." Kennedy responded that "we certainly paid for ours," but indicated that the trustees "wanted a chance for the Stanford community to meet [his new wife] so it did an entertainment and we have taken those costs out of the pool." Was that an adequate response? Should Kennedy or the trustees have worried earlier about how the "entertainment" was funded and whether taxpayers or even the university should have subsidized this event?

5. How would you evaluate the leadership of Representative John Dingle? How might his own political needs have figured in his handling of the indirect cost issue? Is it reasonable to expect him to subordinate those needs to concerns about financial fairness to universities submitting government research proposals? If not, what follows from that fact?

NOTES AND QUESTIONS

1. Analogous scandals have surfaced at other institutions concerning the use of university funds to support what appear to be excessively lavish life-styles.[183] A case in point was the 2010 disclosure of some $700,000 to renovate the private residence of Mark Yudof, President of the University of California. At a time when the university was facing massive financial cutbacks, many observers were outraged that large amounts of money and staff time were consumed by the upkeep of a palatial rental home that was not even the official president's house.[184] Are such problems primarily due to inadequate oversight procedures or to lack of ethical sensitivity? Are they an illustration of the claim by the President of the American Association of Governing Boards of Universities and Colleges that we do a "terrible job of preparing presidents to be president"?[185]

2. Related problems surfaced for British members of Parliament ("MPs") in 2009, when details on their expense reports surfaced in the press. "How many politicians does it take to change a light bulb?" was a common quip. "The answer seems to be 'one,' albeit with the help of a team of workmen" whose home repair jobs included changing twenty-four light bulbs, all funded by the taxpayer to the tune of more than $3,000. Other items claimed as part of the MPs' second home allowance included items such as an ironing board, hedge trimming, and moat cleaning.[186] The House Speaker became the first man ousted from the job in over 300 years, 381 MPs were forced to pay back an average of £3000, and nearly two-thirds of taxpayers thought that those who claimed unauthorized expenses should lose their seats and face criminal prosecution.[187] As was true with the Stanford scandal, part of the problem was attributable to arcane and poorly designed rules, but part was also due to ethically tone-deaf decision making. Why do you suppose that leaders used to being in the public eye were so seemingly oblivious to how such expenses would appear to the public?

3. Could the same questions be asked about the bonuses to AIG employees after the federal bailout? Joining a chorus of outraged taxpayers, President Obama stated the obvious: "This is a corporation that finds itself in financial distress due to recklessness and greed. . . . Under these circumstances, it's hard to understand how derivative traders at AIG warranted any bonuses, much less $165 million in extra pay. I mean, how do they justify this outrage to the taxpayers who are keeping the company afloat?"[188] That question was presumably rhetorical, but if you had been AIG's CEO or general counsel, how would you have responded? Would it be enough to claim that "retention bonuses" were necessary to hold on to the talent that would make the company profitable and justify the taxpayers' investment?[189]

MEDIA RESOURCES

Ample coverage of the bonus issue is available.[190] An amusing discussion is available concerning a British politician who claimed compensation for rental of pornographic videos.[191] National Public Radio's *This American Life* aired interviews with Wall Street investment bankers in a 2010 segment "Money Never Weeps," in which they justify their high earnings.

G. SEX

Just about everyone loves a sex scandal, except, of course, the leaders who are experiencing one. In the following excerpt, Ari Adut explores the extent of America's fascination with celebrity sex and some of its causes and consequences.

ARI ADUT, ON SCANDAL: MORAL DISTURBANCES
IN SOCIETY, POLITICS, AND ART

(New York: Cambridge University Press, 2008),
pp. 175-183 and 208-222

Sex and the American Public Sphere

The American public sphere was "All Monica, All the time" in 1998. The nation spent an entire year engrossed in a lewd narrative about adulterous sex in the Oval Office between President Clinton and a sprightly White House intern. It was a cheap but very lucrative story for the media, which, to keep the plot moving, fed the public daily with a steady stream of fresh allegations. . . . For most Americans, it was hard not to be interested, not to be amused. The Starr Report, the lurid account of the illicit liaison . . . by the Independent Counsel's office that was investigating the president, was downloaded an estimated nine million times in two days after it hit the Internet.

But the scandal was serious business, too. The revelation of Bill Clinton's affair with Monica Lewinsky and the legal complications that arose thereof plunged the American democracy in a drawn-out constitutional crisis, making the satyrical politician, already embattled by a sexual harassment suit, the second impeached president in history and pushed him to the brink of resignation. Recall the generalized outrage among the political and intellectual elite. Conservatives clobbered Clinton for having contaminated the White House; liberals rejoined that it was precisely the unscrupulous Republican onslaught on the office of the presidency that was responsible for the pollution. And the maelstrom soon implicated numerous third parties in a quite direct way [including Robert Livingston who resigned after *Hustler* exposed his own extramarital activity.] . . .

The United States has since been blessed with a sexually demure president, and these are sober times of war and terrorism. Public discourse is nonetheless still steeped in sex scandals. Just for a small sample, consider all the sleaze that has been alleged or revealed in public in the recent years about [Michael Jackson, Paris Hilton, Arnold Schwarzenegger, former New Jersey governor James McGreevey, the mayor of Detroit Kwame Kilpatrick, television host Bill O'Reilly, and Senator Larry Craig.] . . . Jack Ryan withdrew from the senatorial race in Illinois in 2004, ensuring that the GOP would lose a seat, after the *Chicago Tribune* obtained divorce documents divulging that the Republican politician had propositioned his actress wife to have sex with him in a club. Eliot Spitzer resigned in March 2008 from the office of the governor of New York after a federal investigation caught him contacting an expensive prostitute for an assignation. Allegations of pedophilia by Catholic priests peaked in 2003 and 2004, disgracing the entire Church. The revelation of Mark Foley's off-color Internet communications with Congress pages in October 2006 [and inadequate response by the House speaker] . . . was a factor in the Republican wipeout in the 2006 midterm elections. . . .

What accounts for the high frequency of sex scandals in American public and political life? Two different constructivist arguments are usually offered to answer this question: societal puritanism and moral activism by elites. . . . Americans—or at least an appreciable and vociferous portion of them—are simply too uptight about sex, too eager to make a disproportionate fuss of pedestrian peccadilloes. . . .

[However,] it is unclear whether Americans are more straitlaced about sex than others. . . . In a CBS 1992, poll—conducted in the wake of allegations by Gennifer Flowers that she had had sex with the presidential candidate Bill Clinton—only 14 percent of Americans said that they would not vote for an adulterer. . . . A January 24-25, 2006, poll conducted in France by TNS Sofres for *Le Figaro* found that 17 percent of the Gallic sample would not vote for a presidential candidate guilty of extramarital affairs. . . . There is no evidence that the French are not interested in the private lives of public figures. President Nicolas Sarkozy's affair with the supermodel-turned-singer Carla Bruni that ended with marriage was closely followed by the French media. The main reason there are few sex scandals in contemporary French politics are the legal protections that Gallic politicians enjoy against the unfavorable publicization of their private lives in the form of tough privacy and defamation laws. . . .

Sex scandals luxuriate in settings in which the publicity of sex has lost a good deal of its embarrassing, shameful, discomfiting quality for audiences. I call this declining modesty. The relative attenuation of the puritanism of

Americans since the early sixties has dramatically lowered the threshold of shame associated with the publicity of sexuality. . . . A by-product of the relative ease with which contemporary Americans talk about — and especially listen to and read about — sex in public is that the symbolic and emotional costs of public accusations of sexual misconduct both for accusers and audiences have dwindled. . . .

Sex and Scandal

What accounts for the close association, since time immemorial, between sex and scandal? . . . [A] celebrity sex scandal — and contemporary politicians are often celebrities — gratifies on several levels. We are afforded intimate peeks into the lives of important people, whom we often find to be fascinating. We are offered an opportunity to live vicariously through the sexual experiences that are not ordinarily accessible for want of opportunity, moral qualms, lack of imagination, or maybe cowardice. Simultaneously, a sex scandal slakes our all-too-natural resentfulness by giving us a chance to see those, whose better fortunes are frequently unforgivable, to get their comeuppance. And finally, unlike an accounting scandal, a sex scandal is fairly simple and features a cast we can easily identify with or react against. We find it much more natural to adjudicate on sexual matters: the capacity to judge does not call for special expertise because we have all in various ways tackled moral issues regarding our or others' sexual behavior. . . . Sex is not just absorbing. It also lends itself readily to moralizing. . . .

Moreover, sexual liberalization has paradoxically transformed private morality into political capital. Private rectitude has become a diacritical public marker to be used predominantly, but not exclusively, by conservatives. This has, however, given a pretext to the media and political opponents to hunt for hypocrisy. Politicians who capitalize on private morality are generally fair game, and sex scandals with consequences in the United States are usually not simply about sexual sins but hypocrisy or other transgressions committed to cover them up. . . .

We are now in a better condition to understand the Lewinsky scandal. . . . [In a deposition in the sexual harassment case by Arkansas state employee Paula Jones, Clinton denied that he had sexual relations with Monica Lewinsky. In a later grand jury proceeding brought by Independent Counsel Kenneth Starr, Clinton acknowledged an "improper physical relationship" with Lewinsky but denied having lied in his deposition because he had not consider receiving oral sex to constitute sexual relations. On recommendation by the independent counsel, the House of Representatives impeached Clinton on two grounds: lying under oath and obstructing justice. The Senate lacked the two-thirds votes to convict. An Arkansas judge dismissed Jones's sex harassment case but found the president in contempt for lying to the grand jury and imposed a fine.]

The standard verity about scandals is that cover-ups always backfire. This is patently wrong. Given the first poll figures[, which found that almost half of voters wanted the president out of office if he had engaged in a sexual affair, lied about it, and had asked Lewinsky to lie as well], Clinton was astute to keep the truth from the public; opinion turned soon after. The main reason

Americans were mostly with Clinton was the economy, which had been doing swimmingly throughout his second term. . . . As the scandal dragged on and eventually palled on the public, most Americans (60 to 70 percent) blamed Starr. The job approval rating of Clinton actually reached 68 percent while Clinton was being impeached, and the Democrats gained five House seats in the 1998 midterm elections.

For the majority of the public, the scandal was primarily about sex. Clinton perjured himself and obstructed justice, but most Americans were not all that outraged by these legal transgressions and, to the exasperation of the Republicans in Congress, refused to see the matter as something much more than lying about sex. . . .

Clinton's allies also acted strategically. Feminists would have definitely gone after the president had he not been a Democrat who had done much to advance their agenda. So they took his side even though Clinton's lie technically obstructed the course of justice in a sexual harassment case and even though feminists are highly skeptical about the legitimacy of relationships involving power differentials, however consensual they may be. Feminist activists and politicians were more concerned with the political costs of Clinton's demise than with his individual transgression. . . .

In contemporary America, sex norms are not strong enough to make public discussion of sex scandalous, but not weak enough for us to be indifferent to the sexual behavior of others.

PROBLEM 7-6

1. If you had been President Clinton, with his sexual history, what might you have done differently?

2. Before the Lewinsky affair became public through her exposure as a witness in Paula Jones's sexual harassment lawsuit, Clinton offered to settle the suit for $700,000. Although that amount was far in excess of any likely verdict had the case gone to trial, Jones rejected the offer. Prodded by her husband and other politically motivated advisors, she insisted on an apology admitting wrongdoing, which Clinton refused to give.[192] If you had been counsel to the president or White House chief of staff, would you have advised him to make the apology? Alternatively, should you have advised him to refuse to testify and accept a default judgment in the case?

3. As the scandal unfolded, Clinton reported "having to become quite an expert in this business of asking for forgiveness."[193] Compare the following attempts. Which are most and least effective? What would you have said in his place?
   - I did have a relationship with Miss Lewinsky that was not appropriate. In fact, it was wrong. It constituted a critical lapse in judgment and a personal failure on my part for which I am solely and completely responsible. . . . [However, the Independent Counsel investigation] has gone on too long, cost too much, and hurt too many innocent people. . . . Now this matter is between me, the two people I love most—my wife and our daughter—and our God. It's nobody's business but ours. Even Presidents have private lives.[194]

- I have acknowledged that I made a mistake, said that I regretted it, asked to be forgiven, spent a lot of very valuable time with my family in the last couple of weeks, and said I was going back to work.[195]
- What I want the American people to know, what I want the Congress to know, is that I am profoundly sorry for all I have done in words and deeds. . . . Mere words cannot fully express the profound remorse I feel for what our country is going through and for what members of both parties in Congress are now forced to deal with.[196]
- I agree with those who have said that in my first statement after I testified, I was not contrite enough. I don't think there is a fancy way to say that I have sinned. It is important to me that everyone who has been hurt know that the sorrow I feel is genuine: first and most important my family; also my friends; my staff, my Cabinet; Monica Lewinsky and her family, and the American people. I have asked all for their forgiveness. But I believe that to be forgiven, more than sorrow is required, at least two more things. First, genuine repentance; a determination to change, to repair breaches of my own making. I have repented. Second what my Bible calls a "broken spirit": an understanding that I must have God's help to be the person that I want to be. . . .[197]

In her autobiography, Hillary Clinton recalls that most commentators and some of Clinton's most trusted advisors thought that his initial decision to criticize Independent Counsel Kenneth Starr instead of just apologizing had been a mistake. But, she notes, her husband's "standing in public opinion polls remained high. His standing with me had hit rock bottom."[198]

According to many experts, the last apology, given at a White House National Prayer Breakfast, was the one "he should have given all along."[199] Do you agree? If so, why do you think it took so long in coming?

NOTES AND QUESTIONS

1. As information about the affair began to trickle out and Clinton initially denied his involvement, his primary pollster found that 60 percent of voters believed that if he had committed perjury or obstructed justice by asking Lewinsky to lie, he should be removed from office.[200] But by the close of his term, when a court found that he had indeed lied under oath, his approval ratings remained high. How do you account for the inconsistency? Was it just about the economy, as Adut suggests? Or are there other lessons for scandal management?

2. Whether other nations are more tolerant of leaders' sexual misconduct remains open to dispute. As one *Wall Street Journal* commentator noted, at the same time that South Carolina governor Mark Sanford watched his career tank in the wake of lies concerning an extramarital affair, another country's prime minister, "was cheerily waving off the latest set of allegations about his relationships with young girls. . . . [Also,] in Paraguay, the president[,] Fernando Lugo[,] was accused of sexual assault by a former housekeeper. He has already admitted to being the father of one illegitimate child and is alleged to have fathered others. Oh, and by the way, he is a

former Catholic bishop."[201] If these examples point to significant cultural differences, which voters have it right?

3. Why are almost all of the leaders embroiled in sexual scandals men? Is it mainly because fewer women are leaders? Or are they more risk averse, partly due to lingering double standards of morality, which make promiscuity more costly for women than men (particularly if they are married and have children)? Or, as anthropologist Lionel Tiger argues, is it that women have fewer sexual opportunities because power is not as alluring in women as in men?[202] Or do women have less interest in, or less of a sense of entitlement to, extramarital sex? As the world moves toward greater gender equality in leadership roles, should we expect to see more sex scandals involving women, or fewer involving men? Are wronged husbands likely to play the same role as wronged wives at press events where leaders acknowledge "pain" in their marriages?

4. What enables some leaders to survive sex scandals while others never recover? Consider the following factors. Which are most important? Which should be?

   - *Hypocrisy.* The greater the disparity between the public image and private conduct, the more judgmental the public is likely to be. Eliot Spitzer, the New York governor who was caught with a high-priced call girl, suffered from having supported increased penalties for patronizing prostitutes and from having cast himself as a moral crusader while attorney general. David Vitter, the Louisiana Senator who purchased services from the "D.C. Madam," was pummeled by the press because of his prior stand on "family values," including his condemnation of then-president Bill Clinton as "morally unfit to govern."[203] Many voters agree with the observation of Barney Frank, a liberal Massachusetts Ccongressman who survived a scandal involving sex with a gay prostitute because he was out and open about his mistake: "Everyone in public life is entitled to privacy but no one in public life is entitled to hypocrisy."[204] Do you agree? Do voters? Note that Vitter won reelection in 2010 despite the scandal.

   - *Deception.* The received wisdom among crisis management professionals is that ineffective attempts to conceal misconduct compound its consequences. South Carolina Governor Mark Sanford was condemned less for having an affair than for lying about it; his claims to be hiking the Appalachian trail while he was actually AWOL in Argentina with his mistress made him a target of late-night comedy as well as resentment from voters and staff. John Edwards's bungled efforts to evade tabloid reporters and to have his campaign manager assume paternity of Edwards's own illegitimate child contributed to his political free fall. Is Clinton's experience an example or counterexample of this point?

   - *Apology.* Edwards added nails to his coffin by suggesting that a mitigating circumstance during his affair was that his wife's fatal cancer was in remission. Mark Sanford's public confessional was a textbook case of what not to do. He opened his press conference by promising not to "begin in any particular spot," and to provide "more detail than you'll ever want," and delivered on both claims. As *New York Times* columnist

Gail Collins noted, his rambling narrative, confessing " 'love for the Appalachian trail' (where he didn't go)," "his fondness for 'adventure trips' (clearly a personal specialty)," and his desire for a "soulmate," made him appear "a complete loony."[205] Eric Dezenhall captured prevailing reactions: "[L]ess would have been more."[206] Clinton's initial statements, by contrast, were criticized as too little too late. Can you identify a politician who seemed to have struck the right balance?

- *Allies.* One critical factor in surviving a sex scandal is the extent to which others rally around the leader. Clinton benefitted from the continued support of feminists. However much they deplored his personal sexual history, women's rights activists felt that he had been good on their issues, and that his impeachment would set them back. By contrast, Spitzer's fall was partly attributable to a governing style that had alienated political colleagues.[207] Wives' clenched-teeth stoicism can often be critical, while a tell-all memoir or interview invites further disaster.[208] Former wives can also precipitate as well as quell concerns. Jack Ryan's Illinois Senate race was derailed by his ex-wife's revelations that he had taken her to sex clubs and pressured her to have sex with patrons.[209] Yet, while a spouse's support is critical, is having her at a press conference always desirable? Laura Kipnis describes Spitzer's resignation, with his demonstrably mortified wife standing beside him, as "like watching someone swallow a hand grenade in real time."[210]
- *Related Misconduct.* The misuse of campaign funds or taxpayer dollars to finance an affair can also play a role, as was the case with Edwards and Sanford. Ohio representative Wayne Hays inflamed voters by employing a secretary whose primary duty was sex; Elizabeth Ray, by her own admission, did not know how to type. Soliciting a minor, or in Congressman Larry Craig's case, an undercover police officer, is generally political suicide.

As these examples, and countless others make clear, multiple factors affect the outcome of sexual scandals. Not all are fatal. But few end happily ever after. And in this world of increasing technological transparency, leaders need to recognize that their digital footprints will be hard to conceal.[211]

MEDIA RESOURCES

Bill Clinton's grand jury testimony is worth reviewing, as are clips of his various apologies.[212] Other press conferences are also available on YouTube, including those by Mark Sanford, Eliot Spitzer, and Larry Craig. *Client Nine: The Rise and Fall of Eliot Spitzer*, offers a number of scenes worth excerpting. Jon Stewart's treatment of many of these events can also supply a cautionary tale. The satirical newspaper *The Onion* produced a video parody in which a politician calls a press conference to apologize before he engages in a sex scandal.[213] Film versions of sexual and political scandals include *The American President*, starring Michael Douglas and Richard Dreyfuss, and *Primary Colors*, explored in Chapter 12.

END NOTES

1. Laura Kipnis, How to Become a Scandal (New York: Henry Holt and Company, 2010), 8, 21.

2. Id. at 14.

3. Ari Adut, On Scandal: Moral Disturbances in Society, Politics, and Art (New York: Cambridge University Press, 2008), 80.

4. Peter Firestein, Crisis of Character: Building Corporate Reputation in the Age of Skepticism (New York: Union Square Press, 2009), 41.

5. Leslie Gaines-Ross, Corporate Reputation (Hoboken, NJ: John Wiley and Sons, 2008), 7, citing Weber Shandwick, Safeguarding Reputation (KRC Research, 2006).

6. Jacob A. Stein, Legal Spectator, Washington Lawyer, January 2011, 48 (quoting Maugham).

7. G.R. Goethals, David W. Messick, and S.T. Allison, The Uniqueness Bias: Studies of Constructive Social Comparison, in Jerry M. Suls and Thomas Ashby Wills, eds., Social Comparison: Contemporary Theory and Research (Hillsdale, NJ: Erlbaum, 1991), 149, 161-162.

8. John Schwartz, Resumes Made for Fibbing, New York Times, May 23, 2010, WK5.

9. Piercarlo Valdesolo and David DeSteno, The Duality of Virtue: Deconstructing the Moral Hypocrite, Journal of Experimental Social Psychology 44 (2008):1334.

10. Joris Lammers, Diederick A. Stapel, and Adam D. Galinsky, Power Increases Hypocrisy: Moralizing in Reasoning, Immorality in Behavior, Psychological Science 21(2010):737.

11. See surveys cited in Lammers, Stapel, and Galinsky, Power Increases Hypocrisy, 738; Adam D. Galinsky, Joe C. Magee, Deborah H. Gruenfeld, Jennifer A. Whitson, and Katie A. Lijenquist, Social Power Reduces the Strength of the Situation: Implications for Creativity, Conformity and Dissonance, Journal of Personality and Social Psychology 95 (2008):1450.

12. Dennis Thompson, Hypocrisy and Democracy, in Dennis Thompson, Restoring Responsibility: Ethics in Government, Business and Healthcare (Cambridge University Press, 2005), 216-217.

13. Ruth Grant, Hypocrisy and Integrity (Chicago: University of Chicago Press, 1997), 26. See also Judith Shklar, Ordinary Vices (Cambridge, MA: Harvard University Press, 1984), 54 (arguing that to fail in aspirations is not hypocritical).

14. Id. at 178.

15. Id. at 53.

16. Id. at 181.

17. Shklar, Ordinary Vices, 70.

18. Alan Ehrenhalt, Hypocrisy Has Its Virtues, New York Times, February 6, 2001, A19.

19. Marvin Kitman, Supersource for Scandal: Reporters Are Wasting Time and Money on Politicians' Dirty Secrets. Let's Get It All Organized in a "Sin Bin," Los Angeles Times, April 6, 2008, 9.

20. Peter Furia, Democratic Citizenship and the Hypocrisy of Leaders, Polity 41 (2009): 114, 123.

21. Suzanne Dovia, Making the World Safe for Hypocrisy, Polity 34 (2001):3.

22. David Runciman, Political Hypocrisy: The Mask of Power, From Hobbes to Orwell and Beyond (Princeton, NJ: Princeton University Press, 2008), 53-54.

23. Andrew Young, The Politician (New York: St. Martin's Press, 2010), 206-207.

24. Maureen Dowd, Running with Scissors, New York Times, April 21, 2007, A25.

25. Maureen Dowd, Feliz Cumpleanos and Dios, New York Times, August 8, 2010, WK9.

26. Jay Leno, Laugh Lines, New York Times, August 15, 2010, WK2.

27. Dowd, Feliz, WK9 (quoting Axelrod).

28. See Rush Limbaugh, Kerry's "I Didn't Inhale" SUV Moment, April 23, 2004, http://www.rushlimbaugh.com.

29. Some critics faulted Whitman less for hypocrisy than for her callous dismissal of an employee she described as part of her extended family. Susan Estrich, Meg Whitman's Housekeeper Hypocrisy, October 1, 2010, http://www.newsmax.com/Estrich/MegWhitmanGloriaAllred/2010/10/01/id/372216.

30. Isabel MacDonald, Lou Dobbs, American Hypocrite, The Nation, October 15, 2010, 11.

31. Time Magazine, November 22, 2010, 27 (quoting Hayward).

32. Bankers and the Bonus, New York Times, February 6, 2011, Week Review, 7.

33. Calvin Trillin, Goldman's Chief's $9 Million Bonus Seen by Some as Show of Restraint, The Nation, March 1, 2010, 6.

34. Bill Clinton, My Life (New York: Knopf, 2004), 385.

35. Id. at 387.

36. Ken Gormley, The Death of American Virtue (New York: Crown Publisher, 2010), 4-5 (quoting Livingston and Flynt).

37. Gormley, Death of Virtue, 6 (quoting Hyde).

38. Vandesolo and DeSteno, The Duality of Virtue, 1334 (quoting Foley).

39. Gerard Baker, Sex Americana, Wall Street Journal June 27-28, 2009, W1 (quoting Bennett).

40. Stephen J. Rubenzer and Tom R. Faschingbauer, Personality, Character and Leadership in the White House: Psychologists Assess the Presidents (Washington, D.C.: Brassey's, 2004); S.E. Dingfelder, A Presidential Personality, Monitor on Psychology, American Psychological Association, November 26-28, 2004, discussed in Roger Gill, The Theory and Practice of Leadership (Thousand Oaks, CA: Sage, 2006), 15.

41. Jonah Lehrer, The Power Trip, Wall Street Journal, August 14-15, 2010, W1.

42. Arjit Chatterjee and Donald C. Hambrick, It's All about Me: Narcissistic CEOs and Their Effect on Company Strategy and Performance, Administrative Science Quarterly 52 (2007):351; Mark Maremont, Scholars Link Success of Firms to Lives of CEOs, Wall Street Journal, Sept 5, 2007, A1, A15.

43. Lehrer, The Power Trip, W2.

44. Carlin McEnroe, Downsizing the Horse Guard, Funny Times, July 2010, 14.

45. Todd S. Purdum, Washington, We Have a Problem, Vanity Fair, September 2010, 339 (quoting Lauer and Obama).

46. For examples, see Keith Michael Hearit, Crisis Management by Apology (New York: Lawrence Erlbaum, 2006), 26-27. The quote is from Bill Clinton, concerning allegations of his relationship with White House intern Monica Lewinsky. For mistakes made, see Carol Tavris and Elliot Aronson Mistakes Were Made (but not by me) (New York: Harcourt, 2007); The American Presidency, www.presidency.ucsb.edu/ws/index.php; and Charles Baxter, Dysfunctional Narratives: Or "Mistakes were Made," in Charles Baxter, ed., Burning Down the House: Essays on Fiction (Saint Paul, MN: Graywolf Press, 1997). Lack of knowledge was what Mark Hurd claimed following the Hewlett Packard pretexting scandal described in Chapter 3. Notorious examples of buck passing between corporate entities include the Ford Explorer–Firestone tire recall and the BP Gulf oil spill. Examples of blame placed on consumers involved the Firestone tire and the Toyota "pedal misapplication" accelerator scandal. Many Toyota Recalls, Little Toyota Recall, Washington Post, February 24, 2010, A2.

47. Hearit, Crisis Management by Apology, 80.

48. Peter H. Kim, Removing the Shadow of Suspicion: The Effects of Apology versus Denial for Repairing Competence versus Integrity-Based Trust Violations, Journal of Applied Psychology 89 (2004):107.

49. Donald L. Ferrin, Peter H. Kim, Cecily D. Cooper, and Kurt T. Dirks, Silence Speaks Volumes: The Effectiveness of Reticence in Comparison to Apology and Denial for Responding to Integrity- and Competence-Based Trust Violations, Journal of Applied Psychology 92 (2007): 893, 894.

50. Hearit, Crisis Management by Apology, 207.

51. Id. at 208; Ferrin, Kim, Cooper, and Dirks, Silence Speaks Volumes, 89.

52. David Mankoff, New Yorker, February 1, 2010, 70.

53. Ferrin, Kim, Cooper, and Dirks, Silence Speaks Volumes, 906.

54. Noam Cohen, Word for Word/Mixed Messages: Swimming with Stock Analysts, or Sell Low and Buy High . . . Enthusiastically, New York Times, May 5, 2002, 4, 7; McGeehan, $100 Million Fine for Merrill Lynch, New York Times, May 22, 2002, A1.

55. Steven J. Scher and John M. Darley, How Effective Are the Things People Say to Apologize? Effects of the Realization of the Apology Speech Act, Psycholinguistic Research 26 (1997):127, 130.

56. Deborah Tannen, The Power of Talk: Who Gets Heard and Why, Harvard Business Review (September-October 1995):143.

57. Douglas A. Cooper, CEO Must Weigh Legal and Public Relations Approaches, Public Relations Journal 48 (1992):40.

58. Jennifer K. Robbennolt, Apologies and Legal Settlement: An Empirical Examination, Michigan Law Review 102 (2003):460, 469, 491-499.

59. Jennifer Robbennolt, Attorneys, Apologies, and Settlement Negotiations, Harvard Negotiation Review 13 (2008):349, 362; Ken-ichi Ohbuchi, Masuyo Kameda, and Nariyuki Agarie, Apology as Aggression Control: Its Role in Mediating Appraisal of and Response to Harm, Journal of Personality and Social Psychology 56 (1989):219, 224-226.

60. Graham Dobbs, Political Apologies: Chronological List, http://reserve.mg2.org/apologies.htm.

61. Lisa Belkin, Unforgivable, New York Times Magazine, July 4, 2010, 10 (noting that hospitals have found that a disclose and apologize policy has reduced litigation costs); Jennifer Robbennolt, Apologies and Settlement Levers, Journal of Empirical Legal Studies 3 (2006):333; Robbenalt, Attorneys, Apologies, and Settlement Negotiation, 354-355.

62. Robbenalt, Attorneys, Apologies, and Settlement Negotiation, 356; Robbennolt, Apologies and Settlement Levers, 336-337.

63. Jennifer K. Robbennolt, Apologies and Settlement Levers.

64. Scher and Darley, How Effective Are the Things People Say, 132; Hearit, Crisis Management by Apology, 69; Paul Vitello, I Apologize. No, Really, I'm Serious, I . . . , New York Times, February 21, 2010, WK2; David De Cremer and Barbara C. Schouten, When Apologies for Injustice Matter: The Role of Respect, European Psychologist 13 (2008):239.

65. David D. Kirkpatrick, In Secretly Taped Conversations, Glimpses of the Future President, New York Times, Feb. 20, 2005, 1.

66. Dodds, Political Apologies.

67. Mark D. West, Secrets, Sex, and Spectacle: The Rules of Scandal in Japan and the United States (Chicago: University of Chicago Press, 2006), 285, 294, quoting Shozo Shibuya, Techniques of Apology (2003), 152.

68. Id. at 319.

69. Hearit, Crisis Management by Apology, 175.

70. Id. at 176-186.

71. Id. at 146.

72. Hiroko Tabuchi and Bill Blasic, Toyota's Top Executive under Rising Pressure, New York Times, February 6, 2010, B4 (quoting Tuck School of Business professor Paul Argenti); Micheline Maynard, The Family Face of Toyota, New York Times, February 24, 2010, B4.

73. Weber Shandwick, Safeguarding Reputation; Gaines-Ross, Corporate Reputation, 51.

74. Caroline E. Mayer and Frank Swoboda, "I Come . . . to Apologize": Firestone CEO Hears Coverup Allegations on Hill, Washington Post, September 7, 2000, A1.

75. Diana B. Henriques and David Barstow, Red Cross Pledges Entire Terror Fund to Sept. 11 Victims, New York Times, November 15, 2001, A1, B10.

76. Gaines-Ross, Corporate Reputation, 80-82.

77. Id. at 119.

78. Firestein, Crisis of Character, 262; Gaines-Ross, Corporate Reputation, 85-89.

79. Linda Kleve Trevino, Out of Touch: The CEO's Role in Corporate Misbehavior, Brooklyn Law Review 79 (2005):1195, 1209; Elizabeth Wolfe Morrison and Frances Milliken, Organizational Silence: A Barrier to Change and Development in a Pluralistic World, Academy of Management Review 25 (2000):706, 707.

80. William George, Tragedy at Toyota: How Not to Lead in Crisis, http://hbswk.hbs.edu/cgi-bin/print?id=6381.

81. Presidential Address to the Nation on the Oil Spill in the Gulf of Mexico, Daily Comp. Pres. Doc. 2010 DCPD No. 0502 (June 15, 2010), available at http://www.gpoaccess.gov/presdocs/2010/DCPD-201000502.pdf.

82. Peter Robison and James Gunsalus, Boeing Chief Tackles Ethics, All-New Jet, Seattle Post-Intelligencer, May 29, 2006, 4, available at http://www.seattlepi.com/business/271937_boeing mcnerney29.html.

83. See the discussion of Chip Heath and Dan Heath, Made to Stick, in Chapter 4.

84. Lisa Belkin, Unforgivable, New York Times Magazine, July 4, 2010, 10 (quoting Hayward)

85. Peter S. Goodman, In Case of Emergency: What Not to Do, New York Times, August 22, 2010, BU1 (quoting Hayward).

86. Steven K. May, George Cheney, and Juliet Roper, The Debate over Corporate Social Responsibility (New York: Oxford University Press, 2007), 173.

87. Jim Lentz, Testimony to House Committee on Oversight and Government Reform, http://www.toyota.com/about/news/corporate/2010/02/24-1-testimony.html; Alex Altman, Congress Puts Toyota (and Toyoda) in the Hot Seat, Time/CNN, February 24, 2010, http://www.time.com/time/tprintout/0,8816,1967654,00.html.

88. Caroline E. Mayer and Frank Swoboda, "I Come . . . to Apologize": Firestone CEO Hears Coverup Allegations on Hill, Washington Post, September 7, 2000, A1.

89. Andrew S. Grove, Craig R. Barrett, and Gordon E. Moore, To Owners of Pentium Processor-Based Computers and the PC Community, Wall Street Journal, December 21, 1994, A7.

90. Tavris and Aronson, Mistakes Were Made, 1 (quoting Kissinger).

91. http:www.jfklibrary.org/Research/Ready-Reference/JFK-Speeches/The-President-and-the-Press-Address-before-the-American-Newspaper-Publishers-Association.aspx.

92. Steve Pendlebury, Helen Thomas Joins Long Line of Pubic Figures Apologizing, http://www.aolnews.com/the-point/article/helen-thomas-joins-the-apology.com (quoting Blumenthal); Maureen Dowd, Lies as Wishes, New York Times, May 23, 2010, WK9.

93. Pendlebury, Helen Thomas (quoting Kirk).

94. Id. (quoting Knotts).

95. Ashlee Vance, Hewlett-Packard Ousts Chief for Hiding Payments to Friend, New York Times, August 7, 2010, A1 (quoting Hurd).

96. Eric Dash, So Many Ways to Almost Say "I'm Sorry," New York Times, April 18, 2010, WK 4 (quoting Prince).

97. Pages 2-3 (point 2), available at http://www.vatican.va/holy_father/benedict_xvi/letters/2010/documents/hf_ben-xvi_let_20100319_church-ireland_en.html.

98. J.V. Grimaldi, Firestone CEO Says Apology Wasn't Admission of Fault, New York Times, October 10, 2000, E2.

99. Hearit, Crisis Management by Apology, 143.

100. Ben Heineman, HP's CEO, Mark Hurd: How Could He Do Something So Stupid?, Atlantic Monthly, Aug 7, 2010.

101. Joe Nocera, The Real Reason H.P.'s Board Ousted its Chief, New York Times, Aug 14, 2010, B7.

102. Richard Waters, Moral Hazards, Financial Times, August 15, 2010, 5 (quoting Coffee).

103. Ben Heineman, HP's CEO, Mark Hurd: How Could He Do Something So Stupid?, Atlantic Monthly, Aug 7, 2010.

104. Scandal Gets Juicier: Tech Mogul Assails H.P., San Jose Mercury News, Aug 10, 2010, A1 (quoting Ellison). Ellison also claimed that this was the worst personnel decision since the idiots on the Apple board fired Steve Jobs many years ago." Id.

105. Joe Nocera, H.P.'s Blundering Board, New York Times, September 11, 2010, B1, B6. California forbids agreements not to compete, so inevitable disclosure suites are the only option and they are difficult to win. Richard A. Booth, National Law Journal, October 25, 2010, 42.

106. Robert A. Guth, Ben Worthen, and Justin Scheck, Accuser Said Hurd Leaked an H-P Deal — CEO Lost Out as Board Lost Faith, Wall Street Journal, November 6, 2010, A1.

107. Vance, Hewlett-Packard Ousts Chief, A1 (quoting Michael Hurst).

108. Charles C. Manz, Vikas Anand, Mahendra Joshi, and Karen P. Manz, Emerging Paradoxes in Executive Leadership: A Theoretical Interpretation of the Tensions between Corruption and Virtuous Values, Leadership Quarterly 19 (2008):385, 387. See also the discussion of moral leadership in Chapter 5.

109. Nocera, The Real Reason, B1.

110. Eric Dezenhall, Not All Publicity Is Good Publicity, Ethical Corporation, July-August 2010, 42, 43.

111. Andy Borowitz, The Borowitz Report, Funny Times, July 2010, 19.

112. Laurence H. Summers, Remarks at NBER on Diversifying the Science and Engineering Workforce, January 14, 2005, available at http://www.president.harvard.edu/speeches/2005/nber.html.

113. Id.

114. Harvard Standing Committee on Women, quoted in Stanley Fish, Clueless in Academe, Chronicle of Higher Education, February 23, 2005, available at http://chronicle.com/jobs/2005/02/2005022301c.htm.

115. Rebecca Winters, Harvard's Crimson Face, Time, January 31, 2005, 52.

116. The Revenge of Ellen Swallow, New York Times, February 20, 2005, C8.

117. Alan Dershowitz, The Crimson Controversy, Nightline, ABC News, February 21, 2005; Richard Freeman, quoted in Fish, Clueless.

118. Dershowitz, The Crimson Controversy.

119. Stanley Fish, Clueless in Academe, Chronicle of Higher Education, February 23, 2005, available at http://chronicle.com/jobs/2005/02/2005022301c.htm.

120. Van Jones, http://www.vanjones.net/vanjones.html (last visited Nov. 28, 2009). A biographical website outlining Van Jones's career and achievements.

121. John M. Broder, White House Official Resigns after G.O.P. Criticism, New York Times, Sep. 7, 2009, at A1.

122. Maura Judkis, Obama Drafts Van Jones as Green Jobs Adviser, U.S. News & World Report, Mar. 10, 2009, http://www.usnews.com/money/blogs/fresh-greens/2009/03/10/obama-drafts-van-jones-as-green-jobs-adviser.html.

123. Sarah Wheaton, White House Adviser on "Green Jobs" Resigns, New York Times, Sep. 6, 2009, at A17.

124. Broder, White House Official Resigns, at A1. The petition demanded "a call for immediate inquiry into evidence that suggest high-level government officials may have deliberately allowed the September 11th attacks to occur."

125. Mary Snow, Obama Did Not Order Van Jones' Resignation, Adviser Says, Cable News Network (CNN), Sep. 6, 2009, http://www.cnn.com/2009/POLITICS/09/06/obama.adviser.resigns/index.html.

126. Id.

127. Glenn Beck of Fox News led the campaign. White House Official Resigns after G.O.P. Criticism, at A1.

128. Michael Burnam, Embattled Van Jones Quits, but "Czar" Debates Rage On, New York Times, Sep. 9, 2009, http://www.nytimes.com/gwire/2009/09/08/08greenwire-embattled-van-jones-quits-but-czar-debates-rage-9373.html?scp=1&sq=embattled%20van%20jones%20quits,%20but%20%27czar%27%20debates%20rage%20on&st=cse.

129. Burnam, Embattled Van Jones Quits.

130. Color of Change, http://colorofchange.org (last visited Nov. 28, 2009). Color of Change is an organization dedicated to strengthening the black political voice and committed to ensuring that all Americans are "represented, served, and protected — regardless of race or class. Van Jones cofounded the organization in 2005. Although criticism of Jones predated the campaign, it accelerated after some of Beck's sponsors withdrew their ads. Wheaton, White House Official Resigns, at A1; Burnam, Embattled Van Jones Quits, but "Czar" Debates Rage On. The campaign was triggered by Beck's characterization of Obama as a racist. Id. For attacks on Jones by Beck's defenders see Defend Glenn, http://www.defendglenn.com/bec and http://gatewaypundit.firstthings.com.

131. Burnam, Embattled Van Jones Quits.

132. Broder, White House Official Resigns, at A1.

133. Wheaton, White House Advisor, at 17.

134. Broder, White House Official Resigns after G.O.P. Criticisms, at A1.

135. Id.

136. Id.

137. Van Jones, Shirley Sherrod and Me, New York Times, June 25, 2010, WK10.

138. The Brian Lehrer Show: ACORN Reacts, New York National Public Radio broadcast, Sep. 18, 2009.

139. Association of Community Organizations for Reform Now (ACORN), http://www.acorn.org/index.php?id=12342 (last visited Sep. 25, 2009).

140. Christopher Drew and Eric Lipton, G.O.P. Anger in Swing State Eased Attorney's Exit, New York Times, March 18, 2007, 1.

141. Clark Hoyt, Tuning In Too Late, New York Times, Sep. 26, 2009, WK12. The most unconscionable advice was to claim some of the Salvadoran girls as dependents. Christopher Hayes, ACORN and Accountability, The Nation, Oct. 12, 2009, 4.

142. The Brian Lehrer Show.

143. Id.

144. "Defund ACORN Act," H.R. 3571, 111th Cong. (2009).

145. Sarah Wheaton, Acorn Sues over Video as I.R.S. Severs Ties, New York Times, Sep. 23, 2009, at A22.

146. The Brian Lehrer Show.

147. Id.

148. Id.

149. Christopher Hayes, ACORN and Accountability, The Nation, Oct. 12, 2009, 4.

150. Id.

151. Carl Hulse, House Prohibits Federal Money to Acorn, New York Times, Sep. 18, 2009, A15.

152. Carol D. Leonnig, Progressive Coalition Come Out for ACORN, Washington Post, Oct. 1, 2009, http://voices.washingtonpost.com/44/2009/10/01/progressive_coalition_comes_ou.html.

153. Jeremy Scahill, The ACORN Standard, The Nation, Nov. 2, 2009, at 4. For abuses by other companies that retain contracts, see Hayes, ACORN and Accountability.

154. Thomas Brom, Stinging Acorn, California Lawyer, February 2010, 11.

155. Vera v. O'Keefe, U.S. District Court, Southern District of California, 10 CV1 422 L, filed July 8, 2010; Ed O'Keefe, Activist James O'Keefe Alleges Census Bureau Fraud, Washingtonpost.com, June 1, 2010.

156. Susan Kinzie, ACORN'S Capitol Hill Office Shutting Down: National Group Making Broad Closures but Hasn't Dissolved, Washington Post, March 25, 2010, B1 (quoting Michael McCray).

157. Kinzie, ACORN's Capitol Hill Office Shutting Down, B1 (quoting Issa).

158. Sandhya Somashekhar, Planned Parenthood Fires Worker Caught on Video, Washington Post, February 2, 2011, available at Washingtonpost.com.

159. In the Matter of Representative Charles B. Rangel, Adjudicatory Subcommittee from the Committee on Standards of Official Conduct, U.S. House of Representatives, November 16, 2010.

160. Eric Lipton, Lawmakers Linked to Centers Endowed by Corporate Money, New York Times, August 6, 2010, A1.

161. David Kocieniewski, Rangel Censured over Violations of Ethics Rules, New York Times, December 3, 2010, A1.

162. David M. Herszenhorn and Carl Hulse, In Personal Ethics Battles, A Partywide Threat, New York Times, August 2, 2010, A11 (quoting McConnell).

163. Lipton, Lawmakers Linked to Centers, A3 (quoting Ornstein).

164. Dennis Thompson, Ethics in Congress: From Individual to Institutional Corruption (Washington, D.C:Brookings, 1995), 135-137. See also Dennis St. Martin and Fred Thompson, eds., Public Ethics and Governance: Standards and Practices in Comparative Perspective (Oxford: Elsevier, 2006).

165. Patrick Wintour, Party Funding Row, The Guardian (London), March 21, 2006, 6.

166. Brendan O'Neill, Don't Moan about the House of Lords: Abolish It, http://www.spiked-online.com/index.php/site/article/264.

167. For Acorn workers, see http://www.youtube.com/watch?annotation_id=annotation_714205&feature=iv&v=LtTnizEnC1U; http://www.youtube.com/watch?feature=iv&annotation_id=annotation_872007&v=TNYU9PamIZk. For Shirley Sherrod's edited speech, see http://www.youtube.com/watch?v=t_xCeItxbQY; http://www.cnn.com/video/#/video/us/2010/07/20/sherrod.naacp.speech.dctv?iref=videosearch. For Rangel's press statements, see http://www.cnn.com/video/#/video/politics/2010/07/23/sot.rangel.investigation.cnn?iref=videosearch; http://www.cnn.com/video/#/video/politics/2010/07/29/sot.rangel.overzealous.cnn?iref=videosearch; http://www.cnn.com/video/#/video/politics/2010/08/17/pkg.soledad.rangel.exclusive.cnn?iref=videosearch; http://www.cnn.com/video/#/video/politics/2010/08/12/bts.rangel.presser.cnn?iref=videosearch. For Fox News's coverage of Van Jones, see http://www.youtube.com/watch?v=tJAz8D14wDQ; http://www.youtube.com/watch?v=VYlx9evcMoA. For Glenn Beck, see http://video.foxnews.com/v/3938743/who-is-van-jones.

168. The Hayward segment aired June 21, 2010, and one of the Rangel segments aired November 16, 2010.

169. For Lewis, see The Brian Lehrer Show; for Runciman, with David Willets MP and Executive Editor of the Evening Standard Anne McElvoy, BBC Night Waves, http://www.bbc.co.uj/radio3/nightwaves/pip/dugr6. ACORN Reacts, New York National Public Radio broadcast, Sep. 18, 2009.

170. Alison Leigh Cohen, Lawyer Seen as Bold Enough to Cheat the Best, New York Times, December 14, 2008, A1.

171. Nathan Koppel and Mike Esterl, Lawyer Crashes after a Life in the Fast Lane, Wall Street Journal, November 19, 2009, A16; John Pacenti, Why Suspicions about Fla. Firm's Alleged Ponzi Scheme Weren't Voiced, Law.com, December 7, 2009, http://www.law.com/jsp/law/sendEmail.jsp?content=a&id=1202436126736.

172. Brtittany Wallman, Life in the Fast and Secret Lane, South Florida Sentinel, November 6, 2009; A Video Tour of Scott Roth Rothstein's Office, Miami Herald, November 6, 2009.

173. A Video Tour of Scott Roth Rothstein's Office, Miami Herald, November 6, 2009, http://www.youtube.com/watch?v=9Bmp_4zcrGM. For Dreier, see http://www.youtube.com/watch?v=JEH4fNOqIjM.

174. http://www.veoh.com/browse/videos/category/educational_and_howto/watch/v19638349cJsADswp.

175. http://feedroom.businessweek.com/index.jsp?fr_story=ea8af491b21c54bd997cd11457e69f15cab88d02.

176. For a roundtable discussion with Bernard Madoff, see http://www.youtube.com/watch?v=ab1NTIlO-FM&p=472F217D3868451B; For a news account, see http://www.youtube.com/watch?v=SsSGZezvuSg.

177. Donald Kennedy, Academic Duty (Cambridge, MA: Harvard University Press, 1997), 165.

178. Id. at 170.

179. Kennedy, Academic Duty.

180. Id. at 170-172.

181. David Folkenflik, What Happened to Stanford's Expense Scandal, Baltimore Sun, November 20, 1994, 4F.

182. Kennedy, Academic Duty, 174-175.

183. See Harry Jaffe, Ben Ladner's Years of Living Lavishly, Washingtonian, April 1, 2006, www.washingtonian.com/articles/people/1714.html (describing the downfall of an American University president for grossly excessive expenses and possible fraud, such as a personal chauffer and chef).

184. In response to adverse publicity, the university appointed an official charged with oversight of expenditures. Steve Fainaru, University to Manage Home Costs of President, New York Times, August 27, 2010, A17. See also Steve Fainaru, University Head's Housing Raises Ire and Expense, New York Times, August 22, 2010, A23 (quoting official's claim that Yudof had "turned the Office of the President into his personal staff").

185. Goldie Blumenstyk, Outside Chance for Insiders, Chronicle of Higher Education, November 4, 2005, 28 (quoting Richard Ingram).

186. Ben Quinn, British Parliament Finds Steep Cost in "Expense" Scandal: Credibility, Christian Science Monitor, May 13, 2009, http://www.csmonitor.com/2009/0513/p06s07-woeu. html; "Mr. and Mrs. Expenses" Stand Down as Tory Veterans Become the Latest Casualties, The Times (London), May 26, 2009, 16, 17.

187. David Hughes, Dangerous Gulf between the People and the Political Class, The Daily Telegraph (London), May 18, 2009, 6; Robert Winnett, This Rotten Parliament: Half of MPS Guilty of Overclaiming Expenses, The Daily Telegraph (London), February 5, 2010, 1.

188. Michael Kranish, Obama Seeks to Stop AIG Bonuses; Amid Outrage, Geithner Tries to Recoup Cash, Boston Globe, March 17, 2009, 1, available at http://www.boston.com/news/nation/washington/articles/2009/03/17/obama_seeks_to_stop_aig_bonuses.

189. Investment Banks Defend Bonus Payouts, UPI Business News, February 28, 2009.

190. For Obama on Wall Street's "shameful" bonuses, see http://www.youtube.com/watch?v=_qfWqmmlmXU.

191. For Jacqui Smith scandal, see http://www.youtube.com/watch?v=msBa0jDtVbw.

192. Gormley, The Death of American Virtue, 257-259.

193. West, Secrets, Sex, and Spectacle, 296 (quoting Clinton).

194. New York Times, Last Night's Address: In his Own Words, New York Times, August 18, 1998, A12.

195. John M. Broder, Testing of a President: In Moscow, Clinton Defends His TV Admission on Lewinsky Case, New York Times, September 3, 1998, A1.

196. John M. Broder, Another Apology but G.O.P. Appears Unmoved, New York Times, December 12, 1998, A1.

197. New York Times, President Clinton's Address at the National Prayer Breakfast, New York Times, September 12, 1998, A12.

198. Hillary Clinton, Living History (New York: Simon and Schuster, 2003), 468.

199. Hearit, Crisis Management by Apology, 93.

200. Gormley, The Death of American Virtue, 413.

201. Gerard Baker, Sex Americana, Wall Street Journal, June 27-28, 2009, W1.

202. Rebecca Dana, Why Women Don't Have Sex Scandals, The Daily Beast, December 11, 2009 (quoting Tiger's view that "[w]omen tend to prefer males who are more powerful than they [are] and not vice versa").

203. E.J. Dionne Jr., Give Him a Break: Sen. Vitter Has Sinned, But It's Time to Stop Nosing into our Politicians' Private Lives, Pittsburgh Post Gazette, July 13, 2007, B7.

204. Paul Farhi, Bad News Travels Fast, and Furiously, Washington Post, March 14, 2008 (quoting Frank).

205. Gail Collins, The Love Party, New York Times, June 25, 2009, A23.

206. The Sins of Governor Sanford, National Public Radio, June 25, 2009 (comments by Dezenhall).

207. Peter Elkind, Rough Justice: The Rise and Fall of Eliot Spitzer (New York: Portfolio, 2010); Lloyd Constantine, Journal of the Plague Year: An Insider's Chronicle of Eliot Spitzer's Short and Tragic Reign (New York: Kaplan Publishing, 2010); Kristi Keck, Surviving a Political Sex Scandal, CNN.com, July 14, 2009, 1, available at http://www.cnn.com/2009/POLITICS/07/14/political.sex.scandal.survival/index.html.

208. Jenny Sanford, Staying True (New York: Ballantine Books, 2010); Elizabeth Edwards, Resilience: Reflections on the Burdens and Gifts of Facing Life's Adversities (New York: Broadway Books, 2009).

209. Paul Farhi, Bad News Travels Fast, And Furiously, Washington Post, March 14, 2008, C1.

210. Kipnis, How to Become a Scandal, 5.

211. Susan Dominus, Doing Something Sketchy? It's Harder to Cover Up Now, New York Times, March 21, 2008, B6; Farhi, Bad News Travels Fast.

212. For Clinton, see http://www.youtube.com/watch?v=ClfpG2-1Bv4; for Kilpatrick, Dateline on Kwame Kilpatrick, http://www.youtube.com/watch?v=YLQ02-pbRB0 (from beginning to 3:15).

213. http://www.youtube.com/watch?v=jNX518hfghU. The Huffington Post also posted the video at http://www.huffingtonpost.com/2009/03/04/congressman-offers-preemp_n_172000.html.

PART IV

LEADERSHIP CHALLENGES

8

DIVERSITY IN LEADERSHIP

Prior discussion has focused on what constitutes leadership and what qualities, skills, and organizational dynamics make it effective. This chapter explores who exercises leadership, and how characteristics such as race, ethnicity, and gender matter in the selection and performance of leaders. We focus on these characteristics not because they are the only relevant dimensions of diversity, but because these are the ones that affect most individuals and that have generated the most research. Our approach highlights how different identities intersect to structure the leadership experience.[1] Although constraints of space and research make it necessary to generalize, that should not obscure important differences within and between particular groups.

What these groups share, however, is a history of exclusion. For most of recorded history, women and minorities seldom figured in leadership positions. When commentators spoke of the "great man" theory of leadership, they were not using the term generically. A comprehensive review of encyclopedia entries published at the turn of the twentieth century identified only about 850 eminent women, famous or infamous, throughout the preceding 2000 years. In rank order, they included queens, politicians, mothers, mistresses, wives, beauties, religious figures, and women of "tragic fate."[2] Most of these women acquired their influence through men. Even when successful, female leaders were often discounted: the counselors of Queen Elizabeth I pressured her to marry so the country could avoid the unnatural aberration of her "petticoat government."[3] In the United States, the few women who obtained leadership positions were almost entirely white, Anglo-Saxon, and protestant, as were the "great men" who occupied similar roles.

That began to change in the mid-twentieth century in response to broader social, economic, and political forces, which the law reflected and reinforced. Presidents Roosevelt, Truman, and Eisenhower made efforts to desegregate the military, and Presidents Kennedy and Johnson promulgated executive orders requiring affirmative action by government contractors. In 1964, Congress passed Title VII of the Civil Rights Act, which extended equal opportunity requirements to all employers with more than fifteen workers, and created the Equal Employment Opportunity Commission (EEOC) to pursue complaints and monitor compliance.[4] State and local governments enacted similar legislation and often created their own enforcement agencies.

These mandates, and the broader forces they reflected, prompted significant efforts to level the playing field. Many employers began actively recruiting women and minorities, formalizing hiring, promotion, and compensation criteria; establishing identity-based affinity groups; and creating mentoring and training programs. Government contractors set goals and timetables for the employment and promotion of underrepresented groups. Government agencies reviewed the results, filed discrimination lawsuits, and mediated complaints. Such enforcement action, together with litigation by private parties, resulted in substantial expansion of the pipeline to leadership.

As these efforts evolved, and government pressure waned under more conservative administrations, the justifications for equal opportunity initiatives shifted from legal and ethical principles to economic grounds. Employers increasingly emphasized the "business case for diversity." Equalizing opportunity for women and minorities was not only the right thing to do and necessary for legal compliance, it was also good for the bottom line. Greater inclusiveness, particularly at leadership levels, was said to improve decision making, enhance reputation and recruitment, and expand customer and client bases.

Despite continuing diversity efforts, women and minorities remain significantly underrepresented at leadership levels. For example, as this book went to press, when blacks, Asian Americans, Latinos, and Native Americans constituted about a third of the American population, they accounted for 22 percent of the United States Supreme Court, 17 percent of the House of Representatives, 12 percent of the Senate, 8 percent of state governors, 6 percent of partners in major law firms, and 3.8 percent of Fortune 500 CEOs.[5] Women, although over half the adult population, accounted for 34 percent of the United States cabinet, 17 percent of the Congress, 24 percent of state legislators, 12 percent of state governors, 15 percent of equity partners in major law firms, and 3 percent of Fortune 1000 CEOs.[6] For women of color, the underrepresentation is even more pronounced. For example, although women of color constitute 15 percent of the population, they account for 5 percent of federal appellate judges, 4 percent of Cabinet officials, 3 percent of seats on Fortune 500 boards of directors, 0.4 percent of Fortune 500 CEOs, and no governors.[7]

The readings that follow explore why such underrepresentation might constitute a problem and what should be done to address it. Which arguments appear most and least persuasive? Why have they had only limited success in changing the landscape of leadership? Does it matter? What implications should we draw for future leadership initiatives?

A. THE CASE FOR DIVERSITY

DAVID A. THOMAS AND ROBIN J. ELY, "MAKING DIFFERENCES MATTER: A NEW PARADIGM FOR MANAGING DIVERSITY"

Harvard Business Review, 74(5) (Sept.-Oct. 1996):79-90

What will it take for organizations to reap the real and full benefits of a diverse workforce? A radically new understanding of the term, for starters.

Why should companies concern themselves with diversity? Until recently, many managers answered this question with the assertion that discrimination is wrong, both legally and morally. But today managers are voicing a second notion as well. A more diverse workforce, they say, will increase organizational effectiveness. It will lift morale, bring greater access to new segments of the marketplace, and enhance productivity. In short, they claim, diversity will be good for business.

Yet if this is true — and we believe it is — where are the positive impacts of diversity? Numerous and varied initiatives to increase diversity in corporate America have been under way for more than two decades. Rarely, however, have those efforts spurred leaps in organizational effectiveness. Instead, many attempts to increase diversity in the workplace have backfired, sometimes even heightening tensions among employees and hindering a company's performance.

This article offers an explanation for why diversity efforts are not fulfilling their promise and presents a new paradigm for understanding — and leveraging — diversity. It is our belief that there is a distinct way to unleash the powerful benefits of a diverse workforce. Although these benefits include increased profitability, they go beyond financial measures to encompass learning, creativity, flexibility, organizational and individual growth, and the ability of a company to adjust rapidly and successfully to market changes. The desired transformation, however, requires a fundamental change in the attitudes and behaviors of an organization's leadership. And that will come only when senior managers abandon an underlying and flawed assumption about diversity and replace it with a broader understanding.

Most people assume that workplace diversity is about increasing racial, national, gender, or class representation — in other words, recruiting and retaining more people from traditionally underrepresented "identity groups." Taking this commonly held assumption as a starting point, we set out six years ago to investigate its link to organizational effectiveness. We soon found that thinking of diversity simply in terms of identity-group representation inhibited effectiveness.

Organizations usually take one of two paths in managing diversity. In the name of equality and fairness, they encourage (and expect) women and people of color to blend in. Or they set them apart in jobs that relate specifically to their backgrounds, assigning them, for example, to areas that require them to interface with clients or customers of the same identity group. African American M.B.A.'s often find themselves marketing products to inner-city communities; Hispanics frequently market to Hispanics or work for Latin American subsidiaries. In those kinds of cases, companies are operating on the assumption that the main virtue identity groups have to offer is a knowledge of their own people. This assumption is limited — and limiting — and detrimental to diversity efforts.

What we suggest here is that diversity goes beyond increasing the number of different identity-group affiliations on the payroll to recognizing that such an effort is merely the first step in managing a diverse workforce for the organization's utmost benefit. Diversity should be understood as the varied perspectives and approaches to work that members of different identity groups bring.

Women, Hispanics, Asian Americans, African Americans, Native Americans —
these groups and others outside the mainstream of corporate America don't
bring with them just their "insider information." They bring different, important, and competitively relevant knowledge and perspectives about how to
actually do work — how to design processes, reach goals, frame tasks, create
effective teams, communicate ideas, and lead. When allowed to, members of
these groups can help companies grow and improve by challenging basic
assumptions about an organization's functions, strategies, operations, practices, and procedures. And in doing so, they are able to bring more of their
whole selves to the workplace and identify more fully with the work they do,
setting in motion a virtuous circle. Certainly, individuals can be expected to
contribute to a company their firsthand familiarity with niche markets. But
only when companies start thinking about diversity more holistically — as
providing fresh and meaningful approaches to work — and stop assuming
that diversity relates simply to how a person looks or where he or she comes
from, will they be able to reap its full rewards.

Two perspectives have guided most diversity initiatives to date: the discrimination-and-fairness paradigm and the access-and-legitimacy paradigm.
But we have identified a new, emerging approach to this complex management issue. This approach, which we call the learning-and-effectiveness
paradigm, incorporates aspects of the first two paradigms but goes beyond
them by concretely connecting diversity to approaches to work.

Our goal is to help business leaders see what their own approach to diversity currently is and how it may already have influenced their companies'
diversity efforts. Managers can learn to assess whether they need to change
their diversity initiatives and, if so, how to accomplish that change. . . .

The Discrimination-and-Fairness Paradigm

Using the discrimination-and-fairness paradigm is perhaps thus far the
dominant way of understanding diversity. Leaders who look at diversity
through this lens usually focus on equal opportunity, fair treatment, recruitment, and compliance with federal Equal Employment Opportunity requirements. The paradigm's underlying logic can be expressed as follows:

Prejudice has kept members of certain demographic groups out of
organizations such as ours. As a matter of fairness and to comply with federal
mandates, we need to work toward restructuring the makeup of our
organization to let it more closely reflect that of society. We need managerial
processes that ensure that all our employees are treated equally and with
respect and that some are not given unfair advantage over others.

Although it resembles the thinking behind traditional affirmative-action
efforts, the discrimination-and-fairness paradigm does go beyond a simple
concern with numbers. Companies that operate with this philosophical orientation often institute mentoring and career-development programs specifically for the women and people of color in their ranks and train other
employees to respect cultural differences. Under this paradigm, nevertheless,
progress in diversity is measured by how well the company achieves its recruitment and retention goals rather than by the degree to which conditions in the
company allow employees to draw on their personal assets and perspectives to

do their work more effectively. The staff, one might say, gets diversified, but the work does not. . . .

Without doubt, there are benefits to this paradigm: it does tend to increase demographic diversity in an organization, and it often succeeds in promoting fair treatment. But it also has significant limitations. The first of these is that its color-blind, gender-blind ideal is to some degree built on the implicit assumption that "we are all the same" or "we aspire to being all the same." Under this paradigm, it is not desirable for diversification of the workforce to influence the organization's work or culture. The company should operate as if every person were of the same race, gender, and nationality. It is unlikely that leaders who manage diversity under this paradigm will explore how people's differences generate a potential diversity of effective ways of working, leading, viewing the market, managing people, and learning. . . .

As an illustration of the paradigm's weaknesses, consider the case of Iversen Dunham, an international consulting firm that focuses on foreign and domestic economic-development policy. (Like all the examples in this article, the company is real, but its name is disguised.) Not long ago, the firm's managers asked us to help them understand why race relations had become a divisive issue precisely at a time when Iversen was receiving accolades for its diversity efforts. Indeed, other organizations had even begun to use the firm to benchmark their own diversity programs.

Iversen's diversity efforts had begun in the early 1970s, when senior managers decided to pursue greater racial and gender diversity in the firm's higher ranks. . . . Women and people of color were hired and charted on career paths toward becoming project leaders. High performers among those who had left the firm were persuaded to return in senior roles. By 1989, about 50% of Iversen's project leaders and professionals were women, and 30% were people of color. The 13-member management committee, once exclusively white and male, included five women and four people of color. Additionally, Iversen had developed a strong contingent of foreign nationals.

It was at about this time, however, that tensions began to surface. Senior managers found it hard to believe that, after all the effort to create a fair and mutually respectful work community, some staff members could still be claiming that Iversen had racial discrimination problems. The management invited us to study the firm and deliver an outsider's assessment of its problem.

We had been inside the firm for only a short time when it became clear that Iversen's leaders viewed the dynamics of diversity through the lens of the discrimination-and-fairness paradigm. But where they saw racial discord, we discerned clashing approaches to the actual work of consulting. Why? Our research showed that tensions were strongest among midlevel project leaders. Surveys and interviews indicated that white project leaders welcomed demographic diversity as a general sign of progress but that they also thought the new employees were somehow changing the company, pulling it away from its original culture and its mission. Common criticisms were that African American and Hispanic staff made problems too complex by linking issues the organization had traditionally regarded as unrelated and that they brought on projects that seemed to require greater cultural sensitivity. White male project leaders also complained that their peers who were women and people of color were undermining one of Iversen's traditional strengths: its hard-core quantitative orientation. For instance, minority project leaders had suggested that Iversen consultants collect information and seek input from others in the client company besides senior managers — that is, from the rank and file and from middle managers. Some had urged Iversen to expand its consulting approach to include the gathering and analysis of qualitative data through interviewing and observation. Indeed, these project leaders had even challenged one of Iversen's long-standing, core assumptions: that the firm's reports were objective. They urged Iversen Dunham to recognize and address the subjective aspect of its analyses; the firm could, for example, include in its reports to clients dissenting Iversen views, if any existed.

For their part, project leaders who were women and people of color felt that they were not accorded the same level of authority to carry out that work as their white male peers. Moreover, they sensed that those peers were skeptical of their opinions, and they resented that doubts were not voiced openly.

... Iversen's discrimination-and-fairness paradigm had created a kind of cognitive blind spot; and, as a result, the company's leadership could not frame the problem accurately or solve it effectively. Instead, the company needed a cultural shift — it needed to grasp what to do with its diversity once it had achieved the numbers. If all Iversen Dunham employees were to contribute to the fullest extent, the company would need a paradigm that would encourage open and explicit discussion of what identity-group differences really mean and how they can be used as sources of individual and organizational effectiveness.

Today, mainly because of senior managers' resistance to such a cultural transformation, Iversen continues to struggle with the tensions arising from the diversity of its workforce.

The Access-and-Legitimacy Paradigm

In the competitive climate of the 1980s and 1990s, a new rhetoric and rationale for managing diversity emerged. If the discrimination-and-fairness paradigm can be said to have idealized assimilation and color- and gender-blind conformism, the access-and-legitimacy paradigm was predicated on the acceptance and celebration of differences. The underlying motivation of the access-and-legitimacy paradigm can be expressed this way:

We are living in an increasingly multicultural country, and new ethnic groups are quickly gaining consumer power. Our company needs a demographically more diverse workforce to help us gain access to these differentiated segments. We need employees with multilingual skills in order to understand and serve our customers better and to gain legitimacy with them. Diversity isn't just fair; it makes business sense.

Where this paradigm has taken hold, organizations have pushed for access to — and legitimacy with — a more diverse clientele by matching the demographics of the organization to those of critical consumer or constituent groups. In some cases, the effort has led to substantial increases in organizational diversity. In investment banks, for example, municipal finance departments have long led corporate finance departments in pursuing demographic diversity because of the typical makeup of the administration of city halls and county boards. Many consumer-products companies that have used market segmentation based on gender, racial, and other demographic differences have also frequently created dedicated marketing positions for each segment. The paradigm has therefore led to new professional and managerial opportunities for women and people of color. . . .

Again, the paradigm has its strengths. Its market-based motivation and the potential for competitive advantage that it suggests are often qualities an entire company can understand and therefore support. But the paradigm is perhaps more notable for its limitations. In their pursuit of niche markets, access-and-legitimacy organizations tend to emphasize the role of cultural differences in a company without really analyzing those differences to see how they actually affect the work that is done. Whereas discrimination-and-fairness leaders are too quick to subvert differences in the interest of preserving harmony, access-and-legitimacy leaders are too quick to push staff with niche capabilities into differentiated pigeonholes without trying to understand what those capabilities really are and how they could be integrated into the company's mainstream work. To illustrate our point, we present the case of Access Capital.

Access Capital International is a U.S. investment bank that in the early 1980s launched an aggressive plan to expand into Europe. Initially, however, Access encountered serious problems opening offices in international markets; the people from the United States who were installed abroad lacked credibility, were ignorant of local cultural norms and market conditions, and simply couldn't seem to connect with native clients. Access responded by hiring Europeans who had attended North American business schools and by assigning them in teams to the foreign offices. This strategy was a marked success. Before long, the leaders of Access could take enormous pride in the fact that their European operations were highly profitable and staffed by a truly international corps of professionals. They took to calling the company "the best investment bank in the world."

Several years passed. Access's foreign offices continued to thrive, but some leaders were beginning to sense that the company was not fully benefiting from its diversity efforts. Indeed, some even suspected that the bank had made itself vulnerable because of how it had chosen to manage diversity. A senior executive from the United States explains:

> If the French team all resigned tomorrow, what would we do? I'm not sure what we could do! We've never attempted to learn what these differences and cultural competencies really are, how they change the process of doing business. What is the German country team actually doing? We don't know. We know they're good, but we don't know the subtleties of how they do what they do. We assumed—and I think correctly—that culture makes a difference, but that's about as far as we went. We hired Europeans with American M.B.A.'s because we didn't know why we couldn't do business in Europe—we just assumed there was something cultural about why we couldn't connect. . . . We knew enough to use people's cultural strengths, as it were, but we never seemed to learn from them.

Access's story makes an important point about the main limitation of the access-and-legitimacy paradigm. . . . [O]nce the organization appears to be achieving its goal, the leaders seldom go on to identify and analyze the culturally based skills, beliefs, and practices that worked so well. Nor do they consider how the organization can incorporate and learn from those skills, beliefs, or practices in order to capitalize on diversity in the long run.

Under the access-and-legitimacy paradigm, it was as if the bank's country teams had become little spin-off companies in their own right, doing their own exotic, slightly mysterious cultural-diversity thing in a niche market of their own, using competencies that for some reason could not become more fully integrated into the larger organization's understanding of itself. Difference was valued within Access Capital — hence the development of country teams in the first place — but not valued enough that the organization would try to integrate it into the very core of its culture and into its business practices.

Finally, the access-and-legitimacy paradigm can leave some employees feeling exploited. Many organizations using this paradigm have diversified only in those areas in which they interact with particular niche-market segments. In time, many individuals recruited for this function have come to feel devalued and used as they begin to sense that opportunities in other parts of the organization are closed to them. . . .

The Emerging Paradigm: Connecting Diversity to Work Perspectives

Recently, in the course of our research, we have encountered a small number of organizations that, having relied initially on one of the above paradigms to guide their diversity efforts, have come to believe that they are not making the most of their own pluralism. These organizations, like Access Capital, recognize that employees frequently make decisions and choices at work that draw upon their cultural background — choices made because of their identity-group affiliations. The companies have also developed an outlook on diversity that enables them to incorporate employees' perspectives into the main work of the organization and to enhance work by rethinking primary tasks and redefining markets, products, strategies, missions, business practices, and even cultures. Such companies are using the learning-and-effectiveness paradigm for managing diversity and, by doing so, are tapping diversity's true benefits.

A case in point is Dewey & Levin, a small public-interest law firm located in a northeastern U.S. city. Although Dewey & Levin had long been a profitable practice, by the mid-1980s its all-white legal staff had become concerned that the women they represented in employment-related disputes were exclusively white. The firm's attorneys viewed that fact as a deficiency in light of their mandate to advocate on behalf of all women. Using the thinking behind the access-and-legitimacy paradigm, they also saw it as bad for business.

Shortly thereafter, the firm hired a Hispanic female attorney. The partners' hope, simply put, was that she would bring in clients from her own community and also demonstrate the firm's commitment to representing all women. But something even bigger than that happened. The new attorney introduced ideas to Dewey & Levin about what kinds of cases it should take on. Senior managers were open to those ideas and pursued them with great success. More women of color were hired, and they, too, brought fresh perspectives. The firm now pursues cases that its previously all-white legal staff would not have thought relevant or appropriate because the link between the firm's mission and the employment issues involved in the cases would not have been obvious to them. For example, the firm has pursued precedent-setting litigation that challenges English-only policies—an area that it once would have ignored because such policies did not fall under the purview of traditional affirmative-action work. Yet it now sees a link between English-only policies and employment issues for a large group of women—primarily recent immigrants—whom it had previously failed to serve adequately. As one of the white principals explains, the demographic composition of Dewey & Levin "has affected the work in terms of expanding notions of what are [relevant] issues and taking on issues and framing them in creative ways that would have never been done [with an all-white staff]. It's really changed the substance—and in that sense enhanced the quality—of our work."

Dewey & Levin's increased business success has reinforced its commitment to diversity. In addition, people of color at the firm uniformly report feeling respected, not simply "brought along as window dressing." Many of the new attorneys say their perspectives are heard with a kind of openness and interest they have never experienced before in a work setting. Not surprisingly, the firm has had little difficulty attracting and retaining a competent and diverse professional staff. . . .

Eight Preconditions for Making the Paradigm Shift

. . . Hence the question arises: What is it about the law firm of Dewey & Levin and other emerging third-paradigm companies that enables them to make the most of their diversity? Our research suggests that there are eight preconditions that help to position organizations to use identity-group differences in the service of organizational learning, growth, and renewal.

1. The leadership must understand that a diverse workforce will embody different perspectives and approaches to work, and must truly value variety of opinion and insight. . . .
2. The leadership must recognize both the learning opportunities and the challenges that the expression of different perspectives presents for an organization. In other words, the second precondition is a leadership that is committed to persevering during the long process of learning and relearning that the new paradigm requires.
3. The organizational culture must create an expectation of high standards of performance from everyone. . . . Some organizations expect women and people of color to underperform—a negative assumption that too often becomes a self-fulfilling prophecy. To move to the third paradigm, a company must believe that all its members can and should contribute fully.
4. The organizational culture must stimulate personal development. Such a culture brings out people's full range of useful knowledge and skills— usually through the careful design of jobs that allow people to grow and develop but also through training and education programs.

5. The organizational culture must encourage openness. Such a culture instills a high tolerance for debate and supports constructive conflict on work-related matters.
6. The culture must make workers feel valued. If this precondition is met, workers feel committed to — and empowered within — the organization and therefore feel comfortable taking the initiative to apply their skills and experiences in new ways to enhance their job performance.
7. The organization must have a well-articulated and widely understood mission. Such a mission enables people to be clear about what the company is trying to accomplish. It grounds and guides discussions about work-related changes that staff members might suggest. Being clear about the company's mission helps keep discussions about work differences from degenerating into debates about the validity of people's perspectives. A clear mission provides a focal point that keeps the discussion centered on accomplishment of goals.
8. The organization must have a relatively egalitarian, nonbureaucratic structure. It's important to have a structure that promotes the exchange of ideas and welcomes constructive challenges to the usual way of doing things — from any employee with valuable experience. . . .

[P]erhaps more than anything else, a shift toward [our new] paradigm requires a high-level commitment to learning more about the environment, structure, and tasks of one's organization, and giving improvement-generating change greater priority than the security of what is familiar. This is not an easy challenge, but we remain convinced that unless organizations take this step, any diversity initiative will fall short of fulfilling its rich promise.

PROBLEM 8-1

You are the faculty chair of a search committee for the dean of the preeminent public university law school in your state. The search process has narrowed the selection to two final candidates, and the committee now needs to make a recommendation of one of them to the university president.

The first candidate, James Dawson, has been teaching at the law school for fifteen years. He is a highly regarded teacher and scholar, and one of the faculty's best-known members. He is a dynamic speaker and is expected to be a very capable fund-raiser based on his outgoing personality and his name recognition. He has no significant academic administrative experience, but he has served on some outside boards of directors. Dawson is white, Episcopalian, and married. He has no children and no time-consuming pursuits outside of work. He has more conservative views on most issues than those held by the faculty generally. One concern for the committee involves his extensive outside consulting projects. Some colleagues have raised questions about whether his work exceeds the university's rules limiting external involvement to one-fifth time. A few students who have assisted him on these projects have received academic credit for their work. In articles related to his consulting, he has not always disclosed his paid position. In response to these questions, Dawson has insisted that he has remained within the university guidelines on outside commitments, but has produced no time records. He has also claimed that the student research had legitimate academic value, that he did not believe his consulting work was relevant to the positions that he took in the articles, and that no university ethical rules required his disclosure.

A second concern about Dawson's candidacy involves interpersonal sensitivity. Dawson has a reputation of being flirtatious with female students and dismissive toward certain female staff and junior colleagues. No formal complaints have been made regarding inappropriate behavior.

A final concern for the committee is how to weight Dawson's own concerns about his reputation. He is widely regarded as the front-runner in the process. If he is not selected as dean, Dawson is expected to leave the law school faculty.

The second candidate, Kim Chang, is an Asian alumna of the law school who has been on the faculty for twelve years. She is currently an associate dean. She has also held a midlevel administrative position at the Federal Trade Commission in Washington, D.C. She has a reputation for being a very skilled administrator and consensus builder in a school in which faculty disagreements can be contentious. She has an impressive list of publications and is very highly regarded among those in her field. Chang has also done significant pro bono consulting work, although not at levels that would come close to exceeding the university's limits.

Some members of the faculty have raised concerns about whether Chang is dynamic enough to be a successful fund-raiser, and whether her pro bono activities, including work for pro-choice and immigrant rights organizations, as well her Buddhist Temple, would sit well with alumni. Chang also has two young children, which some alumni fear might discourage extensive travel. Although she has been mentioned as a likely candidate at other schools conducting searches, she has family ties that are likely to keep her from leaving even if she is not selected as dean.

The law school has an underrepresentation of women and minorities in tenured faculty and upper-level administrative positions. There are bitter divisions among some groups within the faculty around diversity issues. The law school is in the middle of a major fund-raising campaign to support student financial aid and a new classroom building.

The committee believes that a majority of the law school alumni favor Dawson. A vocal group of students strongly favors Chang. Eight student groups have sent a letter to the committee and the president expressing concern about Dawson's record on diversity issues. The letter stated that Dawson has consistently supported increased dependence on test scores and grade point averages in student admissions, which the groups believe would have adverse effects on the law school's ability to admit minorities. Dawson has stated in interviews that he agrees with current admissions policies. The student body, which is 55 percent female and 45 percent male, seems to tip slightly in favor of Chang, but most male law students appear to favor Dawson. A slight majority of the faculty also support Dawson, but a group of female faculty is strongly opposed. The alumni who have registered views generally prefer Dawson.

1. How do you proceed?
2. What, if any, further information would you seek and what process would you put in place to collect it?
3. How would you weight the candidates' different strengths and weaknesses? Why?
4. If you were the university president, and these were the facts you had on each candidate, which candidate would you select? How would you justify your decision to the law school community?

NOTES AND QUESTIONS

Although the business case for diversity is widely accepted in principle, it is often marginalized in practice. Part of the reason may be that findings on its impact are not uniformly favorable. Not all social science research reflects strong, positive benefits from diversity on group performance. If poorly managed, it can heighten conflict and communication problems, or cause outsiders to suppress divergent views.[8] Nor do all studies find a correlation between diversity and profitability.[9] In those that do, it is unclear which way causation runs. As the following discussion of corporate boards indicates, it may well be that financial success sometimes enhances diversity rather than the converse. Organizations that are on strong financial footing are better able to invest in diversity initiatives or have sound employment practices that promote both diversity and profitability.[10]

Moreover, in skeptics' view, even if diversity has quantifiable advantages in enhancing decision making, the benefits need to be weighed against the adverse effects of lowering standards and provoking backlash based on "identity politics" and "special" treatment."[11] In a recent study by the Minority Corporate Counsel Association, many white men agreed that "diversity should take a back seat to performance and capability."[12] In their view, too much "reverse discrimination" causes resentment, and "stretch hires of minorities who are not qualified sometimes does much to undermine . . . acceptance of diversity and inclusion."[13] As one participant put it, "Taking opportunities . . . from those with merit and giving [them] . . . to people based upon race, gender, or sexual identity is forcing us apart not bringing us together. . . . I can think of few things worse for an ostensibly color blind and meritocratic society."[14]

Supporters of diversity initiatives, relying on research summarized in sections C and D below, argue that they are necessary to counteract the unconscious biases that shape assessments of performance and that limit opportunities for qualified women and minorities to develop leadership capabilities. Pretending that we already live in a strictly meritocratic society will not bring us closer to achieving one. Advocates of diversity also believe that it promotes effective leadership by ensuring difference in backgrounds and perspectives, and by enhancing the legitimacy of decision making processes.

1. What is your response? How compelling is the business case for diversity?
2. What diversity initiatives have you encountered in the workplace? How effective have they been? What might have improved their effectiveness?

B. A CASE STUDY ON THE CASE FOR DIVERSITY: CORPORATE BOARDS

One context in which pressures for diversity have been steadily increasing has been corporate boards of directors. The following excerpt explores the arguments for increasing women's and minorities' board representation, the obstacles that stand in the way, and some plausible responses. The challenges facing corporate boards are similar to those arising in other corporate, nonprofit, legal, and government workplaces.

DEBORAH L. RHODE AND AMANDA K. PACKEL, "DIVERSITY ON CORPORATE BOARDS: HOW MUCH DIFFERENCE DOES DIFFERENCE MAKE?"

Rock Center for Corporate Governance at Stanford
University Working Paper No. 89, 2010

> To serve as director on the board of a leading American corporation is to hold a position of exceptional power and influence. Indeed, the decisions made in corporate boardrooms affect the lives of hundreds of thousands of employees and consumers, as well as the performance and policies of other corporations, the ebb and flow of economic activity, the dealings of the global marketplace, and international strategies. Yet, even today, the players at the highest level of corporate governance are for the most part a homogenous group.
>
> Mary C. Mattis, *Women on Corporate Boards, Two Decades of Research*

. . . Members of corporate boards of the largest American companies are primarily white men. According to the most recent data, women hold only approximately 15 percent of the seats on Fortune 500 boards and only 15 percent of key board committee chairs. Minorities account for only 12 percent of Fortune 500 board seats, and minority women for only 3 percent of board seats. Almost two-thirds of Fortune 500 companies have no women of color serving as directors.

Although the overall percentage of women and minorities on corporate boards remains small, the number has been growing. By some measures, diversity has increased substantially. In 1973, only seven percent of Fortune 1000 boards had any minority directors; now 78 percent have at least one minority director. Similarly, the number of Fortune 100 boards with at least one woman increased from 11 percent in 1973 to 97 percent in 2006. By other measures, however, progress—especially in the past decade—has stalled. At current rates of change, it will take almost seventy years before women on corporate boards reach parity with men. And increases in minority representation appear to have slowed substantially. Total minority seats on Fortune 100 boards have barely increased since 2003, and the representation of women of color has grown less than 1 percent over the last decade. Moreover, some of the most encouraging numbers on board diversity may conceal less promising trends. Much of the increase in women and minority board directors over the last decade has reflected the same individuals sitting on more boards. Many commentators worry that these "trophy directors" are spread too thin to provide adequate oversight.

The Business Case for Diversity

The growing consensus among corporate leaders is that ensuring board diversity is an important goal. Not only is it the "right thing to do," especially as corporations' employees, customers, and clients become increasingly diverse, it also pays off at the bottom line. The "business case" for diversity rests on two primary claims. The first is that it improves outcomes, particularly financial performance. The second is that it improves decision-making processes, which may in turn improve firm performance.

Diversity and Firm Performance

Despite increasing acceptance of the business case for diversity, empirical evidence on the issue is mixed. . . . One of the most significant constraints is the shortage of studies on racial and ethnic diversity. Most of the research focuses on gender, from which commentators often generalize without qualification.

Studies using regression analyses have also found a positive relationship between board diversity and various measures of firm performance in samples of U.S. and foreign companies. . . . Of course, such correlations do not demonstrate causation. A few studies have claimed to show that board diversity leads to improved financial performance, but causal linkages are extremely difficult to prove. As other studies have suggested, it could be that better firm performance leads to increased board diversity rather than the reverse. More successful firms may also be more able to attract the female and minority candidates in high demand for board service. Larger and better-performing firms may have more resources to devote to pursuing diversity and may face more pressure from the public and large institutional investors to increase diversity on the board. Finally, some omitted third factor could be causing both improved performance and greater board diversity.

Several other studies of U.S. and foreign firms have found no relationship or a negative relationship between board diversity and firm performance. . . . Adams and Ferreira concluded in a 2009 study that "the positive correlation between performance and gender diversity documented in prior literature is not robust to any method of addressing the endogeneity of gender diversity. If anything, the relationship appears to be negative." . . .

In sum, the empirical research on the effect of board diversity on firm performance is inconclusive, and the results are highly dependent on methodology. The mixed results reflect the different time periods, countries, economic environments, types of companies, and measures of diversity and financial performance selected. The relationship between board characteristics and firm performance likely varies by country because of the different regulatory and governance structures, economic climate and culture, and size of capital markets. Some researchers attribute the varied findings to the methodological shortcomings of many of the studies, including small sample size, short-term observations of performance, and the difficulty of controlling for reverse causation, endogeneity, and other omitted variables that may be affecting both board diversity and firm performance. Moreover, with so many different measures of firm performance from which to choose, researchers are likely to find some values that show a positive relationship with board diversity and others that show a negative relationship. Scholars also question whether focusing on short-term accounting measures of financial performance is the best way to measure the impact of diversity. Research is lacking on the relationship between board diversity and long-term stock price performance, which is the "gold standard" measure of shareholder value.

These mixed quantitative results may reflect not only differences in research methodology, but also differences in the context in which diversification occurs. For example, some studies suggest that the influence of minority directors on corporate boards is heavily shaped not only by the prior experience of the directors, but also the "larger social structural context in which demographic differences are imbedded." The failure to include a critical mass of women or minorities may in some cases prevent the potential benefits of diversity. Those benefits may also be dampened by corporations' well-documented tendency to appoint women and minorities who are least likely to challenge the status quo, or who are "trophy directors," with too many board positions to provide adequate oversight.

Perhaps it should not be surprising that studies of the relationship between board diversity and financial performance are inconclusive, given that a direct relationship between various other aspects of board composition and performance has been similarly difficult to establish. . . . The relationship between board characteristics, including diversity, and company performance may be "complex and indirect." Because boards perform multiple and varied tasks, diversity may affect different functions in different ways, making it difficult to establish any consistent relationship between board diversity and firm performance.

Although empirical research has drawn much-needed attention to the underrepresentation of women and minorities on corporate boards, it has not convincingly established that board diversity leads to improved financial performance. Given the limitations of these studies, many commentators believe that the case for diversity rests on other grounds, particularly its effects on board decision-making processes, corporate reputation, and governance capacities.

Diversity and Board Process, Corporate Reputation, and Good Governance

A common argument by scholars, as well as board members of both sexes, is that diversity enhances board decision-making and monitoring functions. This assertion draws on social science research on small-group decision making, as well as studies of board process and members' experiences. The basic premise is that diversity may lessen the tendency for boards to engage in groupthink — a phenomenon in which members' efforts to achieve consensus override their ability to "realistically appraise alternative courses of action."

The literature on board decision making reflects three different theories about the process through which diversity enhances performance. The first is that women and men have different strengths, and that greater inclusion can ensure representation of valuable capabilities. For instance, some empirical evidence suggests that women generally are more financially risk averse than men. For that reason, many commentators have speculated that women's increased participation in corporate financial decision making could have helped to curb tendencies that caused the most recent financial crisis. A widely discussed panel at a World Economic Forum in Davos put the question: "Would the world be in this financial mess if it had been Lehman Sisters?" Many Davos participants believed that the answer was no, and cited evidence suggesting that women were "more prudent" and less "ego driven" than men in financial management contexts. Other research points in similar directions, including studies from researchers at Harvard and Cambridge Universities, which find a correlation between high levels of testosterone and an appetite for risk.

Some commentators also cite evidence indicating that women have higher levels of trustworthiness or collaborative styles that can improve board dynamics. As one female director put it, "Women are more cooperative and less competitive in tone and approach. When there's an issue, men are ready to slash and burn, while women are ready to approach. . . . Women often provide a type of leadership that helps boards do their jobs better." So too, racial and ethnic minorities' experience of needing to relate to both dominant and subordinate groups is thought to provide a form of bicultural fluency that may enhance decision making.

A second argument is that women and minorities have different life experiences than white men do and bring different concerns and questions to the table, which allows the board to consider "a wider range of options and solutions to corporate issues."[15] Diversity is productive by generating cognitive conflict: "conflicting opinions, knowledge, and perspectives that result in a more thorough consideration of a wide range of interpretation, alternatives, and consequences."[16] For example, Phillips, Liljenquist, and Neale's study of group decision making found that when new members were "socially similar" to existing team members, subjective satisfaction was high but actual problem solving results were not. Although team members rated productivity much lower when newcomers were socially dissimilar, in fact the more heterogeneous group was much better at accomplishing the problem-solving task. A diverse board can also enhance the quality of a board's decision-making and monitoring functions because diverse groups are less likely to take extreme positions and more likely to engage in higher-quality analysis.

Some scholars have also suggested that diverse boards can help prevent corporate corruption because they are "bold enough to ask management the tough questions." According to one study, female directors expanded the content of board discussions and were more likely than their male counterparts to raise issues concerning multiple stakeholders. Research has found that heterogeneous groups are associated with broader information networks and increased creativity and innovation. One study concluded that board racial diversity increased innovation by expanding access to information and networks, and prompting more thorough evaluation. Studies on the relationship between board diversity and its capacity for strategic change have reached conflicting results.

Although research suggests that functionally or occupationally diverse groups may solve problems more quickly and effectively than homogeneous teams, demographic diversity may not improve decision making processes and outcomes in the same ways. The educational, socioeconomic, and occupational backgrounds of women and minority directors tend to be quite similar to those of other directors. Studies on the extent to which gender influences leadership behavior are mixed, but some suggest that men and women who occupy the same role tend to behave similarly. Moreover, in some studies, demographic diversity leads to increased conflict and poor communication, which tend to counteract or dominate the benefit of broader perspectives. Research also shows mixed effects of gender diversity on problem-solving abilities. Diverse teams may also experience increased levels of anxiety and frustration. One study found that racial (but not gender) diversity increased the risk of emotional conflict and that such interpersonal clashes characterized by anger, frustration, and other negative feelings adversely affect performance. As Scott Page summarizes the evidence, demographically diverse groups tend to outperform homogeneous groups "when the task is primarily problem solving, when their identities translate into relevant tools, when they have [little or no difference in what they value], and when their members get along with one another."

A third claim is that the very existence of diversity alters board dynamics in ultimately positive ways. Mannix and Neale, for example, argue that the presence of visibly diverse members enhances a group's ability to handle conflict by signaling that differences of opinion are likely. A group that lacks diversity is less likely to handle conflict well because it is not expected. Other scholars have drawn on signaling theory to argue that "a diverse board conveys a credible signal to relevant observers of corporate behavior." Board diversity can convey a commitment to equal opportunity, responsiveness to diverse stakeholders, and a general message of progressive leadership, which can enhance the corporation's public image. Empirical evidence is limited, but some findings are consistent with this theory. Catalyst has found a relationship between the proportion of female directors and the proportion of female officers a corporation is likely to have in the future. Other studies have indicated that in some sectors, the presence of female or minority directors can enhance a firm's reputation with consumers. In explaining these findings, researchers have suggested that board diversity may enhance firm reputation by sending signals to investors "about the robustness of the governance mechanisms in place and the quality of the firm." Yet the significance of such claims should not be overstated. Employees, consumers, and the general public are typically unaware of board composition. . . .

A cluster of empirical studies have identified a positive correlation between diversity and various other measures of good governance. Adams and Ferreira, for example, found that firms that have a higher representation of women hold more meetings, have higher attendance rates, experience greater participation in decision making, engage in tougher monitoring, and are more likely to replace a CEO when the stock performs poorly. Ibrahim and Angelidis' survey of nearly 400 corporate directors concluded that female directors exhibit a stronger commitment to corporate social responsibility. A study by the Conference Board of Canada found that, on average, organizations whose boards have two or more women adopt a greater number of accountability practices and regularly review more non-financial performance measures than organizations with all-male boards. The study further found that boards with more women paid greater attention to audit and risk oversight than all-male boards. However, as in many of the preceding studies, correlation does not indicate causation, and it could be that well-governed corporate boards are more committed to diversity and seek greater gender parity. Moreover, in Adams and Ferreira's 2009 study, although a higher proportion of women correlated with better board monitoring, it had a negative effect on financial performance in well-governed firms.

Given the competing findings and methodological limitations of these studies, the financial benefits of board diversity should not be overclaimed. But neither should boards understate other justifications for diversity, including values such as fairness, justice, equality of opportunity, as well as the symbolic message it sends to corporate stakeholders.

Challenges and Barriers to Achieving Diversity

Given the growing support for diversity on corporate boards, why has it been so difficult to achieve? One obvious explanation is that the research on performance is too mixed to make diversification a priority. . . . Other explanations involve unconscious bias and the counterproductive effects of tokenism. These factors both directly impede appointment of qualified female and minority candidates, and prevent others from gaining the leadership experience that would make them attractive choices. A third explanation is resistance to "special preferences." As with other forms of affirmative action, opponents believe that selecting members on the basis of race or gender reinforces precisely the kind of color consciousness and sex stereotyping that society should be seeking to eliminate.

Experience

One of the most common reasons for the underrepresentation of women and minorities on corporate boards is their underrepresentation in the traditional pipeline to board service. The primary route has long been experience as a CEO of a public corporation. Indeed, one study found that over one-half of male Fortune 500 board directors were CEOs or former CEOs. Given the low representation of women and minorities in top executive positions, their talents are likely to be underutilized if selection criteria are not broadened. For example, women account for fewer than 3 percent of CEOs in Fortune 500 corporations, and minorities for fewer than 4 percent of Fortune 500 CEOs. Of senior corporate officers, only 14 percent are female, and 3 percent are black. Even women and minorities who reach upper-level management positions often do so through routes other than profit and loss responsibility, which provides crucial experience for board positions.

Bias

One obvious form of bias impeding diversity on corporate boards and in corporate management is "in-group" favoritism, the preference that individuals feel for those who are like them in important respects, including race, ethnicity, and sex. Such bias is particularly likely in contexts where selection criteria are highly subjective, as is often true in board appointments. Indirect evidence for the importance of such favoritism comes from research showing that when CEOs are more powerful than their boards, new board directors are likely to be similar to the CEO. Conversely, when the board is more powerful, new directors are more likely to be similar to the board.

In-group favoritism also influences perceptions of competence and access to support networks. Members of in-groups tend to attribute accomplishments of fellow members to intrinsic characteristics, such as intelligence, drive, and commitment. By contrast, the achievements of out-group members are often ascribed to luck or special treatment. Even in experimental situations where male and female performance is objectively equal, women are held to higher standards, and their competence is rated lower. As one Australian study concluded, "women's competence has to be widely acknowledged in the public domain or through family connections before boards . . . will be prepared to 'risk' having [them] on the board." So too, in-group preferences often exclude women and minorities from the informal networks of mentoring, contacts, and support that are critical for advancement. As a consequence, they are less likely to have the experience and credentials necessary for board appointments.

For women, traditional gender stereotypes compound the problem. Men continue to be rated higher than women on most of the qualities associated with leadership. People more readily credit men with leadership ability and more readily accept men as leaders. What is assertive in a man may seem abrasive in a woman, and female leaders risk seeming too feminine or not feminine enough. In effect, it is more difficult for women to be both liked and respected in contexts like corporate boards, which require both.

Minorities also confront traditional stereotypes, and women of color are doubly disadvantaged. The stereotypes vary somewhat across different racial and ethnic groups, but share common features. The most common is the devaluation of competence; minorities who reach positions that might qualify them for board leadership are often assumed to be the beneficiaries of "special treatment" rather than meritocratic selection. Class poses further obstacles. For example, Westphal and Stern have found that minorities from underprivileged backgrounds must engage in a higher level of ingratiating behavior toward CEOs than non-minorities and economically privileged individuals in order to obtain recommendations for board positions where the CEO is the lead director, or on boards on which the CEO is a member.

Tokenism and Critical Mass

It is also unclear whether the appointment of only one or two female or minority directors will make a significant improvement in board decision making. Rosabeth Moss Kanter's pathbreaking research, confirmed in multiple subsequent studies, found that token members often encounter "social isolation, heightened visibility, . . . and pressure to adopt stereotyped roles. They are less likely to do well in the group, especially if the leader is a member of the dominant category." They also find themselves representing the "woman's" or the "minority's" point of view, as if that were a monolithic position. Thus, tokenism may make it more difficult for women and minorities to be heard on an equal basis with other board members. Outsiders also may have limited opportunities to influence group decisions, particularly in the context of corporate boards where much of the real discussion takes place outside of official meetings.

Research on corporate boards suggests that a "critical mass" is necessary to fully realize the benefits of diversity. As a report by the Wellesley Center for Women notes, "the magic seems to occur when three or more women serve on a board together. Suddenly having women in the board room becomes a normal state of affairs. . . . [They] are no longer seen as outsiders and are able to influence the content and process of board discussions more substantially."

However, many women and minorities who have served on boards take issue with the notion that it takes a critical mass of three to make a significant impact because it implies that "one is doomed to fail." They also fear that such claims may discourage women and minorities from accepting nominations when they are the first, and that boards will feel complacent when they reach the magic number. Already, some companies lose their sense of urgency once they appoint even a single outsider. As one board member noted, "When you're the only woman on the board and talk about adding another woman, they say, 'but we've got you.'"

The marginalization that token members experience may also impair their performance, which discourages further appointment of outsiders. For example, a director may "make herself socially invisible to avoid disrupting perceived group harmony and alleviate discomfort felt by the rest of the (all male) board." As a result, her strengths may go unrecognized, and her silence may reinforce "antiquated beliefs that a woman brings nothing new to the table." Alternatively some directors may fall into the role that sociologists identify as the "Queen Bee" syndrome: they "revel in the notoriety of token status, enjo[y] the perceived advantages of being the only woman in the group and excessively criticize potential women peers."

Strategies: What Works and What Doesn't

Strategies to counteract these dynamics and increase board diversity fall into three main categories. One cluster of initiatives focuses on increasing individuals' capacity for service. A second group includes legal strategies that might expand the pool of qualified members and level the playing field for their appointment. A third set of approaches targets institutions, and attempts to increase the pressure on boards to broaden their appointments through enhanced disclosure requirements and investment strategies.

Strategies for Individuals

One obvious way to expand the number of women and minorities on corporate boards is to increase the pool of qualified applicants. Formal mentoring programs, leadership workshops, diversity advisors or coaches, and related strategies can all help interested applicants shape their career paths, refine their resumes, develop networking strategies, and overcome barriers to self-promotion. In recent years, mentoring and networking programs targeted toward increasing women's representation on boards have become more prevalent in some countries, including the UK, Canada, and France. Providing mentors who themselves have had board experience may be especially critical in bringing qualified candidates to the attention of board nominating committees.

Legal Strategies

Law could also play a greater role in reducing the obstacles to women and minorities who seek leadership positions, including both board appointments and the managerial experience that makes candidates attractive. One common proposal is to require corporations over a certain size to disclose data on recruitment, retention, and promotion of women and minorities. A number of countries mandate such disclosures, and obligating U.S. companies to supply such information would make it easier for corporations to benchmark their performance relative to other similarly situated organizations, and for stakeholders to hold poor performers accountable. The government could also require transparency surrounding the board search process, requiring companies to disclose whether women and minority candidates were considered or interviewed for open positions.

Another strategy would be to increase enforcement resources for anti-discrimination initiatives. Although in theory individuals can sue for sex or racial discrimination in leadership positions, the difficulties of proof and the threat of blacklisting make such litigation extremely rare. However, state and federal equal opportunity agencies could be more proactive in investigating organizations with poor performance in gender and racial equity.

Another possibility would be to follow the example of some European countries that have established quotas for board membership. Norway led the way by requiring firms to have corporate boards with a minimum of 40 percent of female directors by 2008, or face dissolution. The Norwegian government has reported full compliance with the program, which increased women's share of board seats from 7 percent in 2002 to over 40 percent. Spain and the Netherlands have recently followed suit with legislation requiring firms to meet a 40 percent female director minimum by 2015, and France, Belgium, Germany, and Sweden are also debating similar legislation.

Critics contend that quotas do not address the problems that prevent underrepresented groups from obtaining leadership experience, and that the focus should be on eliminating those obstacles and enhancing the qualifications of women and minorities. According to some commentators, the dramatic increase in Norwegian female directors "has done little — yet — to improve either the professional caliber of the boards or to enhance corporate performance." The increase has also had no meaningful impact on the number of female CEOs, which remains stuck close to 5 percent. Critics are also concerned that quotas will simply lead to more unqualified directors, either because of an insufficient supply of well prepared women, or because boards will fill seats with women who won't speak up. In France, where a 40 percent quota is being debated, "[i]n private, chief executives say they will look for female board members . . . who will look decorative and not rock the boat. . . ."

For these reasons, some advocates of diversity prefer a "comply or explain" approach: "companies with a lower proportion [than 30 percent women on their boards] would have to explain [in their annual reports] if they proposed to fill a vacancy with a man." Similarly, companies with no or a very small percentage of minority directors would have to explain if they intended to fill a vacancy with a non-minority. Research from other diversity contexts suggests that requiring individuals to give reasons for particular actions reduces reliance on stereotypes and helps to level the playing field for underrepresented groups. . . . Such voluntary quotas and comply or explain approaches are more politically palatable than mandatory quotas, but they still encounter criticism and their effectiveness remains uncertain, as companies may have no obligation to explain if they choose not to comply. Future research will be needed to see if these approaches actually produce higher rates of female representation on boards.

Institutional Initiatives

Boards themselves could intensify their diversity efforts. One option is to set their own goals or requirements for new appointments. Some advocate a "structured search" that starts with an analysis of the board's functional needs and then identifies female and minority candidates who could fill them. Whatever the process, companies need to expand their searches beyond the traditional pool of CEOs and consider other corporate executives, nonprofit directors and officers, and academic presidents and experts. Many commentators believe that the current pool of potential members is large enough to achieve diversity if qualifications are appropriately broadened. Professional consultants, who now conduct approximately half of board searches, can help identify promising candidates outside the board's network or from less traditional backgrounds. Companies could also institute age limits and term restrictions, which open up seats for women and minorities. These and other efforts to demonstrate a commitment to diversity could help boards make service seem more attractive to well qualified members of underrepresented groups.

Another strategy is to reduce the influence of CEOs in the membership selection process. Some commentators argue that the interests of top corporate executives may be skewed by their desire to maintain control and high levels of compensation. Such considerations can lead them to prefer candidates who share their interests — socially similar, fellow CEOs. Simply giving the board more power over the appointment process could expand the pool of potential candidates.

A final cluster of strategies should focus on making board diversity (or a lack of diversity) more visible, and enlisting pressure from stakeholder groups to hold organizations accountable for their progress. Some empirical research has demonstrated a significant increase in women and minority directors when companies include pictures of the board in annual reports. Large institutional investors could demand such disclosure.

The Securities and Exchange Commission has recently enacted two rules that may affect board diversity. The first rule requires increased transparency regarding director qualifications and the board appointment process. Companies are required to disclose "whether, and if so, how, the nominating committee (or the board) considers diversity in identifying nominees for director." In addition, companies whose boards have a diversity policy must explain how it is implemented and how they assess its effectiveness. The SEC allows companies to define diversity "in ways that they consider appropriate," and acknowledges that some may focus on racial, ethnic, and gender diversity, while others may "conceptualize diversity expansively to include differences of viewpoint, professional experience, education, skill and other individual qualities and attributes that contribute to board heterogeneity."

An analysis of the first four months of disclosures filed under these new rules found that companies' statements were "not very specific, thorough, or revealing." Most statements express support for diversity or claim to make it a consideration in board appointments, while defining it broadly to include diversity of background, experience, and skills, as well as age, geographic location, national origin, race, gender, and ethnicity. Although these disclosure requirements are a significant symbolic step in recognizing the importance of board diversity, they may not of themselves do much to increase racial, ethnic, and gender diversity.

The second rule, approved in August 2010, enables longstanding shareholders with significant holdings to nominate a certain number of directors and place them in the company's proxy materials. Under previous rules, shareholders had to bear the burdens of launching a proxy fight and distributing their own materials. With these new requirements, large investors, including hedge funds, pension funds, and unions, may exercise greater influence over board composition. Because large institutional investors have been among the most vocal advocates of board diversity, their candidates are likely to be more diverse than those traditionally proposed by the company.

Investors could also act, individually and collectively, to make board diversity a higher priority in investment decisions. For example, in 2009, the Women's Leadership Fund was created to invest up to $2 billion in publicly listed companies with a high percentage of women in senior positions, including board members, and to take activist positions in companies lacking such gender representation. More investors should pursue such investment strategies to reward and reform companies based on their diversity records. In addition, organizations that publish indexes for socially responsible investing and corporate social responsibility could include measures of diversity in leadership. Only a few publications now include information along these lines, despite evidence that some investors are interested in receiving it. If diversity on boards becomes part of the standard criteria for measuring corporate social responsibility, that would increase the ability of investors, consumers, and public-interest organizations to hold corporations accountable.

Conclusion

As this overview makes clear, board membership remains a significant site in the struggle for more equitable and effective leadership structures. The gains in diversity that corporate America has made over the last quarter century testify to our capacity for progressive change. But the distance we remain from truly inclusive corporate boards reminds us of the progress yet to be made.

NOTES AND QUESTIONS

1. If you were the only woman or person of color on a board of directors, how might you try to persuade your fellow members to make diversity a higher priority? Role-play your arguments with someone taking a skeptical position. If board members claimed to value diversity, but consistently found female and minority candidates to be either "unqualified" or "unavailable," how would you proceed?

2. Suppose that you are successful in your efforts at persuasion, and the board identifies two women of color as potential candidates. You believe that the first is almost certain to decline, given her other commitments. The second is almost certain to accept, but she is widely viewed as a trophy director whose full-time occupation is to sit on boards where she makes no waves on gender- and race-related issues. Your support of other candidates has been unsuccessful. What should you do? Is this a fight worth having? What factors would be most relevant to your decision? Is it demeaning to suggest that all female or minority directors should have to share the same "politically correct" view on issues that affect their group? Or do you see legitimate reasons to oppose diversity candidates on the ground that they will not be supportive of diversity initiatives?

3. How important is diversity on corporate boards relative to other diversity-related strategies? Damien O'Brien, chief executive of Egon Zehender International, a leading executive search company, argues that the focus on boards is a distraction from the more critical task of getting women into influential line positions. As he notes, since Norway introduced a 40 percent quota for women on boards in 2004, there has been almost no increase in the number of women in senior line-management positions.[17] What is your view? What might account for the lag between board leadership and executive leadership?

4. Nonprofit as well as corporate boards suffer from an underrepresentation of minorities. A recent study found that, on average, 86 percent of nonprofit board members are non-Hispanic whites, and 51 percent of boards are composed solely of white non-Hispanic directors.[18] Although most nonprofit boards are fairly equally balanced in terms of gender, women comprise only

29 percent of board members of nonprofits with annual expenses of over $40 million.[19] What accounts for these inequalities? Are the barriers or strategies to address them any different from those arising in corporate contexts?

C. MANAGING DIVERSITY

Even in organizations that are committed to diversity in leadership, the best path to achieving it is not always clear. In the following article, Dobbin, Kalev, and Kelly explore which strategies are most and least effective in increasing women and minority representation in upper-level positions. Getting more women and minorities into the leadership pipeline is, of course, only the first step toward equity and inclusion. Organizations also need to help them advance and succeed. Manzoni, Strebel, and Barsoux, in the second excerpt below, describe why "diversity goes awry" on corporate boards and what can be done to prevent it.

FRANK DOBBIN, ALEXANDRA KALEV, AND ERIN KELLY, "DIVERSITY MANAGEMENT IN CORPORATE AMERICA"

Contexts 6(4) (Fall 2007):21-27

In the fall of 1996 a tape of two Texaco executives joking about the "black jelly beans" working for the company hit the airwaves in the course of a discrimination suit. Texaco settled almost immediately for $176 million. Of that, $35 million was to fund diversity efforts. Texaco revamped training, expanded feedback to managers through diversity audits and diversity evaluations, and set up mentoring programs and affinity networks for women and minorities. Texaco's report on its progress after five years championed the programs but did not make clear whether diversity had actually increased.

Coca-Cola's 2000 race-discrimination settlement promised similar improvements. Under its consent decree, Coca-Cola agreed to pay $192.5 million, $35 million of which was to fund half a dozen major diversity programs. In 2005, Coca-Cola reported to the court that women and minorities held 64 percent of salaried jobs, up from 61 percent in 2000.

Should Texaco and Coca-Cola be models for the rest of corporate America? How can we judge which of their programs should be copied elsewhere? Proponents of equal opportunity and diversity have faced this question for decades. Case studies and theories offer a variety of prescriptions for ending workplace inequality, but, as in medicine, discovering which remedies work best requires a large number of cases observed over time.

In the decades since Congress passed the Civil Rights Act of 1964, firms have experimented with dozens of diversity measures. Consultants have been pushing diversity training, diversity performance evaluations for managers, affinity networks, mentoring programs, diversity councils, and diversity managers, to name a few. But some experts question whether diversity programs are counterproductive, raising the hackles of white men who, after all, still do most of the hiring and firing. Certain programs even seem to get firms into trouble — Texaco executives were recorded talking about "black jelly beans" after hearing the term in diversity training seminars.

Until recently, no one had looked systematically at large numbers of companies to assess which kinds of programs work best, on average. Our research shows that certain programs do increase diversity in management jobs — the best test of whether a program works — but that others do little or nothing.

The good news is that companies that give diversity councils, or diversity managers, responsibility for getting more women and minorities into good jobs typically see significant increases in the diversity of managers. So do companies that create formal mentoring programs. Much less effective are diversity training sessions, diversity performance evaluations for managers, and affinity groups for women and minorities. There is no magic bullet for the problem of inequality. Programs that work in one firm may not work in another. Programs that fail on average may be just what the Acme Rocket Co. needs. But we are beginning to understand what works in general and what does not. . . .

The Study

Texaco and Coca-Cola spent more than $7 million a year on diversity programs created under their consent decrees. Even Fortune 500 companies not under consent decrees can spend millions of dollars a year on trainers alone, without accounting for lost work time or travel expenses. Yet it is not easy to determine whether these programs actually improve opportunity for women and minorities.

Our challenge was to get accurate data on workforce diversity and on diversity programs for enough companies, over a long enough period of time, so that we could use sophisticated statistical techniques to isolate the effects of, say, diversity training on the percentage of black women in management. . . .

We surveyed 829 of the companies covered in the EEOC's massive data file, putting together a life history of employment practices at each. We asked companies whether they had used dozens of different programs, and when those programs had been in place. Our research question was simple: if a company adopts a particular diversity program, what effect does it have on the share of women and minorities in management? To answer the question, we conducted statistical analyses on the 829 firms over 31 years. . . . Our analyses considered more than 60 workplace characteristics that might affect diversity so as to isolate the effects of diversity taskforces, training, and so on.

Changing Managers' Behavior

One source of gender and racial inequality in the workplace is stereotyping and bias among managers who make hiring and promotion decisions. Research shows that educating people about members of other groups may reduce stereotyping. Such training first appeared in race-relations workshops conducted for government agencies and large federal contractors in the early 1970s. An industry of diversity trainers emerged in the 1980s to argue that people were unaware of their own racial, ethnic, and gender biases and that sensitivity training would help them to overcome stereotypes. . . .

Some diversity experts dismissed training, arguing that attitudes are difficult to alter but that behavior can be changed with feedback. Instead they
supported performance evaluations offering feedback on managers' diversity
efforts. Laboratory experiments support this idea, showing that subjects who
are told that their decisions will be reviewed are less likely to use stereotypes in
assigning people to jobs. General Electric first created equal opportunity
performance evaluations in 1969, arguing that the key to achieving equal
opportunity is a "measurement system with rewards and penalties designed
to produce behavioral changes in managers." Nearly 30 years later, Texaco's
settlement called for a new Leadership Performance Factor (LPF) system for
evaluating each manager's progress on diversity. Bonuses were tied to the LPF
score. . . .

The current enthusiasm for training and evaluations has made them
widely popular. Four in ten of the firms we surveyed offered training, and
one in five had diversity evaluations. But these programs did not, on average,
increase management diversity.

[Our research determined] the percentage change in the proportion of
managers from each group as a consequence of each program — holding the
effects of other factors constant. Because minorities are rare in management to
begin with, for them the [percentage changes] represent small numerical
changes. African-American men held about 3 percent of management jobs
in 2002, and so a 25 percent increase does not translate into big numerical
gains. For white women, the numerical changes are more dramatic. But for all
groups, an increase is an increase. Where the effect is not statistically significant, [we represented the numerical change] as a zero.

Training had small negative effects for African-American women and small
positive effects for Hispanic women. Evaluations had only small negative
effects on black men. In very large workplaces, with 1,500 or more workers,
diversity training has a small positive effect on other groups, but nothing like
the effects of the mentoring programs and taskforces discussed below. Evaluations were no more effective in large workplaces.

Some psychological research supports our finding that training may be
ineffective. Laboratory experiments and field studies show that it is difficult
to train away stereotypes, and that white men often respond negatively to
training — particularly if they are concerned about their own careers. If training cannot eliminate stereotypes, and if it can elicit backlash, perhaps it is not
surprising that, on average, it does not revolutionize the workplace.

We suspect that the potential of diversity performance evaluations is
undermined by the complexity of rating systems. The diversity manager at a
giant communications company told us that diversity performance makes up
5 percent of the total score. With so much of the score riding on other things,
like sales performance, perhaps putting diversity into an employee's annual
evaluation score is not enough to change behavior.

Overall, companies that try to change managers' behavior through training and evaluations have not seen much change. That is disappointing,
because training is the single most popular program and, by most accounts,
the most costly, and because many companies have put their money on diversity evaluations in recent years.

Creating Social Connections

Another way to view the problem of inequality in management jobs is from the supply side. Do women and minorities have the social resources needed to succeed? Many firms have well-educated white women and minorities in their ranks who fail to move up, and some sociologists suggest this is because they lack the kinds of social connections that ambitious white men develop easily with coworkers and bosses. . . .

Consultants argued that formal programs could help women and minorities develop social networks at work. Company affinity networks became popular. . . . Under these affinity networks, people gather regularly to hear speakers and talk about their experiences.

Many companies also put in formal mentoring programs that match aspiring managers with seasoned higher-ups for regular career-advising sessions. These programs can target women and minorities but are often open to all employees. . . .

When it comes to improving the position of women and minorities in management, network programs do little on average, but mentor programs show strong positive effects. In the average workplace, network programs lead to slight increases for white women and decreases for black men. Perhaps that is not surprising, as studies of these network programs suggest that while they sometimes give people a place to share their experiences, they often bring together people on the lowest rungs of the corporate ladder. They may not put people in touch with what they need to know, or whom they need to know, to move up.

Mentor programs, by contrast, appear to help women and minorities. They show positive effects for black women, Latinos, and Asians. Moreover, in industries with many highly educated workers who are eligible for management jobs, they also help white women and black men. Mentor programs put aspiring managers in contact with people who can help them move up, both by offering advice and by finding them jobs. This strategy appears to work.

Making Someone Responsible

. . . The best way to bring about change, management theorists argue, is to make new programs the responsibility of a person or a committee. . . . Now that is the job of the diversity manager, or chief diversity officer. Recently firms have also put in taskforces, or diversity councils, comprising managers from different departments and charged with finding ways to increase diversity. The accounting giant Deloitte and Touche set up taskforces responsible for analyzing the gender gap, recommending remedial steps, and establishing systems for monitoring results and holding managers responsible. Both Texaco and Coca-Cola have diversity managers, and both set up external taskforces to oversee their settlements. . . .

Our analyses show that making a person or committee responsible for diversity is very effective. Companies that establish taskforces typically see small decreases in the number of white men in management, and large increases for every other group (white men dominate management to begin with, so a small percentage decrease for white men can make space for big percentage gains in other groups). Firms that put in diversity managers see increases for all groups of women, and for black men.

In interviews, executives tell us that diversity managers and taskforces are effective because they identify specific problems and remedies. If the taskforce sees that the company has not been recruiting African-American engineers, it will suggest sending recruiters to historically black colleges. If a company has trouble retaining women, the diversity manager may talk to women at risk of leaving and try to work out arrangements that will keep them on the job. Managers and taskforces feel accountable for change, and they monitor quarterly employment data to see if their efforts are paying off. If not, it is back to the drawing board to sketch new diversity strategies. Taskforces may be so widely effective, some tell us, because they cause managers from different departments to "buy into" the goal of diversity.

Lessons for Executives

What are the most cost-effective strategies for increasing diversity? [Our data from 2002 shows that m]any companies were not investing in the strategies that have proven most effective. Three of the four most popular programs—diversity training, evaluations, and network programs—have no positive effects in the average workplace. The two least popular initiatives, mentoring and diversity managers, were among the most effective.

On average, programs designed to reduce bias among managers responsible for hiring and promotion have not worked. Neither diversity training to extinguish stereotypes, nor diversity performance evaluations to provide feedback and oversight to people making hiring and promotion decisions, have accomplished much. This is not surprising in light of the research showing that stereotypes are difficult to extinguish.

There are two small caveats about training. First, it does show small positive effects in the largest of workplaces, although diversity councils, diversity managers, and mentoring programs are significantly more effective. Second, optional (not mandatory) training programs and those that focus on cultural awareness (not the threat of the law) can have positive effects. In firms where training is mandatory or emphasizes the threat of lawsuits, training actually has negative effects on management diversity. Psychological studies showing backlash in response to diversity training suggest a reason: managers respond negatively when they feel that someone is pointing a finger at them. Most managers are still white and male, so forced training focused on the law may backfire. Unfortunately, among firms with training, about three-quarters make it mandatory and about three-quarters cover the dangers posed by lawsuits.

Our findings suggest that firms should look into how they can make training and evaluations more effective. Some experts suggest that training should focus on hiring and promotion routines that can quash subjectivity and bias. Others suggest that diversity performance evaluations based on objective indicators (minority hiring and retention, for instance) and tied to significant incentives (attractive bonuses, or promotions) would work. But few companies follow that model.

... [M]entor programs appear to be quite effective. Such programs can provide women and minorities with career advice and vital connections to higher-ups. While mentoring can be costly—involving release time for mentors and mentees, travel to meetings, and training for both groups—the expense generally pays off. One reason mentoring may not elicit backlash, as training often does, is that many companies make it available to men and women and to majority and minority workers. The theory is that women and minorities less often find mentors on their own (if they did, there would be less of a problem to start with), and thus benefit more from formal programs.

... [C]ompanies that assign responsibility for diversity to a diversity manager, or to a taskforce made up of managers from different departments, typically see significant gains in diversity. Management experts have long argued that if a firm wants to achieve a new goal, it must make someone responsible for that goal. To hire a diversity manager or appoint a taskforce or council is to make someone responsible. Both managers and taskforces scrutinize workforce data to see if their efforts are paying off, and both propose specific solutions to the company's problems in finding, hiring, keeping, and promoting women and minorities. Taskforces have the added advantage of eliciting buy-in—they focus the attention of department heads across the firm who sit together with a collective mission.

... If companies regrouped and put their time and energy into programs known to work elsewhere, they would likely see small but steady increases in the representation of women and minorities in management jobs. ... Managers might also spend more time assessing programs that don't seem to be working and trying to figure out how to make them effective. ...

JEAN-FRANCOIS MANZONI, PAUL STREBEL, AND JEAN-LOUIS BARSOUX,
"WHY DIVERSITY CAN BACKFIRE ON COMPANY BOARDS"

WSJ Business Insight Report, Wall Street Journal, Jan. 25, 2010

When it comes to corporate boards and diversity, the conventional wisdom is simple: Diversity is good. When directors are too alike, the thinking goes, they look at problems—and solutions—the same way. There's no one to challenge prevailing ideas, or to speak out on issues important to certain groups of customers and employees.

By contrast, diversity leads to more innovation, more outside-the-box thinking and better governance.

Sounds great. And it is, in theory. Unfortunately, few boards that pursue diversity ever see the wished-for returns. Many report no significant change in their performance, while others bog down in conflict and gridlock.

Why the gap between potential and reality? Why does it appear to be a lot easier to appoint a diverse board than to make it function well?

Blame it on human nature: As much as diversity is something we prize, the truth is that people often feel baffled, threatened or even annoyed by persons with views and backgrounds very different from their own. The result is that when directors are appointed because their views or backgrounds are different, they often are isolated and ignored. Constructive disagreements spill over into personal battles.

But the solution is not to give up and avoid diversity. Rather, boards need to minimize the friction that diversity often introduces. To unlock the benefits, in short, boards must learn to work with colleagues who were selected not because they fit in—but because they don't.

Our research sheds light on some of the hurdles that diverse boards face, and on solutions for maximizing the benefits such boards offer.

Where Diversity Goes Awry

Initial Encounters. The problems start from Day One. At the very first meeting, directors will scrutinize the words and behavior of new and atypical colleagues for signals about their competence and personality. Depending on why they were appointed to the board, the newcomers run the risk of being saddled with all sorts of stereotypes. "Typical minority." "Typical accountant." "Politician." "Activist." And so on.

If the new member asks too many basic questions, for instance, he becomes "clueless" or "high maintenance." If she says nothing, she's "insecure." Unbridled enthusiasm, meanwhile, particularly coming from a specialist, could be seen as "posturing" or posing a threat to an existing director's expertise in a given area.

A company we work with added a woman designer to its board—the only woman on the board—with a background attuned to the future of the industry but very different from its present. After the first meeting, during which she took an oblique perspective on many issues, some directors were already expressing doubts about her contributions. After just one meeting, she already had been pigeonholed.

Impressions Last. Once a label is on, it can be all but impossible to remove. Directors who quickly take a dim view of a colleague will tend to process all subsequent information in ways that support their initial opinion—and to block information that doesn't fit. If a new member's commitment is doubted, for example, a non-reaction might be read as disinterest, even though the member actually agreed.

Cultural Differences. Signals easily get crossed due to cultural differences. Directors with broadly different experiences will behave in unexpected ways that may be misinterpreted—as disruptive or aggressive, for example. . . .

Confirmation from Others. Current board members also will compare notes about the newcomer in an attempt to define his or her character. That makes perfect sense. But it's important to realize that they are usually turning to like-minded colleagues, who often not only confirm the view but reinforce it with observations of their own that support the bias.

Reinforcing Behavior. When people are regarded as difficult—or unimportant—some of their colleagues may begin to interact with them in a brusque or forceful manner. Once judged unfavorably, such people usually are excluded from informal interactions that take place before and after meetings, which further limits their involvement. Having contact only when it's required also means there's less opportunity for directors to develop more rounded views of that individual.

The reactions of the new members themselves can be a source of friction, as well. They may be defensive or overly sensitive to stereotyping—seeing slights where none were meant (or where they were). And they may succumb to stereotyping themselves.

The bottom line is, when a lack of trust or respect develops, the new director can become more reluctant to contribute — or more strident. In either case, such behavior is likely to move them to fringe status on the board.

Groupthink. Conflicts that at first affect only a few members can spread to and impair the performance of the entire board — inhibiting discussion, innovation and decision-making. In the worst cases, the situation turns into a vicious circle that can't self-correct. Part of the problem is that boards typically gather infrequently, and in rather formal settings, leaving few opportunities to correct false impressions and iron out the tensions.

Existing directors may unite in defensive reaction to the new member and become more entrenched in groupthink. For example, studies show that lone women on boards often report feeling isolated and ignored. Adding a second woman seems to make the problem worse, leading to false perceptions of collusion between the two. Only when there are at least three women do their colleagues accept them as something more than "female directors." The women, too, say they feel less self-conscious and less concerned about representing "their gender."

A War Between Factions. Sometimes, boards become polarized or split into factions determined by how the different members perceive the new director and his or her contributions. For instance, the appointment of a foreign national may sharpen differences between domestic and overseas directors. Over time, a pattern of "us-and-them" relations evolves.

Avoiding the Conflict

The good news is there are ways to handle all of these potential conflicts. Most of the friction can be avoided, or at least kept to a minimum, by following some simple strategies.

Choose Members Carefully. When board members are choosing a new director who will bring diversity, they should think carefully about personality. Newcomers need to be savvy and aware of how they come across to others. The more different they are from the rest, the more they'll need to work at winning over skeptical colleagues.

Ability to disagree constructively should be high on the list of desired characteristics, as well as experience dealing with new kinds of people and situations. The newcomer needs to become part of the group even as he or she challenges it.

Board members looking to hire a new director should also guard against biased thinking — by themselves and their colleagues — as early as the interview stage. When interviewers catch themselves thinking "she/he just doesn't get the business," they can also remind themselves that this will also allow the newcomer to ask questions the board stopped asking long ago.

Assist Newcomers. The chairman or chairwoman should pay close attention to the way new directors are introduced, especially if they have divergent profiles. Newcomers must have a chance to make a favorable first impression and to connect with others in a benign setting — before their first official board meeting.

The chairman should identify the board member likely to connect best with the incoming director and ask him or her to make a friendly phone call or meet for coffee. Giving newcomers insights into the board's operating philosophy and culture up front can help avoid gaffes early on. Debriefings after meetings can help, too.

At the first official board meeting, the chairman can help the newcomer get off to a good start by calling on him or her to comment about a particular issue. This can signal the new director's area of expertise, helping them make contributions right away without seeming presumptuous. But the chairman must be careful not to pigeonhole the new director—for example, by inviting the newly appointed female director to "give us the women's perspective on this issue."

Don't Give In to Get Along. Dissenting voices can be necessary to pick up on issues that chief executives may be missing. But sometimes diversity inhibits pushback. Some directors, for example, may hold their tongues in order not to trigger hostilities between warring factions.

Diverse boards must not be afraid of conflict, as long as it is constructive and civil. Boards that have difficulty discussing their differences, or reconciling them, make it easy for the CEO either to dismiss what they are saying or to listen exclusively to their supporters on the board. The board thus fails in its governance role.

Encourage Initial Dissenters. New directors sometimes tire of the struggle of making themselves heard. Feeling isolated and ignored, they end up self-censoring.

Sometimes they won't speak up for fear of being alone in their opinion, even though they were put on the board for their unique perspective. Other members may have the same opinion but also remain silent, not realizing another person thinks the same thing.

The chairman or lead director must go out of his or her way to make it easy for board members to express vague concerns as a way of finding out whether those views are more widely shared.

NOTES AND QUESTIONS

1. Why do companies persist in investing so many resources in diversity training programs that have little demonstrable payoff? Consider the description of an initiative by BP America that included four two-day "Race Summits" involving 750 diverse "thought leaders" from all levels of the company at different cities across the country. "Participants reported very high levels of satisfaction" and "an independent survey estimated that between 8,000 and 13,000 employees in BP had engaged in a conversation about race as a result of the summit activity."[20] How adequate are those measures of cost-effectiveness? Why would BP advertise its success on those grounds? What other evaluation strategies might be preferable?

2. Diversity consultants Frederick Miller and Judith Katz argue that "[i]nclusion can be built only through inclusion. . . . Change needs to happen in partnership *with* the people of the organization not *to* them."[21] From this perspective, white men need to be treated not as a source of problems but as

critical parts of the solution. They need to be engaged in the problem-solving process and convinced that they will benefit from organizational change. Many problems confronting women and minorities should be seen as symptomatic of broader organizational problems. Building a constituency for reform will require evaluating organizational and individual performance on a "balanced scorecard" that includes diversity as well as short-term profitability. Supervisors need to be judged by their success in advancing female and minority employees and managing inclusive environments.[22]

In principle, those recommendations seem likely to attract broad agreement. In practice, what is likely to stand in the way?

3. Consider an experience that you have had or observed regarding "diversity gone awry." How could it have been handled more effectively?

4. Another increasingly important diversity-related issue is how to prepare leaders to deal with cultural and regional differences. As noted in Chapter 2, nationalities vary across multiple dimensions, including the importance they place on context and relationships in their business dealings. In "low-context" societies, such as the United States, candor and directness are key values; leaders generally want to make the assumptions of transactions explicit and cover contingencies in legal detail. By contrast, in "high-context" societies, including Japan, China, Saudi Arabia, and Spain, leaders tend to rely on personal relationships and shared cultural understandings to provide the backdrop for commercial arrangements.[23] The clash of styles emerges in many settings, in which Americans perceive their counterparts as slow and evasive, and their counterparts see Americans as pushy, distrustful, and overly legalistic. Individuals who are negotiating in a multicultural setting need to be aware of such differences and remember that the "message that ultimately counts is the message that the other person creates in her mind, not the one [they] intended to send."[24]

Have you been in situations in which such differences emerged? How well were they handled? What might have been done differently?

MEDIA RESOURCES

Films, television series, news programs, and training videos offer a wealth of examples of bias and misplaced efforts to combat them. Examples include:

- Stephen Colbert's parody of the role of race and gender in the nomination of Sonia Sotomayor;
- Caricatures of a "diversity day" and a "racial segregation mindset" from *The Office;*
- Tom Hanks's portrayal in *Philadelphia* of an associate with AIDS who sues his firm for discrimination;
- Will Ferrell's portrayal in *Anchorman* of tensions surrounding diversity;
- Eddie Murphy's attempt in *Imagine That* to counter a corporate executive's attempts to capitalize on his Native American identity; and
- Law firms' use of racial and gender stereotypes.[25]

Such caricatures offer a window on why ill-designed diversity training and preferential treatment can provoke backlash, and how such resentment might be avoided. It can also be useful to analyze the effectiveness of promotional videos that corporations and law firms use to showcase their diversity commitment.

D. GENDER AND LEADERSHIP

The materials that follow seek a deeper understanding of the gender dynamics that play out in leadership contexts. As you consider the research summarized below, what seem to be the most significant obstacles confronting women who seek positions of influence? How can they best be addressed? How much does it matter? Why? What role does gender play for male leaders? How might changing the gender composition of leadership influence its effectiveness?

1. WOMEN

DEBORAH L. RHODE AND BARBARA KELLERMAN, "WOMEN AND LEADERSHIP: THE STATE OF PLAY"

Barbara Kellerman and Deborah L. Rhode, eds., Women and Leadership: The State of Play and Strategies for Change (San Francisco: Jossey-Bass, 2007), pp. 1-35

Over the last several decades, we have [identified the problem of leadership for women] . . . and created a cottage industry to address it. . . . Yet while we have made considerable progress in understanding the problem, we remain a dispiriting distance from solving it.

The Underrepresentation of Women in Leadership Roles

The facts are frustratingly familiar. Despite almost a half century of equal opportunity legislation, women's opportunities for leadership are anything but equal. To be sure, the situation has improved significantly over this period, particularly if leadership is broadly defined to include informal as well as formal exercises of authority. By that definition, the percentage of women in leadership roles is substantial and is increasing dramatically. That is particularly true in management and the professions, where women now occupy roughly half of all jobs. Women also hold positions of power in a wide range of government, nonprofit, and religious contexts. But they are still grossly underrepresented at the top and overrepresented at the bottom of the most influential leadership hierarchies. . . .

From an international perspective, the United States is by no means atypical. However, as subsequent discussion makes clear, neither is it a world leader, at least in the number of women political leaders. At this writing, the United States ranks sixty-ninth in female legislative representation, behind Cape Verde, Singapore, Turkmenistan, Zimbabwe, and the Philippines. Overall, the percentage of women in elective office has grown substantially over the last quarter century, but . . . progress remains sluggish. Women hold about 16 percent of the seats in parliamentary bodies and about 11 percent of the presiding officer positions. At current rates of change, it would take about a century for women to reach equal representation in legislative offices. A similar pattern is apparent with heads of state. About 6 percent of the world's top political leaders are female, up from less than 1 percent in 1950. . . .

Comprehensive international data is unavailable for women's representation in leadership roles in business and the professions, but the limited information that has been compiled suggests ample room for progress. For example, across Europe, women make up only about a third of high-level decision makers, including legislators, senior government officials, and business managers. Only 8 percent of directors and 5 percent of top executives in the two hundred largest companies are female. . . . [I]n some countries, no woman has ever headed a large global corporation. In many nations in Asia, Africa, and the Mideast, women have difficulty walking unescorted or working in any setting outside their homes or fields, let alone ascending a leadership ladder. Despite significant national variations, the global workforce is highly gender-segregated and gender-stratified, and progress toward equity at the highest levels has been slow and uneven.

This introduction explores the reasons for these persistent and pervasive inequalities. . . . An initial issue for consideration involves the role of women's own choices in explaining women's underrepresentation in leadership positions. Although these choices play an important part, they cannot be understood in isolation from broader cultural constraints. These include gender biases in leadership opportunities, gender roles in families, inflexibility in workplace structures, and inadequacies in social policies.

Women's Choices

The most common—and for many constituencies, most convenient—explanation for women's underrepresentation in leadership positions is women's choices. Prominent news publications, television talk shows, and employee chitchat all offer variations on a long-standing theme: women who opt out of full-time professional work to keep the home fires burning. . . . [For example,] Lisa Belkin's cover story in the *New York Times Magazine* laid blame in similar places. In her account of the "opt-out revolution," women are underrepresented in leadership positions less because "the workplace has failed women" than because "women are rejecting the workplace." "Why don't women run the world?" asks Belkin. "Maybe it's because they don't want to."

Such explanations capture a partial truth. Women, including those with leadership credentials, do on average make different choices from men; more opt out for at least some period and more who stay in remain childless. In a study by the Center for Work-Life Policy of some three thousand high-achieving American women and men (defined as those with graduate or professional degrees or high honors undergraduate degrees), nearly four in ten women reported leaving the workforce voluntarily at some point over their careers. The same proportion reported sometimes choosing a job with lesser compensation and fewer responsibilities than they were qualified to assume so they could accommodate family responsibilities. By contrast, only one in ten men left the workforce primarily for family-related reasons. Although other surveys find some variation in the number of women who opt out to accommodate domestic obligations, all these studies report substantial gender differences. Almost 20 percent of women with graduate or professional degrees are not in the labor force, compared with only 5 percent of similarly credentialed men. . . . The overwhelming majority of these women do, however, want to return to work, and most do so, although generally not without significant career costs and difficulties. The same is true in other advanced industrial nations for which data is available.

Findings on career aspirations and expectations are also mixed, but gender differences typically emerge. A survey of some twelve hundred executives in various regions of the world found that substantially more women than men reported reducing career aspirations to accommodate personal and family concerns. . . . In most, although not all, studies, fewer highly qualified women than men described themselves as very ambitious, or interested in a CEO position or elective political office. . . .

Yet what is too often missed or marginalized in discussions of women's "different choices" is the extent to which the choices are socially constructed and constrained. What drops out of the opt-out narrative are the complex forces that drive women's decisions. Equally noticeable for their absence are the choices that men make, as spouses, policy leaders, and employers that limit the choices available to women. As subsequent discussion makes clear, explanations focusing solely on women's preferences understate the subtle, often unconscious, biases that both shape the priorities of those who opt out and limit the opportunities for those who opt in. Over the last quarter century, a growing number of women have aspired to leadership on the same terms as men; they have made the same choices as their male counterparts but confront an additional set of obstacles. These barriers deserve greater public attention and policy initiatives.

Gender Bias in Leadership Opportunities

Obstacles in women's path to leadership take several forms. Careers are waylaid by gender stereotypes, gender bias in evaluation and mentoring, gender differences in family responsibilities, and inadequate workplace structures and public policies.

Gender Stereotypes

One of the most intractable obstacles for women seeking positions of influence is the mismatch between the qualities traditionally associated with women and those traditionally associated with leadership. . . . Most characteristics associated with leaders are masculine: dominance, authority, assertiveness, and so forth. In recent years, this disjuncture between femininity and leadership has lessened somewhat. Women are becoming more like men in their career aspirations and achievements, and they are more willing to see themselves as having qualities associated with authority. More women now occupy highly visible leadership roles, and recent theories of leadership have stressed the importance of interpersonal qualities commonly attributed to women, such as cooperation and collaboration.

Yet despite these trends, traditional gender stereotypes still leave women with a double standard and a double bind. Men continue to be rated higher than women on most of the qualities associated with leadership. People more readily credit men with leadership ability and more readily accept men as leaders. What is assertive in a man can appear abrasive in a woman, and female leaders risk appearing too feminine or not feminine enough. On one hand, they may appear too "soft"—unable or unwilling to make the tough calls required in positions of greatest influence. On the other hand, those who mimic the "male model" are often viewed as strident and overly aggressive or ambitious. . . . An overview of more than a hundred studies confirms that women are rated lower as leaders when they adopt authoritative and seemingly masculine styles, particularly when the evaluators are men, or when the role is one typically occupied by men. Yet other research finds that individuals with masculine styles are more likely to emerge as leaders than those with feminine styles. In effect, women face trade-offs that men do not. Aspiring female leaders risk being liked but not respected, or respected but not liked, in settings that may require individuals to be both in order to succeed.

Other gender-related stereotypes are inconsistent with leadership roles. Having children makes women, but not men, appear less competent and less available to meet workplace responsibilities. The term "working father" is rarely used and carries none of the adverse connotations of "working mother." Attitudes toward self-promotion reflect a related mismatch between stereotypes associated with leadership and with femininity—women are expected to be nurturing, not self-serving, and entrepreneurial behaviors viewed as appropriate in men are often viewed as distasteful in women.

Because such stereotypes operate at unconscious levels and selections for leadership positions involve subjective and confidential judgments, the extent of bias is hard to assess. It is, however, instructive that in experimental settings, resumes are rated more favorably when they carry male rather than female names. And in large-scale surveys of senior executive women, the most frequently cited obstacle to advancement is "male stereotyping and preconceptions." . . .

Many women also internalize these stereotypes, which creates a psychological glass ceiling. On average, women appear less willing to engage in self-promoting or assertive behaviors, or to take the risks that may be necessary for leadership roles. So too, as one comprehensive overview of gender in negotiations puts it, "Women don't ask." An unwillingness to seem too pushy or difficult and an undervaluation of their own worth often deter women from negotiating effectively for what they want or need. In workplace settings, the result is that female employees may be less likely than their male colleagues to gain the assignments, positions, and support necessary for leadership roles.

Other cognitive biases compound the force of these traditional stereotypes. People are more likely to notice and recall information that confirms their prior assumptions than information that contradicts those assumptions; the dissonant data is filtered out. For example, when employers assume that a working mother is unlikely to be fully committed to her career, they more easily remember the times when she left early than the times when she stayed late. So too, [those] . . . who assume that women of color are beneficiaries of preferential treatment, not merit-based selection, will recall their errors more readily than their insights. A related problem is that people share what psychologists label a "just world" bias. They want to believe that, in the absence of special treatment, individuals generally get what they deserve and deserve what they get. Perceptions of performance frequently are adjusted to match observed outcomes. If women, particularly women of color, are underrepresented in positions of greatest prominence, the most psychologically convenient explanation is that they lack the necessary qualifications or commitment.

These perceptions can, in turn, prevent women from getting assignments that would demonstrate their capabilities, and a cycle of self-fulfilling predictions is established. In managerial contexts, decision makers generally see women as more suited for jobs involving human relations than those involving line responsibility for profits and losses. The absence of such line experience is the major reason given by CEOs in the United States and abroad for women's underrepresentation in leadership positions. Gender stereotypes also help explain why women are less likely to be viewed as leaders than similarly situated men. For example, in studies where people see a man seated at the head of a table for a meeting, they typically assume that he is the leader. They do not make the same assumption when the person in that seat is a woman.

In-Group Favoritism: Gender Bias in Evaluations and Mentoring Networks

A related problem involves in-group favoritism. Extensive research documents the preferences that individuals feel for members of their own groups. Loyalty, cooperation, favorable evaluations, and the allocation of rewards and opportunities all increase in likelihood for in-group members. A key example is the presumption of competence that dominant groups accord to their members but not to outsiders. Members of in-groups tend to attribute accomplishments of fellow members to intrinsic characteristics, such as intelligence, drive, and commitment. By contrast, the achievements of out-group members are often ascribed to luck or special treatment. Even in experimental situations where male and female performance is objectively equal, women are held to higher standards, and their competence is rated lower. Moreover, for women, effective performance does not necessarily suggest leadership potential. In one recent study of twenty-eight hundred managers, supervisors who rated female subordinates somewhat higher than men in current competence rated the women lower in long-term leadership potential.

Again, women often internalize these stereotypes; they generally see themselves as less deserving than men for rewards for the same performance and less qualified for key leadership positions. In male-dominated settings, aspiring female leaders are also subject to special scrutiny and polarized assessments. Gender stereotypes are particularly strong when women's representation does not exceed token levels, and too few counterexamples are present to challenge conventional assumptions. A small number of superstars will attract special notice and receive higher evaluations than their male counterparts, but women who are just below that level tend to get disproportionately lower evaluations. At the same time, the presence of a few highly regarded women at the top creates the illusion that the glass ceiling has been shattered for everyone else. And when superstars fail or opt out, their departures attract particular notice and reinforce stereotypes about women's lesser capabilities and commitment.

In-group favoritism is also apparent in the informal networks of mentoring, contacts, and support that are critical for advancement. People generally feel most comfortable with those who are like them in important respects, including gender. Women in traditionally male-dominated settings often remain out of the loop of advice and professional development opportunities. Women of color also experience particular difficulties of isolation and exclusion. Surveys of upper-level U.S. managers find that almost half of women of color and close to a third of white women cite a lack of influential mentors as a major barrier to advancement. . . .

A similar problem confronts potential leaders in other professional and political settings in the United States and abroad. The relatively small number of women who are in positions of power often lack the time or the leverage, or in some cases the inclination, to assist all who may hope to join them. Differences across race, ethnicity, and culture compound the problem. White men who would like to fill the gaps in mentoring often lack the capacity to do so or are worried about the appearance of forming close relationships with women, particularly women of color. Although a growing number of organizations are attempting to respond by establishing formal mentoring programs and women's networks, the playing field is still far from level.

Gender Roles in Family Settings

Ironically, the home is no more an equal opportunity employer than the workplace: only in domestic matters the presumptions of competence are reversed, which creates unequal family burdens. Women are, and are expected to be, the primary caregivers, especially of the very young and the very old. In principle most men support gender equality—but in practice they fail to structure their lives to promote it. Despite a significant increase in men's domestic work over the last two decades, women continue to shoulder the major burden. In one representative survey of high-achieving women, four of ten felt that their husbands created more domestic work than they contributed. In another survey of well-educated professional women who had left the paid workforce, two-thirds cited their husbands' influence on the decision, including their lack of support in child care and other domestic tasks, and their expectation that wives should be the ones to cut back on employment. Most male leaders in business and professional positions have spouses who are full-time homemakers, or who are working part time. The same is not true of female leaders, who, with few exceptions, are either single or have partners with full-time jobs. Few of these husbands are willing to subordinate their own careers to assist their wives. . . .

Double standards in domestic roles are deeply rooted in cultural attitudes and workplace practices. Working mothers are held to higher standards than working fathers and are often criticized for being insufficiently committed, either as parents or professionals. Those who seem willing to sacrifice family needs to workplace demands appear lacking as mothers. Those who take extended leave or reduced schedules appear lacking as leaders. These mixed messages leave many women with the uncomfortable sense that whatever they are doing, they should be doing something else.

The gender imbalance in family roles reinforces gender inequalities in career development. Women with demanding work and family commitments often lack time for the networking and mentoring activities necessary for advancement. As former Catalyst president Sheila Wellington notes, at the end of the day, "Men head for drinks. Women for the dry cleaners." Men pick up tips; women pick up kids, laundry, dinner, and the house. Although women on leadership tracks can often afford to buy their way out of domestic drudgery, not all family obligations can be readily outsourced. When asked how women can solve the work-family conflict, Gloria Steinem aptly answered: "Women can't, until men are asking that question too." If women are choosing not to run the world, it's partly because men are choosing not to run the washer and dryer.

Inflexible Workplace Structures and Inadequate Public Policies

All these problems are compounded by inadequacies in the workplace and the public policies that address them. Gender inequalities in family roles pose particular challenges for women in leadership positions, which typically require highly demanding schedules. Hourly requirements in most professions have increased dramatically over the last two decades, and what has not changed is the number of hours in the day. For leaders in business, politics, and the professions, all work and no play is fast becoming the norm rather than the exception; sixty-hour workweeks are typical. Technological innovations have created as many problems as they have solved. Although they make it increasingly possible for women to work at home, they also make it increasingly impossible not to. Many high-achieving women remain tethered to their office through their e-mail, fax, beeper, and BlackBerry. Unsurprisingly, most women in upper-level professional and business positions report that they do not have sufficient time for themselves or their families. Some feel they cannot manage a goldfish, much less a child. . . .

Part of the problem is the wide gap between formal policies and actual practices concerning work-family conflicts. Although most women in top managerial and professional positions have access to reduced or flexible schedules, few of these women feel able to take advantage of such options. For example, over 90 percent of U.S. law firms report policies permitting part-time work, yet only about 4 percent of lawyers actually use them. Most women believe, with good reason, that any reduction in hours or availability would jeopardize their career prospects. A wide variety of research finds that even short-term adjustments in working schedules such as leaves or part-time status for less than a year result in long-term reductions in earnings and advancement.

Workplace inflexibility and unmanageable time demands play a major role in women's decisions to step off the leadership track both in the United States and abroad. Although many of these women return to high-powered careers, others find reentry blocked, or less appealing than volunteer work or starting a small-scale business in which they can control their own hours. Some of these alternatives present leadership opportunities of another sort, but for too much talent falls by the wayside. . . .

Equal opportunity laws have also proven inadequate to ensure equality in leadership positions. Legal remedies for gender bias generally require either proof of intentional discrimination or a pattern and practice that has broad discriminatory impact and is not justified by business necessity. Neither remedy is well suited for those in upper-level professional and management positions. The difficulties of proof and costs of legal proceedings prevent most women who experience gender bias from seeking legal remedies. These remedies are even less accessible outside the United States, because most nations lack anti-discrimination enforcement structures and class-action procedures. . . . Even in countries like the United States, which have relatively well-developed legal protections, few individuals want to incur the risks of retaliation or the reputational injuries that accompany formal complaints. Unless liability is clear and damages are substantial, discrimination claims are simply too expensive to litigate. Yet liability is seldom clear for women on leadership tracks, where the criteria for advancement are subjective, and the pool of similar employees is too small to permit meaningful statistical comparisons.

Winning such cases frequently demands fairly explicit evidence of bias, but those who harbor intentional prejudice generally have the sense not to express it publicly. To be sure, a few high-profile cases involving egregious facts continue to arise, and their large damage awards have prompted much-needed changes, particularly in fields such as financial services. But for the vast majority of women who are stymied by subtle bias and inflexible schedules, lawsuits make no sense. "Career suicide" is a common description. . . .

The Social Costs of Gender Inequalities

Women's unequal representation in leadership positions poses multiple concerns. Most obviously, the barriers to women's advancement compromise fundamental principles of equal opportunity and social justice. These barriers impose organizational costs as well. Researchers consistently find a positive correlation between the representation of women in leadership positions and business performance measures such as market share and return on investment. Although correlation does not always imply causation, there are strong reasons to believe that diversity in leadership has tangible payoffs.

The most obvious reason is demographic. Women are now a majority of college graduates and a growing share of the talent available for leadership. Organizations that create a culture of equal opportunity are better able to attract, retain, and motivate the most qualified individuals. Reducing the obstacles to women's success also reduces the costs of attrition. It increases employees' morale, commitment, and retention, and decreases the expenses associated with recruiting, training, and mentoring replacements.

A second rationale for ensuring equal access to leadership positions is that women have distinct perspectives to contribute. To perform effectively in an increasingly competitive and multicultural environment, workplaces need individuals with diverse backgrounds, experiences, and styles of leadership.

The point is not that there is some single "woman's point of view" or woman's leadership style, but rather that gender differences do make some difference that needs to be registered in positions of power.

Women's Leadership Styles and Priorities

Assumptions about gender differences in leadership styles and effectiveness are widespread, although the evidence for such assumptions is weaker than commonly supposed both in the United States and abroad. The conventional wisdom is that female leaders are more participatory and interpersonally oriented than male leaders and are more likely to adopt empathetic, supportive, and collaborative approaches. This view is consistent with women's self reports and some small-scale laboratory studies. However, most research reveals no gender differences, particularly when it involves evaluations of leaders by supervisors, subordinates, and peers in real-world settings. Nor do most surveys reveal significant gender differences in the effectiveness of leaders. Indeed, contrary to popular assumptions, large-scale research generally finds that women slightly outperform men on all but a few measures.

What accounts for the inconsistency in findings and the disconnect between conventional wisdom and recent data? Gender socialization and stereotypes play an obvious role; they push women to behave, and to describe their behavior, in ways that are consistent with traditional notions of femininity. Yet the force of these cultural norms is constrained in organizations where advancement requires conformity to accepted images of leadership. It is not surprising that women's styles are similar to those of male counterparts, particularly since recent trends in leadership education have encouraged both sexes to adopt more collaborative, interpersonally sensitive approaches. Nor is it surprising that some studies find superior performance by women leaders, given the hurdles that they have had to surmount to reach upper-level positions and the pressures that they have faced to consistently exceed expectations. Whatever else can be inferred from this research, it is clear that a society can ill afford to lose so many talented women from its leadership pool. To the extent that female leaders gravitate toward a collaborative, interpersonally sensitive approach, it will prove an asset in many leadership settings.

Similar points are applicable to gender differences in leadership priorities. The most systematic research involves commitment to women's issues, and here again, the findings are mixed. For example, most, although not all, evidence indicates that female judges are more supportive than their male colleagues on gender-related issues. And many women judges, both through individual rulings and collective efforts in women's judicial organizations, have spearheaded responses to women's concerns in areas such as domestic violence, child support, and gender bias training. The same is true of women in management and public office, who have often championed causes of particular concern to women. . . .

Yet not all female leaders share such commitments. Examples such as Margaret Thatcher remind us that electing women is not always the best way to advance women's concerns. Extensive research on U.S. legislatures finds that party affiliation is more important than gender in predicting votes on women's issues, and that ideology is more important in predicting sponsorship of legislation on these issues. . . .

The same point could be made about professional and managerial contexts. Many women leaders have made a crucial difference in promoting women's issues and in creating institutional structures that will do the same. For example, female university presidents and managing partners of law firms have been at the forefront of efforts to promote gender equity through fairer evaluation processes, improved work-family policies, and related initiatives. Yet surveys also find large numbers of women leaders who do not actively advocate women's interests. Underlying these different priorities are differences in personal experiences, risks, and influence.

For some female leaders, their own experiences of discrimination, marginalization, or work-family conflicts leave them with a desire to make life better for their successors. Because these women have bumped up against conventional assumptions and workplace structures, they can more readily question roles that men take for granted. Other women end up as advocates partly by default. They may be asked to represent the "woman's view" or be enlisted by colleagues to serve that role.

But not all female leaders are willing to accept that responsibility. They have internalized the values of the culture in which they have succeeded and have little interest in promoting opportunities that they never had. They have "gotten there the hard way," and they have "given up a lot"; if they managed, so can anyone else.

Women's willingness to raise women's issues may also depend on the likely consequences. It matters whether leaders feel secure in their positions and safe in raising gender-related concerns, and whether they expect to benefit directly from the changes in policy or climate that may result. All too often, the risks outweigh the rewards. . . .

In short, the difference that gender difference makes depends on context. Putting women in positions of power is not the same as empowering women. But the influence of women holding leadership positions can make a crucial difference in promoting gender equality and improving organizational performance. The challenge remaining is to identify strategies that will assist and encourage women to play that role.

Strategies for Change

To reach greater gender equality in leadership will require expanding opportunities for talented women and enabling them to perform effectively in positions of power. As is obvious from the preceding discussion, such a reform agenda will require strategies on the individual, institutional, and societal levels. . . . [T]he effectiveness of individual strategies often depends on institutional reform. For example, women receive endless advice to find the right mentors and maintain a healthy work-life balance, but their chances of doing so may depend partly on organizational culture. Moreover, the jazzed-up, dumbed-down approach of many how-to publications may lead individuals to focus too much attention on fixing themselves and too little on fixing the institutional and societal structures that are at the root of the problem.

Individual Strategies

Both self-help publications and scholarly research underscore certain basic strategies for women who seek a leadership position. They need to understand their own objectives and capabilities, to develop leadership qualities, to obtain mentors, and to balance personal and professional needs.

Self-Awareness. A necessary first step on the path to leadership involves self-reflection. Women need to be clear about their goals and values: What do they want, why do they want it, and what are they prepared to sacrifice to get it? Clarifying those priorities can then help women identify where they want to be in the short and long term and what it will take to get there. Individuals also need to consider their managerial strengths and weaknesses and to obtain adequate feedback from others about necessary improvements.

Leadership Styles and Capabilities. To reach their desired goals, women must demonstrate leadership abilities. To that end, they should seek challenging assignments, acquire appropriate job experience, develop informal relationships with influential colleagues and clients, and cultivate a reputation for effectiveness that exceeds expectations. They also need an authentic leadership style that fits their organization. According to a survey of women managers and professional consultants, that includes finding a "style that men are comfortable with." In many contexts, projecting a decisive and forceful manner without seeming arrogant or abrasive is an essential skill. But as most experts emphasize, women also need a style with which they are comfortable. If the style they can employ most effectively does not mesh with their workplace culture, it may be prudent to find a different workplace.

Formal leadership training and coaching can sometimes help in developing interpersonal styles and capabilities such as risk taking, conflict resolution, and strategic vision. . . . Women who wait passively for their work to be valued may benefit from expert advice on how to highlight their abilities or how to find others who can do it for them.

Models, Mentors, and Networks. Guidance can come from both role models and mentors. These can but need not be the same individuals. Aspiring leaders need multiple sources of support, contacts, and career development opportunities from both men and women and from both inside and outside their organizations. Leaders themselves can also benefit from mentoring relationships. Quite apart from the satisfaction that comes from assisting those most in need of assistance, upper-level professionals may receive more tangible payoffs from fresh insights and from the loyalty and influence that their efforts secure. . . .

The most effective mentoring relationships typically arise naturally among individuals who share important similarities, such as sex, race, ethnicity, background, and interests. This presents problems in organizations that have too few women in leadership positions to aid all those seeking assistance and too few powerful men who are comfortable filling the gaps. The problems are compounded when senior women are already overextended with work and family responsibilities, and are worried about the appearance of favoritism if they direct all their mentoring to junior women. The result is often a form of "managerial cloning," in which a largely white male leadership unreflectively replicates itself.

Some organizations have responded to these challenges with women's networks and with formal mentoring programs that match employees or allow individuals to select their own pairings. Other employers have diversity officers who help groom talented women for advancement. Such initiatives serve a variety of useful functions, but they are no substitute for the mentoring that occurs more naturally during collaborative projects and shared activities. . . .

Time Management and Work-Family Choices. Setting priorities and managing time effectively are also critical leadership skills. Setting boundaries, delegating domestic tasks, and developing effective reduced hour, flextime, or telecommuting arrangements are obvious strategies. Women who temporarily opt out of the workforce need to stay involved in their fields. They can assist the transition back to paid employment through participation in professional associations and development of expertise through continuing education courses, volunteer activities, and reentry programs specially targeted to their needs. . . .

Organizational Strategies

The most important factor in ensuring equal access to leadership opportunities is a commitment to that objective, which is reflected in workplace priorities, policies, and reward structures. That, in turn, requires accountability for results and strategies that will assess progress on gender issues.

Commitment and Accountability. A necessary first step is commitment from the top. An organization's leadership team needs to acknowledge the importance of diversity and equity, to assess its progress in achieving them, and to hold individuals at every level of the organization accountable for improvement. . . .

Measuring and Monitoring Results. To make such progress, employers need concrete assessments of results. On this point, conventional wisdom is right; organizations get what they measure. And too few organizations adequately measure gender equity. Employees should compile information on recruitment, hiring, promotion, and retention, broken down by sex as well as by race and ethnicity. Surveys of current and former employees can also provide valuable information on equity and quality-of-life issues. Decision makers need to know whether men and women are advancing in equal numbers and whether they feel equally well supported in career development. Where possible, employers should assess their own progress in comparison with similar organizations and the best practices identified by experts. . . .

Quality of Life and Work-Family Initiatives. Any serious commitment to expand women's leadership opportunities requires a similarly serious commitment to address work-family conflicts that stand in the way of advancement. Best practices and model programs are readily available on matters such as flexible and reduced schedules, telecommuting, leave policies, and child care assistance. . . . Most of these women rate schedule flexibility as more important than compensation. Although the details of effective policies vary across organizations, two important factors are mutual commitment and flexibility. Technologies that blur the boundaries between home and work can help, but not if individuals remain constantly on call, hostage to schedules not of their own making.

Organizations also need to ensure that women who seek temporary accommodations do not pay a permanent price. Stepping out should not mean stepping down: individuals on reduced or flexible schedules should not lose opportunities for challenging assignments or eventual promotion. Nor should women who temporarily opt out lose all contact with the workplace. Part-time consulting arrangements and employer-supported career development opportunities can build loyalty and assist the transition back.

Finally, and most important, family and quality of life concerns need to be seen not just as women's issues but also as organizational priorities. Options like parental leave and flexible schedules should be gender neutral in fact as well as in form, and men should be encouraged to take advantage of them. Time should be available for both sexes to acquire the broad experience that comes from family and civic pursuits. Policies need to be monitored to ensure that options are available in practice as well as in principle, and that individuals at the highest leadership level feel able to use them. . . .

[Other useful strategies include formal mentoring programs and women's networks.]

Societal Strategies

Women's access to leadership is influenced by a broad range of public and private sector initiatives. Regulatory agencies, stakeholder organizations, and professional associations should hold employers more accountable for performance on gender equity issues. Public policy should do more to reduce work-family conflicts. Professional associations should take additional steps to identify and reward best practices, support members' career development, and press for societal and workplace reforms. . . .

Conclusion

> It has long since come to my attention that people of accomplishment rarely . . . [stayed] back and let things happen to them. They went out and happened to things.
>
> *Elinor Smith*

It has come to our attention in preparing this overview that more and more women share Smith's conclusion. Fewer women are content to stay back, and those who advance are changing the landscape of leadership. . . . The challenges are substantial, but so too are the talents of women leaders and the men who support them.

Herminia Ibarra and Otilia Obodaru, "Women
and the Vision Thing"

Harvard Business Review (Jan. 2009)

Many believe that bias against women lingers in the business world, particularly when it comes to evaluating their leadership ability. Recently, we had a chance to see whether that assumption was true. In a study of thousands of 360-degree assessments collected by Insead's executive education program over the past five years, we looked at whether women actually received lower ratings than men. To our surprise, we found the opposite: As a group, women outshone men in most of the leadership dimensions measured. There was one exception, however, and it was a big one: Women scored lower on "envisioning"—the ability to recognize new opportunities and trends in the environment and develop a new strategic direction for an enterprise.

But was this weakness a perception or a reality? How much did it matter to women's ability to lead? And how could someone not perceived as visionary acquire the right capabilities? As we explored these issues with successful female executives, we arrived at another question: Was a reputation for vision even something many of them wanted to achieve? . . .

Vision Impaired

Our research drew on 360-degree evaluations of 2,816 executives from 149 countries enrolled in executive education courses at Insead. As with most 360-degree exercises, these managers filled out self-assessments and invited subordinates, peers, supervisors, and other people they dealt with in a professional context, such as suppliers and customers, to evaluate them on a set of leadership dimensions. In total 22,244 observers participated. . . .

The first surprise for us, given prior published research, was that we found no evidence of a female "modesty effect." Quite the opposite: Women rated themselves significantly higher than men rated themselves on four of the 10 GELI [(Global Executive Leadership Inventory)] dimensions we analyzed. And on the remaining dimensions, the women and men gave themselves ratings that were about the same.

Our analyses of how leaders were rated by their male and female associates—bosses, peers, and subordinates—also challenged the common wisdom. Again based on prior research, we'd expected gender stereotypes to lower the ratings of female leaders, particularly those given by men. That was not the case. If there was a gender bias, it favored female leaders: Male observers scored female leaders significantly higher than they scored male leaders on seven dimensions, and female observers scored them significantly higher on eight. . . .

Ratings on one dimension, however, defied this pattern. Female leaders were rated lower by their male observers (but not by women) on their capabilities in "envisioning." That deficit casts a large shadow over what would otherwise be an extremely favorable picture of female executives. The GELI instrument does not claim that the different dimensions of leadership are equal in importance, and as other research has shown, some do matter more than others to people's idea of what makes a leader. In particular, the envisioning dimension is, for most observers, a must-have capability.

Intrigued by this one apparent weakness, we looked more closely at the observers' ratings. Was a particular group responsible for bringing the envisioning scores down? Indeed one was. . . . [T]he male peers (who represented the majority of peers in our sample) rated women lower on envisioning. Interestingly, female peers did not downgrade women, contrary to the frequently heard claim that women compete rather than cooperate with one another. Our data suggest it's the men who might feel most competitive toward their female peers. Male superiors and subordinates rated male and female leaders about the same.

What It Means to Be Visionary

George H.W. Bush famously responded to the suggestion that he look up from the short-term goals of his campaign and start focusing on the longer term by saying, "Oh—the vision thing." His answer underlines vision's ambiguity. Just what do we mean when we say a person is visionary? . . .

[Vision] encompasses the abilities to frame the current practices as inadequate, to generate ideas for new strategies, and to communicate possibilities in inspiring ways to others. Being visionary, therefore, is not the same as being charismatic. It entails "naming" broad-stroke patterns and setting strategy based on those patterns. . . .

Perception or Reality?

. . . When we asked how [women executives] would interpret our data, we heard three explanations. . . .

THEORY 1: Women are equally visionary but in a different way. Several of the women who had taken the GELI survey argued that it is not that women lack vision but that they come to their visions in a less directive way than men do. One executive put it like this: "Many women tend to be quite collaborative in forming their vision. They take into account the input of many and then describe the result as the group's vision rather than their own." Another said, "I don't see myself as particularly visionary in the creative sense. I see myself as pulling and putting together abstract pieces of information or observations that lead to possible strategies and future opportunities." . . .

Interestingly, the processes these women describe do not hinge just on a collaborative style. They also rely on diverse and external inputs and alliances. At BP Alternative Energy, [Vivienne] Cox spent much of her time talking to key people outside her business group and the company in order to develop a strategic perspective on opportunities and sell the idea of low-carbon power to her CEO and peers. Her ideas were informed by a wide network that included thought leaders in a range of sectors. She brought in outsiders who could transcend a parochial view to fill key roles and invited potential adversaries into the process early on to make sure her team was also informed by those who had a different view of the world. Our results hint at an interesting hypothesis: By involving their male peers in the process of creating a vision, female leaders may get less credit for the result.

THEORY 2: Women hesitate to go out on a limb. Some women responded to our findings by noting that they need to base their marching orders on concrete facts and irrefutable analysis, not unprovable assertions about how the future will take shape. . . .

A common obstacle for female leaders is that they often lack the presumption of competence accorded to their male peers. As a result, women are less likely to go out on a limb, extrapolating from facts and figures to interpretations that are more easily challenged. When a situation is rife with threat — when people, male or female, expect that they are "guilty until proven innocent" — they adopt a defensive, often rigid, posture, relying less on their imagination and creativity and sticking to safe choices. . . .

THEORY 3: Women don't put much stock in vision. . . . We suspect women may not value envisioning as a critical leadership competency to the same extent that men do or may have a more skeptical view of envisioning's part in achieving results. Over and over again in our discussions with women, we heard them take pride in their concrete, no-nonsense attitude and practical orientation toward everyday work problems. We were reminded of a comment made by Margaret Thatcher: "If you want anything said, ask a man; if you want anything done, ask a woman." Many of the women we interviewed similarly expressed the opinion that women were more thorough, had a better command of detail, and were less prone to self-promotion than men.

Making the Leadership Transition

Women may dismiss the importance of vision — and they may be reassured by the many claims made over the years about their superior emotional intelligence — but the fact remains that women are a minority in the top ranks of business organizations. Our findings suggest to us that the shortfall is in no small part due to women's perceived lack of vision.

The findings of a 2008 study by Catalyst researchers Jeanine Prime and Nancy Carter and IMD professors Karsten Jonsen and Martha Maznevski concur. In it, more than 1,000 executives from nine countries (all alumni of executive education programs) were asked for their impressions of men and women in general as leaders. Both men and women tended to believe that the two genders have distinct leadership strengths, with women outscoring men on some behaviors, and men outscoring women on others. But here's the catch: When people were asked to rate the behaviors' relative importance to overall leadership effectiveness, the "male" behaviors had the edge. Across countries, "inspiring others" — a component of our envisioning dimension — landed at the top of the rankings as most important to overall leadership effectiveness. And what of the areas of leadership where men agreed that women were stronger? Let's take women's standout advantage: their much greater skill at "supporting others." That one ranked at the bottom of the list. As a component of overall leadership effectiveness, it was clearly not critical but merely nice to have.

It's often observed that the very talents that bring managers success in midlevel roles can be obstacles to their taking on bigger leadership roles. . . . Having had the message drummed into their heads that they must be rational, nonemotional, and hyperefficient, they might actually place a higher value than men on knowing the details cold and getting the job done. That, in turn, makes their leadership transition more difficult, because they stick with what they know longer. . . .

The challenge facing women, then, is to stop dismissing the vision thing and make vision one of the things they are known for. In a senior leadership role, it's the best use of their time and attention. It's a set of competencies that can be developed. And of all the leadership dimensions we measured, it's the only thing holding women back.

NOTES AND QUESTIONS

1. What are the greatest barriers to women seeking leadership positions? Have you observed any of the problems that the readings describe? How did the individuals and organizations respond?

2. What appear to be the most promising strategies for gender equity at individual, institutional, and policy levels?

3. How can women cope with the "too assertive/not assertive enough" dilemma? Linda Babcock and Sara Laschever suggest being "relentlessly pleasant" without backing down. Strategies for increasing "likeability" include: frequently smiling; maintaining constant eye contact; appearing fully engaged; expressing appreciation and concern; mentioning common interests; focusing on others' goals as well as your own; and taking a problem-solving rather than critical approach.[26] Think of women leaders whose styles you found effective. What was distinctive about their approaches?

4. Some research suggests that greater familiarity with individual women's performance reduces the penalties associated with an assertive style. For example, in one study MBA students read a Harvard Business School case study about a Silicon Valley entrepreneur described in such terms as "aggressive," "an outspoken critic," and "a captain of industry." Half the students received the original case, in which the leader was identified as Heidi Roizen. The other half received a version that described the fictional Howard Roizen. Students liked Heidi less and showed less likelihood of hiring her compared with Howard, although they did not rate her lower in competence or effectiveness. In follow-up studies, researchers showed that the backlash effect diminished when subjects rated women with whom they were familiar. Researchers hypothesized that greater knowledge counteracted the tendency to link assertiveness with selfishness and lack of concern for others.[27] From a policy standpoint, do such findings suggest that gender equity is more likely under hiring and promotion systems that rely on in-depth, individualized assessments rather than impressionistic data about personal styles? What other implications might you draw?

5. Apart from vision, one other area in which women leaders are thought to differ from men is in attitudes toward risk. In the wake of the recent economic recession, a widely discussed *New York Times* article ran under the title "Where Would We Be If Women Ran Wall Street?" The article discusses a question put by the moderator at a World Economic Forum panel in

Davos. "Would the world be in this financial mess if it had been Lehman Sisters?"[28] Many Davos participants believed that the answer was no, and cited evidence suggesting that women were "more prudent" and less "ego driven" than men in financial management contexts.[29] Other research points in similar directions, including studies from researchers at Harvard and Cambridge universities, which find a correlation between high levels of testosterone and an appetite for risk.[30] Given that testosterone levels are significantly higher in men than women, some commentators have argued that competitive male-dominated management cultures may be overly prone to risky behaviors. Is that a plausible argument for greater gender diversity in corporate management and boards of directors?

Other commentators, however, note that although greater risk aversion would have been advantageous in the run-up to recent economic recession, that tendency also discourages other highly profitable behavior.[31] One obstacle to women-owned businesses is women's reluctance to seek substantial credit. Such cautiousness keeps female entrepreneurs from applying for the loans they need, and reinforces lenders' perceptions that they are "not serious about growth."[32] Are these tendencies that training and mentoring could overcome? How else might gender-based differences regarding risk play out in leadership contexts? Eleanor Roosevelt once observed that "[w]omen who are willing to be leaders must stand out and be shot at. . . ."[33] What might encourage more women to do that?

2. MEN

NOTES AND QUESTIONS

Women are not the only ones who pay a price for gender norms at leadership levels. Men also bear the costs of pressures to be the primary breadwinner, and to conform to the hypermasculine work ethic that characterizes many upper-level positions. In her study of the gender dynamics in high-powered, high-tech work cultures of Silicon Valley, Marianne Cooper documents men's perception of what is necessary to be a successful "go-to guy." As she notes, a "masculine mystique permeates descriptions . . . of work. It's as if these men are digital warriors, out conquering enemies, surmounting insurmountable odds in their quest to win. . . . The pace is intense. If you stop to take a breath, you may miss out."[34] One man explained, "[G]uys try to out macho each other. . . . There's a lot of 'see how many hours I can work.'" Other comments included: "He's a real man, he works 90 hours a week. He's a slacker; he works 50 hours a week."[35] Another observed that those who "conspicuously overwork are guys and I think it's usually for the benefit of other guys."[36] None of those Cooper interviewed questioned the inevitability of these demands. Two weeks of paternity leave seemed all that was "capitalistically fair for the company to offer."[37] "I hate to sound like a capitalist," said one man, "but at the end of the day, the company shareholders aren't holding shares so that we can have flexible lives."[38] Another was equally resigned: "I signed up for this life, right . . . and you pay a price if you have a high paying job, or a career you are really fulfilled by. So my price is that I'm exhausted."[39]

Another price is time with family. A vice president who was on the road for a month earned this description: "[H]e doesn't have two kids and a wife, he has people that live in his house."[40] Another described the "emotionally downsized" life of the CEO of his former start-up company.

> [He] had three kids—4, 7, and 10—nice kids but he never ever sees them because he's at work 7 days a week. He does triple sevens. He works from 7:00 in the morning until 7:00 in the evening seven days a week. He thought he was a good father because once a year he'd go camping for a week with his kids or one day on a weekend he would take them out . . . for two hours and he'd say it's not the quantity of time, it's the quality of time.[41]

One father who had taken only two days off at the birth of his second child and then gone through a year of seeing his family "almost not at all" finally left his position as vice president. That required renegotiating his identity. He had a new job he liked, decent pay, and an ability to spend time with the family he loved, but he no longer could feel "famous in [my] field."[42]

The trade-off he identified is not one many male leaders feel comfortable making. Derek Bok, former dean of Harvard Law School and president of Harvard University, described a partner in a San Francisco firm who "was always complaining about how hard he worked, so I asked 'Then why don't you just work 3/5 as hard and take 3/5 the salary?' He was tongue tied. But of course the real reason he couldn't is that then he feared he wouldn't be a 'player.'"[43] Those fears are widely shared. In one longitudinal study of elite law school graduates, only 1 percent of fathers had worked part-time or had taken parental leave, compared with 47 percent of women who had worked part-time and 42 percent who had taken a leave.[44] In another study by the American Bar Foundation, female lawyers were about seven times more likely than male lawyers to be working part-time or to be out of the labor force, primarily due to child care.[45] Part of the reason for those disparities is that the small number of fathers who opt to become full-time caretakers suffer even greater financial and promotion costs than female colleagues who make the same choice.[46]

The same dynamics play out in the corporate as well as professional sector. C.K. Wilson, the founder of Holiday Inns, captured conventional wisdom: "You cannot be successful unless you tell your wife not to expect you home for dinner."[47] Few companies offer fathers the same options for paid parental leaves as mothers, and few of those who do find many takers. It is virtually impossible to identify male CEOs who have taken time out of the workforce for family reasons.

These patterns are deeply rooted in traditional gender roles. Men with family responsibilities generally feel considerable pressure to provide their primary financial support, whatever the personal sacrifices. Yet these long-standing norms are also coming under increasing challenge. Growing numbers of men are expressing a desire for better balance between their personal and professional lives. And examples of those who insist on it are in increasingly visible supply, including at the highest levels. Bill Clinton while president once put off an important trip to Japan so he could help his daughter, then a high school junior, prepare for her midterms.[48] A *New York Times* article titled

"He breaks for Band Recitals," reported that Barack Obama was willing to leave key meetings in order to "get home for dinner by 6 or attend a school function of his 8 and 11 year old daughters." According to senior advisor David Axelrod, certain functions "are sacrosanct on his schedule—kid's recitals, soccer games. . . ."[49] Yet one frequently noted irony is that President Obama's commitment to a family-friendly schedule in his own life makes it harder for others to do the same. When he adjourns a meeting at 6 and resumes at 8 to allow his dinner break, other participants who do not "live over the shop" end up extending their own work day well past their children's bedtimes. Obama's first White House chief of staff, Rahm Emanuel, was known for his "Friday-afternoon mantra: 'Only two more workdays until Monday.'"[50] And while Obama may control his schedule now, his commitment is to some extent payback for two years on the campaign trail, when he could not.

1. Hypermasculine work ethics penalize women as well as men by reinforcing domestic roles that are separate and unequal. Mothers still are held to higher parental standards and suffer more personal anxiety and social pressure for falling short. Mary Matalin famously resigned her White House position as Dick Cheney's top aide after two years because the "job [took] over" and unduly compromised her relationship with her two young daughters. A tipping point came when she was in the Middle East arranging meetings between the vice president and local leaders, and her children called to let her know that their hamsters had died and it was her fault.[51] Does it follow that those aspiring to leadership positions cannot always have it all, at least not all the time?

2. Is part of the problem for leaders of their own making? Joe Flomm, the legendary lawyer who built Skadden Arps into a Wall Street powerhouse, was famously unable to take a vacation. As one commentator noted, "a part of him was afraid the firm was going to collapse and a part that it wasn't."[52]

3. According to some experts, a piece of the solution lies in making it easier for individuals who temporarily opt off the fast track to opt back in.[53] What other strategies would you propose?

PROBLEM 8-2

You are a lawyer who co-directs the Energy Program for the Natural Resources Defense Council, one of the world's leading environmental public-interest organizations. For much of the last two years, you have been working to secure passage of major energy conservation and global warming legislation that would establish California as a model for the nation and the international community. Negotiations over the bill's content are likely to continue at a frenetic pace during the final weeks of the August legislative session. You are leading a fragile coalition of consumer and environmental organizations, which is negotiating with industry representatives, legislative leaders from both parties, and officials from the governor's office.

You also are facing major difficulties on the family front. For years, your elderly and ailing mother-in-law has attempted to arrange a family reunion of you, your wife, and your sister-in-law and her two nephews at her summer home in upper Wisconsin. Until now you have resisted, because the home is difficult to reach, and a long weekend requires a day of travel on each end. But your mother-in-law's health—both physical and mental—is declining, and you agreed a year ago to make a trip in mid-August when your sister-in-law could get vacation time.

It now turns out that the weekend you chose is the worst possible one in terms of your work obligations. It coincides with the final days of the legislative session, and no one from your office believes that you are expendable. You are the only one who knows all the major players. Your principal staff on the project—a female attorney and a female scientist—are extremely gifted, but also relatively young and inexperienced, and lack your judgment, self-confidence, credibility, and contacts. Some members of the coalition have difficulty taking these women seriously. Neither they, nor the female president of the organization, believe that you should take your vacation as planned. Although they are all extremely sensitive to work/family issues, the public's stake in this legislation seems too important to be sacrificed.

Your wife and her family see the issue differently. Your mother-in-law simply does not get it. She has never really understood your job, and her growing dementia makes rational discussion impossible. Your sister-in-law is sympathetic, but she is struggling to cope with her own work and family conflicts and cannot shift the vacation. As a single mother and partner in a major Chicago firm, it is all she can do to carve out a short stint in Wisconsin, and it is too late to reschedule for a different time. Your wife, also a lawyer, is equally empathetic, but equally insistent that you come. She is unwilling to make the trip without you. Getting there requires extensive driving on unfamiliar freeways and rural roads. Since her recent eye surgery, she has not wanted to risk that kind of travel behind the wheel. Your wife also believes that the reunion means a great deal to her eighty-five-year-old mother, who might not be physically or mentally able to appreciate it next summer. As spouses go, yours has been fairly understanding of your sweatshop work hours in recent years. Now she refuses to believe that the fate of global warming depends on your presence in Sacramento on this particular August weekend.

Neither your family's summer home, nor the small inn nearby where you are staying, has Internet access. You do not know what the cell phone reception will be like. If you go, and want to advise from a distance, you may need to do so from the closest town. This will make some of the weekend activities impossible, and you anticipate a steady stream of "Why can't Uncle Ralph go fishing now?" It's equally unclear whether you can get to key players in time without actually being in the room. What is clear is that if you do not go, you are likely to hear about it from your family for the foreseeable future.

Divide into groups and assign members various roles: the male energy program director, his female staff, his wife, and other members of his coalition. After arguments by all the stakeholders, the director should make a decision and be prepared to defend it before the class as a whole.

MEDIA RESOURCES

An interview with Madeleine Albright on women and leadership, and discussion of Margaret Thatcher's reputation as the "iron lady" raise issues of gender bias and gender differences in leadership style.[54] Examples of gender stereotypes are in ample supply in major films and television series. Scenes of abrasive women are available in *The Devil Wears Prada*, *The Proposal*, and *Legally Blonde*.[55] David Letterman also had an interesting exchange with *Vogue* editor Anna Wintour, about her reputation as an "ice queen," which reportedly inspired Meryl Streep's character in *The Devil Wears Prada*.[56] Work-versus-family conflicts are equally common. A segment from *Sex and the City* suggests why a lawyer believes that having her pregnancy outed is comparable to a gay colleague's having his sexual orientation exposed; a scene from *Erin Brockovich* shows the ways in which children punish mothers for working late; and excerpts from *Imagine That* show Eddie Murphy as a divorced executive trying to fit child care into his overscheduled life.[57] A National Public Radio interview of Jon Stewart by Terry Gross also includes a semiserious account of his efforts to balance a demanding job with parenting two small children.[58]

E. RACIAL AND ETHNIC IDENTITY

Diversity initiatives targeting race and ethnicity serve several objectives. One is to counteract the unconscious biases that restrict equal opportunity in the workplace and to ensure the full utilization of the nation's talent pool. A second is to expand the effectiveness of leadership by ensuring a broad range of perspectives and experiences among those who exercise it. A third is to ensure the legitimacy and responsiveness of powerful institutions in an increasingly multicultural society. A fourth is to create leaders who can serve as role models and use their influence to combat racial and ethnic injustice. Whether diversity also translates into improved financial performance is subject to debate for many of the same reasons discussed earlier concerning corporate boards.[59] But the growing consensus is that diversity promotes important social and organizational goals regardless of whether they can be readily quantified in terms of short-term economic gain.

The readings below explore the justifications for racial and ethnic diversity and the challenges to achieving it in the legal profession. Ironically enough, although lawyers have been at the forefront of this nation's struggle for racial justice, their own workplaces have lagged behind, and typify the problem in many public- and private-sector organizations.

ABA Commission on Women in the Profession, Visible Invisibility:
Women of Color in Law Firms, Executive Summary

(2006)

This report on the ABA Commission on Women's Women of Color Research Initiative [attempts to] further our understanding of the professional lives of women of color [including those of] . . . African-American, Native American, Hispanic/Latina, Asian, or of mixed background. . . . The career experiences of women of color in this study differed dramatically from those of their peers and from white male counterparts in particular. Nearly half of women of color but only 3% of white men experienced demeaning comments or harassment. Unlike white men, many women of color felt that they had to disprove negative preconceived notions about their legal abilities and their commitment to their careers. Seventy-two percent of women of color but only 9% of white men thought others doubted their career commitment after they had (or adopted) children.

Nearly two-thirds of the women of color but only 4% of white men were excluded from informal and formal networking opportunities, marginalized and peripheral to professional networks within the firm. They felt lonely and deprived of colleagues with whom they could share important career-related information. Women of color had mentors, but their mentors did not ensure that they were integrated into the firm's internal networks, received desirable assignments (especially those that helped them meet their required billable hours) or had substantive contacts with clients. Sixty-seven percent of women of color wanted more and/or better mentoring by senior attorneys and partners, whereas only 32% of white men expressed a similar need.

Women of color often became stuck in dead-end assignments, so that as third- and fourth-year associates, their experience lagged behind their white male counterparts, limiting their advancement potential and career trajectories. Forty-four percent of women of color but only 2% of white men reported having been denied desirable assignments. Differential assignments, in turn, affected the ability of women of color to meet the number of billable hours required of them. Forty-six percent of women of color but 58% of white men were able to meet required billable hours.

Forty-three percent of women of color but only 3% of white men had limited access to client development opportunities. Women of color stated that they met with clients only when their race or gender would be advantageous to the firm; they frequently were not given a substantive role in those meetings. This kept them from developing business contacts that they could use to develop a book of clients or as resources for finding subsequent positions.

Nearly one-third of women of color but less than 1% of white men felt they received unfair performance evaluations. Sometimes their accomplishments were ignored by the firm or were not as highly rewarded as those of their peers; sometimes their mistakes were exaggerated. Many women of color complained that they received "soft evaluations" which denied them the opportunity to correct deficits and gain experiences that could lead to promotions and partnership. Twenty percent of women of color but only 1% of white men felt they were denied promotion opportunities. . . .

In addition to these career hurdles, women of color in the survey and focus groups felt they could not "be themselves"; they downplayed and homogenized their gender and racial/ethnic identities. Some tried to act like the men in their firms, become "one of the boys"; others played down their femininity and tried to "mannify" themselves. The effort to minimize the impact of their physical differences was stressful to many women of color, an added burden to the long hours and hard work demanded by their firm. Many complained that they often felt invisible or mistaken for persons of lower status: secretaries, court reporters, paralegals.

The stress of second-class citizenship in law firms led many women of color to reconsider their career goals. The retention rates of women of color and white men reflected their lopsided experiences: 53% of women of color and 72% of white men chose to remain in law firms. Many women of color left firms to work in settings (especially corporations) that were lucrative, where they thought others' decisions about their careers would be less idiosyncratic, based on more merit, and where they had more flexibility to balance personal life, family, and work. . . .

Recommendations

Based on the research from the focus groups and the survey, the ABA Commission on Women proposes the following recommendations. . . .

1. Address the success of women of color as a firm issue not a women of color's issue.
2. Integrate women of color into existing measurement efforts.
3. Integrate women of color into the firm's professional fabric.
4. Integrate women of color into the firm's social fabric.
5. Increase awareness of women of color's issues through dialogue.
6. Support women of color's efforts to build internal and external support systems.
7. Stay compliant with anti-discrimination and anti-harassment policies and hold people accountable for non-compliance.

NOTES AND QUESTIONS

Following this report, other organizations, including the Minority Corporate Counsel Association, Catalyst, and the Hispanic National Bar Association, reported similar findings concerning racial and ethnic bias.[60] Its consequences are particularly apparent in law firms. As noted earlier, racial and ethnic minorities account for only about 6 percent of large-firm partners, a proportion almost three times lower than their representation in elite law schools. About half of the lawyers of color leave firms within three years, an attrition rate substantially higher than that for white attorneys.[61]

To address the issue, increasing numbers of corporate clients are making diversity a factor in allocating work. Some companies have signed the Call to Action: Diversity in the Legal Profession, which obligates them to "end or limit . . . relationships with firms whose performance consistently evidences a lack of meaningful interest in being diverse."[62] In widely publicized actions, Wal-Mart has required that a least one woman and one person of color be among the top five relationship attorneys who handle its business, and it has terminated relationships with two firms that failed to meet its diversity standards.[63] How much difference this pressure will make is not yet clear. As partners in one in-depth survey noted, so long as prestigious firms generally resist changes that would significantly increase diversity, then "where are [the clients] going to go?"[64] Few seem willing to risk abandoning those firms as long as they appear to be making a "good faith effort."[65] Regional and local businesses do not seem to be making diversity a priority, and even the largest national companies that have pledged to reduce or end representation in appropriate cases have been extremely reluctant to do so.[66] For example, Wal-Mart still continues to give much of its work to firms with poor diversity records.[67]

There are, moreover, downsides to client pressure when it results in race matching by firms—that is, when lawyers of color receive work because of their identity, not because of their interests, in order to create the right "look" in courtrooms, client presentations, recruiting, and marketing efforts. Although this strategy sometimes creates helpful opportunities, it can also place minority lawyers in "showhorse" or "mascot" roles in which they have no substantive function and develop no useful skills.[68] The practice is particularly irritating when lawyers of color are pulled from desirable work and trotted out to attract a client whom they never see again, or when they are assumed to have skills and affinities that they in fact lack.[69] Examples include a Korean associate who was given Chinese materials to review, a Japanese American asked to a meeting to solicit a Korean client, and a Latina who was assigned documents in Spanish even after she explained that she was not fluent in the language. "Oh, you'll be fine," she was told. "Look [anything unfamiliar] up in a dictionary."[70] However, when it comes to conventional assignments with client development possibilities, lawyers of color are about twice as likely as their white counterparts to report exclusion from such opportunities.[71]

In responding to these challenges, American Bar Association's Commission on Racial and Ethnic Diversity in the Legal Profession, together with other experts in the field, has issued a broad set of recommendations. They focus on increasing accountability and racial comfort, and challenging racial bias.[72] For example, employers should intensify their efforts in hiring, retaining, and promoting lawyers of color. In particular, employers should reassess evaluation procedures and criteria that have a disproportionate racial impact. Recruiters should make greater contact with law schools that have substantial minority enrollments, either through on-site interviews or letters to minority student associations and visits to regional minority placement conferences. Hiring standards should avoid excessive reliance on first-year grades, LSAT scores, and law review experience, which disproportionately exclude students of color and do not measure the full range of skills that are necessary for successful practice. Promotion criteria such as collegiality and ability to attract client business need to take into account the special obstacles facing minorities. Employers should also ensure a favorable working environment for underrepresented groups. Providing adequate mentoring and opportunities for challenging assignments, supervisory experiences, and client contact should be key priorities.[73]

1. Is that agenda sufficient? What stands in its way?
2. Although most discussions of diversity generalize about the "minority" experience, that experience varies significantly within and across racial

and ethnic groups. For example, Asian American women confront different stereotypes than African American men, and first-generation immigrants from low-income communities face different challenges than counterparts coming from privileged economic backgrounds. How can diversity initiatives take account of these variations?

3. If you were the general counsel of a large corporation, would you join the diversity Call to Action? If so, what evidence of good-faith efforts at diversity would you require? How would you respond to concerns about race matching?

4. If you were the managing partner of a prominent law firm, what strategies would you propose to address diversity issues? How would you respond to situations such as the one described in problem 8-3 below?

PROBLEM 8-3[74]

Paul Barrett's profile *The Good Black* provides a case history of the profession's difficulties in addressing diversity-related issues. It chronicles the efforts of Lawrence Mungen, an African American graduate of Harvard College and Harvard Law School, to fit the model that Barrett's title invokes. As a senior associate, Mungen joined the Washington, D.C., branch office of a Chicago law firm, Katten, Muchen and Zavis, and attempted to "play by the rules." After being hired to do complex bankruptcy work in an office that generated too little of it, he fell through the cracks, and landed off the partnership track. But until late in the process, Mungen failed to complain or to raise race-related concerns. He did not want to be typecast as the "angry black." Nor did he take responsibility for supporting or mentoring any of the small number of other minority lawyers at the firm. When his difficulty in obtaining work became clear, some partners made a few well-meaning but ineffectual responses. They slashed his billing rate, which enabled him to take over some routine matters, but also undermined his reputation as someone capable of demanding partnership-caliber work. Although the senior partners eventually offered to relocate him to another office, they did not provide assurances of opportunities that would lead to promotion. He sued for race discrimination and alleged multiple examples, such as the firm's failure to provide formal evaluations, informal mentoring, invitations to client meetings, or help with business development. A largely black District of Columbia jury found in his favor, but a divided appellate panel reversed. Unable to find another comparable position, Mungen made do with temporary, low-level assignments at other firms and, by the end of the book, was contemplating an alternative career.

As many commentators have noted, the case was a kind of "racial Rorschach test" in which observers saw what they expected to see. To lawyers in the firm and sympathizers outside it, including the appellate court, this was a morality play in which no good deed went unpunished. From their perspective, Mungen was treated no worse than white associates, and in some respects considerably better. The slights and oversights that he alleged at trial were "business as usual mismanagement." And the extra efforts that the firm made to keep Mungen were evidence of a commitment to equal opportunity. By contrast, critics, including Barrett, saw this as a textbook case of "reckless indifferent affirmative action." From their vantage, the firm's efforts were too little, too late. Unsurprisingly, these competing perceptions usually divided along racial lines and typified attitudes within the profession generally. In an ABA survey around the time, only 8 percent of black lawyers, but 41 percent of whites, believed that firms had a genuine commitment to diversity.[75]

Much, of course, depends on what counts as commitment. Katten's management, like that at many firms, undoubtedly did want minority lawyers to succeed. Even from a purely pragmatic standpoint, it helps in recruitment and business development if a firm includes more than the single black lawyer that Katten's Washington office had during Mungen's employment. But while many attorneys want to achieve greater diversity, they do not necessarily want to rethink the structures that get in the way.

1. If you had been managing partner at Katten, what would you have done when Mungen's problems surfaced? Would you have settled the case? What would you have done after the litigation ended?
2. Psychologist Claude Steele and colleagues have extensively documented a dynamic that they label "stereotype threat." Racial and ethnic minorities underperform in circumstances in which they believe that their performance will be taken as evidence of their abilities and in which members of their group are stereotyped as less proficient.[76] Could this dynamic play out in law firms? How might racial stereotypes have affected Lawrence Mungen's performance?
3. Was Lawrence Mungen a "good black" in the sense that David Wilkins describes below? Should it matter?

DAVID B. WILKINS, "TWO PATHS TO THE MOUNTAINTOP?
THE ROLE OF LEGAL EDUCATION IN SHAPING THE VALUES
OF BLACK CORPORATE LAWYERS"

Stanford Law Review 45 (1993):1981, 1984-1985, 1990-2002,
2011-2013, and 2026

Introduction

[My argument in this essay is that black professionals such as corporate lawyers] . . . have moral obligations running to the black community that must be balanced against other legitimate professional duties and personal commitments when deciding on particular actions and, more generally, when constructing a morally acceptable life plan. I call this strategy the obligation thesis. . . .

Something like the obligation thesis has [long] been a standard part of the rhetoric of racial solidarity. . . . Advocates of this approach are always careful to stress the limited nature of their claim. The obligation thesis in no way diminishes the responsibility that *whites* have to work towards remedying the continuing harmful effects of past and present injustices against blacks. Nor should anyone believe that if all black lawyers adopted the obligation thesis (or all black professionals for that matter), the desperate problems of racism and poverty that have haunted the black community for so long would suddenly disappear or even be substantially abated. Nevertheless, black corporate lawyers do have strategic access to power, money, and influence. Standing in the shadow of Thurgood Marshall's towering legacy, many of today's black attorneys view the obligation thesis as a coherent way to reconcile their expanding opportunities with the black bar's historic connection to the struggle for racial justice.

Notwithstanding this pedigree, proponents of the obligation thesis must respond to . . . powerful critiques that expose the many complexities lurking behind the seemingly straightforward propositions outline above. The first, which I will call the universalist challenge, asserts that any effort to define the moral obligations of "black" corporate lawyers to members of the "black community" is either premised on false claims of racial essentialism or places unjustified moral weight on the mere fact of racial identity. The second, which I call the political correctness challenge, asserts that even if one were to recognize the existence of such a race-based obligation, any attempt to give content to this duty will inevitably rest on contested political assertions about the "interests" of the black community and how best to serve them. . . .

Each of these critiques is powerful. . . . Nevertheless, there are good moral and empirical reasons for believing that the obligation thesis is as effective at mediating the inherent tension between the twin goals of equal opportunity and substantive justice as any of its plausible rivals. . . . [Although some critics suggest that black professionals might be better off avoiding corporate practice where their presence could legitimate practices that disadvantage communities of color, this argument] ignores the potential social justice benefits of having at least some black corporate lawyers. . . . Five such benefits seem plausible. First, if nothing else, the presence of blacks within these elite ranks undermines the stereotype of black intellectual inferiority. It therefore becomes somewhat more difficult to justify policies and practices that retard black achievement on the express or implicit assumption that blacks are inherently unqualified to perform the work. Second, as a corollary to the first point, the achievements of black corporate lawyers might inspire other young black women and men to strive harder to become successful in their own right. Indeed, in addition to being passive role models, black corporate lawyers might work actively to open up additional opportunities for blacks, in law or elsewhere. Third, corporate law practice gives black lawyers access to money and other resources that can be directed toward projects to benefit the black community. Fourth, in addition to offering material rewards, corporate law practice traditionally has been a stepping stone to politics and political influence. As a result, black corporate lawyers may be able to translate their private power into public power in ways that benefit the black community. Finally, the very fact that corporations have such power to impose costs on the black community underscores the benefits that could accrue if black lawyers are able to persuade corporations to act in ways that are less harmful (and perhaps even beneficial) to the black community. . . .

This is not to suggest that corporate law practice is the *best* arena for pursuing the cause of racial justice. . . . Nevertheless, the claim that *all* black lawyers should avoid *all* forms of corporate law practice is not plausible even from a purely social justice perspective.

We are left, therefore, with a paradox. On the one hand, a primary goal of the civil rights movement was to ensure that blacks have an equal opportunity to participate in every aspect of the mainstream economy. Precisely because these new opportunities are located in the mainstream, however, they will often be closely linked with the very structures that have contributed to the oppression of blacks in the first instance. As a result, the more blacks take advantage of these new opportunities, the more they may find themselves separated from, and perhaps even opposed to, the demands of other blacks for substantive justice.

The obligation thesis offers one potential way out of this paradox. By positing that successful blacks have a duty to consider the interests of other blacks when performing their new roles, proponents of this thesis seek to ensure that the progress of individual blacks will not unduly impede the advancement of the black community as a whole. However, before examining whether this approach provides a workable means of accomplishing this goal, it is first necessary to confront the universalist challenge that the "paradox of opportunity" is premised on either empirically or morally false claims about the significance of racial identity. . . .

The charge of racial "essentialism" is frequently leveled at anyone who attempts to use racial categories as a means of distributing social goods. The gist of this charge is that racial categories, regardless of their intended purpose, inevitably stereotype blacks, either as all sharing a distinctive viewpoint or ideology or as being victims who are incapable of helping themselves. . . . [But] the obligation thesis does not assume that blacks have any essential interests or character traits. Nor does it portray all blacks as victims.

Although defenders of the obligation thesis sometimes talk in terms of the importance of bringing a "black perspective" to the inner sanctums of the American elite, the argument need not depend upon any essentialist claims about the conduct of black professionals. At its core, the obligation thesis is a moral theory: Its ultimate goal is to establish what black lawyers *ought* to do, not what they inevitably *will* do because of who they are or where they come from. Indeed, one of the reasons black leaders have always stressed the obligation thesis — and one of the reasons I am pressing it here — is the serious danger that black professionals *will not* pay sufficient attention to their duties to the black community. In this respect, obligation theory is the opposite of essentialism.

Nor can this theory be accused of reinforcing the stereotype that all blacks are victims. While the economic and social deprivation of certain parts of the black community is part of the theory's justification, the obligation thesis expressly states that successful blacks can and should play an important role in ameliorating these problems. This thesis constitutes precisely the kind of self-help program that those who oppose racial preference on the ground that it "victimizes" all blacks ought to support. . . .

From the perspective of comprehensive universalism, the obligation thesis must answer one fundamental question: What is the *moral* justification for focusing on the obligations blacks in corporate law firms allegedly owe to other blacks? For example, if it would be morally wrong (or at least morally troubling) for a black lawyer to assist a real estate developer to sell houses at double their market value by exploiting the ignorance of moderate income buyers, wouldn't it be equally wrong for a white lawyer to do so? Would the moral calculus be any different if the prospective homebuyers were all poor whites? Indeed, to the extent that race is relevant at all, shouldn't *whites*, as the perpetrators (or the descendants of the perpetrators) of racist oppression, have the greatest obligation to rectify the results of past injustices to blacks? Why should those few blacks who have finally managed to squeak past the unjust barricades of a hostile and racist world be required to carry the additional burden of worrying about whether their actions will "uplift the race"? . . .

Certain relationships create special moral obligations. Parents have special obligations to care for their own children, just as citizens have obligations running to their own state. . . . In the United States today . . . blacks must take account of the pervasive influence of race.

America was built on race. . . . This legacy has two important consequences for the present inquiry. First, despite all of our many differences, black Americans continue to be joined by an identifiable common culture that overlaps with, but is distinct from, mainstream American culture. . . . Moreover, and this is the second point, although individual blacks undoubtedly participate in and identify with this common cultural community in many different ways, no one can escape it altogether. In *today's* America, "race matters" in ways that go beyond individual choice. . . .

Two aspects of this reality support the move from the "is" of race consciousness to the "ought" of the obligation thesis. First, for many blacks (including many black corporate lawyers), the bonds of solidarity and community with other blacks constitute an important source of strength and well-being. In order to be sustained, however, these bonds must be nurtured. . . . Second, regardless of whether one values the bonds of racial solidarity, the actions of individual blacks and the well-being of the black community are inextricably linked. This is true on both the micro and the macro scale. At the level of personal opportunity, the actions of one black person are often attributed to other blacks. The most obvious example of this common phenomenon is the familiar and pernicious lament by white employers that "we had a black once and he didn't work out." But it can also take more benign forms, such as the "role model" argument that publicly acknowledging the success of one black person will inspire others to do likewise. . . .

[T]he interdependency between individual blacks and blacks as a group gives black professionals a moral reason for valuing the interests of other blacks even in circumstances where they do not see group membership as central to their own identity. Given the link between individual opportunity and group advancement, even those blacks who ultimately care only about their own moral right to be free from racist constraints ought to recognize a moral responsibility to participate in collective projects to end racist oppression. Moreover, moving beyond self-interest, black professionals must also recognize that they have *already* benefitted from the group-based struggles of others.

Moral principles of fair play and reciprocity thus support a corresponding moral obligation to repay this debt by participating in actions that will further the cooperative scheme. This obligation is strengthened by the historical evidence indicating that the participation of black professionals in this cooperative scheme will play a significant role in determining whether the unjustified oppression of blacks in the United States is ever brought to a close.

Finally, morality requires that individual blacks take account the unintended but nevertheless predictable consequences of their actions. Consider, for example, a black corporate lawyer who is asked to defend a company accused of discriminating against blacks in employment. No matter how much that lawyer protests that his race is irrelevant to the performance of his professional role, his very presence at the counsel table sends a message to the jurors (both black and white) about the merits of the discrimination claim. To the extent that this implicit message (i.e., a company that discriminated would not hire a black lawyer) helps the company defeat a valid claim of discrimination, the black lawyer has helped inflict a moral wrong on the black plaintiffs. . . .

What must [that lawyer] do to discharge his obligation to the black community? Must he refuse the case or perhaps even resign from the firm? Can he take the case so long as he has reasonable grounds to believe that the company did not in fact discriminate? Should he refrain from engaging in certain tactics (e.g., vigorously cross-examining the plaintiff) that he otherwise would be prepared to do? What happens if he vigorously defends the case but then makes a substantial contribution to a job retraining program catering primarily to a black clientele? Or can the lawyer discharge his entire obligation by being the best lawyer that he can be, thereby continuing to shatter racist stereotypes?

From a cursory glance at these options, it is apparent that there is no a priori method for choosing among them. Moreover, before one reached a definitive judgment, one would want to know a range of other information about the lawyer, the client, and the situation. What is needed, therefore, is a forum where black lawyers can investigate and debate the range of concrete alternatives for balancing their obligations to the black community against other legitimate professional obligations and personal commitments. . . .

NOTES AND QUESTIONS

1. Do members of groups who are underrepresented in positions of leadership have some special obligation to advance the interests of those groups? On what basis could you argue for such an obligation? What would be the objections? Why shouldn't members of privileged groups have the same obligations?

2. Do Wilkins's arguments suggest that women also have special responsibilities to help other women? If not, why? If so, what forms of assistance are appropriate? Is it fair for women leaders to single out women subordinates for special opportunities and mentoring when they criticize men for doing the same for other men?

3. Wilkins argues that if a black lawyer allows his identity to help a client "defeat a valid claim of discrimination, the black lawyer has helped inflict

a moral wrong on the black plaintiffs." But typically when lawyers accept a case, they do not know whether a claim is valid. Moreover, psychological evidence suggests that once individuals have taken on an advocacy role, they tend to identify with that position and to discount competing evidence.[77] Does that suggest that lawyers of color should avoid accepting the very kinds of cases in which they are likely to be in greatest demand? Or might minority lawyers sometimes have enhanced leverage to persuade clients to do the right thing in responding to valid discrimination claims?

4. Consider the dilemma of the only black partner in a prominent San Francisco firm who was asked to help solicit a new client whose general counsel was black. The client's legal needs were not in an area in which she had substantive expertise, although a colleague pointed out that she had worked for the Department of Transportation while a law student and the client's business was shipping. But business was slow and she felt enormous pressure to respond as she did. "No problem. . . . You know I'm always willing to help with anything that will be good for the firm." She later regretted the decision. At the meeting in which her colleague "made the pitch about the firm's relevant expertise, none of which I possessed, it was clear that the only reason I was there was to tout the firm's diversity, which was practically nonexistent. In that moment, I wanted to fling myself through the plate glass window of that well-appointed conference room overlooking the port of Oakland."[78]

   Would you have felt the same? What would you have done in her position? What would you have done if you had been her colleague? Would it have mattered whether the client had signed the Call to Action pledge concerning diversity?

5. How should leaders respond to concerns of white men who are preempted from certain work because of clients' commitments concerning diversity? In a letter to the editor of the *National Law Journal*, a self-described "young, white straight male attorney who happens to be politically progressive" protested employment-termination decisions attributable to "meeting an important client's newly asserted diversity demands."[79] From his perspective, "surely firing people even partially on the basis of an immutable characteristic is as unjust when done in the name of increasing diversity as it is when done to maintain homogeneity."[80] Do you agree? If not, how would you respond?

6. Can even "positive" race-based characterizations work against the stereotyped group? What barriers might confront Asian Americans who are cast as the "Model Minority" based on their intelligence and hard work?[81] Consider the description Senator Joseph Biden offered of Barack Obama during the presidential campaign, as the "first mainstream African-American who is articulate and bright and clean and a nice-looking guy."[82] Psychologists refer to this as the "flower blooming in winter" effect.[83] Although it can provide special recognition for the individual who is deemed an exception, it can also leave the underlying stereotype intact.

7. Research on diversity in other organizational contexts apart from law suggests similar challenges. For example, Catalyst's surveys, *Women of Color in Accounting* and *Women of Color in U.S. Securities Firms*, found that minority

women were the group least satisfied with their workplaces on multiple dimensions, including access to influential mentors, challenging assignments, client development opportunities, and an inclusive, supportive work environment.[84] Among members of securities firms, 38 percent of men of color and 35 percent of women of color felt that diversity efforts failed to address subtle racial biases.[85] Among accountants, only 45 percent of men of color and 41 percent of women of color believed that senior leadership demonstrated a commitment to diversity by placing qualified women of color in leadership positions.[86]

In another survey, involving minority female corporate executives, only half felt accepted and only a fifth felt that their company was truly committed to advancing people of color.[87] Racial tokenism was a significant problem, particularly when managers were steered to positions that were good for the company's public image but not for their own careers.[88] The lone black woman manager in the manufacturing plant of a Fortune 500 company described her experience as

> just a brutal environment. It was sometimes a lonely demoralizing experience. I never had peers to talk with. I'd go into the executive dining room. Imagine a big room full of big tables, full of big white men. . . . [T]here might be seventy-five people in there eating and of that seventy-five, there might be one or two friendly faces.[89]

What coping strategies might you advise for that environment? In his account of "covering" by sexual, racial, and ethnic minorities, Columbia law professor Kenji Yoshino details the pressure that these individuals feel to suppress aspects of their identity to fit in the dominant culture. Self-help advice to aspiring leaders is to avoid everything from Afro hairstyles to clothing that has "Hispanic associations."[90] Yoshino argues that such advice mischaracterizes the problem and the solution. In his view, the answer is for the culture to become more tolerant, not for minorities to become more mainstream. Minority professionals should feel "emboldened" to challenge conformist pressures in the "everyday places where tolerance is made and unmade."[91] Is that the advice you would provide? If not, what would you suggest to break down patterns of isolation and exclusion such as the one described above?

PROBLEM 8-4[92]

In their *Harvard Business Review* article "Rethinking Political Correctness," professors Robin Ely, Debra Meyerson, and Martin Davidson describe coping strategies for what they term "identity abrasions." These are situations in which individuals believe that they have been targets of bias or unfair accusations of bias—situations that breed resentment, conflict, and mistrust. A case history involves Brianna, an African American CEO of a start-up that provided consulting services. The company's white founder, Jay, remained a close advisor to her leadership team, but his "autocratic style rubbed Brianna the wrong way." The problem came to a head during a team meeting when Jay told her that she needed to "'lighten up' on her push to market more vigorously to clients of color. He told her that she was being 'too aggressive.' Brianna's immediate impulse was dismissive; it seemed to her that Jay just couldn't bear the authority of a strong black woman."[93]

Two friends with whom Brianna discussed Jay's behavior agreed with her interpretation, but that did not get her "any closer to finding a way to work with him."[94] Another advisor, a black professor from her MBA program, suggested instead that Brianna approach Jay as if he had her best interests at heart, and attempt to learn from his views. Pursuing that advice, Brianna found that Jay had understandable doubts about the firm's ability to connect with minority clients, in part because he had doubts about his own ability. That acknowledgment made it easier for Brianna to share her own insecurities, and the resulting conversation suggested that her forceful style may have inhibited other team members from raising concerns. As a result, Brianna began to realize that "her investment in being seen as a powerful black woman had gotten in the way of actually being a powerful black woman."[95]

Building on such examples, Ely, Meyerson, and Davidson generalize five principles that can guide leaders in navigating cultural difference:

- *Pause* to short-circuit the emotion and reflect.
- *Connect* with others in ways that affirm the importance of relationships.
- *Question yourself* to help identify your blind spots and discover what makes you defensive.
- *Get genuine support* that doesn't necessarily validate your point of view but, rather, helps you gain a broader perspective.
- *Shift your mind set* from "*You* need to change" to "What can *I* change?"[96]

Leaders can also foster a climate for such dynamics by creating safe spaces for dialogue and visibly modeling these strategies in their own behavior. Ely, Meyerson, and Davidson note that

> the most difficult—and rewarding [principle] is that of questioning oneself. This principle is challenging for managers because it runs counter to the image of the confident, decisive leader. As it turns out, however, leaders who question themselves and learn from others in the service of clear goals do not bespeak a lack of confidence; rather, they demonstrate humility, clarity, and strength. Indeed, the leaders we have observed who exemplify this principle generate fierce respect and loyalty from their followers. They model vulnerability, respond nondefensively to questions and challenges, are aware of their own biases and emotional triggers, demonstrate resilience in the face of identity abrasions, and openly rely on others to test the validity of their perspective. . . .[97]

Break up into teams and construct an "identity abrasion," built on an experience from film, literature, or personal experience. Assign team members roles as participants and advisors, and attempt to apply the principles set forth above. Then reflect on your experience. What challenges did you confront? What might you have done better?

MEDIA RESOURCES

For examples of pressures for conformity, see *Hollywood Shuffle*, in which Robert Townsend describes techniques that enable actors to conform to racist stereotypes, and *Strictly Business*, in which a black business executive explains to a black mail room clerk why he needs to act "less black" in order to get a promotion. For an example of "benign" stereotyping, Joe Biden's description of Obama is also available.[98]

END NOTES

1. Intersectional approaches start from the premise that different identities overlap or combine to contribute to unique experiences of disadvantage and privilege. See Association for Women's Rights in Development (AWID), Intersectionality: A Tool for Gender and Economic Justice, Women's Rights, and Economic Change 9 (Aug. 2004), 1.

2. Karin Klenke, Women and Leadership: A Contextual Perspective (New York: Springer Publishing Co., 1996), 27.

3. Alison Weir, The Life of Elizabeth I (New York: Ballentine, 1998), 45 (quoting Sir William Cecil).

4. 42 U.S.C. §2000. For a history, see Erin Kelly and Frank Dobbin, How Affirmative Action Became Diversity Management, American Behavioral Scientist 41 (1998):960, 963-964.

5. For the percentage of minorities in the population, see http://www.census.gov/prod/cen2000/dp1/2kh00.pdf. For the cabinet, see http://www.whitehouse.gov/administration/cabinet. For the United States Congress, see http://www.ethnicmajority.com/congress.htm. For governors, see http://ncsl.typepad.com/the_thicket/2009/07/racial-and-ethnic-minority-governors.html. For corporations, see Diversity Inc., Fortune 500 Black, Latino, Asian CEOs, July 22, 2008, http://www.diversityinc.com/content/1757/article/3895. For law firms, see National Association for Legal Career Professionals (NALP), Women and Minorities in Law Firms by Race and Ethnicity, NALP Bulletin, January 2010.

6. For Congress, see http://womenincongress.house.gov/historical-data/representatives-senators-by-congress.html?congress=111. For the cabinet, see http://www.whitehouse.gov/administration/cabinet. For women-owned businesses, see Center for Women-Owned Business, cited in Sharon G. Hadary, What's Holding Back Women Entrepreneurs, Wall Street Journal, May 17, 2010, R1. For Fortune 1000 CEOs, see http://www.catalyst.org/publication/322/women-ceos-of-the-fortune-1000. For state governors, see http://ergd.org/Governors.htm. For women in the federal judiciary, see www.nwlc.org/pdf/factsheetnumberofwomeninjudiciary.pdf.

7. For governors, see http://www.whitehouse.gov/administration/cabinet. For the United States Congress, see http://www.ethnicmajority.com/congress.htm. For law firm partners, see http://nawl.timberlakepublishing.com/files/NAWL%202010%20Final(2).pdf. For corporations, see http://www.diversityinc.com/content/1757/article/3895. For the cabinet, see http://www.whitehouse.gov/administration/cabinet. For the federal judiciary, see www.nwlc.org/pdf/factsheetnumberofwomeninjudiciary.pdf. For directors, see Rachel Soares, Nancy M. Carter, and Jan Combopiano, 2009 Catalyst Census: Fortune 500 Women Board Directors (2009), available at http://www.catalyst.org/file/320/2009_fortune_500_census_women_board_directors.pdf.

8. See studies discussed in David Wilkins, From "Separate Is Inherently Unequal" to "Diversity Is Good for Business": The Rise of Market-Based Diversity Arguments and the Fate of the Black Corporate Bar, Harvard Law Review 117 (2004):1548, 1588-1590; Douglas E. Brayley and Eric S. Nguyen, Good Business: A Market-Based Argument for Law Firm Diversity, Journal of the Legal Profession 35 (2009):1, 7; Frank Dobbin and Jiwook Jung, Corporate Board Gender Diversity and Stock Performance: The Competence Gap or Institutional Investor Bias?, North Carolina Law Review (forthcoming 2010), available at http://www.wjh.harvard.edu/~dobbin/cv/workingpapers/Board_Diversity_and_Performance_07_01_10.pdf; Susan E. Jackson and Aparna Joshi, Diversity in Social Context: A Multi-Attribute, Multi-Level Analysis of Team Diversity and Sales Performance, Journal of Organizational Behavior 25 (2004):675, 676; Jonathan S. Leonard, David I. Levine, and Aparna Joshi, Do Birds of a Feather Shop Together? The Effects on Performance of Employees' Similarity with One Another and with Customers, Journal of Organizational Behavior 25 (2004):731; Katherine Y. Williams and Charles A. O'Reilly, Demography and Diversity in Organizations: A Review of 40 Years of Research, in Research in Organizational Behavior 20 (1998):77, 94-95.

9. See studies discussed in Deborah L. Rhode and Amanda K. Packel, Diversity on Corporate Boards: How Much Difference Does Difference Make?, Rock Center for Corporate Governance at Stanford University Working Paper no. 89, October 2010.

10. Brayley and Nyugen, Good Business, 34; Rhode and Packel, supra note 9.

11. Paula M.L. Moya and Hazel Rose Markus, Doing Race: An Introduction, in Hazel Rose Markus and Pula M. Moya, eds., Doing Race (New York: Norton, 2010), 1, 6-10.

12. Minority Corporate Counsel Association (MCCA), Sustaining Pathways to Diversity (New York: MCCA, 2009), 16.

13. Id. 25.

14. Id. 15.

15. Lisa M. Fairfax, Clogs in the Pipeline: The Mixed Data on Women Directors and Continued Barriers to Advancement, Maryland Law Review 65 (2006):579, 589-590.

16. Lynne L. Dallas, The New Managerialism and Diversity on Corporate Boards of Directors, Tulane Law Review 76 (2002):1363, 1393.

17. Emily Mychasuk, The Quandary of Quotas, Financial Times, December 8, 2010, 10.

18. Francie Ostrower, Nonprofit Governance in the United States: Findings on Performance and Accountability from the First National Representative Study (Washington, D.C.: The Urban Institute, Center on Nonprofits and Philanthropy, 2007), 18-19.

19. Id. at 19.

20. Deepali Bagati, Women of Color in U.S. Securities Firms (New York: Catalyst, 2008), 47.

21. Frederick A. Miller and Judith H. Katz, The Inclusion Breakthrough: Unleashing the Real Power of Diversity (San Francisco: Berrett-Koehler, 2002), 37-38.

22. Id. at 82, 102, 173.

23. Adaptive Coaching (Mountain View: Davies-Black, 2003), 240-241.

24. Id. at 244.

25. The Colbert clip is available at http://www.colbertnation.com/the-colbert-report-videos/229349/june-01-2_0/sonia-sotomayor-s-nominationo_jeffrey-toobin. *The Office* clips are available at http://www.youtube.com/watch?v=-j7wr-wsmcI&feature=related and http://www.youtube.com/watch?v=0YI7Q0ZGvIc. For law firms, see a training clip at http://www.youtube.com/watch?v=alEH4NyTvWc&feature=PlayList&p=32CC01BB949DD0D8&index=5, and http://www.youtube.com/watch?v=4U21I0pZop8.

26. Linda Babcock and Sara Laschever, Ask for It (New York; Bantam, 2008), 252-262.

27. Francis J. Flynn, Cameron Anderson, and Sebastien Brion, Too Tough, Too Soon: Familiarity and the Backlash Effect (working paper, Stanford Business School, 2011).

28. Katrin Bennhold, Where Would We Be If Women Ran Wall Street?, New York Times, Feb. 1, 2009, http://www.nytimes.com/2009/02/01/business/worldbusiness/01iht-gender.3-420354.htm.

29. Id.

30. Sheelah Kolhatkar, What If Women Ran Wall Street?, New York Magazine, March 29, 2010, 36, available at http://nymag.com/news/nusinessfinance/64950.

31. Id.

32. Hadary, Why Are Women-Owned Firms Smaller than Men-Owned Ones?, Wall Street Journal, March 17, 2010, R1, available at http://online.wsj.com/article/SB100014240527487046886045751255543191609632.html.

33. Blanche W. Cook, Eleanor Roosevelt, Vol. 1 (New York: Penguin, 1992), 5-6.

34. Marianne Cooper, Being the "Go-to Guy": Fatherhood, Masculinity and the Organization of Work in Silicon Valley, Qualitative Sociology 23 (2000):379, reprinted in Naomi Gerstel, Dan Clawson, and Robert Zussman, Families at Work: Expanding the Bounds (Nashville: Vanderbilt University Press, 2002), 5, 10, 13.

35. Id. at 7 (quoting Scott Webster).

36. Id. at 9 (quoting Kirk Sinclair).

37. Id. at 24 (quoting Eric Salazar).

38. Id. (quoting Chris Baxter).

39. Id. at 20.

40. Id. at 21 (quoting Rich Kavelin).

41. Id. at 25 (quoting Rich Kavelin).

42. Id. at 26 (quoting Kirk Sinclair).

43. Joan C. Williams, Reshaping the Work-Family Debate (Cambridge, MA: Harvard University Press, 2010), 89 (quoting Derek Bok).

44. Mary C. Noonan and Mary E. Corcoran, The Mommy Track and Partnership: Temporary Delay or Dead End?, Annals of the American Academy of Political and Social Science 596(2004):130, 137.

45. Ronit Dinovitzer, Robert Nelson, Gabriele Plickert, Rebecca Sandefur, and Joyce S. Sterling, After the JD II: Second Results from a National Study of Legal Careers (Chicago, IL: American Bar Foundation; Dallas, TX: NALP Foundation for Law Career Research and Education, 2009), 62.

46. Nancy Levit and Douglas O. Linder, The Happy Lawyer: Making a Good Life in the Law (New York: Oxford University Press, 2010), 12, 13; Kenneth G. Dau-Schmidt et al., Men and Women

of the Bar: The Impact of Gender on Legal Careers, Michigan Journal of Gender and Law 16 (2009):49, 112-113 (2009).

47. William Safire and Leonard Schir, Leadership (New York: Simon & Schuster, 1990), 106.

48. Sheryl Gay Stolberg, He Breaks for Band Recitals, New York Times, February 14, 2010, S11.

49. Id. at S1, S10.

50. Todd S. Purdum, Washington, We Have a Problem, Vanity Fair (September 2010):290.

51. Family First: Mary Matalin, An Ex-White House Heavy, Tells Why She Quit Dick Cheney to Stay Home with Her Two Kids, People Magazine, March 17, 2003, available at http://www.people.com/people/archive/article/0.20,,20139543,00.html.

52. Lincoln Caplan, Skadden: Power, Money, and the Rise of a Legal Empire (New York: Farrar Straus Giroux, 1993), 7.

53. See, e.g., Sylvia Ann Hewlett, Off-Ramps and On-Ramps: Keeping Talented Women on the Road to Success (Cambridge: Harvard Business School Press, 2007).

54. For Albright, see http://www.youtube.com/watch?v=oF-iUTvPRJc; for Thatcher, see Ladyhttp://www.youtube.com/watch?v=4O6NZ4PRh_0&feature=related.

55. For a particularly good clip from The Devil Wears Prada in which Streep interviews a possible assistant, see http://movieclips.com/Awo5D-andys-interview.

56. http://www.youtube.com/watch?v=gEiDR4qtVZc&feature=fvst.

57. For Sex and the City, see http://www.youtube.com/watch?v=x1duLhDN1_0&feature=related (start time: 4:15).

58. Jon Stewart, Interview, The Most Trusted Name in Fake News, Fresh Air, Oct. 4, 2010.

59. Wilkins, From "Separate Is Inherently Unequal" to "Diversity Is Good for Business"; Brayley and Nguyen, Good Business, 7.

60. Deepali Bagati, Women of Color in U.S. Law Firms (New York: Catalyst, 2010); Minority Corporate Counsel Association, Sustaining Pathways; Jill L. Cruz and Melinda S. Molina, Hispanic National Bar Association National Study on the Status of Latinas in the Legal Profession, Few and Far Between: The Reality of Latina Lawyers, Pepperdine Law Review 37 (2010):971; Gladys Garcia Lopez, "Nunca Te Toman en Cuenta [They Never Take You into Account]": The Challenges of Inclusion and Strategies for Success of Chicana Attorneys, Gender & Society 22 (2008):590, 601-603, 609 (2008); Brittany Hutson, The Legal Face of Diversity, Black Enterprise (January 2010):60.

61. Nancy Levitt and Douglas Linder, The Happy Lawyer (New York: Oxford University Press, 2009), 250.

62. A Call to Action: Diversity in the Legal Profession Commitment Statement, http://www.tools.mcca.com/CTA/commitment_statement.html.

63. Claire Tower Putnam, Comment: When Can a Law Firm Discriminate among Its Own Employees to Meet a Client's Request? Reflections on the ACC's Call to Action, University of Pennsylvania. Journal of Labor and Employment Law 9 (2007):657, 660; Karen Donovan, Pushed by Clients, Law Firms Step Up to Diversity Efforts, New York Times, July 21, 2006, C6.

64. John M. Conley, Tales of Diversity: Lawyers' Narratives of Racial Equity in Private Firms, Law and Social Inquiry 31 (2006):833, 845-846 (2006).

65. Id. at 846.

66. Id.

67. Brayley and Nyugen, Good Business, 37 (concluding that "[t]there is no evidence here that Wal-Mart is choosing its law firms with an eye to measured levels of diversity").

68. ABA Commission on Women in the Profession, Visible Invisibility: Women of Color in Law Firms (Chicago: American Bar Association, 2006), 21; LeeAnn O'Neill, Hitting the Legal Diversity Market Home: Minority Women Strike Out, The Modern American (Spring 2007):7, 10.

69. Garner Weng, Racial Bias in Law Practice, California Lawyer Magazine (January 2003):37, 39; Wilkins, From Separate Is Inherently Unequal, 1594; Lopez, They Never Take You into Account, 596.

70. ABA Commission on Women in the Profession, Visible Invisibility 22; Wilkins, From Separate Is Inherently Unequal, 1595; ABA Commission on Women in the Profession, Visible Invisibility, 26.

71. MCCA, Sustaining Pathways, 23.

72. Devon Carbado and Mitu Gulati, Race to the Top of the Corporate Ladder: What Minorities Do When They Get There, Washington and Lee Law Review 61 (2004):1645, 1662-1663.

73. Elizabeth Chambliss, Miles to Go: Progress of Minorities in the Legal Profession (Chicago: American Bar Association Commission on Racial and Ethnic Diversity in the Legal Profession, 2004), 97-98; Sam Reeves, The Carrot Didn't Work So Let's Apply the Stick, National Law Journal (Oct. 23, 2006):S6, S8; Edgardo Ramos and Lynn Anne Baronas, What Works: Ways to Increase Diversity at Law Firms, National Law Journal, Jan. 16, 2006, at 13. David Wilkins and Mitu Gulati, Why Are There So Few Black Lawyers in Corporate Law Firms? An Institutional Analysis, California Law Review 84 (1996):493.

74. This problem is adapted from the discussion in Deborah L. Rhode and David Luban, Legal Ethics (New York: Foundation Press, 5th ed. 2009), 98-99.

75. Walter La Grande, "Getting There, Staying There," ABA Journal, February 1999, 54.

76. For an overview, see Hazel Rose Markus, Claude M. Steele, and Dorothy M. Steele, Colorblindness as a Barrier to Inclusion: Assimilation and Nonimmigrant Minorities, Daedelus 29 (2000):233, 250.

77. Lawyers are not of course unique in this respect. See the discussion of confirmation bias and tendencies toward reduction of cognitive dissonance discussed in Chapter 3.

78. Linda A. Mabry, The Token, California Lawyer (July 2006):76.

79. Ben Martin, Letter to the Editor, National Law Journal, Nov. 6, 2006, at 23.

80. Id.

81. Mirand O. McGowne and James Lindgren, The First Century: Celebrating 100 Years of Legal Scholarship Essay: Testing the Model Minority Myth, Northwestern University Law Review 100 (2006):331; Pat Chew, Asian Americans: The "Reticent" Minority and Their Paradoxes, William & Mary Law Review 36 (1994):1, 24.

82. Lynette Clemetson, The Racial Politics of Speaking Well, New York Times, February 4, 2007, Sec. 4, at 1.

83. Ella L.J. Edmondson Bell and Stella M. Nkomo, Our Separate Ways: Black and White Women and the Struggle for Professional Identity (Boston: Harvard Business School Press, 2001), 145.

84. Katherine Giscombe, Women of Color in Accounting (New York: Catalyst, 2008); Deepali Bagati, Women of Color in U.S. Securities Firms (New York: Catalyst, 2008).

85. Bagati, Women of Color in U.S. Securities Firms, 41.

86. Giscombe, Women of Color in Accounting, 17.

87. Edmondson Bell and Nkomo, Our Separate Ways, 127.

88. Id. at 146.

89. Id. at 123.

90. Kenji Yoshino, The Pressure to Cover, New York Times Magazine, January 15, 2006.

91. Id.

92. This problem is adapted from a discussion in Robin J. Ely, Debra Meyerson, and Martin N. Davidson, Rethinking Political Correctness, Harvard Business Review (September 2006):79.

93. Id. at 84.

94. Id. at 85.

95. Id. at 84.

96. Id. at 80.

97. Id. at 87.

98. "Hollywood Shuffle" is available at http://www.youtube.com/watch?v=xKX4LktBI5o (start time: 3:23). "Strictly Business" is available at http://www.youtube.com/watch?v=ex3whZnk170 &feature=related. For Joe Biden's comments, see Jason Horowitz, Biden Unbound: Lays into Clinton, Obama, Edwards, New York Observer, February 4, 2007, available at http://www.observer.com/ 2007/politics/biden-unbound-lays-clinton-obama-edwards.

9

LEADERSHIP FOR SOCIAL CHANGE

A. INTRODUCTION

Leaders are, by definition, at the forefront of social change. As heads of government, nonprofits, and social change movements, they play a critical role in cultural transformation. Their formal positions vary considerably. Nelson Mandela led from a prison cell, Martin Luther King persuaded from a pulpit, and Lyndon Johnson issued orders from the Oval Office. Yet, whatever their position, they also confronted some common challenges in defining goals, forging coalitions, mobilizing followers, proposing policy, attracting resources, and engaging public attention.

Social movements are a key drivers of change, and despite the importance of leadership in such movements, its role has only recently received systematic analysis.[1] This chapter draws on that emerging research, as well as on other historical and contemporary portraits of cultural transformation.[2] Broadly defined, social movements involve a desire for change, driven by general public sympathy and participants who contribute resources to the effort.[3] The discussion below begins with an overview of the conditions that are likely to yield such movements and the role of leaders in creating or capitalizing on such conditions. More in-depth analysis then explores two American civil rights campaigns that have brought about major cultural transformations over the last half century—campaigns challenging discrimination based on race and on sexual orientation. The focus is on the leaders involved in those struggles, as heads of movement organizations, lawyers for their causes, or government officials sympathetic to their agendas.

1. THE CONDITIONS OF SOCIAL CHANGE AND THE CENTRALITY OF LEADERS

Social movements result from a complex interrelationship of factors whose relative importance is subject to debate. Clearly leaders both influence and are influenced by external conditions. Yet how much leadership matters relative to other structural conditions is difficult to assess. Research on the same social movements often comes to different conclusions. For example, some accounts of Martin Luther King's role in the American civil rights campaign insist that "the movement made Martin; Martin did not make the movement."[4] According to Clayborn Carson, director of Stanford University's Martin Luther King Papers Project, even without King "the black struggle would have followed a course of development similar to the one it did."[5] King himself famously suggested as much before a mass meeting during the 1995 Montgomery bus boycott: "If M.L. King had never been born, this movement would have taken place. I just happened to be here. You know there comes a time when time itself is ready for change."[6] Yet others believe that the skills King brought to the movement were critical in shaping its early successes; the "times were ready for King," but so also "King was ready for the times."[7] Cross-cultural research similarly underscores the importance of such leadership capabilities. Similar public policy initiatives in similar circumstances have different outcomes depending on leaders' skills and strategies.[8]

In any event, whatever the relative importance of structures or agency in accounting for particular social changes, there is no doubt that one of the key characteristics of successful leaders is their ability to create or capitalize on conditions conducive to progress. A vast literature explores such conditions and debates their role in the context of particular struggles. For present purposes, a few overarching themes bear emphasis.

The first involves the importance of social, economic, and political dynamics. For example, the contemporary American women's movement arose at a time when traditional gender roles had become increasingly out of step with social realities. Increasing longevity and access to birth control meant that women in the 1960s could anticipate spending about two-thirds of their lives without children under eighteen. These changes in family patterns, together with the economy's rising demand for trained workers, propelled growing numbers of women into the workforce. The prejudice they encountered there, as well as in civil rights and other political activities, became catalysts for change.[9] A related factor was President Kennedy's appointment of a Commission on Women with the official mandate of recommending changes to further the "full realization of women's rights." An unofficial purpose was to discharge political debts to his female campaign workers, none of whom obtained other significant administration posts. Leaders of the commission took full advantage of their opportunity. Not only did they recommend legislation such as the Equal Pay Act, they also created task forces and a Citizen's Advisory Council that began documenting problems of discrimination and placing them on the political agenda.[10]

Another catalyst for social change is disaster, crisis, violence, or some equally pivotal event that captures widespread attention. For example, media coverage of southern police brutalizing peaceful civil rights protesters in the early 1960s helped build the necessary coalitions for antidiscrimination statutes.[11] Coastal oil spills, accidents at Three Mile Island and Chernobyl nuclear reactors, and mounting evidence of global warming have all raised the public's environmental consciousness and laid foundations for policy responses.[12] The 1991 televised hearings at which Anita Hill made claims of sexual harassment by Supreme Court nominee Clarence Thomas before an almost entirely male Senate Judiciary Committee galvanized the women's movement and advanced its agenda.[13] That same year, an announcement by the Cracker Barrel restaurant chain that it would terminate employees whose sexual orientation failed to match "normal heterosexual values" raised awareness of homophobia, and prompted formation of gay and lesbian workplace task forces.[14]

A further impetus for social change comes from widespread recognition of injustice and some general consensus about causes and potentially effective responses.[15] Those perceptions of grievances typically arise less from objective circumstances than from a sense of relative deprivation—peoples' conviction either that their circumstances have fallen short of expectations or that they are disadvantaged relative to another relevant reference group.[16] Social movements often draw on this indignation as well as a sense of collective identity based on shared characteristics, experiences, or ideology.[17] To inspire activism as well as sympathy, movements also need foundations of group solidarity. Participants must see their own status and interests connected to those of a broader group.[18]

2. LEADERSHIP CHARACTERISTICS

As Chapter 1 suggested and studies of social change confirm, what makes for successful leadership of social change depends on context. Movements have different needs at different times, stages, and levels. Typically, they benefit from a combination of what sociologists label universal cultural capital, local cultural capital, and symbolic capital.[19] Universal cultural capital, as French theorist Pierre Bourdieu famously described it, refers to individuals' general knowledge, capabilities, and social networks: education, background, analytic and communication abilities, ties to government, media, funders, and so forth. Leaders need to understand the values of the broader constituencies they seek to engage, and to work effectively in multiple settings with widely different audiences. Local cultural capital refers to individuals' knowledge of the particular groups they are seeking to lead and their relationships with members. A personal history that is shared with the group can be invaluable. Symbolic capital refers to the legitimacy conferred by particular affiliations or positions, such as being a pastor of a church, an elected head of an organization, a member of a leader's family, or a target of government repression.

No single individual may be strong on all these dimensions, but movements generally need leadership that combines them. National social movement organizations often have three tiers of leaders; those who hold the top position, those who advise that individual, and those who form bridges to local groups.[20] As Harvard professor Marshall Ganz notes, developing leadership all the way down needs to be a central priority. For example, the Sierra Club pursues its environmental agenda through 750,000 members and 380 local groups with 12,500 leadership positions, all of which need individuals adept at mobilizing resources and public support.[21]

Martin Luther King is a leader who exemplified many of these characteristics. His preparation and practice as a minister honed his speaking skills and understanding of the Baptist traditions that would resonate with the southern black communities he sought to mobilize. He also had knowledge of non-violent protest techniques and exceptional interpersonal abilities that enabled him to connect with diverse constituencies, including not just black congregations but also union members, urban gangs, and white politicians.[22] King also built on a network of southern black clergy who had deep knowledge of, and credibility with, local communities. His status as a minister and his courage in facing violence and imprisonment conferred further symbolic authority.

Yet even the most exceptional leaders have their limitations, and King's critics point to several. One was his failure to understand that the rhetorical styles and strategies that had worked effectively in challenging overt racism in the South did not translate into combating the structural inequalities in the more secular North. Nor was King always receptive to hearing dissenting views or to sharing power, particularly with women. In one celebrated incident, after an advisor suggested that King had failed to understand the power structure of Chicago, his response was to walk away and pray. Colleagues such as Bayard Ruskin were infuriated by "this business of King talking to God and God talking to King."[23] The result, according to critics, was that King offered a "leader-centered movement," when what was needed was a "movement-centered leader."[24]

3. LEADERSHIP CHALLENGES AND STRATEGIES

Leaders seeking to secure major social change confront many of the same obstacles, and need many of the same strategies concerning influence and innovation described in Chapter 4. However, leaders in this context also face certain distinctive challenges. One involves the diffusion of authority. In *Leadership for the Common Good*, Barbara Crosby and John Bryson note that "anyone who tries to tackle a public problem . . . sooner or later comes face to face with the dynamics of a shared power world."[25] Leaders of social movements typically lack coercive authority. Even heads of state or government agencies who seek to advance movement objectives cannot rely simply on command and control styles of leadership. American presidents who have achieved major social policy victories have succeeded only by persuading key constituencies of the necessity of change and of their own stake in achieving it. In confronting major social issues where "no one is in charge," leaders need to rely on soft power and collaborative networks, often involving both governmental and nongovernmental organizations.[26]

Leaders also need to work on multiple levels and focus resources strategically in light of "windows of opportunity."[27] Effective policy entrepreneurs know when to assume the risks of seeking "big wins" and when to settle for incremental "small wins" that can build confidence, test solutions, and lay foundations for broader change.[28] That requires knowing when to wait for the right moment. Moving too early on an issue can entrench opposition, as then President Clinton learned in his early unsuccessful efforts to end sexual orientation discrimination by the military. Premature escalation of conflict can also demoralize supporters; it deprives them of the small victories that sustain hope and make the ends of activism seem worth its price.[29]

So too, overreliance on a single lever of change can be disabling. Leaders often need to "venue shop," and work in multiple legislative, administrative, legal, media, business, funding, and activist arenas. For example, focusing too much on litigation can result in "victory in the courts but . . . not victory in practice."[30] Judges may lack the legitimacy, expertise, and enforcement resources necessary for meaningful social reform.[31] Leaders of public-interest legal organizations such as the American Civil Liberties Union, the NAACP Legal Defense Fund, the Natural Resources Defense Council, the Western Center on Law and Poverty, and the National Women's Law Center all have ample experience with legal rights gone wrong.[32] Judicial decisions without a political base to support them are vulnerable to chronic noncompliance, public backlash, and statutory or doctrinal reversal.[33] Litigation is most successful when used in tandem with other strategies to gain public attention, mobilize group support, impose costs, and increase policy leverage. As Ralph Nader once summed it up, "You have to deal with the adversary on all the fronts on which the adversary deals with you."[34]

That requires resources—both time and money. The ability to mobilize support quickly in response to opportunities is often a key strategy in building social movements. Representative examples are bus boycotts and sit-ins during the 1950s and 1960s civil rights campaigns. Some of the precipitating incidents arose without advance planning. Rosa Parks's refusal to move to the back of a segregated Montgomery bus was not a product of a coordinated strategy. Nor was a similar decision by two black Tallahassee college students; unlike Parks, they did not even have a history of prior involvement with any civil rights organizations. But once these events occurred, leaders quickly sought to organize boycotts. That required volunteer efforts to supply alternative transportation systems and money to pay the legal fees of activists arrested for organizing and operating such systems without a license.[35] In some cases, involvement in protests led to a broadening of their agenda. In Montgomery, many organizers initially had been wary of being too far out in front of public opinion, and of asking for more than a fairer system of allocating seats on public transit.[36] But resistance stiffened their resolve, and like other activists, they quickly saw the need to challenge segregation head-on. That, in turn, required seeking support beyond the local communities involved and developing coordinated protest strategies. In addition to bus boycotts and restaurant sit-ins, civil rights leaders organized sleep-ins at motels, wade-ins at beaches, and knee-ins at churches that excluded blacks.[37]

Part of their success in that effort came from the capacity to frame the struggle in ways that resonated both with racial minorities and with the broader public. Martin Luther King was particularly gifted in combining appeals based on black experiences and spiritual traditions with invocations of broader American ideals of liberty and justice.[38] As Chapter 4 notes, his "I have a Dream" speech and "Letter from a Birmingham Jail" were effective in mobilizing support across a broad range of audiences. Such appeals, together with strategies offering credible responses to injustice, gave meaning to the promise that "we shall overcome."

Cesar Chavez had similar success in framing the struggle to organize farm workers in ways that built group solidarity and attracted widespread public support. Prior organizing efforts by the predominantly white leaders of national labor organizations had been unsuccessful. Intransigence by growers, intimidation by police, and recruitment of immigrant replacements had doomed initial strike efforts.[39] Chavez, who had deep knowledge of the local community as well as ties to potential support groups outside it, reframed the struggle to appeal to both constituencies. He stressed racial injustice, recruited clergy and college students, and organized dramatic protests. One of the most celebrated examples was a pilgrim-like march through farm worker communities timed to arrive on Easter at the California governor's mansion. The national union affiliate declined to join; its leaders insisted that the struggle was a "labor union dispute, not a civil rights movement or a religious crusade."[40] Chavez and his advisors cast the campaign as all three and recognized the expressive value of social activism. Although they had far fewer financial and organizational resources than the nationally affiliated union, they had wider aspirations, more inspiring strategies, and more enduring successes.

As that example illustrates, organizations differ in their "strategic capacity," and leaders can help lay the institutional foundations for success.[41] That requires striking the right balance in decision-making processes. Either too much or too little structure can be disabling.[42] Movements can be stifled by what social theorist Robert Michels termed the "iron law of oligarchy," that is, the tendency of leaders to resist challenges to their power, and to close off channels for diverse views and grassroots engagement.[43] But movements can also suffer from the "tyranny of structurelessness," in which the absence of authoritative decision making leads to schisms and prevents coherent coordinated actions.[44] To avoid these pathologies, effective leaders need to create open but authoritative deliberative processes that draw on resources from diverse constituencies and that ensure accountability for results.[45]

Recent technologies of social networking have created new opportunities and new challenges. Online organizing can increase participation in social movements by lessening the efforts that it requires. People can become armchair activists by pushing a few buttons. But building deep and sustained support remains difficult. The Save Darfur Coalition has 1.2 million members, but they have contributed only an average of nine cents.[46] So too, because online organizing networks tend to lack strong centralized leadership, they have difficulty reaching consensus and developing coherent long-term strategies. As Malcolm Gladwell notes, these new technologies "make it easier for activists to express themselves and harder for that expression to have any impact."[47]

When used strategically, however, social media represent an extraordinarily efficient way of achieving what Jennifer Aaker and Andy Smith describe as the "dragonfly effect."[48] The dragonfly is the only insect able to propel itself in any direction when its four wings act in concert. Aaker and Smith use the term to symbolize the importance of integrated efforts in achieving a ripple effect. The method "relies on four essential skills or wings: 1) *focus*: identify a single concrete and measurable goal; 2) *grab attention*: cut through the noise of social media with something authentic and memorable; 3) *engage*: create a personal connection, accessing higher emotions such as compassion and empathy; and 4) *take action*: enable and empower others to take action."[49]

A striking example of the dragonfly effect involves two young South Asian American professionals who suffered from a rare form of leukemia. Their only hope for survival was to secure, within a matter of months, a transplant from a donor with similar bone marrow. Matches are most likely to be found within the patient's own ethnic group, and only 1 percent of some 8 million donors registered in America's National Marrow Donor Program are South Asian. India, the country of origin for the patients' families, has no national registry. To increase the pool of South Asian donors, the patients' friends organized online campaigns through Facebook, Google Apps, and YouTube. They asked recipients of their e-mail messages to register as donors and submit to a single-cheek swab test, spread the word, become engaged by going to a website explaining more about the disease, and organize a donor drive. After eleven weeks, some 24,000 individuals had registered, 3500 had volunteered their help, and successful matches for both patients had emerged.

A similar effort propelled an eight-year-old girl to national prominence for her fundraising efforts on behalf of childhood cancer research. After being diagnosed with an aggressive form of pediatric cancer, Alex Scott established a neighborhood lemonade stand with the proceeds going toward research. In her first summer she raised $2000, word spread, and similar stands began emerging in all fifty states. After appearances on the Oprah Winfrey Show and the Today Show, Scott set a $1 million goal and reached it before dying of cancer before her ninth birthday. The Alex's Lemonade Stand Foundation has raised more than $27 million dollars in her name and inspired over 10,000 volunteers.[50]

Another strategy for attempting to leverage modest resources is to scale small successes. Psychologists Chip Heath and Dan Heath describe this approach as "looking for bright spots"; other experts describe it as searching for "positive deviants."[51] An example is Jerry Sternin's campaign to fight child malnutrition in Vietnam during the early 1990s. At the root of the problem was poverty and the resulting inadequacies in food, sanitation, and clean water. Sternin found such explanations TBU, "true but useless."[52] His organization, Save the Children, lacked the capacity to make significant inroads on poverty. However, in touring rural villages, he noticed that some children managed to fare reasonably well despite their circumstances, and he began searching for reasons why. He found that the mothers of these children fed them more frequently in smaller amounts than was customary, and they also provided a more varied diet. His strategy then was to organize local cooking classes for mothers, which could be replicated throughout the country. The result was to improve the life chances of some 2.2 million children. Similar "bright spot" strategies have brought significant social change in a wide variety of contexts.[53] Generalizing from these examples, Heath and Heath conclude that leaders facing seemingly intractable social problems may sometimes do best by focusing less on underlying causes and more on scaling successes.[54]

It may also be important to appeal to people's sense of identity as well as interests. A case history is that of Paul Butler, who pioneered efforts to save an endangered species of parrot, found only on the Caribbean island of St. Lucia. Hunters, pet seekers, and environmental degradation had put this bird on a path to extinction. The only solutions — steep criminal penalties and creation of a parrot sanctuary — would require a groundswell of public support that was notably lacking. Butler, "fresh out of college, working with the forestry department, and armed with a budget in [only] the hundreds of dollars, had to figure out a way to rally the people of St. Lucia behind a parrot that most of them took for granted (and some of them ate)."[55] His answer was an appeal to national pride through "made to stick" messages. He organized puppet shows, distributed tee shirts, enlisted local businesses in printing bumper stickers and calling cards, and convinced ministers to preach environmental stewardship. One card featured a gorgeous parrot next to a homely American bald eagle, making it obvious whose bird looked better. The message was clear: "This parrot is ours. Nobody else has this but us. We need to cherish it and look after it." The people agreed. They passed tough laws, established a sanctuary, virtually ended illicit trade, and preserved the parrots. The conservation organization Rare has now replicated that strategy in about 120 campaigns to save endangered species.[56]

That example points up the challenges in securing change on issues that involve "common action" problems on which no individual has a significant personal stake. The problems are compounded in many environmental contexts, such as global warming, in which solutions seem technical, consequences are long-term, and actions by any single person or political entity are unlikely to have significant impact. To motivate change in these circumstances, it is helpful to

- build a sense of urgency through vivid, dramatic messages that appeal to core values and concerns (polar bears on melting ice caps, financial savings from energy conservation);
- harness peer pressure to create social norms of responsibility (telling people that their neighbors have reduced energy consumption);
- appeal to people's self-image as socially responsible individuals (link consumer choices to environmental stewardship); and
- advocate specific, readily achievable behavioral changes and reduce their costs (suggest home improvements and provide rebates and lists of contractors).[57]

Once leaders get a "foot in the door" and convince people to take small steps toward social responsibility, their commitment is likely to escalate.[58]

In seeking large-scale social change, leaders also must build collaborations among a broad range of nonprofit, private, and government organizations. Such "collective impact initiatives" need centralized staff and decision-making structures, shared evaluation systems, continuous communication, and mutually reinforcing activities.[59] For example, Strive, a nonprofit subsidiary of Knowledge Works, achieved dramatic improvements in Cincinnati students' educational performance through such collaboration. Organizers coordinated a collective effort by 300 leaders of local organizations, including heads of influential private and corporate foundations, city government officials, school district representatives, university presidents, and executive directors of hundreds of education-related nonprofit groups.[60]

In principle, all of these strategies seem straightforward. In practice, the challenge lies in knowing how best to pursue them, and in determining which will be most cost effective in particular contexts. Politicians, activists, and lawyers involved in social movements often agree on goals but divide sharply on strategies. What litigation, legislation, or policy initiatives make most sense? When should leaders wait for greater public, political, or judicial support? How can they prevent ill-conceived lawsuits or precipitous government action from derailing a coherent national strategy? Those issues are the subject of the case studies that follow.

QUESTIONS

1. Consider a social movement with which you are familiar. What were the major challenges facing its leaders? What strategies did they most effectively pursue? What could they have done differently?
2. Compare the websites and public outreach strategies of three different social-change organizations that focus on a similar issue. What seem to be the most and least effective approaches? If you were the leader of one of these organizations, what changes would you make?

PROBLEM 9-1

Divide into teams and select an issue on which you would like to see major social change. Identify the fundamental challenges and devise a strategy for overcoming them. What allies do you need to enlist? Where and how will you obtain resources and political support? What communication initiatives will you pursue? What external opposition and internal conflicts do you anticipate? How will you address them?

B. CIVIL RIGHTS IN SOCIAL CONTEXT

The readings that follow explore leadership challenges in two phases of the American struggle for racial justice. They begin with dilemmas facing the NAACP Legal Defense Fund in orchestrating litigation challenges to racial discrimination in the mid-twentieth century. Discussion then turns to President Johnson's efforts to build a coalition for civil rights legislation.

Starting in the 1930s, NAACP lawyers launched a plan to end state-sponsored segregation, which gradually moved from bringing isolated lawsuits to "treat[ing] each case in a context of jurisprudential development."[61] That strategy required assessing any particular challenge in light of multiple factors, such as whether the facts were sufficiently favorable, resources were available to develop the case, courts were ready to rule favorably on the issue, lead lawyers were effective advocates, and so forth. The excerpt from *Simple Justice* describes that process in the context of litigating one of the major school desegregation cases leading to the Supreme Court's landmark decision in *Brown v. Board of Education.* How far to push the Supreme Court was one of the key considerations. Conventional wisdom is that the Court is never too far ahead of public opinion, particularly on volatile social issues.[62] Surveys at the time indicated that slightly over half of Americans favored segregated public facilities, but 89 percent thought that blacks should have equal opportunities to get a good education.[63] Consider how public attitudes shaped the strategies of early civil rights leaders. What assumptions did different leaders make about the best way to influence opinion? How did differences of class complicate the struggle for racial justice and what strategies were most effective in bridging them? What lessons can be drawn for contemporary struggles?

RICHARD KLUGER, SIMPLE JUSTICE: THE HISTORY OF BROWN V. BOARD
OF EDUCATION AND BLACK AMERICA'S STRUGGLE FOR EQUALITY

(New York: Vintage Books, 1977), pp. 511, 513-518, 521, 530, 535-536, and 580

The Negro schools in the [District of Columbia] were more nearly equal to the white schools than in any of the segregating states, but they were scarcely palaces of learning. . . . It was widely understood in Washington that any family which could afford it would send its children to private school. Few black families could afford such an expenditure, but those at the top of the Negro social scale, and especially those with federal jobs, often succeeded in getting their children transferred to the newer or least crowded colored schools in the District. Worst off of all, of course, were the plain black people, the ones without a pipeline to the white community and without stature in the highly stratified world of colored Washington.

One such plain black man [Gardner Bishop], who ran a barbershop on U Street near 15th in the Northwest section, got angry enough at the haughty whites who controlled the city and at the Negroes who he felt lorded over the black rabble to defy both groups and start a minor revolution. . . . What made the situation particularly galling was that nearby Eliot Junior High for whites had several hundred unoccupied places as more and more white families put their children in private schools or began the exodus to the Maryland and Virginia suburbs that would turn Washington into a city two-thirds black within twenty years. Enough Browne Junior High parents were sufficiently angered by the reduced quality of education being offered blacks throughout Washington to file a suit in the name of Marguerite Carr, daughter of the president of the Browne PTA. Black attorney Belford Lawson, who had first won fame in colored Washington for his work with the New Negro Alliance in the late Thirties, was hired to handle the case, and a mass meeting of the Browne PTA was summoned to seek wide support and financial backing for the legal action. Gardner Bishop, the U Street barber, went to that meeting, and he was not impressed.

The truth was that Bishop had never before been to a PTA meeting, was not even a dues-paying member of the PTA, and deeply resented the sort of upper-crust blacks who ran the PTA with the blessing of the teachers. They were the same sort who belonged to the NAACP and the other civic and social-uplift organizations — professional people, government people, people with jobs in white neighborhoods, people with learning. They spoke grandly, the way

Belford Lawson did in explaining the lawsuit that charged white officials with illegally preventing black children in badly overcrowded schools from being transferred to schools for whites that had plenty of room. Nothing in the laws Congress had passed made segregated schools obligatory in Washington, Lawson argued. The case was duly filed in the spring of 1947 against the superintendent of schools and bore the title of *Carr v. Corning.* Gardner Bishop and the poor people with him were unconvinced by the legal tactics. "We knew the case wasn't going to work," he says of their gut reaction, "but nobody asked us what we thought because we were nothin'! Nobody gave us a chance to speak. What we wanted was relief, not lawsuits with $500 fees for the lawyers."

Over the summer, an effort was made to relieve the overcrowding at Browne Junior High by designating two rundown white schools in the vicinity as annexes, but the colored children who took shop and other classes in the satellite buildings had to travel many blocks to and from the main building in every sort of weather. Resentment ran deep among the poorer Browne parents, who groped for a way now to organize and act. . . . Denied access to the school building itself because they were not members of the PTA, Bishop's followers found a hospitable church to meet at and set to work. "We didn't have no president, we didn't have no vice president, we didn't have no nothin'—and we were mad at everyone—the whites, the highfalutin' blacks, the Board of Education—everyone." They took the name Consolidated Parents Group, Inc., puzzled over the same numbers the PTA had compiled showing the inequities of black education in the District, and then went along with Bishop's conclusion: "We needed whites on our side to oppose whites if we were going to get anywhere."

With winter coming on, Bishop piled forty youngsters into taxis that had been volunteered for their use and drove them down to the offices of the Board of Education, whose members were about to begin their weekly deliberations at three in the afternoon. The arrival of so many colored children was disconcerting enough, but when the large, angry black man who was leading them asked, without any prior warning, to address the board, confusion reigned. No, he could not just barge in and obtain a hearing from the august school board, Bishop was told—and anyway, what was so confounded important? "These are children from the Browne Junior High School," the barber explained, "and there's not going to be a one of them—or anyone else—at that school tomorrow, so I just wanted to explain who was doin' it and why." They let him speak, Bishop recalls, "but they sat there like a bunch of fools, not believing a word they heard." That night, the ragtag legion that Bishop headed was on the telephone and knocking on front doors to organize people who had never taken concerted civic action before. The next day, almost all the 1,800 students who normally attended Browne Junior High stayed home. And they stayed home the next day, too, and the day after that.

Pickets were out, demanding better schools, insisting that half-empty white schools be turned over to the black community, and soon the white press began to cover the uprising and comment sympathetically on it. The Board of Education started to feel the hot breath of civic resentment and began to treat Bishop's group like full-fledged citizens with legitimate grievances. Negotiations were opened. The Consolidated Parents held fast.

Membership rose to nearly 300, despite efforts by the NAACP to discourage the strike. The president of the school board, a white woman who had never before had contact with the poor colored community, found Bishop a devoted and sincere leader and asked to address his group. "A charming woman," Bishop recalls, excepting her from his gallery of hated white-establishment types. She looked around the packed meeting room at the burbling, curious colored crowd and remarked to Bishop, "These are fine-looking people" — as if relieved that they had not all just been shanghaied from the Congo bush, the cotton fields of Alabama, the gutters of the "Gold Coast," or some other blighted section of the capital.

Winter deepened, the strike went into its second month, the Board of Education was growing increasingly embarrassed, and the black parents began to lose enthusiasm. . . . Then, one evening late in February of 1948, Gardner Bishop steeled himself for a visit to the enemy camp. The enemy was not white but blacks attending an NAACP meeting in a Methodist church to hear a talk by Charles Houston, the well-known and widely admired civil-rights lawyer. These were the high and mighty of his own race, and Bishop resented them fiercely, but he needed help. He waited until the meeting was over, caught Houston on the way out, introduced himself, and told the lawyer he had a problem. "I know you, Bishop," Houston said warmly, "and I'd like to help." He wrapped an arm around the barber, who welcomed the gesture as a sign both of respect and of warning to the others in the crowd not to come between the two men. . . .

They went to Houston's home that very evening and met again the next day. "He wanted to know everything about us," Bishop recalls, "how we got our printings and mailings done, who paid for what, what we were really after. He seemed terribly concerned — and terribly ignorant about us. He had never been associated with our kind of people before." Finally, Houston asked Bishop how much money his group had in its treasury. The answer was $14. "Well, you've got yourself a lawyer," Houston said, and proceeded to work out a face-saving scheme whereby Bishop would convene a mass meeting of his group and call the strike off on the understanding that Houston would file a whole series of lawsuits and take other actions aimed at winning equal facilities for the black schoolchildren of Washington. It was as if Houston, who once had been a member of the school board, suddenly legitimized the efforts of Bishop's group. The end of the strike marked the beginning of an unlikely collaboration between the outspoken, unlettered barber and the formidable lawyer who was even then preparing to argue before the Supreme Court of the United States that residential covenants against blacks violated the Constitution.

"Charlie became us — a part of our group," recalls Bishop. . . . They would meet or talk three or four times a week as Bishop began to devote himself to a wide range of protest activities planned by or with Houston, whose standing as a lawyer prevented his taking to the barricades in so open a manner. Houston explained to Bishop that . . . the Fourteenth Amendment's promise of equal protection pertained only to the usurpation of citizens' rights by state governments; it did not cover residents of the District of Columbia. Houston's strategy, then, was to file a series of equalization suits calling for improvement at every level of learning: kindergarten classes had to be offered to black children if they were offered to white children; elementary-school class sizes had to be the same; colored junior-high schools could not be on double sessions when the white ones were not; colored senior-high schools were entitled to all the equipment, courses, classroom space, and athletic facilities that the white ones had. Petitions and legal briefs proliferated. Gardner Bishop was all over black Washington, gathering depositions from people who had never heard the word before.

It was a cumbersome process, and many who participated in it were discouraged by the failure to obtain overnight results. "A lot of people thought you filed a case and bing! the next morning it was all settled." The ranks of the Consolidated Parents thinned, and Bishop had only a few dozen ardent members still working with him. . . .

Late in 1949, Houston was [twice] hospitalized with a heart ailment. . . . An orderly telephoned the dying lawyer's request to Bishop that he come to his bedside. "He told me that it looked as if he wasn't ever going to practice again the way he had," the barber recalls, "and that the important thing was for us to carry on the fight. He told me to go see Jim Nabrit at Howard to take over the equalization cases he'd been working on for so long. Well, I didn't want to do that. Nabrit was a big shot, and I didn't know him — and I didn't want to know him. I figured that our man was dyin' and we had no money and I was tired. . . ." But his colleagues in what was left of Consolidated Parents set up the appointment, and Bishop reluctantly made his way to the Howard campus, a place where he felt singularly uncomfortable, and to the office of James Madison Nabrit, Jr., professor of law, secretary of the university, and its next president.

"I explained it all to him," says Bishop, "including Charlie's wish that he should take over the lawsuits and continue the fight." None of the equalization cases had yet reached the hearing stage, but several of them were due to be heard imminently. Nabrit thought they were bad cases to pursue and that the equalization strategy was a lost and wasteful cause. He turned Bishop down, and the barber, unsurprised, concluded that few Charlie Houstons were put on this earth. But Nabrit interrupted Bishop's swift exit to say that if the barber wanted to arrange for a group of plaintiffs to challenge segregation itself, he would be happy to handle it. . . . In short, James Nabrit thought the time had come to take larger legal risks than either Charles Houston or Thurgood Marshall in New York had thought prudent.

Gardner Bishop considered the matter, then shook hands with his new lawyer. . . . A member of the NAACP Legal Defense Fund's inner circle of advisors, Nabrit watched the agonizing progress of Spottswood Robinson and Oliver Hill in their Virginia campaign to equalize the black schools, and soon the Howard professor began to press Thurgood Marshall to strike at segregation itself. It was a position that Marshall's younger assistants, including Carter and Franklin Williams, urged on their chief, but Marshall was not eager to push the Supreme Court for decisions he feared it was not yet ready to render. [But Nabrit acted on an opposing view.] . . .

Nowhere in the pleadings of *Bolling v. Sharpe,* which Nabrit filed in early 1951 in U.S. District Court, was any claim made that young Bolling and the other plaintiffs were attending schools unequal to those provided white children. [One school had a science lab consisting of a single Bunsen burner and a bowl of goldfish.] Their plainly inferior facilities were entirely beside the point, as Nabrit framed the case. He based it entirely upon the fact of segregation itself. The burden of proof, he argued, was not upon the black plaintiffs but upon the District government to show that there was any reasonable basis for or public purpose in racial restrictions on school admission. . . .

[Trial court findings in the Brown litigation also pushed the NAACP toward a frontal assault on segregation. However, advisors such as Columbia law professor Herbert Wechsler raised troubling issues.] [W]as it so plain, Wechsler countered, that a Negro child attending a segregated school was worse off than a Negro child attending a non-segregated school where he might feel the full brunt of white prejudice? . . .

A cautionary tale was told as well by one of Thurgood Marshall's newer and most astute outside advisors, John P. Frank, then an associate professor at Yale Law School. . . . [After noting at an NAACP Strategy Conference that] "[a] judge cannot be blamed if he shrinks from precipitating a race riot," John Frank told the Howard crowd it was plain that the Supreme Court was stalling on both *Briggs* and *Brown* and he wondered if the Justices were not likely to delay a good deal longer in a presidential election year. Unquestionably, the NAACP "should not hesitate in its just demands for fear of reaping the whirlwind" because "judicial victories will not be won without asking for them." But "Vigor is not recklessness," Frank asserted. "The most daring army guards its lines of retreat. So should a litigation strategist." It would be a mistake to push the attack on segregation itself to the exclusion of victories won on lesser grounds (that is, equalization). For if the Court were pushed "inescapably" to a decision on the validity of school segregation where no other element of discrimination is present, "it may decide in behalf of segregation; and the morale and prestige loss to the anti-segregation forces from such a decision would be incalculable." . . .

[James Nabrit responded with passion.] Of those who said blood would run in the streets if the segregation fight was waged in the face of intransigent white-supremacists, Nabrit demanded, "Suppose it does? Shall the Negro child be required to wait for his constitutional rights until the white South is educated, industrialized, and ready to confer these rights on his children's children?" No, he thundered. . . .

. . . [Nabrit returned to this position at the oral argument in *Brown v. Board of Education*. In closing, he stated:]

> The basic question here is one of liberty. . . . We submit that in this case, in the heart of the nation's capital, in the capital of democracy, in the capital of the free world, there is no place for a segregated school system. This country cannot afford it, and the Constitution does not permit it, and the statutes of Congress do not authorize it.

NOTES AND QUESTIONS

Similar issues continue to arise in various civil rights contexts. Some widely publicized examples involved large school desegregation lawsuits filed by the

NAACP Legal Defense Fund in Boston and other major cities. As certified, the classes included all black children who were then or would be attending public schools. Conflicts arose between the parents who favored integration through busing and those who preferred improvements in their de facto segregated neighborhood schools. Derrick Bell, then a prominent litigator for the NAACP, published a landmark law review article criticizing NAACP lawyers for "serving two masters," and placing their own integration ideals over the desires of class members for quality local education. "Idealism," he maintained, "though perhaps rarer than greed, is harder to control."[64]

1. Related controversies emerged over the next several decades in both desegregation and school finance cases. Such disputes pose difficult issues for leaders of civil rights organizations. How much risk of an adverse ruling should leaders assume? Who should decide remedial priorities: lawyers or class members? How can or should class preferences be assessed when members are constantly changing and often poorly informed over the long duration of a lawsuit?
2. Are there lessons from the early civil rights strategies that are generalizable to other public interest contexts? How might these lessons guide activists in the gay marriage debate, discussed in the readings and problem below?
3. In the following excerpt, Harvard professor Ronald Heifetz explores a related question: when should leaders take a principled stand on civil rights, when should they compromise, and when should they stay their hand in the hope of forcing others to act responsibly? Consider Lyndon Johnson's efforts to reshape and respond to public opinion in the context of the Selma protest discussed below. What would you have done in his place?

MEDIA RESOURCES

Many documentaries on civil rights movements are available; among the best is *Eyes on the Prize*.[65] Footage of antidiscrimination protests, an interview with Martin Luther King, and his last speech can also give context to the campaign for social justice.[66] For an account of the quest for Native American rights, see Modern Day Warriors.[67] For more information about farm workers' rights, see *The Fight in the Fields*, as well as *Harvest of Shame*.[68] For an examination of the history of the U.S. environmental rights movement, see *American Experience's Earth Days*.[69] For the history of women's rights, see *A History of Women's Achievement in America*, and *One Woman One Vote*.[70] For the disability rights movement, consult *Beyond Affliction: The Disability History Project*.[71]

RONALD A. HEIFETZ, LEADERSHIP WITHOUT EASY ANSWERS

(Cambridge, MA: Belknap Press of Harvard University Press, 1994),
pp. 129-149

Prelude: The Ripening of the Issue

. . . Of his many initiatives, perhaps Johnson's most successful were in civil rights. At his best, Lyndon Johnson built for himself the opportunity for leadership by listening intently to the nation, identifying its internal contradictions, and transforming the dialogue of competing interests into legislation and programs. He encouraged Martin Luther King Jr.'s civil rights vision, and he encouraged what he viewed as George Wallace's populist vision of economic justice. Progress would be made by pushing people to engage with one another to adjust their views or reach compromises. The parties would be made to do the work.

Indeed, in his legislative program Johnson routinely put the pressure on the people who asked him for help. Thus, Johnson put the pressure on black leaders to persuade reluctant conservatives. The key to success on civil rights, in Johnson's opinion, lay in the hands of the minority party, the Republicans headed by Senator Everett Dirksen. Without their support, no new legislation could get past Senator Richard Russell and the block of Southern Democratic senators committed to its defeat. They would filibuster it to death, as they had done with nearly every civil rights bill for nearly a century. Yet Johnson was not going to do the lobbying work alone. To win the Republicans over, Johnson called on Roy Wilkins, head of the National Association for the Advancement of Colored People (NAACP), as prelude to introducing the Civil Rights Act of that year. He placed the call on January 6, 1964, six weeks after assuming the presidency.

Johnson: ". . . I think you are going to have to sit down with Dirksen and persuade him this is in the interest of the Republican party, and you think that if the Republicans go along with you on cloture, why you'll go along with them at elections. And let them know that you're going with the presidential candidate that offers you the best hope and the best chance of dignity and decency in this country, and you're going with a senatorial man who does the same thing. *I'm no magician.* Now I want to be with you, and I'm going to help you any way I can. But you're going to have to get these folks in here, and the quicker you get them the better. If we lose this fight we're going back ten years."

Indeed, the Senate went through seventy-five days of filibuster over the Civil Rights bill—the longest in its history. But on June 10, 1964, it was ready to vote on cloture. The key, as Johnson had said, was Dirksen. In response to Russell's protest that "the bill simply involves a political question and not a moral issue," Dirksen finally took his stand. Declaring "civil rights is an idea whose time has come . . . we are confronted with a moral issue," he had turned around. Dirksen's priorities had shifted in the course of his conversations with Wilkins and others. The issue had been made to ripen. As Johnson later described the problem to his biographer Doris Kearns: "The challenge was to learn what it was that mattered to each of these men, understand which issues were critical to whom and why. Without that understanding nothing is possible. Knowing the leaders and understanding their organizational needs let me shape my legislative program to fit both their needs and mine." In pursuing domestic policies in general, Johnson sought to induce the relevant parties— business leaders, educators, labor, the media—to get involved with one another. Some authorities might concentrate on getting people to acquiesce to their commands. Johnson sought to educate people to cooperate with one another, respecting one another's goals. He corralled people into collaborative work. As he described it, "I wanted each of these men to participate in my administration in a dozen different ways. The key was to get men from different groups so involved with each other on so many committees and delegations covering so many issues that no one could afford to be uncompromising on any one issue alone."

Johnson intended to mobilize the nation as a whole to work on issues that had been avoided for nearly two hundred years. Yet mobilizing the society to tackle hard problems and learn new ways required far more than fashioning deals in the legislature; it required public leadership. Johnson had to identify the adaptive challenges facing the nation, regulate the level of distress, counteract work-avoiding distractions, place responsibility where it belonged, and protect voices of leadership in the community. Nowhere did he illustrate this strategy of leadership better than during events in Selma, Alabama.

Selma — Eight Days in 1965

On Sunday, March 7, 1965, black Americans set out to march from Selma to the state capital at Montgomery in an all-out drive for voting rights. Selma, a city of about 29,000, had slightly more black people than white, but only 3 percent of the people on its voting rolls were black. Out of 15,000 black citizens, 325 were registered to vote. The county had used time-worn methods to prevent black citizens from registering to vote, including lengthy written examinations and tricky oral questions like: Recite the Thirteenth Amendment to the Constitution, and what two rights does a citizen have after indictment by a grand jury? Governor Wallace of Alabama had declared during his campaign in 1962: "From this cradle of the Confederacy, this very heart of the great Anglo-Saxon Southland . . . , segregation now! Segregation tomorrow! Segregation forever!"

In response to the voting rights march, Governor Wallace sent the state police against the 600 unarmed black people as they reached the city limits. Americans throughout the country witnessed with shock and fury the televised scenes of black men, women, and children being beaten with billy clubs, stricken with tear gas, and bull-whipped by troopers on horseback. As loud as the screaming was the yelling of white onlookers, "Git 'em! Git 'em!" In reaction, spontaneous demonstrations sprang up across the land as massive pressure focused on President Johnson to mobilize the national guard.

Johnson, however, refused to move. In fact, he faced contrary pressures from Sunday's bloodshed, each with its own long history. On one hand, the outraged public called on the President to act forcefully at once to protect the marchers in Selma. People marched and sat-in at the White House; they marched and sat-in at the Justice Department; they berated him in the press nationwide. Dr. Martin Luther King Jr., "dismayed and discouraged," accused the federal government of "timidity." On the other hand, many others wanted Johnson to keep out of the matter. They expressed great fear of federal interference in their own state affairs. White Southerners, among others in the nation, were tired of federal government intervention into their way of life and wanted to maintain local norms and control. Johnson was faced with a conflict between two different constituencies with two opposing values: states' rights, which represented white supremacy, and voting rights.

This conflict was nothing new. It dated back to the Civil War era. What should be the balance of power between local and central government in determining civil rights? No one knew better than Johnson, a long-time Texas politician, how sensitive this question remained in the South. And no one knew better than Johnson, as former Senate Majority Leader and Vice-President, that the balance of power between local and central governments had been shifting on the rights issue. The Supreme Court ruled in 1954 that segregated schools were illegal. President Eisenhower felt obliged to back up that ruling in 1957 when he sent federal troops to Little Rock, Arkansas, to integrate Central High School. Five years later, in 1962, John F. Kennedy sent federal troops to protect James Meredith as he enrolled at the University of Mississippi. Just months before the march in Selma, Johnson and Congress had passed the historic Civil Rights Act of 1964, which further strengthened the power of the central government over local affairs. Black people could no longer be discriminated against in most places of public accommodation, like hotels, restaurants, and bathrooms. Employers and unions had to provide equal employment opportunities for minorities. Schools were given financial and technical assistance to speed desegregation.

The country had spent years deliberating and testing the issue and, by and large, had come down on the side of protecting civil rights against local transgression. But not fully. The previous year, Congress had been unable to agree on a voting rights provision for the 1964 Civil Rights Act. Johnson had floated the idea, but Congress rejected it. Too many white people found it hard enough to integrate restaurants and schools. They refused to give blacks political power. The Congressional stalemate on voting rights indicated that the country as a whole was not yet ready to enfranchise minorities. Urgency over the issue was far from widespread; voting rights had not yet fastened in people's minds. The steps taken in 1964 toward guaranteeing civil rights were as large as the public seemed able to take at that moment.

Legislators were not about to take pains unless constituents demanded it. Taking pains for a legislator meant making costly bargains with other legislators, giving in on one issue in exchange for support on another, and paying the price back home. These bargains were least painful and risky if the legislator had multiple goals with varying importance to his or her district. A minor goal could be traded away for an urgent one, particularly if other legislators had complementary priorities, without much cost. Such was the case with civil rights legislation. Until Selma, white citizens across the nation generally gave voting rights low priority. . . .

In private meetings in early 1965, Johnson, knowing the constraints of his role, encouraged King in his plans to ripen the voting rights issue. Although he hoped there would be no violence, he thought public pressure might set the stage for legislative action. As did King. By generating nationwide urgency, the civil rights movement aimed to change the public's priorities and throw Congress into motion. King and his strategists had learned through decades of effort that the federal government would protect the rights of black Americans when public pressure forced it to. So the civil rights movement would turn up the heat. Through the carefully scripted presence of television reporters, the brutality of racism would be transmitted into living rooms throughout the land. Demonstrations would force the nation to pay attention. On Sunday, March 7, after the televised beatings in Selma, Dr. King announced:

> In the vicious maltreatment of defenseless citizens of Selma, where old women and young children were gassed and clubbed at random, we have witnessed an eruption of the disease of racism which seeks to destroy all of America. . . . The people of Selma will struggle for the soul of the Nation, but it is fitting that all Americans help to bear the burden. I call, therefore, on clergy of all faiths, representative of every part of the country to join me in Selma for a minister's march on Montgomery Tuesday morning.

In anticipation of Tuesday's march, the pressure on Johnson grew enormously. Marches and demonstrations proliferated across the country. Busloads and planeloads of priests, ministers, rabbis, nuns, and lay people descended on Selma. In Washington, D.C., sit-ins at the Justice Department continued to block Attorney General Katzenbach's office. The White House was deluged with telegrams and calls to take action. A group of demonstrators sat-in during a White House tour, yelling angry epithets at whoever passed by. Clearly, the public did not relish the prospect of more televised beatings, this time with King and the nation's clergy at the forefront. The public looked to President Johnson to restore order. As he described it, "Everywhere I looked I was being denounced for my 'unbelievable lack of action.'"

On Monday afternoon, King's lawyers appealed to the federal court in Montgomery for an injunction forbidding local and state authorities from interfering with Tuesday's march. Instead, Judge Frank Johnson issued a restraining order to delay the march entirely for a few days until proper safety precautions could be made. In light of this order, President Johnson felt compelled to step in. He quietly sent LeRoy Collins from the Justice Department aboard Air Force One to negotiate a middle path with King that would keep the public pressure on without going farther than any President could legally allow. At the very last minute, on Tuesday morning as the march itself was moving, they made a deal. King avoided clashing with local and State police, and with the federal court, and turned the march back after a dramatic moment of prayer at the site of Sunday's violence. The nation held its breath as it lived through the encounter on television. And though momentarily relieved, the acute level of tension remained very high. Dr. King insisted that the full three-day march to Montgomery still lay ahead.

Johnson continued to hold steady. He neither quelled nor inflamed the situation. Rather than take dramatic public action or a clear stand, Johnson issued a lukewarm statement Tuesday afternoon deploring the brutality in Selma and urging leaders on all sides to "approach this tense situation with calmness, reasonableness, and respect for law and order." He added that he would be sending a voting rights bill to Congress by the weekend. Privately, however, after seeing the televised beatings and judging their public impact, he called in the Justice Department and asked them to draft the strongest bill that would have any chance of surviving a constitutional challenge.

On Tuesday night, Reverend James J. Reeb, a white Unitarian minister from Boston, was beaten badly by a group of white people in Selma; he died two days later. His was the second death. Jimmy Lee Jackson, a seventeen-year-old black man, had been shot by state troopers two weeks before while marching in nearby Marion, Alabama. Reverend Reeb's fatal beating added more fuel to the demonstrations and the urgency. "But," as Kearns described it, "Johnson refused to be pushed. Pickets surrounded the White House, carrying placards calculated to shame him into action: 'LBJ, open your eyes, see the sickness of the South, see the horrors of your homeland.' Telegrams and letters demanding action streamed into the President's office." Still, Johnson held steady through Tuesday night, Wednesday, Thursday, and Friday. At one point, a presidential aide interjected, "We have to do something." Johnson replied, "We will. Keep the pressure on. Make it clear we're not going to give an inch. Now that Wallace . . . it's his ox that's in the ditch, let's see how he gets him out."

Finally, on Friday, Wallace asked to meet with the President, and Johnson granted the request at once. As Johnson understood the situation, Wallace had national aspirations. He had run briefly for President in 1964. He could ill afford more bloodshed broadcast nationwide from his state. As much as he hated to give in on civil rights, Wallace also had to maintain law and order. Thus, Johnson had something Wallace needed. He could help Wallace back out of his corner because he, Johnson, had refused to back into one himself. "On Saturday, in the Oval Office, they discussed the question of troops. Johnson appealed to the large ambition and the populist strain that he perceived in Wallace: How could there be any fixed limits, he suggested, to the political career of the first Southern governor to combine economic and social reform with racial harmony? Why not Wallace?"

The meeting resulted in an arrangement. Johnson would rescue Wallace from his obligations to maintain the law and protect innocent black people, for which he would have paid dearly with his own white constituents, but Wallace would have to ask Johnson publicly to mobilize the national guard. Following the meeting, Johnson took Wallace into a prearranged press conference where he made sure that Wallace was still publicly on the hook, that is, accountable for protecting all citizens, black and white. Johnson announced: "If local authorities are unable to function, the federal government will completely meet its responsibilities."

The next day, Sunday, while 15,000 demonstrators outside the White House sang "We shall overcome," and chanted: "LBJ, just you wait, See what happens in '68," Johnson solicited an invitation to appear before a joint session of Congress the next evening, Monday, March 15, and he began to prepare for his now historic speech.

Principles of Leadership

. . . Identifying the Adaptive Challenge. . . . No authoritative presidential decision would "fix" this kind of problem. This problem existed in the minds and hearts of citizens, and only adjustments *there* would resolve the value conflict. What the President could do was animate and prod people across the nation to address the internal contradiction between the values of freedom and equality they espoused and the mode of suppression they lived or permitted. Although laws, political stands, and programs could not mandate adaptive

change, they could fix attention on the need for adjustment. They could begin to change institutions to create new norms and set new limits on behavior. As Johnson commented after passage the previous year of the Civil Rights Act, "I understand that a law doesn't change people's feeling. But it's a beginning. It shows the way."

. . . Johnson did not have the final answers. But his responses to Selma illustrate at least four conditions for stimulating adaptive change after the challenge has been identified: *managed stress,* disciplined by *attention to the issues,* with *pressure* on those who need to take responsibility for the changes in their midst, and *protective cover* for threatened leadership voices.

Regulating Distress. In the midst of crisis, the first priority is to evaluate the level of social distress, and, if it is too high, take action to bring it into a productive range. Confronted by overwhelming distress, a society and its factions may fall back on extreme measures to restore direction, protection, and order: authoritarian rule, suppression of dissent, fragmentation into smaller identity groups (ethnic, religious, regional), and war (civil and otherwise). Thus, Johnson had to assess the level of disequilibrium in the society in order to determine whether or not emergency actions were called for, like sending in the National Guard. Could the nation sustain the storm without breaking apart? . . .

King and his organizers turned up the heat, but Johnson let the stew simmer. By his calm demeanor and lukewarm statements, Johnson communicated that the crisis was no emergency. But by inaction, Johnson raised the level of tension so that people could no longer ignore their own responsibility for the harsh reality of black people being beaten for requesting an equal right to vote.

Directing Disciplined Attention to the Issues. By having waited over a week to make a move, Johnson allowed television images of racial brutality to settle into the public consciousness. He prevented premature closure. When he finally announced during his press conference with Wallace that, if necessary, he would take decisive action, he merely relieved the immediate source of distress. The underlying issue had now fastened in people's minds, where it would continue to generate dissonance. Dissonance would call for more action. The issue would ripen: people would come to see the issue as a public priority. And therein lay the opportunity. Johnson waited to seize that moment when he could address the issue of racial justice rather than merely diffuse the dissonance. He took the event and gave it meaning that would have been lost before.

Had Johnson intervened as the nation demanded, by mobilizing the National Guard, he would surely have reduced the public's distress over police brutality against black Americans. Johnson's action would have directed the nation's attention to a side issue: protecting the marchers' right to express their demands. Yet as Johnson unbundled the issues, the point was not the right to march; the point was the right to vote. Had Johnson intervened immediately, the issue might have been understood the wrong way—the easy way.

Worse, his intervention would also have diverted the nation's attention from the issue of racism to the issue of states' rights. Johnson, the Southern politician, knew better than to let that happen.

> If I just send in federal troops with their big black boots and rifles, it'll look like Reconstruction all over again. I'll lose every moderate, and not just in Alabama but all over the South. Most southern people don't like this violence; they know, deep in their hearts, that things are going to change. And they'll accommodate. They may not like it, but they'll accommodate. But not if it looks like the Civil War all over again. That'll force them right into the arms of extremists, and make a martyr out of Wallace. And that's not going to help the Negroes. . . . I may have to send in troops. But not until I have to, not until everyone can see I had no other choice.

Had he intervened immediately, Johnson would probably have survived quite well, personally. As a Southerner intervening with federal troops to protect innocent black people, he would likely have gained considerable popularity throughout much of the nation. There were good precedents for federal interference into racial disturbances: Kennedy in Mississippi, Eisenhower in Arkansas. And *they* were Northerners.

Stepping in decisively to resolve the crisis, however, would have interrupted the work being done in the polity. By letting the distress persist for over a week, Johnson provided the nation with no choice but to face the issue of racism itself. The appalled public would not permit Southern whites to frame the issue as states' rights. Furthermore, voters throughout the nation had witnessed from their own living rooms that the marchers longed for the right to vote, not the right to march. The issue would not be mistaken as states' rights or the right of black people to march. By refusing to be pushed by the public, Johnson pushed people to face the internal contradictions of *their* society, embodied in the sights they could not avoid watching on television.

Giving the Work Back to People. Johnson's long experience taught him to be wary of the trap that Wallace had set — shifting all responsibility to the highest authority. By stepping in with troops, Johnson would have presented himself and his office as a receptacle for blame or credit. Either would be a diversion from working on the problem of equality. The solution to the crisis would have become "Johnson's solution," framed as federal interference in states' affairs, or federal protection of the right to march. Instead, Johnson did nothing to divert responsibility until the public's will had crystallized. He let the people with the problem bear weight. He let blacks carry the major responsibility for provoking change. He waited for Wallace to request federal troops. And he waited until voters across the nation had done enough work to reveal to themselves, and to him, the outlines of a solution — their solution. As Kearns described it, "When Johnson finally sent troops to Alabama [two weeks after the crisis began], the act was generally regarded, not as an imperious imposition of federal power, but as a necessary measure to prevent further violence. By waiting out his critics and letting the TV clips make their own impression on the country, he had succeeded in persuading most of the country that he had acted reluctantly and out of necessity, not because he was anxious to use federal power against a guilty South."

The civil rights movement had focused attention and ripened the issue. Johnson's task was to restrain himself from absorbing the attention and responsibility. The tactic of holding steady shifted the feeling of necessity to the public so that it would face the issue with its costs and its gains. The public and its representatives were made to do the work of changing their attitudes and priorities about justice.

Thus, by keeping the spotlight on the persons embodying the issues, Johnson gave the work of adjustment back to the people with the problem: the civil rights activists, George Wallace, Congress, and the general public. For example, he encouraged King in private meetings to arouse public attention. Animated constituents would generate the political will and leeway for legislative action. Moreover, he let Wallace stew for awhile, appealing to him at the White House in his moment of distress to adjust his own view of himself. To paraphrase Johnson: "Wallace could be a statesman, not just for Alabama, but for the nation. He could help his people adjust to the demands for economic and social reform. Social justice might make sense to a populist like Wallace in the context of economic justice." Johnson's authority as President gave him a grip on Wallace, but only because he had refrained from stealing the limelight and shifting the responsibility for law and order away from the governor. When Wallace finally asked for federal assistance (on the grounds that Alabama could not afford the cost of protecting the marchers), Johnson let everyone know that he was acting on Wallace's initiative. He made sure that the debate remained focused on civil rights and not on states' rights, and that Wallace had borne the burden. . . .

Protecting Voices of Leadership in the Community. Johnson provided protection to King and his colleagues in the form of encouragement, guidance, and warning. . . . To avoid a confrontation between King and the federal government, Johnson tried to dissuade King from marching that day; King insisted, however, and they reached a compromise. In essence, Johnson made clear to King the limits of the cover he could provide. The march went on in truncated form, and Johnson held steady through it. . . .

The Speech

By waiting, Johnson raised the stakes, not only for the nation but for himself. If, as President, he failed to act decisively after what seemed so prolonged a time of crisis, the public would hold him accountable. Public expectations constrained him. As with any person in a position of senior authority, a President eventually has to provide a clear focal point to restore a sense of direction and order. Johnson did that eight days after the crisis in Selma had begun. By that time, the nation looked to Johnson with ever heightened anticipation. But by that time, the nation was ready to hear what it needed to hear, and not just what it wanted to hear. Johnson spoke before a joint session of Congress during prime evening television. The speech, excerpted at length, captures Johnson's strategy.

> I speak tonight for the dignity of man and the destiny of democracy. . . . At times history and fate meet at a single time in a single place to shape a turning

point in man's unending search for freedom. So it was at Lexington and Concord. So it was at Appomattox. So it was last week in Selma, Alabama. . . . There is no cause for pride in what has happened in Selma. There is no cause for self-satisfaction in the long denial of equal rights of millions of Americans. But there is cause for hope and for faith in our democracy in what is happening here tonight. . . .

Last time a President sent a civil rights bill to Congress it contained a provision to protect voting rights. That bill was passed after eight long months of debate. And when that bill came to my desk for signature, the heart of the voting provision had been eliminated. This time, on this issue, there must be no delay, no hesitation, no compromise with our purpose. . . .

But even if we pass this bill, the battle will not be over. What happened in Selma is part of a far larger movement which reaches into every section and state of America. It is the effort of American Negroes to secure for themselves the full blessings of American life. Their cause must be our cause too. It is not just Negroes, but all of us, who must overcome the crippling legacy of bigotry and injustice. *And we shall overcome.* As a man whose roots go into Southern soil I know how agonizing racial feelings are. I know how difficult it is to reshape attitudes and the structure of society. . . . I say to all of you here and to all in the Nation tonight, that those who ask you to hold on to the past do so at the cost of denying you your future.

This great, rich, restless country can offer opportunity and education to all—black and white, North and South, sharecropper and city dweller. These are the enemies—poverty and ignorance—and not our fellow man. And these too shall be overcome. Let no one, in any section, look with prideful righteousness on the troubles of his neighbors. There is no part of America where the promise of equality has been fully kept. In Buffalo as well as Birmingham, in Philadelphia as well as Selma, Americans are struggling for the fruits of freedom. This is one nation. What happens in Selma or in Cincinnati is a matter of legitimate concern to every citizen. But let each of us look within our own communities and our own hearts, and root out injustice there. . . .

The real hero of this struggle is the American Negro. His actions and protests—his courage to risk safety and even life—have awakened the conscience of the Nation. His demonstrations have been designed to call attention to injustice, to provoke change and stir reform. He has called upon us to make good the promise of America. And who among us can say we would have made the same progress were it not for his persistent bravery, and his faith in American democracy. For at the heart of battle for equality is a belief in the democratic process.

Historic in its sweep and claim, this speech inspired much of the country. It also demonstrates and helps summarize our principles of leadership. First, Johnson spoke clearly to the orienting values of the nation, the values that had made it one nation: freedom, equality, and democracy. The issue of civil rights was to be seen in that context. He identified the adaptive challenge by identifying the discrepancy between our values and behavior. Indeed, he identified the next adaptive challenge as well: poverty.

Second, by speaking in so dramatic a fashion—before a joint session of Congress—Johnson tried to maintain the level of urgency at the same time that he addressed its causes. Taking charge might have reduced the pressure had Johnson not demanded immediate Congressional action. Moreover,

Johnson pointed out that Congress had failed to complete its work on voting rights in the earlier civil rights legislation. These acts kept the pressure on.

Finally, Johnson exercised leadership in one of the few ways that authority figures can — by protecting the voices of those who lead with little authority, even though such voices often will be both deviant and annoying. He credited the civil rights movement for provoking the nation to face the large gap between what we stood for and the way we lived.

In exercising leadership on civil rights, was Johnson advancing his own vision for the country? Not really. As a Southern congressman since 1937 and senator since 1949, Johnson came out in favor of civil rights only in 1956 when he saw the issue ripening and saw himself as a national contender. For nearly twenty years he had voted against every civil rights bill before Congress — laws to end the poll tax, segregation in the armed services, and lynching. In 1960 he opposed liberal proposals for federal voting registrars in favor of the middle-of-the-road proposal for voting referees, which had not worked. As Vice-President, he had decided against liberalizing Senate rules, which distressed civil rights advocates. During the debate over the Civil Rights Act of 1964, he backed a moderate conception for a voting rights clause. When Congress seemed unready even for that, he did not push it.

It seems then that the civil rights movement and the events in Selma had their impact on Johnson's conscience, as well as that of the nation. As he described in his memoirs, "Nothing makes a man come to grips more directly with his conscience than the Presidency. . . ."

We often think that leadership means having a clear vision and the capacity to persuade people to make it real. In this case, Johnson had authored no vision. Events acted on him to shape the vision to which he then gave powerful articulation. He *identified the nation's vision* and put it into words. . . .

Johnson signed the Voting Rights Act into law on August 6, 1965. Within one week, federal registrars set up shop; six months later, 9,000 black people were registered to vote in Selma.

QUESTIONS

1. With the benefit of hindsight, Johnson's decision to delay sending federal troops to Selma seems clearly justified. But at the time that he made it, was that outcome clear? What risks was he assuming? Suppose Judge Johnson had not delayed the march, violence had broken out, and hundreds of protestors had been injured. Suppose Wallace had refused to ask for federal help and Johnson had been forced to respond belatedly.
2. Compare Johnson's address on civil rights legislation with Barack Obama's historic speech on race, discussed in Chapter 4. What rhetorical strategies do they share that make them effective?
3. One lesson from the Selma decision is the importance of a leader's understanding of the motives and constraints of other key players, and his or her willingness to accept criticisms and risks of short-term costs in pursuit of larger goals. How might this lesson inform the contemporary struggle for racial justice and gay marriage?

PROBLEM 9-2

Consider a contemporary social issue on which leaders are divided. What accounts for their conflict? Have they created appropriate structures for handling it? What lessons do the readings suggest about how you might respond to these challenges?

C. CONFLICTING VIEWS OF COMMON INTERESTS

The following materials explore a recurring question in civil rights movements: when should activists force an issue into the courts and when should they pursue broader political strategies while waiting for a more favorable case or judicial climate? In the excerpt below, Harvard Law School professor William Rubenstein addresses that question in the context of racial discrimination and gay marriage litigation. To resolve disputes over that question, Rubenstein proposes a model of collective decision making. In principle, his framework has much to recommend it. In practice, what complications arise when any litigant who takes a different view holds keys to a courthouse door? Consider those difficulties in light of the following readings and problem on the California same-sex marriage case.

WILLIAM B. RUBENSTEIN, DIVIDED WE LITIGATE: ADDRESSING DISPUTES AMONG GROUP MEMBERS AND LAWYERS IN CIVIL RIGHTS CAMPAIGNS

106 Yale Law Journal 1623 (April 1997)

Should political processes control the kinds of litigation a private attorney general can institute? Groups are messy. They are, by definition, comprised of many individuals and thus encompass a range of desires and agendas. Any group must generate ways to reach decisions among these competing possibilities. Typically, groups develop formal and informal mechanisms to define their goals and strategies. . . .

But consider litigation. . . . [T]wo questions [] lie at the heart of more informal groups' decisionmaking about litigation: Why is any individual group member able to step forward in the litigation arena and unilaterally claim to represent, and indeed bind, all similarly situated group members to a particular legal position? Further, why can any single attorney litigating one of many cases brought on behalf of a group decide alone what tactics and strategies to employ in pursuing that case? There is one immediate answer to both of these questions: Group decisions about litigation are structured by the rules of litigation, that is, by the rules of civil procedure and professional ethics, and those rules currently adhere to an individualist model. . . .

I. The Problem: Disputes among Group Members and among Lawyers in Civil Rights Campaigns

A. The Story of Shelley v. Kraemer

In the spring of 1947, Thurgood Marshall was annoyed. The source of his frustration was an attorney from St. Louis named George Vaughn. Vaughn had just done something Marshall did not want him to do: He had filed a petition for certiorari with the United States Supreme Court in a case called Shelley v. Kraemer, one of the many cases pending throughout the country in which the constitutionality of racially restrictive housing covenants was at issue. Marshall did not want Vaughn to file this petition because he did not think that the black community's legal position in the many restrictive covenant cases was sufficiently developed to be heard by the Supreme Court; Marshall and his NAACP colleagues had been working on developing that position for many years. Marshall also did not believe Vaughn's factual record in the Shelley case was the best that could be brought before the Court; he and the NAACP attorneys had been working closely with social scientists to generate a compelling policy analysis of the effects of these covenants.

Marshall was also worried about Vaughn's legal abilities. Vaughn was not a constitutional scholar. He was an able municipal court lawyer in St. Louis, and, in part because of his political influence within the Democratic party, had prevailed in the Shelley case in municipal court. But Vaughn's 1945 victory was shortlived; by the end of 1946, the Missouri Supreme Court had overturned it. . . .

Marshall's intent in convening this conference was to try to develop the right theory and case for Supreme Court review. In the following year, however, the cases reached uniformly bad outcomes in the lower courts. Marshall grew worried and called a second conference in January of 1947. By the end of the conference, Marshall was convinced that the ideal case had not yet been developed and that the time was still not right. . . . Vaughn's filing of the petition that spring forced Marshall's hand. He and other NAACP staff took over the appeal of a case pending in Michigan, which Marshall had deemed not the right test case at the January conference, and filed a petition for certiorari. Better to argue a less than perfect Michigan case than to have Vaughn argue the issue alone in the Supreme Court. . . .

The restrictive covenant cases were argued for seven hours in the Supreme Court. Philip Elman, an attorney in the Solicitor General's office who helped produce the government's brief in Shelley v. Kraemer — and who would write the government's brief in Brown v. Board of Education — was present for the argument. He tells this story of George Vaughn's argument:

> [H]e made an argument that as a professional piece of advocacy was not particularly distinguished. You might even say it was poor. He mainly argued the thirteenth amendment, which wasn't before the Court. He tried to distinguish cases when it was clear that the cases were indistinguishable and the only way to deal with them was to ignore or overrule them. He didn't cut through all the underbrush; he got caught in it. And the Justices didn't ask many questions. It was a dull argument until he came to the very end. He concluded his argument by saying . . . "Now I've finished my legal argument, but I want to say this before I sit down. In this Court, this house of law, the Negro today stands outside, and he knocks on the door, over and over again, he knocks on the door and cries out, 'Let me in, let me in, for I too have helped build this house.'"
>
> All of a sudden there was drama in the courtroom, a sense of what the case was really all about rather than the technical legal arguments. . . . [It was] the most moving plea in the Court I've ever heard.

Vaughn's speech was so compelling that he was invited to repeat it at the 1948 Democratic National Convention.

In May 1948, the Supreme Court ruled in the black litigants' favor, holding in Shelley v. Kraemer that court enforcement of racially restrictive covenants would violate the Equal Protection Clause of the Constitution. Legend has it that Thurgood Marshall argued Shelley. Legend does not say much about George Vaughn.

B. The Lessons of Shelley v. Kraemer

The story of the litigation campaign that culminated with Shelley exemplifies the central concerns that motivate this Article: the difficulty the NAACP attorneys had "controlling" civil rights litigation even at a time when so few lawyers were involved that control seemed plausible, and, more importantly, the intriguing question of what values are furthered by such control. Before turning to the exploration of these themes, it is necessary to state several key premises, each of which also flows from the Shelley story. First, this Article talks of "communities" pursuing "goals," despite the fact that civil rights campaigns are not waged by easily identifiable "communities" pursuing settled, concrete goals. The restrictive covenant cases reflected the interests of a particular segment of the African-American community, the black middle-class home-buyers, and the extent to which such cases represented an important element of the civil rights struggle was contested among the various factions struggling to define that movement. Similarly, there is not a fixed "lesbian and gay 'community.'" Indeed, if anything, the fact that lesbians, gay men, and bisexuals are generally not visually identifiable makes the boundaries of this "community" especially amorphous. . . .

C. Disputes about Goals: Lessons from the Same-Sex Marriage Debate

In the fall of 1989, a lesbian/gay intellectual journal called Out/Look published a debate concerning same-sex marriage. On one side of the debate was Tom Stoddard, then the executive director of Lambda; on the other side of the debate was Paula Ettelbrick, then Lambda's legal director. Stoddard's contribution, entitled Why Gay People Should Seek the Right to Marry, set forth a practical, political, and philosophical argument for gay marriage and urged the gay community to give marriage priority as an issue: "I believe very strongly," Stoddard wrote, "that every lesbian and gay man should have the right to marry the same-sex partner of his or her choice, and that the gay rights movement should aggressively seek full legal recognition for same-sex marriages." Ettelbrick dissented. In her article, entitled Since When Is Marriage a Path to Liberation?, Ettelbrick stated that:

> [M]arriage will not liberate us as lesbians and gay men. In fact, it will constrain us, make us more invisible, force our assimilation into the mainstream and undermine the goals of gay liberation. . . . Marriage runs contrary to two of the primary goals of the lesbian and gay movement: the affirmation of gay identity and culture; and the validation of many forms of relationships. . . ,
>
> The moment we argue, as some among us insist on doing, that we should be treated as equals because we are really just like married couples and hold the

same values to be true, we undermine the very purpose of our movement and begin the dangerous process of silencing our different voices. . . .

We will be liberated only when we are respected and accepted for our differences and the diversity we provide to this society. Marriage is not a path to that liberation.

The Stoddard/Ettelbrick exchange was a "marriage announcement" of sorts, a declaration that the issue of marriage was moving from the margin to the center of the lesbian/gay movement. Yet from the moment of its reintroduction, the marriage issue produced controversy among community members. The Stoddard/Ettelbrick debate exposed one fissure, whether the community ought to prioritize and pursue marriage at all, and reflected a discussion within Lambda about how the organization should respond to increasing demands that it file a same-sex marriage case. This was not the only contentious issue. The community also disputed when such cases ought to be filed, where such filings might be made, and on whose behalf. The community generally, and the lawyers at Lambda specifically, were confronted by a significant conundrum: What constituted a satisfactory response to these divisions?

Stoddard and Ettelbrick's response was to air their debate publicly, first in the pages of Out/Look and then "on the road." The two leaders traveled around the United States to debate in front of community audiences. By taking their debate to the community, Stoddard and Ettelbrick apparently envisioned that some resolution of their disagreement would emerge from the community discussion, perhaps that some consensus would evolve to guide their actions.

A similar attempt to gauge community consensus occurred at the outset of a marriage challenge in Hawaii. In 1990, some individuals in Hawaii approached the ACLU affiliate in that state, asking the organization to file a challenge to Hawaii's marriage laws on their behalf. The local ACLU affiliate contacted the ACLU's National Lesbian and Gay Rights Project in New York seeking guidance. Nan Hunter, then Director of the Project, suggested that the Hawaii affiliate measure support for the case within the lesbian and gay community in Hawaii before pursuing the issue. The ACLU's Hawaii affiliate translated Hunter's advice into an informal poll of gay community leaders. By letter, the Hawaii affiliate attorney sought input from the community about whether there was "broadly based support for such litigation" in Hawaii, writing that the "ACLU would not want to act in a manner inconsistent with the opinion of a substantial number of gays and gay rights activists." The ACLU was attacked for taking this approach: A community activist in Hawaii wrote that "[i]ndividuals or civil rights should never be construed as a popular opinion issue, but rather a right of each human being."

The internal community debate largely subsided after lesbians and gay men, without support from the legal experts, proceeded with their own legal actions. In late 1990, Craig Dean, a gay lawyer, filed his own case challenging the District of Columbia's marriage law on behalf of himself and his lover. In May 1991, three lesbian and gay male couples in Hawaii filed an action in Hawaii state court without the support of the ACLU; they were represented by a former staff attorney at the ACLU of Hawaii. After the cases were filed, the community legal organizations ultimately provided support for them, thus quelling the internal community drama. All of the actors had different perspectives on how this resolution was accomplished: The professionals viewed it as a rebuke of their expertise, or of some community consensus, by rogue individuals; the individuals defended their actions either as in the best tradition of courageous individuals, or as capturing a community consensus while their leaders fiddled. Notwithstanding these differing perspectives, what seems clear is that the legal capacity of any individual, or group of individuals, within the community to end the debate about litigation by resorting to litigation proved to be an important factor in concluding the community's marriage debate. Once filed, such litigation changed the terms of the debate from an intracommunity struggle of self-definition to an intercommunity struggle of self-preservation. . . .

III. The Democratic Model

Group members and attorneys could address disputes concerning the conduct of impact litigation by employing more democratic means of decisionmaking. Democratic values would lend significant legitimacy to goal-based decisions, but would have less applicability to the more technical decisions about legal strategies.

A. Democracy in the Pursuit of Goals

Our procedural system could assign litigation decisions concerning group rights to those groups, rather than to any individual within the group, and could promote group-based decisionmaking about litigation. Under such a regime, individuals would not be authorized to litigate the group's rights on their own; instead, their role would be to participate in the group's decisionmaking about its litigation options. The question of whether to file a marriage case would be decided by the group collectively. Such a group decision could be achieved either through a formal vote or according to a more informal democratic process, and could be practically implemented by any number of possible procedural innovations.

Democratic decisionmaking quickly cures the downsides of the individualist and expertise models; rather than one, indeed any, individual or elite group of experts deciding for the entire group when and how to proceed in the litigation arena, democracy ensures that litigations undertaken for groups have the assent of those whose rights are at issue. Those individuals governed by the outcome of the case each possess an opportunity to participate in the decisionmaking that sets the community's goals. Litigants representing groups thereby have a stronger claim to legitimacy, and their litigative activities evoke more confidence from their communities and from other legal actors. Further, whereas individual filings promote competition among plaintiffs and cases in the legal arena, democratic decisionmaking envisions community discord before filing and ideally constructs it as a meaningful, not competitive, discourse. . . . Perhaps most importantly, the process of democratic decisionmaking involves the community more closely in the decisions affecting its life. If the community members actually controlled the filing and pursuit of litigation, they would be forced into a more active engagement with one another about these issues. This obligation could counter the alienation that results from dependence on lawyer-experts, increase the individuals' sense of belonging to the community, and could further the civic republican's much-idealized community discourse. . . .

Limited to a strict voting approach, however, the democracy model confronts several significant hurdles. Given the ambiguous contours of the "communities" at issue and the often complicated and fluid nature of litigation decisionmaking, it would be nearly impossible to identify a meaningful voting constituency and to conduct a worthwhile vote. Moreover, only an insignificant percentage of the "electorate" may be interested or informed enough to involve itself in the "election." Permitting filing only after a community vote also limits some individuals' autonomy and threatens to disenfranchise permanent minorities within the community. These types of problems with voting mechanisms have largely constrained their application to problem-solving in the related context of complex class action jurisprudence. In determining whether a proposed representative will adequately represent the interests of a class, courts generally have not relied on community sentiment in support of or against certification, but have engaged in an independent (albeit cursory) analysis of the quality of the proposed representative. Similarly, in determining whether to approve a proposed settlement, courts rarely rely on voting devices like surveys of class members, nor weigh majority sentiment heavily. Relatively few class members respond to court mailings and those who do are not representative. Even more disturbing, few class members attend meetings convened by their attorneys in civil rights cases. Those who do respond or attend are often neither knowledgeable nor unbiased observers, and their views are typically shaped by the attorneys presenting the issues to them. . . .

[Yet in many contexts, the issues at stake in filing a lawsuit] are neither complicated nor beyond intelligent community discourse. . . . [If we ask members generally] whether they believe gay people should file lawsuits seeking the right to marry, or blacks to integrate their local schools, or women to enter the Citadel [military academy], . . . chances are they will have opinions. Most importantly, democratic values can be embodied in procedural rules without requiring reliance on formal voting mechanisms. For instance, rules that enhance community dialogue, increase individual participation, or "rectify the antidemocratic exclusion of chronically disadvantaged groups from the theatre of politics," serve democratic values. Rules of procedure could be constructed around these values of democracy without requiring formal voting processes. Rules that required individuals or experts filing group-based cases to demonstrate that some level of community dialogue preceded the decision to file, or to show some level of community participation in the filing, or to establish approval for their filings from democratically elected representatives, could capture some of the benefits of democracy without falling prey to the unworkability of elections about litigation. . . .

MARGARET TALBOT, "A RISKY PROPOSAL: IS IT TOO SOON
TO PETITION THE SUPREME COURT ON GAY MARRIAGE?"

The New Yorker, Jan. 18, 2010, pp. 40-51

On January 11th, a remarkable legal case opens in a San Francisco courtroom—on its way, it seems almost certain, to the Supreme Court.

Perry v. Schwarzenegger challenges the constitutionality of Proposition 8, the California referendum that, in November 2008, overturned a state Supreme Court decision allowing same-sex couples to marry. Its lead lawyers are unlikely allies: Theodore B. Olson, the former solicitor general under President George W. Bush, and a prominent conservative; and David Boies, the Democratic trial lawyer who was his opposing counsel in Bush v. Gore. The two are mounting an ambitious case that pointedly circumvents the incremental, narrowly crafted legal gambits and the careful state-by-state strategy that leading gay-rights organizations have championed in the fight for marriage equality. The Olson-Boies team hopes for a ruling that will transform the legal and social landscape nationwide, something on the order of Brown v. Board of Education, in 1954, or Loving v. Virginia, the landmark 1967 Supreme Court ruling that invalidated laws prohibiting interracial marriage.

Olson's interest in this case has puzzled quite a few people. What's in it for him? Is he sincere? Does he really think he can sway the current Court? But when I spoke with Olson, . . . he sounded confident and impassioned; the case clearly fascinated him both as an intellectual challenge and as a way to make history. "The Loving case was forty-two years ago," he said, perched on the edge of his chair in the law offices of Gibson Dunn & Crutcher, in Washington, D.C., where he is a partner. "It's inconceivable to use these days to say that a couple of different racial background can't get married." . . . He said, "Separate is not equal. Civil unions and domestic partnerships are not the same as marriage. We're not inventing any new right, or creating a new right, or asking the courts to recognize a new right. The Supreme Court has said over and over and over again that marriage is a fundamental right, and although our opponents say, 'Well, that's always been involving a man and a woman,' when the Supreme Court has talked about it they've said it's an associational right, and it's a liberty right, it's a privacy right, and it's an expression of your identity, which is all wrapped up in the Constitution." The Justices of the Supreme Court, Olson said, "are individuals who will consider this seriously, and give it good attention," and he was optimistic that he could persuade them. (The losing side in San Francisco will likely appeal to the Ninth Circuit, and from there the case could proceed to the Supreme Court.) Olson's self-assurance has a sound basis: he has argued fifty-six cases before the high court — he was one of the busiest lawyers before the Supreme Court bench last year — and prevailed in forty-four of them. . . .

If the Perry case succeeds before the Supreme Court, it could mean that gay marriage would be permitted not only in California but in every state. And, if the Court recognized homosexuals as indistinguishable from heterosexuals for the purposes of marriage law, it would be hard, if not impossible, to uphold any other laws that discriminated against people on the basis of sexual orientation. However, a loss for Olson and Boies could be a major setback to the movement for marriage equality. Soon after Olson and Boies filed the case, last May, some leading gay-rights organizations — among them the A.C.L.U., Human Rights Campaign, Lambda Legal, and the National Center for Lesbian Rights — issued a statement condemning such efforts. The odds of success for a suit weren't good, the groups said, because the "Supreme Court typically does not get too far ahead of either public opinion or the law in the majority of states." The legal precedent that these groups were focused on wasn't Loving v. Virginia but, rather, Bowers v. Hardwick, the 1986 Supreme Court decision that stunned gay-rights advocates by upholding Georgia's antiquated law against sodomy. It was seventeen years before the Court was willing to revisit the issue, in Lawrence v. Texas, though by then only thirteen states still had anti-sodomy statutes; this time, the Court overturned the laws, with a 6-3 vote. . . .

Seventeen years was a long time to wait. "A loss now may make it harder to go to court later," the activists' statement read. "It will take us a lot longer to get a good Supreme Court decision if the Court has to overrule itself." Besides, the groups argued, "We lost the right to marry in California at the ballot box. That's where we need to win it back." Plenty of gay-marriage supporters agreed that it was smarter to wait until the movement had been successful in more states — and, possibly, the composition of the Supreme Court had shifted. (During the last year of a second Obama term, Scalia would be eighty-one.)

By August, the inevitability of the Olson-Boies suit had become clear, and several of the groups decided, grudgingly, to support the effort. But, when they petitioned to be intervenors in the suit, Olson and Boies opposed the move. Olson told me that their inclusion would have made the case too fragmented, and he wanted a "unified, controlled, consistent, on-message approach." The presiding judge in the case, Vaughn Walker, sided with Olson and Boies, though he did allow the City of San Francisco to join their suit.

Nobody seems to be saying anymore, as some skeptics did initially, that Olson was deliberately setting up the gay-marriage movement for a fall. But doubts remain. William Eskridge, a professor of constitutional law at Yale University, and a prominent advocate of same-sex marriage, says that he is now "even more pessimistic" about the lawsuit's chances, given that, in recent months, voters in Maine approved a referendum overturning same-sex-marriage law, and the state senates of New York and New Jersey opted not to allow gay marriages. "A question that so evenly but intensely divides the country is not one that should be decided by the courts nationwide," Eskridge said. "It's the mirror image of the mistake the Bush Administration made by trying to introduce a constitutional amendment to define marriage as between a man and a woman." He added, "It is just not something that this Supreme Court is going to deliver on at this point." It's a peculiar situation: while gay-rights activists advocate judicial restraint, solicitude for the popular will, and a gradual, state-centric approach, Ted Olson argues, in the urgent language of civil rights, for a sweeping, federal solution on their behalf.

At present, only the District of Columbia and five states — Massachusetts, Vermont, New Hampshire, Connecticut, and Iowa — permit gay couples to marry. (Five others, including California, have civil-union or domestic-partnership laws, which confer benefits and some official recognition without the title, and freighted significance, of marriage.) Since 1993, when the Supreme Court of Hawaii surprised just about everybody by finding that a state ban on gay marriage was discriminatory, twenty-nine states have passed amendments prohibiting gay marriage. (Most states had seen no need to be explicit on that point before.) And in 1996 Congress passed, and President Bill Clinton signed, the Defense of Marriage Act, which defined marriage as between a man and a woman. Seen from this angle, an incipient movement has been countered by a formidable backlash.

Yet there is a countervailing story, one that points to an inevitable shift toward acceptance of same-sex marriage. In 1993, few Americans had heard of same-sex marriage. Now some forty percent of Americans support marriage for gay couples, and more than fifty percent support civil unions. Many more people condone gay marriage today than condoned interracial marriage at the time of Loving v. Virginia, when only twenty per cent of Americans told Gallup that they approved of it.

Younger Americans endorse gay marriage at strikingly higher rates than older ones. According to a 2009 study underwritten by the Pew Charitable Trusts, fifty-eight per cent of Americans between the ages of eighteen and twenty-nine support gay marriage. . . .

Patrick Egan, a political scientist at New York University, and Nathaniel Persily, a law professor at Columbia University, who together have studied public opinion on gay rights, believe that in five years a majority of Americans will favor same-sex marriage — the result of generational replacement and what Persily calls "attitude adjustment." When people change their mind on this issue, they tend to change it toward marriage equality. The more striking conversion stories of the past couple of years conform to this pattern: Bill Clinton saying that he was "wrong" in opposing gay marriage; Dick Cheney, whose daughter Mary is a lesbian with a partner and two children, declaring that "people ought to be free to enter into any kind of union they wish." . . .

In some ways, though, this trend makes the Oslon-Boies suit more complicated. Why push the Court far ahead of public opinion if public opinion is moving in that direction anyway? Even a victory for Olson and Boies could cut one of two ways. It could be like Brown v. Board of Education, which accelerated a gradual shift in public opinion. Or it could be like Roe v. Wade, in 1973, which interrupted a move toward abortion rights, and froze public opinion in two polarized camps. Olson is undaunted. "I have spent a fair amount of time reading Dr. King's response to people who said, 'People aren't ready for this,' " he said. "His 'Letter from a Birmingham Jail,' one of the more moving documents in history, addresses this. If people are suffering and being hurt by discrimination, and their children and their families are . . . then who are we as lawyers to say, 'Wait ten years'?"

The case that became Perry v. Schwarzenegger would probably never have materialized had it not been for a young political strategist in Hollywood named Chad Griffin. . . . Griffin and Olson agreed that federal lawsuits were inevitably going to be filed on this issue, and that gave them a sense of urgency. As Olson told me, "There are millions of people in this country who would like to be married — in California, in Arkansas, wherever. Some couple is going to go to some lawyer and that lawyer is going to bring the case. And that case could be the case that goes to the Supreme Court. So, if there's going to be a case, let it be us. Because we will staff it — we've got fifteen, twenty lawyers working on this case and we have the resources to do it, and we have the experience in the Supreme Court." . . . Proposition 8 was the basis for a shrewd lawsuit, he reasoned, because it had created three unequal classes of people in California: "The eighteen thousand or so gay couples who were already married got to remain married. But if they get divorced they can't get remarried! Is that irrational, or what? Then you have heterosexual couples who can get married, and gays and lesbians who didn't get married before Prop. 8 and now can't." . . .

. . . [Olson and Boies] will also try to convince the Court that sexual orientation is a suspect classification, and that gays and lesbians have been subject to a history of discrimination, are defined by an immutable characteristic that "bears no relation to their ability to perform or contribute to society," and are "politically powerless," in this case, to win marriage equality. This argument is trickier. Though gays and lesbians lost at the polls in California, can they really be said to be politically powerless? Just how immutable homosexuality is remains a hotly contested question. And the Court has never before defined sexual orientation as a suspect classification.

Even if the Court declined to apply strict scrutiny, Boies told me, he could still argue that Proposition 8 fails the much more commonly applied "rational basis" scrutiny. Under that test, a law is considered valid as long as it is logically related to a plausible state interest. But, Boies says, "There is overwhelming evidence of damage to gay and lesbian couples who cannot marry—and to their children—and no evidence that permitting gays to marry damages heterosexual couples. . . . Olson and Boies will aim to show that the motivation for Proposition 8 could only have been animus—a rationale that the Court does not look kindly on. In the 1996 case Romer v. Evans, for instance, it ruled that a Colorado amendment that excluded gays and lesbians from anti-discrimination laws was motivated by anti-gay feeling, and was therefore unconstitutional. . . .

The legal team on the other side will be led by Charles Cooper, a Washington lawyer who succeeded Olson as assistant attorney general under Reagan, and by the Alliance Defense Fund, a sort of Christian-conservative counterpart of the A.C.L.U. (The State of California, in the person of Governor Arnold Schwarzenegger, declined to defend Proposition 8, leaving it to private lawyers to fill in.) Cooper will argue that California indeed has a rational interest in upholding "procreative marriage." As Cooper told the Judge at a pretrial hearing, in October, the traditional definition of marriage has "prevailed in every civilized society throughout the ages" and "still prevails everywhere in the world, with the exception of five American states, and seven foreign countries." (Since then, Portugal has become the eighth country to legalize gay marriage.) With Proposition 8, Cooper said, California voters merely defended that tradition. A court, therefore, "should not lightly conclude that everyone who held this belief was irrational, ignorant, or bigoted." . . .

The case has involved some unexpected staking out of positions—as though both sides had been reading up on the work of postmodern academics and come to opposite conclusions. Olson's team will argue that marriage is a malleable institution, shaped by shifting notions of gender, race, and property, while sexual orientation is innate. And the defendants will likely argue that marriage is immutable, and sexual orientation is a performative act, a chosen identity.

Nan Hunter, a law professor at Georgetown University, is skeptical about Olson and Boies' chances. "As a purely formal matter, one could argue that Olson and Boies are correct," Hunter said. "But invalidating roughly forty state laws that define marriage as between a man and a woman is an awfully heavy lift for the Supreme Court, and especially for Justices who take a limited role of the scope of the judiciary." She added, "I fear that their strategy is: Ted Olson will speak, Anthony Kennedy will listen, and the earth will move. I hope I'm wrong about this — they're excellent lawyers — but I fear, frankly, that there's more ego than analysis in that."

Proposition 8 won by only four percentage points, and some believe that if the opposing side had waged a better campaign California might still have gay marriage. Three statewide organizations . . . are now leading efforts to bring Proposition 8 back onto the ballot and repeal it. . . . Whatever happens with the Perry lawsuit, these groups are waging a campaign to persuade reluctant Californians to embrace gay marriage, and they are basing their approach on the power of personal stories.

After Proposition 8 passed, many gays and lesbians complained that the ads that political consultants had come up with for their side did not show any couples. They did not counter the other side's claims that gay marriage would not be taught in schools with their own images of gay families who would be hurt by the denial of marriage rights. The ads were not visceral or urgent. They didn't show enough love. Instead, they were abstract and a little arid, if sometimes wry. One, based on the "Mac vs. P.C." ads, featured a portly, middle-aged guy in a brown suit, who represented "Yes on 8"; a young hipster in skinny jeans was "No on 8." Another showed a woman talking to her friend about attending her niece's wedding, but never showed the wedding pictures (or the niece).

Eugene Hedlund, a media consultant in Southern California who . . . is working on new ads for the gay-marriage side, says of the last media campaign, "It was too intellectual. And though that might have worked for some people, it wasn't a strong enough argument against 'They want our children.' I remember thinking, Where are the ads with the couples? . . . How can you have a campaign based on equality and then hide what it would look like? Can you send a clearer message that there is something to hide? This time around, we'd better be serious about getting emotional." . . .

Hedlund now plans to make ads in support of gay marriage that are . . . microtargeted: one might be aimed at Latinos in San Diego, and another at churchgoing African-Americans in South L.A. One ad that he's put together, titled "Family Values," features a man named Frank Reifsnyder, who is a retired naval submarine commander and a devout Catholic. The ad begins with him speaking of his and his wife's long-held dream of grandchildren, and of their happiness when twins came along. "Watching our son become a wonderful father has been an amazing gift," he says. Reifsnyder then explains that his son is gay and has a husband, and that the two of them are raising their children with "strong morals, compassion, and love." The ad, which has the intimacy of a home movie, shows the babies being baptized; their two fathers walking down a tree-lined street, with the kids on their shoulders; and the whole family, including the grandparents, saying grace before dinner. The montage ends with Reifsnyder saying, "It may not be the family we had imagined, but it is the family we have — and love." For Hedlund, that's a seductive sentiment, because "nobody gets quite the family they imagine."

This fall, the spot was tested by H.C.D., a New Jersey–based advertising research firm, found Republicans were surprisingly receptive: fifty-five per cent of them called the ad "effective," even though only twenty-nine per cent of them supported gay marriage. Glenn Kessler, the head of research for H.C.D., told me, "That suggests a useful dissonance." The ad didn't change many minds after one viewing, he noted, but the reaction "suggests that if you tell that kind of story over and over you could get some movement." . . .

Perry v. Schwarzenegger is not the only federal lawsuit for gay marriage. Another one, Gill v. Office of Personnel Management, is thought by some scholars to stand a better chance of success, though it has been overshadowed by Olson and Boies's effort. Gill was filed last March, by a public-interest law firm, Gay & Lesbian Advocates & Defenders (GLAD), in Boston. One of the GLAD lawyers on the case is Mary Bonauto — the attorney who successfully argued the case that legalized same-sex marriage in Massachusetts. (That case is heralded by gay activists but is seen by others as a cautionary tale: the ruling, announced in the run-up to the 2004 Presidential election, served as a rallying cry for evangelical voters, and may have helped Bush win a second term.) Gill is not the damn-the-torpedoes case that Perry is. It challenges a section of the Defense of Marriage Act which prevents same-sex couples from receiving the many benefits accorded to married couples at the federal level — from joint tax filing to health insurance for federal employees' families — even though in the state of Massachusetts those couples are lawfully married. Gill insists not on the constitutionality of same-sex marriage but on the unconstitutionality of denying federal benefits to a class of citizens whose marriages are recognized by the state. . . . GLAD could have brought the suit that Olson and Boies did but feared "pushing the ball too far and potentially having a setback." . . .

As seemingly modest as the Gill case is, it could help create a favorable climate for more ambitious challenges, including the Perry case. . . . As [Bonauto's co-counsel] Gary Buseck told me, ". . . You have to approach the Supreme Court in an incremental way." For Buseck, this, and not the "Letter from a Birmingham Jail," was the relevant lesson from the civil-rights movement. He recalled that the N.A.A.C.P. Legal Defense and Education Fund had recognized it would be a stretch to try to desegregate the public schools first — it would be too sweeping and provocative an effort. "So they first won cases about a law school and a university, to make it inevitable that when they brought the case that became Brown the chances of winning would be so much better."

Maybe the Perry case stands a better chance than skeptics are willing to admit, given that public opinion is more in favor of gay marriage than it was of interracial marriage when the Court ruled in Loving. But Bonauto notes that in 1967 only sixteen states, most of them in the South, had anti-miscegenation laws, whereas thirty-nine states now have laws against gay marriage. A more aggressive strategist like Chad Griffin would counter that state laws are often anachronistic. . . . And who would make a serious argument that the Court should have postponed a decision on Loving until the Southern states were in line with it? . . .

CHULEENAN SVETVILAS, "ANATOMY OF A COMPLAINT: HOW HOLLYWOOD ACTIVISTS SEIZED CONTROL OF THE FIGHT FOR GAY MARRIAGE"

California Lawyer, Jan. 20, 2010, pp. 20-27, 50

. . . For months, the people backing the [*Perry v. Schwarzenegger*] suit had worked in the shadows. They wanted the complaint to be *the* challenge to the constitutionality of Proposition 8, the November 2008 statewide ballot initiative that declared, "Only marriage between a man and a woman is valid or recognized in California." . . .

"We didn't want there to be an explosion of lawsuits around the country," says Theodore Boutrous, Jr., a partner in Gibson Dunn's Los Angeles and Washington, D.C., offices who helped draft the complaint. The litigation group was mindful, however, that many lesbian, gay, bisexual, and transgender (LGBT) advocacy groups were pursuing a different strategy to legalize same-sex marriage, taking a state-by-state approach and avoiding a federal challenge. "We did not want to have a big debate about what we felt was the right strategy," Boutros explains. "We did not want that debate to break out before we launched our suit." . . .

The announcement [of the lawsuit] produced the national headlines [its supporters] had hoped to generate. But it caught many LGBT advocacy groups by surprise. "It was a very high-stakes move," said attorney Kate Kendell, executive director of the San Francisco–based National Center for Lesbian Rights (NCLR). Kendell's group had worked closely with the American Civil Liberties Union and the Los Angeles office of Lambda Legal, the nation's oldest and largest LGBT legal organization, in litigating [other same-sex marriage cases]. "This federal case has the potential to be a total game changer," she added. "But it also has the potential to have devastating consequences. You hope that it will be the former."

Nan Hunter, founder of the ACLU's LGBT Project, shared Kendell's concerns. She called the lawsuit "reckless" because "there is a significant chance of failure if the case reaches the U.S. Supreme Court." Hunter, now a professor at Georgetown University Law Center in Washington, D.C., also noted that LGBT legal groups had been following a "very careful and deliberate, collaborative" strategy for many years, only to have it "thrown off by an organization with a small number of people who are wealthy enough to pay for a major litigation effort." . . .

Fast-forward to June 2008: Nine LGBT legal and advocacy organizations spelled out their evolving strategy in a statement entitled "Make Change, Not Lawsuits." "We were encouraging people to continue to work in the states," [Lambda lawyer Jennifer] Pizer says, "and to not think that the federal courts were going to be a quick route" to success.

The six-page joint statement specifically warned same-sex couples against filing federal cases, or suing "their home state or their employer to recognize their marriage or open up the health plan" until there is a "critical mass of states recognizing same-sex relationships." Losing court cases, the groups argued, would actually make it "take longer to win the right to marry" in those states than if they had waited. . . .

[After the Perry case was filed, Judge Walker issued an order suggesting] more than a dozen issues for the parties to consider. He named potential factors needed to "establish the appropriate level of scrutiny under the Equal Protection Clause," such as "the history of discrimination gays and lesbians have faced" and "the relative political power of gays and lesbians, including successes of both pro-gay and anti-gay legislation." He suggested further that the record may need to establish evidence such as "the longstanding definition of marriage in California [and] whether a married mother and father provide the optimal child-rearing environment . . . whether excluding same-sex couples from marriage promotes this environment," and "the history of development of California's ban on same-sex marriage." . . .

Walker's order prompted the ACLU, Lambda Legal, and NCLR to consider formally intervening in the case. The three groups advised the plaintiffs' lawyers of their intent: "Between our organizations, we've litigated in a trial setting almost every single one of those issues," Kendall said. "That's invaluable experience, and these issues are difficult." . . .

The hearing convinced the ACLU, Lambda Legal, NCLR, and — separately — the San Francisco City Attorney's office that they *must* intervene. But the plaintiffs' legal team strongly opposed it. "I respect their interest in intervening, and we told them that we very much wanted their help and support," Olson later said. "But we represent clients, and we have to retain control of the case — not only the strategic decisions but also the pace of litigation. As soon as you have five captains of the ship, it's very hard to control the ship."

On July 8, Griffin wrote a startling three-page letter addressed to Kendell, Pizer, and Rosenbaum in an attempt to stop them. "You have unrelentingly and unequivocally acted to undermine this case even before it was filed," Griffin stated. "In light of this, it is inconceivable that you would zealously and effectively litigate this case if you were successful in intervening."

Pizer calls Griffin's letter, "an extremely negative, combative rewriting of history" that "most of us working in this movement wouldn't do because we're all in this together. We do have opponents, but they're not each other."

Ignoring Griffin's letter, the ACLU, Lambda Legal, and NCLR moved to intervene on behalf of Our Family Coalition; Lavender Seniors of the East Bay; and Parents, Families, and Friends of Lesbians and Gays. They asserted a "unique ability to develop a factual record." The city of San Francisco separately requested to join the case, citing "its interest as a public entity required to enforce an unconstitutional law." . . .

But Walker denied the LGBT groups' motion, stating that their interests were "indistinguishable from those advanced by the Plaintiffs." He granted the city of San Francisco's motion, however, citing its position as "the only governmental entity seeking to present evidence on the effects of Proposition 8 on governmental services and budgets." Walker then set a trial date of January 11, 2010.

Though spurned by the court, the LGBT legal groups chose to cooperate with the *Perry* team. They have provided background material that includes expert witnesses who had been used in other cases, and briefs from gay-rights litigation. "We are interested in doing whatever we can to make sure their case is as successful as possible," says James Esseks, co-director of the ACLU's LGBT Project. "And we wish the plaintiffs' legal team the best. We know they're doing everything they can to put together a great case." . . .

NOTES AND QUESTIONS

1. In 2010, Judge Walker held that Proposition 8 violated the plaintiff's constitutional rights, but the effects of the decision were stayed pending appeal.[72] Does that result alter your views of the decision to sue?

2. A *New York Times* account of the Olson and Boies suit describes the consensus of the gay community that the litigation was "the wrong claim in the wrong court in the wrong state at the wrong time."[73] Do you agree? One reason for the opposition to the suit, in addition to those reviewed in the readings, was that many activists felt that the focus on marriage was deflecting attention from issues that were equally critical and less controversial, such as workplace discrimination, hate crimes, and harassment. How should leaders of social movements make and implement priority decisions?

3. The California controversy was set in motion by San Francisco Mayor Gavin Newsom's decision to allow city authorities to provide marriage licenses to same-sex couples. Legal challenges to that decision led to the lawsuit overturning California's marriage law on state constitutional grounds, which in turn laid the groundwork for Proposition 8. In their comprehensive overview of the marriage-law controversy, law professors Scott Cummings and Douglas NaJaime note that Newsom did not involve LGBT leaders in his decision, and that many questioned its motives. In their view, Newsom was using the issue to shore up his political base, which had been put at risk by a progressive challenger in the mayoral election. He also may have been hoping to be perceived as the "Rosa Parks" of a movement that voters ultimately would support.[74] However, his famous prediction that gay marriage was coming "whether you like it or not" also galvanized opposition, especially when it was replayed in Proposition 8 campaign adds. How would you evaluate Newsom's leadership on this issue? What would you have done in his place?

4. In commenting on the secrecy before the filing of the California lawsuit, one of the plaintiffs' lawyers Thomas Boutros explained, "We did not want to have a big debate about what we felt was the right strategy." Why not? What would have been the advantages and disadvantages of involving the coalition of gay rights groups that had been active on the issue? If you had been in Boutros's place, what would you have done? If you had been a member of the coalition, how would you have responded to Olson's desire to file the case?

5. In defending the decision to bring the California lawsuit, Olson reasoned that millions of gay couples would like to be married, and one was bound to file a constitutional challenge. "So if there's going to be a case, let it

be us . . . because we have the resources [and experience] to do it." Are you persuaded? Given Olson's own self-interest, was he in a good position to assess who would have been the best lawyers to lead the charge? What cognitive biases might have influenced his judgment? One difference between the early civil rights cases and the contemporary gay-marriage dispute involves the number of litigants willing and able to bring constitutional challenges. In the 1940s and 1950s, filing a racial discrimination lawsuit often exposed parties and attorneys to substantial physical and financial risks, and brought little favorable public recognition. By contrast, today's litigants have more to gain and less to lose. In the contemporary climate, how can national strategies be forged? Would Rubenstein's proposal of procedural reforms have helped in the California gay-marriage dispute?

6. Supreme Court Justices are leaders with enormous power, but that power comes not from the "sword or the purse" but from the credibility of the Court as an institution. That credibility depends in part on keeping judicial interpretations of the law within bounds that the public will perceive as legitimate. On issues of constitutional rights, the Court can sometimes effectively prod the nation to live up to its own aspirations, as it did in cases involving interracial marriage and racially segregated schools. But when the Justices push too far too fast, legislators and government officials often push back, and that backlash may derail the progress that the original decision was designed to secure. Many, though not all, commentators view the *Roe v. Wade* decision recognizing women's right to an abortion as an example. If you were a leader of the gay rights movement, how would you assess the risks and advantages of asking the Supreme Court to play a leadership role in deciding whether same-sex marriage should be available? To what extent would your answer depend on whether you thought that the state legislative campaign had "run its course"?[75]

PROBLEM 9-3

1. Assume that you are the leader of a national gay/lesbian rights organization. You learn from a confidential source that Theodore Olson is planning to bring a constitutional challenge to California's ban on same-sex marriage. You discuss the matter with the directors of two other organizations whose confidentiality you trust. They are both incensed. What infuriates them is not only the substance of the decision but the fact that a "right-wing" "publicity-hungry" straight conservative is about to undermine the carefully planned strategy that the gay/lesbian community has struggled for a decade to develop. One director proposes that your organizations beat Olson to the courthouse door by filing a similar suit first. Alternatively, she suggests trying to pressure him to drop the case by threatening to reveal extremely embarrassing information about firm lawyers.

   The other director finds both of these responses problematic. If you file suit, other coalition members would feel betrayed and there is not time to build a united front. If someone is going to sue, he sees advantages in having an experienced conservative such as Olson in the lead advocate position.

As for threats of disclosing personal information, the director points out that this tactic has long been used with devastating consequences against gay, lesbian, and bisexual individuals; your organizations should not stoop to the same strategy even in a good cause.

What do you do?

2. Assume that you are one of the leading lawyers working with Olson in the *Perry* case. After the suit is filed, gay rights organizations that had opposed the litigation want to intervene. Olson opposes sharing control and publicity. Other members of your litigation team disagree. They believe that it would be a politically constructive gesture that would also generate additional support and expertise. Olson responds that the expertise will be available in any case; the groups will have no choice but to cooperate. And he is less concerned about the long-term political consequences for the gay rights community than about the immediate outcome of the litigation. What is your view?

Assume that the other members of the litigation team agree to oppose the intervention. You and Chad Griffin have responsibility for conveying that decision to the groups. Griffin presents you with a draft of the letter, which is quoted in the Svetvilas article above. If he refuses to tone it down, how do you respond?

3. You are the chief media strategist for a conservative public-interest organization that opposes same-sex marriage. You have read about the advertisements that gay rights advocates are planning to run in a new ballot proposition campaign to overturn California's ban on gay marriage. How would you counter their messages? Consider the discussion of "made to stick" messages in Chapter 4. What is likely to work best for your position and for theirs?

MEDIA RESOURCES

Many documentaries on the gay-marriage struggle are available, as are advertisements from the Proposition 8 campaign.[76] Olson and Boies justify their strategy in an interview with Rachel Maddow.[77] Clips from Harvey Milk's speeches and the film *Milk* also can provide interesting historical context.[78] In the film, Sean Penn portrays Milk, the San Francisco assemblyman who led a statewide movement to oppose a ban on gay school teachers. A documentary, *The Times of Harvey Milk*, is also available. It includes a powerful recording of him reading part of his will shortly before his murder, acknowledging the risk of assassination, and his sense of his role less as a "candidate" than as a "candidacy" and a "cause."[79]

END NOTES

1. For inattention, see Sharon Erickson Nepstad and Clifford Bob, When do Leaders Matter? Hypotheses on Leadership Dynamics in Social Movements, Mobilization: An International Journal 11 (2006):1; Aldon D. Morris and Suzanne Staggenborg, Leadership in Social Movements, in David A Snow, Sarah A. Soule, and Hanspieter Kriesi, eds., The Blackwell Companion to Social Movements (Oxford, UK: Blackwell Publishing, 2004), 171; Colin Barker, Alan Johnson, and Michael

Lavalette, Leadership Matters: An Introduction, in Colin Barker, Alan Johnson, and Michael Lavalette eds., Leadership and Social Movements (Manchester, UK: Manchester University Press, 2001),1.

2. Thomas R. Rochon, Culture Moves: Ideas, Activism, and Changing Values (Princeton, NJ: Princeton University Press, 1998); Gary T. Marx and Douglas McAdam, Collective Behavior in Oppositional Settings: The Emerging Social Movement, in Gary T. Marx and Douglas McAdam, eds., Collective Behavior and Social Movements (Englewood Cliffs, NJ: Prentice Hall, 1993); Doug McAdam, Political Opportunities: Conceptual Origins, Current Problems, and Future Directions, in Doug McAdam, John D. McCarthy, and Mayer N. Zald eds., Comparative Perspectives on Social Movements: Political Opportunities, Mobilizing Structures, and Cultural Framings (New York: Cambridge University Press, 1996); Enrique Larana, Hank Johnston, and Joseph R. Gusfield, eds., New Social Movements: From Ideology to Identity (Philadelphia, PA: Temple University Press, 1994).

3. John D. McCarthy and Mayer N. Zald, Resource Mobilization and Social Movements: A Partial Theory, in Russell L. Curtis and Benigno A. Aguirre eds., Collective Behavior and Social Movements (Boston, MA: Allyn and Bacon, 1993), 40, 43.

4. Alan Johnson, Self Emancipation and Leadership, in Colin Barker, Alan Johnson, and Michael Lavalette, eds., Leadership in Social Movements (Manchester, UK: Manchester University Press, 2001), 96, 99 (quoting civil rights activist Ella Baker).

5. Clayborne Carson, Reconstructing the King Legacy: Scholars and National Myths, in Peter J. Albert and Robert Hoffman, eds., We Shall Overcome: Martin Luther King and the Black Freedom Struggle (New York: De Capo Press, 1993), 243, 246.

6. David J. Garrow, Bearing the Cross: Martin Luther King, Jr. and the Southern Christian Leadership Conference, 1st Perennial Classics ed. (New York: Perennial, 2004), 56 (quoting King).

7. Aldon Morris, A Man Prepared for the Times: A Sociological Analysis of the leadership of Martin Luther King, Jr., in Albert and Hoffman eds., We Shall Overcome, 36.

8. Joe Walls and Brian Dollery, Market Failure, Government Failure, Leadership and Public Policy (London: MacMillan, 1999), 119.

9. Deborah L. Rhode, Justice and Gender (Cambridge, MA: Harvard University Press, 1989), 54-55.

10. Id. at 56; Thomas R. Rochon, Culture Moves: Ideas, Activism and Changing Values (Princeton, NJ: Princeton University Press, 1998), 207.

11. McAdam, Culture and Social Movements, 40.

12. Rochon, Culture Moves, 8; McAdam, Culture and Social Movements, 40.

13. Rochon, Culture Moves, 190-198; Deborah L. Rhode, Sexual Harassment, Southern California Law Review 65 (1992):1459.

14. Nicole C. Raeburn, Working It Out: The Emergence and Definition of the Workplace Movement for Lesbian, Gay, and Bisexual Rights, in Daniel J. Myers and Daniel M. Cress, eds., Research in Social Movements: Conflicts and Change (Oxford and San Diego: Elsevier, 2004), 187.

15. Bert Klandermans, The Demand and Supply of Participation: Social-Psychological Correlates of Participation in Social Movements, in Snow, Soule, and Kriese, eds., The Blackwell Companion, 360, 362; Marshall Ganz, Leading Change: Leadership Organization and Social Movements, in Nitin Nohria and Rakesh Khurana, eds., Handbook of Leadership Theory and Practice (Boston, MA: Harvard Business Press, 2010):527, 533; McCarthy and Zald, Resource Mobilization and Social Movements, 40.

16. Joan Neff Gurney and Kathleen J. Tierney, Relative Deprivation and Social Movements: A Critical Look at Twenty Years of Theory and Research, in Curtis and Aguirre eds., Collective Behavior and Social Movements, 141. See also Herbert Buner, Social Problems as Collective Behavior, in Curtis and Aguirre, eds., Collective Behavior and Social Movements, 54 (noting that harmful conditions are not sufficient to mobilize a movement; they need to be legitimated as a problem that can be addressed by social action).

17. Scott A. Hunt and Robert D. Benford, Collective Identity, Solidarity, and Commitment, in Blackwell Companion, 433, 439; Rochon, Culture Moves, 124-161.

18. Rochon, Culture Moves, 104.

19. Morris and Staggenborg, Leadership in Social Movements, 174-175; Sharon Erickson Nepstad and Clifford Bob, When Do Leaders Matter? Hypotheses on Leadership Dynamics in Social Movements, Mobilization: An International Journal 11 (2006):1.

20. Barker, Johnson, and Lavalette, Leadership Matters, 3.

21. Ganz, Leading Change, 527-528.

22. Alan Johnson, Self-Emancipation and Leadership: The Case of Martin Luther King, in Barker, Johnson, and Lavalette, Leadership Matters, 96-101.

23. Garrow, Bearing the Cross, 455 (quoting Rustin); Johnson, Self Emancipation, 107.

24. S.B. Oates, Let the Trumpet Sound: A Life of Martin Luther King (Edinburgh: Payback Press, 1982), 123-128; Johnson, Self Emancipation, 106.

25. Barbara C. Crosby and John M. Bryson, Leadership for the Common Good (San Francisco: Jossey Bass, 2005), 3.

26. Ricardo S. Morse, Integrative Public Leadership: Catalyzing Collaboration to Create Public Value, Leadership Quarterly 21 (2010):231, 243.

27. Joe Walls and Brian Dollery, Market Failure, Government Failure, Leadership and Public Policy (London: MacMillan Press, 1999), 145.

28. Crosby and Bryson, Leadership for the Common Good, 275-278.

29. Id. at 122.

30. Deborah L. Rhode, Public Interest Law: The Movement at Midlife, Stanford Law Review 60 (2008):2027, 2043 (quoting Barbara Olshansky, Center for Constitutional Rights and citing sources).

31. Gerald N. Rosenberg, The Hollow Hope: Can Courts Bring About Social Change? (Chicago, IL: University of Chicago Press, 1991); Ross Sandler and David Schoenbrod, Democracy by Decree: What Happens When Courts Run Government (New Haven, CT: Yale University, 2003); Kenneth Lee, Where Legal Activists Come From, American Enterprise, June 2001, 50.

32. Rhode, Public Interest Law, 2043.

33. Stuart A. Scheingold, The Politics of Rights (Ann Arbor: University of Michigan, 2004), xxiv; Kevin R. Den Dulk, In Legal Culture, but Not of It: The Role of Cause Lawyers in Evangelical Legal Mobilization, in Austin Sarat and Stuart Scheingold, eds., Cause Lawyers and Social Movements (Stanford, CA: Stanford University Press, 2006), 199-200; Ann Southworth, Lawyers and the "Myth of Rights" in Civil Rights and Poverty Practice, Boston University Public Interest Law Journal 8 (1999):469.

34. Nan Aron, Liberty and Justice for All: Public Interest Law in the 1980s and Beyond (Washington, D.C.: Council for Public Interest Law, 1989), 90 (quoting Nader).

35. Lewis M. Killian, Organization, Rationality and Spontaneity in the Civil Rights Movement, in Curtis and Aguirre, Collective Behavior and Social Movements, 209, 214-216.

36. Gail Collins, When Everything Changed (New York: Little, Brown, 2009), 110.

37. Rochon, Culture Moves, 7.

38. McAdam, Culture and Social Movements, 36, 38. See generally Johnston, Laranna, and Gusfield, Identities, Grievances, and New Social Movements in Larrana, Johnston, and Gusfield, eds., New Social Movements, 10, 189-190.

39. J. Craig Jenkins and Charles Perrow, Insurgency of the Powerless: Farm Workers Movements (1946-1972), in Curtis and Aguirre, eds., Collective Behavior and Social Movements, 341, 351-352; Mashall Ganz, Resources and Resourcefulness: Strategic Capacity in the Unionization of California Agriculture, 1959-1966, American Journal of Sociology 105 (2000):1003, 1033-1043.

40. Ganz, Resources and Resourcefulness, 1039.

41. Id. at 101-114.

42. Morris and Staggenborg, Leadership and Social Movements, 189-190.

43. Colin Barker, Robert Michels and the "Cruel Game," in Barker, Johnson, and Lavelette, eds., Leadership and Social Movements, 24.

44. Barker, Johnson, and Lavalette, Leadership Matters, 12-14.

45. Ganz, Resources and Resourcefulness, 1014-1016,

46. Malcolm Gladwell, Snatch, New Yorker, October 4, 2010, 42. See Andy Smith and Jennifer Aaker, The Dragonfly Effect: Quick, Effective, and Powerful Ways to Use Social Media to Drive Social Change (San Francisco: Jossey-Bass, 2010).

47. Gladwell, Snatch, 42.

48. Jennifer Aaker and Andy Smith, The Dragonfly Effect (New York: John Wiley and Sons, 2010).

49. Jennifer Aaker and Andy Smith, The Dragonfly Effect, Stanford Social Innovation Review (Winter 2011):31, 32.

50. Aaker and Smith, The Dragonfly Effect, 35.

51. Chip Heath and Dan Heath, Switch: How to Change Things When Change Is Hard (New York: Broadway Books, 2010), 28.

52. Id. at 28 (quoting Sternin).

53. See the work summarized by the Positive Deviance Initiative at Tufts, http://www.positivedeviance.org/materials/bib_subj.html.

54. Heath and Heath, Switch, 29-39, 40.

55. Id. at 150.

56. Id. at 151. For a history, see http://rarreconservation.orgh/about/page.php?subsection=history.

57. Deborah L. Rhode and Lee D. Ross, Environmental Values and Behaviors: Strategies to Encourage Public Support for Initiatives to Combat Global Warming, Virginia Environmental Law Journal 26(2008):161, 167-187.

58. For examples, see Heath and Heath, Switch, 159-161; Rhode and Ross, Environmental Values, 181.

59. John Kania and Mark Kramer, Collective Impact, Stanford Social Innovation Review (Winter 2011):36, 38.

60. Kania and Kramer, Collective Impact, 36.

61. Derrick A. Bell Jr., Serving Two Masters: Integration Ideals and Clients' Interests in School Desegregation Litigation, Yale Law Journal 85 (1976):470, 473.

62. See generally Barry Friedman, The Will of the People (New York: Farrar, Straus and Giroux, 2009).

63. Michael Murakami, Desegregation, in Nathaniel Persily, Jack Citrin, and Patrick J. Egan, eds., Public Opinion and Constitutional Controversy (New York: Oxford, 2008), 18, 19-20. Eighty-five percent of Americans thought that "Negros who lived in their town [did] have the same chance as whites to get a good education." Id., at 20.

64. Derrick A. Bell, Serving Two Masters: Integration Ideals and Client Interests in School Desegregation Litigation, Yale Law Journal 85 (1975-1976):470, 504.

65. Eyes on the Prize: America's Civil Rights Years 1954-1965 (Alexandria, VA: PBS Video, 2006).

66. For a 1957 interview with King discussing strategies, see http://www.youtube.com/watch?v=-Ll4QmvnGcU (Part 1) and http://www.youtube.com/watch?v=HXlfeeh_Wqg (Part 2). For King's last speech, see http://www.youtube.com/watch?v=o0FiCxZKuv8.

67. Modern Day Warriors (Boulder, CO: Native American Rights Fund, 2008).

68. The Fight in the Fields: Cesar Chavez and the Farmworkers' Struggle (Berkeley, CA: Paradigm Productions, 1997); Harvest of Shame (New York: Columbia Broadcasting System, 1960).

69. American Experience: Earth Days (Alexandria, VA: PBS Distribution, 2010).

70. A History of Women's Achievement in America (New York: Ambrose Video Pub., 2006); One Woman One Vote (Alexandria, VA: PBS Home Video, 2005).

71. Beyond Affliction: The Disability History Project (Conway, MA: Straight Ahead Pictures, 1998), available at http://www.npr.org/programs/disability.

72. *Perry v. Schwarzenegger*, 921 F. Supp. 921 (N.D. Cal. 2010).

73. Adam Liptak, In Battle on Marriage, The Timing May Be Key, New York Times, October 27, 2009, A14.

74. Scott L. Cummings and Douglas NeJaime, Lawyering for Marriage Equality, University of California Law Review 57 (2010):1235, 1276 (quoting anonymous member of the San Francisco Board of Supervisors).

75. Abby Goodnough, Gay Rights Rebuke May Change Approach, New York Times, Nov. 5, 2009, A25 (quoting Richard Socarides).

76. Proposition 8 ads are available at http://laist.com/2008/10/15/new_ads_say_no_on_prop_8_more_effec.php and http://www.afterellen.com/blog/trishbendix/prop-8-videos. For a parody of an antigay marriage advertisement see http://www.youtube.com/watch?v=exPoH1JX0Q8&feature=related.

77. Ted Olson and David Boies, The Case for Gay Marriage, The Rachel Maddow Show, January 12, 2010, available at http://www.msnbc.msn.com/id/26315908/vp/34833785#34833785.

78. Milk (Studio City, CA: Universal Studios Home Entertainment, 2009). For a Harvey Milk speech on hope, see http://www.youtube.com/watch?v=pzQ3NFXwpV8.

79. The Times of Harvey Milk (New York: New Yorker Films, 1984). The excerpt from Harvey Milk's actual tape-recorded will is also available at http://www.youtube.com/watch?v=_x4jPGEr HIM#t=62.

10

LEADERSHIP IN A GLOBAL CONTEXT: CORPORATE SOCIAL RESPONSIBILITY AND INTERNATIONAL HUMAN RIGHTS

A. INTRODUCTION

This chapter explores leadership challenges in promoting socially responsible practices and respect for human rights in an increasingly interdependent world. We link these subjects because they have overlapping histories and present overlapping issues. The rise of corporate social responsibility has been prompted in part by business involvement in human rights abuses such as sweatshop conditions and child labor. But we treat the topics sequentially because they also present some distinctive concerns. Corporate social responsibility encompasses domestic as well as international practices, and a range of social and environmental concerns apart from individual rights. So too, many international human rights issues involve states, individuals, and nongovernmental organizations rather than corporations. The materials that follow offer an overview of leadership challenges that arise in both settings.

Common to all of these issues is their complexity and importance. Often the goals are clear but the means are not. How best to end child labor in ways that respect cultural context, acknowledge competitive pressures, and do not exacerbate child poverty is more complicated than conventional wisdom acknowledges. The human stakes in these efforts are enormous. Leadership decisions affect not only the physical safety, security, and welfare of millions of individuals but also the conditions for a just society. Preparing private- and public-sector leaders for these challenges should be a central global priority.

B. CORPORATE SOCIAL RESPONSIBILITY

1. DEFINITIONS AND PRINCIPLES

The corporate enterprise dates to early Rome, but in the last half century, changes in its scale and impact have dramatically altered understandings of its social responsibilities. Of the 100 largest economies in the world, about half are companies rather than countries, and the influence of even moderately sized companies often touches all corners of the globe.[1] In an increasingly interdependent and interconnected world, the actions of multinational corporations assume new significance.

Concerns about the corporation are also long-standing, but they too have increased in tandem with the widening impact of business organizations. Seventeenth-century philosopher Thomas Hobbes compared corporations to "worms in the entrails" of the Commonwealth, which weakened its ability to regulate for the common good.[2] Commentators today express similar concerns about corporations' "pathological" pursuit of profit and their capacity to evade, capture, or co-opt oversight institutions.[3] What distinguishes recent critiques is the extent to which they have been institutionalized through social responsibility initiatives both within and across corporations. As a result, increasing numbers of leaders in business, nonprofit, and governmental organizations are focusing on the issue.

There is no single, widely accepted definition of "corporate social responsibility." The term is used more or less interchangeably with corporate citizenship, corporate ethics, and corporate social performance. Modern understandings are generally traced to Howard Bowen's 1953 publication, *Social Responsibilities of the Businessman*, which stressed companies' obligations to act in ways consistent with the "objectives and values of our society."[4] In the late 1970s, Professor Archie Carroll offered one of the first and most influential definitions of responsibilities that corporations owe to society: economic profitability, legal compliance, ethical conduct, and philanthropic contributions, the last of which he viewed as discretionary, and we consider in Chapter 11.[5]

More recent definitions generally stress accountability to stakeholders for the consequences of corporate actions.[6] An influential Green Paper by the Commission of the European Communities lays out a framework for social responsibility calling on companies to "integrate social and environmental concerns in their business operations and in their interaction with their stakeholders on a voluntary basis."[7] Different countries and industries give different weights to particular concerns, and experts hold different views about whether the term encompasses only "voluntary" efforts.[8] However, the general principle is captured by Business for Social Responsibility, an organization providing resources for those working in the field. It defines corporate social responsibility as the pursuit of "commercial success in ways that honor ethical values and respect people, communities, and the natural environment."[9]

Core principles of social responsibility include engagement of stakeholders, transparency in reporting conduct, consistent and sustainable best practices regardless of location, and accountability for results. Promotion of these principles has occurred through multiple strategies: codes of conduct, reporting and monitoring structures, stakeholder pressure, social responsibility agreements, and liability judgments. One of the most important international agreements is the United Nations Global Compact, which requires its approximately 3,000 signatory companies to commit to broad principles in ten areas involving human rights, labor conditions, anticorruption measures, and environmental practices.[10] Another influential framework is the Organisation for Economic Co-operation and Development's Guidelines for Multinational Enterprises, which sets forth voluntary standards for responsible business conduct in areas such as employment, human rights, the environment, bribery, consumer interests, competition, taxation, and information disclosure.[11]

2. THE BUSINESS CASE FOR SOCIAL RESPONSIBILITY

What is driving these initiatives? In its early phase, the campaign for social responsibility met with considerable skepticism. A common objection was that the business of business was business. Critics maintained that corporate executives lacked the expertise and accountability to make broader judgments about the public good, and that it was illegitimate for them to appropriate shareholder assets for that end. As economist Milton Friedman famously put it in a 1970 *New York Times* article, "there is one and only one social responsibility of business [namely to] . . . increase its profits."[12]

Three decades later, a McKinsey survey of over 4000 business leaders worldwide found that only one in six agreed with Friedman that the corporation's sole responsibility was profit maximization. Over four-fifths believed that shareholder returns had to be balanced against the higher public good.[13] In other surveys, over three-quarters of surveyed business leaders reported that social responsibility enhances profitability, and most thought that the benefits of environmentally sustainable practices outweigh the costs.[14] Chip Goodyear, CEO of HHP Billiton, expresses widespread views: "Social responsibility has a dollar value." It is not a question of "stockholder versus stakeholder . . . but is a critical part of maximizing shareholder returns. Simply, corporate social responsibility is in the best interest of our stakeholders and is fundamental to profit creation and sustainability."[15]

Empirical evidence for that view is mixed, and plagued by methodological difficulties. However, meta-analysis and overviews of more than 100 systematic studies from the last three decades generally reveal a modest positive correlation between social and financial performance.[16] Of course, causation may run in both directions and strategies for enhancing profitability and responsibility may be mutually reinforcing. Financially well-managed companies may be more willing and able to invest in socially desirable practices than their competitors, and their investments may have long-term economic payoffs.

The "business case" for social responsibility rests on multiple considerations. The first is a need to manage "social risk." As the scope and visibility of corporate conduct has grown, so too have the social, legal, and reputational consequences of undesirable practices. Writing in the *Harvard Business Review*,

Christopher Marlow and Julia Kirby argue that "leadership in the age of transparency" must take account of rapid increases in "scale," "sensors," and "sensibilities."[17] Environmental externalities such as pollution have escalated along with the growth of commercial activity, and now can have a devastating global impact. The effect of leaders' decisions has expanded accordingly, in potentially positive as well as negative directions. Companies such as Hewlett Packard and Wal-Mart have enormous leverage over not only their own decisions but also those of the companies and customers with whom they deal. H-P's $50 billion procurement budget enables it to impose a Supplier Code of Conduct demanding sustainable practice from other businesses throughout the world.[18]

As the impact of corporate activities has grown, so too has society's capacity to measure them, and to demand accountability for the consequences. The United States Air Quality System stores data from 5000 monitors on 188 pollutants, and its data are readily accessible online. The increasing size and sophistication of organized stakeholder interests has made it easier to hold corporations accountable for socially irresponsible conduct. Consumer, environmental, labor, and human rights organizations have become more influential through boycotts, protests, media outreach, lobbying, and litigation.[19] Technological advances, including the ready availability of visual images and organizing strategies, have increased capacities for naming and shaming; corporations can pay a substantial price for behaviors that activists target.[20] A case in point involved Nike's disastrous experience after offering purchasers the opportunity to customize their sneakers with a personal name. When the company refused to honor an order with the word "sweatshop," its e-mail was circulated to 10 million Internet users.[21]

As professor Jeffrey Pfeffer puts it in the *Harvard Business Review*, today's world is one of "stakeholder capitalism," and shareholder profits are only part of the balance sheet for measuring performance.[22] A reputation for integrity and social concern can be important to both workers and consumers. Most employees want to work for a responsible company. In one recent Aspen Institute survey, MBA students ranked "having a positive impact on society" as important as earning a high income.[23] About four-fifths of young Americans entering the labor force want to work for companies that care about how they affect or contribute to society and over 90 percent of British employees feel that their employer's social responsibility is important.[24] The vast majority of customers also prefer buying from a socially and environmentally responsible company.[25] Of course, whether those preferences translate into purchasing behavior is another matter, and most evidence suggests that only a relatively small percentage of consumers make choices dependent on the basis of positive or negative social performance.[26] Much depends on the egregiousness of corporate conduct; the public's knowledge and commitment concerning the issue; the availability of an alternative that meets their cost and quality concerns; and the positive reinforcement that comes from acting on principle. However, in a growing number of contexts, ethical performance, particularly abusive practices, can be a key factor in purchasing decisions and can also affect brand image and long-term customer loyalty.[27]

Another driver of corporate social responsibility is pressure from investors and lenders. An increasing number of individuals and institutions are committed to socially responsible investment (SRI), which includes ethical screening of financial opportunities and shareholder advocacy. In the United States alone, an estimated $2.7 trillion—about a ninth of total investments—are under management using at least one of the core SRI strategies.[28] In addition, many mainstream (and especially large institutional) investors now routinely consider environmental, social, and governance (ESG) issues. To assist investor decisions, various sustainability indexes track corporate performance on environmental and social matters.[29] A growing number of financial institutions also consider social responsibility in loan decisions. Many of the world's leading lenders have adopted the Equator Principles, which require signatories to ensure that the projects that they finance reflect socially responsible and environmentally sustainable practices.[30]

Other economic pressures encourage such practices. Many environmental initiatives reflect a desire for long-term cost savings through greater efficiency and technological innovation. Reforms in working conditions often yield gains in employee health, safety, productivity, and retention. Adoption of international standards concerning matters such as labor conditions and corruption can help prevent a race to the bottom, and losses to rogue competitors.[31]

Finally, corporate social responsibility can reduce the risks of litigation and legal liability and prevent the need for more intrusive regulatory oversight. Multimillion-dollar judgments for environmental, human rights, and product safety violations have prompted many companies both to overhaul their own practices and to require similar reforms by suppliers and subcontractors with whom they deal. In the United States, administrative agency requirements and white-collar criminal sentencing guidelines have prompted adoption of internal ethics codes.[32] So too, much of the impetus for voluntary international standards comes from a conviction that if businesses fail to devise effective regulatory mechanisms themselves, the government will do it for them.[33]

In the following excerpt, Ben Heineman, former general counsel of General Electric and lecturer on Leadership at Harvard, defends the "business case" for high integrity and identifies some structural initiatives by corporate executives and in-house counsel to make that commitment a reality in global corporations.

BEN W. HEINEMAN JR., HIGH PERFORMANCE WITH HIGH INTEGRITY

(Boston: Harvard Business Press, 2008), pp. 1-3, 9-11, 25,
31-35, 39-42, 89-90, 96-98, 109-111, and 138-139

In an era characterized by accelerating change, economic dislocation, and—all too often—highly visible scandals . . . contemporary corporations should strive to fuse high performance with high integrity—the twin goals of capitalism.

This calls for some definitions.

- High performance means
  - Strong, sustained economic growth

- That is based on superior products and services, and
- That provides durable benefits both to shareholders and to other stakeholders
- High integrity means
  - A tenacious adherence on the part of the corporation to the spirit and the letter of the formal rules, financial and legal
  - Voluntary adoption of global ethical standards that bind the company and its employees to act in its enlightened self-interest
  - Employee commitment to the core values of honesty, candor, fairness, reliability, and trustworthiness — values which infuse the creation and delivery of products and services and which guide internal and external relationships

High-performance corporations put relentless financial pressures on their employees to increase net income, cash flow, stock price — pressures that can often cause corruption when unconstrained by high integrity. Meanwhile, the dramatic changes in laws, regulations, stakeholder expectations, and media scrutiny over the past decade can now make a major integrity lapse not just damaging, but devastating. The CEO is fired in disgrace. Billions are squandered through fines, penalties, and lost business. In the worst cases, the company simply implodes.

Combining high performance with high integrity reduces such risks. . . . But combining high performance with high integrity isn't just about avoiding evils. It also has strong, affirmative benefits for the company: internally, in the marketplace, and in the broader society. Ultimately, it creates the fundamental trust of shareholders, creditors, employees, recruits, customers, suppliers, regulators, communities, and the public at large. Such trust is needed to sustain corporations' enormous power and freedom (even under current regulation): to allocate capital, to hire and fire people, to drive productivity, to invest in new geographies and communities, and to innovate with new products or services.

So this is not a frill or a nice-to-have. It is not the initiative of the month. The fusion of high performance with high integrity is the very foundation of the corporation. . . .

Top-performing companies apply relentless internal pressure on their people to hit basic financial goals for net income, cash flow, and stock price. Other targets, too, may be critically important: achieving specific returns on investment, equity, or assets; hitting sales or service goals; meeting product development or product launch schedules; and attaining productivity increases, to name a few.

Pressure begets more pressure. "Stretch targets" may put numbers on steroids. The explicit "nice to hit" target becomes an implicit "must do."

Personal incentives are driven by "making the numbers" and therefore create ubiquitous temptations. Employees at all levels may feel that their bonuses and promotions — and perhaps even their job security — depend on falsifying accounts, cutting corners, skipping key process steps, or worse.

Far-flung global enterprises face external pressures, which also create ever-present and illicit temptations. Many non-U.S. markets — from Russia to Brazil, from the Middle East to Asia — suffer from a weak rule of law, endemic corruption, and pervasive conflicts of interest. Yet these same markets are now a critical source of growth for global corporations. Whether that growth is organic or comes through acquisitions, new employees are predominantly local nationals. Not surprisingly, these individuals often come from cultural or business backgrounds that tolerate practices intolerable to a transnational company, such as bribes, shoddy accounting, channeling business to family members.

In most of those nations, moreover, dealing with government is a major element of doing business, because the state defines markets, procures goods and services, taxes income, and makes countless other decisions that decisively affect firm performance. Official extortion and misappropriation are clear and present dangers in places where the rule of law is tenuous, at best.

Local customers, too, may request that companies bend or break rules to facilitate customers' own private- or public-sector relationships. Similarly, using third-party distribution may be a local or regional necessity, but it tends to raise a host of legal and ethical issues. And with the dramatic enhancement of global supply chains, multinational corporations must increasingly worry about the financial, legal, and ethical practices of their sourcing partners. . . .

The key to achieving sustained high performance with high integrity lies in creating the right CEO-led corporate culture — the shared principles (values, policies, and attitudes) and the shared practices (norms, systems, and processes) that influence how people think and therefore how they behave. . . . The way chief executives exercise moral judgment is much more important than company policy. Specifically, the CEO must make it clear that the top executives of the corporation will not be spared nor favored, but will be held every bit as accountable for lapses in integrity as they are for other performance failures — and that in fact, the "generals" will be held to even higher standards than the "troops."

One example was uncovered [at General Electric] in the early '90s, while Jack Welch was CEO; a second surfaced a decade later, early in Jeff Immelt's tenure. The former involved a fraud against the U.S. government in an Israeli Air Force jet fighter procurement financed by U.S. funds. The latter involved a Japanese customer who insisted that GE employees falsify documents relating to safety issues; these documents, in turn, were submitted by the customer to in-country regulators.

Both matters grew out of the dark side of customer satisfaction. Both were understood to be wrong by many in the organization. Both involved many individuals who either engaged in improper conduct themselves or failed to have it investigated or stopped. . . . [T]he most painful and difficult [company] actions involved the senior officers who led the business units. They had had long careers with the company and were widely regarded as "good guys" by other senior leaders. They had no personal knowledge of the bad acts. But they had failed, in a most dramatic way, to create a performance-with-integrity culture. Far too many in their organizations were indifferent to intolerable acts for far too long.

The executives were asked to leave the company. The message was clear: there is no favoritism. The CEO holds top leaders to high standards, and those who are indifferent to creating an integrity culture will be gone. . . .

[D]elivering a positive message to the top leadership group is equally effective. Shortly after becoming CEO in 2001, Jeff Immelt instituted Chairman's Leadership Awards. . . . [Some awards recognize profitability, b]ut other awards go to the internal audit staff, or to a successful environmental program, or to a person who has made a contribution to governance — and this speaks volumes to company leaders about the core value of high performance with high integrity. . . .

[Another key to effective leadership involves] building the integrity infrastructure: developing rigorous systems and processes to prevent, detect, and respond. . . . [Such a structure:]

- Prevents ethics and compliance misses . . . and when prevention fails . . .
- Detects misses as soon as possible . . . and once they are detected . . .
- Responds quickly and effectively . . .

The first critical step in prevention is risk assessment. This involves taking an inventory of the important financial and legal rules in all product lines and in all places where the corporation does business. . . . The second critical prevention step is risk abatement or mitigation. In general, this means building information tracking and control processes in all business functions . . . for key risks.

. . . [A second strategy involves r]obust internal systems for detecting possible improprieties as soon as possible. . . . Of course, general management oversight and control processes help surface questions about integrity issues. But giving employees voice — through an ombuds system or other means — is also critical to detection. . . .

Responding to concerns about possible improprieties has four basic dimensions:

- Investigation
- Individual discipline
- Remediation within the business unit
- Remediation across the company, when appropriate . . .

[One] way to give employees voice is an annual "bottom-up" review: an important component of each business's broader, periodic integrity review. At GE, this review starts with on-the-ground employees in each nation. Either finance, legal, or their managers ask them about risks they perceive or issues they might have with the integrity infrastructure. This review then builds up through localities, countries, and regions, giving employees higher in the organization the same opportunity to assess the business's integrity efforts. . . . It culminates in a report on results . . . that identifies in rank order which risks, policies, and processes have registered the most questions or comments. . . .

Cross-unit comparisons on financial and legal integrity issues are a powerful way to evaluate and motivate business leaders — especially when the company's top leaders, at their regular meetings, review charts comparing their performance. How do the leaders rank on the number of audit adjustments required in a year, and how quickly do they close open audit items? How do they compare on the number of actionable concerns registered in the ombuds system, or on the audit staff's review of integrity programs? . . .

Another key comparative tool for assessing leadership is the annual employee survey. In 2006, more than 127,000 professional employees across GE were asked in an anonymous survey (that generated a 95 percent response rate) whether they agreed or disagreed with the statement "There are no compromises around here when it comes to conducting business in an ethical way." For GE as a whole, 85 percent agreed, [but in some units, where a significant number of employees] . . . said leaders were more concerned with results than compliance, change came swiftly: new leaders, a new compliance staff, a reorganized ombuds system, and more visits by the audit staff. . . .

Multinational corporations will always experience tensions between local practices and global standards. These tensions often lead to hard choices. One such choice arises when local customer practices are at variance with local laws. For example, using ultrasound technology for abortions on the basis of the gender of the fetus is against the law in both China and India—but is nonetheless widely practiced, due to the importance placed in those cultures on male offspring. This is a hot-button issue in parts of those societies—and around the world. Medical equipment manufacturers like GE had to determine how to sell ultrasound equipment, which of course has many legitimate medical purposes, into a market characterized by its illegal use.

Steps included educating customers, putting warning labels on equipment, writing product manuals that highlighted legal requirements, selling only to physicians licensed and certified in compliance with the law, and providing sales data to appropriate state and central authorities who are just now beginning to enforce the law. GE could not guarantee that its ultrasound equipment was not being used illegally for sex-selection abortions, but it could point to serious, good-faith efforts to forestall that outcome.

A second kind of hard choice arises when local law—which multinationals are required to obey—comes into conflict with a company's global standards. . . . In one recent notable case, Google—determined to compete with a Chinese search engine—chose to abide by Chinese censorship law, which was in conflict with its broad ethical principles against such governmental restrictions. . . .

A third kind of hard choice arises when corrupt practices in a nation are so pervasive that conflicts with global rules or global standards cannot be resolved, and the corporation has to ask whether it must exit particular industries—or leave the country entirely. At various times, for example, GE has chosen not to do business in Iran (an alleged state sponsor of terrorism and supporter of insurgents in Iraq), in Colombia (where employees' safety cannot be guaranteed and money laundering is rife), and in "cash-flow businesses" in Russia (a locus of widespread organized crime and money laundering). . . .

Although performance is the core of a company's reputation, so is its integrity. . . . It's an oft-repeated truism—but it's still true that reputation, like a forest, takes years to grow but can burn down overnight.

3. CHALLENGES AND CONCERNS

NOTES

In principle, few leaders would disagree with the need to combine high performance and high integrity. But for those heading corporate, governmental, and nongovernmental organizations, the practical challenges of ensuring socially responsible practices can be daunting. Consider the sheer scale of the effort required. Today's world includes an estimated 77,000 transnational corporations, some 770,000 subsidiaries, and millions of suppliers.[34] A threshold issue is the extent to which these corporations should be responsible for the sins of others. On that issue, Dow Chemical took the position that it was not accountable for cleanup and compensation costs connected with a disastrous gas explosion in Bhopal, India, simply because it had later acquired the company that was responsible. Much as Dow leaders would like to "see the issue resolved in a humane and satisfying way," they were unwilling to set a precedent that could expose multinational corporations to billions of dollars in liability costs.[35] Of course, responsibilities are greater for corporations in a position to prevent misconduct. But even companies that themselves have rigorous ethical and environmental standards are often unwilling or unable to impose them on others with which they deal. A 2007 survey of Global 2000 companies found that almost four-fifths did not require suppliers to enforce a code of conduct and only about a fifth regularly assessed ethical conduct in their supply chains.[36] Although recent attention to the problem has increased monitoring, progress remains uneven at best.

A further set of challenges arises from the lack of uniform standards to assess social performance. In the environmental area alone, some 300 frameworks are available, and one corporate officer recently reported filling out 130 annual surveys concerning sustainable practices.[37] The difficulties in assessing performance in this universe are reflected in the emergence of frameworks such as AccountAbility, which are designed to evaluate evaluation measures. Information technology is gradually addressing these challenges, as common computer language formats are increasingly allowing the sharing and comparison of disparate sustainability and corporate social responsibility data.[38] In addition, efforts to improve and consolidate existing standards and stakeholder initiatives are reflected in the Global Social Compliance Program (GSCP) and the recently established Integrated International Reporting Committee (IIRC).[39]

The largely voluntary nature of corporate social responsibility measures poses additional challenges. The only official compliance mechanism for the UN Global Compact and similar frameworks is annual reporting. Although some accountability initiatives monitor compliance, critics note that many companies can "cheerfully sign up to [the compact] and even more cheerfully ignore it."[40] A similar option is available with corporations' own corporate codes of conduct, which seldom include independent oversight.[41] However, growing legal and social enforcement initiatives are increasing the risks of noncompliance. About 2300 organizations in approximately sixty countries participate in Social Accountability 8000, which monitors human rights performance. Still, the companies that fail to participate are the ones most likely to need oversight. The quality and independence of some monitoring agencies is also subject to criticism.[42]

Moreover, in purely voluntary regimes, companies that make the effort to ensure responsible practices can be undercut by less ethical competitors. Nike's experience is a case in point. Its overseas labor conditions were singled out for media coverage and consumer protest not because they were the worst in the industry, but because Nike was the most prominent and vulnerable target — a practice some commentators label the brand boomerang effect.[43] Yet, once the company began rigorous efforts to monitor supplier conduct, it found that many consumers and investors were not rewarding initiatives that failed to deliver reduced prices and higher profits. Worse still, its efforts to rehabilitate its image left it even more vulnerable to charges of hypocrisy when occasional abuses continued. The company ended up paying over $1 million to settle a lawsuit charging that its public relations efforts fraudulently represented its success in preventing sweatshop labor conditions.[44] In the long term, Nike's success in fusing high integrity and high performance required more fundamental changes in its production expectations, and buy-in from other apparel manufacturers willing to adhere to comparable labor standards.[45] Although not all companies have the capacities and competitive leverage to secure such reforms, the standards set by leading companies often can encourage and enable others to follow suit.

However, for some critics, such as Berkeley political economist Robert Reich, the limitations of voluntary frameworks make many corporate social responsibility efforts counterproductive; they forestall government regulation and "deflect public attention from the need for stricter laws. . . ."[46] A wide array of evidence suggests that in many competitive contexts, the possibility of sanctions is necessary to ensure adequate compliance.[47] For example, an Organisation for Economic Co-operation and Development (OECD) report focusing on voluntary environmental standards found that a majority had failed to bring about significant change.[48] Studies of voluntary labor codes come to similar conclusions, leading critics to claim that these efforts crowd out more effective government and union efforts.[49] Examples of hypocrisy and greenwashing are in ample supply, and experts are particularly incensed when corporations publicly pledge allegiance to socially responsible action and then privately lobby against measures that would promote it.[50] Criticism has also focused on social responsibility awards, which are too often based on partial information and sponsored by organizations funded by corporations that they honor.[51] Although critics acknowledge that it is the absence of effective governance that makes voluntary action necessary, they believe that the solution lies in building regulatory capacity, not settling for aspirational stopgaps.

Defenders of corporate social responsibility initiatives offer several rejoinders. First, they deny that these initiatives undermine support for regulatory alternatives. Rather, supporters point to examples in which such efforts have become the basis for mandatory reporting frameworks, or have laid the foundations for legal liability and legislative requirements.[52] In other contexts, voluntary action may hold advantages over less flexible regulatory regimes. Legal mandates may be over- or underinclusive, or incapable of adapting to rapidly changing circumstances. For transnational corporations, uniform international standards present fewer compliance difficulties than inconsistent national requirements. Those requirements are also more expensive to enforce, and more likely to encounter resistance than self-imposed codes. According to some experts, the best solution is frequently "metaregulation," or "enforced self-regulation," in which companies work with governmental and nongovernmental organizations to develop standards, and the law backs them up.[53] These commentators reject the dichotomy between "mandatory" and "voluntary" regulation, and underscore the complementarities of various approaches.[54] Even in the absence of legal enforcement structures, corporations often have reason to work in collaboration with governments as well as other stakeholders. A model is ExxonMobil's alliance with the Chad and Cameroon governments, the World Bank, several nongovernmental organizations, and indigenous populations to address issues concerning one of its pipeline projects.[55]

In any event, whatever would be the ideal solutions in the long term, social responsibility initiatives are unquestionably necessary in the short term. Particularly in developing nations, conflict, corruption, and lack of resources often hobble regulatory efforts. In the absence of more effective state enforcement, there is little choice but to rely on corporate self-governance.

QUESTIONS

1. In *Capitalism and Freedom*, Milton Friedman asked:

> If businessmen do have a social responsibility other than making maximum profits for stockholders, how are they to know what it is? Can self-selected private individuals decide what the social interest is? Can they decide how great a burden they are justified in placing on themselves or their stockholders to serve the social interest? Is it tolerable that these public functions of taxation, expenditure, and control be exercised by the people who happen at the moment to be in charge of particular enterprises, chosen for those posts by strictly private groups?[56]

How would you respond?

2. By the early 2000s, Nike had invested considerable resources in auditing labor conditions of its approximately 900 suppliers. When abuses persisted, the company decided to expand its focus. Rather than trying simply to improve the sanctioning process for noncompliance, management began looking for underlying causes. It found them in the standard industry practice of awarding performance incentives to procurement teams based on price, quality, and delivery time. This system had the unintended effect of encouraging buyers to circumvent code compliance structures in order to hit their targets and secure bonuses. So too, the company's tight inventory management often led to shortages when forecasting errors occurred. That led to pressure on suppliers to increase production by violating maximum hour protections. Contract requirements that suppliers pay air freight rates to make delivery targets had a similar effect; if orders arrived late, suppliers stepped up production, sometimes using temporary workers and not disclosing their substandard conditions. When abuses surfaced, the legal and reputational costs were passed on to the central organization, not to those who had caused the problem in the first instance.[57]

If you were Nike's general counsel, or head of its social responsibility division, how would you respond? What lessons might you draw from Heineman's strategies?

3. Several years after Nike conducted its internal review, an independent study of approximately 800 of its suppliers in fifty-one countries concluded that monitoring had only a small effect in improving labor conditions.[58] In some countries such as China, overviews of factory conditions in a wide range of industries found that employees typically worked over six times the legal monthly overtime limits, often twelve hours, seven days a week.[59] If you were the head of a human rights organization concerned with this issue, what strategies would you pursue for apparel manufacturers?

4. In McKinsey's global survey of executives, only 8 percent believed that large corporations champion social or environmental causes out of "genuine concern." Almost 90 percent agreed that they were motivated by public relations, profitability, or both. Only 3 percent of surveyed leaders reported that their companies were doing a "good job" in anticipating social pressure, including criticism of their efforts. Almost half saw "substantial room for improvement."[60] If those perceptions are reasonably accurate, how might they be effectively addressed? Does the motive of corporate decision makers matter?

5. In elaborating on the role of general counsel in enforcing high-integrity cultures, Heineman recommends that lawyers develop multiple ways for employees to give voice to values.[61] Among his suggestions is appointment of an ombudsperson who can receive confidential concerns by phone, e-mail, and letter. Under what, if any, circumstances can you imagine contacting such a person? What strategies might increase your willingness?

6. If you were part of a business, labor, and governmental coalition on improving workplace conditions in East Asia, what priorities would you pursue? Your research indicates that the issues that are of most concern to consumers in the developed world, such as sweatshops and child labor, are not those of most concern to workers in the developing world, whose priorities are wages and job security.[62] Consider that issue in light of the materials below.

MEDIA RESOURCES

A Duke Business School professor discusses new research in corporate social responsibility that sheds light on the problems discussed in the text.[63] *The Simpsons'* biting parody of a sugar company CEO raises serious issues about the limits of social responsibility initiatives.[64] *Thank You for Not Smoking* opens with an illuminating scene of how a tobacco lobbyist is able to spin antisocial conduct. A discussion with CEO Jeff Immelt offers perspectives on corporate social responsibility in the recent financial crisis.[65]

C. HUMAN RIGHTS

1. INTRODUCTION

Although human rights concerns have figured in religion, law, philosophy, and politics since antiquity, it was only after World War II that they became a major force in the international community. The sheer scale of atrocities during a war involving some 50 million casualties inspired a vast body of laws and institutions seeking to promote fundamental rights. As a consequence, a growing number of leaders in government, business, and nongovernmental organizations (NGOs) are focusing on how to make those rights a reality.

Widely recognized entitlements are set forth in the United Nations' Universal Declaration of Human Rights (1948), the International Covenant on Civil and Political Rights (1966), and the International Covenant on Economic, Social, and Cultural Rights (1966). Related treaties and conventions elaborate these rights in specific areas including warfare, torture, labor, and discrimination. Although the complexities of human rights enforcement are beyond the scope of this volume, some introduction to the topic is important for leaders in an increasingly globalized world order. Even leaders operating in primarily national contexts need to be sensitive to the competing values and multicultural concerns that inform international human rights work.

Such work poses certain distinctive leadership challenges. A threshold issue is how to define which rights deserve protection, and how they should be enforced. A common approach among contemporary theorists such as Martha Nussbaum is to identify core capabilities that are "of central importance in any human life."[66] The problem, as Charles Betz notes, is that theories focused on which interests should be protected "deflect attention from what are frequently the more difficult questions." At what point does violation of a right such as adequate nutrition constitute a basis for intervention by outsiders, and when do they have a justification or responsibility for action?[67] Unlike other subjects of international law, human rights violations are generally rooted within a single state. When and why they should be a matter of international or corporate concern raises complicated questions of national sovereignty, humanitarian principles, multilateral security, and economic development. Those who argue for strong protections of human rights point out that widespread violations often have transnational consequences. So, for example, one government's persecution of an ethnic minority can create a large refugee problem, provoke hostilities by foreign groups that share that ethnicity, destabilize the region, and compromise widely shared moral principles. In addition, widespread violations of labor standards in one country can help create a race to the bottom that puts ethical businesses in other countries at a competitive disadvantage.

A second complication in human rights work arises from the challenges it can pose to cultural identity, religious values, family authority, and community practices. As Professor Sally Merry puts it, "human rights [are] embedded in cultural assumptions . . . [that] do not translate easily from one setting to another."[68] Supporters of the human rights movement respond that its core values, including those recognized in the Universal Declaration of Human Rights, have been repeatedly reaffirmed in national constitutions and legal systems, as well as at international conferences throughout the world. Yet leaders often face charges of ideological imperialism when they attempt to impose assertedly "universal" values on a group that does not share them.[69] Finding ways to institutionalize human rights while respecting local traditions requires considerable cultural sensitivity.

A third challenge in human rights work involves accountability of the movement itself. Human rights leaders often view their ethical responsibilities in terms of broad concepts of individual liberty and social justice. Many lawyers and heads of nongovernmental organizations work on behalf of large numbers of people whose rights have been violated, or on behalf of the broader principles at stake; they may lack direct responsibility to any identifiable constituency, such as clients, shareholders, or democratically chosen officials.

2. STANDARDS GOVERNING CORPORATE RESPONSIBILITY FOR HUMAN RIGHTS

The application of human rights principles to businesses is relatively recent and rapidly evolving. Historically, human rights and corporate law evolved along separate tracks, although concerns regarding accountability date back to the emergence of this new form of concentrated commercial power.[70] International law was concerned primarily with relations between states, and human rights law was concerned primarily with the rights of individuals in relations with state officials. Corporate law, by contrast, was primarily focused on the regulation of financial organizations by national governments. However, the growth and influence of transnational corporations has made clear the need to develop ways to hold them accountable for human rights violations, and international law provides some basis for doing so. The Universal Declaration of Human Rights, which established the first authoritative definitions in the field, referred to the obligation of "every organ of society" to respect such rights. So too, the International Covenant on Civil and Political Rights, a treaty ratified by 167 nations, including the United States, requires governments to ensure respect for rights recognized in the covenant. Protection from corporate violations has been widely assumed to fall within the covenant's reach, and the same is true of other treaties providing safeguards from specific human rights abuses.[71]

However, efforts to impose more specific human rights requirements on transnational corporations have met with little success. In 2003, a working group of the UN Subcommission on the Promotion and Protection of Human Rights drafted a set of Norms on the Responsibilities of Transnational Corporations and Other Business Enterprises with Regard to Human Rights.[72] It spelled out a broad range of responsibilities regarding civil, political, social, economic, labor, and environmental concerns. Although reception from some business organizations (such as the Business Leaders Initiative on Human Rights (BLIHR) and the International Business Leaders Forum) was positive, the response from other business organizations (such as the International Chamber of Commerce and the International Employees Organization) was highly negative. Some respected policy experts also criticized the Norms as ambiguous and unenforceable. The UN Commission on Human Rights therefore "welcomed" the Norms but decided not to act further on them, and instead asked the UN secretary-general to appoint a special representative to review issues of human rights and transnational corporations. Then Secretary-General Kofi Annan appointed Harvard professor John Ruggie to this role.

In follow-up reports, Ruggie both documented corporate violations of human rights and proposed a three-part framework—"protect, respect, and remedy"—to address them.[73] Under the category of "protect" came state responsibilities to strengthen pressure on corporations to prevent involvement in human rights abuses. For example, states can require reporting on human rights compliance, and can incorporate protections in their own criminal and civil law. International organizations can also supply pressure. The International Labor Organization's Declaration of Principles concerning Multinational Enterprises and Social Policy, and the OECD Guidelines for Multinational Enterprises can provide appropriate guidance, although as Ruggie notes, these Guidelines would benefit from revisions strengthening their application, a process now underway. Another illustration comes from the International Finance Corporation of the World Bank Group, which imposes performance standards involving human rights as a condition of receiving investment funds.

The second prong of Ruggie's framework calls on corporations to respect human rights by exercising due diligence and creating systems capable of ensuring compliance. Efforts to promote such internal policies on human rights issues are long-standing. The first prominent initiative came in the 1970s, when the Sullivan Principles established ethical norms for companies doing business in South Africa under the apartheid regime. By the late 1980s, however, the consensus was that the initiative had been unsuccessful and its authors urged companies to cease doing business in South Africa.[74] Around the same time, a growing number of voluntary corporate responsibility standards began to emerge in other areas. For example, the Kimberly Process Certification Scheme labels diamonds that have not contributed to international conflicts; Rugmark certifies carpets that have not been created through child labor; and the Voluntary Principles in Security and Human Rights guide extractive industries. Although these efforts have promoted significant progress, questions have been raised about the effectiveness of monitoring and compliance procedures.[75] According to Ruggie's reports, most corporations lack adequate systems to ensure compliance.[76]

The third obligation set forth in Ruggie's framework involves access to remedies for human rights violations. One model is the U.S. Alien Torts Claims Act, which gives foreign citizens rights to sue Americans for illegal actions committed abroad. Although its applicability to corporations remains contested, the act has been extended to American companies for egregious violations of international human rights abroad.[77] However, as Ruggie notes, most countries provide inadequate remedies, and companies need to establish their own grievance mechanism to ensure compliance.[78]

As noted earlier, corporations have a variety of reasons for responding to these concerns. Effective human rights protections can reduce legal risks; address stakeholder concerns; appeal to consumers; improve worker health, safety, and morale; and build a reputation for integrity.[79] In an opinion poll of some 21,000 people in twenty countries, eight out of ten respondents assigned corporations at least part of the responsibility for reducing human rights abuses.[80] Yet the extent to which performance on human rights issues has long-term financial benefits is not always clear. In some cases, enough consumers have been willing to pay higher prices for products carrying fair-labor or fair-trade labels so that the items remain profitable.[81] But in other circumstances, companies have been forced to abandon efforts to market socially responsible products; price and quality concerns trump other customer commitments.[82] Whether corporations will do well by doing good depends on multiple factors, including the likely detection and visibility of abuses, the threat of legal and consumer sanctions, and the accountability of competitors for similar conduct. However, research over the past decade, including metastudies (which aggregate findings of other studies), increasingly finds a positive correlation between corporate social responsibility (including human rights compliance) and corporate success.[83]

Still, as Berkeley business professor David Vogel notes, the "market for virtue" is clearly lacking in many human rights contexts. Ruggie agrees, and points out that "few if any voluntary [human rights] efforts have reached a scale where they can move markets." The absence of accessible dispute resolution procedures and "widely accepted, . . . [effective, and credible] accountability mechanisms . . . has created mounting frustrations all around."[84] How best to respond to those challenges is a matter of debate. As noted earlier, some experts believe that corporate social responsibility initiatives are a diversion from the more critical work of building governance capacity, particularly among developing nations. Others respond that in the absence of such capacity, corporations should step in to fill the gap. In most states, human rights victims now have no realistic prospect of legal remedy.[85] The evolution of uniform international human rights norms could reduce the difficulties that arise for corporations facing inconsistent national standards, while also deterring abuses and enhancing effective remedies.

PROBLEM 10-1

In 2003, a shift in power in the Chinese government brought a new crackdown on freedom of expression, including peaceful political comment on the Internet. Despite such repression, Google in 2006 launched a Chinese search engine. After much internal debate, Google's leaders concluded that "the benefits of increased access to information for people in China" outweighed the costs of complicity in censorship.[86] As required by the government, the search machine filtered coverage of matters such as the 1989 Tiananmen Square massacre, Human Rights Watch, and the Dalai Lama. Other American companies, including Microsoft and Yahoo, made similar decisions, all of which received substantial criticism from the civil liberties community. As Harvard professor Jonathan Zittrain noted, these actions offered a "near-textbook case study on the deep question of how much assistance, if any, companies chartered in free societies should render to regimes that censor political and cultural expression."[87]

The issue sparked congressional hearings and a heated public debate. In 2006 House Subcommittee Hearings, Representative James Leach of Iowa accused Google of serving as a "functionary of the Chinese government," and added that if "we want to learn how to censor, we'll go to you."[88] Google's CEO Eric Schmidt responded, "I think it's arrogant for us to walk into a country where we are just beginning operations and tell that country how to run itself."[89] Rather, the company announced to users that its China service did not "accord fully with its principles," and it disclosed when search results were censored.[90] Reaction within the human rights community was mixed. According to Human Rights Watch, the Chinese system of electronic surveillance had become the most advanced in the world, and it had been significantly aided by American corporations.[91] Others took the view expressed by Harvard researcher Rebecca Mackinnon: "Bottom line, it's good they're in China. . . . But there's a lot more they can do" to protect users, such as publicizing sites that were delisted and collaborating with other U.S. Internet firms to lobby for more "transparency and accountability" in Chinese government practices.[92]

The issue arose again in 2010 when Google discovered that Chinese hackers had illegally breached its security, along with that of some twenty other companies, and had accessed the accounts of American, Chinese, and European advocates of human rights in China. In response, the company refused to continue filtering censored material from its Chinese language search engine, and began rerouting Chinese users to an uncensored Hong Kong site. The Chinese government then used its Internet filter to block banned material.[93]

The issue involved more complex trade-offs of profit and principle than were commonly acknowledged. About forty countries routinely censor the Internet, and more than twenty-five have blocked Google service over the last decade.[94] Google's cofounder Sergey Brin saw its China decision as a signal to other nations.[95] According to Arvind Ganesan, director of Human Rights Watch's business and human rights program, "[a] transnational attack on privacy is chilling, and Google's response [in China] sets a great example."[96] That example appeared particularly commendable given the huge potential market at stake. China has 400 million Internet users, more than any other nation and a fifth of the global market, and Google provides the second-largest search engine for those individuals.[97]

Yet, as others pointed out, Google's current profit levels from the Chinese market are relatively inconsequential—only about 1 percent of its total revenues. Most of that profit comes from advertising on sites other than its Chinese search engine, and such profit would not be lost if the company shut down that service but was allowed to keep a sales force in the country.[98] In the view of many experts, toleration of censorship poses a far greater financial risk than the loss of a single market because the company's "entire business model [depends on] a free and open Internet."[99]

1. Does that analysis, together with the risk to its intellectual property, suggest that Google's China position has always been influenced more by profits than principle and that its change of heart in 2010 simply reflected a reassessment of the financial stakes? Or is that an overly cynical view of a

company trying to do the "right" thing for its global users over the long term?

2. Google identifies three principles that inform its decisions to operate in new markets:

   • Access: maximizing information flow;
   • Transparency: informing users when information has been removed at government demand; and
   • Trust: protecting users' privacy and security.[100]

   If you were the CEO or general counsel of Google, how would you assess the trade-offs between those principles in China? If the government threatens to oust Google entirely if it will not continue filtering information, what would you do?

3. In 2010, the chair of the Senate Judiciary Subcommittee on Human Rights announced plans to introduce legislation requiring Internet companies to take reasonable steps to protect human rights or to face civil or criminal liability.[101] Would you support such legislation? Who should decide what information should be available on Chinese search engines: the Chinese government, the United States government, or leaders of companies such as Google?

3. CHILD LABOR

A case study in the complexities of global human rights enforcement involves child labor. Since 1919, the International Labor Organization (ILO) has adopted ten conventions regarding minimum ages for work in different sectors.[102] The vast majority of nations have signed treaties committing them to the abolition of child labor. The 1989 Convention on the Rights of the Child, which includes various labor protections, has the most ratifications of any human rights document; only the United States and Somalia have not ratified the document.[103] The Convention concerning the Prohibition and Immediate Action for the Elimination of the Worst Forms of Child Labour (ILO No. 182) (1990), which has been ratified by 169 nations, including the United States, obligates signatories to take "immediate and effective measures to secure the prohibition and elimination of the worst forms of child labor, such as work involving coercion, bondage, sexual exploitation and hazardous conditions." Despite such governmental commitments, the ILO estimates that about one out of seven children in the world today is involved in child labor.[104] Much of that work, particularly when combined with domestic tasks within the family, can severely compromise children's educational opportunities, as well as psychological development.[105] Most child labor occurs in agriculture, mining, forestry, and fishing, but for transnational corporations, the best-publicized abuses have occurred in the garment, shoe, and carpet trades. In the Indian hand-knotted rug industry alone, estimates suggest that over a fifth of the workforce is underage, and in the country as a whole, an estimated 13 million children work.[106] Contributing causes include poverty, inadequate education, gender and caste discrimination, and long-standing cultural norms.

Although India has not ratified the Convention on the Worst Forms of Child Labour, it has both constitutional and statutory prohibitions on the employment of children in hazardous occupations, which include the carpet industry. In the mid-1980s, widespread violations of these prohibitions in India, along with related abuses in surrounding nations, prompted the formation of the South Asian Coalition on Child Servitude. This Coalition, which now has over 400 organizational members, joined with various human rights groups and trade unions to pressure consumers and retailers to demand carpets made without child labor. In 1995, the Rugmark Foundation was established to certify hand-knotted rugs in India, Pakistan, and Nepal that are produced only by adults who are paid a minimum wage. To finance inspections and rehabilitate illegally employed children, the foundation collects a license fee from exporters, who pay .25 percent of the value of the product, and importers, who pay 1.75 percent.[107]

The effectiveness of the labeling program is subject to dispute. One study estimated that the incidence of child labor in looms not covered by social labeling was about 24 percent, compared to 7 to 18 percent in looms subject to labeling requirements.[108] But the high incidence of abuse has made many retailers wary of a label promising "no child labor." For example, IKEA, a Scandinavia-based home furnishing company, declined to join Rugmark's consortium because it was skeptical that the foundation could effectively monitor such a fragmented production process. IKEA estimated that there were some 175,000 looms alone in one Indian carpet belt, each accommodating two or three workers, and many located in small workshops or homes. Moreover, the company worried that a strategy focused solely on prohibition could have unwelcome by-products. For example, a crackdown on child labor in the Bangladeshi garment industry in the 1990s led to the ouster of an estimated 50,000 underage factory workers, who were then pushed into more hazardous and lower-paying occupations, including prostitution.[109] An ILO initiative to eliminate child labor in stitching soccer balls had similarly unintended consequences; home labor was eliminated to facilitate monitoring, and because cultural norms prevented women from working outside the home, some 20,000 adult female employees lost their livelihood.[110]

To address the issue, IKEA developed its own auditing system, along with a community development initiative aimed at addressing the root causes of the problem. Partnering with UNICEF, the company set up alternative learning centers for the 24,000 children in the heart of India's carpet belt who were unable to attend government-run schools. Because illness and debt were often responsible for forcing children into paid labor, the initiative also provided vaccinations and supported microenterprise.[111]

Despite the program's substantial success concerning education, health, and financial security, the company faced continued criticism for child labor. At a time when annual audits revealed between nine and thirteen cases of underage workers among some 1500 suppliers, and resulted in at least ten terminations of suppliers for ethical reasons, a British survey of trade practices gave IKEA only a half-star rating in its five-star scale. The study also encouraged consumers to consider boycotting the worst-performing stores.[112] Other companies faced similar criticism for abuses revealed in public audit procedures.

Apple's 2010 revelation of three facilities with workers under age sixteen led to significant adverse publicity.[113] Although the companies claimed that such reports revealed that their audit procedures were effective, the media coverage was largely negative.

PROBLEM 10-2

You are the vice president in charge of compliance and social responsibility for a North American corporation that sells inexpensive home furnishing products. One of your profitable product lines is carpets designed by Toronto studios and woven in India and Nepal. Rugmark Foundation has recently launched a "Most Beautiful Rug" campaign in major metropolitan areas to raise awareness about child labor in the industry.[114] An increasing number of customers have asked why all your carpets do not carry the Rugmark label. You have been unwilling to impose this requirement because you do not believe that the label can in fact ensure the absence of underage workers. Nor are you confident that children banned from looms in some of the poorest areas of your supply chain are better off as a consequence; informal reports by NGOs suggest that many end up in more hazardous occupations.

You have suggested that the company follow IKEA's audit and prevention model, but your CEO questions whether you have the resources and expertise to make such a project successful. He has preferred to direct corporate philanthropy to local community development projects that have widespread support among customers and employees. He suggests that you drop the product line entirely, which would minimize the risk of bad publicity from audits or media exposés. That would hardly be an optimal solution for impoverished workers in Nepal and India, but it might make your job easier.

1. You are preparing a report with recommendations on this issue. How should you proceed? What options might you consider? What further information would you need to make the decision? Is there anything that you could do to make consumers more aware of the complexity of the issues?
2. If you were the director of Rugmark, how would you respond to the concerns shared by this vice president and IKEA?

MEDIA RESOURCES

Many excellent movies and documentaries are available concerning transnational corporations and human rights. *Blood Diamonds, Diamonds of War,* and *Blood Diamond* examine violent conflicts financed by the diamond trade.[115] *Total Denial* recounts the history of *Doe v. Unocal,* a landmark victory under the Alien Tort Claims Act. The case involved forced labor, rape, torture, and other abuses in Burma in the 1990s, committed by government troops that provided "security" for Unocal's gas pipeline construction. An essay by lawyers representing Burmese victims in the litigation provides additional material on the human face of corporate complicity.[116]

Documentaries on child labor include:

- *A Kind of Childhood,* which documents six years in the lives of working children in Bangladesh;

- *Stolen Childhoods*, which chronicles child labor Brazil, India, the United States, Mexico, Indonesia, Kenya, and Nepal;
- *India: The Little Serfs*, which explores bonded child labor in the rug, jewelry, and mining trades;
- *Tomorrow We'll Finish*, which follows the lives of three girls in the Nepal rug trade;
- *Slavery: A Global Investigation*, which portrays bonded labor in rug-making sectors of India, in cocoa plantations in the Ivory Coast, and at the homes of World Bank officials in Washington, D.C.[117]

4. GOVERNMENTAL AND NONGOVERNMENTAL ORGANIZATIONS IN INTERNATIONAL CONFLICTS

Leaders in human rights organizations as well as in governmental and other nongovernmental organizations also confront difficult issues of principles and priorities. In a world of scarce resources, which rights are most critical to enforce? When should leaders compromise moral principles in the face of practical political imperatives? When should they privilege immediate humanitarian needs at the expense of longer-term values in reinforcing rights and deterring abuse? How should leaders reconcile universal principles with countervailing cultural norms, and when do the security concerns of activists on the ground trump broader values? How should leaders balance their own personal or organizational concerns involving reputation and legitimacy against the interests of particular victims or groups? For lawyers, how should obligations to named clients be reconciled with the concerns of broader communities, or with universal human rights principles? The following excerpts explore those dilemmas. Consider not only how you would resolve the issues raised but also the process that you believe leaders should use in making their decisions.

THOMAS POGGE, "MORAL PRIORITIES FOR INTERNATIONAL HUMAN RIGHTS NGOS"

Daniel A. Bell and Jean-Marc Coicaud, eds., Ethics in Action: The Ethical Challenges of International Human Rights Nongovernmental Organizations (New York: Cambridge University Press, 2007), pp. 218-220

We inhabit this world with large numbers of people who are very badly off through no fault of their own. The statistics are overwhelming: some 850 million human beings are chronically undernourished, 1,037 million lack access to safe water, and 2,747 million lack access to improved sanitation. About 2,000 million lack access to essential drugs. Roughly 1,000 million have no adequate shelter and 2,000 million lack electricity. Some 799 million adults are illiterate and 250 million children between ages five and fourteen do wage work outside their household—often under harsh or cruel conditions: as soldiers, prostitutes, or domestic workers, or in agriculture, construction, textile, or carpet production. Some 2,735 million people, 44 percent of humankind, are reported to be living below the World Bank's US $2/day international poverty line. Roughly one-third of all human deaths, 18 million annually or 50,000 each day, are due to poverty-related causes, readily preventable through better nutrition, safe drinking water, cheap hydration packs, vaccines, antibiotics, and other medicines. People of color, females, and the very young are heavily overrepresented among the global poor and hence also among those suffering the staggering effects of severe poverty. . . .

Seeing how much human deprivation there is and how little money to reduce it, INGOs [international nongovernmental organizations] face difficult moral decisions about how to spend the funds they collect. . . . How should [an INGO] spend such funds? This question points to an awesome responsibility because, in the world as it is, any decisions it makes are likely to affect many lives severely. To put it bluntly, an INGO must often make decisions that will certainly lead to many deaths because spending one's limited funds on trying to protect some is tantamount to leaving others to their fate.

Neera Chandhoke, "Thinking through Social and Economic Rights"

Daniel A. Bell and Jean-Marc Coicaud, eds., Ethics in Action: The Ethical Challenges of International Human Rights Nongovernmental Organizations (New York: Cambridge University Press, 2007), pp. 181-185

[S]ocial and economic rights are neither easily defined nor easily implemented. What is the degree of malnourishment, it is asked, which can be considered a violation of the right to nutrition? . . . Second, in a globalized interdependent world, where the power of governments over national resources has been drastically curtailed, which agency, it is asked, has the responsibility to uphold or implement these rights — governments, international institutions, global civil society, or the United Nations? Third, can governments be obliged to uphold social and economic rights even if they don't have the resources to do so? In that case, is the international community or, more precisely, the affluent West, obliged to furnish the individual government with resources to implement social and economic rights? . . . [Such] rights, it is argued, are not rights; they are merely a desirable state of affairs. . . .

My arguments . . . are built around the following presuppositions. First, the defense of particular human rights simultaneously articulates and validates those rights. These acts of validation serve, perhaps unintentionally, to downgrade other rights. This point may be important because given the political economy of the global order, human rights movements based in the West happen to exert an inordinate amount of influence in the way human rights movements based in the South do or do not privilege certain rights. Second, many countries in the world are characterized by such dire hunger, poverty, and homelessness that any talk of human rights that does not take these issues into account can be considered unfinished and inadequate. There may of course be a fine conceptual difference between a young person dying as a result of intentional action by the state, such as torture, and a person dying because the state refuses to heed the problem of silent hunger that stalks many countries of the South. Yet both "intentional" and "unintentional" actions of the state lead to similar outcomes: loss of human life. Do not acts of omission as well as those of commission constitute violations of the basic right to life? Third, I assume that the state has obligations that are far deeper and far more morally compelling than those of nonintervention in the affairs of its citizens. These obligations lie in the realm of providing for its own people.

I assume that the legitimacy of states resides in their ability to provide the minimal conditions that allow citizens to live with some modicum of dignity. . . .

The issue at hand is simply this: which human rights do human rights INGOs consider worthy of defense, and which human rights do they consider possible to defend? Or do they defend only those rights that these organizations find it possible to defend? This question is important given the great power of human rights INGOs over the setting of the human rights agenda.

NOTES AND QUESTIONS

1. How should human rights organizations establish priorities for their work? Who should play a role in the decision-making process? How should organizations be held accountable for their choices? Little information is available on those issues. To the extent that these INGOs are similar to other public-interest groups, leaders and upper-level staff are likely to play a dominant role. In one study of fifty prominent public-interest legal organizations in the United States, only about a quarter reported that their priority-setting process made efforts to include the organization's members or other stakeholders such as clients or community groups. Only a third reported extensive or even moderate influence from their boards of directors, and about two-fifths reported moderate influence from funders.[118] Such independence gave leaders and their staff considerable discretion in determining what constituted the public interest and how best to advance it. Among the common criteria considered were:
   • Where could the group make the most impact?
   • What problems were most urgent?
   • What were the chances for success?
   • What· could the organization do that other groups could not?
   • Would the work attract support from the public, donors, and funders?[119]
     What other questions might be relevant for human rights leaders? Do they help resolve the dilemmas that Bell and Carens describe below?
2. To what extent can social and economic rights be institutionalized in impoverished nations? What strategies are most likely to be effective?
3. How should leaders with influence over prosecutorial policy set priorities in contexts such as Darfur, described in problem 10-4 below? How should officials balance the values of bringing perpetrators of abuse to justice against the risks of prolonging abuse? Consider such issues in light of the materials that follow.

DANIEL A. BELL AND JOSEPH H. CARENS, "THE ETHICAL DILEMMAS OF INTERNATIONAL HUMAN RIGHTS AND HUMANITARIAN NGOS: REFLECTIONS ON A DIALOGUE BETWEEN PRACTITIONERS AND THEORISTS"

Human Rights Quarterly 26 (2004):300-329

I. Introduction

International human rights and humanitarian nongovernmental organizations (INGOs) are major players on the world stage. They fund human rights projects, actively participate in human rights and humanitarian work, and criticize human rights violations in foreign lands. They work in cooperative networks with each other, with local NGOs, and with international organizations. They consult and lobby governments and international organizations, sometimes participating in high level negotiations and diplomacy for global policy development. They cooperate and negotiate with the same economic and political organizations in the field for the implementation of their projects, whether this be monitoring or assistance. In short, they are generating a new type of political power, the purpose of which is to secure the vital interests of human beings on an international scale, regardless of state boundaries.

Needless to say, good intentions are not always sufficient to produce desirable results. In an imperfect and unpredictable world, INGOs often face ethical dilemmas that constrain their efforts to do good in foreign lands. This paper draws upon a recent dialogue between leading representatives of different kinds of human rights and humanitarian INGOs and academics of different backgrounds and disciplines who work on the subject of human rights in order to identify some of the typical ethical dilemmas encountered by INGOs during the course of their work, and to discuss some of the advantages and disadvantages associated with different ways of dealing with those dilemmas. We identify four kinds of ethical dilemmas frequently faced by INGOs: conflicts between human rights principles and local cultural norms; the tension between expanding the organization's mandate to address more fundamental problems and restricting it for the sake of providing immediate help or for the sake of feasibility; whether and how to collaborate with governments, including ones who are themselves responsible for human rights violations; and how to raise the money required for the organization's work without compromising or subverting the organization's mission in the process. . . .

II. Dilemma One: The Conflict between Human Rights and Local Cultural Norms

Most human rights and humanitarian INGOs are based in the West. With their executives and offices centralized in key Western cities, program officers and coordinators are then sent to the field. . . . From a practical point of view, this may pose a special challenge in foreign lands where detailed knowledge of different linguistic, social, cultural, and economic circumstances is more likely to ensure success. INGO workers are not always familiar with these, or trained beforehand to face unexpected complications, or to deal with subtle behavioral nuances of people who have different social and political customs. It is not merely a strategic matter of understanding "the other" for the purpose of promoting one's views, however. INGO representatives also experience ethical conflicts where they must decide between promoting their versions of human rights norms and respecting local cultural norms that may differ from these. There are different ways of dealing with this conflict, and below we list some of the possible responses along with their associated advantages and disadvantages.

A. Tolerating Clashing Beliefs

Ndubisi Obiorah, Senior Legal Officer of HURILAWS in Lagos, Nigeria, noted that many Nigerian NGOs work with INGOs but pointed out that, in relation to the subject of advocacy activities undertaken by INGOs in Nigeria, it would be very difficult, given local cultural and religious beliefs widely prevalent at the present time in Nigeria, to press vigorously for gay and lesbian rights in Nigeria. In such cases, representatives of human rights INGOs that would otherwise try to promote gay and lesbian rights need, in the immediate to medium term, to refrain from a high-decibel "naming and shaming" approach in acting upon (or speaking about) this aspect of their mandate. They would need to tolerate, without respecting, the negative views of many people in Nigeria on gay and lesbian rights. This approach carries the advantage that other aspects of their mandate may stand a greater chance of success. The cost, however, is that it sends the message that gay and lesbian rights can be sacrificed on the altar of other values. Strong defenders of these rights may well question why the INGO needs to work in Nigeria as opposed to other places where they needn't suppress an important part of their ethical mandate. . . .

B. Challenging Local Cultural Norms

Habitat for Humanity is an INGO that was founded in the U.S. in 1976 with the goal of helping people to acquire adequate housing, which the organization sees as a basic human right and a prerequisite for the effective enjoyment of many other human rights. According to Steven Weir, the Asia and Pacific Director of Habitat, the organization's best practice standards require that local boards be diverse and representative of the community at large, including 30 percent representation by women. Moreover, many affiliates require that the women's names be included on the land title as a condition of the loan. But Weir adds that these requirements can be contrary to cultural norms and legal regulations in some countries. Still, he suggests that challenging these norms can be effective:

> In most developing countries, reaching gender equity and full participation is a slow process. A typical local affiliate (governing board) begins with the women serving tea, sitting quietly in the back, and evolves to their participation on the family selection and support subcommittees, finally developing into full participation on all committees, often including chairing the family selection and support committees. Some affiliates in traditionally male-dominated societies even eventually elect women as board presidents.

Weir's account here paints a happy outcome. At the same time, he acknowledges that the organization does make compromises with local communities. It does not simply come into a place and insist that it conform to the organization's norms in every respect, including its practices with regard to gender, not only because such a demand would be impractical but also because it would conflict with the organization's commitment to local participation and control over the process. . . . [T]here may also be some resistance given the developing world's history of experience with "cultural imperialism." . . .

III. Dilemma Two: The Tension between Expanding and Limiting the Organization's Mandate

Many humanitarian and human rights INGOs begin with a particular focus and then feel pressure to expand their concerns so as to deal with the broader, underlying forces that give rise to the particular problem they are addressing. For example, Oxfam, as the name suggests, began as a famine relief organization. The organization gradually came to believe, however, that it was not enough to relieve the immediate suffering of those caught up in a famine situation. It was equally or more important to address the underlying conditions that gave rise to situations where people found themselves in desperate need for food. Consequently, much of Oxfam's work today deals with problems of economic and social development. Yet, no organization can do everything, and if an organization fails to focus on concrete tasks where it can actually make a difference, its activities may be scattered and ineffective. Moreover, if one focuses only on the big picture, one risks losing sight of real human beings in need. . . .

A. Amnesty International and Human Rights Watch

Amnesty International is the oldest and largest human rights INGO. AI had traditionally concentrated exclusively on violations of civil and political (CP) rights. In 2001, it officially expanded its mission to include economic, social, and cultural (ESC) rights within its ambit of concern. This was not a simple decision for the organization. It followed lengthy internal discussions. . . .

First, the focus on civil and political rights had sometimes led to misguided priorities that implicitly downplayed or ignored the sometimes more serious areas of human suffering. [Curt Goering, executive director of Amnesty International, USA] mentions two cases: One example frequently cited in internal debates was Sudan, where in 1994 the government engaged in massive displacement of local populations and destruction of their crops and food reserves. It was difficult to explain why AI treated the shooting and torture of a few victims as human rights violations and the manufactured starvation of thousands as background. Another example was Afghanistan. The warring factions opposed to the government imposed a total road blockade on Kabul in 1996. AI denounced the indiscriminate killings from daily bombings, but said little about the starvation resulting from the blockade. . . .

Second, there was strong support for an expansion of AI's mandate among its branches in the "South." As Goering notes,

> [a]s an international human rights organization, AI has taken important steps over the past several years to become a truly multicultural organization. Yet, the focus of its work — the selection of which categories of human rights violations to actively research and campaign against reflected, some felt, a "Northern" bias or preference for work civil and political rights, instead of ESC rights. Many people and NGOs in the "Global South" and a growing number in the "North" felt that AI's narrow mandate with its limited serious work on violations of ESC rights was a barrier to inclusion of people whose views on this issue differed from the prevailing "Northern consensus." And importantly to an organization that strived to be truly international, the civil and political focus was also seen as a barrier to development of AI's structure and membership in the South. This was seen to undermine AI's credibility in general with important audiences.

. . . Third, AI responded to the argument that its CP focus was biased towards male concerns. To quote Goering once again: "Some noted that women's experience of human rights is often different to men's: property rights and reproductive rights, and the rights to health, education and nutrition were some of these areas. In addition, by maintaining the distinction, AI limited its opportunities for cooperation with other civil society and human rights groups at a time when coalition work was becoming ever more critical in advancing a human rights agenda."

In the end, the vast majority of AI members found the arguments for expanding the formal mission of the organization to include ESC rights more persuasive than the arguments for the status quo. But expanding the formal mission does not eliminate the tensions reflected in this debate; it simply moves them to another forum, namely, the question of how best to promote ESC rights. This was illustrated by the contribution to the conference from Ken Roth, the Executive Director of Human Rights Watch. . . . .

Like AI, HRW had traditionally focused exclusively on civil and political rights, and like AI it expanded its concerns to include ESC rights. . . . In Roth's view, international human rights organizations like HRW (as distinct from national and local ones) tend to be most effective when they employ the methodology that he calls "shaming": investigating, documenting, and publicizing behavior by states (and some non-state actors) that conflicts with widely accepted public moral expectations. As Roth puts it,

> [i]n my view, the most productive way for international human rights organizations like Human Rights Watch to address ESC rights is by building on the power of our methodology. The essence of that methodology . . . is not the ability to mobilize people in the streets, to engage in litigation, to press for broad national plans to realize ESC rights, or to provide technical assistance. Rather, the core of our methodology is our ability to investigate, expose, and shame. We are at our most effective when we can hold governmental (or, in some cases, nongovernmental) conduct up to a disapproving public.

For the shaming methodology to work, Roth says, "clarity is needed around three issues: violation, violator, and remedy. That is, we must be able to show persuasively that a particular state of affairs amounts to a violation of human rights standards, that a particular violator is principally responsible, and that there is a widely accepted remedy for the violation." . . .

In some circumstances in which ESC rights are involved, however, Roth thinks that the three preconditions of effective shaming cannot be met, and in those circumstances international human rights organizations should cede the field to local and national NGOs, because the INGOs will not be able to have any significant impact on the problem. If people lack adequate food or health care, for example, one can say that their human rights are not being respected, but unless one can trace these lacks to the arbitrary or discriminatory actions of a government, intergovernmental organization, or organized nongovernmental actor such as a corporation or a rebel group, it will not be possible to use the shaming methodology to bring about change. Roth puts it this way:

> [G]iven that respect for ESC rights often requires the reallocation of resources, the people who have the clearest standing to insist on a particular allocation are usually the residents of the country in question. Outsiders such as international human rights organizations are certainly free to have a say in

such matters, but in an imperfect world in which the fulfillment of one ESC right is often at the expense of another, their voice has less legitimacy in insisting on a particular tradeoff than does that of the country's residents. Why should outsiders be listened to when they counsel, for example, that less be spent on health care and more on education—or even that less be spent on roads, bridges or other infrastructure deemed important for long-term economic development, and more on immediate needs?

Roth is careful to point out that his argument applies only to international human rights organizations working in countries away from their organizational base, not to local and national NGOs which often employ other methodologies besides shaming (such as political mobilization) and have clearer standing to speak out about the proper direction of politically contested national policies in their own states. Roth specifies that his argument does not apply to INGOs addressing the domestic or foreign policy of their "home" governments, where they have standing comparable to that of a local human rights group.

It is striking how many of the concerns that appeared in the internal AI debate as reasons not to expand AI's concerns to include ESC rights reappear here as reasons to limit the scope of the activities of international human rights organizations. In both cases we find a concern about the effectiveness of the organization's work being undermined by overreaching. There are the same worries about a lack of normative consensus on principles, a lack of clarity about standards, the absence of expertise, the depletion of moral capital, the loss of focus, and the same sense that the organization will waste scarce resources unless it sticks to what it is good at and leaves certain problems and issues to others.

In many ways, the reactions to Roth's line of argument at the conference mirrored the reactions to the arguments in favor of limiting Amnesty's concerns to civil and political rights. The critics at the conference did not accept Roth's view that there is such a tight link between the effectiveness of international human rights organizations and the methodology of shaming. What Roth saw as pragmatic, they saw as unduly cautious and conservative. They feared that restricting the activities of international human rights organizations in the way Roth recommended might impede rather than contribute to the development of the international human rights movement and might fail to address the most important human rights issues of our times. . . .

One problem with relying on shaming is that people in the South often understandably resent any apparent claim of moral superiority from the North, given the role of the North, past and present, in the South. If international human rights organizations spend their energies in the South on exposing the moral failings of those in the South, this is apt to be experienced as carrying with it a tone of moral superiority, even if the failings are real, there is no intention to claim moral superiority, and the same INGOs also criticize Northern states (as HRW, for example, clearly does). Equally important, as Roth's critics at the conference argued, if human rights NGOs in the South rely primarily on methods other than shaming in their work (and Roth himself says that this may be appropriate for them), they will have less basis for cooperative work with international human rights organizations that focus exclusively on shaming activities in the South than for ones that take a broader approach to their human rights work there. This could undermine the sense that there is a genuinely *international* human rights movement in which participants in both the North and the South share common projects and common agendas. . . .

The second set of objections to Roth's approach was concerned with the danger that a focus on what international human rights organizations can do well might draw attention away from what is really important. If the most severe and extensive violations of human rights stem not from the misbehavior of authoritarian rulers but from the global maldistribution of wealth and power and from structural features of the international political and economic systems, then to limit the activities of international human rights organizations to problems where there are clear standards, a clear culprit, and a clear remedy may render the organizations irrelevant to the most important struggles for justice today. . . .

B. Humanitarian INGOs

. . . [H]umanitarian INGOs often experience tensions between the aim of doing good by helping in an emergency and the aim of promoting justice by reforming institutions or policies. [Médecins Sans Frontières (MSF), also known as Doctors Without Borders,] presents itself as an organization that does not take sides between different political ideologies and institutional arrangements. Its sole purpose is to alleviate suffering and aid those in need. This has the apparent advantage of avoiding controversy and appealing to many individuals and groups of different ideologies. In some cases, however, the policy of "neutrality" can carry a high price.

Such neutrality might mean tolerating, or refraining from criticizing, evil actions that contribute to the suffering in the first place. Eric Dachy, Senior Researcher for the Belgium branch of MSF, raised the hypothetical example of a humanitarian INGO that sets up a nutritional center to feed children. The INGO subsequently finds out that the army only lets members of one ethnic group through a military checkpoint established ten kilometers outside the nutritional center. Should the INGO feed the children, thus tolerating ethnic cleansing, or should it let the children starve? Dachy suggested that MSF should feed the children.

In practice, however, MSF acted differently when faced with an actual choice between confronting an evil government and saving lives in the early 1970s:

> The Ethiopian famines of the early 1970s resulted from government policies of the Derg under Mengistu, which employed starvation as a means of control. Most of the NGOs working to alleviate this humanitarian crisis refrained from publicly challenging the government's human rights record, policies, cover-up of the cholera epidemic, and conduct of civil war in the northern part of the country based on the precept that they should avoid politics. *Médicins sans frontières* (Doctors Without Borders) expressed opposition to the government in this case, and was expelled. Hence, it seems safe to assume that silence in the face of abuses was necessary if the starving were to be fed.

. . . Plunging into the political fray and actively campaigning for institutional reform, however, can carry some costs. It may be more difficult to secure funding from governments and foundations that are keen to avoid political controversy, particularly in areas where, as Roth put it, "respectable arguments" can be marshaled on both sides of the dispute. Such political INGOs may lose their moral authority once they are seen as interested parties. The probability of success is often lower than direct humanitarian relief.

Another disadvantage of the political approach is that INGO representatives themselves can become targets if they are seen to take sides. Rony Brauman, former head of MSF, was critical of food drops by the US military in Afghanistan because they blurred the boundaries between military intervention and humanitarian relief, thus endangering relief workers on the ground: "We are viewed as people coming from abroad, maybe having direct relations with Western powers. If a Western power confirms this impression, then we become really part of the military drive, and we as aid workers can become transformed into war targets."

Perhaps the most serious moral issue for defenders of the political approach is the possibility that some individuals may be sacrificed on the altar of the greater political good. Eric Dachy condemns the institutional donors who are making the resumption of humanitarian aid in the Democratic Republic of Congo conditional upon the resumption of peace negotiations on precisely these grounds: "[This aid] is necessary in the short term in order to prevent deaths from epidemics and because of the lack of basic health care. It is therefore criminal to delay the provision of aid in this way and it constitutes a sort of hostage-taking of the population."

IV. Dilemma Three: Whether or Not to Collaborate with Governments

Human rights INGOs grapple with the question of whether or not to collaborate with governments in order to help remedy human rights violations. Different organizations adopt different strategies, but we can distinguish two basic stances: collaboration and criticism.

A. The Collaborators

Some organizations focus on the necessity of working with governments, even less-than-democratic governments, such as that of China, in order to achieve any improvement in human rights or any success in pursuing humanitarian goals. It is obvious that such governments do not welcome critical perspectives from outside forces (not to mention inside forces), which puts human rights and humanitarian INGOs in a difficult position. Nonetheless, organizations such as the Ford Foundation and the Danish Centre for Human Rights (DCHR) are actively involved in human rights projects in China and other countries with less-than-democratic governments.

In China, the Ford Foundation has been establishing and developing grant-making activities in areas such as judicial reforms, legal aid, and constitutional law research. Such projects are explicitly designed to promote greater awareness and respect for individual rights and concern for the worst-off groups in society. Effective implementation of these projects is premised upon successful collaboration with government officials and institutions, notwithstanding appearances. . . .

The Danish Centre for Human Rights adopts a similar cooperative approach. This government-funded agency (its largest funder is the Royal Danish Ministry of Foreign Affairs) has been funding and supporting various human rights projects in China, including a program concerned with the prevention of the use of torture and ill-treatment by police in the pre-trial phase, another program designed to train Chinese legal scholars and practitioners in European law and practice, a human rights center in a provincial capital, a project providing legal aid to women, and a death penalty study. As with the Ford Foundation, the activities of the DCHR require active collaboration with the government sector: "In authoritarian states, where the local NGOs might be few or non-existent within certain sectors, cooperation with governments might be the only option." It would be a mistake, the DCHR implies, to always view less-than-democratic governments as evil perpetrators of human rights abuses. Sometimes, government officials are sincerely committed to improving the rights situation in selected areas. Where human rights violations do occur, this may be "due to institutional inertia rather than to active state willed perpetration of violations." It could also be due to lack of technical skills and know-how, and the government might welcome INGO aid in this respect. In sum, "the successful cases demonstrate that it is indeed possible to obtain very good results even in authoritarian regimes."

B. The Critics

There are, of course, also disadvantages linked to this partnership with less-than-democratic governments approach. The most obvious is that human rights organizations working in China often choose to "avoid politically sensitive issues" such as labor rights, press freedom, and the political rights of dissidents and "avoid politically sensitive places" such as Tibet and Xinjiang.

Another potential disadvantage is that human rights INGOs that cooperate with less-than-democratic governments may grant moral legitimacy to those governments, thus postponing the day of reckoning. The authors of a report titled "Promoting Human Rights in China" express their doubts regarding those who favor engaging the Chinese government on human rights issues: "In general the Chinese government has succeeded in taking control of standard setting for engagement programs and has shaped these programs so that their impact on human rights practices is slight. . . . In some cases the dialogue process has become a substitute for more critical approaches that could generate real pressure for change." One has only to recall how many corporations and governments opposed policies of disinvestment and other economic sanctions against the apartheid regime in South Africa, arguing instead for policies of constructive engagement. In retrospect it seems clear that constructive engagement was far less effective than sanctions in assisting the transition to a new South Africa. This is not to imply that the current Chinese government ranks on the same scale of injustice as the former apartheid regime, but similar worries may arise.

Another disadvantage of collaboration was raised by Ken Roth of HRW. The DCHR argues for an international "division of labor," with organizations such as AI and HRW adopting a confrontational approach and documenting violations and lobbying for international criticism while "engagers" such as the DCHR and similar organizations cooperate with the government on long-term rights projects. Roth pointed out, however, that there are trade-offs because less-than-democratic governments can use their cooperation with the "engagers" as evidence that their policies on human rights are not so bad and are getting better, thus weakening the force of criticisms put forward by other organizations.

It is inevitable, of course, that any human rights reforms or humanitarian efforts will be trumpeted for public relations purposes, and INGOs must always try to determine whether the substantive merits of the changes are worth the public relations advantage that the targets of their efforts will obtain with a particular reform. . . .

V. Dilemma Four: The Ethical Limits of Fund-Raising

The need to raise funds has also generated debates within human rights and humanitarian INGOs. The source of funding and the means employed to raise funds both raise ethical questions. . . . One important area of controversy is the issue of government funding for INGOs. Many INGOs do accept government funds and the main advantage, of course, is that they can carry out their projects without wasting too much time and money on fund-raising efforts. This raises questions regarding their independence, however. . . . Governments can force agendas onto reluctant human rights organizations. . . .

The INGOs that rely more on confrontational approaches have been particularly wary of dependence on government funding. . . . Human Rights Watch, as Widney Brown explains, "has an absolute prohibition on accepting funds either directly or indirectly from governments. This prohibition is aimed at avoiding even the appearance of undue government influence on any choices or investigations made by Human Rights Watch and to avoid the inference that the organization is implicitly endorsing a government as not being a human rights violator."

NOTES AND QUESTIONS

"Charity creates a multitude of sins," said Oscar Wilde, and recent humanitarian crises have confirmed the truth of that observation. Some of the most agonizing dilemmas for relief organizations arise in war-torn regions when aid to victims fuels the fighting that creates their victimization. Fiona Terry describes this as the "paradox of humanitarian action: It can contradict its fundamental purpose by prolonging the suffering it intends to alleviate."[120] An example occurred in the camps for Rwandan refugees across the border in Zaire, which became staging grounds for guerilla raids and extortionate schemes that diverted humanitarian assistance to military activities.[121] Similar problems have arisen in other conflict zones, including Afghanistan, Biafra, Bosnia, and Somalia.[122] Aid can also reinforce dependency and divert resources from addressing the fundamental social, economic, and political problems that make aid necessary.[123] As Sadako Ogata, the former UN High Commissioner of Refugees, put it, "there are no humanitarian solutions to humanitarian problems."[124] The problems are compounded by the understandable reluctance of NGOs to address them publicly. In the struggle for public sympathy and donor dollars, most leaders find it unproductive to air the abuses and limitations of aid.[125] But that reticence also impedes organizational learning and informed deliberation.

Are there ways to hold NGOs more accountable for the adverse unintended by-products from their assistance? If not, what special obligations does that impose on leaders to engage with the human rights community about second-best solutions to humanitarian dilemmas?

Another of these dilemmas involves policies that condition assistance on political neutrality. For example, as part of the "with us or against us" philosophy of some American presidents, the administration of George H.W. Bush required international NGOs in Iraq to refrain from public criticism of U.S. policy as a condition of retaining government funding and support. Activist Lyal Sunga describes the problem. How would you respond?

Lyal S. Sunga, "Dilemmas Facing NGOs in Coalition-Occupied Iraq"

Daniel A. Bell and Jean-Marc Coicaud, eds., Ethics in Action: The Ethical
Challenges of International Human Rights Nongovernmental
Organizations (New York: Cambridge University Press, 2007),
pp. 99, 110-114.

Not to speak out against the launch of a war—an event that inevitably causes or worsens humanitarian situations—or to refrain from criticizing violations during armed conflict that cause human suffering, in many cases would seem blatantly unethical. However, an NGO's denunciation of a government's violations can undercut the NGO's provision of humanitarian assistance on a politically neutral and impartial basis at ground level.

This ethical dilemma involves also difficult political and practical dilemmas for NGOs. Humanitarian NGOs can work much more effectively where they form part of an overall, integrated approach to reconstruction and relief efforts so as to avoid duplication and maximize the effective use of scarce resources in their totality. . . . At the practical level, coordination and integration in relief efforts requires cooperation among UN agencies, bodies, and programs, country authorities, and humanitarian NGOs. However, highly critical NGO political advocacy can jeopardize such coordination and cooperation, particularly when NGOs have to rely on occupation Powers for security and other forms of logistical support to gain access to people in need of humanitarian assistance. . . . If NGOs are seen as opponents of the war, they risk being shut out of occupying Power operational strategy and planning, as NGOs in fact have been in coalition-occupied Iraq, and this can severely hamper the aid effort. Access under security provided by armed forces almost always comes at a price, and that price can be the image if not the fact of neutrality and impartiality. . . .

One way to solve this dilemma could be to adopt the approach taken by the International Committee of the Red Cross (ICRC), which, although neither an intergovernmental organization nor an NGO, exemplifies a strictly neutral and impartial approach to humanitarian relief operations in war zones. The

ICRC refuses to take any side in hostilities or engage at any time in any political, racial, religious, or ideological controversy whatsoever. On this basis, the ICRC has been more successful than any intergovernmental or nongovernmental body in gaining the confidence and respect of all sides to an armed conflict. This in turn has afforded ICRC delegates an unrivaled degree of access to detainees, prisoners of war, refugees, internally displaced persons, and other persons protected by the Geneva Conventions of 1949. The ICRC's unique history, image, and role make it difficult for humanitarian NGOs to emulate its example, however.

Would humanitarian NGOs be willing to give up political advocacy to guard their neutrality and impartiality in the field? Probably not. Political advocacy forms an essential activity for many NGOs. Aside from its obvious value as an instrument to influence decision making on the part of governments and intergovernmental organizations, it also enhances public visibility, helps to generate funds, and increases membership. Moreover, many humanitarian NGOs might consider that, in any case, armed conflict zones inevitably involve NGOs in politically controversial issues. For any NGO wishing to speak out on political issues, the ICRC's approach of strict neutrality again would be difficult to follow.

PROBLEM 10-3

Darfur is a region in western Sudan that has been plagued by violence for the last two decades. The conflict involves the Janjaweed, Arab camel-herding nomads who migrated to the region in the 1970s, and the local African farming tribes. Tension between the Janjaweed and the tribes escalated in the late 1990s due to increased drought, competition for scarce resources, and the availability of weapons.[126]

In 2003, the government and Janjaweed mounted a full-scale coordinated attack upon the African tribes. While the government forces pursued aerial bombardment, the Janjaweed moved in on horseback. The attackers employed "scorched-earth" tactics, leaving many villages almost entirely destroyed. Between 2003 and 2004, an estimated 200,000-400,000 Africans were killed and 2.5 million displaced. The killings were ethnically motivated and met the international human rights community's definition of genocide.[127]

Those responsible for the killings included officials at the highest levels of the Sudanese government. Relying on eyewitness accounts, on-the-ground investigations, government documents, and secondary sources, human rights workers determined that Sudanese President Omar al-Bashir and other senior government officials were personally involved in orchestrating the violence.[128] It continued despite intense international pressure from the human rights community and efforts from the United Nations, African Union, and the United States.[129]

In March 2005, the Security Council formally referred the situation in Darfur to the Prosecutor of the International Criminal Court.[130] The Prosecutor found reasonable grounds to believe that President Omar al-Bashir was responsible for the violence, and in 2009, a warrant was issued for his arrest for war crimes and crimes against humanity.[131] In retaliation, he expelled twenty-nine foreign NGOs from Sudan. Their departure put an end to projects supplying food, clean water, healthcare, and other essential services. The consequences were devastating because years of protracted violence and displacements had made many Sudanese dependent on humanitarian aid.[132]

1. If you had been the Prosecutor for the International Criminal Court, would you have recommended bringing the indictment against Omar al-Bashir even if you had anticipated that the charges would result in denying essential humanitarian relief? How would you balance the need to deter genocidal campaigns against the need to assist those victimized by violence?

2. Imagine that you represent the United States on the UN Security Council. Two of the five permanent members, Russia and China, are allies of Sudan and are known to supply most of the weapons used by the Sudanese government in Darfur.[133] These members oppose referring the matter to the ICC Prosecutor and invoke concerns about jeopardizing humanitarian efforts. How do you respond and what ethical and strategic considerations would be most relevant?

3. A similar situation arose in Uganda, where the Lord's Resistance Arm (LRA), led by Joseph Kony, orchestrated a rebellion resulting in horrific human rights violations, particularly against the Acholi population. An estimated 30,000 children were abducted for military service or sexual slavery, and over a million people were displaced. In 2003, at the invitation of the Ugandan government, the International Criminal Court began investigating the LRA and in 2005 issued arrest warrants for five LRA leaders, including Kony. A year later, peace talks began and the leaders insisted on amnesty.[134] Government and NGO officials faced not only complicated issues of how best to secure lasting stability for the region, but also of how to decide that question. How much should it matter whether most Acholi people saw prosecution as an important end in itself, or only valuable if it contributed to the peace process? How could their views be adequately registered in the decision-making process?

4. Another issue of how the international community should respond to atrocities arose in Kosovo in 1999. At the time of the crisis, Kosovo was an autonomous province of Serbia, populated mainly by Albanians but considered by Serbians to be at the center of their religious and cultural history. During the 1980s, the growing strength of Albanians in Kosovo prompted Serbian claims of "physical, political, legal, and cultural genocide," and set the stage for the rise of nationalist leader Slobodan Milosevic.[135] His presidency brought a revocation of Kosovo's independent status, and efforts to oust Albanians from the area. The escalating conflict, including mass rapes and murders, failed to prompt action from the United Nations Security Council, which, under the UN Charter, has primary responsibility for international peacekeeping. When it became clear that China and/or Russia were likely to veto any Security Council action, NATO emerged as the only multilateral force able to avert a massacre comparable to the 1994 genocide in Rwanda. There, as the world stood by, some 500,000 to 1,000,000 Tutsis were killed in less than 100 days.[136]

To address the Kosovo crisis, NATO launched a seventy-eight-day air-strike against strategic Yugoslavian targets. Although successful in helping to end the armed conflict, the action also triggered widespread condemnation. The strikes resulted in at least 2000 civilian deaths, with thousands more injured; the casualties exceeded the number of Albanians killed in Kosovo in the months preceding the air war.[137] Although then President Clinton claimed that the action was justified on humanitarian grounds, critics noted his failure to distinguish many other situations of greater atrocities in which no action was taken.[138] Under international law, the only justification for the action was a much debated doctrine of humanitarian intervention. It permits a necessary and proportional invasion of another nation's territory if it is the only way to prevent atrocities. A Ministerial Declaration by the foreign ministers of the Group of 77 spoke for 138 countries in rejecting the doctrine under such circumstances.[139] The Independent International Commission on Kosovo concluded that NATO's intervention was illegal but justified.[140]

How should leaders resolve such issues? Was the governing principle in Kosovo that "force may be used if the United States thinks force would be a good idea"?[141] What would you have done in President Clinton's position? What considerations should inform the process of leaders balancing incommensurable values, such as preventing mass atrocities versus establishing precedents that invite international escalation of internal strife?

PROBLEM 10-4

Since 2000, twelve Nigerian states have added criminal law to the jurisdiction of Muslim Sharia courts. Human rights activists worried that this transfer of authority would violate fundamental rights such as procedural due process, access to legal representation, and protection from coercive interrogation. They were also concerned about widespread judicial corruption and sex discrimination in Sharia courts.[142]

In March of 2002, a Nigerian Sharia court sentenced Amina Lawal to death by stoning for adultery, after she gave birth to a child out of wedlock following her divorce. At the time, Ms. Lawal was thirty years old and already had three children. Although she identified the father, he was not convicted due to lack of evidence. BAOBAB for Women's Human Rights, a Nigerian-based NGO, represented her in the proceedings.[143]

Although Lawal's case was not unique, the human rights community gave it widespread international attention. While the appeal was pending before a state Sharia court, activists employed typical "naming and shaming" tactics, such as letter-writing campaigns and political efforts to pressure the state or federal appellate Sharia courts to overturn her conviction or sentence, or to convince the government to grant her a pardon. The campaign was featured on the Oprah Winfrey show, and several contestants threatened to boycott the Miss World beauty pageant, originally scheduled to be held in Nigeria in 2002.[144]

However, despite the overwhelming international attention Lawal's story brought to human rights violations in general and to Nigerian women in particular, local NGO activists denounced the letter-writing campaign. BAO-BAB released a public statement noting that many of the petitions and letters "are inaccurate and ineffective and may even be damaging to her case and those of others in similar situations."[145] The statement raised several concerns. One was that erroneous facts and stereotypical assumptions about the inherent unfairness of Sharia courts would undermine the credibility of local human rights efforts. Contrary to the assertions of many international activists, Lawal was in no immediate danger and none of the other, similar sentences against women had been carried out. Her case was still on appeal, and Sharia appellate courts were known for greater sensitivity to gender equity issues than lower courts. "If there is an immediate physical danger to Ms. Lawal and others," the statement argued, "it is from vigilante and political . . . (over)reaction to international attempts at pressure." A cautionary example was a case in which an unmarried teenager convicted of extramarital sex was flogged "not despite national and international pressure [but] . . . deliberately to defy it." A local government had ignored a judicial order and carried out the sentence, partly in response to what the governor described as "letters from infidels."[146]

Another concern was that reliance on letter writing for a single victim over the objections of local groups risked "campaign fatigue" and undermined efforts of organizations with greatest legitimacy and expertise. Activists could not target all of those at risk and the Lawal initiative betrayed an "arrogance in assuming that international human rights organizations know better than those directly involved." The BAOBAB statement asked Lawal's supporters "to recognize that an international protest letter campaign is not necessarily the most productive way to act in every situation. On the contrary, women's rights defenders should assess potential backlash effects before devising strategies."[147] According to the statement, a more productive approach in the Lawal case and others like it would be to provide financial support for victims and for local organizations representing them. Safe havens were urgently needed to protect women from vigilante action, and additional resources were essential to support effective legal advocacy.

On appeal, Ms. Lawal's conviction was overturned.[148] After the case was resolved, human rights activists continued to argue about whether the case was illustrative of a successful or counterproductive international effort.[149]

NOTES AND QUESTIONS

1. If you had been in a leadership role at an international women's rights organization, what would you have done about Lawal's case? Would your strategies have changed after reading BAOBAB's press release? Why do you suppose international organizations chose to make the case a cause célèbre rather than to marshal support for local women's groups representing Lawal and similar victims? How should human rights activists balance the sometimes competing goals of raising public awareness and support for human rights violations and of maximizing the likelihood of success in a particular case? How should those decisions be made?

2. If you had been the director of BAOBAB, would you have done anything differently?

3. If you were in a leadership position in the human rights community, what broader lessons would you draw from the Lawal case? Compare the Nigerian case to one involving a Congolese woman who had been repeatedly raped by prison guards. After her escape, she applied for asylum in the United States. A federal appellate court found her story credible, but ruled that asylum law did not apply. A San Francisco lawyer, handling the case pro bono, marshaled human rights activists to register their protest with the Department of Justice. After receipt of some 10,000 letters, the Department agreed to support a motion to reopen the case, and the woman ultimately won asylum.[150] Does a comparison of this case with the Lawal campaign suggest broader lessons about when letter writing is most likely to be effective?

4. Sally Merry notes that in a world of "limited enforcement mechanisms . . . the impact of human rights law is [a] matter of persuasion rather than force, of cultural transformation rather than coercive change."[151] What does this imply in contexts in which international principles of gender equality clash with community practices of gender subordination?

MEDIA RESOURCES

A number of excellent documentaries are available on the Kosovo crisis and subsequent prosecutions.[152] The leadership dilemma for Bill Clinton and Great Britain's prime minister Tony Blair is explored in an HBO docudrama, *The Special Relationship*. Reports on Darfur and on oil wars and human rights issues in Nigeria illustrate the complexities of leading effective intervention efforts.[153]

END NOTES

1. Sarah Anderson, John Cavanagh, and Thea Lee, Field Guide to the Global Economy, Corporate vs. Country Economic Clout: The Top 100 (New York: New Press, 2005), 69.

2. Thomas Hobbes, Leviathan, Part II, Ch. 29 (1651).

3. Joel Bakan, The Corporation: The Pathological Pursuit of Profit and Power (Toronto: Viking Canada, 2004); Robert Reich, Supercapitalism: The Transformation of Business, Democracy, and Everyday Life (New York: Knopf, 2007).

4. Howard R. Bowen, Social Responsibilities of the Businessman (New York: Harper and Row, 1953), 6. For an overview, see Archie B. Carroll, A History of Corporate Social Responsibility: Concepts and Practices, in Andrew Crane, Abagail McWilliams, Dirk Matten, Jeremy Moon, and Donald S. Spiegel, eds., The Oxford Handbook of Corporate Social Responsibility (New York: Oxford University Press, 2008), 19.

5. Archie B Carroll, A Three-Dimensional Conceptual Model of Corporate Performance, Academy Management Review 4 (1979):497, discussed in Dirk Matten and Andrew Crane, Corporate Citizenship: Toward an Extended Theoretical Conceptualization, Academy of Management Review 30 (2005):166, 167.

6. For examples see Michael Kerr, Richard Janda, and Chip Pitts, Corporate Social Responsibility (Canada: Lexis Nexis Canada, 2009), 6-7; John F. Kennedy School of Government, Harvard University, Corporate Social Responsibility Initiative, Our Approach: Defining Corporate Social Responsibility, available at http://www.hks.harvard.edu/m-rcbg/CSRI/init_approach.html. For an overview, see Jill J. McMillan, Why Corporate Social Responsibility, Why Now, How?, in Steve May, George Cheney, and Juliet Roper, eds., The Debate over Corporate Social Responsibility (New York: Oxford University Press, 2007).

7. Commission of the European Communities, Green Paper: Promoting a European Framework for Corporate Social Responsibility (July 2001), 6, available at http://eurlex.europa.eu/LexUriServ/site/en/com/2001/com2001_0366en01.pdf.

8. For differences between European and American conceptions, see Thomas Donaldson, Defining the Value of Doing Good Business, Financial Times, June 2, 2005, 3. For arguments that the concept also encompasses initiatives that are not entirely voluntary, but are prompted by legal regulations, see Kerr, Janda, and Pitts, Corporate Social Responsibility, 560, and Thomas W. Dunfie, Stakeholder Theory: Managing Corporate Social Responsibility in Multiple Action Contexts, in Crane et al., eds., Oxford Handbook, 346, 349.

9. Business for Social Responsibility, Business Brief: Intangibles and CSR (February 2006), 6, available at http://www.bsr.org/reports/BSR_AW_Intangibles-CSR.pdf.

10. UN Global Compact, http://www.unglobalcompact.org.

11. OECD Guidelines for Multinational Enterprises, http://www.oecd.org/about/0,3347,en_2649_34889_1_1_1_1,00.html.

12. Milton Friedman, A Friedman Doctrine—The Social Responsibility of Business Is to Increase Its Profits, New York Times Magazine, September 13, 1970, 126.

13. McKinsey Global Survey of Business Executives: Business and Society, McKinsey Quarterly 2 (2006):23.

14. Grant Thornton LLP, Corporate Responsibility: Burden or Opportunity? (September 2007), 9, available at http://www.gt.com/staticfiles//GTCom/files/About%20us/BusinessLeaders Survey/Grant_Thornton_Corp_Responsibility.pdf; Economist Intelligence Unit, Doing Good: Business and the Sustainability Challenge (London, UK: Economist Intelligence Unit, 2008), 9, 31.

15. Chip Goodyear, Social Responsibility Has a Dollar Value, The Age, July 27, 2006.

16. See Marc Orlizky, Corporate Social Performance and Financial Performance, in Crane et al., eds., Oxford Handbook, 113, 116 (discussing meta-analysis finding positive correlation); Joshua Margolis and James P. Walsh, Misery Loves Companies: Rethinking Social Initiatives by Business, Administrative Science Quarterly 48 (2003):268 (of some 127 studies on financial and social performance, half found a positive correlation and only 7 found a negative correlation; 28 found no significant relationship, and 20 found a mixed relationship). See also Joshua D. Margolis and James P. Walsh, People and Profits?: The Search for a Link between a Company's Social and Financial Performance (Mahwah, NJ: Lawrence Erlbaum Associates, Inc., 2001).

17. Christopher Meyer and Julia Kirby, Leadership in an Age of Transparency, Harvard Business Review (April 2010):41-42.

18. Id. at 41.

19. Sarah A. Soule, Contention and Corporate Social Responsibility (New York: Cambridge University Press, 2009).

20. Kerr, Janda, and Pitts, Corporate Social Responsibility, 45-46; Soule, Contention and Responsibility, 7-8.

21. Graham Knight, Activism, Risk, and Communicational Politics: Nike and the Sweatshop Problem, in Stephen K. May, George Cheney, and Juliet Roper, eds., The Debate over Corporate Social Responsibility, 305.

22. Jeffrey Pfeffer, Shareholders First? Not So Fast, Harvard Business Review (July-August 2009): 90-91.

23. Center for Business Education, Where Will They Lead? MBA Student Attitudes about Business and Society (Aspen, CO: Aspen Institute, 2008), 16. For other surveys, see Kerr, Janda, and Pitts, Corporate Social Responsibility, 45.

24. Sarah E. Needleman, The Latest Office Perk: Getting Paid to Volunteer, Wall Street Journal, April 29, 2008, D5; Doreen McBarnet, Corporate Social Responsibility beyond Law, through Law, for Law: The New Corporate Accountability, in Doreen McBarnet, Aurora Voiculescu, and Tom Campbell, eds., The New Corporate Accountability: Corporate Social Responsibility and the Law (Cambridge, UK: Cambridge University Press, 2007), 9, 19

25. Kerr, Janda, and Pitts, Corporate Social Responsibility, 45-46; Donaldson, Defining the Value of Doing Good Business.

26. Robert Reich, Supercapitalism (New York: Knopf, 2007), 178-179; David Vogel, The Market for Virtue: The Potential and Limits of Corporate Social Responsibility (Washington, D.C.: Brookings Institution Press, 2005), 43-44; N. Craig Smith, Consumers as Levers of Corporate Social Responsibility, in Crane et al., eds., Oxford Handbook, 281, 286-287.

27. See McBarnet, Corporate Social Responsibility, 17; Kerr, Janda, and Pitts, Corporate Social Responsibility, 46; Smith, Consumers as Levers, 294-296; Rosabeth Moss Kanter, How to Do Well and Do Good, Sloan Management Review (Fall 2010):12. In one recent study on fair-trade coffee, consumers reported a willingness to pay an average reward of $1.40 a pound and a penalty of $2.40 a pound, depending on environmental and child labor practices. Remi Trudel and June Cotte, Does It Pay to Be Good?, Sloan Management Review (Winter 2009):61. In another study, three-quarters

of Americans reported willingness to pay 50 cents more for fair-trade coffee. Anand Giridharadas, Boycotts Minus the Pain, New York Times, October 11, 2009.

28. Social Investment Forum, 2007 Report on Socially Responsible Investing Trends in the United States (Washington, D.C.: Social Investment Forum 2007), ii.

29. Examples include the Dow Jones Sustainability Index Series and the FTSE4Good Index Series.

30. See Equator Principles, available at http://www.equator-principles.com.

31. For an overview of these factors, see Kerr, Janda, and Pitts, Corporate Social Responsibility, 290-291, 482-483.

32. McBarnet, Corporate Social Responsibility, 35-36; Kerr, Janda, and Pitts, Corporate Social Responsibility, 331, 437.

33. See David L. Levy and Rami Kaplan, Corporate Social Responsibility and Theories of Global Governance, in Crane et al., eds., Oxford Handbook, 433, 436.

34. Report of the Special Representative, ¶65.

35. http://www.dowethics.com/r/about/corp/bhopal.htm, discussed in Soule, Contention and Corporate Social Responsibility, 123.

36. Mathew Bishop and Michael Green, Philanthrocapitalism: How the Rich Can Save the World (New York: Bloomsbury Press, 2008), 184.

37. AccountAbility, http://www.accountability.org/default.aspx?id=124; Meyer and Kirby, Leadership in the Age of Transparency, 43.

38. GRI's XBRL is an example. See http://www.globalreporting.org/ReportingFramework/G3Guidelines/XBRL.

39. http://www.gscpnet.com; http://www.integratedreporting.org.

40. Daniel Franklin, Just Good Business, The Economist, January 19, 2008, 21.

41. Kristen Bell DeTienne and Lee W. Lewis, The Pragmatic and Ethical Barriers to Corporate Social Responsibility Disclosure: The Nike Case, Journal of Business Ethics 60 (2005):359, 371 (reporting findings that only a minority of surveyed companies reported annually on their social performance and only a fifth of those had any independent monitoring).

42. Richard M. Locke, Fei Quin, and Alberto Brause, Does Monitoring Improve Labor Standards? Lessons from Nike, Industrial and Labor Relations Review 61 (2007):3; Duncan Pruett, Looking for a Quick Fix: How Weak Social Auditing Is Keeping Workers in Sweatshops (Amsterdam: Clean Clothes Campaign, 2005), available at http://cleanclothes.org/documents/05-quick_fix.pdf.

43. See McBarnet, Corporate Responsibility, 15; Simon Zadek, The Path to Corporate Responsibility, Harvard Business Review (December 2004):127-132

44. *Kasky v. Nike*, 27 Cal. 4th 939, 95 P.2d 243 (Cal. Sup. Ct. 2002).

45. Zadek, The Path to Corporate Responsibility, 127-132. For discussion of the Nike boycotts, see Soule, Contention and Corporate Social Responsibility, 110-119.

46. Reich, Supercapitalism, 170. See also Aneel Karnani, The Case against Corporate Social Responsibility, Sloan Review, August 22, 2010.

47. See research discussed in Thomas McInerney, Putting Regulation before Responsibility: Toward Binding Norms of Corporate Social Responsibility, Cornell International Law Journal 40 (2007):171, 186. For an overview of the debate, see Lars Thoger Christensen, The Discourse of Corporate Social Responsibility, in May, Cheney, and Roper, eds., The Debate over Corporate Social Responsibility, 448, 455.

48. OECD, Voluntary Approaches for Environmental Policy: Effectiveness, Efficiency and Usage in Policy Mixes (Paris: OECD, 2003), 14.

49. For ineffectiveness, see Jill Esbenshade, Monitoring Sweatshops: Workers, Consumers and the Global Apparel Industry (Philadelphia, PA: Temple University Press, 2004); Locke, Quin, and Brause, Does Monitoring Improve Labor Standards? For preemption of better approaches, see Ebenshade, Monitoring Sweatshops.

50. For greenwashing, see William S. Laufer, Social Accountability and Corporate Greenwashing, Journal of Business Ethics 43 (2003):255-257. For inconsistencies in public and private action, see examples in Kerr, Janda, and Pitts, Corporate Social Responsibility, 561, 611 (n. 3) (discussing opposition to labor standards, remedies for human rights violations, and energy-efficient mass transit).

51. Timothy Kuhn and Stanley Deetz, Critical Theory and Social Responsibility, in Crane et al., eds., Oxford Handbook, 173, 182-183.

52. Jeremy Moon and David Vogel, Corporate Social Responsibility, Government, and Civil Society, in Crane et al., eds., Oxford Handbook, 316 (discussing state-required disclosures); Franklin, Just Good Business, 3 (discussing the United Kingdom's 2006 Companies Act requirement that corporations report on social and environmental performance); David L. Levy and Rami Kaplan, Corporate Social Responsibility and Theories of Global Governance, in Crane et al., eds., Oxford Handbook, 433, 436 (discussing examples of environmental standards that become templates for regulations or that are incorporated in trade and purchasing agreements).

53. For meta-regulation, the regulation of internal corporate regulation, see Christine E. Parker, Meta-Regulation: Legal Accountability for Corporate Social Responsibility, in McBarnet, Voiculescu, and Campbell, eds., The New Corporate Accountability, 207; Ian Ayres and John Braithwaite, Responsive Regulation: Transcending the Deregulation Debate (New York: Oxford University Press, 1992); Kerr, Janda, and Pitts, Corporate Social Responsibility, 603, 609.

54. Joe W. "Chip" Pitts III, Corporate Social Responsibility: Current Status and Future Evolution, Rutgers Journal of of Law and Public Policy 6 (2009):334, 377-381.

55. Patricia H. Werhande, Corporate Social Responsibility/Corporate Moral Responsibility, in May, Cheney, and Roper, The Debate over Corporate Social Responsibility, 450, 469.

56. Milton Friedman, Capitalism and Freedom (Chicago, IL: University of Chicago Press, 1962), 133-134.

57. Zadek, The Path to Corporate Responsibility, 129-130; Doreen McBarnet and Marina Kurkchiyan, Corporate Social Responsibility through Contractual Control?: Global Supply Chains and "Other Regulation," in McBarnet, Voiculescu, and Campbell, eds., The New Corporate Accountability 59, 89.

58. Locke, Quin, and Brause, Does Monitoring Improve Labor Standards?

59. McBarnet and Kurkchiyan, Corporate Social Responsibility through Contractual Control?, 62.

60. McKinsey Global Survey of Business Executives, 2.

61. Ben W. Heineman Jr., The General Counsel as Lawyer Statesman (2010). For giving voice to values, see Mary Gentile, Giving Voice to Values (New Haven, CT: Yale University Press, 2010), discussed in Chapter 4.

62. McBarnet and Kurkshiyan, Corporate Social Responsibility through Contractual Control, 86.

63. http://www.youtube.com/watch?v=iXsaYR1Izqw.

64. Sweets and Sour Marge appears in season 13, episode 8.

65. http://www.gereports.com/immelt-talks-sustainability-at-csr-conference.

66. Martha C. Nussbaum, Human Rights Theory: Capabilities and Human Rights, Fordham Law Review 66 (1997):273, 286. See also Bernard Williams, The Standard of Living: Interests and Capabilities, in Amartya K. Sen, ed., The Standard of Living (Cambridge: Cambridge University Press, 1987), 100; Amartya K. Sen, Elements of a Theory of Human Rights, Philosophy and Public Affairs 32 (2004):315.

67. Charles Beitz, The Idea of Human Rights (New York: Oxford University Press, 2009), 65.

68. Sally Engle Merry, Human Rights and Gender Violence: Translating International Law into Local Justice (Chicago, IL: University of Chicago Press, 2006), 3.

69. For an overview, see Mary Ann Glendon, A World Made New: Eleanor Roosevelt and the Universal Declaration of Human Rights (New York: Random House, 2001).

70. For the evolution on separate tracks, see Ralph G. Steinhardt, Paul L. Hoffman, and Christopher N. Camponovo, International Human Rights Lawyering: Cases and Materials (St. Paul, MN: West Publishing, 2009), 66; David S. Weissbrodt, Business and Human Rights, University of Cincinnati Law Review 74 (2005):59. For the early concerns, see Kerr, Janda, and Pitts, Corporate Social Responsibility, 56-64.

71. Weissbrodt, Business and Human Rights, 55; Report of the Special Representative of the Secretary-General on the Issue of Human Rights and Transnational Corporations and Other Business Enterprises, Business and Human Rights: Mapping International Standards of Responsibility and Accountability for Corporate Acts, UN Doc. A/HRC/4/035/(2007).

72. UN Doc. E/CN.4/Sub.2/2003/12/Rev.2 (2003).

73. Report of the Special Representative of the Secretary General on the Issue of Human Rights and Transnational Corporations and Other Business Enterprises, Promotion and Protection of All Human Rights, Civil, Political, Economic, Social and Cultural Rights, Including the Right to Development, Protect, Respect and Remedy: A Framework for Business and Human Rights (New York: United Nations Human Rights Council, April 2008), and Addendum, Corporations and Human Rights: A Survey of the Scope and Patterns of Alleged Corporate-Related Human Rights Abuse (New York: United Nations Human Rights Council, May 2008).

74. Steinhardt, Hoffman, Camponovo, International Human Rights Lawyering, 677.

75. For problems generally, see David L. Owen and Brendan O'Dwyer, Corporate Social Responsibility: The Reporting and Assurance Dimension, in Crane et al., eds., Oxford Handbook, 384, 405. For the diamond process, see Tom Zoellner, The Heartless Stone: A Journey through the World of Diamonds, Deceit, and Desire (New York: Picador, 2006). For Rugmark, see Christopher A. Bartlett, Vincent Dessain, and Anders Sjoman, IKEA's Global Sourcing Challenge: Indian Rugs and Child Labor (B), Harvard Business School Case Study 9-906-415 (November 14, 2006), 2 (noting the difficulty of policing 177,000 looms in one region alone, given their dispersal in homes and small workshops as well as factories); Ratner, Corporations and Human Rights, Yale Law Journal 111 (2002):443, 532, n. 357.

76. Report of the Special Representative, Protect, Respect, and Remedy, ¶25.

77. *In re South African Apartheid Litigation*, 617 F. Supp. 2d 228 (S.D.N.Y. 2009) (involving claims against companies that did business in apartheid South Africa); *Abdullahi v. Pfizer, Inc.*, 562 F.3d 1663 (2d Cir. 2009) (raising claims that Pfizer violated a customary international law norm prohibiting involuntary medical experimentations when it tested an experimental antibiotic on Nigerian children without their consent). A recent decision by a federal appellate court concluded that corporations cannot be sued under the Alien Tort Claims Act, but left open the possibility of individual claims against directors and officers, or state law claims against the corporation. See *Kiobel v. Royal Dutch Shell*, 621 F.3d. 111 (2d Cir. 2010); Michael D. Goldhaber, Alien Territory, American Lawyer (February 2011), 63.

78. Report of the Special Representative, Protect, Respect, and Remedy, ¶¶88, 93, 94.

79. United Nations High Commissioner for Human Rights, Business and Human Rights: A Progress Report (January 2000), available at http://www.ohchr.org/Documents/Publications/BusinessHRen.pdf.

80. Klaus M. Leisinger, On Corporate Responsibility for Human Rights (Basil, Switzerland, 2006), reprinted in Henry J. Steiner, Philip Alston, and Ryan Goodman, International Human Rights in Context: Law, Politics, Morals (New York: Oxford University Press, 2007), 1394.

81. Franklin, Just Good Business, 16.

82. See Reich, Supercapitalism, 178-179 (describing tuna, Levis, and related products); Vogel, The Market for Virtue, 46-48; Andrew Millington, Responsibility in the Supply Chain, in Crane et al., eds., Oxford Handbook, 363, 369.

83. Kerr, Janda, and Pitts, Corporate Social Responsibility, 22 (n. 50), 42-52; Marjorie Kelly, Holy Grail Found: Absolute, Positive, Definitive Proof CSR Pays Off Financially, Business Ethics Magazine 18 (Winter 2004).

84. Remarks at International Chamber of Commerce Commission on Business in Society, Paris, April 27, 2007, quoted in Steiner, Alston, and Goodman, International Human Rights in Context, 1412.

85. Ratner, Corporate Social Responsibility, 534.

86. Testimony of Nicole Wong, Vice President and Deputy General Counsel, Google, Inc., before the U.S. Senate Judiciary Committee Subcommittee on Human Rights and the Law, Hearing on Global Internet Freedom and the Rule of Law, Part II, March 2, 2010.

87. Michael Bazeley, Google's New Frontier: Firm Says Some Information Is Better than None at All, San Jose Mercury News, January 25, 2006, 2C (quoting Zittrain).

88. Tom Zeller, Web Firms Are Grilled on Dealings in China, New York Times, February 16, 2006, at C1; Joseph Nocera, Enough Shame to Go Around on China, New York Times, February 18, 2006, at B1, B13.

89. Jim Yardley, Google Chief Rejects Putting Pressure on China, New York Times, April 13, 2006, C7.

90. Mure Dickie, Internet Groups "Shirk Human Rights Duties in China," Financial Times (London), July 20, 2006, 10.

91. Human Rights Watch, Race to the Bottom: Corporate Complicity in Chinese Internet Censorship (Human Rights Watch, 2006).

92. Philip P. Pan, U.S. Firms Balance Morality, Commerce; Critics Say Companies Overlook Human Rights, Washington Post, February 19, 2006, A17; Human Rights Watch, Race to the Bottom: Corporate Complicity in Chinese Internet Censorship (New York: Human Rights Watch, August 2006).

93. James Glanz and John Markoff, Vast Hacking by a China Fearful of the Web, New York Times, December 5, 2010, A1; Jessica E. Vascellaro, Brin Drove Google's Pullback, Wall Street Journal, March 25, 2010, A18.

94. Wong, Statement.

95. Vascellaro, Brin Drove Google's Pullback, A18.

96. David M. Dickson, Google Weighs Leaving China over Attacks and Censorship, Washington Times, January 25, 2010, 1 (quoting Ganesan).

97. Dickson, Google Weighs Leaving China.

98. Miguel Helft, Google Tries to Salvage Chinese Activities: Despite Censorship Rift, Company Hopes That Lucrative Business Units Can Stay, International Herald Tribune, January 21, 2010, 17. See Ben Worthen and Siobhan Gorman, Google Prepares to Stop Censoring in China, Wall Street Journal, March 12, 2010 (discussing plans to leave some business in China).

99. Dickson, Google Weighs Leaving China (quoting Rebecca MacKinnon, of the Open Society Institute).

100. Wong, Statement.

101. Chloe Albanesius, Google: We're Committed to Not Censoring in China, PC Magazine, March 2, 2010.

102. Geeta Chowdhry and Mark Beeman, Challenging Child Labor: Transnational Activism and India's Carpet Industry, Annals of the American Academy of Political and Social Science 575 (2001):158.

103. Id. at 163.

104. International Labor Organization, Facts on Child Labor (2008), available at http://www.ilo.org/ipecinfo/product/viewProduct.do?productId=8213.

105. Federico Blanco Allais, Assessing the Gender Gap; Evidence from SIMPOC Surveys (Geneva, International Programme on the Elimination of Child Labour, 2009).

106. Sayan Chakrabarty and Ulrike Grote, Child Labor in Carpet Weaving: Impact of Social Labeling in India and Nepal, World Development 37 (2009):1683; India: Ban on Child Labor in Homes and Hotels, New York Times, August 3, 2006, 6.

107. Chakrabaty and Grote, Child Labor in Carpet Weaving, 1683, 1684.

108. Alakh N. Sharma, Impact of Social Labeling on Child Labour in Carpet Industry, Economic and Political Weekly Vol. 37, No. 52 (Dec. 28, 2002–Jan. 3, 2003):5202.

109. Bartlett, Dessain, and Sjoman, IKEA's Global Sourcing Challenge, 3.

110. Id. at 3.

111. Id. at 4.

112. Id. at 35; Severin Carrell, Shops Score Poorly in Fair Trade Survey, The Independent, June 16, 2002, 4.

113. Apple's Annual Audit Finds Some Violations from Suppliers, March 1, 1010, available at http://blogs.reuters.com/mediafile/2010/03/01/apples-annual-audit-find-some-violations-from-suppliers.

114. For discussion of the campaign and the "relief" of Canadian buyers to learn that the company can "guarantee" the absence of child labor, see Jennifer Hollett, Magic Carpets: Canadian Designers Are Pulling Rug Out from under Child Labour, The Globe and Mail (Canada), June 14, 2008, 19.

115. Blood Diamonds (New York: The History Channel, 2006); Diamonds of War: Africa's Blood Diamonds (Washington, D.C.: National Geographic Video, 2007); Blood Diamond (Burbank, CA: Warner Home Video, 2007).

116. Katie Redford and Beth Stephens, The Story of *Doe v. Unocal:* Justice Delayed but Not Denied, in Deena R. Hurwitz, Margaret L. Satterthwaite, with Doug Ford, eds., Human Rights Advocacy Stories (New York: Foundation Press, 2009), 433.

117. A Kind of Childhood (2002) is distributed by Direct Cinema Ltd., Santa Monica, CA; Stolen Childhoods (2003) is distributed by Galen Films, Vineyard Haven, MA; India: The Little Serfs (2003) is distributed by Films for the Humanities and Sciences, Princeton, NJ; Tomorrow We'll Finish (1994) is distributed by UNICEF (Division of Communications); and Slavery: A Global Investigation (2000) is distributed by Free the Slaves, Washington, D.C.

118. Deborah L. Rhode, Public Interest Law: The Movement at Midlife, Stanford Law Review 60 (2008):2027, 2051.

119. Id. at 2053.

120. Fiona Terry, Condemned to Repeat? The Paradox of Humanitarian Action (Ithaca, NY: Cornell University Press, 2002), 2.

121. Id. Linda Polman, What's Wrong with Humanitarian Aid? (New York: Metropolitan Books, 2010), 10-35. Some NGO leaders estimated that militias stole 60 percent of aid supplies, as well as taxed other assistance and demanded employment of guerillas in relief work. Polman, What's Wrong, 30.

122. For accounts, see Polman, What's Wrong with Humanitarian Aid?; Michael Maren, The Road to Hell: The Ravaging Effects of Foreign Aid and International Charity (New York: Free Press, 1997); Terry, Condemned to Repeat; David Rieff, A Bed for the Night: Humanitarianism in Crisis (New York: Simon and Schuster, 2002).

123. Rieff, A Bed for the Night, 24 (quoting Mary Anderson).

124. Id. at 22 (quoting Sadko Ogata). Some have suggested that this worldview, which sees politics as the source of solutions, may also absolve humanitarian organizations from the adverse consequences of their own assistance. See Philip Gourevitch, Alms Dealers, New Yorker, October 11, 2010, 109.

125. Terry, Condemned to Repeat, 230-237.

126. Jennifer Trahan, Why the Killing in Darfur Is Genocide, Fordham International Law Journal 31 (2008):990, 995-996.

127. Id. at 990-996.

128. Human Rights Watch, Entrenching Impunity: Government Responsibility for International Crimes in Darfur (2005), 1.

129. See Mr. Bush and Genocide, Washington Post, February 12, 2006.

130. S.C. Res. 1593, UN Doc. S/RES/1593 (May, 31, 2005).

131. *Prosecutor v. Omar Hassan Ahmad Al Bashir*, Case No. ICC-02/05-01/09, Warrant of Arrest (March 4, 2009).

132. See, e.g., Sudan: Groups Told to Exit within Year, New York Times, March 17, 2009; In Sudan, Surviving without the Help of NGOs, Ground Report, December 10, 2009.

133. Amnesty International, Sudan: Arms Continuing to Fuel Serious Human Rights Violations in Darfur, May 8, 2007.

134. Human Rights Watch, The Crisis in Northern Uganda, http://hrw.org/campaigns/uganda; Human Rights Watch, Uganda: No Amnesty for Atrocities, July 27, 2006, available at http://www.hrw.org/en/news/2006/07/28/uganda-no-amnesty-atrocities.

135. Independent International Commission on Kosovo, The Kosovo Report (New York: Oxford University Press, 2000), 33-34.

136. *Prosecutor v. Akayesu*, Case No. ICTR-96-4-T (1998), Judgment ¶¶110-111.

137. Jeremy Rabkin, A New World Order: The Clinton Doctrine Could Be Turned against the United States, American Spectator 32 (August 1999):50, 51.

138. Suzanne Dovi, Making the World Safe for Hypocrisy, Polity 34 (2001):3, 8, 16-21.

139. Declaration by the Ministers for Foreign Affairs of the Group of 77 (September 24, 1999). See Ian Brownlie, Principles of Public International Law (New York: Oxford University Press, 7th ed. 2008), 744.

140. Kosovo Commission, 4. For analysis, see Christopher Greenwood, International Law and the NATO Intervention in Kosovo, International and Comparative Law Quarterly 49 (2000):926, 929; Dino Kritsiotis, The Kosovo Crisis and NATO's Application of Armed Force against the Federal Republic of Yugoslavia, International and Comparative Law Quarterly 49 (2000):330.

141. Mary O'Connell, The UN, NATO and International Law after Kosovo, Human Rights Quarterly 22 (2000):57, 87.

142. Human Rights Watch, Political Shari'a?, September 21, 2004.

143. Norimitsu Onishi, Mother's Sentence Unsettles a Nigerian Village, New York Times, September 7, 2002.

144. Somini Sengupta, The World; When Do-Gooders Don't Know What They're Doing, New York Times, May 11, 2003; Can We Save Amina Lawal's Life? The Oprah Winfrey Show, November 2002; Warren Hoge, World Pageant Goes Ahead over Protests; A Turk Wins, New York Times, December 8, 2002.

145. Ayesha Iman and Sindi Medar-Gould, BAOBAB for Women's Human Rights, The Hidden Dangers of Letter Campaigns, May 2003; Sengupta, The World; When Do-Gooders Don't Know What They're Doing.

146. Iman and Medar-Gould, The Hidden Dangers of Letter Writing Campaigns.

147. Id.

148. Somini Sengupta, Facing Death for Adultery, Nigerian Woman Is Acquitted, New York Times, September 26, 2003.

149. Human Rights Watch, Political Shari'a?, September 21, 2004.

150. Emily Heller, Asylum Cases Keep Her on the Cutting Edge, National Law Journal, January 4, 2010, 15 (discussing work of Jayne Fleming of Reed Smith).

151. Merry, Human Rights and Gender Violence, 16.

152. For an Australian documentary on Kosovo, see Of Blood and History at http://www.youtube.com/watch?v=_L7WvJGgHSk. For BBC documentaries, see Kosovo: The Valley of the Dead at http://news.bbc.co.uk/olmedia/390000/video/_393406_dead_mov_vi.ram, and The Killing of Kosovo at http://news.bbc.co.uk/olmedia/video/panorama/kosovo_kil.ram.

153. For Darfur, see the documentary by Refugees International On Our Watch at http://www.youtube.com/watch?v=MdR9SB4yPOo. For a BBC overview, see http://www.youtube.com/watch?v=AcpwzCaoZCM. For Nigeria, see http://www.youtube.com/watch?v=zalqYjcjA2Y and http://www.youtube.com/watch?v=Yzj3rEUEXoo.

CHAPTER 11

PHILANTHROPY AND PUBLIC SERVICE

One context in which leaders exercise increasing influence is the allocation of charitable resources. Private foundations give away about $41 billion and corporate foundations and giving programs about $14.5 billion of the roughly $308 billion annually donated by Americans.[1] Business contributions average between 1 to 2 percent of pretax profits.[2] Corporate and professional organizations also support substantial volunteer work. For example, almost three-quarters of lawyers report donating legal services to persons of limited means or to organizations assisting them, for an average of forty-one hours a year.[3]

Such charitable contributions have made possible some of the nation's greatest achievements in social justice and public welfare.[4] In recent years, the massive investment in global causes, through organizations such as the Bill and Melinda Gates Foundation and multinational corporations, has brought impressive progress on health, environmental, and related issues.[5] Although the value of such philanthropy is widely acknowledged, the cost-effectiveness of many philanthropic initiatives has been widely criticized. This chapter explores the challenges of allocating scarce charitable resources for leaders in three representative contexts: nonprofit organizations, corporations, and law firms. Each setting poses some distinctive issues, but also shares a common goal: developing a strategic philanthropic approach that best accommodates both donor and societal interests. We do not focus on government aid because its relationship to political processes and policy objectives raises other concerns. However, much of the following analysis of strategic philanthropy is applicable to public- as well as private-sector organizations, and calls for collaboration between them.

A. STRATEGIC PHILANTHROPY AND PUBLIC POLICY

In the following excerpt, Paul Brest, former dean of the Stanford Law School and president of the Hewlett Foundation, and Hal Harvey, president of

Climate Works, explore the meaning of strategic philanthropy and the strategies necessary to achieve it.

PAUL BREST AND HAL HARVEY, MONEY WELL SPENT:
A STRATEGIC PLAN FOR SMART PHILANTHROPY

(New York: Bloomberg Press, 2008), pp. 7, 15-17,
145-146, 214-215, and 217-218

What Strategic Philanthropy Is

[A]ccomplishing philanthropic goals requires having great clarity about what those goals are and specifying indicators of success before beginning a philanthropic project. It requires designing and then implementing a plan commensurate with the resources committed to it. This, in turn, requires an empirical, evidence-based understanding of the external world in which the plan will operate. And it requires attending carefully to milestones to determine whether you are on the path to success, with a keen eye for signals that call for midcourse corrections. These factors are the necessary parts of what we regard as the essential core of strategic philanthropy—the concern with *impact.*

"Impact" is obviously not the same as good intentions. Nor is it the same as engaging in the activities called for by your strategic plan. Given the complexities of the world, even well-thought-out activities do not always achieve their goals. Impact is not even the same as seeing the outcome you intended come about—at least not if the outcome would have happened anyway. Simply put, impact is *making a difference*—not in some universal sense, but in terms of your own philanthropic goals. . . .

The idea of a *social return on investment* (SROI) is simply that you want your (inevitably) limited resources to achieve the greatest possible impact. For most objectives—whether improving the graduation rates of disadvantaged youth, feeding the hungry, or preventing AIDS—the more you accomplish the better. The more you accomplish with the same resources, the greater the SROI. . . .

The concept of *expected return* accounts for the risk involved in achieving your goals. It is a function of the magnitude of the impact times the probability of achieving it. The cost of a program and the expected return of its outcome together describe its cost-effectiveness. The impact of some philanthropic activities is pretty certain: if you are supporting a soup kitchen, you and the organizations you are funding will know at the end of the day how many people (who might otherwise have gone hungry) you are feeding and you can predict what the organization will achieve tomorrow. For many if not most not-for-profit activities, however, the impact is anything but certain. How many unwanted pregnancies will a teen-pregnancy-prevention program prevent? Will advocacy for campaign-finance reform result in legislation, will the legislation be implemented, and will it have more good than bad consequences?

Realistically, one can rarely calculate impact and probability with any degree of precision, which has led some people to criticize the ideas of SROI and expected return as misguided efforts to measure things that cannot be quantified. But forget about quantification for now, and consider SROI and expected return as the essence of an attitude that has at least the following benefits:

- It encourages philanthropists and the organizations they support to marshal their resources most effectively to accomplish shared objectives.
- It puts the administrative costs of the foundation and those of the organizations it supports in the proper context; specifically, those costs are justified to the extent, but only to the extent, that they contribute to an organization's impact. (More on this later.)
- It helps philanthropists recognize the risks of strategies and implementation in order to try to mitigate them.
- It justifies risky not-for-profit ventures whose potential benefits are high. Consider the likelihood of an organization succeeding in reducing global warming or of a medical research institute developing an AIDS vaccine. The probabilities are very low, but the potential payoffs are enormous.
- It encourages philanthropists to be realistic and candid about failure. "Failure" is almost a dirty word in our sector—for operating not-for-profits as well as foundations. Yet a large proportion of not-for-profit activities and foundation grants fail, not in the sense of the organizations falling apart—though that happens, too—but by having no impact. Without acknowledging failure, an organization loses one of its most important avenues of learning. At the Hewlett Foundation, we hold an annual contest for "the worst grant from which you learned the most." Because of the foundation-wide learning that comes from it, the prize has become a sought-after honor rather than a mark of opprobrium.
- It helps philanthropists understand their own tolerance for risk. Some funders are prepared to take huge risks of failure. Others are quite risk averse. You can often find effective ways to achieve objectives that fit your tolerance for risk; for example, undertake several projects with different risk levels so that the overall "portfolio" is in line with your appetite for risk or choose different objectives that can be achieved without too much risk. . . .
- [In short, strategic] philanthropy consists of
  - clearly defined goals, commensurate with resources;
  - strategies for achieving the goals;
  - strategies that are based on sound evidence; and
  - feedback to keep the strategy on course.
- Strategic philanthropy deploys resources to have maximum impact—to make the biggest possible difference. This approach is captured by the idea of social return on investment, where "return" refers to improving the world rather than financial gain. . . .

The costs and complexities of evaluating impact may tempt you to throw up your hands and just rely on intuition. Before you yield to the temptation, consider the work of Dr. Joan McCord, a criminologist who evaluated programs for troubled youth. Her best-known work was a longitudinal study comparing participants in programs that provided mentoring, health-care services, and summer camp to high-risk boys with a control group of similar youths. She found that boys in the program were more likely to become criminals, have employment and marital problems, and become alcoholics than those in the control group. The evidence contradicted not only the expected outcome but also the participants' own belief that they had benefited from the program. (Dr. McCord hypothesized that the boys in the treatment group may have felt that they were given the attention because something was wrong with them, making it a self-fulfilling prophecy.) She found similar paradoxical effects from a "just say no" drug education program and from Scared Straight, a program designed to deter young people from following a criminal path.

In sum, if you are a philanthropist with a long-term commitment to a field, it is well worth putting your funds—and lots of them—into evaluation. In any event, if you are about to fund a program, find out what empirical validation lies behind its strategy. . . .

[To make a difference in public policy], here are some considerations to keep in mind: . . .

- *Clarity of your ask.* Is your message, or the policy "ask," clearly articulated and focused? It does no good to generate a huge political force for "better education." You need to advocate for (or against) specific measures: vouchers, teacher certification, statewide standards, longer school days, whatever.
- *Credibility and political weight.* The Hewlett Foundation once received a proposal to organize petition drives to ask the Bush administration to act seriously to reduce climate change. Apart from other problems, the applicant was going to work the campuses and streets in Madison, Wisconsin; Boulder, Colorado; and Boston, Massachusetts. Not to put too fine a point on it, these were not the centers of gravity of the Bush administration's constituencies. Whether you're circulating petitions or buying a newspaper ad, the point is not that the source be credible to you, the funder, but that it be credible to the target audience.

This last point also suggests that you should consider funding across cultural or ideological boundaries. In designing an initiative to reduce unplanned pregnancies among young adults, the National Campaign to Prevent Teen and Unplanned Pregnancy has drawn on leaders from across the political spectrum, including people who disagree about the morality of abortion and of sex outside of marriage but are concerned about the very high abortion rate among women in their twenties. Look for odd bedfellows.

Related to credibility is whether the group has the political weight to make a difference. We recall one organization supporting renewable energy policy in the Northwest. The decision maker was a public utilities commission—the right choice, because it has a big role in determining the state s energy future and it is required to hear arguments on all sides of an issue and make decisions under clear procedures. Our grantee was sophisticated and technically capable. But when we privately asked some savvy observers of the commission whether the organization was effective, we got a resounding "no." The reasons? There were no political consequences to ignoring this group, but the political consequences of ignoring the utility companies were high. The solution was for our grantee to invite local businesses, academics, politicos, and others to testify alongside its experts, to get op-eds in the paper, to undertake polls showing public support, and to add political weight to its persuasive arguments on the merits of the cause. . . .

Sausage Making

Politics isn't nice. It can involve nasty tactics, strange bedfellows, and compromises with opponents. Be ready to take heat from your friends when you make a pact with the devil. The prestigious Environmental Defense Fund roundly criticized the National Commission on Energy Policy (NCEP) for agreeing to a "safety valve" on carbon emissions, which NCEP regarded as essential to garnering sufficient support for a mandatory federal cap-and-trade law. Opponents of junk food in public schools have attacked a leading ally, the Center for Science in the Public Interest, for a compromise with the food industry that would ban selling candy, sugary soda, and salty, fatty food in school snack bars, vending machines, and cafeterias, but allow sales of chocolate milk, sports drinks, and diet soda. . . .

PROBLEM 11-1

1. *Change Philanthropy*, a project sponsored by the Center for Community Change, reviews examples of successful social justice initiatives and draws several lessons for foundations. They should begin by searching for root causes of a problem and identifying a niche for action, based on an issue, identity group, geographic location, or strategy (organizing, education, policy, etc.). They should then look for allies, collaborators, and the strongest possible grantees, and develop evaluation measures to monitor progress.[6]

   Based on these guidelines and the framework Brest and Harvey propose, consider a social issue with which you are familiar and design a philanthropic strategy to address it.
2. You are the chair of the board of your city's natural history museum. You have an opportunity to host a traveling exhibit, The Nature of Diamonds, sponsored by one of the world's leading diamond companies. Your board is divided on whether to accept. Supporters point out that the exhibit has been extremely popular in other cities. They believe that it will bring new visitors to the museum and boost its somewhat stodgy reputation as catering only to "bird and bunny" people. Revenues from tie-in retail opportunities such as jewelry and books could provide much-needed support for other museum renovation projects. Opponents, however, are concerned that the exhibit's content offers a sanitized and highly misleading chronicle of the diamond trade. It makes no mention of "conflict diamonds," or their role in violence, colonialism, and environmental degradation. Nor is the company willing to have those issues highlighted in any parallel exhibits or programs. Although the content of the exhibit has not been subject to protests or adverse press coverage in other cities, some board members think the risk

of that happening in your city is too great. The likely impact would be to alienate the city's African American community and reinforce the museum's elitist image.

How do you resolve the issue? What is the mission of a museum and by what metrics do you measure the social impact of a particular exhibit? How relevant is the financial position of the museum?

Would research on corporate philanthropy summarized below suggest that the exhibit was a good use of the diamond company's resources? If you were the head of its corporate social responsibility office, would you support the exhibit?

3. You are the newly appointed president of the Nature Conservancy. Its mission is to preserve wilderness and the diversity of plants and animals by protecting the habitats of endangered species. Traditionally, it has measured success by the amount of money it has raised and the habitats it has preserved. By this measure, your predecessor was highly successful. Under his leadership, the Conservancy's membership, contributions, and protected land all grew steadily; by the turn of the twenty-first century, it had projects in twenty-eight countries and had preserved some 12 million acres in the United States alone.[7] Yet the diversity of species has continued to decline, even within protected areas. In-depth assessments reveal that species survival rates depend on ecosystem preservation in bordering areas. In your view, effectiveness requires more than "bucks and acres." It will need multifaceted efforts focusing on issues such as land-use planning, pollution, and soil erosion. Not all members of your board agree. They, and large donors, view wilderness preservation in largely aesthetic terms, and are reluctant to acknowledge that prior efforts have been misdirected. How do you proceed?

4. You head a foundation that has long supported women's organizations in Haiti, particularly those focusing on violence and economic development. Haiti has one of the highest sexual assault rates in the world. Estimates suggest that over a third of Haitian women have experienced sexual violence.[8] Poverty traps many individuals in abusive families and unsafe communities, and few shelters or services are available for rape and domestic-violence victims. Research suggests that a necessary condition of progress for Haiti is the kind of policy advocacy, support services, economic development, and law enforcement reform on which your local grantees are working. However, in the aftermath of the hurricane, a majority of your board believes that you should reallocate your aid to disaster relief. The sheer scale of devastation and threats of epidemics make survival-related assistance seem more pressing.

Leaders of local women's groups disagree. As they note, women's vulnerability to assault has grown in the aftermath of the disaster. The stress and lack of security in shanty dwellings creates increasing urgency for violence-oriented programs, and the need to help women secure independent income remains crucial. Many other groups are providing disaster relief, but few have the capacity to replace the work of your grantees.

How do you respond? What evidence should your board consider in making its decision?

NOTES AND QUESTIONS

In principle, the case for strategic philanthropy and for measurable social returns on nonprofit investment is self-evident. Everyone benefits when money is well spent, not just well intentioned. But in practice, such frameworks bump up against significant obstacles. The most obvious involves evaluation. Many nonprofit initiatives have mixed or non-quantifiable outcomes. How do we price due process, wilderness preservation, performing arts, or gay marriage? Dennis Collins, former director of the Irvine Foundation, worries that strategic philanthropy encourages a "pseudo science" of "metrics and matrices" that cannot capture intangible values."[9] Bruce Sievers, former head of the Haas Family Foundation, similarly warns against what Alfred North Whitehead termed the "fallacy of misplaced concreteness." In Sievers's view, "the sheer number and complexity of variables in the realms of social action make it virtually impossible to arrive at rigorously measurable comparisons of performance among competing non-profit activities."[10] In many contexts, nonprofit leaders cannot help but suffer "measurement angst"; they lack the research or methodology on which to make informed assessments of social impact.[11] Moreover, as experts such as Peter Karoff, founder of the Philanthropic Initiative, have noted, insistence on objective performance measures can discourage funders and their grantees from taking on the "tough issues where success is hard to measure."[12] Philanthropists who demand concrete indicators of success may be reluctant to "swing for the fences" on "complicated, seemingly insoluble problems" where charitable funds and creativity are most needed.[13]

1. How would you respond? Consider the programs of a nonprofit organization with which you are familiar. How would you measure effectiveness?
2. Thomas Pogge, Yale professor of philosophy and international affairs, argues that in evaluating the cost-effectiveness of international contributions, philanthropic organizations should measure the value of aid by the amount of harm reduced or benefit received by the individuals affected.[14] Would this framework help resolve the issue of assistance for Haiti or for other nations where incommensurable needs are at stake? If not, how would you set priorities?
3. In the case of the natural history museum exhibit, what measures of success would be most relevant? How would you rank factors such as the number and satisfaction of visitors, the assessment of experts, the revenue raised, and the amount and content of publicity?[15]
4. Brest and Harvey note that the effectiveness of evaluation is likely to increase if organizations become more willing to share information about what works and what does not. However, those who invest significant time and money in social impact initiatives want to feel good about their efforts, and are understandably reluctant to expose poor outcomes. What nonprofit wants to rain on its parade when that might jeopardize its reputation and public support?

   How would you address that reluctance? Can you identify strategies that might encourage nonprofits to pool information and benchmark performance? How can leaders of nonprofit organizations encourage constructive criticism?

5. Does a foundation's commitment to strategic philanthropy and evidence-based evaluation extend to its grantees' advocacy work? How should foundation leaders respond if they see grantees making claims in political and media forums that fail to acknowledge uncertainties, competing evidence, or methodological limitations in the research on which they rely? Can you think of examples where the policy objective seemed worthy but the persuasive tactics necessary for "sausage making" seemed problematic?

6. Some critics of traditional philanthropy object not only to its lack of strategic focus but also to its hierarchical processes. A common approach is for a foundation to identify a goal and then determine which grantees are best able to advance it. An alternative is to engage potential grantees more actively in setting objectives. The Boston Women's Fund, for example, moved to such an approach when it became clear that it was not funding what grassroots women's organizations most "wanted to be doing."[16] What would be the costs and benefits of a more collaborative approach in establishing philanthropic goals? How could the benefits be best achieved?

7. One other trend in the world of strategic philanthropy concerns the role of celebrities. Although some leaders in sports, entertainment, and politics have long used their fame to raise money and attention for social causes, a growing number have become more sophisticated in maximizing the effectiveness of their involvement. A prominent example is rock star Bono, who has infused social activism in his band's lyrics, and has founded organizations and grassroots campaigns to reduce global poverty and disease. Unlike many other celebrities, Bono is credited with a deep understanding of the structural causes of the problems he has targeted and the political obstacles to solutions.[17] Other celebrities have played a more limited role, which consists mainly of providing photo opportunities.[18] How might nonprofit organizations more effectively partner with celebrities?

B. CORPORATE PHILANTHROPY

Until the last several decades, most business leaders exhibited little support for the philanthropy that is now a standard part of "corporate social responsibility." William Vanderbilt once famously responded to a *New York Times* reporter's question about keeping a railroad line open for the public, "The public be damned."[19] Such views would never be expressed openly today. But one question raised by the readings below is whether corporate philanthropy reflects a substantial departure from Vanderbilt's views.

The tradition of corporate philanthropy began with nineteenth-century manufacturers' contributions to the communities of their workers: housing, schools, hospitals, libraries, and so forth.[20] With the rise of the corporate social responsibility movement in the 1970s, many large businesses broadened their philanthropic agenda, and some set up foundations to coordinate their giving and align it with business objectives.

Such donations are not without critics. In the excerpt below, Matthew Bennett and Michael Green summarize claims that corporate philanthropy is a contradiction in terms. In critics' view, to the extent that it serves business objectives, such as enhancing reputation, it is not really philanthropy but an ill-disguised form of public relations. Some corporations spend more on publicizing their contributions than on the good works themselves.[21] According to Berkeley professor Robert Reich, the "only legitimate reason for a corporation to be generous with its shareholders' money is to burnish its brand image, and such a rationale will go only so far."[22]

Alternatively, to the extent that the contributions are genuinely philanthropic, primarily intended to serve the public not the business, what entitles corporate leadership to decide which charities shareholder dollars should support? A McKinsey Global Survey found that the personal interests of the CEO and board members had by far the greatest weight in determining the focus of corporate philanthropy. Only a fifth of corporations used the "highest potential for social impact" as a major factor in setting priorities.[23] All too often, critics note, corporate leaders have used contributions as a form of social currency to buy themselves status or perks, such as seats on prestigious nonprofit boards or preferential treatment at events.[24] An egregious example involved Armand Hammer, the head of Occidental Petroleum, who had the company donate a third of one year's profits to build a museum for his personal art collection.[25] Such donations seem particularly objectionable when companies are undergoing financial hardship. At the same time United Airlines' parent company was in bankruptcy and claiming an inability to pay pension benefits, the company continued to support the Lyric Opera of its home city, Chicago.[26] Moreover, from a policy standpoint, modest corporate charitable assistance may be counterproductive by deflecting attention from the need for broader public responses to the problems it targets, or the need for reforms in the company's own policies. To some critics, it is ironic that Wal-Mart is the nation's top corporate philanthropist, and that it recently made a five-year, 2 billion dollar pledge to fight hunger at the same time that it was fighting efforts by its own workers to achieve living wages.[27]

Defenders of corporate philanthropy acknowledge that many contributions are fairly subject to these criticisms, but argue that properly designed programs can serve both public and business interests. In the excerpt below, Michael Porter and Mark Kramer maintain that corporate philanthropy should be not simply strategic in the sense of focused and aligned with general business objectives, such as enhancing brand image and reputation. Rather, corporations should target their unique assets and expertise to important social goals that also enhance the company's competitive position.[28] So for example, Coca Cola has partnered with Greenpeace to assist conservation of freshwater that is essential for long-term manufacturing needs; DreamWorks has trained low-income Los Angeles youth for careers in the entertainment industry; Grand Circle Travel provides historic preservation assistance to international sites that appeal to its primary customer base; Pfizer and Merck work with world health organizations and foundations to provide pharmaceuticals in developing countries; Home Depot supports Habitat for Humanity; Goldman Sachs works with universities and NGOs to train impoverished women in basic business skills; and FleetBoston Financial supports inner-city economic development where its employees live and lend.

Do such approaches address critics' concerns? Are they consistent with Brest and Harvey's framework? Part of the difficulty in evaluating arguments concerning corporate philanthropy is that evidence of its economic impact is mixed, and subject to considerable methodological limitations.[29] Data are incomplete and show no consistent relationship between giving and financial performance.[30] As with other indices of corporate social responsibility, it is difficult to know whether philanthropy increases profitability or whether more profitable companies can better afford philanthropy. Evaluating the long-term value of contributions that enhance reputation is especially difficult. A case in point involves Merck's pledge to make its drug Mectizan available free of charge to combat a parasitic disease causing river blindness in indigent, mostly African communities. By the turn of the twenty-first century, a combination of the drug and pesticides had largely eliminated the risk for some 200 million people, averted an estimated 600,000 cases of blindness, and set a precedent for free distribution that other companies followed. Although the company earned enormous respect at the time, the boost to its reputation was never shown to have translated into financial value or to have protected it from reputational damage during subsequent product liability litigation.[31]

In the absence of clear data, how would you evaluate the claims set forth in the excerpts below? Would your assessment vary if you were a CEO, the leader of a corporate watchdog organization, the head of a nonprofit consortium, or a public policy maker? Consider a business with which you have some familiarity. What recommendations might you make about its charitable giving program?

MATTHEW BISHOP AND MICHAEL GREEN, PHILANTHROCAPITALISM: HOW THE RICH CAN SAVE THE WORLD

(Bloomsbury Press, 2008), pp. 177-180 and 193

. . . [The] growing interest in corporate giving raises many questions, not least about balance between a firm's duty to its shareholders to make a profit and its responsibility to society to do good. . . . Should companies be aiming for anything but profitability? Does a company deserve credit from the public if its giving is part of a strategy to maximize its profits or only if it makes the firm worse off? Do companies have particular capabilities that can be used to solve societal problems that even wealthy individuals or governments cannot? . . . Certainly, the scale and power of big companies means that they have the potential to be an important force for good. However, the need to make a profit will constrain the ways in which they can do so in ways that their nonprofit-driven partners in any cause need to understand, or risk disappointment.

To antibusiness activists, corporate philanthropy and corporate social responsibility are superficial at best, an attempt to disguise the ugly underlying reality of big business today. In his 2007 book, *Supercapitalism*, Robert B. Reich, a professor at the University of California, Berkeley (and labor secretary in Bill

Clinton's cabinet) writes that corporate social responsibility is "as meaningful as cotton candy. The more you try to bite into it the faster it dissolves." It is not that company bosses are evil, or even less ethical than everyone else, says Reich, but in today's supercompetitive globalized capitalism few firms can afford to be socially responsible, at least not to any significant extent: "Corporations were never set up to be charitable institutions and are less able to operate in that sphere now," he says, pointing out that sums spent by business on "doing good" are dwarfed by what firms spend lobbying politicians to promote their narrow interests, often against the public interest. For Reich, the only meaningful answer to society's problems, and the way to ensure that firms do more social good than harm, is politics—better government, better regulations—not corporate giving.

Reich's disdain for corporate social responsibility, but not his enthusiasm for more government, was shared by the late, great free market economist Milton Friedman, who famously argued in 1970 that "there is one and only one social responsibility of business—to use its resources and engage in activities designed to increase its profits, so long as it stays within the rules of the game." He believed that in these circumstances—that is, engaging in open and free competition without deception or fraud—generating higher profits was a reflection of the benefit that business generated for society. Anything else, he might have said, is cotton candy.

Increasingly, however, even some of those business leaders who are sympathetic to Friedman think he failed to recognize the positive profit-making possibilities that can arise from participating in solving society's biggest problems. As for Reich, they say, perhaps he simply doesn't understand business.

According to Michael E. Porter and Mark Kramer, two of the leading academic observers of philanthrocapitalism, firms looking to maximize long-run profits should use their philanthropic efforts to "improve their competitive context"—that is, "the quality of the business environment in the locations where they operate." Particularly in countries with weak or ineffective governance and infrastructure, firms have a chance to enhance their long-term prospects by using philanthropy (broadly defined) to build a sustainable business environment.

Porter and Kramer would surely applaud [support by General Electric and other aluminum electricity companies for caps on] carbon emissions. This would help create a market for [their environmental] products. . . . [A stable carbon regulation system would also] make the business conditions in which they will operate in future more predictable, reducing the risk involved when they make multibillion-dollar investments in new operations that may take years to build and decades to generate profit.

Likewise, [CEO Marc] Benioff is clear that one of the goals of Salesforce. com's philanthropy is to attract the best talent. Surveys show that college graduates, in particular, increasingly want to work for a company that shares their values and commitment to a better world. Benioff is adamant that he has been able to recruit better employees because of his firm's philanthropic commitment, and that having lots of employees who are motivated by this sense of mission makes Salesforce.com a more successful business. . . .

Reich concedes that there are activities taking place under the banner of corporate social responsibility or corporate philanthropy that are both good for society and profitable for the companies that do them. Indeed, that is why he is underwhelmed by them. "All these steps may be worthwhile but they are not undertaken because they are socially responsible," he writes. They are done to reduce costs or boost profits in other ways. "To credit these corporations with being 'socially responsible' is to stretch the term to mean anything a company might do to increase profits if, in doing so, it also happens to have some beneficent impact on the rest of society."

Reich misses the point, however, about the difficult choices that companies face. Many executives are so focused on dealing with short-term pressures for bigger profits that they do not devote sufficient time to thinking about what is in their long-term-profit-maximizing, enlightened self-interest. Even if they do think about it, it is all too rare that an executive is willing to incur the short-run costs (such as that R&D-like philanthropy) necessary to achieve that more profitable long-term goal. Spending on lobbying against change that may impose a short-term cost is often the reflex reaction. Corporate "doing well by doing good" may provide a win-win for the firm and society, but it is a win that too few firms even attempt — which is why those firms that do try surely deserve the public's encouragement.

The enlightened self-interest case for business to engage fully in society was set out by Klaus Schwab, founder of the World Economic Forum, in the January-February 2008 issue of *Foreign Affairs*. Especially since anticapitalist protesters started to target the WEF's annual meetings in the 1990s, Schwab has thought hard about the need for business to engage more constructively in society — and has led by example in opening up the WEF to more diverse opinions, including from some of the people who would once have supported the activists on the other side of the Davos security fence. In his article, "Global Corporate Citizenship," he calls on international business leaders to "fully commit to sustainable development and address paramount global challenges," including climate change, the provision of public health care, energy conservation, and the management of resources, particularly water, as part of a long-term profit-maximization strategy.

Schwab argues that the emergence of global corporate citizenship is the "inevitable result" of several factors. One is the weakness of government: Schwab would reject Reich's big-government prescriptions because the role of the nation-state is declining and global governance institutions (such as the U.N. and World Trade Organization) are inadequate to address global challenges. He also points to the increasing effectiveness of firms, not least through their mastery of technology. There are things that companies, particularly big multinational firms, can do better than anyone to help solve society's problems, he says. This has brought about what he calls a "fundamental shift in the global power equation": as state power has declined, the influence of corporations on communities, on the lives of citizens, and on the environment has sharply increased. . . .

It is easy to be cynical about corporate attempts to be good, or even not to be evil. Certainly, the public should ensure that politicians properly regulate companies in areas where it is unrealistic to rely on self-regulation or good behavior. Equally, the need to make a profit limits the ability of a firm to devote its resources to solving the world's biggest problems. This is especially true of public companies with a broad base of shareholders to please; privately owned firms may have more discretion, and can sometimes be a funnel for the owner's personal philanthropy. When business conditions get tough, philanthropy can often be the first casualty, and anyone working in partnership with a business should realize that the more closely the firm's philanthropy is bound into its core profit-making strategy, the more sustainable it is likely to be.

Moreover, many good causes will not fit into a firm's core business strategy. To avoid disappointment, it is crucial that philanthropists, governments, NGOs, and others who hope that business will partner with them understand the limitations, as well as the exciting possibilities, of working to achieve good in tandem with a company.

Certainly, companies claiming to do good should be scrutinized at least as carefully as anyone else who makes such claims—especially as firms often have large public relations budgets to spend on making themselves look good. Yet there are many reasons to believe that firms pursuing their enlightened self-interest can play a significant part in tackling the world's biggest problems. . . .

MICHAEL E. PORTER AND MARK R. KRAMER. "THE COMPETITIVE
ADVANTAGE OF CORPORATE PHILANTHROPY"

---

80 Harvard Business Review 12 (2002):58-61, 67-68

Few phrases are as overused and poorly defined as "strategic philanthropy." The term is used to cover virtually any kind of charitable activity that has some definable theme, goal, approach, or focus. In the corporate context, it generally means that there is some connection, however vague or tenuous, between the charitable contribution and the company's business. Often this connection is only semantic, enabling the company to rationalize its contributions in public reports and press releases. In fact, most corporate giving programs have nothing to do with a company's strategy. They are primarily aimed at generating goodwill and positive publicity and boosting employee morale. . . .

Most consist of numerous small cash donations given to aid local civic causes or provide general operating support to universities and national charities in the hope of generating goodwill among employees, customers, and the local community. Rather than being tied to well-thought-out social or business objectives, the contributions often reflect the personal beliefs and values of executives or employees. Indeed, one of the most popular approaches—employee matching grants—explicitly leaves the choice of charity to the individual worker. Although aimed at enhancing morale, the same effect might be gained from an equal increase in wages that employees could then choose to donate to charity on a tax-deductible basis. It does indeed seem that many of the giving decisions companies make today would be better made by individuals donating their own money. . . .

Cause-related marketing, through which a company concentrates its giving on a single cause or admired organization, was one of the earliest practices cited as "strategic philanthropy," and it is a step above diffuse corporate contributions. At its most sophisticated, cause-related marketing can improve the reputation of a company by linking its identity with the admired qualities of a chosen nonprofit partner or a popular cause. Companies that sponsor the Olympics, for example, gain not only wide exposure but also an association with the pursuit of excellence. And by concentrating funding through a deliberate selection process, cause-related marketing has the potential to create more impact than unfocused giving would provide.

However, cause-related marketing falls far short of truly strategic philanthropy. Its emphasis remains on publicity rather than social impact. The desired benefit is enhanced goodwill, not improvement in a company's ability to compete. True strategic giving, by contrast, addresses important social and economic goals simultaneously, targeting areas of competitive context where the company and society both benefit because the firm brings unique assets and expertise. . . .

Corporations can use their charitable efforts to improve their *competitive* context — the quality of the business environment in the location or locations where they operate. Using philanthropy to enhance context brings social and economic goals into alignment and improves a company's long-term business prospects. . . . In addition, addressing context enables a company not only to give money but also to leverage its capabilities and relationships in support of charitable causes. That produces social benefits far exceeding those provided by individual donors, foundations, or even governments. . . .

A handful of companies have begun to use context-focused philanthropy to achieve both social and economic gains. Cisco Systems, to take one example, has invested in an ambitious educational program — the Cisco Networking Academy — to train computer network administrators, thus alleviating a potential constraint on its growth while providing attractive job opportunities to high school graduates. By focusing on social needs that affect its corporate context and utilizing its unique attributes as a corporation to address them, Cisco has begun to demonstrate the unrealized potential of corporate philanthropy. Taking this new direction, however, requires fundamental changes in the way companies approach their contribution programs. Corporations need to rethink both *where* they focus their philanthropy and *how* they go about their giving. . . .

Philanthropic investments by members of a cluster, either individually or collectively, can have a powerful effect on the cluster's competitiveness and the performance of all of its constituent companies. Philanthropy can often be the most cost-effective way — and sometimes the only way — to improve competitive context. It enables companies to leverage not only their own resources but also the existing efforts and infrastructure of nonprofits and other institutions. Contributing to a university, for example, may be a far less expensive way to strengthen a local base of advanced skills in a company's field than developing training in-house. And philanthropy is amenable to collective corporate action, enabling costs to be spread over multiple companies. Finally, because of philanthropy's wide social benefits, companies are often able to forge partnerships with nonprofit organizations and governments that would be wary of collaborating on efforts that solely benefited a particular company. . . .

Adopting a context-focused approach, however, goes against the grain of current philanthropic practice. Many companies actively distance their philanthropy from the business, believing this will lead to greater goodwill in local communities. While it is true that a growing number of companies aim to make their giving "strategic," few have connected giving to areas that improve their long-term competitive potential. And even fewer systematically apply their distinctive strengths to maximize the social and economic value created by their philanthropy. Instead, companies are often distracted by the desire to publicize how much money and effort they are contributing in order to foster an image of social responsibility and caring. Avon Products, for example, recently mobilized its 400,000 independent sales representatives in a high-profile door-to-door campaign to raise more than $32 million to fund breast cancer prevention. Fighting breast cancer is a worthy cause and one that is very meaningful to Avon's target market of female consumers. It is not, however, a material factor in Avon's competitive context or an area in which Avon has any inherent expertise. As a result, Avon may have greatly augmented its own cash contribution through effective fund-raising — and generated favorable publicity — but it failed to realize the full potential of its philanthropy to create social and economic value. Avon has done much good, but it could do even better. As long as companies remain focused on the public relations benefit of their contributions instead of the impact achieved, they will sacrifice opportunities to create social value. . . .

Collective action will often be more effective than a solo effort in addressing context and enhancing the value created, and it helps mitigate the free rider problem by distributing costs broadly. Few companies today work together to achieve social objectives. This may be the result of a general reluctance to work with competitors, but clusters encompass many related partners and industries that do not compete directly. More likely, the tendency to view philanthropy as a form of public relations leads companies to invent their own contributions campaigns, which are branded with their own identities and therefore discourage partners. Focusing on the social change to be achieved, rather than the publicity to be gained, will expand the potential for partnerships and collective action.

Once a company has identified opportunities to improve the competitive context and determined the ways in which it can contribute by adding unique value, the search for partners becomes straightforward: Who else stands to benefit from this change in competitive context? And who has complementary expertise or resources? Conversely, what philanthropic initiatives by others are worth joining? Where can the company be a good partner to others by contributing in ways that will enhance value? . . .

Monitoring achievements is essential to continually improving the philanthropic strategy and its implementation. As with any other corporate activity, consistent improvement over time brings the greatest value. The most successful programs will not be short-term campaigns but long-term commitments that continue to grow in scale and sophistication. . . .

Were this approach to be widely adopted, the pattern of corporate contributions would shift significantly. The overall level of contributions would likely increase, and the social and economic value created would go up even more sharply. Companies would be more confident about the value of their philanthropy and more committed to it. They would be able to communicate their philanthropic strategies more effectively to the communities in which they operate. Their choices of areas to support would be clearly understandable and would not seem unpredictable or idiosyncratic. Finally, there would be a better division of labor between corporate givers and other types of funders, with corporations tackling the areas where they are uniquely able to create value.

Charities too would benefit. They would see an increased and more predictable flow of corporate resources into the nonprofit sector. Just as important, they would develop close, long-term corporate partnerships that would better apply the expertise and assets of the for-profit sector to achieve social objectives. Just as companies can build on the nonprofit infrastructure to achieve their objectives more cost-effectively, nonprofits can benefit from using the commercial infrastructure. . . .

If systematically pursued in a way that maximizes the value created, context-focused philanthropy can offer companies a new set of competitive tools that well justifies the investment of resources. At the same time, it can unlock a vastly more powerful way to make the world a better place.

PROBLEM 11-2

1. You head corporate philanthropy for Chevron, headquartered outside of Oakland, California, with operations in 180 countries. About 10 percent of your budget supports local civic charities, including a family literacy initiative and a training program for disadvantaged high school youth in the health and science fields. The remainder goes to a variety of international and national efforts. For example, the company recently won an award for reaching over 20,000 employees with AIDS/HIV-prevention training in eleven languages. It also has given $18 million for an Energy for Learning project to aid school districts affected by hurricanes Katrina and Rita, and $30 million to help launch a global fund fighting AIDS, tuberculosis, and malaria. Another initiative, Chevron Humankind, matches employee contributions to charities of their choice and supports their volunteer activities.[32] You are currently preparing a report that evaluates the company's giving strategies. What questions would you ask and what evidence would you seek?

2. As part of Chevron's review process, the company convenes a committee that includes the general counsel, the director of public relations, the diversity officer, representatives of employee groups, and an outside expert on corporate philanthropy. Class members should break into small groups and assign roles. For example, suppose that the general counsel sits on the board of the Oakland Symphony and that his wife, along with the company's CEO, sits on the board of the Oakland Art Gallery. The general counsel believes that support for local cultural institutions is critical to cultivating an image of corporate citizenship and creating a community attractive to upper-level managerial and professional employees. By contrast, rank-and-file employee representatives who live in Oakland's inner city are worried about the effects of a recent budget crisis on basic services. They believe that more of the

company's charitable budget should support local education, law enforcement, economic development, and park programs that have lost taxpayer funding. The director of public relations, however, thinks that the BP oil spill is a wake-up call to spend more on partnerships with environmental organizations and academic institutions to expand safety, conservation, and renewable energy efforts. The outside expert is concerned that most of the company's prior grants have not been adequately evaluated and benchmarked. He would like to see the company cease making contributions, including employee-matching donations, to any program unless it can demonstrate a substantial social return on investment, as well as a benefit to the company's competitive context. After role-playing a debate, the committee should try to formulate a general road map for future giving strategies.

3. Consider the following corporate charitable initiatives that have been showcased as model programs. Would they fit Porter and Kramer's definitions of cost-effective approaches? Would they fit yours?

   • In the late 1980s, Reebok spent an estimated $15 million to sponsor a "Human Rights Now" concert tour in Eastern Europe with Sting and Bruce Springsteen. According to Craig Smith, former publisher of the Corporate Philanthropy Report, the tour "probably didn't sell any shoes, but had . . . a huge political impact that inspired the imagination of Reebok employees, suppliers, and franchisees. By thrusting the company into the leadership ranks of the global human rights movement, the concerts gave the company's young stakeholders a reason to be proud of what they do."[33]

   • For over thirty years, the Ronald McDonald House has provided homes for rural families who bring severely ill children to urban hospitals for outpatient care. Much of the money is raised from McDonald's restaurant customers through cause-marketing campaigns run by the franchisees.[34]

   • The high-tech company Intel includes among its leading philanthropic ventures a volunteer program in which employees coach, tutor, and mentor students, and the company provides matching grants to schools in which employees provide assistance. The company has also provided a $100,000 grant to Second Harvest Food Bank, which serves the county in which the company is located.[35]

   • Ford Motor Company recently overhauled its giving program and is partnering with a Detroit community group to sponsor days of volunteer service that come with $5000 cash grants. Employees provide help such as packing holiday baskets, building playgrounds, and planting a community garden.[36]

NOTES AND QUESTIONS

1. What is the "business case" for corporate philanthropy? What are the benefits to individual companies and to the business community as a whole? To what extent does the business case justify initiatives such as those listed in Problem 11-2?

2. Critics claim that shareholders should not have to subsidize the favorite charities of corporate leaders. How would you respond? Can corporations be held accountable for their social contributions?

3. In the wake of the economic recession, corporate giving temporarily declined, more donations were strategically aligned with business objectives, and more took the form of products, services, and volunteer time rather than financial assistance.[37] What are the societal implications of this trend? How should policy and nonprofit leaders respond?

4. Porter and Kramer claim that the enhanced morale from employee-matching grant programs could be equally or better achieved through an "increase in wages that employees could then choose to donate to charity on a tax-deductible basis. It does seem that many of the giving decisions companies make today would be better made by individuals donating their own money. . . ." Do you agree? In what sense would the decisions be "better"?

5. Reich and other critics of corporate philanthropy worry that it will displace government responsibility. But on some problems, might large global corporations have resources and capabilities that governments lack? Consider, for example, the assistance that high-tech companies have provided to the United Nations High Commission on Refugees to implement registration systems, or the medical assistance that pharmaceutical companies have provided to impoverished African nations in the fight against HIV/AIDS.[38] How might Reich respond? How would you?

6. Former Wharton professor Thomas Dunfee argued that in order for corporations to rationally allocate their charitable contributions, they should

> (1) align their social investments with their comparative advantages in providing social goods, (2) treat social investments in a manner similar to their financial investments by specifying social goals and objectives and then evaluating their investments to make sure that the goals and objectives are realized, and (3) be completely transparent in all dimensions of [their giving].[39]

In formulating their strategy, companies should first identify projects in which they can leverage their specific competencies, and then choose among those projects based on where social need is greatest.[40] Is this approach significantly different from Porter and Kramer's? If so, which is preferable? Would both frameworks eliminate corporate funding of arts, civic, antipoverty, and other programs in which the business has no special capacities to bring to the venture? Would that be desirable from a public-policy perspective?

MEDIA RESOURCES

Many foundations have materials on their strategic vision. For an illuminating comparison of the role of diamonds discussed in Problem 11-1, compare the website for the Nature of Diamonds exhibit at the Chicago Field Museum with the documentaries on "blood diamonds" identified in Chapter 10.[41] Another interesting comparison is between a Wal-Mart food drive commercial and an anti–Wal-Mart Christmas carol.[42] Mark Kramer has a discussion of effective philanthropy that amplifies the views discussed above and another perspective is available from a Business Leaders Roundtable.[43] The role of celebrity philanthropists has been thoroughly documented (Brad Pitt in Ethiopia, George Clooney in Haiti and Darfur). Most large corporate websites also include materials on their philanthropic initiatives.

C. PRO BONO SERVICE BY LAWYERS

The bar's tradition of providing unpaid legal assistance *pro bono publico* (for the good of the public) has extended historical roots, reaching back to classical Rome and medieval ecclesiastical courts.[44] How often it occurred, and who benefited, is not entirely clear. Surveys of the American bar in the 1970s and 1980s found that overall levels of assistance were quite modest, averaging only five to fifteen hours a year per lawyer, and that much of the aid went not to the poor but to relatives, friends, middle-class civic organizations, and other potential clients.[45] Recent decades, however, have brought a substantial increase in pro bono commitments, particularly for those most in need. As noted earlier, about three-quarters of lawyers report providing some assistance to low-income clients or to organizations that serve them, and their work on these and other public-interest matters has been central to struggles for social justice.[46]

Leaders can make a difference in several respects. The first is by personal example. As with other ethical issues, the "tone at the top" is critical, and when the busiest managing partners of firms make time for public service, it sends a crucial message. A second form of influence involves setting policy within leaders' own practice settings. As discussion below indicates, legal workplaces vary in how much they value and how effectively they allocate pro bono services. A third context in which leadership matters involves the rules and incentives that the profession collectively establishes for public service.

On all of these dimensions, progress remains to be made. While applauding the dedication of many pro bono lawyers, commentators raise concerns about both the quantity and quality of service. The average for the profession as a whole is well under an hour a week, and fewer than two-fifths of the lawyers in the most profitable firms contribute even a half hour.[47] Most firms also do little, if anything, to monitor the cost-effectiveness of assistance. The following excerpt explores the challenges facing the bar in ensuring that its charitable work best serves the public's, and not just the profession's, interests.

Deborah L. Rhode, "Rethinking the Public in Lawyers' Public Service: Pro Bono, Strategic Philanthropy, and the Bottom Line"

77 Fordham Law Review 1435 (2009)

Introduction

> Law firms . . . do not support pro bono unless there is a business reason to do so. The bottom line on this question is the bottom line.
>
> Chicago law firm partner

The preamble to the American Bar Association's (ABA) Model Rules of Professional Conduct declares, "A lawyer, as a member of the legal profession, . . . [is] a public citizen having special responsibility for the quality of justice." One of those responsibilities is the commitment to provide unpaid service "pro bono publico"—for the good of the public. But in practice, pro bono has never been only about what is good for the public; it has also been about what is good for lawyers. What will enhance their reputation, experience, contacts, and relationships? The occasional disjuncture between public and professional interests in charitable work is the focus of this essay. In particular, the concern is that lawyers' own pragmatic interests have marginalized more socially responsible considerations and resulted in inadequate evaluation, strategic planning, and accountability.

That is not to discount the extraordinary contributions of time and talent that thousands of lawyers make. Nor is it to overlook the equally impressive increase in pro bono contributions over the last decade. But it is to argue against complacency. It is a shameful irony that the country with the world's highest concentration of lawyers has done so little to make legal assistance available to low-income individuals who need it most. Equal justice is what we put on courthouse doors; it does not describe what goes on behind them. Lawyers, both individually and collectively, have a responsibility for the quality of justice that implies a responsibility for effective pro bono assistance. This obligation is too often overlooked in contemporary practice.

I. The Role of Self-Interest

Whether self-interest matters in public service is part of a long-standing debate about the meaning of altruism. Some branches of philosophy and economics deny the possibility of wholly disinterested behavior. Their assumption is that all reasoned action is motivated by some self-interest—after all, why else would someone act? According to this view, when people attempt to benefit another, it is because they derive personal satisfaction from doing so. And from a societal standpoint, why should their motivation matter? To borrow philosopher Bernard Williams's example, when a man gives money to famine relief, why should we care whether his objective is to enhance his standing with the Rotary Club? So too, what difference does it make if law firms volunteer time less out of concern for social justice than a desire to improve their recruitment, reputation, training, and media rankings. The point is to get their contributions.

Yet, to view public service solely in terms of professional interests is troubling on both moral and pragmatic grounds. As a matter of principle, an action taken because benefiting others feels intrinsically rewarding stands on different ethical footing than an action taken because it will bring extrinsic rewards. Part of what individuals find fulfilling about charitable work is a sense that they are expressing moral values and serving broader social objectives. A wide array of evidence suggests that selfless action is good for the self; it enhances satisfaction, health, and self-esteem. Moreover, as a practical matter, encouraging individuals to engage in public service for intrinsic reasons rather than extrinsic rewards serves societal objectives. It is generally less expensive and more effective to rely on internal motivations than on external incentives and sanctions to ensure quality assistance. That is particularly true in contexts like pro bono legal work, where most clients are not in a position to evaluate or challenge the adequacy of aid. Those who provide legal services based on deeply felt values are more likely to do their best than those who are merely fulfilling a firm's hourly quota or improving their legal skills. Some evidence also suggests that lawyers motivated by internalized commitments are the most likely to engage in substantial and sustained service.

Of course, intrinsic and extrinsic motivations are not mutually exclusive; they are often mutually reinforcing. Billable hours credit can ensure that individuals have the time to offer assistance that they are internally motivated to provide. The point is simply that encouraging individuals and employers to view pro bono contributions in terms of their social impact is likely to enhance their performance. A strategic philanthropic orientation also encourages the kind of public service that most benefits the public.

Yet this ethical focus is too often eclipsed by the "business case" for pro bono service. This essay explores the way that lawyers' own pragmatic interests can marginalize more socially responsible considerations. It also chronicles the inadequacies in program design, evaluation, and reporting and accountability standards that have compromised the effectiveness of even the best-intentioned public service initiatives. The full potential of pro bono work is more likely to emerge under a framework grounded in strategic philanthropy. In essence, that framework demands clarity in goals and specific measurements of achievement. Its premise is that those who make philanthropic contributions want the maximum social return on their investment. For lawyers' pro bono programs, that will require a more reflective process for establishing priorities and evaluating progress. . . .

III. Pro Bono for Whom? The Profession's Interest in Public Service

[What exactly should count as pro bono work is a matter of long-standing dispute? Should any unpaid work qualify, including favors for family, friends, and paying clients; service on nonprofit boards; or cases involving deadbeat clients or court-awarded fees?] The lack of consensus about what constitutes pro bono work is partly attributable to the lack of consensus about why lawyers should do it. Attorneys' public service reflects the same mix of motives that underpins other charitable work. People contribute out of a sense of empathy and obligation, and out of a desire for rewards and recognition. Giving makes givers feel good and translates into tangible personal and professional benefits. Lawyers are no exception. When asked about motivating factors for pro bono work, lawyers most often cite personal satisfaction, and then a sense of professional obligation, followed by employer policies and encouragement, and career advancement. For many attorneys, public service offers their most rewarding experiences; it is a way to feel that they are making a difference and to express the values that sent them to law school in the first instance. Work for racial, ethnic, or other disadvantaged groups can also be an important form of "giving back" and affirming identity. So too, for attorneys phasing into retirement, volunteer service is a way to continue making productive use of their skills on a less demanding schedule. Other lawyers cite practical payoffs. Public service can bring recognition, contacts, trial experience, direct client relationships, and expertise in a field in which they would like to obtain paid work. . . .

As bar leaders have also recognized, the profession has a strong self-interest in seeing that its members voluntarily assume such obligations. In a society in which over four-fifths of the legal needs of the poor, and two- to three-fifths of the needs of moderate-income individuals remain unmet, bar pro bono assistance can help relieve pressure for more systemic reforms that would reduce the need for attorneys. . . . In one representative survey, which asked what could improve the image of lawyers, the response most often chosen was "provision of free legal services to the needy"; two-thirds of Americans indicated that it would favorably influence their opinion.

Legal employers, for their part, have comparable interests in supporting pro bono work. Those interests vary somewhat across practice settings. Particularly for junior attorneys in large firms, nonpaying cases can offer training, litigation experience, client contact, intellectual challenge, and responsibility far beyond what is available in their other work. . . .

Such work can also enhance a firm's reputation and visibility in the community. The benefits are particularly great for the largest firms. They have the resources to attract and underwrite high-profile cases, and their pro bono performance is ranked by the American Lawyer based on the number of hours per lawyer and the percentage of lawyers who contribute more than twenty hours. A firm's pro bono rating also accounts for a third of its score in the competition for membership on the American Lawyer's coveted "A-List" of the nation's top twenty firms. A low score also risks relegating the firm to the magazine's occasional profiles of cellar dwellers. Interviews with senior managers leave no doubt that many firms have responded to these rankings by substantially improving their pro bono programs.

IV. Limitations of Existing Programs

These bottom-line concerns have led many bar leaders to stress the business case for pro bono initiatives. As one veteran repeatedly emphasized to American Bar Foundation researchers — "often pounding the table — self-interest, self-interest, self-interest." The risk, however, is that the public interest may become an unintended casualty. Problems arise in several forms: the quality of service, the need for recognition, and the criteria for selection.

One chronic difficulty stems from the inadequacy of oversight and accountability. Law firms and media ranking systems compile information on the quantity, not quality, of pro bono work, and clients often lack the knowledge or leverage to raise concerns. . . . In my own recent survey of leading public interest legal organizations, almost half reported extensive or moderate problems with quality in the pro bono work they obtained from outside firms. . . .

A related problem involves lawyers who "want to do pro bono work in theory but in practice, don't want to make the commitment." Although many firms go to considerable lengths to ensure that public service clients are not treated as second class citizens, others let bottom-line considerations prevail. These employers look for "training and opportunities for bored associates, but don't want to give them the time . . . when other paid work comes up."

In some cases, the difficulty lies with the associates who are disenchanted with their pro bono options, often because the programs do not provide sufficient choice or credit. Here again, American Lawyer rankings may have perverse results if firms pressure attorneys to participate without providing a range of satisfying opportunities. Almost half the lawyers in my pro bono study expressed dissatisfaction with the kind of work their firms permitted. Favors for clients, other lawyers, and their relatives, or partners' "pet organizations" struck many associates as "not truly" pro bono. . . .

A [further] problem involves the lack of strategic focus in formulating selection standards. Despite all the discussion about the business case for pro bono, most firms are strikingly unbusinesslike in the way that they structure their programs. The result is missed opportunities for both the profession and the public. Research on strategic philanthropy in general and public interest legal efforts in particular suggests that the most effective approach is to be systematic in identifying goals, designing cost-effective strategies to address them, and developing criteria to measure their achievement. By this standard, most lawyers' pro bono work falls short. Relatively few firms engage in any systematic assessment of community needs or of the most cost-effective use of resources. Seldom do they even survey their own membership about giving priorities or attempt to monitor the satisfaction of clients or the social impact of particular initiatives. When asked about how effectiveness is measured, one Wall Street partner expressed a common view with uncommon candor: " 'We are not able to answer this question as it is posed. . . . [W]e cannot opine as to which of our pro bono projects most effectively contributes to the community.' " The result is often a mismatch between public needs, partner priorities, and associate satisfaction. . . .

V. A Strategic Approach to Pro Bono Service

Paul Brest, former Stanford law professor, and now president of the Hewlett Foundation, likes to remind nonprofit organizations that "if you don't know where you are going, any road will take you there." Pro bono decision making often lacks that sense of direction. Many lawyers have not thought deeply about their objectives or have no principled way of resolving conflicts among them. The result is often a "spray and pray" approach, which spreads assistance widely in the hope that somehow something good will come of it. Something usually does, but the result is not necessarily the most cost-effective use of resources. . . .

[A well-designed] approach should have at least four critical dimensions:

- A process for identifying objectives and establishing priorities among them;
- A process for selecting projects that will best advance those objectives;
- Policies that encourage widespread participation; and
- A system for overseeing performance and evaluating how well objectives are being met.

In essence, those who make substantial pro bono contributions need to become more strategic in setting goals and monitoring progress in achieving them. . . .

Research on philanthropy in general and pro bono programs in particular leaves no doubt about the strategies most likely to promote involvement. First, organizations need to demonstrate a commitment to public service that is affirmed by their leadership and institutionalized in their policies. According to surveyed lawyers, the reforms most likely to encourage volunteer work included crediting it toward billable hour requirements and valuing it in promotion and compensation decisions. . . .

Enlisting students, clients, and the legal media in efforts to pressure legal employers also makes sense. For example, a student-led group, Building a Better Legal Profession, ranks major firms on measures including pro bono commitments and diversity. If a significant number of students act on that information, many employers will respond accordingly. So too, some government and corporate counsel's offices here and abroad have begun considering pro bono records in allocating legal work. If more clients joined a coordinated campaign, involving a broad spectrum of the legal market, the result might be a significant difference in law firm priorities. And if more legal publications published pro bono rankings of more legal employers, the heightened visibility might help improve performance. . . .

A final group of strategies should focus on evaluation. Employers need to know not simply who contributes and how much, but also how satisfied stakeholders are with their contributions. The ABA Standards for Programs Providing Civil Legal Services to Persons of Limited Means identifies strategies for assessing effectiveness, which include collecting evaluations from participants, clients, referring organizations, and peer review teams.

More effort should also address social impact. It is, of course, true, as Albert Einstein reportedly observed, that "'[n]ot everything that counts can be counted, and not everything that can be counted counts.'" In many charitable contexts, the social return on investment is hard to quantify and evaluate. . . . But that is no reason to avoid the effort, and there are better and worse ways of making such evaluations. As research on philanthropy demonstrates, donors who want to make a difference cannot afford to conflate good intentions with good results. Yet lawyers have a tendency to do just that. They often assume that anything given pro bono is pro bono; representation is taken as a good in and of itself, regardless of cost-effectiveness.

A more strategic approach would incorporate criteria similar to those that public interest legal organizations often use in allocating resources and evaluating their efforts. For example, are they meeting needs that experts or client groups consider most compelling? How many individuals are they assisting? If the matter involves policy or work or impact litigation, what are the chances of a long-term legal or political payoff? Will the work help to raise public understanding or empower clients? Is the assistance filling gaps in coverage or bringing some special expertise to the table? What are the other uses of lawyers' time? Might they find better ways to address the sources rather than symptoms of the problems? . . .

Conclusion: Beyond the Bottom Line

In today's increasingly competitive legal market, it comes as no surprise that pro bono is increasingly presented as a bottom-line issue. Nor is that strategy entirely misplaced. Convincing lawyers that they will do well by doing good is a key strategy in sustaining charitable commitments. But to present public service purely in those terms is to compromise altruistic impulses and societal objectives. When attorneys talk about pro bono, they generally speak in shorthand. "Publico" has dropped out of the discourse. We can afford to lose the Latin, but not the concept.

PROBLEM 11-3

If you were the chair of a law firm pro bono committee, what process would you establish to determine the amount and distribution of your organization's charitable contributions? How would you establish priorities? How much freedom would you give to individuals to choose where to commit time or money? Would you require a minimum commitment from all attorneys? Would you cap the amount of pro bono work that could count toward billable hour quotas? How would you measure cost effectiveness?

NOTES AND QUESTIONS

1. What is the "business case" for lawyers' public service? Is it the same as the case for corporate philanthropy?
2. One virtue of relying on "bottom-line" justifications for pro bono work is that they make it less vulnerable to cutbacks when the economy goes south. During the recent recession, large firms' charitable work went up 15 percent even as other economic indicators went down.[48] Rather than treating pro bono programs as an unaffordable luxury, firms generally relied on them to provide training and professional development for attorneys lacking sufficient paid work. Media ranking systems have also focused firms' attention on pro bono involvement as an important measure of reputation, which matters in recruitment and retention. Yet, as the preceding excerpt notes, that bottom-line focus has not come without costs. One is the absence of incentives for lawyers to focus on measures of performance apart from the number of hours contributed. A recent survey of pro bono counsel at large law firms found that none attempted any systematic analysis of the cost-effectiveness or social impact of their efforts. Nor did any have formal mechanisms for gauging satisfaction among clients and nonprofit organizations that referred or co-counseled pro bono cases.[49] Many pro bono programs seemed to operate on the assumption that any unpaid service is a good in itself, and that its value need not be questioned unless someone actually complains. This reactive approach is particularly ill suited to pro bono contexts. Unlike paying clients, who can vote with their feet if dissatisfied with performance, recipients of aid may lack alternatives or the sense of entitlement to express concerns.

   How should lawyers and law firms be held accountable for the quality and impact of their contributions? What could you do as managing partner of a firm or as a bar association president to promote greater accountability?
3. What might a strategic approach to pro bono involve for a law firm? A growing number of firms are attempting to partner with clients in order to build relationships and expand capacity. For example, Baker McKenzie is collaborating with in-house lawyers and other corporate

employees at companies including Google, Accenture, and Merck to tackle issues in Nepal involving exploitation of women, discrimination, education, and labor abuses.[50] What other approaches might you recommend?

4. Should firms require a minimum contribution in time (or a financial equivalent) from all lawyers? Should courts or bar associations? Or should they require reporting of contributions, which in some jurisdictions has produced a significant increase in services and financial contributions?[51] Would it be possible to ensure reasonable levels of competence and compliance under a mandatory pro bono system? Esther Lardent, president of the Pro Bono Institute, warns that mandatory systems make a "very small dent in a very large problem." In her view, the costs of training participants, administering referrals, and monitoring performance are likely to exceed the benefits.

> Unfortunately, the end product of a successful campaign for a mandatory pro bono program probably will fail to meet the original goals of the program's proponents. Experience demonstrates that the political compromises involved in securing approval of such a program will result in a definition of pro bono service so broad that it encompasses activities already undertaken by virtually all lawyers. All lawyers will be in compliance, yet no additional services to address unmet legal needs will be provided. . . . Mandatory pro bono will not increase services, enhance professionalism, or improve the performance of existing pro bono programs.[52]

Supporters of pro bono requirements respond that even if they were imperfectly administered and enforced, their existence would at least support lawyers who would like to provide more pro bono assistance but whose employers have other priorities. A mandatory program that offered training and support services, and a financial buyout alternative, could also respond to lawyers who lack expertise or interest in addressing unmet legal needs.[53]

What is your view? Should lawyers be subject to pro bono requirements by the bar or their employer? What about law students? Have you participated in organized volunteer work? Did it provide significant personal or professional benefits? How might public service enhance lawyers' performance in leadership positions?

MEDIA RESOURCES

Many law firms include material on their pro bono efforts on their websites. Some legal aid and public interest organizations also have promotional videos.[54] The American Bar Association's Center on Professional Responsibility compiles profiles of the winners of its annual Pro Bono Award.

END NOTES

1. http://foundationcenter.org/getstarted/faqs/html/giveingstats.html.

2. Giving USA, Annual Report. See also Noelle Barton and Caroline Preston, America's Biggest Businesses Set Flat Giving Budgets, Chronicle of Philanthropy, August 7, 2010 (reporting median of 1.2 percent).

3. American Bar Association Standing Committee on Pro Bono and Public Service, Supporting Justice II: A Report on the Pro Bono Work of America's Lawyers (Chicago, IL: American Bar Association, 2009), 10-11.

4. Claire Gaudiani, The Greater Good: How Philanthropy Drives the American Economy and Can Save Capitalism (New York: Henry Holt and Company, 2003).

5. Peter Singer, What Should a Billionaire Give—And What Should You?, in Patricia Illingsworth, Thomas Pogge, and Leif Wenar, eds., Giving Well: The Ethics of Philanthropy (New York: Oxford University Press, 2011), 13, 14; Chip Pitts, Ethical Philanthropy: Review of Giving Well, SSRN, 2011.

6. Alicia Epstein Lorten, Change Philanthropy (San Francisco: Jossey-Bass, 2009), 214-216.

7. John Sawhill and David Williamson, Measuring What Matters in Nonprofits, McKinsey Quarterly (May 2001):99, 100.

8. Michael Justesen and Dorte Verner, Factors Impacting Youth Development in Haiti, World Bank Report No. WPS4110, 4 (January 2007) (sexual abuse of girls); World Bank, Haiti: Social Resilience and State Fragility in Haiti, A Country Social Analysis, 33 (2006) (sexual violence against women).

9. Dennis Collins, The Art of Philanthropy, in H. Peter Karoff, ed., Just Money: A Critique of Contemporary American Philanthropy (Fitchburg, MA: TPI Publications, 2004), 63.

10. Bruce Sievers, Ethics and Philanthropy, in Deborah L. Rhode, ed., Moral Leadership: The Theory and Practice of Power, Judgment, and Policy (San Francisco: Jossey-Bass, 2006), 257.

11. The phrase is Michelle Courton Brown's, based on her experience with Fleet Bank initiatives. Michelle Courton Brown, Making the Case for Corporate Philanthropy, in Karoff, ed., Just Money, 160. See also Fleishman, "Simply Doing Good or Doing Good Well: Stewardship, Hubris, and Foundation Governance," in Just Money, at 118 (discussing the absence of research); William and Flora Hewlett Foundation and McKinsey & Company, The Nonprofit Marketplace: Bridging the Information Gap in Philanthropy, 2008, at 1 (discussing the absence of any central repository for information about performance), available at http://www.givingmarketplaces.org.

12. H. Peter Karoff, Introduction, in Karoff, ed., Just Money, at xxii. See also Karoff, Saturday Morning, in Karoff, ed., Just Money, 13; Collins, The Art of Philanthropy, at 65; Bruce Sievers, Philanthropy's Blindspots, in Just Money, at 134-135.

13. Collins, The Art of Philanthropy, 65.

14. Thomas Pogge, How International Nongovermental Organizations Should Act, in Illingsworth, Pogge, and Wenar, eds., Giving Well, 46, 52.

15. Paul Brest, Strategic Philanthropy and its Malcontents, in Rhode, ed., Moral Leadership, 237, 243; Hal Harvey and Barbara Merz, Problem Solving Philanthropy (unpublished manuscript); Hewlett Foundation and McKinsey & Company, "The Nonprofit Marketplace," at 18 (noting value of proxy information such as views of stakeholders).

16. Susan A. Ostrander, Moderating Contradictions of Feminist Philanthropy, Gender and Society 18 (2004):29, 39.

17. See Nancy Gibbs, The Good Samaritans, Time, December 19, 2005; Eliot Van Buskirk, Is It So Bad that Bono Does Good?, Wired.com, September 3, 2008.

18. See Linda Pulman, The Crisis Caravan (New York: Metropolitan Books, 2010), 185.

19. Richard S. Tedlow, Keeping the Corporate Image: Public Relations and Business, 1900-1950 (Greenwich, CT: JAI Press, 1979), 5 (quoting Vanderbilt).

20. Mathew Bishop and Michael Green, Philanthrocapitalism: How the Rich Can Save the World (New York: Bloomsbury Press, 2008), 182-183.

21. Robert B. Reich, Supercapitalism: The Transformation of Business, Democracy and Everyday Life (New York: Knopf, 2007), 204-207; Mary Lyn Stoll, The Ethics of Marketing Good Corporate Conduct, Journal of Business Ethics 41 (2002):121, 124.

22. Reich, Supercapitalism, 206.

23. Thomas W. Dunfee, The Unfulfilled Promise of Corporate Philanthropy, in Illingsworth, Pogge, and Wenar, eds., Giving Well, 243, 255, 257.

24. Bishop and Green, Philanthrocapitalism, 44; Dunfee, The Unfulfilled Promise, 245, 255; Usha C.V. Haley and Stephen A. Stumpf, Corporate Contributions as Managerial Masques: Reframing Corporate Contributions as Strategies to Influence Society, Journal of Management Studies 28 (1991):485-494.

25. *Kahn v. Sullivan*, 594 A.2d 48, 50-51 (Delaware Sup. Ct. 1991) (affirming a settlement with shareholders who challenged the donation).

26. Patricia H. Werhane, Corporate Social Responsibility/Corporate Moral Responsibility, in Steve May, George Cheney, and Juliet Roper, eds., The Debate over Corporate Social Responsibility (New York: Oxford University Press, 2007), 459, 460.

27. For Wal-Mart's contributions, see Barton and Preston, America's Biggest Businesses. For critiques, see http://walmartwatch.com and http://uspoverty.change.org/blog/view/ironic_philanthropy_walmart_donates_2b_to_fight_hunger.

28. Michael Porter and Mark Kramer, The Competitive Advantage of Corporate Philanthropy, Harvard Business Review (May, 2002):57.

29. For an overview, see M. Todd Henderson and Anup Malani, Corporate Philanthropy and the Market for Altruism, Columbia Law Review 109 (209):571, 579-585. For example, a recent study showing that MBA students will accept $3700 less compensation to work for a company committed to stakeholders does not identify the influence of philanthropy, and empirical evidence on corporate responsibility generally shows substantial disparities between what people say they value and what their behavior shows. See id., at 615, and discussion of studies in Chapter 10.

30. Dunfee, Unfulfilled Promise, 247, 253.

31. Thomas W. Dunfee, Managing Corporate Social Responsibility in a Multiple Actor Context, in Andy Crane, Abigail McWilliams, Dirk Matten, Jeremy Moon, and Donald S. Siegel, eds., The Oxford Handbook of Corporate Social Responsibility (New York: Oxford, 2008), 346, 351.

32. Information on Chevron programs comes from its website and from Sarah Duxbury, Chevron Merged Company Rethinking Its Giving from Top to Bottom, San Francisco Business Times, July 23, 2005.

33. Craig Smith, The New Corporate Philanthropy, Harvard Business Review (May-June 1994):105, 111-112.

34. Smith, The New Corporate Philanthropy, 112.

35. Eilene Zimmerman, How to Match Companies and Causes, New York Times, August 29, 2010, at B7; Intel website.

36. Noelle Barton and Caroline Preston, America's Biggest Businesses Set Flat Giving Budgets, Chronicle of Philanthropy, August 7, 2010.

37. Chris Farrell, Philanthropy: Companies Seek Greater Returns in Tough Times, Business Online, January 15, 2010 (reporting 8 percent drop in 2008); Barton and Preston, America's Biggest Businesses (reporting 7.5 percent drop in 2009 and flat rate in 2010); Rob Blizard, 2009 and Beyond: Seeing Down the Road in a Round World; Corporate Philanthropy, Non-Profit Times, July 1, 2009, 18.

38. For the assistance to the UN High Commissioner, see Joe W. "Chip" Pitts III, Corporate Social Responsibility: Current Status and Future Evolution, 6 Rutgers Journal of Law and Public Policy 334 (2009):369 (text at note 128).

39. Dunfee, Managing Corporate Social Responsibility in a Multiple Actor Context, 360.

40. Dunfee, Unfulfilled Promise, 257-258.

41. For the Nature of Diamonds, see http://www.fieldmuseumk.org/diamonds/highlights.asp.

42. Compare anti–Wal-Mart carol at http://www.youtube.com/watch?v=W3zwFAMc-6I with Wal-Mart food drive commercial at http://www.youtube.com/watch?v=0_qttht03Os.

43. For Kramer, see http://www.youtube.com/watch?v=t0tsnU3vZIw. For the roundtable, see http://www.youtube.com/watch?v=APTFEOzheDE.

44. See Deborah L. Rhode, Pro Bono in Principle and in Practice (Stanford, CA: Stanford University Press, 2005), 3-4.

45. Id. at 14.

46. American Bar Association Standing Committee on Pro Bono and Public Service, Supporting Justice II: A Report on the Pro bono Work of America's Lawyers (Chicago, IL: American Bar Association, 2009), 1.

47. David Bario, Has Pro Bono Become Recession-Proof?, American Lawyer, July 2, 2009.

48. Id.

49. Scott L. Cummings and Deborah L. Rhode, Managing Pro Bono: Doing Well by Doing Better, Fordham Law Review 78 (2010):2357.

50. The Gift of Giving, Financial Times, December 1, 2010.

51. Since Florida has required reporting of pro bono contributions, the number of lawyers providing assistance to the poor has increased by 35 percent, the number of hours has increased by 160 percent, and financial contributions have increased by 243 percent. Florida bar, Standing Committee on Pro Bono Legal Service, Report of the Supreme Court of Florida, the Florida Bar and the Florida Bar Foundation on the Voluntary Pro bono Attorney Plan (2006), 3.

52. Esther Lardent, Mandatory Pro Bono in Civil Cases, The Wrong Answer to the Right Question, Maryland Law Review 78 (1990):100-101.

53. See Rhode, Pro Bono, 29-46.

54. For a documentary by the Legal Aid Foundation of Los Angeles, see http://www.youtube.com/watch?=BbgAzWrtO.

PART V

CONCLUSION— LEADERSHIP THROUGH A WIDER LENS

12

LEADERSHIP IN LITERATURE AND FILM

Courses on leadership can be taught entirely through literature or film, and although that is obviously not the approach of this book, much can be gained from approaching leadership issues through a narrative lens.[1] Prior chapters have included references to relevant materials. In this chapter, we identify books and movies that would be worth discussing in their entirety, but that also could be excerpted in connection with topics addressed earlier.

We begin with a rationale for studying leadership through narrative, focusing on fiction, and then anchor discussion around one novel, Leo Tolstoy's *The Death of Ivan Ilych*. Although the main character is a magistrate, his profession is not central to the narrative and his experience has a universal resonance. The remaining discussion is organized around workplace settings — law, business, and politics — but again, the leadership concerns at issue are not limited to those occupational contexts. By exploring common challenges through these diverse narrative forms, this chapter seeks to deepen understanding of themes that have figured throughout the book and that will arise in any leadership position.

A. LEADERSHIP THROUGH THE LENS OF NARRATIVE

Why analyze leadership through narrative? One reason is that the arts "interpret and amplify experience." In the words of the organizers of the Edinburgh International Festival, artistic works "engage the mind, touch the heart, feed the soul."[2] Because stories speak to our emotion as well as intellect, they give us a broader, sharper, and more intense understanding than what is available through other experiences. As philosophy professor Martha Nussbaum notes, "much of actual life goes by without that heightened awareness that comes through narrative."[3] Stories are, in the metaphor explored in Chapter 4, "made to stick" in ways that other knowledge is not. Social science research makes clear that narratives often shape the moral intuitions that guide decisions, particularly in high-pressure situations.[4]

A related reason for exploring leadership through literature and film is their capacity to engage our moral imagination. Anton Chekov's *Gooseberries* notes that in ordinary life:

> Everything is peaceful and quiet and only mute statistics protest: so many people gone out of their mind ... so many children dead from malnutrition—and such a state of things is evidently necessary; obviously the happy man is at ease only because the unhappy ones bear their burdens in silence. .... Behind the door of every contented happy man there ought to be someone standing with a little hammer and continually reminding him with a knock that there are unhappy people, that however happy he may be, life will sooner or later show him its claws, and trouble will come to him—illness, poverty, losses, and then no one will see or hear him, just as he now neither sees nor hears others. But there is no man with a hammer. The happy man lives at his ease, faintly fluttered by small daily cares, like an aspen in the wind, —and all is well.[5]

Fiction supplies a hammer. Psychiatrist Robert Cole, who taught a celebrated Harvard Business School course on moral leadership through literature, similarly sees fiction as a corrective to our tendency to "shrug off, shake off ... close our eyes to the world of unhappiness." A "compelling narrative is a gift of grace." It can "prick our conscience," and remind us of the moral imperatives that should guide our relationships. Heeding the "call of stories" is, "[a]ll in all, not a bad start for someone trying to find a good way to live this life."[6]

A final justification for looking at leadership through a fictional lens is that it supplies a foundation for lifelong learning. In the final analysis, the best that any single book or course can offer its audience is a greater capacity for continuing professional development. An ability to mine literature and film for broader leadership lessons is an acquired skill that will pay dividends over an entire career. Central to that skill is self-reflection, and here narrative can help. As Harvard professor Sandra Sucher notes, understanding not only why fictional characters act the way they did but also how and why we respond to their actions, is an invaluable way of gaining insight into our own values, aspirations, and moral blind spots.[7]

B. LOST OPPORTUNITIES: *THE DEATH OF IVAN ILYCH*

1. HISTORICAL BACKGROUND

Count Lev Nikolayevich Tolstoy was born in 1828, the son of an aristocratic landowning family. Both parents died during his childhood, and he was raised by a devout aunt. During his childhood, he was at best an indifferent student. In describing his aptitude for learning, a tutor remarked, "Leo neither wishes nor can," a description Tolstoy himself echoed.[8] At a provincial university, he studied law and oriental languages but left without a degree. After several years of a dissolute life in Moscow, he joined an artillery regiment that saw service in the Crimean War. He then began writing and established his reputation in fashionable circles in St. Petersburg. Disillusioned by that life, in his early thirties he returned to his family estate, became a magistrate, and built a school for peasant children. In 1862, he married and for the next fifteen years had a relatively happy life. He wrote two great novels, *War and Peace* and *Anna Karenina*, fathered thirteen children, and achieved considerable fame and fortune.

In his early fifties, he underwent a spiritual crisis. As he later explained in *The Confession*,

> [t]he question, which in my fiftieth year had brought me very close to suicide, was the simplest of all questions — one to make itself heard in the heart of every man from undeveloped childhood to wisest old age: a question without which, as I had myself experienced, life became impossible.
>
> That question was as follows: "What result will there be from what I am doing now, and may do to-morrow? What will be the issue of my life?" Otherwise expressed, it may run: "why should I live? Why should I wish for anything? Why should I do anything?" Again, in other words it is "Is there any meaning in my life which can overcome the inevitable death awaiting me?"[9]

In attempting to answer that question, Tolstoy came to realize that he had not been living by God's values, or even by his own, but by society's. In his social circle, "ambition, love of power, covetousness, lasciviousness, pride, anger and revenge were all respected." But when confronting the notion of death, he doubted the validity of such goals. "Well, I have now six thousand 'desatins' in the government of Samara, and three hundred horses — what then? . . . 'Well, what if I should be more famous than Gogol, Poushkin or Shakespeare, Moliere — than all the writers in the world — well, and what then?' I could find no reply."[10]

Neither his readings of the great philosophers nor the teachings of organized religion offered an answer. In Tolstoy's view, conventional Christian doctrine of damnation and salvation had robbed people of their ability to make moral choices on their own.[11] The only way that he could ultimately make sense of the meaning of life was through a personal belief in the existence of God. Over the next decade, he wrote a series of pamphlets denouncing war, violence, private property, the church, the courts, and the desires of the flesh. By the close of his life he was also indicting his prior fiction, along with *King Lear* and other classic Shakespearean works.[12] His alternative worldview was an "instinctive," "unmediated sense of religious and moral truth," rooted in love and compassion.[13] In 1901, the Russian Holy Synod excommunicated him, and he died nine years later en route to a monastery.

2. NOTES ON THE NOVEL

Ivan Ilych was Tolstoy's first work of fiction after his spiritual conversion, and it is regarded by many, including Vladimirovich Nabokov, as "Tolstoy's most artistic, most perfect, and most sophisticated achievement."[14] The inspiration was not his own experience, although he did at one point suffer from a painful leg ulcer, which left him bedridden for nine weeks, tended by his wife.[15] Rather, the model was the sudden and painful death of Ivan Ilych Mechnikov, a forty-five-year-old prosecutor in a regional court near Tolstoy's estate.[16] According to the memoir of Tolstoy's sister-in-law, she had told him what she had learned from Mechnikov's wife: that the dying man's thoughts had been of the "uselessness of the life he had lived."[17]

In a letter just before the novel's publication, Tolstoy indicated that he had wanted to write a "description of the simple death of a simple man from his point of view."[18] For millions of readers, however, *The Death of Ivan Ilych* has been much more than that.

From the standpoint of leadership, Ilych's life is a cautionary tale. He occupies a leadership position; he is a judge with opportunities to do justice for those who come before him. But the role offers few such satisfactions. As the narrator notes, "[t]he pleasures Ivan Ilych derived from his work were those of pride; the pleasures he derived from society were those of vanity; but it was genuine pleasure that he derived from playing whist."[19] For today's professionals, the functional equivalent might be golf, shopping, or a summer home. Yet, in the face of an agonizing death, these pleasures seldom add up. For Ivan Ilych, the physical pain of his illness is amplified by psychological anguish at the banality of his existence. As he recognizes:

> That what had appeared perfectly impossible before, namely that he had not spent his life as should have done, might after all be true. It occurred to him that his scarcely perceptible attempts to struggle against what was considered good by the most highly placed people, those scarcely noticeable impulses which he had immediately suppressed, might have been the real thing, and all the rest false. And his professional duties and the whole arrangement of his life and of his family, and all his social and official interests, might all have been false. He tried to defend all those things to himself and suddenly felt the weakness of what he was defending. There was nothing to defend.

"What is it all for?" Ivan Ilych asks, which invites readers to do the same. The novel prods us to think about what really matters in life and why, before it is too late.

QUESTIONS

1. In the novel's opening chapter, Ivan Ilych's servant Gerasim makes a common sense point about death: "We all come to it one day." Yet one of Tolstoy's powerful points is the extent to which we generally manage to avoid coming to terms with that fact. At one point in the story, Ivan Ilych recalls Kieswetter's syllogism: "Caius is a man: men are mortal; therefore Caius is mortal." Yet he cannot accept that this logic might apply to him personally. "I Vania, Ivan Ilych, with all my feelings and thoughts" cannot be mortal in the same way as Caius is mortal: that is "how he felt." When you read the syllogism, did you share that emotional response? How might coming to terms with death affect how leaders choose to lead?
2. The author of a distinguished biography of Tolstoy writes of *The Death of Ivan Ilych* that "there are, in fact, few stories whose intended meaning is so abundantly clear."[20] Is it? What meaning do you take from the novel?
3. If you were in Ivan Ilych's place, how would you evaluate your own life to date? What would you most want said at your memorial service? Are you living your day-to-day life with your fundamental values clearly in view?

BIBLIOGRAPHIC AND MEDIA RESOURCES

Many biographies of Tolstoy are readily available, as are books and articles on *Ivan Ilych*.[21] A comprehensive website with pictures and biographical material appears at www.tolstoy.com/etext. A text of *The Confession* and audio of Tolstoy speaking are also available online.[22] Interesting background material appears in the documentary *Alexander II and His Times: A Narrative History of Russia in the Age of Alexander II, Tolstoy, and Dostoevesky*.[23]

C. LAW

1. HARPER LEE, *TO KILL A MOCKINGBIRD* (1960)

Harper Lee was born in 1926 in Monroeville, Alabama, the daughter of a prominent lawyer. She studied law for several years at the University of Alabama, and then as an exchange student at Oxford University, but never earned a degree. Instead, she went to New York to become a writer, and after a brief stint working as an airline reservation clerk, managed to produce the novel that would become her legacy. *To Kill a Mockingbird* is an undisguised portrait of her father, and the racial dynamics of the community in which he practiced. It won a Pulitzer Prize, sold over 12 million copies, and inspired a movie that earned several Academy Awards, including one to Gregory Peck in the starring role.[24]

The book has also generated considerable debate within the legal community. A key dispute is whether the novel's main character, Atticus Finch, is a moral hero. Should the bar honor a lawyer who acted as he did?

The conventional view has been that Finch represents the highest ideals of the profession. Some loyalists have viewed any criticism of his conduct as tantamount to attacks on "God, Moses, Jesus, Gandhi, and Mother Theresa."[25] From his defenders' perspective, Finch does his utmost to provide effective representation in a court-assigned case involving the most unpopular kind of defendant in Jim Crow Alabama: a black man accused of raping a white woman. Finch risks his life to save his client from a lynch mob, treats blacks with respect, and treats his opponents with civility and empathy. As his neighbor concludes, "we trust him to do right. It's that simple."[26]

By contrast, critics fault Finch on multiple grounds. The first is his brutal cross-examination of the rape complainant, his exploitation of sexist stereotypes, and his indifference to her own victimization. He assumes she is lying, which some law professors have found less self-evident than conventional readings suggest.[27] But even if that assumption is correct, commentators note that his defense builds on class and gender prejudices in ways that are gratuitously demeaning and that reinforce her status as a social pariah. He presents her as white "trash," a woman whose uncontrolled sexual desires have led her to violate the community's ultimate moral code. As he sums it up for the jury, "[s]he was white and she tempted a Negro. . . . No code mattered to her before she broke it, but it came crashing down on her afterward," causing her to falsely claim rape.[28] To further impugn her character, Finch elicits testimony suggesting that she had previously been raped by her father. Neither this possibility nor her serious injuries following that sexual encounter elicits any sympathy from Finch or the town's citizens; no one even offered medical treatment.[29] Indeed, Finch's nine-year-old daughter seems to have greater empathy for the complainant than any of the community's respected citizens. Only she recognized that the woman "must have been the loneliest person in the world. . . . [W]hite people wouldn't have anything to do with her because she lived among pigs; negroes wouldn't have anything to do with her because she was white."[30] As Malcolm Gladwell noted in a *New Yorker* review, Finch did not "challenge the foundations of [race or class] . . . privilege. Instead Finch does what lawyers for black men did in those days. He encourages [white male jurors] . . . to swap one of their prejudices for another."[31]

Worse still, according to law professor Monroe Freedman, is Finch's complicity in racism. He tells his children that the leader of a lynch mob "is basically a good man" who "just has his blind spots along with the rest of us."[32] Not only does Finch fail to volunteer to defend a man whom he believed innocent of a capital charge, he acknowledges that he had "hoped to get through life without a case of this kind. . . ."[33] As far as we know, never does Finch once "in his professional life voluntarily tak[e] a case in an effort to ameliorate the evil . . . [of] apartheid. . . ." Neither as a lawyer nor a state legislator did he "voluntarily use his legal training and skills . . . to make the slightest change in the social injustice of his own town."[34]

Finally, and to some critics even more disturbingly, Finch betrays his own professional responsibilities after his children are threatened by the father of the disgraced complainant. A reclusive neighbor saves the children but kills the would-be assailant. Finch and the town sheriff agree to avoid public inquiry by pretending that the assailant died by his own hand, and Finch tells his children to lie about what happened. The result may be rough justice, but the means are not what legal ethics experts expect from a moral icon.[35]

QUESTIONS

1. What is your view? Was Atticus Finch a hero for his times? Deeply flawed? Or, for a white man in small-town Alabama in the 1930s, "probably ahead of the curve?"[36]
2. Could Finch have effectively defended his client without playing to race and class privilege? What did moral leadership require in his situation?

2. ROBERT BOLT, *A MAN FOR ALL SEASONS* (1960)

Robert Bolt (1924-1995) was born in Manchester, England, the son of small shopkeeper. After attending Manchester University, serving briefly in the military, and doing postgraduate work at Exeter, he became a schoolmaster in English literature. In his midthirties, he became a full-time writer, best known for *A Man for all Seasons*. The play won a Drama Critics and two Tony awards, and the film adaptation earned Academy Awards for Bolt for the screenplay and Paul Scofield for best actor. Bolt also achieved recognition as a scriptwriter for *Lawrence of Arabia*, and notoriety during its production when he was arrested in a nuclear arms protest. He initially refused to sign a pledge to keep the peace, which would secure his release from jail. However, after pressure from the studio, he agreed to the condition in order to prevent costly delays in the filming schedule. That decision reportedly left him with a deep sense of guilt, in part because his capitulation compared unfavorably to the resistance of Sir Thomas More (1477-1535), the hero of *A Man for all Seasons*.[37]

More was a lawyer and scholar who became Lord Chancellor of England during the reign of Henry VIII. His conflict with the King over the role of the Roman Catholic Church and the validity of Henry's marriage cost More his life. The conflict unfolded against the backdrop of the Reformation, which responded to doctrinal cleavages and corruption in the Church hierarchy. During that period, popes often were embroiled in scandal, religious offices went to the highest bidder, sinners could purchase indulgences, and taxes were levied for seemingly excessive expenses. Calls for reform intensified with Martin Luther's famous *Ninety-Five Theses* (1517). They supplied the foundation for a Protestant movement, which stressed the individual's direct relationship to God, and made salvation dependent on faith rather than rituals mediated by the Church hierarchy.

In England, this reform movement played out against a complicated and contested split of authority between king and pope. At the turn of the sixteenth century, estimates suggested that the Church controlled as much as a third of all the land in England. However, the Crown exercised authority over taxation and the appointment of high Church officers who were also civil servants. But Rome controlled matrimonial law, which for Henry VIII proved highly inconvenient. He gained the throne in 1509, and soon after married Catherine of Aragon, the daughter of the King of Spain. Although she had formerly been married to Henry's deceased brother, she claimed that the union had never been consummated. But given biblical prohibitions against marrying a brother's widow, a papal dispensation was arranged to safeguard the legitimacy of her marriage with Henry.

By the 1520s, Catherine had failed to produce a male heir, which Henry interpreted as divine retribution for contradicting bans against incest. Although divorces were not then available, he asked for an annulment, a practice common where royalty was involved. In this case, however, the annulment was problematic, both doctrinally (because of the prior dispensation) and politically (because the Pope was under the control of the Holy Roman Emperor, Catherine's nephew). Henry's impatience with the annulment process increased as a result of his infatuation with reformist-leaning Ann Boleyn. To secure his right to remarriage, he appointed a new Archbishop of Canterbury, Thomas Cramner, who granted an annulment. Henry also installed a new chief advisor, Thomas Cromwell, who helped secure Parliament's passage of the 1534 Act of Supremacy. The Act established Henry as the new head of the English church, and he demanded that leading church and political figures swear an oath acknowledging his supremacy.[38] More, a devout

Catholic, refused. After a year of solitary confinement in the Tower of London, he was convicted of treason through perjured testimony and beheaded.

As Bolt describes him in the Preface and portrays him in the play, More had all the qualities of a great leader. Born to a merchant, not noble, family, he earned distinction first as a scholar, then as a lawyer and politician of great wisdom and integrity. He "corresponded with the greatest minds of Europe" and published an important tract, *Utopia*. As Bolt sums it up, More "parted with more than most men when he parted with his life."[39]

In the play, when More asks why he has been chosen as Lord Chancellor, Henry replies:

> Because you are honest. What's more to the purpose, you're known to be honest. . . . There are those like [the Duke of] Norfolk who follow me because I wear the crown, and there are those like Master Cromwell who follow me because they are jackals with sharp teeth and I am their lion, and there is a mass that follows me because they follow anything that moves — and there is you.[40]

Yet the choice turns out to be disastrous for both men: for Henry, because he ultimately values loyalty more than integrity, and for More, because his prominence draws attention to his silence regarding the king's supremacy. As Cromwell puts it at trial, that silence is "booming throughout Europe."[41]

What makes More's decision so illuminating from the standpoint of leadership is not just the personal price he is willing to pay for principle, but also the political costs that he is willing to impose on the nation. The price becomes apparent in a dialogue with Cardinal Wolsey, who argues that More should not let his own religious convictions take precedence over the safety of the country. More responds: "I believe that when statesmen forsake their own private conscience for the sake of their public duties . . . they lead their country by a short route to chaos." Wolsey is not persuaded and reminds More of the consequences if Henry is unable to remarry. "Do you remember the Yorkist Wars? Let him die without an heir and we'll have them back again. Let him die without an heir and this 'peace' you think so much of will go out like that," Wolsey predicts, extinguishing a candle.[42]

Aware of the risk to the country, as well as to himself and his family, More attempts to avoid confrontation with the King. He does not seek martyrdom by openly asserting his principles, and he studiously avoids commenting on the king's plans for remarriage. At one point when More and Wolsey look out a window and see the King turning to the castle, presumably after an evening with Ann Boleyn, Wolsey says to More, "The King wants a son; what are you going to do about it?" More deflects rather than answers the question: "I'm sure the King needs no advice from me on what to do about it." When Wolsey persists, and again asks More how he will help Henry obtain an heir, More responds that he prays for it daily.[43]

But when silence will no longer suffice, More cannot sacrifice principle to pragmatism. After the Duke of Norfolk shows More a list of all the government and Church leaders who have pledged to support the King and entreats More to "do what I did and come with us for fellowship," More resists: "And when we stand before God, and you are sent to paradise for doing according to your conscience, and I am damned for not doing according to mine, will you come with me, for fellowship?"[44]

More's adherence to principle stands in sharp relief to others in the play, who are motivated primarily by their own interests. The clearest example is Richard Rich, an academic who seeks a position in the government and ultimately gives false testimony against More to secure it. More has clues of Rich's possible betrayal, and More's wife, Alice, daughter, Margaret, and son-in-law, William Roper, all urge that Rich be arrested. More declines in what is one of the play's most celebrated exchanges:

Margaret: "That man's bad."
More: "There is no law against that."
Roper: "There is, God's law."
More: "Then God can arrest him. . . . The law, Roper, the law. I know what's legal, not what's right. And I'll stick to what's legal."
Roper: "Then you set man's law above God's!"
More: "No, far below; but let me draw your attention to a fact — I'm not God. The current and eddies of right and wrong, which you find such plain sailing, I can't navigate. . . ."
Alice (exasperated, pointing after Rich):   "While you talk, he's gone!"
More: "And go he should, if he was the Devil himself, until he broke the law."
Roper: "So now you'd give the Devil benefit of law?"
More: "Yes. What would you do? Cut a great road through the law to get after the Devil?"
Roper: "I'd cut down every law in England to do that!"
More (roused and excited):   "Oh?" (advancing on Roper) "And when the last law was down, and the Devil turned round on you — where would you hide, Roper, the laws all being flat." (He leaves him.) "This country's planted thick with laws from coast to coast — man's laws, not God's — and if you cut them down — and you're just the man to do it — d'you really think you could stand upright in the winds that would blow then?" (quietly) "Yes, I'd give the devil benefit of law, for my own safety's sake."[45]

More clearly has the best of the argument, even though it turns out that giving Rich the benefit of the law in fact undermines More's safety. But Rich's betrayal also brings home one of the enduring lessons of the drama. It underscores the contrasting values that earn More sainthood, and leave Rich one of the most detested figures of the English stage. After observing Rich perjure himself at trial with a chain of the Attorney General of Wales around his neck, More invokes scripture to drive home his point: "For Wales? Why, Richard, it profits a man nothing to give his soul for the whole world. . . . But for Wales?"[46]

QUESTIONS

1. Could More have done anything that would have avoided the conflict between personal principle and political loyalty that cost him his life?

2. If More was willing to elevate his view of "God's law" over the Supremacy Act, why was he reluctant to invoke God's law to arrest Rich and prevent his betrayal?

3. Does motive matter? If More's objective was to secure glory in the next life rather than this one, does that make him a moral hero? Is that the same motive that impels suicide bombers? Consider T.S. Eliot's analysis of that issue for Thomas Becket in *Murder in the Cathedral*: "The last temptation is the greatest treason: to do the right deed for the wrong reason."[47]

4. Are there any contemporary leaders who have exemplified More's courage and commitment to principle?

D. POLITICS

1. ROBERT PENN WARREN, *ALL THE KING'S MEN* (1953)

Robert Penn Warren was born in Kentucky in 1905, and earned a graduate degree in literature as a Rhodes scholar. He wrote both poetry and prose, and was named the first Poet Llaureate of the United States. *All the King's Men* is his most famous work. It is also one of the nation's most celebrated political novels, although Warren famously claimed that it was "never intended to be a book about politics."[48] Modeled on the regime of Louisiana Governor and Senator Huey Long (1893-1935), it was a national bestseller, winner of a Pulitzer Prize, and the basis for two movies, the second starring Sean Penn and Jude Law in the lead roles.

The story centers on Willie Stark, who begins as an idealistic lawyer and evolves into a populist demagogue, shedding most of his principles along the way. He loses his initial position as a county treasurer by supporting the low bid on a school-contracting case. A higher bidder gets the contract, cuts corners, and causes a tragic accident, which makes Stark a local hero. He is then duped into running for governor by an aide to the corrupt incumbent, who needs to split the rural vote. When Stark discovers the truth, he drops out of the race and learns some lessons that enable him to win the next election. His story is told by Jack Burden, a political reporter who becomes an aide and similarly loses much of his initial idealism. In analyzing Stark's first failed race, Burden concludes: "[T]oo much talk about principles, and not enough about promises."[49]

That ceases to be a problem as Stark's career evolves. Although he retains concern for the masses, he becomes increasingly ruthless toward any individual who stands in his way. When told that no dirt was available about an opponent, he responds, "There's always something." He is diligent about finding it, and develops a flexible view of ethics. As he observes, "You've got to make good out of bad. That's all you've got to make it with." Moreover, the very concepts of good and bad come to seem less and less like fixed principles in his political world. From his vantage,

> [w]hat folks claim is right is always just a couple of jumps short of what they need to do business. Now an individual one fellow, he will stop doing business because he's got a notion of what is right, and he is a hero. But folks in general, which is society, . . . is never going to stop doing business. Society is just going to cook up a new notion of what is right."[50]

Law suffers from the same deficiency, as it is "always too short and too tight for growing humankind. The best you can do is do something and then make up some law to fit and by the time that law gets on the books you would have done something different."[51]

As Stark's aide, Burden initially comes to a similar view. Unlike reporting, where his goal was to learn the truth, in politics, "the world was full of things that I [Burden] didn't want to know."[52] "Maybe," he notes at one point, "a man has to sell his soul to get the power to do good."[53] But by the end of the novel, that is not the conclusion that Burden ultimately embraces. And even Stark himself, as he dies from an assassin's bullet, insists that "it might have been different. You got to believe that."[54]

The extent to which *All the King's Men* captured a realistic view of politics has been subject to considerable debate. Clearly, many events in the novel are modeled on Long's career, including his initial failed political campaigns and his impeachment and assassination.[55] But Warren himself rejected interpretations that reduced the narrative to political commentary. As he put it in an Introduction to a Modern Library edition,

> On one hand, there were those who took the thing to be a not-so-covert biography of, and apologia for, Senator Long. . . . There is really nothing to reply to this innocent boneheadedness or gospel-bit hysteria. As Louis Armstrong is reported to have said, there's some folks that, if they don't know, you can't tell 'em. . . . But on the other hand, there were those who took the thing to be a rousing declaration of democratic principles and a tract for the assassination of dictators. This view, though somewhat more congenial to my personal political views, was almost as wide of the mark. For better or worse, Willie Stark was not Huey Long. Willie [Stark] was only himself. . . .
>
> [His career suggests] the kind of doom that democracy may invite upon itself. The book, however, was never intended to be a book about politics. Politics merely provided the framework in which the deeper concerns, whatever their final significance, might work themselves out.[56]

QUESTIONS

1. If *All the King's Men* is taken not simply as a book about politics in a given era but as an exploration of leadership, what insights does it suggest?
2. What might have made things different in Stark's career?
3. What would be modern examples of the "dirty hands" dilemmas that "all the king's men" confront?[57]

2. KAZUO ISHIGURO, *THE REMAINS OF THE DAY* (1989)

Kazuo Ishiguro was born in 1954 in Nagasaki, Japan. When he was five, his family moved to Great Britain, where his father, an oceanographer, began work on a North Sea research project. Despite his Japanese heritage, Ishiguro had what he described as a "very typical middle-class southern English upbringing."[58] After working briefly as a grouse beater for the Queen Mother at a Scottish castle, Ishiguro studied English and philosophy at the University of Kent. He then spent a year working on behalf of London's homeless, and another year obtaining a master's degree in creative writing. His first novels were set in Japan, but his first critical success was *The Remains of the Day*, the story of a British butler between the 1930s and 1950s. It won the prestigious Booker Prize and was adapted for an award-winning film produced by Merchant Ivory, with Anthony Hopkins and Emma Thompson in the lead roles.

The story is told through the eyes of Stevens, the butler, in a series of flashbacks. It opens in 1956, after the "great house" in which he served Lord Darlington for most of his life has been sold to an American. To rebuild Britain after World War II, the government imposed such high inheritance taxes that most large ancestral homes were donated to the National Trust, opened to tourists, or put up for sale to developers and foreign investors. The declining appeal of domestic service also created enormous problems in staffing country manors, and Stevens is now faced with the task of running a household with four, rather than twenty-eight, retainers.[59] In all his years of service, Stevens has never taken a vacation. When his new employer gives him the opportunity, Stevens adds a business purpose. He takes Darlington Hall's car to visit its former housekeeper, Miss Kenton. She has married and resettled in the West Country, but a recent letter suggests that she may be open to leaving her husband and returning to service.

Over the course of the trip, Stevens reflects on his professional life and is not entirely happy with how it has played out. His work as a butler provides an ideal way to explore the complexities of leader-follower relationships, because that position puts its occupants in both roles simultaneously. In his relations with his employer, the butler must display unqualified subservience. In his relations with the household staff, he exacts the same obedience from others. For Stevens, both dimensions of this role held moral significance.

> The question was not simply one of how well one practiced one's skills, but to what end one did so; each of us harboured the desire to make our small contribution to the creation of a better world, and saw that, as professionals, the surest means of doing so would be to serve the great gentlemen of our times in whose hands civilization had been entrusted. . . . A "great" butler can only be, surely, one who can point to his years of service and say that he has applied his talents to serving a great gentleman,—and through the latter, to serving humanity.[60]

Ishiguro sees a nobility in this role, and one that is a model not just for butlers. As he explained in an interview, "I chose the figure [of a butler] deliberately, because that is what I think most of us are. . . . For most of us, the best we can hope for is to use our rather small skills in serving people and organizations that really do matter."[61]

The central difficulty for Stevens is that Lord Darlington matters in the wrong way, and from a historical standpoint, does not figure as a "great gentleman" worthy of his staff's unqualified loyalty. He is a Nazi sympathizer who arranges several secret meetings with the German ambassador and British leaders in the hope of forestalling conflict. His appeasement sympathies earn him a warm reception from the Third Reich and a despised status in postwar Britain. Even before the war begins, Stevens sees some evidence of his employer's misplaced moral compass when Darlington demands the dismissal of two German Jewish housemaids. Despite their excellent service and the difficulties that they will face in gaining other work, Darlington explains: "It's regrettable . . . but we have no choice. There's the safety and the well being of my guests to consider. Let me assure you, I've looked into this matter and thought it through thoroughly. It's in our best interests."[62] Stevens conveys this decision to Miss Kenton, who is outraged, and threatens to quit. He responds by reminding her that

> our professional duty is not to our own foibles and sentiments, but to the wishes of our employer. . . . You are hardly well placed to be passing judgments of such a high and mighty nature. The fact is, the world of today is a very complicated and treacherous place. There are many things you and I are simply not in a position to understand concerning, say, the nature of Jewry. Whereas his lordship, I might venture, is somewhat better placed to judge what is best.[63]

Looking back on the incident, Stevens recalls: "[M]y every instinct opposed the idea of their dismissal. Nevertheless, my duty in this instance was quite clear, and as I saw it, there was nothing to be gained at all in irresponsibly displaying such personal doubts. It was a difficult task, but as such, one that demanded to be carried out with dignity."[64]

Miss Kenton recalls the incident differently. The topic arises a year after the maids' dismissal, when Lord Darlington acknowledges to Stevens that "it was wrong what happened," and that he "would like to recompense them somehow."[65] Stevens raises the issue with Miss Kenton in the vain hopes of finding the maids' address. She then confesses her shame at her "cowardice" in not resigning. "Whenever I thought of leaving, I just saw myself going out there and finding nobody who knew or cared about me. There, that's all my high principles amount to. I feel so ashamed of myself. . . . But I just couldn't bring myself to leave."[66] When Stevens then shares his own "distress" and "concern" about the episode, she asks: "[Why] did [you] not tell me so at the time? . . . Do you realize how much it would have helped me? Why, Mr. Stevens, why, why, why do you always have to pretend?"[67]

The same question arises in another scene that captures the ethical dilemmas of the follower's role. At one of Lord Darlington's dinner parties, some guests decide to make a point about the follies of universal suffrage at Stevens's expense. To expose the ignorance of the common voter, they begin grilling Stevens on the nuances of monetary and foreign policies. This forces him repeatedly to acknowledge that he can give no "satisfaction." The film is especially effective in conveying Stevens's repressed anger and humiliation, and in exposing yet another of Darlington's leadership failures in tolerating the abusive exchange.

The personal costs of Stevens's professional role are measured not only in such indignities but also in his total absorption in work. As his father lies dying upstairs, Stevens feels obligated to continue supervising a dinner party. In their final exchange, his father (himself a butler) tells his son: I'm proud of you. . . . I hope I've been a good father to you. I suppose I haven't." Rather than provide reassurance, Stevens replies simply, "I'm afraid we're extremely busy now, but we can talk again in the morning,"[68] which, of course, they cannot. Another forgone opportunity is presented by Miss Kenton, who clearly signals a desire for a deeper relationship.

At the close of the novel, Stevens realizes his loss, and sums it up for another butler that he meets on his travels:

> [Lord Darlington] wasn't a bad man. . . . And at least he had the privilege of being able to say at the end of his life that he made his own mistakes. . . . He chose a certain path in life, it proved to be a misguided one, but there, he chose it, he can say that at least. As for myself, I cannot even claim that. You see, I *trusted*. I trusted in his lordship's wisdom. All those years I served him, I trusted I was doing something worthwhile. I can't even say I made my own mistakes. What dignity is there in that?[69]

QUESTIONS

1. Is there dignity in that? Is it possible to take moral satisfaction from effectively discharging a professional role, independent of the ends that those efforts serve?
2. Was Lord Darlington "not a bad man?" Would he have been better served by less servility? Could actions by Stevens or Miss Kenton have changed his mind about the dismissal? Could either or both have enlisted allies among other staff, or were the risks to their livelihoods too great? What would you have done in their place?
3. Whose conduct seems most ethically problematic in connection with that incident? Is it that of Miss Kenton, who believes that Lord Darlington is wrong and that she should resign, but who lacks courage to do so? Or is the conduct of Stevens, who is distressed by Darlington's decision but refuses to second-guess his moral judgment?
4. Many commentators have drawn parallels between the role of the butler and the role of the lawyer.[70] What are the similarities and differences? To what extent should either be held accountable for the morality of their employer's actions? If a lawyer had been asked to dismiss Jewish employees, would his responsibility have been different than a butler's?

3. *INVICTUS* (2009)

Invictus is a film adaptation of John Carlin's *Playing the Enemy*, a description of Nelson Mandela's early years as South Africa's president, and his relationship with François Pienaar, captain of the nation's rugby team. The movie, produced by Clint Eastwood, stars Morgan Freeman as Mandela and Matt Damon as Pienaar. It begins in 1994, just after Mandela's election as president. Although the formal trappings of apartheid have been dismantled, its legacy of hatred and mistrust remains. Mandela's central leadership challenge is to bridge this racial divide and create a unified South Africa.

As noted in the discussion in Chapter 4 on conflict management, Mandela faces a key dilemma shortly after his inauguration. The new black commander of the presidential body guard resists Mandela's suggestion that the guard include white officers who may have brutalized blacks under the apartheid regime. But Mandela refuses to perpetuate racial segregation in his own administration. "Reconciliation and forgiveness begin here," he reminds the commander.

Mandela sees another opportunity to build bridges through rugby. As Chapter 4 noted, the South African team, the Springboks, had a poor record and was seen by blacks as a symbol of apartheid. When the national rugby association comes under black control, its members want to change the team's name. Mandela believes that the change would alienate the white community. At a meeting of the association, he convinces its members to retain the name. He then reaches out to Pienaar to involve him an alternative strategy to reposition the team, both in its athletic performance and its symbolic impact. By the time South Africa hosts the 1995 rugby World Cup finals, Mandela wants the Springboks to be source of national pride and unity. With Mandela's assistance, Pienaar helps make that happen. To build players' understanding of the legacy of apartheid, he takes them to the prison where Mandela was incarcerated for almost three decades, and has them provide workshops for impoverished black youths. To build unity, he has them learn the lyrics to the Afrikaner anthem played at games. As the team comes to see its symbolic role in the nation's reconciliation, its performance rises to the occasion. The film ends with scenes of how effective leadership can help bridge the deepest cleavages of class and race: black street urchins share a radio broadcast of the final match with white policemen, and a white family brings its black maid to attend the game. The ultimate message is that of the poem by William Ernest Henley, from which the movie title is drawn, and which reportedly sustained Mandela during his incarceration.

> Out of the night that covers me
> Black as the Pit from pole to pole;
> I thank whatever gods may be
> For my unconquerable soul.
> It matters not how strait the fate
> How charged with punishments the scroll,
> I am the master of my fate,
> I am the captain of my soul.

QUESTIONS

1. How does Mandela help Pienaar become an effective leader without ever suggesting what to do? What generalizations can you draw from their joint effort?
2. Consider the qualities of Mandela's leadership as portrayed in the film and book, and in Chapter 4. What makes him so effective? What strategies of influence convince the rugby association to retain the name Springbok?

3. What risks was Mandela taking in allowing the team to keep its name, and in investing so much of his own personal capital in the team's support? Would you have made the same decisions?

4. ANONYMOUS [JOE KLEIN], *PRIMARY COLORS* (1996)

Primary Colors, a best-selling novel by *Newsweek* columnist Joe Klein and an acclaimed film directed by Mike Nichols, views political leadership through a contemporary lens. The story centers on the presidential election campaign of Jack Stanton, and the narrative draws on Bill Clinton's 1992 victory. The narrator is Henry Burton, an idealistic African American campaign worker modeled on George Stephanapoulos. Although key facts have been altered, both the novel and film capture much of the reality of current political life. As Richard Cohen put it in a *Washington Post* review, sometimes only "fiction can do justice to the truth."[71]

From a leadership standpoint, several themes bear emphasis. One involves the qualities of leaders discussed in Chapters 1 and 2. Stanton, played by John Travolta, projects the magnetism that enabled Bill Clinton to connect to voters, despite his many personal failings. The movie opens with an exploration of the Stanton handshake. The scene then moves to a campaign event at an adult literacy class where Stanton exudes empathy (and follows it up in a hotel-room quickie with the class teacher). This link between Stanton's sexual and political charm also comes through in the novel's portrayal of a conversation between Burton and a woman who had had an affair with Stanton during college. In recalling his two-timing behavior, she notes:

> He loved her. He loved me. He loved every stray cat in the quad. That boy is not deficient in the love zone, — he's got more than enough to go around and it's all legit. He's never faking it. . . . I knew I'd never really have him. He was too needy and it wasn't the usual male kind of needy."[72]

Cohen's review observes the same quality, apparent in Clinton as well, and draws connections between these leaders' political strengths and personal weaknesses: "The fictional Stanton is the most indefatigable campaigner of our times, a man whose keenest sexual fantasy is to reach out and hug the American people — touch them all, love them, and have them love him back. If he can't love them that way, he'll just have to love them one at a time."[73] By contrast, Susan Stanton, effectively portrayed by Emma Thompson, captures Hillary Clinton's harder edges but more disciplined strategies. As one reviewer notes, it is the "wronged and humiliated" wife who puts the "steel back in the election effort. Both 'Susan' and Jack Stanton have their eyes on the prize, but Susan/Hillary is the one who keeps her gaze from wandering."[74]

A second theme involves the role of honesty in politics: when and why it sometimes appears expendable. At one campaign event, Stanton tells his audience: "I'm gonna do something really outrageous — tell the truth." The irony of that statement is not lost on Henry Burton, part of the cleanup team for Stanton's indiscretions and deceptions, or on American audiences who hear it through the filter of Clinton's famous falsehoods.

A third theme involves the role of followers, and the extent to which a leader's "dirty hands" inevitably soil those around them. Henry Burton faces difficult ethical trade-offs, including those that place his loyalty to the black community at issue.

An illuminating sidebar involves the dilemma for Joe Klein, who wrote the novel under the pen name "Anonymous," not expecting either that the book would become "A VERY BIG DEAL" or that his initial denials of authorship would be believed.[75] When they were, both Klein and his publisher saw advantages to retaining anonymity, even though it forced Klein into ever more public lies to colleagues and friends. When the truth finally came out, Klein wrote a rueful half apology in which he acknowledged being "sorry and horrified that [his] actions caused pain for people at *Newsweek*." But he also insisted that the "world didn't really need to know who 'Anonymous' was." And most importantly, he learned

> what it's like to live as a politician. . . . It's impossible to think straight. It's very easy to screw up, and it is unrelenting. But [political candidates] do it every day and that is no way for a civilized nation to choose its leaders. Of course, this was one the themes of "Primary Colors" — but I was just imagining what it was like on the other side of the press conference. Now that I've lived it, I hope I'll show a little more mercy on this [*Newsweek*] page for the brave, frail fools and heroes who live our public lives. I hope you will too.[76]

QUESTIONS

1. If voters followed Klein's advice, how might that change political campaigns?
2. Consider the discussion of the Clinton-Lewinsky scandal in Chapter 7, as well as the Gennifer Flowers's affair portrayed in the book through the character of Cashmere McCloud. Does the fictional account give you greater understanding of what drives sexual indiscretions, or their relevance to leadership capabilities?
3. Under what circumstances should private sexual affairs ever become matters of public debate? Under what, if any, circumstances, should lies about those affairs be viewed as disqualifying? How would you have handled the issue if you had been Jack or Susan Stanton?
4. What "dirty hands" dilemmas did the Stantons face? What would you have done in their place?
5. Was Henry Burton a good follower? Did he make trade-offs that you would not?

E. BUSINESS

1. GEORGE BERNARD SHAW, *MAJOR BARBARA*, IN *THE BODLEY HEAD BERNARD SHAW: COLLECTED PLAYS WITH THEIR PREFACES*, VOLUME III (1907)

George Bernard Shaw was born in Dublin, Ireland, in 1856 into genteel poverty. He left school at age fifteen, having found the traditional curriculum stifling. After working briefly as a clerk, he followed his mother to London, and began educating himself at the British Museum. His first successes involved musical and literary criticism, but he went on to win critical acclaim as an essayist, and as the author of some sixty plays. He also became a charter member of the Fabian Society, an organization of middle-class socialists; founded the London School of Economics; and became an active supporter of various social reforms including women's rights, the abolition of private property, electoral reform, and the simplification of spelling. On winning the 1925 Nobel Prize for literature, he accepted the honor but refused the money.

His plays were often didactic but leavened with enough humor to make them palatable to a wide audience. *Major Barbara* is an example of that style, and after initial performances on both sides of the Atlantic between 1905 and 1915, it was made into a film with Rex Harrison and Robert Morley in 1941. The story centers on Andrew Undershaft, a foundling who rises from poverty to become a millionaire arms manufacturer and to marry the daughter of an earl. Inspired in some respects by the German arms merchant Siegfried Krupp, Undershaft is a model employer but unprincipled seller, willing to supply weapons to anyone able to pay his price. As the play opens, his estranged wife has invited him home in the hopes of persuading him to make financial arrangements for his two daughters and son. One of the daughters, Barbara, has become a major in the Salvation Army, and is engaged to marry a fellow Salvationist and Greek scholar. She wants her father to come to see her work at a Salvation shelter, and he agrees on the condition that she visit his munitions factory.

On his trip, Undershaft precipitates a crisis of conscience for Barbara by offering to match the five-thousand-pound charitable donation of a whisky distiller. Barbara is horrified by the prospect that the Salvation Army should take money either from a "merchant of death" or a distiller who contributes to the "poor drink-ruined creatures" she is trying to save.[77] Her superior, a Salvation Army commissioner, has no such scruples: "[T]he distiller has a soul to be saved like any of us. If heaven has found the way to make a good use of his money, are we to set ourselves up against the answer to our prayers? . . . Who would have thought that any good could have come out of war and drink? And yet their profits are brought today to the feet of salvation to do its blessed work."[78] Barbara remains unconvinced. But then, after visiting her father's model town, she and her fiancé both decide to assist him in his work. From a leadership perspective, the play is particularly instructive in the treatment of money, and the morality of means and ends in its accumulation. Accused by his wife of having "got on" because he was "selfish and unscrupulous," Undershaft responds: "Not at all. I had the strongest scruples about poverty and starvation. . . . I had rather be a thief than pauper. . . ."[79] Although acknowledging that, of course, he would rather be neither; he views the eradication of poverty as the ultimate social good, and worth the sacrifice of principle to achieve. In his own life, Undershaft sees the vindication of that priority:

> I moralized and starved until one day I swore that I would be a full-fed free man at all costs; that nothing should stop me except a bullet, neither reason nor morals. . . . I was a dangerous man until I had my will; now I am a useful,

beneficent, kindly person. That is the history of most self-made millionaires, I fancy. When it is the history of every Englishman we shall have an England worth living in.[80]

Asked by his future son-in-law whether there was any place in his world-view for "honor, justice, truth, love, mercy, and so forth," Undershaft responds, "Yes: they are the graces and luxuries of a rich, strong, and safe life." "In your Salvation Army," he tells Barbara and her fiancé, "I saw poverty, misery and cold and hunger. You gave them bread and treacle and dreams of heaven. I give them from thirty shillings a week to twelve thousand a year. They find their own dreams; but I look after the drainage."[81]

Undershaft is equally willing to defend the sale of arms, on the ground that force can contribute to reforming society on better principles. To critics who prefer the persuasive force of religion and morality, he argues: "Poverty and slavery have stood up for centuries to your sermons and leading articles; they will not stand up to my machine guns."[82] To his son, who believes a career in politics will much better serve the public interest than his father's arms' trade, Undershaft asks: "Do you suppose that you and half a dozen amateurs like you . . . can govern Undershaft . . . ? No my friend: you will do what pays us. You will make war when it suits us, and keep peace when it doesn't."[83] In the end, at least his son-in-law is convinced. "People need power more than Greek," he acknowledges. And "you cannot have power for good without having power for evil."[84]

In the play's Preface, Shaw attempts to deflect any misreading of his work as an apology for materialism. To "help my critics out with *Major Barbara* by telling them what to say about it," Shaw explains:

> In the millionaire Undershaft I have represented a man who has become intellectually and spiritually as well as practically conscious of the irresistible natural truth which we all abhor and repudiate, to wit that the greatest of our evils and the worst of our crimes is poverty, and that our first duty, to which every other consideration should be sacrificed, is not to be poor.
>
> The universal regard for money is the one hopeful fact in our civilization. . . . Money is the most important thing in the world. It represents health, strength, honor, generosity, and beauty as conspicuously and undeniably as the want of it represents illness, weakness, disgrace, meanness and ugliness. . . . It is only when it is cheapened to worthlessness for some and made impossibly dear to others, that it becomes a curse.[85]

In response to critics who claimed that the Salvation Army would not, or should not, take tainted money, Shaw noted that Salvationists who had seen his play thought otherwise. "They would take money from the devil himself and be only too glad to get it out of his hands and into God's. . . . [A]ll our money is tainted."[86]

To theater goers who might be appalled by the play's elevation of pragmatism over principle, Shaw wrote in a program note that he was "still of the opinion that the best comedies for British audiences are those which they themselves provide by trying to run an international civilization on the precepts of our village Sunday Schools."[87]

QUESTIONS

1. Read against the backdrop of contemporary financial scandals and misjudgments, how much of Shaw's faith in wealth and its redistribution seems warranted? Do you agree that poverty is the ultimate social evil?[88]
2. Do you share Shaw's view of tainted money? Would his defense of Undershaft extend to contemporary arms dealers who supply perpetrators of atrocities, or to leaders of the tobacco industry who became wealthy philanthropists by marketing the product to underage consumers in impoverished nations?

2. F. SCOTT FITZGERALD, *THE LAST TYCOON* (1965)

Francis Scott Fitzgerald was born in St. Paul, Minnesota, in 1896. His father was a failed manufacturer and salesman; his mother supported the family with income from her father's retail grocery business. Fitzgerald began writing in prep school and continued at Princeton, to the neglect of his academic work. He left without graduating, and enlisted in the army. His first love, a debutante, rejected him for a more sensible marriage, and his second, Zelda Sayre, initially broke off their engagement when he failed to make a sufficient living at a New York advertising agency. Then, as Fitzgerald later recalled, "during a long sense of despair I wrote a novel instead of letters so it came out all right. But it came out all right for a different person. The man with the jingle of money in his pocket who married the girl a year later would always cherish an abiding distrust, an animosity toward the leisure class."[89]

After the instant success of his first novel, Fitzgerald and his new wife romped through Europe with the smart set, "seemingly with a highball in either hand."[90] He published several more novels that earned some critical recognition but no commercial success. Although his short stories for magazines paid well, he and Zelda "spent as fast as he earned."[91] Her mental breakdown in 1930 and subsequent institutionalization added to his bills. In the mid-1930s, the combination of alcohol, financial, and writing difficulties, and several embarrassing confessional publications led to his failed suicide attempt.[92]

The lure of fame and money sent him three times to Hollywood, where his scriptwriting earned him neither. As Billy Wilder described the experience, it was as if a "great sculptor . . . is hired to do a plumbing job," with no idea how to connect the pipes so the water would flow.[93] The third trip did, however, supply material for his posthumously published novel, *The Last Tycoon*. It was only partially written when he died in 1940 of a sudden heart attack, but it was complete enough to be published (with notes edited by literary critic Edmund Wilson), and to be the basis for a movie starring Robert De Niro.

The story's main character, Monroe Stahr, is modeled on Irving Thalberg, who ran Universal City at the age of twenty-one and MGM four years later. Although an admirer of those studios' achievements, Fitzgerald loathed their assembly-line method of screenwriting, in which successive teams of writers tweaked each script, giving no one a sense of creative control. In that system, Fitzgerald found it impossible to achieve his competing desires to be both a

great author and a "Hollywood hot shot."[94] His experience supplied foundations for the broader cultural conflicts between art and entertainment that the
novel explores.

The conflicts become explicit midway through the story, when Stahr
explains to a meeting of studio executives that he plans to make a "quality
picture" that would gross a quarter of a million dollars short of its budget (in
today's dollars, a loss of close to $4 million). "For two years we've played safe,"
Stahr notes. "It's time we made a picture that'll lose some money. Write it off
as good will—this'll bring in new customers. . . . [W]e have a certain duty to
the public, as Pat Brady has said at Academy dinners."[95] Stahr expresses similar
views toward the end of the novel after a chance encounter with a black man
who is collecting fish on the beach. "I never go to movies," the man tells Stahr.
"There's no profit. I never let my children go." Stahr tries to dismiss the
comment with the observation that "[t]hey have pictures of their own," but
it continues to rankle.[96] He concludes that the man "was prejudiced and wrong
and he must be shown somehow, some way. A great many pictures, a decade of
pictures, must be made to show him he was wrong." After reconsidering some
prospects in light of the "judgment of the Negro," Stahr rejects them as "trash."
And he puts "back on the list one that he had tossed to the wolves to get his way
on something else. He resurrected it for the Negro."[97]

A second tension in the novel is between work and relationships. Stahr
seems to have been "born sleepless, without a talent for rest or the desire for
it."[98] His single-minded focus on work is both a cause and consequence of
stunted interpersonal skills that he works hard to overcome:

> [L]ike many brilliant men, he had grown up dead cold. Beginning at about
> twelve, probably, with the total rejection common to those of extraordinary
> mental powers, the "See here; this is all wrong—a mess—all a lie—and a
> sham—" he swept it all away, everything, as men of his type do; and then
> instead of being a son-of-a-bitch as most of them are, he looked around at the
> barrenness that was left and said to himself, 'this will never do.' And so he had
> learned tolerance, kindness, forbearance, and even affection like lessons.[99]

But the effort is only partially successful. As Stahr explains to the daughter of a
partner, "I've got no place to go in the evenings so I just work."[100] He pays the
price in physical health. Although he promises his cardiologist that he will ease
up when work slows down, the doctor knows it is a lie and that efforts to avert
Stahr's impending death would "almost surely be useless."

> You couldn't persuade a man like Stahr to stop and lie down and look at the sky
> for six months. He'd much rather die. He said differently, but what it added up
> to was the definite urge towards total exhaustion that he had run into before.
> Fatigue was a drug as well as poison, and Stahr apparently derived some rare
> almost physical pleasure from working lightheaded with weariness. It was a
> perversion of the life force he had seen before, but he had almost stopped
> trying to interfere with it. He had cured a man or so—a hollow triumph of
> killing and preserving the shell. . . . Did Stahr know [of his condition]? Prob-
> ably. But he did not know when.[101]

The same may well have been true of Fitzgerald, whose alcoholism and lifestyle
doubtless contributed to his heart attack at age forty-four.

Critics note that Fitzgerald had much more sympathy for the "romance of money" and the glitter of Hollywood than other artists of his era. He "immersed himself in the age and always remained close to the business world which [other] writers were trying to evade."[102] Yet, for Fitzgerald and characters such as Stahr, money was always an imperfect symbol of what they were aiming to achieve. In his notes for *The Last Tycoon*, Fitzgerald writes that what he saw in Hollywood was "the history of all aspiration—not just the American dream but the human dream."[103] Fitzgerald's dreams to become a great screenwriter, like Stahr's to bust the box office with "quality" pictures, were equally unrealistic, but also emblematic of what drives the greatest of leaders in both fact and fiction.

QUESTIONS

1. Could Stahr's philosophy survive in contemporary Hollywood? Is there any room for a "duty to the public" outside the context of after-dinner rhetoric?
2. Would it have done any good for the cardiologist to tell Stahr "when"? Have you ever worked with or for someone that driven? How would you evaluate the effects on his or her leadership?

3. ALLAN GURGANUS, "BLESSED ASSURANCE" IN *WHITE PEOPLE* (1991)

Allan Gurganus was born in 1947 in a small, racially segregated town in North Carolina. As he later recalled, his childhood included little interest in reading. He was, rather, one of those "smart-alecky kids who preferred to make up the book report than read the book."[104] That changed when he was drafted and stationed off the Vietnam coast in a ship with a large library and not many other recreational options. After his discharge, he studied writing at Sarah Lawrence College and eventually moved to Chapel Hill, where he wrote fiction and taught occasional university courses. His best-known work is a short story collection, *White People*, a title that many readers felt called for explanation. Its inspiration came from classes on painting.

> I was told that black and white are really not colors, per se. Black is the presence of all colors and white is the absence of all colors. It struck me as strange because, since Caucasians could have chosen any name for ourselves . . . why we would have called ourselves white, when, in fact, I'm looking at my hand and I'm yellow and pink and brown, or rose-colored. I mean, why didn't we call ourselves the Rose People? . . .
>
> What I tried to do is to relate this business of being named for a vacuum to our own crippling perfectionism. . . . If you call yourself the perfect people, you've already set yourself an incredible difficulty, because we're all of us flawed.[105]

In another interview, he elaborated: "I named my book of stories *White People* because I wanted to suggest that we are one people among many. I look at you and I see tans and peach tones, but I don't see white. I look at black people and I see brown and umber and blue, not black. So we're calling each other by only partial truths."[106]

"Blessed Assurance," like other stories in *White People*, features characters who are indeed flawed, and who face vexing moral dilemmas: "[W]hat's decent? And whom am I responsible for saving?"[107] Gurganus likes placing "complex characters in ethical situations" and seeing what they do and how they feel.[108] "Blessed Assurance" focuses on two white people in those situations. The central character is a nineteen-year-old boy, Jerry, who takes a summer job collecting payments on installment contracts for funeral services. The buyers are mainly poor blacks, who remained in small southern towns after the great wave of urban migration in the mid-twentieth century.[109] These individuals have extremely limited job opportunities and correspondingly limited income. Why they spend it on the high-priced funeral services that Jerry is peddling is something that his white manager tries to explain.

> Black people come from Africa. No news, right? But all Africans are big on funerals. It's how your dying tribe-people announce the respect they deserve in their next life, see? *I'm* not buying into this, understand—just laying out why a person who's got no dinner will cough up fifty cents to three bucks per Saturday for a flashy coffin and last party.
>
> Now, times, you might get to feeling—nice boy like you, college material—like maybe you're stealing from them. You take *that* attitude, you'll wind up like . . . like me. No, you've got to accept how another type of person believes. Especially when there's such a profit in it. And remember, Our Founder was a black man. Richest colored family in Ohio, I'm told. Plus, for all we know, they could be right, Jerry. If there *is* the so-called next world, they'll turn up in it, brass bands to announce them. And us poor white guys who sold them the tickets, we'll be deep-fat-frying underneath forever. That'd sure get a person's attention, wouldn't it? Coming to in Hell? For being Bad here?
>
> What I'm saying: You've got to work it out for yourself, and quick. Here's your premium book. Take plenty of change. Four bits to three bucks per week might sound like nothing to a crackerjack like you. But, with most of Colored Town paying, it adds up. And, Jerry, they *do* get it back when they break the bank. Soon as some next-of-kin comes in here with the legal death certificate, I pay off like clockwork. So, yeah, it's honest . . . I see that look on your face: Only thing, buddy, if they miss two weeks running, they forfeit. They lose the present policy and any other Windlass ones they've paid up. I don't care if they've put in thousands, and several of your older clients will have: if they let one, then two (count them) two big Saturdays roll by, their pile becomes the company's.
>
> You getting this? See, that's the catch. I warned them during my own feistier collecting days, I'd go, "Hey, no remuneral, no funeral. No bucks, no box." They'd laugh but they got my meaning. Your client misses two back-to-back Saturdays, it's hello potter's field. Could be worse. I mean, *they* won't be around to suffer through it.
>
> And listen. Jer. No exceptions to our two-week rule, none. Because, Jerry, they'll beg you. Hold firm. Way I see it, anybody who can't come up with fifty cents a week on this plane, they don't deserve the four-star treatment in the next, you know?—No, I lied. That's *not* the way I see it. The way I see it is: I wish I hadn't washed out of dental school. The Organic Chemistry, Jerry. The goddamn Organic Chemistry, I had a sick feeling about it from the first. Like a drink? That's right, you said No. So here's your book, names, addresses, amounts paid to date. See—our clients they've got nothing else—they're hoping for a better shot next go-round. Your middle-class black people wouldn't touch funeral insurance with somebody else's ten-foot pole.

> Jerry, I recommend a early start on Saturday. They mostly get paid Friday night. They've mostly spent every penny by Sunday morning. And, son, they *want* to pay. So, do everybody a favor, especially yourself, grab it while it's in their hot hands.[110]

Jerry disregards part of the advice, and begins to cover payments for Vesta Battle, a former cotton mill worker and favorite customer. But he cannot afford to keep it up. "Look," he tells her,

> [y]ou've paid in so much. I just can't have you lose it. You let the latest policy go, they'll grab all your others. You signed, you agreed to this. . . . I've paid your last three weeks my own self. Look, I'm poor too or else I wouldn't keep this job, believe me. — Now maybe that dollar seventy-one doesn't sound like much to you . . . (no, I'm sorry, of course it's a lot to you or else you'd have paid. I see that). But think, here I am, already lying to my boss. I'm paying out of my own pocket. And for your funeral ma'am. I'd rather give you food money any day. Let's reason together, all right? It can't go on can it? Are you even listening? I mean this. Can you hear me?[111]

She is listening, and explains that a check she normally relied on from her daughter is five weeks late. Jerry telegrams the daughter, and promises himself that

> this'd have to be the final Christian act for soft-headed prelaw really un-Princeton Jerry. My sleep was suffering, gone spotty and shallow. . . . For somebody nineteen, somebody American and intending to be self-made, I was growing pretty cynical pretty early. Funerary Eventualities had started eating me alive. On a night-school pop quiz, one question asked, "define Business Ethics." I wrote, "Business Ethics is a contradiction in terms."
> Then I erased this.
> So I'd pass.[112]

QUESTIONS

1. Is this a job that the manager or Jerry should have refused? Is there anything that Jerry should have done differently, given his values?
2. What would you have done in Jerry's place?
3. Did it matter that the company's founder was black? Or that Jerry and the manager were white?
4. Can you think of any contemporary business practices that might be similar? Subprime mortgages? Penny lending at rates well above usury limits? Others? Under what, if any circumstances, would you refuse to engage in sales practices that are legal but that raise ethical concerns along the lines that "Blessed Assurance" suggests?
5. Was Jerry right about business ethics? How would you define it?

END NOTES

   1. For example, Robert Cole taught a famous course on moral leadership through novels at Harvard that he discusses in The Call of Stories: Teaching and the Moral Imagination (Boston, MA:

Houghton Mifflin, 1989); Sandra Sucher has taught a Harvard course that served as the foundation for her book The Moral Leader: Challenges, Tools, Insights (New York: Routledge, 2008); and Scott McClellan has taught leadership through literature at Harvard and Stanford.

2. Roger Gill, Theory and Practice of Leadership (Thousand Oaks, CA: Sage, 2006), 6 (quoting Hart Leaders Program, Leadership in the Arts, and Edinburgh Festival). For a bibliography on the teaching through fiction, see Pedagogy of Narrative: A Symposium Journal of Legal Education 40 (1990). For its value in teaching law, see Kim L. Scheppele, Forward: Telling Stories, Michigan Law Review 87 (1989):2073; Kathryn Abrams, Hearing the Call of Stories, California Law Review 79 (1991):971.

3. Martha Nussbaum, Love's Knowledge: Essays on Philosophy and Literature (New York: Oxford University Press, 1990), 47-48.

4. Gary Klein, Sources of Power: How People Make Decisions (Cambridge, MA: MIT Press, 1998), 177-196.

5. Anton Chekhov, Gooseberries, in The Russian Master and Other Stories, trans. Ronald Hingley (New York: Oxford University Press, 1984), 132-133.

6. Cole, The Call of Stories, 191, 205.

7. Sucher, The Moral Leader, 12.

8. Aylmer Maude, The Life of Tolstoy, Volume 1 (New York: Oxford University Press, 1987), 29.

9. Lyof N. Tolstoi, My Confession and the Spirit of Christ's Teaching (London: Walter Scott, 1887), 40.

10. Tolstoi, My Confession, 27.

11. George J. Gutsche, Moral Fiction: Tolstoy's Death of Ivan Il'ych, in Gary R. Jahn, ed., Tolstoy's The Death of Ivan Il'ich: A Critical Companion (Evanston, IL:. Northwestern University Press, 1999), 55, 57.

12. Leo Tolstoy, Tolstoy on Shakespeare, trans. V. Tchertkoff and Isabella Fyvie Mayo (New York: Funk & Wagnalls, 1907).

13. Gutsche, Moral Fiction, 61.

14. Vladimirovich Nabokov, Lectures on Russian Literature (New York: Harcourt Brace Jovanovich, 1981), 238.

15. A.N. Wilson, Tolstoy (New York: Norton, 1988), 368.

16. Richard Pevear, Introduction, in Tolstoy, The Death of Ivan Ilych and Other Stories, trans. Richard Pevear and Larissa Volokhonsky (New York: Knopf, 2009).

17. Gary R. Jahn, Introduction, in Jahn, ed., Tolstoy's The Death of Ivan Il'ich, 22.

18. Robert Russell, From Individual to Universal: Tolstoy's "Smert" Ivana Il'icha, Modern Language Review 76 (1981):629, 639 (quoting Tolstoy's 1885 letter).

19. Leo Tolstoy, The Death of Ivan Ilych, 22.

20. Gary Jahn, The Role of the Ending in Leo Tolstoi's The Death of Ivan Il'ich, Canadian Slavonic Papers 24 (1982):229, 237.

21. See Donna T. Orwin, The Cambridge Companion to Tolstoy (Cambridge, UK: Cambridge University Press, 2002); Romain Rolland, The Life of Tolstoy, trans. B. Bial (New York: E.P. Dutton & Company,1911); Jahn, Tolstoy's The Death of Ivan Il'ich: A Critical Companion; Vladimir Vladimirovich Nabokov, Lectures on Russian Literature (New York: Harcourt, 1981).

22. http://www.thegodlight.co.uk/god10htm.

23. http://www.emich.edu/public/history/moss.

24. Timothy Hoff, Influences on Harper Lee: An Introduction to the Symposium, Alabama Law Review 45 (1994):389, 390-401, n. 75.

25. Monroe Freedman, Finch: The Lawyer Mythologized, Legal Times, May 18, 1992, 25.

26. Harper Lee, To Kill a Mockingbird (1960), 216.

27. Steven Lubet, Reconstructing Atticus Finch, Michigan Law Review 97 (1999):1339, 1345-1350.

28. Lee, To Kill a Mockingbird, 216.

29. During Finch's cross-examination of Sheriff, Finch asks, "Did anybody call a doctor?" The sheriff responds, "It wasn't necessary," while also acknowledging that "[s]he was mighty banged up." Lee, To Kill a Mockingbird, 169-170.

30. Lee, To Kill a Mockingbird, 185,

31. Malcolm Gladwell, The Courthouse Ring: Atticus Finch and the Limits of Southern Liberalism, New Yorker, August 10, 2009, available at http:www.newyorker.com/reporting/2009/0810fa_fact_gladwell.com.

32. Lee, To Kill a Mockingbird, 168. See Monroe Freedman, Atticus Finch—Right and Wrong, Alabama Law Review 45 (1993):473, 476.

33. Lee, To Kill a Mockingbird, 62.

34. Freedman, Atticus Finch, 481.

35. William H. Simon, Moral Icons: A Comment on Steven Lubet's Reconstructing Atticus Finch, Michigan Law Review 97 (1999):1376, 1378.

36. Randolph N. Stone, Atticus Finch, In Context, Michigan Law Review 97 (1999):1378, 1381.

37. See Sucher, The Moral Leader, 117-118. See Sarah Lyall, Robert Bolt Is Dead at 70: Oscar-Winning Screenwriter, New York Times, February 23, 1995, 10.

38. For overviews, see Sucher, The Moral Leader, 111-119; Peter Ackroyd, The Life of Thomas More (New York: Anchor Books, 1998); Brigden, New Worlds, Lost Worlds: The Rule of the Tudors, 1485-1603 (New York: Viking, 2000).

39. Robert Bolt, Preface, A Man for All Seasons (New York: Vintage International, 1990), xv.

40. Id. at 55.

41. Id. at 115.

42. Id. at 22.

43. Id. at 20.

44. Id. at 132. For an overview of the conflict, see Joseph L. Badaracco, Questions of Character (Boston: Harvard Business Press, 2006), 141-150.

45. Bolt, A Man for All Seasons, 65-66. For a review of the exchange and its importance, see Patrick J. Whitely, Natural Law and the Problem of Certainty: Robert Bolt's A Man for all Seasons, Contemporary Literature XLIII (2002):760.

46. Bolt, A Man for all Seasons, 158.

47. T.S. Eliot, Murder in the Cathedral (New York: Harcourt Brace, 1935).

48. Robert Penn Warren, Introduction, All the King's Men (New York: Modern Library, 1953), vi.

49. Robert Penn Warren, All the King's Men (New York: Harcourt Brace, 1946), 75.

50. Id. at 257-258.

51. Id. at 136.

52. Id. at 142.

53. Id. at 418.

54. Id. at 400.

55. Warren began the novel as a verse play in the 1930s, when Long was in his prime. See Keith Perry, Huey P. Long and the Modern American Novel (Baton Rouge: Louisiana State Press, 2004); Ladell Payne, Willie Stark and Huey Long: Atmosphere, Myth or Suggestion, American Quarterly XX (1968):580. There are also important differences between Stark's and Long's careers, including the circumstances of their assassinations. For Stark, the cause was an affair; for Long, it was politics.

56. Warren, Introduction, vi.

57. For a critical commentary, see Joyce Carol Oates, All the King's Men — A Case of Misreading, New York Review of Books, March 28, 2002; Steven D. Ealy, Corruption and Innocence in Robert Penn Warren's Fiction, Modern Age 47 (2005):139; John Blair, The Lie We must Learn to Live By: Honor and Tradition in All the King's Men, Studies in the Novel 25 (1993):457.

58. Kazuo Ishiguro, Writer 16 (2001), 24. For other bibliographic information, see sources cited in Sucher, The Moral Leader, 103-105.

59. For women, domestic service was one of the largest categories of work available during the early twentieth century, and the time-intensive work connected with heating, cooking, laundry, and cleaning made servants a necessity for a comfortable middle- or upper-class life. The opening up of job opportunities during the war and postwar periods, coupled with the development of labor saving technologies, led to a dramatic decline in domestic work. See generally Frank Dawes, Not in Front of the Servants: A True Portrait of Upstairs Downstairs Life (London: Century Hutchinson, 1989); Sucher, The Moral Leader, 101-105.

60. Kazuo Ishiguro, The Remains of the Day (New York: Knopf, 1989), 115-117.

61. Patricia Highsmith, Reminiscences of a Gentleman's Gentleman: The Remains of the Day by Kazuo Ishiguro, Los Angeles Times, October 1, 1989 (quoting Ishiguro).

62. Ishiguro, The Remains of the Day, 147.

63. Id. at 149.

64. Id. at 148.

65. Id. at 151.

66. Id. at 153.

67. Id. at 153-154.

68. Id. at 97.

69. Id. at 243.

70. Robert Atkinson, How the Butler Was Made to Do It: The Perverted Professionalism of The Remains of the Day, Yale Law Journal 105 (1995-1996):177.

71. Richard Cohen, Who Wrote This Book?, Washington Post, January 30, 1996, A15. For some of the differences between fact and fiction, see Robert Stam, Primary Colors: Adapting the President, http://www.girlsaresmarter.com/laura/papers/PrimaryColors.html.

72. Kerry Dougherty, Washington's Mystery Novel: The Nation's Leaders Are Buzzing about a Clinton Book by an Unnamed Author, Virginian-Pilot, February 18, 1996, 12 (quoting Primary Colors).

73. Cohen, Who Wrote this Book?, A15.

74. Alex Beam, Anonymous'Bedtime Reading Fits the Bill; Book Review: Primary Colors, Boston Globe, February 6, 1996, 53.

75. Joe Klein, A Brush with Anonymity, Newsweek, July 29, 1996.

76. Id.

77. George Bernard Shaw, Major Barbara, The Bodley Head Bernard Shaw: Collected Plays with Their Prefaces, Vol. III (London: Max Reinhardt, 1971 ed.), 132.

78. Id. at 132, 134.

79. Id. at, 173-174.

80. Id. at 173.

81. Id. at 171.

82. Id. at 174-175.

83. Id. at 151.

84. Id. at 181.

85. Shaw, Preface, Major Barbara, 23, 30.

86. Id. at 35.

87. George Bernard Shaw, Author's Note, from the program of the production at Wyndham's Theatre, London, March 5, 1929, reprinted in The Bodley Head Bernard Shaw, 198, 200.

88. See Charles A. Bearst, The Devil and "Major Barbara," Publications of the Modern Language Association of America 83 (1968):71.

89. Malcolm Cowley, The Romance of Money, in F.S. Fitzgerald, Three Novels (New York: Charles Scribner, 1957), xvi (quoting Fitzgerald).

90. Arthur Krystal, Slow Fade: F. Scott Fitzgerald in Hollywood, New Yorker, November 16, 2009, 37.

91. Cowley, The Romance of Money, xi.

92. The articles were published posthumously as The Crack-Up (New York: New Directions Books, 1993), edited by Edmund Wilson. An indiscreet interview ran under the title "The Other Side of Paradise," New York Post, September 25, 1936. For general biographies, see Arthur Mizener, The Far Side of Paradise: A Biography of F. Scott Fitzgerald (Boston, MA: Houghton Mifflin, 1951); Mathew Joseph Bruccoli, Some Sort of Epic Grandeur: The Life of F. Scott Fitzgerald (Columbia: University of South Carolina Press, 2002).

93. Krystal, Slow Fade, 36 (quoting Wilder).

94. Id. at 38.

95. F. Scott Fitzgerald, The Last Tycoon (New York: Penguin, 1965), 59.

96. Id. at 113.

97. Id. at 116.

98. Id. at 19.

99. Id. at 117.

100. Id. at 31.

101. Id. at 131.

102. Cowley, The Romance of Money, x. For other critical commentary, see Brian Diemart, The Death of the Author: F. Scott Fitzgerald and The Last Tycoon, Journal of Narrative Technique 28 (1998):134; John F. Callahan, The Unfinished Business of The Last Tycoon, Literature Film Quarterly 6 (1978):204; John F. Callahan, F. Scott Fitzgerald's Evolving American Dream: The "Pursuit of Happiness" in Gatsby, Tender Is the Night, and The Last Tycoon, Twentieth Century Literature 42 (1996):374.

103. Krystal, Slow Fade, 41 (quoting Fitzgerald).

104. Jan Malone, Gurganus Tackles Moral Issues, Writes Funny Books at Same Time, Richmond Times Dispatch, November 7, 2004, G1.

105. Id. at G1.

106. Susan Ketchin, When I'm Fog on a Coffin Lid: An Interview with Allan Gurganus, Southern Review 29 (1993):645.

107. Malone, Gurganus Tackles Moral Issues, G1 (quoting Gurganus).

108. Ketchin, When I'm Fog (quoting Gurganus).

109. For background, see Sucher, The Moral Leader, 46-48.

110. Allan Gurganus, Blessed Assurance, in White People (New York: Knopf, 1991), 194-195

111. Id. at 209.

112. Id. at 222.

CHAPTER 13

CONCLUSION

"We have all occasionally encountered top persons who couldn't lead a squad of seven year olds to the ice cream counter," noted John Gardiner.[1] This book has attempted to keep you from becoming one of those persons. In that spirit, we close with a review of key insights and thoughts on the legacy that your skills make possible.

A. THE NATURE OF LEADERSHIP

Our discussion began in Chapter 1 with the meaning of leadership and the importance of seeing it as a process, not a position, and as a relationship, not a status. A title may give someone subordinates, but not necessarily followers. To borrow Joseph Nye's metaphor, having a fishing license does not mean you will catch fish.[2] Leadership is earned.

The qualities and styles necessary to the task vary somewhat across circumstances. Yet although research reveals no uniform profile of the ideal leader, certain characteristics do appear effective for most leadership situations.[3] They cluster in five categories:

- values (such as integrity, honesty, trust, and an ethic of service);
- personal skills (such as self-awareness, self-control, and self-direction);
- interpersonal skills (such as social awareness, empathy, persuasion, and conflict management);
- vision (such as forward looking and inspirational);
- technical competence (such as knowledge, preparation, and judgment).[4]

The need for such qualities has never been greater. Contemporary leaders confront a landscape of increasing competition, complexity, scale, pace, and diversity. Many decisions play out on a wider stage, with less time for informed deliberation. What further complicates these challenges is the "leadership paradox": the frequent disconnect between the qualities that enable individuals to attain positions of power and the qualities that are necessary to perform effectively once they get there. Successful leadership requires subordinating interests in personal achievement to creating the conditions for achievement by others. Empowering subordinates is generally the best way to maximize talent in the service of organizational objectives and public interests.

How then do leaders develop the necessary strategies and skills? Experience is critical, as is being reflective about experience—both their own and others'. Mark Twain made the point with his famous metaphor of a misguided cat who will not sit on a hot stove twice, but will not sit on a cold one either. Aspiring leaders need to seek opportunities for exercising influence, obtaining candid feedback, and learning from research and educational initiatives. Those who have obtained positions of power can assist the process by creating "learning organizations" that will effectively create, transfer, and incorporate knowledge, as well as develop new leaders.[5]

B. LEADERSHIP SKILLS

What are the key skills that leaders need to learn? One involves decision making. Leaders are deciders, and those who are most effective have developed the habit of practicing conscious deliberation before and after they act. Rather than simply reacting to events, successful leaders consider what they most want to achieve, and they anticipate what might stand in the way. After they act, these leaders reflect on what worked and what did not, and what they might do differently in the future.[6] Skilled decision makers also recognize that even the most thoughtful processes are subject to biases in perception, memory, and problem solving. Sound judgment depends on recognizing bounded rationality and building in appropriate correctives. Information that is vivid or consistent with stereotypes and self-interest will be disproportionately "available" to skew decision making unless leaders make conscious adjustments. In cost-benefit calculations, psychic numbing, and the salience of individual victims and immediate consequences can lead to overinvestment in short-term remedial responses and underinvestment in long-term preventative strategies. Groupthink and related dynamics can also sabotage effective policy making and risk management. Creating processes that will ensure independent and diverse points of view is an essential leadership skill.

Mastering strategies of influence is equally critical. Power comes in multiple currencies, and often the most obvious rewards and sanctions are less available or effective than other persuasive approaches, such as reciprocity, peer pressure, or association. These techniques are essential in building relationships in a world in which boundaries separating leaders and followers are increasingly blurred. Most managers, professionals, and policy makers "lead from the middle," and encouraging responsible behavior among subordinates is a key part of ensuring responsible behavior among superiors. Leaders also need strategies for innovation and conflict management. They need to overcome inertia, chart a path for change, and create environments that will sustain it. In dealing with conflict, avoidance is generally to be avoided. In most cases, the preferable approach is collaborative problem solving, in which parties build on shared concerns and respect in search of mutual gain. Leaders can facilitate the process, not only by assisting individual dispute resolution, but also by creating "conflict competent" organizations that can do the same.

Finally, leaders need effective communication skills. That requires knowing their objectives, their audience, their occasion, and their substance. To create messages "made to stick," speakers should look for material that is succinct, unexpected, credible, emotional, and that tells a story. They should avoid the curse of knowledge; less is often more, and visual images may be the most powerful persuasive strategy.

C. VALUES IN LEADERSHIP

Effective leadership depends not only on skills but also on values. Challenges often arise because values are in conflict, or because ethical commitments are in tension with situational pressures. Leaders face trade-offs between immoral means and moral ends, and difficulties in institutionalizing principles that come at a cost.

Dilemmas of "dirty hands" are particularly common in political life, and those that Machiavelli described five centuries ago play out in similar forms in contemporary settings. Although many of these dilemmas lack clear answers, leaders need to be accountable for their responses, and their choices need to serve public, not just personal interests. In law, business, and policy contexts, it is also critical to find ways of reinforcing moral behavior. That, in turn, requires addressing the peer pressures, cognitive biases, structures of authority, and diffusion of responsibility that compromise moral judgment. Ethical conduct is highly situational, and research on the banality of evil makes clear how readily minor missteps or mindless conformity can entrap individuals in major misconduct. To maintain their moral compass, leaders as well as followers should consult widely, enlist allies, observe bright-line rules, and cultivate self-doubt. Those in leadership positions can also foster ethical conduct by setting the tone at the top, establishing appropriate reward structures, and strengthening regulatory oversight.

Leaders also need private lives that are consistent with public and organizational responsibilities. Power both imposes special obligations and creates special temptations. Leaders not only have more than the customary opportunities for abuse, they are surrounded by subordinates reluctant to challenge it. Self-serving biases can further reinforce leaders' sense of entitlement and invulnerability. The result is a steady stream of scandal, fed by media eager to fill a continuous news cycle, and equipped with technological resources to make it possible. In this climate, crisis management has become a critical part of the leadership tool kit, and the art of apology is an essential skill. So too is the capacity to use disasters as catalysts for necessary corrective action. Market meltdowns, environmental disasters, or product defects can supply the urgency for organizational and regulatory reform. Where personal conduct is at issue, leaders need to be attentive to even the appearance of impropriety. In an era of increasing transparency and instant notoriety, those in positions of power need to consider how private conduct would play in public settings, before it is too late to change.

D. LEADERSHIP CHALLENGES

Contemporary leaders face a host of challenges, and diversity is high among them. Appropriate responses require understanding how characteristics such as race, ethnicity, and gender matter in the selection and performance of leaders. Despite considerable progress over the last half century, women and minorities are significantly underrepresented in positions of influence. Unconscious stereotypes, in-group biases, and inflexible workplace structures remain substantial obstacles. There are strong reasons to address them. Women and minorities constitute an increasing share of today's talent, and effective performance in an increasingly multicultural environment demands an equal playing field. When well managed, diversity also can enhance the quality and legitimacy of decision making. To that end, leadership strategies should proceed on three levels: helping women and minorities enhance their qualifications, promoting diversity-related legal and policy initiatives that address bias and barriers, and increasing transparency and stakeholder pressure.

Another set of challenges involves corporate responsibility and human rights in an increasingly interdependent world. The growing power of multinational corporations has fueled growing efforts to hold them accountable. The result has been to strengthen the "business case" for responsible business practices. Reputation matters to a substantial number of customers, employees, investors, and organized interest groups. Adoption of voluntary standards can help enhance a corporation's image, reduce the risks of legal liability, preempt more intrusive regulation, and prevent a race to the bottom among competitors. Although such standards can also help address chronic human rights abuses, they can sometimes bring unintended consequences. Leadership dilemmas arise when adherence to principle imposes costs on people who are powerless to address them. Restrictions on child labor can increase poverty or force children into even more dangerous but less well-regulated occupations. Refusal to cooperate with abusive regimes can mean denial of aid or restriction of Internet access for their subjects. Humanitarian organizations face agonizing trade-offs when their intervention risks provoking backlash or prolonging conflict. The absence of external structures of accountability imposes a special obligation on leaders to think deeply and consult widely about the trade-offs that intervention poses.

Similar points can be made about those who spearhead movements for social change. Leaders play a pivotal role in creating or capitalizing on conditions for progress. Their ability to inspire hope, enlist allies, attract public support, and reinforce shared identities can provide the foundations for social transformation. However, the best path forward is seldom self-evident. Conflicts often arise about timing or strategies, such as when to litigate, which cases to bring, and who should decide. One distinguishing feature of great leaders is the ability to mediate such disputes and build a coherent unifying strategy in pursuit of social justice.

E. THE LEGACY OF LEADERSHIP

Leadership not only poses special challenges and special obligations, it can also bring exceptional rewards. Those that are most fulfilling are generally not, however, the extrinsic perks that accompany positions of power. A wide array of psychological research suggests that satisfaction with work depends on feeling effective, exercising strengths and virtues, and contributing to socially valued ends that bring meaning and purpose.[7] As one British military leader put it, "You make a living by what you get; you make a life by what you give."[8] Individuals who are motivated by "intrinsic aspirations" such as personal growth and assisting others tend to be more satisfied than those motivated primarily by extrinsic aspirations, such as wealth or fame.[9] Part of the reason is that desires, expectations, and standards of comparison tend to increase as rapidly as they are satisfied. Leaders can become trapped on a "hedonic treadmill": the more they have the more they need to have.[10] So too, money and status are positional goods; individuals' satisfaction depends on how they compare relative to others, and increases in wealth or position are readily offset by changes in reference groups.[11] The recent arms race in executive compensation reflects this dynamic. Leaders who look hard enough can always find someone getting more.

How then can individuals with high needs for achievement and recognition find greatest fulfillment? Laura Nash and Howard Stevenson of the Harvard Business School studied leaders who by conventional standards had achieved "success that lasts."

> Our research uncovered four irreducible components of enduring success: happiness (feelings of pleasure and contentment); achievement (accomplishments that compare favorably against similar goals others have strived for); significance (the sense that you've made a positive impact on people you care about); and legacy (a way to establish your values or accomplishments so as to help others find future success).[12]

The challenge for leaders is how to set priorities that strike a balance among all four domains.

What constitutes "legacy" is often the hardest measure of accomplishment to assess. The philosopher William James insisted that the greatest use of life is to spend it on something that outlasts it. Leadership expert J. Patrick Dobel agrees but warns against confusing fame with legacy.[13] As Chapter 1 noted, a focus on ensuring recognition of one's legacy can get in the way of achieving it; leaders can be tempted to hoard power, status, and credit. Dobel underscores the distinction between "making a difference" and "making 'my' difference and making sure everyone knows it."[14] Leaders can never control how others will ultimately interpret their contributions; pigeons may nest on their monuments. Thinking about legacy is helpful only if it directs attention to ultimate goals and values, not if it diverts energy into futile quests for lasting glory.

When asked how he wished to be remembered, Supreme Court Justice Thurgood Marshall responded: "He did what he could with what he had."[15] Leaders have many ways to leave a legacy. For most, it is less through grand triumphs and historical events than through smaller cumulative acts that improve the lives and institutions that surround them. Our hope is that this book will aid your leadership, and prompt deeper reflection about what your own legacy will be.

END NOTES

1. John Gardiner, On Leadership (New York: Free Press, 1990), 2.

2. Joseph S. Nye Jr., The Powers to Lead (New York: Oxford University Press, 2008), 19.

3. See Robert Goffee and Gareth Jones, Why Should Anyone Be Led by You?, Harvard Business Review (Sept.-Oct. 2000):63, 64; Jay Lorsch, A Contingency Theory of Leadership, in Nitin Nohria and Rakesh Khurana, eds., Handbook of Leadership Theory and Practice (Cambridge, MA: Harvard Business Press, 2010):411-424.

4. For values, see Warren Bennis, On Becoming a Leader (Reading, MA: Addison Wesley, 2d ed. 1994), 32-33 (citing integrity, trust); Montgomery Van Wart, Dynamics of Leadership in Public Service: Theory and Practice (Armonk, NY: M.E. Sharpe, 2005), 16, 92-119 (citing integrity and an ethic of public service); James M. Kouzes and Barry Posner, The Leadership Challenge (San Francisco: Jossey-Bass, 4th ed. 1995), 21 (citing honesty). For personal skills, see Daniel Goleman, Richard Boyatzis, and Annie McKee, Primal Leadership: Realizing the Power of Emotional Intelligence (Boston, MA: Harvard Business Press, 2002), 253-256 (citing self-awareness, self-management); Van Wart, Dynamics, 16 (citing self-direction). For interpersonal skills, see Goleman, Boyatzis, and McKee, Primal Leadership, 253-256 (citing social awareness, empathy, persuasion, and conflict management). For vision, see Bennis, supra, at 33 (citing vision); Kouzes and Posner, Leadership Challenge, 21 (citing forward looking, inspiring). For competence, see id.; Lorsch, A Contingency Theory, 417. For judgment, see Noel M. Tichy and Warren G. Bennis, Judgment: How Winning Leaders Make Great Calls (New York: Portfolio, 2007).

5. D.A. Gavin, Building a Learning Organization, Harvard Business Review (July-Aug. 1993):78, 79.

6. Linda A. Hill and Kent Linebeck, Being the Boss: The Three Imperatives for Becoming a Great Leader (Boston, MA: Harvard Business Review Press, 2011), 215.

7. David G. Myers, The Pursuit of Happiness: Who Is Happy—and Why (New York: W. Morrow, 1992), 32-38; David G. Myers and Ed Diener, Who Is Happy, Psychological Social Science 6 (1995):10, 17; Christopher Peterson and Martin E.P. Seligman, Character Strengths and Virtues: A Handbook and Classification (New York: Oxford University Press, 2004); William C. Compton, Introduction to Positive Psychology (Belmont, CA: Wadsworth, 2004), 48-49, 53-54; Ed Diener et al., Subjective Well-Being: Three Decades of Progress, Psychological Bulletin 125 (1999):276.

8. Air Vice-Marshal Sir Norman Duckworth Kerr MacEwen, http://www.quotatio.com/m/macewen-norman-quotes.html.

9. Christopher P. Niemiec, Richard M. Ryan, and Edward L. Dei, The Path Taken: Consequences of Attaining Intrinsic and Extrinsic Aspirations, Journal of Research in Personality 43 (2009):291.

10. Martin E.P. Seligman, Authentic Happiness: Using the New Positive Psychology to Realize Your Potential for Lasting Fulfillment (New York: Free Press, 2002), 49; Ed Diener, Richard E. Lucas, and Christie Napa Scollon, Beyond the Hedonic Treadmill: Revising the Adaptation Theory of Well-Being, American Psychologist 61 (2006):305.

11. Robert H. Frank, How Not to Buy Happiness, Daedalus 133 (2004):69, 69-71; Myers, The Pursuit of Happiness, 39.

12. Laura Nash and Howard Stevenson, Success That Lasts, Harvard Business Review (Feb. 2004):102, 104.

13. J. Patrick Dobel, Managerial Leadership and the Ethical Importance of Legacy, in Denis Saint-Martin and Fred Thompson, eds., Public Ethics and Governance: Standards and Practices in Comparative Perspective (Oxford, UK: Elsevier, 2004):195, 200-203.

14. Dobel, Managerial Leadership, 201.

15. Ruth Marcus, Plain-Spoken Marshall Spars with Reporters, Washington Post, June 29, 1991, A1, A10.

INDEX